MW00648181

WAGNER & CINEMA

Wagner

& CINEMA

EDITED BY

Jeongwon Joe & Sander L. Gilman

FOREWORD BY *Tony Palmer*

INTERVIEW WITH *Bill Viola*

Indiana University Press

Bloomington & Indianapolis

This book is a publication of

Indiana University Press
601 North Morton Street
Bloomington, IN 47404-3797 USA

www.iupress.indiana.edu

Telephone orders   800-842-6796
Fax orders   812-855-7931
Orders by e-mail   iuporder@indiana.edu

© 2010 by Indiana University Press
All rights reserved

No part of this book may be reproduced
or utilized in any form or by any means,
electronic or mechanical, including photo-
copying and recording, or by any information storage and retrieval system, without
permission in writing from the publisher.
The Association of American University
Presses' Resolution on Permissions constitutes the only exception to this prohibition.

♾ The paper used in this publication meets
the minimum requirements of the American National Standard for Information
Sciences—Permanence of Paper for Printed
Library Materials, ANSI Z39.48-1992.

Manufactured in the United States of
America

Library of Congress Cataloging-in-Publi-
cation Data

Wagner and cinema / edited by Jeongwon
Joe and Sander L. Gilman ; foreword by
Tony Palmer.
    p. cm.
  Includes bibliographical references and
index.
  ISBN 978-0-253-30030-0 (cloth : alk. paper) — ISBN 978-0-253-22163-6 (pbk. : alk.
paper)
  1. Wagner, Richard, 1813–1883. 2. Motion
picture music—History and criticism. 3.
Motion pictures and opera. 4. Operas—
Film and video adaptations. I. Joe, Jeongwon. II. Gilman., Sander L.
  ML410.W12W34 2010
  782.1092—dc22

                              2009025718

1 2 3 4 5   15 14 13 12 11 10

CONTENTS

FOREWORD

TONY PALMER

Richard Burton once asked me why I wanted him to play the role of Wagner in my epic film. "Easy," I said. "Both of you have the gift of the gab, drink more than you should, have had more women than hot dinners, talk rubbish most of the time, are often thoroughly unpleasant, even offensive, but can be, when the mood takes you, effortlessly charming and seductive. Oh, and you also both happen to be, in your different ways, blessed with genius." "Good," he replied. "As long as I know."

Well, the interesting thing is that when you look back over the endless attempts to portray Wagner on film, how often most of these attributes are missing. I'm not comparing my film (*Wagner*, 1983) with anyone else's, but to portray Wagner as merely an effete rascal who happened to write some good tunes is a disservice to music history, to the social and political history of the nineteenth century, and above all to that monster Wagner himself. Yes, he was anti-Semitic, racist, avaricious, dishonest, unscrupulous, unreliable, a thief, and a braggart, and that's just on Wednesdays. But it is necessary to understand and accept this about him before you can even begin to come to terms with his music and what he achieved.

Eisenstein, no less, toyed with a Wagner film project for years before abandoning it, no doubt because Stalin hated Wagner, performances of whose works were banned after the Nazi invasion of 1941 (*Parsifal* was not performed on stage again until 1997). William Dieterle's 1955 film *Magic Fire* had Alan Badel as Wagner, with music conducted (and arranged) by Erich Korngold—yes, see the *Ring* in five minutes! The studio thought it too "arty," re-titled it *Wagner and His Women* (with Yvonne de Carlo as Minna), emasculated it, and was "surprised" when it flopped at the box office. Most critics said it was incomprehensible. (Ironically, an idiot American producer offered me a small fortune to re-cut my own seven-hour-and-forty-minute film into two hours, provided it was called "Wagner's Women—the Secret Lives").

Actually, the earliest known portrayal of Wagner in film is Leopoldo Fregoli in *L'Homme Protée,* directed by Georges Méliès in 1899, a ten-minute silent. Wagner in ten minutes!—well, at least that's an improvement on Dieterle and Korngold's version. Ken Russell in *Lisztomania* had Paul Nicholas (better known as a pop singer) "doing" Wagner as if he were a character out of *Mad Magazine.* Syberberg in *Ludwig: Requiem for a Virgin King* (1972) had Wagner as a puppet and/or dwarf, not a bad idea in itself. Lyndon Brook appeared in 1959 with Dirk Bogarde as Liszt in *Song without End,* directed by Charles Vidor (better known for *Hans Christian Andersen*), who died in the effort and was replaced by George Cukor (as in *My Fair Lady* and the re-cutting of *The Wizard of Oz*). Michel Vitold, speaking no known language, appeared in Joscé Dayan's 1975 *La Mort du Titan* about Wagner's last days in Venice attended by innumerable doctors, but no Flower Maidens, so something wrong there. And of course there is Visconti's 1973 *Ludwig* with the great Trevor Howard as "Wagner the opportunist." Visconti was a visionary, intelligent director who should have known better. The others—especially those from Hollywood—it could be argued were beholden to the Hollywood system which nurtured them: happy endings, no sex or violence, and, given that all the studios were Jewish controlled, certainly no anti-Semitism.

When I first discussed my own film with Wolfgang Wagner, Wagner's grandson, he gave me two crucial pieces of advice, although I confess I did not fully appreciate their importance at the time. "First, never forget that the world is full of Wagner 'experts,'" he said, "who know for certain how many eggs my grandfather had for breakfast on the third Thursday of the fourth month of 1875, and what's more, many of them know how long he boiled the eggs! To this universal truth," he added, "there is one exception. Me. His grandson. And I don't know or care."

Second, he added, "If my grandfather were alive today, he would undoubtedly be working in Hollywood. He would not have been able to resist the technical wizardry at his disposal, nor the hordes of workers, nor the money. The money especially. He always headed straight for the money." He might have added the beautiful women, or at least the sex. And don't forget this advice was given to me in 1977. Just think of the digital effects that are possible now. Wagner would have been like a crazy kid in a paint shop. You want a dragon? No problem. Dwarfs? Easy. Flood the stage? Well, we did *Titanic* . . . And you'll get a great musical soundtrack as part of the deal.

In the end, or even at the beginning, you absolutely must understand that Wagner's lunatic genius encompassed all of this and more. To portray him as an ordinary bloke in the street who happened to write rather long and often tedious "operas" is to miss the point completely. And not to come to terms with the revolutionary fervor of Germany in the mid-nineteenth century, with its bitter squabbles between Bavaria and Berlin, its brutal loathing of the French, its hatred of the Jews (no wonder Marx, the son of Herschel Mordechai, chose to live in London), its poverty and filth and arrogance and Lutheran hypocrisy, is a complete failure to realize the swamp from which Wagner emerged. And yes, he was a loathsome little man, but also a man of indomitable courage and physical bravery, who read more, certainly wrote more, and knew more than almost all the buffoons he had to deal with. The fact that he managed to trick them into giving him their money, their wives, and even their lives, and do so with brazen effrontery, I find wholly admirable. In this instance he reminds me of what Peter Sellars, the great American stage director, once said to me about his own career. "You have to kick the door in of the various so-called artistic institutions such as the Salzburg Festival or the National Theater in Washington, do what you believe in, and keep doing so until they find out what you're up to and throw you out again." Wagner would have understood that attitude.

There is another element central to portraying a great composer (or any great artist, for that matter) on screen or on stage. Treat the life as fiction, not fact. Of course, it helps to try and get most of the historical detail accurate. But in our everyday conversation, for example, we do not speak in joined-up sentences, let alone paragraphs. Yet most film scripts have their actors doing just that. Moreover, we don't know precisely what Ludwig said to Wagner, or what Wagner said to Cosima as he was pulling off her knickers. We know what Cosima would *like* us to think they said to each other, and she wrote about their relationship endlessly in her diaries, which must rank as some of the most pernicious, self-justifying, racist drivel ever committed to print. If we are to believe her, they discussed Schopenhauer and the finer points of vegetarianism while having sex. Well, bollocks to that, as I'm sure Wagner would have said. The point is that to rely on what appear to be "the facts" in reconstructing historical truths is a blind alley for the dumb. You have to face "the fact" that you are dealing with fiction, and all the risks that this entails.

Worse, I have never known a great composer—and I've personally known quite a few—who "composed" while walking through a forest, by a stream, up a mountain, etc., etc., and who suddenly claps hand on forehead, with a beatific expression on his or her face, saying/thinking/emoting, "My God, I hear a tune!" That's not how it works—creativity. I've no idea *how* it works, and nor do most of those who do it. Most sit pole-axed in front of a blank page struggling with the blankness of the page. But that of course would make for an exceptionally dull film. So it is incumbent on the director to find a way to express the magic of creativity without even beginning to show "the process," even if we knew what it was.

So this is the dilemma: how to create something out of nothing. You have to ignore (more or less) the facts, or at least not make them the priority. You have to paint an act of creation which has no face, no explanation. You have to make the unlikable likable, which in Wagner's case is difficult, but without it no one will want to watch. You have to encapsulate a lifetime of endeavor, of disappointments and suffering, with all its attendant muddle and false turns and confusion, into something approaching coherence, even purpose. Above all, in the case of composers at least, you have to find a way to make the music "live," just as the composer himself or herself did. You also have to ask yourself, what is the point of this film? Cinema, after all, for all its flummery, has I believe a profoundly moral purpose, namely to tell stories which ennoble us as individuals and the human condition in general. Otherwise it is merely cheap and worthless entertainment, and no film director that I have ever met would subscribe to such a tawdry purpose. So film, like all art, seeks to enrich our understanding of ourselves, our world, our times. And Wagner, for all his vile behavior and preposterous theories, sought to do just that—and boy, did he succeed. The filmmaker, therefore, owes it to Wagner to attempt the same, as nothing less will do.

One last thought. In my (fictional) film about Shostakovich, *Testimony,* the character Shostakovich (Ben Kingsley), in reply to yet another denunciation by the Soviet State, says: "To reach the people. But how is it done? That is the question. I expect to receive instruction from you. I will study it with deep interest." That is the question which preoccupies all artists, however much they publicly deny it. I'm sure it confronted Wagner, and it's the most important question that anyone daring to portray Wagner on film must confront also.

This excellent collection of essays makes clear the scale of the task and the difficulty of answering that question. Jeongwon Joe and Sander Gilman have initiated a fascinating symposium on the thickets of Wagner scholarship, and done so with remarkable clarity in spite of the subject himself doing his best at obfuscation. One of the earliest facts I learned about Wagner on my own particular journey was that there existed in every known language more books about Wagner than any other historical person, with the possible exceptions of Jesus Christ and Napoleon. Although as a matter of principle I would be against the burning of books, much of what passes as Wagner "scholarship" might serve a better purpose fuelling the pyre. On my desk at present, for instance, as I prepare for a new film about the Wagner family (the most anti-Semitic of whom were English, I am not proud to report), I have before me ten newly published "definitive biographies." Is there anything new to say? I am happy to report that this volume does add to our understanding of this lunatic, and is definitely on the list of those books which should be preserved from the flames.

WAGNER & CINEMA

Why Wagner and Cinema?
Tolkien Was Wrong

JEONGWON JOE

Both rings were round, and there the resemblance ceased.

J. R. R. TOLKIEN

Nietzsche, in his youthful enthusiasm, failed to
recognize the artwork of the future in which we witness
the birth of film out of the spirit of music.

THEODOR ADORNO, *IN SEARCH OF WAGNER*

If you're an artist, it's hard to avoid Wagner's latent presence.

BILL VIOLA

Richard Wagner has been a continuing source of artistic inspiration and
ideological controversy in literature, philosophy, and the visual arts, as
well as in music. Cinema is no exception. For Hans-Jürgen Syberberg,
film is "the music of the future," the ultimate fulfillment of the Wagnerian *Gesamtkunstwerk*.[1] American cinematographer Morton Heilig's
"cinema of the future" in the 1950s, too, is an evocation of Wagnerian

aesthetics, especially its enhancement of the audience's "immersive experience"—or what Theodor Adorno calls phantasmagoria.[2] Although Wagner's Gesamtkunstwerk is prevalently, although too simplistically, considered to have anticipated cinematic art, the composer's cinematic imagination can be found at more detailed levels of his music-dramas.

> [T]he first notes of the ritornello in the aria accompany the Dutchman's first step on shore . . . with the first crotchet of the third bar he takes his second step—still with folded arms and bowed head; the third and fourth steps coincide with the notes of the eighth and tenth bars.[3]

Thus reads Wagner's stage direction for the Dutchman's entrance aria in Act 1 of *Der fliegende Holländer*. This "mimomaniac" correspondence between music and bodily gestures certainly resembles what is known as "Mickey-Mousing" in film technique. Another example of Wagner's cinematic imagination is the visual effect he intended for the transformation scene in Act 1 of *Parsifal*. In this scene, the transition from the forest to the Grail temple—where time becomes space ("Du siehst, mein Sohn, zum Raum wird hier die Zeit!")—was accomplished by using a kind of "panorama mobile," that is, a moving image created by manually scrolling painted cloth between the two rollers on each side of the stage (while Parsifal and Gurnemanz pretend to walk in front of this moving image).[4] Some of Wagner's scenic descriptions can also be regarded as cinematic, as they focus on visual effects, which are hard to realize on stage but are much easier with cinematic techniques.

> From the ruins of the fallen hall the men and women watch with profound emotion as the flames leap up high into the sky. When the glow reaches its brightest intensity, the hall of Valhalla suddenly becomes visible, with the gods and heroes all assembled there. Bright flames seem to seize upon the hall of the gods. As the gods become entirely hidden by the flames, the curtain falls.

This is Wagner's description of the last scene of *Götterdämmerung*, which motivated Martin van Amerongen's claim that "[i]f Wagner had lived a century later, his home would not have been Bayreuth but Beverly Hills." Wagner, continues Amerongen, would be composing not music-dramas but the soundtracks for disaster movies such as *The Towering Inferno*.[5] At a more abstract and subtle level, Friedrich Kittler finds Wagner's "media technology" in the "Liebestod" in *Tristan und Isolde*: he argues that the aria's climactic point at the word "Weltatem" (World-Breath) is the moment the dead Tristan experiences an "acoustic erection," which is effectuated by the orchestral surge, an aesthetic amplifier.[6] In an extended context, Randall Packer and Ken Jordan trace multi-medial practice to Wagner's music-drama in their collection *Multi Media: From Wagner to Virtual Reality* (2001). Similarly, Matthew Wilson Smith demonstrates in *The Total Work of Art: From Bayreuth to Cyberspace* (2007) how Wagner's operatic aesthetics have served as a driving engine for twentieth-century artists in cinema, experimental happenings, and digital media.[7] Perhaps, then, Steve Reich's use of the "Transformation Music" of *Das Rheingold* at the opening of his video-opera *Hindenberg* (2002) is not only a predictable musical reference to a German product—the Zeppelin, LZ 129 Hindenberg—but also an acknowledgment of Wagner's anticipation of cinematic, multi-medial, and digital innovation.

Wagner's cinematic imagination is not entirely unprecedented or unique: the Mickey-Mousing on stage was also practiced in melodrama, and the use of the panorama mobile in the theater dates back to the Baroque era.[8] However, many cineastes have glorified Wagner's music-drama—although not without ambivalence—as a paradigm for filmmaking, film scoring, and silent film accompaniment. "Every man or woman in charge of the music of a moving picture theatre is, consciously or unconsciously, a disciple or follower of Richard Wagner." So declared W. Stephen Bush in an article published in *The Moving Picture World* in 1911.[9] Bush, a film critic and reformer, idolized Wagner primarily because of the composer's tight integration of music and drama, which he considered to be an essential element for filmmaking. For Bush, the libretto before Wagner was an "excuse for clever orchestration."

> Strictly speaking, the modern school before Wagner (to distinguish it from the music of the ancient Greeks) did not as its primary object seek to give "musical expression to the drama," but subordinated the drama to the music and the libretto became more or less of an excuse for clever orchestration . . . As a result we have some of the finest operas, supported by librettos that border on the idiotic.[10]

Wagner's leitmotif technique, however simplistically and superficially it may have been understood, drew particular attention from many early film artists and critics. "'Leit Motiv' . . . is the one which can best be applied in scoring pictures," noted Erno Rapée, the compiler of *Encyclopedia of Music for Pictures* (1925), a selection of pieces for film accompaniment covering fifty-two moods and situations. In the preface to the volume, Rapée extolled Wagner as "the greatest dramatic Composer of all ages."[11]

That Wagner's music-dramas are among the earliest operas to have been turned into film is another testimony to early filmmakers' fascination with the composer. In 1904, Edwin S. Porter directed *Parsifal*, a twenty-five-minute silent screened in New York City.[12] It consists of eight scenes from the opera, including "Magic Garden" and "Return of Parsifal."[13] Other early silent films associated with Wagner's work include Franz Porten's *Lohengrin* (1907), in which the director played the title role and his daughter played Elsa;[14] Pathé's *Tristan et Yseult* (1909), directed by Albert Capellani;[15] Ugo Falena's *Tristano e Isotta* (1911), which starred Francesca Bertini, one of the most celebrated silent film stars;[16] and Mario Caserini's *Parsifal* (1912) and *Sigfrido* (1912). While Porten's *Lohengrin* and Capellani's *Tristan* are silent shorts that can be called "opera music videos," between three and ten minutes long, Falena's *Tristan* and both of Caserini's films are much longer, ranging from twenty-five to forty minutes.[17] In 1921, Max Reinhardt produced another Wagner silent film, *Parzifal*, a *Kinoweihfestfilm* (a festival film for the consecration of a screen), a sarcastic challenge to the sacred status of Wagner's *Parsifal,* which he called *ein Bühnenweihfestspiel* (a festival play for the consecration of a stage).[18]

Wagner's resonance has been continuous, if not stronger, during the sound era. He is one of the most frequently quoted composers on the soundtracks of blockbuster titles.[19] As the filmography of this volume shows, Wagner's music has been resonant in a variety of film genres, ranging from comedy (e.g., Chaplin's *The Great Dictator* [1940]) and cartoon (e.g., *What's Opera, Doc?* [1957] and some shorts of the *Private Snafu* series in the early 1940s) to fantasy (e.g., John Boorman's *Excalibur* [1981]) and horror (e.g., Werner Herzog's *Nosferatu the Vampyre* [1979] and E. Elias Merhige's *Shadow of the Vampire* [2000]). The use of Wagner's "Ride of the Valkyries" in Francis Ford Coppola's *Apocalypse Now* (1979) was so memorable that it served as an inspiration for the U.S. aerial attack on Iraq on June 21, 2003. According to a report by Reuters:

U.S. troops psyched up on a bizarre musical reprise from Vietnam war film "Apocalypse Now" before crashing into Iraqi homes to hunt gunmen on Saturday, as Shi'ite Muslims rallied against the U.S. occupation of Iraq. With Wagner's "Ride of the Valkyries" still ringing in their ears and the clatter of helicopters overhead, soldiers rammed vehicles into metal gates and hundreds of troops raided houses in the western city of Ramadi after sunrise as part of a drive to quell a spate of attacks on U.S. forces.[20]

Lesser-known and more recent examples of the prominence of Wagner's music in soundtracks include Russell Mulcahy's science-fiction film *Highlander II: The Quickening* (1991) and Jonathan Glazer's mystery *Birth* (2004). In Glazer's film, the entire Prelude to the first act of Wagner's *Die Walküre* accompanies the most crucial moment of the film: the heroine Anna (Nicole Kidman) is at the opera house, but her mind is occupied with the ten-year-old boy she has just left behind, who claims that he is the reincarnation of her dead husband; the close-up of Anna's face—a long take with a fixed camera for about two minutes—shows us that she becomes convinced by the boy. Accompanying this opera-house scene is the diegetic performance of Wagner's turbulent Prelude played by the unseen (i.e., voice-off) orchestra. Wagner's music makes an equally indelible impression in *Highlander II*. The film begins with a slow pan toward the theater's red neon-lit signboard, which reads "OPERA," and in the middle of the panning, the first orchestral interlude of Act 1 of *Götterdämmerung* begins. When the panning pauses on an extreme close-up of "OPERA" on the signboard, it cuts to a close-up of the mouth of a singer who is performing Brünnhilde's song "Zu neuen Taten, teurer Helde" (To new deeds, dear hero). The camera pans from the stage to the balcony of the auditorium and shows the protagonist Connor MacLeod (Christopher Lambert) in a close-up. What follows is a series of cross-cuts between the opera performance and flashbacks as the protagonist recalls a past battle. The final flashback to the battle is accompanied by the concluding orchestral music of the "Immolation Scene": "bright flames" are everywhere in the battle, evoking what Wagner described for the last scene of *Götterdämmerung*, quoted above.[21]

Wagner's ambience extends to such a rare Showtime title as *The Twilight of the Golds* (1997), directed by Ross Kagan Marks. Based on Jonathan Tolins's Broadway play, the story of the film centers around the Gold family: gay director David Gold (Brendan Fraser) is staging Wagner's *Ring*, a "mini-Ring," and his parodic production of *Das Rheingold* appears as a diegetic performance near the end of the film. In children's film, too, Wagner is sonorous beyond the oft-cited cartoon *What's Opera, Doc?* In Danny DeVito's *Death to Smoochy* (2002), the "Ice Show Scene," the climax of the film which is entirely accompanied by an opera collage, opens with the "Liebestod," and "The Ride of the Valkyries" enters in the middle of the scene. BBC's animation *Operavox* (1996) contains another homage to Wagner. Similar to Don Boyd's *Aria* (1987), it consists of six abbreviated animated operas, each of which is directed by a different director, and *Das Rheingold* is one of the six operas. Directed by Graham Ralph, this twenty-seven-minute miniature *Rheingold* shows a radical visualization of the opera—"radical" for children—as Freia appears in a tight kinky-looking bikini costume. Another screen use of Wagner in the children's domain, although not a film but made for television, is "Pigoletto": an opera put on by the Muppets and Beverly Sills in episode 409 of *The Muppet Show* (1979), in which "The Ride of the Valkyries" is sung by Sills and Miss Piggy in their "battle" of the voice.[22]

Wagner's aura is not limited to film screen or soundtrack but also resonates in film ceremonies: at the 2004 Academy Awards, Julia Roberts presented a special video tribute to Katharine Hepburn in commemoration of her death in 2003, and it was the concluding orchestral music of *Götterdämmerung* that accompanied the final few minutes of the video. Even when Wagner's music is not heard, his inaudible presence looms large in such celebrated box-office hit film epics as George Lucas's *Star Wars* series (1980–2005), which the director called "space operas,"[23] and more recently, in Peter Jackson's trilogy *The Lord of the Rings* (2001–2003). In spite of Tolkien's adamant refusal of Wagner's influence on his work in declaring, "Both rings were round, and there the resemblance ceased," Jackson's trilogy made a significant contribution to the popularization of Wagnerian ambience in cinema for the general audience. On November 13, 2005, Carnegie Hall featured a "Double Ring" concert, consisting of excerpts from Wagner's *Ring* cycle and Howard Shore's score for the film trilogy; and Alex Ross's *New Yorker* article "The Ring and the Rings" saluted the affinities between Tolkien's/Jackson's epic and Wagner's tetralogy.[24] Also indicative of Wagner's kinship with cinema is Bayreuth's invitation of film directors to stage productions: for instance,

Werner Herzog, who directed *Lohengrin* in the late 1980s, and Lars von Trier, although he declined his invitation in 2004. Patrice Chéreau, who staged the much-discussed, controversial centennial production of the *Ring* cycle, is also a film director, renowned for *Queen Margot,* the winner of the Jury Prize at the 1994 Cannes Film Festival, and for *Son frère,* which earned him Best Director at the 2003 Berlin International Film Festival.

Given the historical manifestations of cinema's conspicuous evocation of Wagner and Bayreuth's attraction to film directors, Theodor Adorno's belligerent charge that film is the heir of Wagnerian music-drama has proven to be more than an ideologically biased diagnosis.[25] Despite the century-long aura of Wagner's influence in cinema, critical and analytical inquiries into this phenomenon were not active until the 1980s. More specifically, the year 1983, the centennial of the composer's death, stimulated scholarly and public attention to Wagnerism in cinema. The Wagner Film Festival was held in Venice, coinciding with the publication of Hansjörg Pauli's book *Wagner e il cinema* (Wagner and Cinema) and Ermanno Comuzio and Giuseppe Ghigi's ninety-three-page anthology, *L'Immagine in me nascosta—Richard Wagner: un itinerario cinematografico* (The Image Hidden within Me—Richard Wagner: A Journey in Film).[26] It was also in 1983 that Tony Palmer's nearly eight-hour epic biopic *Wagner* was produced and Norbert J. Schneider's article "Der Film—Richard Wagners 'Kunstwerk der Zukunft'?" (Film—Richard Wagner's 'Artwork of the Future'?) appeared.[27] Since the 1980s, the scholarship on Wagner and cinema has been steadily growing: to cite a few recent studies, Christoph Henzel's "Wagner und die Filmmusik" (2004); Carolyn Abbate's "Wagner, Cinema, and Redemptive Glee" (2006); Matthew Wilson Smith's "American Valkyries: Richard Wagner, D. W. Griffith, and the Birth of Classical Cinema" (2008);[28] and most recently, the special issue, "Wagner und Fantasy/Hollywood," of the journal *Wagner Spectrum* (November 2008).[29] David Levin's *Richard Wagner, Fritz Lang, and the Nibelungen* (1998) remains one of the few book-length studies.[30]

Recent studies tend to reconsider and demystify Wagner's apotheosized position in the genealogy of cinema: Scott D. Paulin deconstructs the "fetishistic Wagnerism" in cinema in his essay "Richard Wagner and the Fantasy of Cinematic Unity," while Christoph Henzel demonstrates how cinematic leitmotifs work differently from those of Wagnerian opera, suggesting that the recourse to Wagner among film music apologists is a handy legitimization of film as the "seventh muse" of the bourgeoisie rather than a cheap entertainment for the masses.[31] Because of the composer's pronounced anti-Semitism, which was amplified by the Nazis' appropriation of it, Wagner's resonance in cinema has been not only musical and aesthetic but also ideological. Perhaps that explains why the topic of Wagner in film music studies has drawn more attention and controversy than, say, Puccini, despite the more frequent appearance of the latter composer's "Nessun dorma" on blockbuster soundtracks than any of Wagner's excerpts over the past few decades.[32] The degree of racial implication suggested by Wagner's presence in film varies, ranging from the crude association with the K.K.K. in G. W. Griffiths's *The Birth of a Nation* (1915) to a subtle reference in Barbet Schroeder's *Reversal of Fortune* (1990): an almost inaudible cameo appearance (less than thirty seconds) of the "Liebestod" is followed shortly by a sarcastic racial compliment from the protagonist Claus von Bülow (another reference to Wagner!) to his Jewish attorney: "I should tell you that I have the greatest respect for the intelligence and the integrity of the Jewish people."

David Huckvale admits that it is hard to de-politicize Wagner,[33] but some scholars have shown how Wagner on soundtrack can be dissociated from his ideology. As Scott Paulin notes in his essay in this volume, Lutz Koepnick's reading of *Interrupted Melody* (1955), directed by Curtis Bernhardt, is one such example. In this biopic of Marjorie Lawrence, an Australian diva best known for her Wagnerian roles, the "Liebestod" is used at the end of the film for the moment when the diva overcomes her struggle with polio: she is performing *Tristan und Isolde* on stage in a wheelchair, and when she sings the climactic point of the "Liebestod"—"Weltatem" (World-Breath)—she stands up from the chair and walks a few steps toward Tristan's corpse. For Koepnick, this scene challenges Hollywood's "essentializing" treatment of Wagner as a signifier of ideological decadence, for his music here serves as a "cure" for the diva's physical decay (and for me, it is a visualization of what Friedrich Kittler has described Tristan's "acoustic erection").[34] Lawrence Kramer's essay "The *Lohengrin* Prelude and Anti-anti-Semitism" also provides an alternative reading of Wagner's ideological resonance on soundtrack.

He suggests that Chaplin's famous use of the *Lohengrin* prelude in *The Great Dictator* (1940) could be taken as "a flat refusal to hand Wagner's music over to his ideology," although it does not result in the complete disappearance of that ideology.[35]

The essays in this collection engage in a critical dialogue with existing studies, deconstructing and reconstructing Wagner's ambience in cinema—whether musical, ideological, or technological—extending and renovating current theories, and also proposing unexplored topics and new methodological perspectives. This volume does not attempt to provide some master narrative for researching Wagner and cinema: rather, you will find disagreement on certain issues even among its contributors. In this volume, the term "cinema" is used in the broad sense, not limited to film as a technique or medium but encompassing screen and multimedial engagement with Wagner, as in works such as Bill Viola's *Tristan Project*, Steve Reich's *Three Tales,* and *The Muppet Show.* It should also be noted that the term "opera" is sometimes used synonymously with "music-drama," and that the usage of "film score," "film music," and "film music studies" in this volume is much more flexible than that suggested in the inaugural issue of *The Journal of Film Music.*[36] Considering the growing academic and popular attention to Wagner and cinema, this collection must be a timely appearance: "Die Zeit ist da!" (The time is now!), to borrow Klingsor's words in *Parsifal.*

The collection is divided into five parts. Part 1 considers issues related to Wagner's presence in silent film. The first two essays focus on the affinities between Wagner's operatic technique and silent film practice in general, while the last two analyze Wagner's resonance in particular films. James Buhler attributes the popularity of Wagnerian-style accompaniment in silent film to the new demand for continuity editing (i.e., unobtrusive editing that creates the impression of logical and smooth shot changes, using time and space coherently), which was established around 1910 during the transition from what Tom Gunning has called the "cinema of attractions" to the "cinema of narrative integration."[37] Matthew Wilson Smith has also examined increasing calls for Wagnerian-style accompaniment during the same time period. While Smith situates "Wagner enthusiasm" in the context of steady "bourgeoisification" of the cinema,[38] Buhler focuses more on technical reasons, namely, how "the idea of the leitmotif helped musicians (and audiences) negotiate certain conceptual challenges posed by continuity editing." Buhler finds the greatest affinities between Wagnerian-style silent film accompaniment and the leitmotivic web of Wagner's music-drama in the "extra-diegetic reflection" of the music: "Just as the music to the silent film remained external to the world screened," he argues, the Wagnerian orchestra, when narrating through leitmotivs, occupies "a space outside the mimetic world of the stage." In chapter 2, Peter Franklin proposes that Wagner's aesthetics and works can be considered as forerunners of, although not models for, techniques associated with the construction of cinematic narrative in the early twentieth century. He traces Wagner's cinematic imagination to such materials as his stage directions and to descriptions of his operatic music and other composers' music, most notably Beethoven's symphonic work. For instance, Franklin points out how Wagner's account of the *Eroica*'s Scherzo is "intensely visualized," encouraging the reader and audience to "see" the music and permitting music "not only to narrate but also to acquire a . . . metadiegetic voice." He also demonstrates a link between Wagnerian "preludial" music and cinematic "titles."

Paul Fryer's essay is the first substantial study of Carl Froelich's feature-length (about ninety minutes) silent biopic, *The Life and Works of Richard Wagner* (1913). Giuseppe Becce (1877–1973), one of the most prolific early film music composers, not only scored the film but also played the title role.[39] According to the film's producer, Oskar Messter, Becce's score was the first music in Germany specifically written for film accompaniment. In the *Allgemeines Handbuch der Film-Musik* (1927), a guide to film music, Becce described the function of music in silent film as an element added "not organically, as an artistic device in its own right, but rather as an expedient solution to a practical problem."[40] Currently Froelich's film is not commercially available, but Fryer has reconstructed it from a print housed in a private film collection and added English subtitles and a new soundtrack scored by British composer Barry Seaman. Fryer's essay provides detailed historical and technological background about Froelich's biopic and the reconstruction process. He also compares the film to other Wagner- and opera-related silent films, such as Edwin S. Porter's *Parsifal* (1904), which is notable for its attempted musical synchronization by using the Edison Kinetophone—a primitive sound-mix system that provided recorded music on a cylinder phonograph.

Adeline Mueller examines three versions of Fritz Lang's two-part film *Die Nibelungen* (1924), focusing on their different scores: Gottfried Huppertz's original score that accompanied the premiere of the entire film (Part 1, *Siegfried,* and Part 2, *Kriemhilds Rache*); Hugo Riesenfeld's compilation score used for the American premier of Part 1 in 1925; and the soundtrack Huppertz revised for the 1933 German re-release of Part 1. Through her comparative analysis of the film's three versions, Mueller traces how the change in music demonstrates a different attitude to Wagner and in so doing sheds light on the complicated political milieu of the interwar period. She proposes that if the 1924 original film and Huppertz's original score can be associated with the spirit of German national pride, the American version and Riesenfeld's compilation score reflect "the postwar rehabilitation of Wagner." Pointing out Huppertz's changed characterization of Hagen in his 1933 revised score, which evokes Wagner's demonization of the character in contrast to the sympathetic portrayal of Gunther, Mueller suggests that this change makes sense when one considers the political change in Germany at that time—the emergence of the Third Reich.

Part 2 is devoted to Wagner's influence on specific film music composers. David Neumeyer focuses on Max Steiner, one of the best-known composers during the golden era of Hollywood's studio system (approximately 1930–60). Steiner was thoroughly conversant with the post-Wagnerian operatic milieu, for his grandfather owned an opera house and Richard Strauss and Gustav Mahler were among family friends when he lived in Vienna. Based on the comments that Steiner left in his sketches about specific passages in relation to operas by Wagner and Puccini, Neumeyer's essay explores how Steiner balanced the Wagnerian and post-Wagnerian conceptions of opera with underscoring methods derived from melodrama and operetta. One of the examples he investigates is *A Dispatch from Reuters* (1940), which contains an "operatic" scene created by maximizing the effect of the synchronized symphonic background music as a voiceover narrator—i.e., the Wagnerian symphonic web. Eva Rieger, too, discusses Wagnerian elements in Max Steiner's work but in a different context: the inheritance of Wagner's gendered musical language, especially its harmony and orchestration. Challenging Jean-Jacques Nattiez's claim for Wagner's "androgynous" treatment of his characters,[41] Rieger finds a strongly gender-laden semiotics of music in Wagner's operas. She argues that to the extent that gender studies are concerned with "male- and female-coded spheres" rather than simply "male or female figures," one can see interesting intersections between film music and Wagner's operas. Among the film scores Rieger analyzes are Max Steiner's *Mildred Pierce* (1945), Franz Waxman's *Rebecca* (1940), Bernard Herrmann's *Vertigo* (1958), and the score to Charlie Chaplin's *City Lights* (1931) that the director himself composed with help from Alfred Newman and Arthur Johnson.[42]

In the last chapter of part 2, William H. Rosar examines two science-fiction films from 1951: *The Thing from Another World,* scored by Dimitri Tiomkin, and *The Day the Earth Stood Still,* scored by Bernard Herrmann. Rosar traces Wagnerian influences in these scores from the perspective of the "numinous" in music. In the phenomenology of religion, Rudolf Otto defines the "numinous" as a sense of the otherworldly, exemplified in its crudest forms by awe and fear of the demonic, the uncanny, and the monstrous. Drawing on Otto's theory, Rosar regards the viewing of science-fiction films as a uniquely twentieth-century numinous experience and demonstrates how sci-fi film composers of the 1950s modeled their scoring on Wagner's music-dramas for the musical expression of the numinous.

As in part 2, the films considered in part 3 are also Hollywood products, but the focus is on those soundtracks which use Wagner's music more explicitly, if not as actual quotation or arrangement. Marcia J. Citron examines Jean Negulesco's Warner Bros. film *Humoresque* (1946), a noir melodrama about the obsessive and tragic love of Helen Wright (Joan Crawford) for the violinist protagonist Paul Boray (John Garfield). Citron's essay focuses on the film's final scene, which consists of a series of cross-cuts between Helen's beach house and Boray's diegetic concert; Helen commits suicide by walking into the ocean while Boray is performing the *Tristan and Isolde Fantasy,* Franz Waxman's arrangement of the "Liebestod" for violin and orchestra for the film. In this scene, Helen first hears the *Fantasy* from a radio broadcast at her beach house, but the music soon becomes non-diegetic. Citron examines an intriguing parallelism between the opera and the film in the characters of Isolde and Helen—specifically, between the opera heroine's ambiguous hearing, as suggested in the libretto ("Höre ich nur / diese Weise" [Do I alone hear this melody]), and that of the cinematic heroine—and shows how the visuals of the film's "Liebestod" sequence serve as a literal representation of the text and images of Wagner's song, and how the cinematic heroine "hears" what the operatic heroine is singing through the violin's wordless voice. Like Isolde, Helen hears what others cannot. So she speaks to Paul during her last telephone conversation with him before the "Liebestod" performance: "Oh listen, listen . . . What—you didn't hear."

The next three essays in part 3 explore ideological interactions between Wagner's music on soundtrack and on-screen events in light of Hollywood's politicization of Wagner. Marc A. Weiner's essay investigates how Ridley Scott's *Gladiator* (2000) establishes its central themes of a lost political utopia and the abuse of power within a modern dictatorship through visual and musical references to the Weimar Republic and Nazi Germany. Weiner's analysis of the film demonstrates that Wagner's music is the most prominent component of those references. There is no actual quotation in Hans Zimmer's film score, but some passages bear striking resemblance to Wagner's work: for instance, the music that accompanies the protagonist's crucial announcement, "My name is Gladiator," is an unmistakable evocation of Wagner's "Funeral March" from *Götterdämmerung*. Weiner demonstrates how Wagnerian-sounding passages support the film's references to modern German history not only through their typical underscoring function but also sometimes by serving as an "ironic, judgmental narrator." Weiner argues that *Gladiator* constitutes only one example of Hollywood blockbusters' use of Wagner, at least over the past quarter century, "as an emblem of his nation and of things associated with it in the modern American imagination."

Neil Lerner draws attention to the not-infrequent use of Wagner in Hollywood cartoons. Extending Daniel Goldmark's study, which focuses on *What's Opera, Doc?* and *Herr Meets Hare*, Lerner investigates Wagner's ideologically charged presence in another Warner Bros. cartoon, *Bugs Bunny Nips the Nips* (1944), which centers around Bugs Bunny's encounter with a series of Japanese soldiers on a Pacific island. The soundtrack of this cartoon contains two excerpts from *Die Walküre*—"The Ride of Valkyries" and the Tragic motif. Unlike *Gladi-*

ator and many other Hollywood-produced films, including the cartoons Goldmark analyzed, *Bugs Bunny Nips the Nips* associates Wagner not with Germany but with the United States—the victory of Bugs (symbolic of the United States) over the Japanese soldiers. Reading this idiosyncratic association as a reappropriation of Wagner in the context of U.S. nationalism during the war, Lerner suggests that the use of Wagner in *Bugs Bunny Nips the Nips* can fit within the larger project of dehumanizing and racializing the war enemy, which, according to John W. Dower's study, was not applied to European foes.

Scott D. Paulin provides another example of Hollywood's "revisionist" use of Wagner that moves away from the ideological clichés attached to the composer: Mitchell Leisen's Paramount feature *Golden Earrings* (1947), starring Marlene Dietrich. By analyzing Victor Young's score to the film, especially its explicit borrowings from Wagner's *Ring*, Paulin demonstrates how Leisen's film participates in the postwar denazification of Wagner, "piercing" the much-presumed assumptions about Wagner's ideological role in Hollywood film (hence Paulin's title, "Piercing Wagner: The *Ring* in *Golden Earrings*"). For a better contextualization of how Wagner's work is used in Leisen's film, Paulin provides a concise history of the cinematic association of Wagner with "loathsome Deutschtum," which predates the rise of National Socialism. The films included in his discussion range from such U.S. propaganda documentaries as Frank Capra's *Prelude to War* (1943) and *Your Job in Germany* (1945) to wartime feature films, including *Arise, My Love* (1940), *Reunion in France* (1942), and *Edge of Darkness* (1943). Paulin also reveals that according to silent-era cue sheets from around 1915 to the late 1920s in America, the "Nibelungen-Marsch," a potpourri of Wagner's leitmotifs created by Bayreuth bandmaster Gottfried Sonntag (1846–1921), was one of the most frequently used pieces of music in film accompaniment.

Part 4 continues with the focus on Wagner's ideological presence in film but shifts its geographical and cultural focus from Hollywood to German cinema. Roger Hillman investigates the New German Cinema, with particular attention to Syberberg's *Hitler, a Film from Germany* (a.k.a. *Our Hitler*, 1977), Edgar Reitz's three *Heimat* series (1984–2004), and selected documentaries of Werner Herzog, who has continued to engage with Wagner beyond the lifetime of the New German Cinema. Hillman argues that these films evoke Wagner, musically or otherwise, to redeem him from "Americanization" (most conspicuously through "The Ride of the Valkyries") and nazification. As an example, he analyzes Herzog's use of Wagner at the end of *Wings of Hope* (2000). In re-injecting Wagner with primordial mythical content, contends Hillman, "the music transcends the constraints of Germanic myth, and above all its reception as proto-Nazi and pan-Germanic."

Jeremy Tambling's essay focuses on Alexander Kluge, another director associated with the New German Cinema. Drawing on Kluge's notion of war as the caesura of emotions ("War, as a sensual-practical critic of emotion, defeats our feelings at all levels," wrote Kluge), Tambling explores two related topics: opera and cinema as a "power plant of emotions," and the city experience, especially of wartime cities. He re-reads Wagner's operas from these two perspectives and suggests that despite the wartime "devastation" of emotions evoked in Wagner's works, especially the *Ring* cycle, Kluge does not leave the composer behind; instead, the director uses Wagner to redeem cinema from the hegemony of feeling manufactured by Hollywood and show why emotions are not powerless. One of the examples Tambling discusses is Kluge's *The Power of Emotions* (1983): in its opening scene, accompanied by the *Parsifal* Prelude, Wagner's music demonstrates the power of emotions ironically through the coalition between the opera's mythical time and the time of the modern city—Frankfurt—depicted in the visuals.

In the last essay of part 4, Joy H. Calico examines Joachim Herz's cinematic production of *Der fliegende Holländer* (1964), the first feature-length Wagner opera on film. Drawing attention to the historical singularity of Herz's film as an East German cultural artifact (produced by DEFA, East Germany's state-owned and only film company), Calico provides at the beginning of the essay an overview of opera and film culture in East Germany up to the mid-1960s and Wagner's place in it. Her analysis of the film focuses on Herz's re-gendered portrayal of Senta and the film's affinities with horror film, especially F. W. Murnau's silent *Nosferatu* (1922). After demonstrating how Herz rescues Senta from "the bourgeois constraints of patriarchal expectation," Calico discusses horror film elements—the undead—in Herz's film with reference to studies of the relationship between Wagner and vampires, as explored by such scholars as Slavoj Žižek, Simon Williams, and David Huckvale.[43] She argues for the function of Wagner's opera as a Trojan horse: horror was not among DEFA's approved genres but it was acceptable when it entered the East German screen in the guise of German high culture.

Part 5 addresses issues regarding Wagner's cinematic presence beyond the soundtrack. Elisabeth Bronfen traces such a presence in film noir, focusing on the *Liebestod* trope. Her concept of film noir follows that of Paul Schrader, who uses the term less as a genre than as a product of a specific period of film history—the 1940s and '50s—which not only portrayed the dark world of crime and corruption but also harked back to gangster films and German Expressionist crime films of the 1930s. Extending her previous study "Noir Wagner," which investigated how Wagner's *Tristan und Isolde* has been translated into the scripts and visual language of Hollywood film noir,[44] Bronfen in this volume explores not only the cultural survival of the Wagnerian couple in film noir but also the influence of the late romantic pathos of Wagner's *Tristan und Isolde* on film noir's negotiation of the transition between wartime and peace. Giorgio Biancorosso examines Luchino Visconti's *Ludwig* (1971), a biopic of Wagner's devoted patron, in which the composer himself appears as a character played by Trevor Howard. Visconti's film is another site where *Tristan* looms large beyond the sonic realm of soundtrack: here as both a historical event (Wagner's struggle to have it staged) and a symbolic, oblique presence in the narration. By investigating the interactions between the two layers of *Tristan*'s presence, Biancorosso analyzes how Wagner's music contributes to Visconti's nostalgic reconstruction of nineteenth-century aristocratic culture. He contextualizes his analysis of *Tristan* in *Ludwig* in the larger issue that film music studies has been engaged with: far from merely recycling ready-made meanings, he argues, preexisting music participates in "the process of emergence that characterizes the meaning of music/image relationships in multimedia."

The final two essays in part 5 are devoted to Bill Viola's *Tristan Project,* which was first produced as a concert performance in Los Angeles in 2004 and in 2005 was staged by Peter Sellars at the Paris Opera. Jeongwon Joe's essay addresses Viola's aesthetic and philosophical focus on time and sound, which creates a special kinship between his visual art and music. "Music is all about the rhythmical structuring of time," states Viola, and he identifies Sellars's masterly understanding and handling of the time-based arts as a major motivation for his decision to collaborate with this stage director for *The Tristan Project,* Viola's first venture into opera. It is in this context that Joe explores the interplay between Wagner's musical rhythm and Viola's visually articulated temporality. Drawing on Jonathan Kramer's theory of time in music and Adorno's ideologically charged critique of Wagner's temporal world, she argues that Viola's images can be considered a visual articulation and underscoring of Wagner's temporality, as expressed in his music, libretto, and ideology. In his *New Yorker* article, Alex Ross wrote: "Viola's images seemed to arise from the subconscious of the score." For Joe, the subconscious of the score is the temporal elements of the opera. She traces the temporal affinities between Wagner and Viola to the commonality in their artistic and philosophical—and by extension, ideological—positions, one of which is their privileging of myth over history and the consequent emphasis on universality.

Lawrence Kramer's essay focuses on a different aspect of the interaction between Wagner's *Tristan und Isolde* and Viola's *Tristan Project*: how the sensorial world of Wagner's opera is translated into Viola's *Project,* which he calls the "double *Tristan.*" Like Citron in part 3, Kramer addresses the delirious interplay, or rapturous rupture, between hearing and seeing in the "Liebestod," in which Isolde sees through her ears: "Freunde! Seht! / Fühlt und seht ihr's nicht? / Höre ich nur diese Weise / Die so wundervolle und leise?" (Friends! Look! / Do you not feel and see it? / Can it be that I alone / Hear this mild and wondrous tune?). For Kramer, Wagner's *Tristan* is the opera "par excellence about that which cannot be seen," and in a sense this opera cannot be seen at all. He finds it an irony that in *The Tristan Project,* sight remains a sound in spite of Viola's gigantic moving images, and contextualizes this irony in the Lacanian intervention in the field of perception: the double *Tristan* "opens onto the Lacanian threshold of the visible world because it is no longer a presentation of its amatory narrative or the symbolic repercussions thereof, at least not primarily, but an intervention that touches on the field of vision, besieged by music, just where the view is blocked." Kramer argues that the true author of the double *Tristan* is neither Wagner nor Viola but "the logic of the senses by which both of them were inexorably drawn."

Joseph Horowitz defines "Wagnerism" as the multifarious "faces" of Wagner: "Wagner is a bewilderingly protean figure. Is there another artist who wears so many faces?"[45] Cinema is certainly one of those faces, and it has brought Wagner closer to our everyday life, making him sometimes unabashedly resonant (as in Elmer Fudd's "Kill the Wabbit") or sometimes surreptitiously looming (as in the cameo appearance of the "Liebestod" in *Reversal of Fortune*). As mentioned earlier, Wagner's cinematic imagination is not unprecedented, and in movie theaters during the sound era and television, Puccini's "Nessun dorma" and Bizet's *Carmen* have been as sonorous as, if not more than, Wagner's "Ride of Valkyries." (Denyce Graves sings "Habanera" as a bedtime lullaby for Elmo in Episode 4078 of *Sesame Street,* and "Nessun dorma" was Paul Potts's winning song at the 2007 premiere season of *Britain's Got Talent,* a British equivalent to *American Idol*).[46] If Wagner's presence in cinema has been the most widely recognized, celebrated, and deconstructed, then it is a meaningful task to direct our inquiry into "Why Wagner?" as Sander Gilman titled the symposium he organized in Chicago in 1997. This volume provides several possible answers (in the case of *Carmen,* for instance, it's not the composer Bizet but his work *Carmen* that has been the focus of study).[47] The filmography of this volume shows that myriad titles remain to be explored. Although not complete by any means, it is quite extensive, including about 150 titles. It does not include silent films, but Scott Paulin's postscript provides some information about the cue sheets and cinema music collections relevant to research on Wagner in the silent era.[48] In the postlude, Warren M. Sherk introduces invaluable archival sources available at libraries associated with the film industry, focusing on the Margaret Herrick Library of the Academy of Motion Picture and Sciences. In so doing he sheds light on how those sources can illuminate research on Wagnerism in cinema, with occasional reference to the use of opera in film in general. Sherk even suggests some possible research topics related to certain specific archival materials—for instance, censorship issues related to the making of *Magic Fire* (1955), a biopic of Wagner directed by William Dieterle, which can be traced through the documents from the Production Code Administration (PCA).

One of the joys in researching cinema-related topics is that a variety of people can be your informants and supporters, as cinema is such a prevalent and powerful popular entertainment that permeates everybody's life. The informants for this volume range from the then director of the International Office at the University of Nevada in Reno, Margaret Hellworth, who brought to my attention Ross Kagan Marks's rare title *The Twilight of the Golds,* to my full-time-housewife friend Sookim Lee in Korea, who introduced me to the BBC animation *Operavox,* which is still little known in academia. Looking back, my job interview with the then dean of my school, Douglas Lowry, was prophetic, for he brought up the topic of Wagner and cinema, on which we spent almost the entire time of the interview.

I finished the final editing of this volume in a hospital room while nursing my mother after her emergency surgery. Her principal doctor, a devoted opera and movie fan, was so intrigued by my topic that he made special arrangements to move a spare desk in his office into my mother's room, so that I could put my laptop on it and have a proper work station (but on the condition that I give him a summary of each essay in the collection, one per day until my mother was released from the hospital). He even let me view his copy of *Revenge of the Sith,* the only episode of the *Star Wars* series I had not watched, mentioning that after hearing about my project he could see some Wagnerian elements in this episode, such as a parallelism between the two pairs of twins: Sigmund and Sieglinde in Wagner and Luke and Leia, Darth Vader's (and Padmé's) twin children in *Star Wars.* Despite Tolkien's rigid denial of Wagner's influence on *The Lord of the Rings,* or even in a film unrelated to Wagner, such as Bastian Clevé's ten-minute short *Götterdämmerung* (1974), it seems that people can hear and see multifaceted resemblances between Wagner and cinema—between the *Ring* and the *Rings*—beyond the roundness of the rings. Tolkien was wrong; Viola is right: "It's hard to avoid Wagner's latent presence." This volume intends to promote more dialogue for the growing community of people who are interested in Wagnerism in cinema, pro or contra—or, one might say, to promote "The Fellowship of the *Ring* and the *Rings.*"[49]

NOTES

I wish to thank my research assistants Tom Kernan, Leah Branstetter, and Regina Compton for their invaluable help—intellectual, technological, and much else—in the preparation of this volume.
    The first epigraph is quoted in Alex Ross, "The Ring and the Rings—Wagner vs. Tolkien," *The New Yorker,* December 22, 2003, 161. The second epigraph is from

Theodor Adorno, *In Search of Wagner,* trans. Rodney Livingstone (London: NLB, 1981), 107 (originally published as *Versuch über Wagner* [Berlin: Suhrkamp Verlag, 1952]). The third epigraph is quoted from my interview with Bill Viola on May 4, 2007, at the Rubin Museum in New York City. For the full interview, see the appendix of this volume.

1. Hans-Jürgen Syberberg, *Hitler, a Film from Germany,* trans. Joachim Neugroschel (New York: Farrar, Strauss and Giroux, 1982), 19.

2. Randall Packer and Ken Jordan, eds. *Multi Media: From Wagner to Virtual Reality* (New York: W. W. Norton & Co., 2001), xxi–xxii.

3. Quoted in Mary Ann Smart, *Mimomania: Music and Gesture in Nineteenth-Century Opera* (Berkeley: University of California Press, 2004), 177.

4. Patrick Carnegy, *Wagner and the Art of the Theatre* (New Haven, Conn.: Yale University Press, 2006), 111–12.

5. Martin van Amerongen, *Wagner: A Case History,* trans. Stewart Spencer and Dominic Cakebread (New York: George Braziller, 1984), 44.

6. Friedrich Kittler, "World-Breath: On Wagner's Media Technology," in *Opera through Other Eyes,* ed. David Levin (Stanford: Stanford University Press, 1994), 231.

7. Matthew Wilson Smith, *The Total Work of Art: From Bayreuth to Cyberspace* (New York: Routledge, 2007); for Packer and Jordan, see n. 2.

8. Carnegy, *Wagner and the Art of the Theatre* (New Haven and London: Yale University Press, 2006), 111.

9. W. Stephen Bush, "Giving Musical Expression to the Drama," *The Moving Picture World,* August 12, 1911, 354. Bush was a major contributor to *The Moving Picture World,* one of the first motion picture trade papers published in the United States. In this journal, Clarance E. Sinn, a film accompanist, had a regular column, "Music for the Picture," from 1910 to 1916. For more information about Bush's contribution to the journal, see Richard Stromgren, "The Moving Picture World of W. Stephen Bush," *Film History* 2, no. 1 (Winter 1988): 13–22.

10. Quoted in Matthew Wilson Smith, "American Valkyries: Richard Wagner, D. W. Griffith, and the Birth of Classical Cinema," *Modernism/Modernity* 15, no. 2 (April 2008): 229.

11. Quoted in ibid., 230.

12. A good source for the American reception of Wagner is Joseph Horowitz, *Wagner Nights: An American History* (Berkeley: University of California Press, 1994).

13. For detailed information about Porter's film, see Kevin J. Harty, *The Reel Middle Ages* (Jefferson: McFarland & Company, Inc., Publishers, 1999), 383–84; and the same author's "Cinema Arthuriana: An Overview," in *Cinema Arthuriana,* ed. Kevin J. Harty (Jefferson: McFarland & Co., 2002), 7–8. Porter's film is briefly discussed in chapter 3 of this volume.

14. Porten produced another *Lohengrin* short in 1910.

15. While Capellani's film is dated 1909 in Ken Wlaschin's *Encyclopedia of Opera on Screen* (New Haven, Conn.: Yale University Press, 2004), both the Internet Movie Database (http://www.imdb.com) and another online source, The Complete Index to World Film (http://www.citwf.com), date it as 1911.

16. Bertini's popularity continued during the sound era. After the end of World War II, the Fox Film Corporation in Hollywood offered a contract to her but she declined. She made her last appearance in Bernardo Bertolucci's *Novecento* (1976).

17. Ulrich Müller includes Porten's 1907 *Lohengrin*, which is about three minute long, in the listing of the film versions of Wagner's stage works, but considering its length, this information is misleading. See Ulrich Müller, "Wagner in Literature and Film," in *Wagner Handbook,* ed. Ulrich Müller and Peter Wapnewski (Cambridge, Mass.: Harvard University Press, 1992), 390. The music-video type of opera short was quite popular in both Europe and the United States during the first three decades of the twentieth century. Among the U.S. examples are *Caro nome* (1926, sung by Marion Tolley), *Vesti la giubba* (1926, sung by Giovanni Martinelli), and *Between the Acts at the Opera* (1926, sung by The Howard Brothers, Wille and Eugene Howard), all of which were directed by Edwin B. DuPar and produced by the Vitaphone Corporation. For more information about the Vitaphone project, see Ron Hutchinson, "The Vitaphone Project: Answering Harry Warner's Question, 'Who the Hell Wants To Hear Actors Talk?'" *Film History* 14, no. 1 (2002): 40–46.

18. Richard Evidon, "Film," in *Oxford Music Online: The New Grove Dictionary of Opera,* http://www.oxfordmusiconline.com (accessed September 10, 2008). Adeline Mueller informed me of the following four titles of pre-Lang adaptations of Nibelungen: 1) *Siegfried: Schmiedelied* (Forging Song) (1905), an experimental sound film directed by Oskar Messter; 2) *Die Nibelungenring* (1912), produced by Express Film Co.; 3) *I Nibelunghi* (1910, unknown director); and 4) Arrigo Frusta's *L'Epopeia dei Nibelunghi* (1913). Mueller's sources are http://www.filmportal.de for the first two titles, and Andreas Wirwalski, *Wie macht man einen Regenbogen? Fritz Langs Nibelungenfilm: Fragen zur Bildhaftigkeit des Films und seiner Rezeption* (Berlin: Peter Lang, 1994) for the last two titles.

19. Based on the information in http://www.bohemianopera.com/classicmov home.htm, a website about the use of classical music in film (accessed September 14, 2006).

20. Quoted in Smith, "American Valkyries," 221.

21. The flashbacks explain how Connor became exiled from the planet Ziest, his homeworld, and degenerated from immortal status to mortal; hence a narrative as well as musical connection to Wagner's *Götterdämmerung.*

22. "Pigoletto" is available on YouTube, http://www.youtube.com/ watch?v=f4jXBpPwJvo (accessed September 11, 2008).

23. Quoted in Gary Tomlinson, "Film Fantasy, Endgame of Wagnerism," in *Metaphysical Song: An Essay on Opera* (Princeton: Princeton University Press, 1999), 145. A good source for the study of the Wagnerian elements in the *Star Wars* series is Kristian Evensen's online article, "The *Star Wars* Series and Wagner's *Ring*: Structural, Thematic and Musical Connections," http://www.trell.org/wagner/ starwars.html (accessed September 11, 2008). In Graham Ralph's "Rheingold" episode in *Operavox,* Wagner is evoked through *Star Wars,* as the episode's opening intertitles imitate the signature perspective intertitles of the *Star Wars* episodes, which move and disappear into the galaxy.

24. Alex Ross, "The Ring and the Rings—Wagner vs. Tolkien," 161–62, 164–65.

25. Adorno, *In Search of Wagner,* 107.

26. Hansjörg Pauli, *Wagner e il cinema* (Torino: Assessorato all Cultura, 1983); Ermanno Comuzio and Giuseppe Ghigi, *L'Immagine in me nascosta—Richard Wagner: un itinerario cinematografico* (Venice: Comune di Venezia, 1983). Among the essays included in Comuzio and Ghigi's collection are "Wagner, Verdi e il film" by Darius Milhaud; "Genealogia dell'avvenire e musica dell'inesprimible: il cinema secondo Syberberg" by Paolo Bertetto; and "Visconti e Wagner" by Comuzio. It also includes Ghigi's eleven-page filmography (60–70).

27. Norbert J. Schneider, "Der Film—Richard Wagners 'Kunstwerk der Zukunft'?" in *Richard Wagner und die Musikhochschule München, die Philosophie, Die Dramaturgie, die Bearbeitung, der Film,* Schriftenreihe der Hochschule für Musik München 4 (Regensburg: Gustav Bosse, 1983), 123–50.

28. Christopher Henzel, "Wagner und die Filmmusik," *Acta Musicologica* 76, no. 1 (2004): 89–115; Carolyn Abbate, "Wagner, Cinema, and Redemptive Glee," *The Opera Quarterly* 21 (2005): 597–611; Smith, "American Valkyries," 221–42.

29. The essays in the special issue of *Wagner Spectrum* are Alex Ross, "Der Herr der Ringe und Der Ring des Nibelungen—Tolkien und Wagner"; Albrecht Riethmüller, "'All in the Family'—Cosima und Richard Wagner auf der Leinwandbühne von William Dieterle und Ken Russel"; Tobias Plebuch, "Richard Wagner im Film bis 1945"; Claudius Reinke, "Richard Wagner im Film nach 1945"; Rüdiger Görner, "Rheintöchter an der Themse—oder: zur Bedeutung von G. B. Shaws Wagner-Kritiken"; Holger Reiner Stunz, "Richard Wagners Partituren als Spielball der Zeitgeschichte—Eine Spurensuche"; Johanna Dombois, "Das Auge, das sich wechselnd öffnet und schließt—Zur Szenographie des Wagner-Vorhangs"; and Sue Cole and Kerry Murphy, "Wagner in the Antipodes."

30. David J. Levin, *Richard Wagner, Fritz Lang, and the Nibelungen: The Dramaturgy of Disavowal* (Princeton: Princeton University Press, 1988). Solveig Olsen produced a book-length study on Syberberg's *Parsifal* (1982); see Olsen, *Hans Jürgen Syberberg and His Film of Wagner's* Parsifal (New York and Toronto: University Press of America, 2006). Olsen regards this opera-film as a turning point in Syberberg's oeuvre. She explores the film in light of Wolfram von Eschenbach's medieval romance as well as Wagner's opera, especially its staging history. In her hermeneutic approach, Olsen draws upon diverse theories, including Jungian psychology, Lucien Dällenbach's mirror theory, Masonic studies, Hindu mythology, alchemical symbolism, and Jewish mysticism; in so doing, she provides a wide range of perspectives from which not only Syberberg's film but also Wagner's opera can be interpreted.

31. Scott D. Paulin, "Richard Wagner and the Fantasy of Cinematic Unity: The Idea of the *Gesamtkunstwerk* in the History and Theory of Film Music," in *Music and Cinema,* ed. James Buhler, Caryl Flinn, and David Neumeyer (Middletown, Conn.: Wesleyan University Press, 2000), 58–84. For Henzel, see n. 28.

32. Based on information from a website on the use of classical music in film; see n. 19.

33. David Huckvale, "The Composing Machine: Wagner and Popular Culture," in *A Night in at the Opera: Media Representations of Opera,* ed. Jeremy Tambling (London: John Libby & Co., 1994), 134.

34. See n. 6.

35. Lawrence Kramer, "Contesting Wagner: The *Lohengrin* Prelude and Anti-anti-Semitism," *19th-Century Music* 25, nos. 2–3 (Autumn 2001–Spring 2002): 205.

36. William H. Rosar, "Film Music—What's in a Name?" *The Journal of Film Music* 1 (2002): 1–18

37. Tom Gunning, "The Cinema of Attraction: Early Film, Its Spectators and the Avant-Garde," *Wide Angle* 8, nos. 3–4 (1986): 63–70.

38. Smith, "American Valkyries," 227.

39. Ludwig II was played by Ernst Reicher, Cosima by Olga Engl, Minna Planer by Manny Ziener, and Mathilde Wesendonck by Miriam Horwitz.

40. Quoted in Susanne Aschenbrandt, "Of Fitting Music and Music Made to Fit," trans. Clive Williams, in the program note for *Giuseppe Becce: Music for the Silent Movie* (1913) (CD), KOCH International GumH 3-6495-2, 1997. Although there is no actual quotation, Becce's score makes use of some of the materials from Wagner's operas, including the Prelude to *Das Rheingold* and the "Funeral March" from *Götterdämmerung*.

41. Jean-Jacques Nattiez, *Wagner Androgyne: A Study in Interpretation* (Princeton: Princeton University Press, 1993).

42. Chaplin's original score was partially restored and arranged in 1989 by Timothy Brock, who restored and conducted other Chaplin scores, including *Modern Times* (1936), *The Circus* (1928), and *A Dog's Life* (1918). Brock provided a complete restoration and rearrangement of *City Lights* in 2004. For an interview with Brock, see http://www.charliechaplin.com/en/categories/7-Music/articles/133-Restoration-of-City-Lights-score (accessed November 14, 2008). Chaplin wrote, "The day I completed my current picture *City Lights* was one of extreme relief. After fretting and stewing for almost two years, to see the end in sight was like the finish of a marathon. Usually after each picture I go to bed for a day or two to replenish my nerves, but this time there was another task ahead—the composing of music and synchronizing it to the picture" (ibid.). For more information about Chaplin's film scoring, see Marc Shulgold, "Composer Restores Chaplin's Score to Not-So-Silent Film *City Lights*," *Rocky Mountain News*, http://www.rockymountainnews.com/news/2008/nov/12/composer-restores-chaplins-score-to-not-so-film/ (accessed November 14, 2008).

43. See chapter 14, n. 37 through n. 41.

44. Elisabeth Bronfen, "Noir Wagner," in *Sexuation*, ed. Renata Salecl (Durham, N.C.: Duke University Press, 2000), 170–215.

45. Horowitz, *Wagner Nights*, 1. A recent testimony to Wagner's "bewildering" presence in popular culture is Manowar's 2002 heavy metal album *Warriors of the World*, which contains two tributes to Wagner: "Valhalla" and "The March." The band cites Wagner as "the father of heavy metal." The band's bassist Joey DeMaio notes, "Wagner's music changed my life many years ago. I don't know if I could live another day without the feeling his music gives me. He was the greatest composer ever. He invented metal." Quoted in the draft of Leah Branstetter's master's thesis, "Angels and Arctic Monkeys: A Study of Pop-Opera Crossover" (in progress at the University of Cincinnati). For the original quote, see Manowar, "Biography," http://manowar.com/biography.html (accessed February 17, 2009).

46. For YouTube clip of Graves's "Habanera," see http://www.youtube

.com/watch?v=zZFmNJjv1LM; for Paul Potts, see http://www.youtube.com/watch?v=1ko8yxu57NA&NR=1 (accessed May 25, 2008).

47. One of the most recent and comprehensive studies on *Carmen* on screen is Chris Perriam and Ann Davies, eds., *Carmen: From Silent Film to MTV* (New York: Rodopi, 2005).

48. The filmography is an expansion of the fifty-nine titles included in http://www.bohemianopera.com/classicmovhome.htm (accessed September 14, 2006).

49. The "Wagner and Cinema Festival" is scheduled for June 5–6, 2009, at the University of Cincinnati's College-Conservatory of Music. Festival events include the screening of Carl Froelich's 1913 Wagner biopic, as reconstructed by Paul Fryer, and a cinema-concert conducted by Mark Gibson, in which a selection of Wagner's music will be performed with a film montage created by Tony Palmer. The musical excerpts and the film montage will focus on the theme of "Redemption through Love," as expressed in Wagner's work.

PART ONE

Wagner and the Silent Film

ONE

Wagnerian Motives:
Narrative Integration and the Development
of Silent Film Accompaniment, 1908–1913

JAMES BUHLER

It was around 1910 that the idea of accompanying films à la Wagner first became prominent in the trade paper discourse. Indeed, Wagner's name was invoked almost as soon as the trade papers started to give regular attention to music. In April 1910, for instance, an article in *The Moving Picture World* optimistically stated: "Just as Wagner fitted his music to the emotions, expressed by words in his operas, so in the course of time, no doubt, the same thing will be done with regard to the moving pictures."[1] Later that year, the paper began running a regular column on accompanying film. In an early column, one reader wrote:

> When playing the pictures myself, I follow the rules laid down by the great R. Wagner in his splendid music dramas, by using the leading motives of the "Nibelungen Ring," "Tristan und Isolde," etc. I attach a certain theme to each person in the picture and work them out, in whatever form the occasion may call for, not forgetting to use popular strains if necessary.[2]

Responding to this letter, Clarence Sinn, the author of the column, was somewhat circumspect. First of all, he noted the problem of finding a good definition of leitmotivic technique: "The letters of Richard Wagner, and his biographers, are voluminous on his [thematic] methods, but I can find nothing sufficiently condensed to quote in this page, or in several pages, for the matter of that." He then ventured a general definition.

> Boiled down, it amounts to something like this: To each important character, to each important action, motive, or idea, and to each important object (Siegmund's sword, for example), was attached a suggestive musi-

cal theme. Whenever the action brought into prominence, any of the characters, motives, or objects, its theme or motif was sung or played.[3]

While on the surface Sinn seemed approving of the technique,[4] he recognized a thoroughly practical difficulty: "To apply it thoroughly, one must know his pictures thoroughly beforehand. . . . Given an analytical mind, five years of experience, and opportunity to study the pictures beforehand, any informed pianist ought to be able to get good results."[5] But pianists rarely had such time to *see* the films before they played them the first time, much less study them. Programs often changed daily, and rarely played at a theater more than three consecutive days.[6] The course of his discussion took a turn away from Wagner at this point and toward melodrama, a closer antecedent and better model, he seemed to believe, to the accompaniment practice under debate. Sinn wrote:

> I have touched upon this thematic idea several times in previous articles, although I was merely following the old melodramatic form of attaching a certain easily remembered melody to each of the principal characters. The germ of the idea is much the same, though of a simple and primitive form. . . . The "leading lady" had some pathetic melody, which accompanied her throughout the play. Likewise the leading man in scenes when he was the central figure. The villain also came in for his share of "heavy" music for his entrances and big scenes. Other music was neutral or descriptive, according to scenes and action.[7]

Here, even as the practice of accompanying films was in the process of being defined, Sinn already recognized both the difficulty of drawing a method of leitmotivic accompaniment from Wagner's writings and the much closer affinity playing the pictures had with melodrama technique than with Wagner (leaving aside the issue of whether and to what extent Wagner might have drawn on such melodramatic codes and practices).[8]

It is hardly by chance that calls for Wagnerian-style accompaniment coincided with the establishment of continuity editing, a means of regulating cuts so that segments of film were joined into seemingly logical sequences that served to give perspective to the story world. Such editing, part of the evolving system of narrative integration,[9] transformed film from a mimetic image of a world reproduced into a diegetic image of a represented world. As attested to by many period accounts complaining about the difficulty of following films, this shift was quite disorienting and challenged filmgoers' understanding of the medium. "What is it all about? Very fine, but what does it mean?" one patron to Edison's *Ingomar the Barbarian* (1908) mused.[10]

Narrative integration displaced an earlier system of filmic storytelling based on recording events placed before the camera. With a filmed (reproduced) stage drama under that earlier system, the coherence of the story existed in the staging, not in the filmmaking, which served only to make as clear a recording of the performance as possible. The world was captured in the camera rather than constructed through it, for ideally the pictures spoke for themselves. If the film was incoherent, the story unclear, that was the fault of the actors and directors, not the passive and objective camera. This objectivity of *filmic* meaning was vested in what James Lastra calls "an ontology of recording,"[11] and one barrier to recognizing the representational capacities of the camera lay in the fact that any turn to representation destabilized this objectivity.[12]

The gain in perspective of the new system of storytelling brought with it a loss of objectivity. When the concept of editing film replaced that of joining film strips, the camera was no longer objectively anchored in one spot; it began to move around. Such editing broke down space, analyzed it on the basis of diegetic representation. Edits, gaps between shots marked by the cut, became fissures across which meaning had to leap. Moreover, with the introduction of editing patterns and subjective framings, the means of presenting a story became open to choice; many different shots could serve the same basic narrative function.[13] Such functional equivalency, however, is another name for subjectivization. The emergence of rhetoric and style at the level of technique and the concomitant shift of the status of the director from technician to that of an artist were indications that film was becoming a medium of self-expression and subjective articulation rather than one of objective presentation. Where the reduction of the filmic to the pro-filmic offered a stable meaning, objective and determined, the understanding of the filmic as diegetic opened the Pandora's box of meaning. What had once seemed orderly and harmonious now seemed mobile, chaotic, contingent. Subjectivity seemed to portend incoherence.[14]

The early system of narrative film relied for the most part on long, static shots, and used distant shot scales that focused on the tableau rather than the presence of character. The system of narrative integration, by contrast, generally used somewhat closer shots, which brought more focus to character and so by extension emphasized the character's muteness. There were two basic responses to this muteness. One was a turn to the voice.[15] Vernon C. Lee, among others, urged the adoption of the lecturer:[16]

> Let the picture theater, therefore, keep in its place; not show what is being shown every day on the stage, but entertain its patrons with pictures which will hold their interest from the time they enter until they leave. But also, let them *understand* what they see; let them fully comprehend the meaning of every link of the film as it is being shown, and this can only be accomplished by the aid of a lecture.[17]

Yet the lecturer was a problematic figure whose presence belied film's loss of objectivity. The lecturer spoke, therefore the pictures did not speak for themselves, and narrative sense appeared external to the film, a product of the lecturer rather than the film.[18]

The other response to the muteness was music, which proved more effective in disguising its work of narrative integration. Whereas the lecturer still talked to the audience, the musician played to the picture. Music therefore allowed narrative sense to appear internal to the film since (instrumental) music lacked words even when a musician was also present in the theater making the notes. In other words, music accomplished its work in such a way that the narrative simply seemed to make sense; the pictures spoke for themselves. In this way, music allegorized the loss of voice as an affective value: it acknowledged the inability of the screen to speak for itself while also refusing to speak for the screen.

But the sound in the theater was at first too noisy to hear the muteness of the film. Indeed, as the system of continuity editing began to emerge, musical accompaniment, when it played the picture at all, at first underscored the ontology of recording. In fact, music was generally understood as an "added attraction" rather than the form of accompanying the images that it would later become. Rick Altman has made the point that when conceived as an added attraction, music was basically indifferent to the film.[19] Players might link music to the pictures through song titles or it might be deployed as a sound effect, what we would now characterize as "diegetic" music.[20] A shot of a dance, marching soldiers, or a piano playing in a saloon, for instance, would be accompanied by appropriate music (e.g., a waltz, march, or rag, respectively). In either case, the player scanned the image, looking for opportunities to add music, a mode of accompaniment that accorded with what Noël Burch refers to as "topographical reading."[21] A similar approach was taken by the drummer (the person responsible for the sound effects). This procedure, though obviously imperfect, worked well enough under the ontology of recording. In essence, the accompaniment simply attempted to reproduce sounds the image suggested. The important thing here is that this placed no demand on the player to choose details pertinent to the story. It was the relationship to the image, not to the story or character, that counted.

Whatever its appeal in the theater, topographical reading did not, really could not, address the disorientations of continuity editing. Indeed, it often compounded the disorientation by drawing attention to arbitrary details.[22] In 1910, H. F. Hoffman pointed to a love scene for which the drummer chose to render the sound of horses walking in the background "with a keenness that soon attracts the attention of the audience to the horse's feet and away from the actors."[23] Instead, Hoffman thought the drummer should parse the image for narrative pertinence so as not to distract or confuse the audience. Indeed, Hoffman went on to add: "[I]f you err in sound effects it is better to err on the side of silence."[24] No effects were preferable to those that confused the story, no matter how realistically suited they might be for the image. W. Stephen Bush was even more explicit: "Each picture must be studied by itself and only such effects introduced as have a psychological bearing on the situation as depicted on the screen."[25] The role of sound reflected the changing ontology of film: what was important was clarity of the representation, not fidelity to the reproduction. As Bush astutely noted, this ontology of representation also entailed a turn to the psychological subject.

The shift in music was even more pronounced. Like Hoffman, Sinn sought to break musicians of the habit of reading the image topographically for possibilities of sound illustration and instill in them a dedication to the narrative point. "I have noticed a tendency among some pianists to play to the *details* of a picture rather than to the *story* itself."[26] Instead, music should underscore a narrative line that enforces a hierarchical organization of the image space, where the image is decoded musically for narrative pertinence. The player, Sinn suggested, "must fix on the predominant theme of a picture and work to that."[27] Thus what a player should look for in a scene is its thematic focal point (usually a character) and bring that to the fore, leaving non-pertinent details musically unmarked. Elements that are mere "accessories" to a scene—the contingent details—should not receive the undue attention of being marked musically.

Sinn offered as an example a scene where a general and his staff briefly receive an Indian messenger. The music, Sinn said, should acknowledge the Indian only if his presence was important to the narrative. Otherwise music would be drawing the spectator's attention to something that was not central. The basic rule was this: "[Y]ou should not withdraw the observers' attention from the *important* parts of the story or direct it to the unimportant parts. But whenever an element enters which has a bearing on the story, cater to that if you can."[28]

The issues of negotiating cross-cutting, one of the major innovations of narrative integration and also one of its more disorienting features, were similar. "Our photoplays are often composed of short and rapidly changing scenes and at first glance an alert mind will frequently note the most conspicuous object and give it an unmerited prominence. [The player] thus throws his picture out of balance and destroys an impression it might have otherwise have retained."[29] Playing to the cuts will tend to distract, leading the audience to observe details of the individual shots at the expense of the overall story line. In such alternating scenes, it was important to determine the dominant factor uniting the alternation and play to that.

Generally, playing to the psychology of character was an effective strategy for handling cross-cutting because then the character organized the sequence as a whole. Sinn presented an example from *A Dixie Mother* (1910) to illustrate his point:

> In the first part of the story . . . one of her sons is killed. The father vows eternal hatred to the North. After the war is over the other son marries a Northern girl and is thereby cut off from his parents. These incidents all develop toward the one point, viz.: the Spartan mother's pride has kept her silent, though her heart is hungry for her boy. Later she receives a letter saying her son and his wife are waiting at a nearby station, asks for a reconciliation, and that a carriage will be sent for them. The father refuses but finally, unknown to her, he relents and drives away. The next scenes alternate quickly, showing the despairing and half crazed "Dixie mother" and the carriage on its way; its arrival, the meeting between father and

son, the return trip and the arrival at home. This journey is shown in a number of scenes, and after each one the mother is shown.[30]

Sinn argued for playing the entire sequence to the mother's point of view, since the narrative point was figured around her. "The meeting between father, son and daughter-in-law may not look pathetic, nor the drive forth and back, but you are not playing to them; they are only details whose sole value lies in their relationship to the central idea. You are playing to the 'Dixie mother' and all interest about her must be sustained; a stop or a change in the music would break this tension, which is something you have been trying to hold throughout the latter half of the picture." It was upholding and playing to the psychological bearing of the mother, her anguish, that mattered.

By comparison, the leitmotif received surprisingly little attention in Sinn's column. Early in 1913, however, Sinn briefly revisited the issue. He suggested that a recent Gaumont three-reel feature, *The Vengeance of Egypt* (1912), was effectively accompanied with the "'thematic' treatment," his term for a leitmotivic accompaniment.

> Some musical theme may be chosen to represent the mummy's ring and its malignant power (as Wagner uses a motif for the Shield, Fire, Sword, or other important object), and this theme should be repeated each time the ring changes hands—that is, when it is developed that the ring has found a new victim. This theme should be of a weird, mysterious character.[31]

The initial statement of the theme coincides with the first passing of the ring. The music thus marks the ring as a significant object; we understand its weirdness as a musical style topic. But initially it is only a momentary figure, a narrative detail whose importance may be only local. The theme requires repetition to become a motif: its larger significance only becomes clear with subsequent repetitions, as we come to recognize the nature of the ring's power. As Sinn noted, the theme is not in fact associated with the ring so much as its action, its ability to develop the narrative; or rather the narrative develops around the ring, which remains the same throughout—the bringer of death. It is also worth noting that Sinn nevertheless conceived the music as a full-fledged theme—he suggested the *doloroso* from Theodore Bendix's "Hindoo Priest's Incantation"—rather than a shorter motif more characteristic of Wagner.

Yet the effect is akin to the description of the leitmotif as an agent of foreboding that Wagner hints at in *Oper und Drama*. For Wagner, such foreboding occurs when a motif is stated before its dramatic meaning is clear: it seems to know its future significance. In this case, the initial association of the ring with the musical style topic of "weirdness" seems to operate similarly: the theme already knows that the first event is not, in fact, the first; or at least not the only event of its kind. It seems to intuit the curse. Yet we feel the presence of the theme at first only as a foreboding, its weirdness suggesting the possibility that this event might be endowed with narrative significance. The return of the theme transforms it into a motif in the sense of Wagnerian foreboding and redeems that possibility: foreboding turns into dread at the appearance of the theme, an effect enhanced by Sinn's recommendation that this ring theme be followed with a "plaintive" "for the death of each victim of the ring." Using the same plaintive theme, he thought, will reinforce the continued cycle of the ring from transfer to death. The result serves to "emphasize the dominant idea of the picture—the vengeance following the ring."

Though Sinn's approach to *The Vengeance of Egypt* was leitmotivic, his accompaniment to *A Dixie Mother* was not. The difference in approach nevertheless highlights a consistent underlying principle: allegiance to the "predominant theme of the film." Determining this theme, Sinn realized, required an analytical intelligence: players not only needed to follow the main story line, they also had to recognize that just as some characters held more narrative significance than others, so too some scenes, even (as in the case of cross-cutting) some shots, were more important than others. Moreover, musicians needed to be able to determine which aspect of a scene—character, mood, event, and so on—should be played to in order to best aid the presentation of that narrative idea. Analysis, in other words, entailed discerning a hierarchy in the film, sometimes even imposing one. In playing the picture, the musician must first make sense of it.

One common mode of analysis involved determining the moods of the various scenes and choosing music based on that. Indeed, moods were a far more common basis for accompaniment than were leitmotifs. Inasmuch as it was understood as playing to something other than on-screen cues or the objective setting of location, playing to the basic mood of a scene was a step toward following a narrative line and breaking with topographical reading. But moods were only a first step in this break. An accompaniment practice using moods was perfectly suitable for accompanying the tableau orientation of the earlier form of story films, even if this practice did not correlate especially with the realism of topographic reading. For until moods had been integrated under a system of narrative representation, their status remained ambiguous. Though they did not resist the linearizing work of narrative integration and remained a basis for accompaniment throughout the silent era, in and of themselves moods did not create a narrative hierarchy; they did not wind a narrative thread through the story. On a theoretical level, moods were insufficient to establish a conception of film as narratively integrated.

This is where the idea of the leitmotif proved so useful to conceptualizing silent film accompaniment: playing leitmotivically required just such a conceptual reorientation insofar as it fixed on the narrative integration of plot and aided the audience in following the underlying story. Using leitmotifs, musical accompaniment became an obvious red thread of orientation within the confusing field of narrative integration. A recurring musical theme enhanced the narrative hierarchy characteristic of continuity editing. The leitmotif not only emphasized "the dominant idea of the picture" but also clarified it. Obviously, such a theme would only be used for someone or something of narrative importance, and the theme would not be chosen arbitrarily (on the basis, say, of a song title) but because it was "appropriate" to the narrative point. Moreover, the presence of a theme for a character would fix attention on him or her, despite any discontinuity of cutting, movement in the frame, or even a brief cutaway to another narrative strand. Though it is doubtful that Sinn would have taken a leitmotivic approach to *A Dixie Mother,* accompanying it thus and playing the "mother's theme" for the climactic scene of cross-cutting would have clearly accomplished the goal of making her character and, if the theme was appropriately chosen, her anguish the dominant features of the sequence. Indeed, such an accompaniment choice might well have intensified it. A shift from the theme for one character to that for another, by contrast, would mark a new point of narrative emphasis. A musical theme's recurrence would reflect the course and theme of the narrative, and accompanying the film with leitmotifs thus required that the player analyze and interpret the film narratively in playing it. The degree to which the leitmotif showed up in actual silent film practice or the degree to which its use, when it did show up, resembled Wagner's motivic web is in this sense irrelevant.[32] What was important was the conceptual model the leitmotif provided for binding music to narrative. That is, the leitmotif served less as a practice to emulate than as a model of narrative *synchronization*—this word will later in the silent era come to define the dominant practice of scoring films with compilations. Synchronization through motives thus placed narrative under a hierarchy of pertinence that in the case of the leitmotif was determined by the presence (or absence) of motifs. But synchronization, which may or may not have included leitmotivic synchronization by recurring themes (there are other modes of synchronization), is the key term. The leitmotif allowed the conceptual redefinition of synchronization under the sign of narrative integration: music could no longer be synchronized topographically to the outward, visible screen world; instead it was bound to the inner world of characters, where the mood of a place, its ambience, reflected or was determined by psychology. Music was thus "synchronized" to the drama of interiority. Here, the conception is closer to Wagner's leitmotif than to the melodramatic model of lyrical reflection.

Through such synchronization, music could thus serve as a red thread for following narrative—helping moviegoers negotiate the cuts and editing patterns of continuity editing—while nevertheless simply seeming to mark a story line that was already there. The coherence of the filmic narrative could in this way be reinforced by—or even borrowed from—the music. Insofar as the music seemed to relate to the picture *and* the music seemed to make sense, the music suggested that there was sense to be had in the film. It helped clarify what the film was about and what might be meaningful in it. Following the narrative as marked out by the music, the spectator could follow the narrative in terms of its themes and supporting hierarchy.

Synchronization was the sign of an analytical intelligence at work: the music knew where the story was and where it was headed. Sinn's suggestion for accompanying *The Vengeance of Egypt* required an analysis of the film that was hardly trivial, however obvious it might appear.[33] Synchronization in this sense was not identity, not mechanism. It was, however, a measure of distance: the analytic activity of the performer along with the divide of the performance from the screen assured that the music could only come so close. Synchronization revealed the accompaniment's extra-diegetic placement vis-à-vis narrative. Music's affiliation rested with the diegetic representation, not the pro-filmic staging. What now became essential was knowing on the one hand what not to play to that was contained in the picture, but on the other hand what to include that was not in the picture but implied by the diegesis—most particularly the psychological interiority of character. In choosing the pertinent details, in aligning foreground and background, in separating the essential from the inessential and contingent, the music demonstrated its prescience. In concept, it did not simply describe the world screened; it knew the world and the fate of those who acted within it. Yet whatever interiority it could reveal, music was also fated to be a reflection of that world, to reflect consciously on it. Herein lay its moment of resignation. This tension between prescience and resignation may help explain a certain contradiction in accompaniment manuals that would proliferate later in the silent film era: music should reflect the mood of the scene, but the player should play slightly ahead of the image—players should not be reflective or look backward, but anticipate and know where the story is going. Large-level structure (where the story is) was to be reflective and synchronized; low-level structure was to be prescient, anticipatory, and always slightly ahead of synchronization. This division gave the large-scale reflection its analytical power; or perhaps it would be better to say that it allowed such synchronization to seem purposeful, posited, as though it came from an intelligence external to the diegesis. Silent film music, in other words, demanded an "imaginative diegetic competency" similar to that which Thomas Grey argues is demanded of the Wagnerian leitmotivic web.[34]

Music could not bear the same relationship to the characters in film as to those in opera, because the music heard at the exhibition of the film was not the medium of characters' self-expression as it is in opera.[35] The musical themes in silent film described character, took psychological bearings perhaps, but unlike the aria in opera, they did not offer the character a moment of lyrical reflection. Music to the silent film—like the orchestra in Wagner's dramatic theory—occupied the position of the narrator, or rather the status of narration. And the muteness of film assured this status, even as the presence of the music, of music *in* the theater and so literally outside the diegesis, allegorized the loss of voice, which thereby also presented the capacity to unlock the interiority of the character. Absent from the film but present to the audience, the musical narration remained unspoken, unsung—nowhere more so than when the instrumental versions of vocal music (either popular songs or opera arias) were used.[36] Music in silent film had an allegorical character: it marked a recognition that we know what the characters do not; that we know what we cannot say to them or even to ourselves; in any case, that we empathize though we cannot intervene.[37]

It was at this point of allegorizing muteness that silent film accompaniment practice showed the greatest affinities to Wagner, particularly with respect to the extra-diegetic reflection also characteristic of his motivic web. Because Wagner divided voice from orchestra, in that the orchestra was not merely support for the voice and indeed the voice was often abandoned to endless declamation, the leitmotivic web came to occupy a space outside the mimetic world of the stage. Just as the music to the silent film remained external to the world screened, the external place of commentary in Wagner's music transmuted the mimetic stage into a diegetic representation, the orchestra occupying an extra-diegetic, narrating space. What held this space of diegesis open in Wagner's drama, what prevented it from collapsing back into the lyrical expression of opera, was the very presence of the leitmotif, or rather the non-identity of the motivic web with the stage action, a non-identity that created the impression that the orchestra knew something other than was visible or could be sung, though it was not in the nature of the orchestra to say it.

The "imaginative diegetic competency" shared by silent film music and Wagner's dramas can be staked on the analogy of the face in silent film to the word in Wagner's aesthetics. Dramatically with respect to music, the face in the silent picture was analogous to the word in opera.[38] Insofar as music took a subsidiary role in opera to the word in the name of drama, so too was it with the face in silent film. Though scoring the face might seem incompatible with a Wagnerian aesthetic, the silence of the face, its lack of word, maintained an irreducible distance, however small that might be. In watching silent film, in seeing the face speak, "we are asked to look at sound and to see voices," as Isabelle Reynauld puts it;[39] what the film represented was precisely the voice absented.

In that sense, the absence of speech, the muteness of the film, spoke only to the inability of speech to cross the boundary of the screen, to the impossibility of translation, rather than to the more common conception of transcendence into universal language. Music did not substitute for the missing voice, as one common theory has it, so much as it underscored the absence of the voice, the muteness of the apparatus, the failure of translation. The face could not say what it would express. The silence of the cinema was in this sense a sign of its absolute rootedness within a speech the audience did not—could not—hear. The muteness of the film then marked the limit of universal expression as silence. As the sound of the voice's absence, music played the face's displaced presence to plumb the depths of diegetic interiority. And the displacements of the voice in silent film gave it the capacity to cut through the reactionary entanglement of Wagner's conception. In playing to the picture, in scoring the silent face, music of the silent film thus gave voice to a humanity that would leap across the screen, a leap that Wagner's nefarious commitment to the gravity of language did not allow him to make.

NOTES

1. "The Music and the Picture," *The Moving Picture World*, April 16, 1910, 590. *The Moving Picture World* (henceforth abbreviated *MPW*) was the leading trade paper during the period between 1908 and 1913, when techniques of continuity editing and narrative integration were just beginning to emerge and procedures for "playing the picture" were being codified.

Most histories of film music make reference to the relationship between Wagner and silent film accompaniment. These accounts, however, are based on the mature practice of the 1920s. For other accounts that address, in a general way, the transition to playing the picture in connection with Wagner, see especially Charles Merrell Berg, *An Investigation of the Motives for and Realization of Music to Accompany the American Silent Film, 1896–1927* (New York: Arno Press, 1976) and Rick Altman, *Silent Film Sound* (New York: Columbia University Press, 2004). Scott D. Paulin also makes important contributions to understanding Wagner's influence on the codification of playing the picture; see his "Richard Wagner and the Fantasy of Cinematic Unity: The Idea of the *Gesamtkunstwerk* in the History and Theory of

Film Music," in *Music and Cinema,* ed. James Buhler, Caryl Flinn, and David Neumeyer (Middletown, Conn.: Wesleyan University Press, 2000), 58–84. In an essay
that appeared after this chapter was drafted, Matthew Wilson Smith gives a general
overview of Wagnerian influences on early accompaniment practices in "American
Valkyries: Richard Wagner, D. W. Griffith, and the Birth of Classical Cinema,"
Modernism/Modernity 15, no. 2 (2008): 221–42, esp. 222–31. Though Smith covers
some of the same sources as do I, he sees invocations of Wagner in the trade press
as part of a general "bourgeoisification" of the cinema. I do not disagree with that
interpretation but see Wagner invoked for technical reasons as well: the idea of the
leitmotif helped musicians (and audiences) negotiate certain conceptual challenges
posed by continuity editing. While a good overview of silent film accompaniment
practices in general, Martin Miller Marks's *Music and the Silent Film: Contexts and
Case Studies, 1895–1924* (New York: Oxford University Press, 1997) does not address
Wagner except in a discussion of Carl Breil's score for *The Birth of a Nation* (1915),
139–41 and 146–47.

2. G. H. Hummel, letter quoted in Clarence Sinn, "Music for the Picture,"
MPW, January 14, 1911, 76.

3. "Music for the Picture," *MPW,* January 21, 1911, 135.

4. Paulin's contention that Sinn "enthusiastically embraced Wagner and the
leitmotif" is misleading to say the least. Sinn generally ran his column in a collegial
manner. Much as he does here, Sinn is supportive of an idea but then in the course
of discussing it, he channels it in what he sees as more productive directions. In a
footnote, Paulin does acknowledge Sinn's subtle understanding of the issues involved: "The clarity of Sinn's conclusions shows that, at least initially, his reading of
Wagner was less a misunderstanding than a pragmatic and deliberate adoption of
certain limited aspects of Wagner" ("Richard Wagner and the Fantasy of Cinematic
Unity," 70; 82, n. 43). Smith likewise sees Sinn as more supportive of Wagner's technique than the columnist in fact is. This is at least in part because Smith does not
seem to have a clear understanding of the late nineteenth-century practice of accompanying melodrama ("American Valkyries," 228).

5. "Music for the Picture," *MPW,* January 21, 1911, 135.

6. A typical program around 1910 consisted of three reels of film, which would
last roughly 45 minutes, though the program could be made considerably longer or
shorter depending on the speed of projection. Films were exhibited as soon as they
arrived at the theater, so the first show was often the first time that even the manager of the theater had seen the film. In late 1910, in only his second column, Sinn
noted, "Our problems are more complex than they seem to be. We have no rehearsals; we know nothing of the pictures until we see them at the first show, during
which we must 'play something' and at the same time determine on the most fitting
music. This entails good guessing and a good memory" ("Music for the Picture,"
MPW, December 3, 1910).

7. "Music for the Picture," *MPW,* January 21, 1911, 135. "Melodrama" is a confusing term, as it refers to two distinct, albeit related theatrical forms, as well as a
characteristic stage technique of combining music and dialogue (actually, usually,
a monologue). Sinn is undoubtedly using the term to refer to the popular late-
nineteenth-century form, which featured sensational situations, stock characters,
and the staging of a clear moral worldview (good vs. evil). Though it did not deploy

music to the same extent as the earlier form (which is usually said to originate in Rousseau's *Pygmalion,* first performed in 1770), the later form of melodrama did use music for stock and characteristic situations ("hurrys," "livelys," "agitatos," "tremolos," etc.) and to delineate character by type (heroine, hero, villain, etc.). Peter Branscombe's article on "Melodrama" in *Grove Music Online* (http://www.ox-fordmusiconline.com/public/book/omo_gmo) is misleading in saying that the later form was "more commonly without a musical accompaniment." In fact, it was most commonly performed with a stock musical accompaniment assembled by a local music director; because it was left unspecified in the script and so left wholly to the discretion of the local production, music would obviously be less integrated with the play than in the earlier form of melodrama. Some easily obtainable exemplars of this stock melodramatic music can be found in Alfred Edward Cooper, David Mayer, and Matthew Scott, *Four Bars of "Agit": Incidental Music for Victorian and Edwardian Melodrama: Authentic All-Purpose Music* (London: Samuel French, 1983) and from the "Music for the Nation: American Sheet Music" section of the American Memory project at the Library of Congress, http://memory.loc.gov/am-mem/mussmhtml/mussmhome.html (accessed March 22, 2009); search "melodra-matic." This stock music was also used by film accompanists, and it is featured in many early anthologies. For a historical overview of the "hurry," a melodramatic cue type particularly important for accompanying film, see Anne Dhu Shapiro, "Action Music in American Pantomime and Melodrama, 1730–1913," *American Music* 2, no. 4 (1984): 49–72. On the general relationship between melodrama and early silent film, see especially A. Nicholas Vardac, *Stage to Screen: Theatrical Method from Garrick to Griffith* (Cambridge: Harvard University Press, 1949) and Ben Singer, *Melodrama and Modernity: Early Sensational Cinema and Its Contexts* (New York: Columbia University Press, 2001).

8. Christine Anne Frezza describes melodrama's association of music with character thus:

> A typical melodramatic situation is this: music announces the heroine; by its quality (sad, hopeful, cheerful, ominous, etc.) we not only know her state of mind, but also what is about to happen to her. Our anticipation is heightened and our knowledge increased, all before she says a word. When she speaks, each phrase is punctuated by a musical phrase, not as a comment, an outside voice, but an expansion of her own voice, both outer and inner, a lifting of already emotional declaimed speech into a realm where words are incapable of expressing emotion. "Music as an Integral Design Element in Theatrical Production" (Ph.D. diss., University of Pittsburgh, 1981), 54.

If we accept Frezza's analysis, music serves a similar function in melodrama to what it does in opera—a lyrical voice of the character, albeit here divided from the bodily voice of speech. What divides melodrama from opera, however, is that the speech cannot lift itself into song. The voice falls silent, in other words, so that we can hear the lyrical outpouring of pure feeling. From the standpoint of my analysis, it is significant that the relationship to the stage is lyrical rather than (extra) diegetic.

9. Tom Gunning, "The Cinema of Attraction: Early Film, Its Spectator and the Avant-Garde," *Wide Angle* 8, nos. 3–4 (1986): 63–70; Gunning, *D. W. Griffith and the Origins of American Narrative Film: The Early Years at Biograph* (Urbana and Chicago: University of Illinois Press, 1991), esp. 41–43; and Noël Burch, *Life to Those Shadows* (Berkeley: University of California Press, 1990).

10. Editorial, *MPW*, September 26, 1908, 231.

11. James Lastra, *Sound Technology and the American Cinema: Perception, Representation, Modernity* (New York: Columbia University Press, 2000), 65.

12. This does not mean that such objectivity demanded documentary fidelity. The use of the camera to produce tricks through substitution cuts, scale mismatches, and the occasional cut-in had occurred nearly from the beginning, but in general they remained that—tricks, special effects that enhanced but did not fundamentally alter the notion of what film was. When they were not used for such tricks or special effects, such camera work was generally denounced. See, for instance, the *MPW* editorial from July 3, 1909 complaining about changing image size in films of the time (7–8). The author seems particularly concerned about the fact that the camera has changed positions in the course of filming the scene. In this respect, it seems that a commitment to the objective, reproducing capabilities of the camera was fundamental to the understanding of filmic sense.

13. On narrative, functional equivalency, and continuity editing, see David Bordwell, Janet Staiger, and Kristin Thompson, *The Classical Hollywood Cinema: Film Style and Mode of Production to 1960* (New York: Columbia University Press, 1985), 5.

14. The situation is not unlike that which the other universal language, music, confronted in the early modern period. Instrumental music, especially the Italian sonatas that began to come to prominence in the seventeenth century, posed a challenge to the claims of universal understanding to the extent that functional equivalency derived from vocal practice demanded that instrumental music be constructed around a "wordless rhetoric" not unlike that of film. Daniel Chua explains:

> The Baroque had no problem lip-reading this kind of instrumental music as a dumb copy of the voice; there were standardised figures that could decode the grammar and meaning of the music; instrumental music could just about "speak." The real problem with it was epistemological; instrumental music "deconstructed" the very basis of musical knowledge. What the sonata reveals is the *linguistic relativity* inherent in the trivium. With music no longer tied to the harmony of the spheres, its melodies simply drifted on the currents of the rhetorical will. This may have enabled humanity to colonise and define new meanings for itself, but there was no way of stabilising these meanings as eternally valid truths. Rhetorical relativity risks meaninglessness, and it was the sonata that made audible this uncontrollable semiosis. Fontenelle confronted the sonata not because it signified nothing, but because it signified too much. The excesses of signification spilled over into an indeterminate relativism that decentered the vocal ontology of the ego and destabilised the trivium as the ground of meaning. *Absolute Music and the Construction of Meaning: New Perspectives in Music History and Criticism* (Cambridge: Cambridge University Press, 1999), 62–63.

The similarity between music and film in this regard is hardly coincidental, since it is bound up in each case with a seeming universal language being confronted by the emergence of a rhetorical and stylistic system that is inherently relativistic.

15. Though I do not discuss it here, in 1908 in particular, attempts were made to put actors behind the screen to deliver the lines of the characters; it was thought that such "talking pictures" would make the films more comprehensible. Clearly, such a practice is very labor-intensive, and after a brief period of novelty the practice fell out of use. For a brief account of this practice, see Altman, *Silent Film Sound,* 166–73.

16. Though mostly a minority practice, at least in the United States, lecturers were a common accompaniment to film all through the silent era, and *MPW* frequently advocated in their favor. From the nineteenth century until the advent of radio and the sound film, illustrated lectures were a popular form of middle-class entertainment. While most lecturers traveled with lantern slides, a number, most notably Lyman H. Howe, built their lectures around film exhibition. For a good overview of the film lecturing business, see Charles Musser, *High-Class Moving Pictures: Lyman H. Howe and the Forgotten Era of Traveling Exhibition, 1880–1920* (Princeton, N.J.: Princeton University Press, 1991). On the use of music and sound effects in these shows, see Altman, *Silent Film Sound,* 133–55.

17. "The Value of a Lecture," *MPW,* February 8, 1908, 93. Around the same time, W. Stephen Bush makes a similar and more elaborate case for the narrator.

18. The discussion here is indebted to Noël Burch, who argues similarly that the lecturer "linearized" films by drawing narrative lines through their stories. He also notes that the presence of the lecturer in the theater ran contrary to aims of narrative integration (*Life to Those Shadows,* 154–55).

19. Altman, *Silent Film Sound,* 182.

20. The term "diegetic" is not only anachronistic, it is also conceptually misleading inasmuch as it belongs to the system of narrative integration that emerged with continuity editing. Rick Altman's alternate term of "cue" music is likewise misleading in that melodrama and other forms of incidental theater music had a long tradition of "cues" that were not understood as onstage music; see "The Living Nickelodeon," in *The Sounds of Early Cinema,* ed. Richard Abel and Rick Altman (Bloomington: Indiana University Press, 2001), 234–35.

21. Burch, *Life to Those Shadows,* 152.

22. For accounts of the disciplining of sound effects to narrative, see Tim Anderson, "Reforming 'Jackass Music': The Problematic Aesthetics of Early American Film Music Accompaniment," *Cinema Journal* 37, no. 1 (1997): 3–22; Stephen Bottomore, "The Story of Percy Peashaker: Debates about Sound Effects in the Early Cinema," in *The Sounds of Early Cinema,* 129–42; Rick Altman, *Silent Film Sound,* 236–40; and Smith, "American Valkyries," 225–27.

23. "Drums and Traps," *MPW,* July 23, 1910, 184.

24. Ibid., 185.

25. "When 'Effects' are Unnecessary Noises," *MPW,* September 9, 1911, 690.

26. *MPW,* December 31, 1910, 1531.

27. *MPW,* December 10, 1910, 1345.

28. Ibid.

29. *MPW,* December 31, 1910, 1531.

30. Ibid.

31. *MPW,* January 25, 1913, 352.

32. Certainly, Wagner's name in general was invoked disproportionately to the actual practice of leitmotivic accompaniment, even in simplified form. There can be little doubt that writers sought to claim cultural legitimacy for the motion picture by associating his music with films. But it would be a mistake to dismiss silent film leitmotifs because they appear for the sake of cultural legitimacy or seem "crude" compared to Wagner's practice. It should be remembered that they are crude in the same way as Wolzogen's guides to Wagner's operas are crude—and for similar reasons. These guides were not, Thomas Grey notes, "designed for students of musical composition or analysis, but to serve the uninitiated as a guiding or leading 'thread' through the labyrinth of Wagner's music dramas"; Grey, *Wagner's Musical Prose: Texts and Contexts* (Cambridge: Cambridge University Press, 1995), 351. In the same way, we might say that the "leitmotivic" accompaniment practice of the silent film was not designed from a musical standpoint; rather it was one means of guiding spectators through the disorienting field of the silent drama. The leitmotifs were a musical means of narrative integration, linearizing the plot and so assimilating the audience to continuity editing.

33. Sinn's analysis is in fact rather subtle: as mentioned above, he recognizes that it is not the ring that needs to be treated with the leitmotif but rather its action. This prevents the association from becoming mechanical.

34. Thomas Grey, ". . . *wie ein rother* Faden: On the Origins of 'Leitmotif' as Critical Construct and Musical Practice," in *Music Theory in the Age of Romanticism,* ed. Ian Bent (Cambridge: Cambridge University Press, 1996), 207.

35. Music was, for one thing, not strictly speaking necessary for silent film—in the extreme case, it was perfectly acceptable if less than ideal to screen the film in silence. In general, my description here presumes live performance, which though the norm in the United States was by no means universal even by the 1920s. Many theaters, for instance, "synchronized" films using phonographs or player pianos. The situation with respect to mechanically reproduced music differed significantly inasmuch as it rendered the place of the music and so also its distance from the screen (and/or affiliation with the audience) somewhat indeterminate. This latter case became formalized in the sound film, in which music was incorporated into the sound track and so became a part of the film (and the apparatus). This is not the place to develop the notion, but my sense is that music moved from an allegorical to a symbolic register as it became incorporated into the sound track.

36. On this point, see Michal Grover-Friedlander, *Vocal Apparitions: The Attraction of Cinema to Opera* (Princeton, N.J.: Princeton University Press, 2005), 20–22.

37. Stanley Cavell makes a related point in *The World Viewed: Reflections on the Ontology of Film,* enlarged edition (Cambridge, Mass.: Harvard University Press, 1979): "In viewing a film, my helplessness is mechanically assured: I am present not at something happening, which I must confirm, but at something that has happened, which I must absorb" (26). If this melancholic interpretation seems overdrawn, too contemporary to be applicable to silent film, it is worth noting that during the period that playing to the pictures developed, there were frequent complaints about the large number of dour films being released. Americans prefer happy endings, the trade papers proclaimed, even as dramatic tragedies and gruesome

melodramas proliferated; interestingly enough, these latter sorts of films initially drove the process of narrative integration.

38. The analogy, in other words, is not directly of the word to dialogue or of drama to narrative.

39. Isabelle Reynauld, "Dialogues in Early Screenplays: What Actors Really Said," in *The Sounds of the Early Cinema,* 75. Reynauld takes the key phrase from Oliver Sacks, *Seeing Voices* (New York: Harper Collins, 1990).

TWO

Underscoring Drama—Picturing Music

PETER FRANKLIN

Wagner's ultimate role in discourse on film and music is akin to
that of the magic *Tarnhelm* in his *Ring* operas: draped rhetorically
over the products of cinema, the figure of Wagner allows film's
illusory transformation into an artwork that has succeeded in
fulfilling its wish, achieving its goals of unity and totality.

SCOTT D. PAULIN, "RICHARD WAGNER AND THE
FANTASY OF CINEMATIC UNITY"

Like Bayreuth, Hollywood promotes complete audience identification
and an unabashedly subjective experience. Wagner's darkened
auditorium proved entirely prophetic, while the invisible pit
has found a successor in "surround sound" speakers. That so
much film music preserves the language, timbre, and leitmotivic
organisation of music drama only makes the connection explicit.

CHRISTOPHER MORRIS, *READING OPERA BETWEEN THE LINES*

In his contribution to the Buhler, Flinn, and Neumeyer collection *Music
and Cinema* (2000), Scott Paulin might almost have been setting out to
head off Christopher Morris at the pass. Indeed, these two quotations
mark something of a factional rift that has developed within film music
studies: between those who accept and those who reject the notion of any

relevant historical continuities between Wagner and mass-entertainment film. My own sympathies are with the Morris faction (if one could even call it that),[1] but Paulin's essay merits serious consideration and has inspired much of what follows. One could hardly quarrel with him when he points out that references to Wagner and the leitmotif were among the most overused items of theoretical equipment of early commentators on film music. He also convincingly explains that these references were (and have continued to be) wielded by critics with often little or no direct experience of the composer's theoretical writings or music dramas. That the deployment of recurring material in popular Italian operas by Verdi, Puccini, or Mascagni might have been as relevant a model for what those underscoring films in the 1930s or '40s were actually doing is something that has rarely been addressed.[2] Perhaps it was because so many high-profile emigré composers and practical musicians working in Hollywood spoke German that Wagner was the pre-cinematic composer most often invoked for the kind of "high-culture" validation of film-scoring practices that Paulin's essay targets. Anti-Hollywood mass-culture critics like Theodor Adorno could nevertheless readily turn those tables on the Master of Bayreuth and disparagingly accuse him of writing "film music" in all but name before film even existed.[3] Adorno's critique of Wagnerism was, of course, rooted in cultural anxiety about the affiliation of Wagnerism and Nazism, but there are assumptions in all this that need to be questioned, not least those concerning categories like "high culture"—and even "art."

Wagner criticism of the Adornian kind may paradoxically hold the key to a more decentered, cultural-historical approach to reasserting the relevance of the composer to film practice, avoiding the *Gesamtkunstwerk* and leitmotivic theory-mongering otherwise aptly criticized by Paulin, who nevertheless appears to sense that Adorno's *In Search of Wagner* threatens some of the very distinctions upon which his thesis relies.[4] I shall propose here that Wagner's ideas and works might appropriately be considered not as models for, but as *forerunners* of techniques associated with the construction of cinematic narrative in the early twentieth century—techniques once discussed by film historians as if they were forged out of nothing by Eisenstein or D. W. Griffith, as new technology facilitated what could be regarded as a new art form. In fact, a good deal of historical work has now been done on cinema's debt to various kinds of nineteenth-century novelty entertainments like the diorama or the "magic lantern" and to the tradition of theatrical melo-drama and the stage effects upon which it relied.[5] Interest in opera as a source of cinematic techniques has nevertheless waxed and waned, with its supposed formality, stylization, and high-cultural status often being cited as impediments to meaningful historical comparison.

One immediate problem here is linked to that absence of Italian opera from historical discussions of cinema's sources. The increasing popularity of Italian *verismo,* and of Puccini, from the 1890s onwards seriously compromises the historiography of opera as essentially or uni-formly high status and high culture. The energetically scorned popular-ity of the more recent Italian opera, not least in the criticism of conser-vative Wagnerians, was even a specific goad to younger anti-modernist German and Austrian opera composers after World War I. Erich Wolf-gang Korngold evidently saw it as something of a mission to engage with the ever-expanding, popular middle-class audience that would be aban-doned by modernists like Alban Berg and Arnold Schoenberg, or, rather differently, by the Weimar period political avant-garde represented by playwright Bertold Brecht and the composers with whom he worked, such as Hindemith, Kurt Weill, or Hanns Eisler.[6]

Korngold remained technically a "post-Wagnerian" composer, and to bring opera back into the frame of film's historical sources must be to move beyond Paulin in reconsidering the multivalent significance of Wagner, most specifically in three areas: his musico-dramatic theory; the way in which he wrote about music (symphonic as much as operatic); and of course, his own compositional and theatrical practice. Recurring and specifically referential leitmotivic material, for all that Paulin has to say about it, will here be assigned a relatively low level of importance. I shall be suggesting that Wagner's mid-nineteenth-century account of what he wanted to achieve in the music drama, radically distinguished from "opera" as a cultural form, involved theorizing a technique of orchestral "underscoring" in a theatrical presentation. We must also bear in mind the longer-term need to question the historical stability of that category "artwork," which Paulin—relying also upon a rather arbitrary distinction between Wagnerian "myth" and cinematic "real-ism"[7]—implicitly distances from the fragmented and un-unified nature of film.

MUSICO-DRAMATIC THEORY

... where gesture lapses into rest, and the melodic discourse of the
actor hushes—thus where the drama prepares its future course in
inner moods as yet unuttered—there may these still unspoken moods
be spoken by the orchestra in such a way that their utterance shall
bear the character of a foreboding necessitated by the poet's aim.

RICHARD WAGNER, *OPERA AND DRAMA*

This quotation from Part 3 of Wagner's *Opera and Drama* (1850–51)[8] is
indicative of the loquacious complexity of his thought in its many antici-
pations of future attempts to explain the role of music in film. Wagner's
own project was to create an ideal type of music drama, freed from the
trivialities of high-status social entertainment and modeled on his image of ancient Greek drama as a quasi-religious and socially inclusive
experience. Yet beyond the darker historical ironies of the culturally empowered nationalism of his later position lies the further irony, *pace* both
Adorno and Paulin, that Wagner's notions about the role of the orchestra
in those parts of his music dramas where the stage characters ceased to
sing (and by extension elsewhere) were closely relevant to the subsequent
development of classical Hollywood underscoring technique.

Wagner's revolutionary aim was that the orchestra should be freed
from its normally accompanying role, in what he always conceived to be
an innovatory bringing together of the previously separate forms of opera and the symphony—specifically the symphony of Beethoven. While
retaining its mimetic and pantomimic aspect as the aural equivalent of
physical gesture, the orchestra's liberated role in the music drama was
based on its additional ability to "materialize thoughts . . . as no longer
merely recollected, but made present."[9] It was here that he went on to
refer to the clarifying role of the motif that had previously been linked
to a "definite object" in the sung stage drama.[10] But his underlying idea
that the orchestra should provide a foundational discourse of emotion,
presentiment, foreboding, and recollection—albeit one that needs cor-
roboration from the visual pictures of the stage action—is fascinating

in that he saw it not only supplying unity to the dramatic fantasy ("the unity of the symphonic movement")[11] but also as constructing what we might now call a "metadiegetic" voice (able to suggest foreboding and so on) that is specifically linked to "the poet's aim."

In a series of bold theoretical moves, subsequently put into practice in the construction and technology of his Bayreuth Festspielhaus, Wagner thus moved well beyond any crude linkage of the metadiegetic voice to that of "the composer," instead positioning it as a tool whereby the composer-poet realizes his larger aim: influencing, encouraging, and even manipulating the audience to experience the drama as he wishes. It is true that this led him to describe the underscoring orchestra of *Tristan*—"the most beautiful of all my dreams"—as the voice of inwardness underpinning that work as enacted wish-fulfillment.[12] Yet its dialectical implications also as a perceived tool already look forward to Mann's *Doctor Faustus* and Adrian Leverkühn's disillusioned and parodic comprehension of the Act 3 *Meistersinger* Prelude's techniques of manipulation.[13]

For Wagner, such comprehension was no disappointment, of course, but rather an insight into how he, as overseeing creator-poet, might awaken "presentiment"—and this is achieved, as he emphatically stresses in the original, "*in order, through its longing, to make us necessary sharers in the creation of his artwork.*"[14] The discourse of the unseen orchestra would underpin the enacted and sung drama on stage in the darkened auditorium at Bayreuth—an initially accidental discovery of how to dematerialize the social spectacle of the audience in conventional French and Italian opera theaters. In this way Wagner perfected the technology of dreamlike theatrical fantasy. He did so in order to make us, the audience, willing collaborators in the new practice of the supreme bourgeois art of inwardness constructed and experienced in public; that is, what would come to be called "transparent narrative," in which both the machinery and materiality of the realization are effectively obliterated and hidden from our perception.

WRITING ABOUT MUSIC

From an Adornian perspective, what might be called the proto-cinematic aspects of Wagner's musico-dramatic innovations would be unequivocally disparaged for their evident anticipation of the mass-cultural form in which the audience comprised victims of, rather than sharers in the creation of his artwork. Class played a role in this. For Adorno, Wagner was indeed the bourgeois artist par excellence: the self-styled "author of his collective works,"[15] who demonstrated the enterprise of his class by leaping across the footlights to become the supreme entrepreneurial conductor-composer, "beating time" while beating his massed listeners into submission.[16] However, the criticism backfires somewhat if Wagner is viewed from a broader historical perspective as a no less key bourgeois appropriator and redistributor of the aesthetic accoutrements of aristocracy. In the process he problematized some of the ideological tenets of orthodox aesthetic discourse, relishing in the revelation of secrets hidden beneath the official language of "art." In the various versions of the Venusberg scene at the beginning of *Tannhäuser* (its "bacchanal" ballet famously imposed by the cultural manners and requirements of a Parisian elite), Wagner heightens the titillating aspects of the erotic play of classical mythological representatives of love and lust—Bacchantes, satyrs, fauns, and cherubs—who would have been found disporting in the internal decorative schemes of innumerable palaces and grand retreats of the powerful. As if to us, the audience, Wagner's sirens sing:

Approach the beach,
approach the shore,
where in the arms
of passionate love
blissful warmth
satisfies your desires![17]

Not only was the bacchanal ballet placed too early for Parisian taste, its erotic implications seemed overemphasized by being located in a romantic drama that thematized the tension between carnal lust and idealized love.[18]

Romanticism was itself an artistic movement that could be seen as a site in which multiple appropriations of this kind were managed and imperfectly policed. No better demonstration of what I mean could be found than in the area of Romantic discourse about music—often seen there as a paradigm of aesthetic idealism, its nature conceived as a "pure" or "autonomous" art form. Yet overestimation of those ideas can drastically underestimate the cultural work done by the language of such idealism in the battle with its ever-present converse: the appropriating discourse of programmaticism. "Programmatic" explanations advertised the psychological, allegorical, or narrative meaning of symphonic music (for example), which the equally Romantic discourse of idealism vainly sought to obscure or deny in the interest of "taste."

Significant in this context is the fact that one of the foundational nineteenth-century statements of musical Romanticism—E. T. A. Hoffmann's 1813 essay, "Beethoven's Instrumental Music"—is often taken as an early credo of idealism, and yet its reliance in key moments upon graphic, and gripping, visual metaphor is significant:

> Beethoven's instrumental music opens up to us also the realm of the monstrous and the immeasurable. Burning flashes of light shoot through the deep night of this realm, and we become aware of giant shadows that surge back and forth.[19]

The issue of programmaticism, of the interpretation (whether by the composer or his subsequent critics) of instrumental music as in some way descriptive and/or narrative in character, is central to the nineteenth-century tension between music's construction as abstract or "absolute" on the one hand (albeit linked to models variously natural or metaphysical), and on the other, as a subjectively expressive and meaningful discourse in its own right. While presented in intellectual debate as a question to which there was a true or false answer, the conundrum about whether music could or could not express or represent anything outside itself was largely hot air. There is a wealth of evidence to indicate that symphonic music was publicly idealized while being privately experienced as vividly meaningful. Wagner's own descriptive evaluations of his and other people's music offers just one source of such evidence, demonstrating that the reception of symphonic works provided intimate opportunities for the generation and development of accompanying internalized scenarios. These were often strongly visual in character and could also be startlingly anticipatory of cinematic narrative techniques.

When writing about Beethoven's *Eroica* symphony in 1852, Wagner sounds the standard registers of descriptive interpretation that Beethoven's music in particular inspired. The first movement embraced for him "all the emotions of a richly-gifted nature in the heyday of unresting youth."[20] It was, in a sense, a condensed emotional self-portrait, its expressed succession of feelings springing "from one main faculty—and that is Force."[21] By the Finale, however, Wagner has Beethoven harnessing music's potential for the construction of an allegorical drama unfolding the tension between "firm-set Manly individuality" (represented by the main theme) and its attendant retinue of "all tenderer and softer feelings . . . evolving to a proclamation of the purely Womanly element":

> [T]o the manlike principal theme—striding sturdily through all the tone-piece—this Womanly at last reveals itself in ever more intense, more many-sided sympathy, as the overwhelming power of *Love*.[22]

That Wagner is adumbrating an idea that would be central to his own work is of less immediate relevance than that his descriptive registers are here permitting music not only to narrate but also to acquire a purposeful metadiegetic voice of consciousness that can strategically shape its dramatic narrative to signify something cumulative beyond its individual events or moments. This is most obvious in his still more intensely visualized descriptive account of the *Eroica*'s Scherzo:

> [W]e have before us now the lovable glad man, who paces hale and hearty through the fields of Nature, looks laughingly across the meadows, and winds his merry hunting-horn from woodland heights; and what he feels amid it all, the master tells us in the vigorous, healthy tints of his tone-painting . . .[23]

Note that the music expresses not what Beethoven, the "master," directly feels but what his projected character feels: the idealized romantic wanderer whose emotional world may be deliberately simpler than that of Beethoven himself. Already here we have in essence a miniature film scenario generated by music in a way that permits it to tell us something about the interiority of its constructed subject.

I have elsewhere observed that in his 1846 account of the second movement of Beethoven's Ninth Symphony, Wagner had proposed a more specifically cinematic montage of musical inter-cut and cross-faded scenes, where the inter-cutting is associated with a metadiegetic voice or directing consciousness with which we, the audience, are clearly invited to identify when it wilfully directs or manipulates such editing.[24]

Where on the operatic stage Wagner may re-employ a standard device for explaining the presence of a formal aria—as in Act 1, Scene 2 of *Tannhäuser,* when the hero responds to Venus in a diegetic "song"—so in his description of the Scherzo of Beethoven's Ninth, he explains the formal succession of the Scherzo and Trio's generic component sections as wilfully appropriated and "edited" for a more than structurally conventional purpose:

> With the abrupt entry of the middle section there suddenly opens out to us a scene of earthly jollity . . . But we are not disposed to view this banal gaiety as the goal of our restless quest . . . our gaze clouds over and we turn from the scene to trust ourselves anew to that untiring force which spurs us on . . . once again, at the movement's close, we are driven to that early scene of jollity, and now we thrust it with impatience from us as soon as recognized.[25]

Here Wagner implicitly and rather interestingly glosses what he might have meant in *Opera and Drama* by that emphasized insistence on the music-dramatist's need *"to make us necessary sharers in the creation of his artwork."* By giving us a model for how we might "see" the music here, Wagner reveals how complex were the later, officially reviled practices of narrative or programmatic listening, which on occasion he could demonstrate with a richness of proto-cinematic imagery. For the Zürich Festival of 1853 he wrote a detailed account of the *Fliegender Holländer* Overture, which keeps fairly closely to the plot which it evidently rehearses in brief (as we can retrospectively judge from its deployment of significant musical material from the opera to come). In common with many such descriptive accounts, Wagner's shares the language both of grand operatic stage directions and of romantic-literary "visions" or "dreams" of the kind that were strategically employed by writers, such as the novelist Jean Paul Richter (1763–1825):

> A ray divides the gloom of night; like a lightning-flash it pierces through his tortured soul. It fades, and leaps to life once more: the seaman keeps his lodestar firm in eye and stoutly steers through waves and billows toward it.[26]

One of the most elaborate realizations of one of Wagner's works as an internally viewed cinematic scenario is found in his short piece on the *Lohengrin* Prelude. After an introductory passage explaining the ethical and symbolic significance of the Holy Grail, he explains how the music evokes its descent and arrival on earth:

> At the beginning, the clear blue air of Heaven seems to condense to a mysterious vision, scarce traceable by the eye of over-earthly yearning, yet holding the enraptured gaze with magic spell; in infinitely soft, but gradually distincter outlines, appears the wonder-bringing host of angels, descending slowly from ethereal heights, and bearing in its midst the sacred vessel. As the vision waxes plainer still and plainer, and hovers down toward this vale of earth, the sweetest fragrance wells from out its wings: entrancing vapours stream from it in clouds of gold, usurping every sense with hallowed awe.[27]

Romantic music was always potentially *seen* as well as heard, and without any need for theoretical explanations of excess or redundancy.

COMPOSITIONAL PRACTICE AND STAGECRAFT

The *Lohengrin* vision was not intended to be staged in any way (something not unlike it would be at the end of *Parsifal*); it was played before the curtain in the conventional manner. It is nevertheless clear that Wagner expected audience members to draw on their symphonic experience and "see" with their inner eye what the music was depicting, varied though the details of their inner narratives might be. In that sense, Wagner draws on the tendency of Romantic opera to turn the Overture into something between a mood-setting trailer for the musico-dramatic events to come and a brief précis of its plot in musical terms (like Weber's *Der Freischütz* Overture or that to his own *Der fliegende Holländer*). I will return to the links between preludial music and cinematic "titles." For the moment the issue of music being used for more practically proto-cinematic purposes might usefully be addressed with respect to the open-stage scene-change interludes in *Das Rheingold*. Here the programmatic question of whether the music is describing what we see or whether what we see is a scenic realization of the music's implicit content is intriguingly unanswerable. The first scene-change interlude provides an instructive example.

As is so often suggested of film, music evidently plays a continuity role here in smoothing over a disjuncture in the narrative. We move, as in an elaborate upward panning shot, from the depths of the Rhine to a peaceful mountain vantage point from which the newly built home of the gods, Valhalla, can be seen on a distant prominence (the Rhine is assumed to flow in the unseen chasm between foreground and background). Here music certainly helps to supply the illusion of unity and continuity—rather as Wagner himself is positioned as a conceptual supplier of unity and "art" status to the "material heterogeneity of the cinematic apparatus" in Scott Paulin's argument.[28] Never was there a clearer example of such heterogeneity in Wagnerian opera, which abounds in it.

In live performances, like those of the notorious 1876 premiere of the complete *Ring* cycle at Bayreuth (which inaugurated the new theater's innovatory equipment and seating arrangement), the physical and technological challenges that Wagner set his scene designers and stage crew were as mercilessly tangible as anything facing the camera crew, cutting editors, and special-effects departments of film studios to come. Here the "material heterogeneity" is unified no less (or more?) by Wagnerian wish-fulfillment than Paulin's cinematic apparatus. But the nature of the highly detailed musical component of that operation bears consideration. I reproduce below the full stage direction, whose visionary poetry could be compared with the explanation of the *Lohengrin* Prelude. In the score of *Das Rheingold,* some of the sentences are precisely located at the relevant points in the music. The described effects and the music are clearly intended to be closely synchronized (the interested reader is recommended to listen to this music, which no printed example could properly evoke; its seamlessly modulated transformation achieves a startling verisimilitude):

> [Alberich] tears the gold from the rock with terrible force and plunges with it hastily into the depths, where he quickly disappears. Thick darkness falls suddenly on the scene. The [Rhine] maidens dive down after the robber. The waters sink down with them. From the lowest depth is heard Alberich's shrill mocking laughter. The rocks disappear in thickest darkness, the whole stage is filled from top to bottom with black waves, which for some time seem to sink downwards . . . The waves have gradually changed into clouds which little by little become lighter, and at length disperse into a fine mist. As the mist disappears upwards in little clouds, an open space on a mountain height becomes visible in the twilight . . . At one side, on a flowery bank lies Wotan with Fricka near him. Both asleep. / Second Scene:/ The dawning day lights up with growing brightness a castle with glittering pinnacles which stands on the top of a cliff in the background.[29]

Paulin is quite right is in his insistence, *pace* would-be Hollywood Wagnerians' reliance on poorly grasped versions of his early theory, that Wagner's ideas and practice developed from a vision of Music as the handmaid of Drama to one where Music is its dominant, maternal progenitor.[30] There are questions about "which comes first" in the scene-change music just alluded to; elsewhere the dramatic precedence or subservience of the orchestra may be more clearly marked. In the second opera of the cycle, *Die Walküre*, Wagner employs a form of opening gambit that is closer by some measure to the action-titles sequence of films to come. In the short and powerfully evocative storm prelude before the curtain rises, Wagner sharpens and compresses *Das Rheingold*'s initiating experiment with a seamless musical linkage between "overture" and "action." The music at first dominates but then recedes to adopt a more conventionally supportive or accompanying role; but one that repays analysis.

Proto-cinematic features of the overture's programmaticism are at first strongly in evidence, signaled by an item of recollected material from the music of the previous evening's "preludial drama." The citations of Donner's cloud- and rainbow-summoning invocation at the end of *Das Rheingold* ("Heda! Heda! Hedo!") have the effect of flashbacks overlaid onto the inwardly visualized naturalistic storm, or rather *seen through it,* as in the Hollywood effect of image superimposition, where glimpses of the past are seen through the evoked present. The dissolution and transformation of that motif, as the storm dies down, into a figure that marks the dissipation of the storm, proves, however, to signal something else: what we might rather describe as a deliberate muting or fading out of the storm's sound as the music, apparently effortlessly, manages a striking effect of focalization. The implicit camera of the unseen film turns its gaze away from the elements to focus on the running man who has been subject to their violence. In fact, the apparent waning of the storm proves to be not only an acoustic alteration of the sound "mix" but also a mimetic paralleling of Siegmund's increasing weariness. The curtain is required to go up as the rising and falling "storm" figuration is still dying away and gradually slowing in the lower orchestral strings. We see (now literally) a stage depiction of the interior of Hunding's dwelling, built around "the stem of a great ash tree." The external door opens. Siegmund enters, exhausted, and is announced by, or calls forth, an evidently new orchestral figure. Fashioned out of the dying storm motif, but with a fanfare-like repeated note initiating its ponderous downward arc and stacked appoggiatura sighs, it provides a mimetic depiction of Siegmund's mood of sorrowful exhaustion and generates a quasi-cinematic subject position (the storm has not really died down, but Siegmund has distanced himself *from* it and its effects).

This is "parallel" underscoring of a rather particular kind. Paulin implies that Wagner's introduction of motifs in the orchestra, as here (rather than connected to sung text, as he had once advocated), indicates musical dominance and the abandonment of any genuine synthesis of music and drama in the way that Wagner had earlier theorized. Paulin goes on to don the mantle of an implicitly more historical, more sophisticated interpreter of Wagner's actual leitmotivic practice when he mocks Erno Rapée's enthusiastic 1925 characterization of Wagner's technique as one of "accompanying" action with music "in the minutest detail."[31] It is true that Wagner's leitmotivic practice assumed a discursive freedom of utterance that he associated with the Beethovenian symphony, whose union with operatic techniques (Paulin seems to forget) had always been an ideal goal of Wagner's innovations. We have seen how cinematic and subjectively focalized his readings of symphonies could be. It is also true, however, that Wagner's practice was frequently *ad hoc,* and marked by fractures in the attempt to maintain centered subjectivity, even meta-subjectivity, and that on closer inspection his music's dominant "symphonic" approach (a term as widely used by film composers and publicists as "leitmotif") often accommodated highly literal passages of mimetic or descriptive parallelism to the stage action, derived not least from the shifting and fragmented accompanying gestures associated with the older operatic recitative. That the first scene of *Die Walküre* is an extended example of what Wagner had referred to as gesturally driven "pantomime" becomes even clearer when Sieglinde enters. Myth gives way to realism for quite some time.

Her initial role as a stranger on stage (albeit in "her" home) leads Wagner perhaps unconsciously to "depict" her and her actions in a way that seems more limited to gestural fidelity than Siegmund's music, whose darkly foreboding manner had focalized his as the presiding subject position. By contrast, Sieglinde's movement toward his slumped form ("Sie tritt näher") is depicted by a mincing little succession of three tripping dotted-note steps that comprise nothing if not an early version of Mickey-Mousing. She then asks aloud who the prone stranger might be. "His" motif reminds us of our now prior sympathetic knowledge of him. When she subsequently "bends over him and listens," Wagner provides as minutely detailed a musical parallelism as one could wish for. The slow downward curve of Siegmund's motif is now attended by an upward arcing figure that quite literally bends over his. This illustrative technique continues, but significantly emphasizes the dominance of Siegmund's subject position as he rouses himself and requests a drink. Sieglinde selects a drinking horn and goes out to fill it; her "bending over" motif is still heard above a sequentially and emotionally intensified extension of Siegmund's motif, whose climax is reached precisely at the point where the stage directions read, "Sie kommt zurück und reicht das gefüllte Trinkhorn Siegmund" (She comes back and offers the filled drinking-horn to Siegmund). As he drinks he gestures thanks with a movement of his head, accompanied by further sequentially rising statements of his motif. When his eyes then fix upon her "mit steigernder Theilnahme" ("with intensifying interest"), the third and highest statement of his motif gives into an extended cello melody that is characterized by "revelatory," chromatically side-stepping harmony. While presented and almost inevitably understood, at first, as *him* growing interested in *her,* the theme famously becomes associated with that first significant meeting of their gaze, and thus of their "inner selves," so that the subject position is now complicated and doubled—or perhaps the music begins to take on the role of a more mythically inclined metadiegetic voice. All of these techniques will be found in classic-era film scoring practice, realistic or "mythic," however critical we may be about it, or about Wagner.[32]

Without embarking upon more extended analysis, which would require the usual plethora of musical examples, the complexity and often inevitably fractured nature of Wagner's musical practice may be characterized as relying on the construction of successive waves of accumulation and intensification: accumulation of signifying musical material and intensification of its metadiegetic invitation to us to become sharers in the larger experience, if not exactly of the creation of the artwork, whose goal had precisely been conceived as a new kind of democratic experience. There is a double irony in Paulin's mockery of the "'demo-cratic' cinema" being valorized by pseudo-Wagnerians "for its artistic progress towards a sort of *Musikdrama*."[33]

CONCLUSION

> Each one of [the] dissevered arts, nursed and luxuriously tended for the entertainment of the rich, has filled the world to overflowing with its products; in each, great minds have brought forth marvels; but the one true Art has not been born again, either in or since the Renaissance. The perfect Art-work, the great united utterance of a free and lovely public life . . . is not yet born again: for reason that it cannot be *re-born*, but must be *born anew*.
>
> Only the great Revolution of Mankind, whose beginnings erstwhile shattered Grecian Tragedy, can win for us this Art-work.
>
> RICHARD WAGNER, "ART AND REVOLUTION"

It would be wrong to suggest too great a degree of correspondence be-tween the idealized "perfect Art-work" of the revolutionary Wagner in 1849[34] and the more nearly "democratic" art of film. But there is a problem in blaming earlier theorists for hoping that there might be such a correspondence on the grounds of a modern film scholar's skepticism about the claims of film to art-authenticity. That is potentially to invest too readily in the Wagnerian music drama as itself embodying that authenticity. We may justly bemoan the overzealous amateurishness of cinematic appropriations of Wagner and Wagnerian theory (while wondering whether misunderstood ideas have not always been the most influential), but let us also beware overlooking the long tradition of critical skepticism about Wagner's own claims to art-authenticity, even about theater in general. One of the founding fathers of such skepticism was Wagner's erstwhile friend Friedrich Nietzsche, who wrote in 1888 (in *Der Fall Wagner*):

> [O]ne should tell the Wagnerians a hundred times to their faces what the theatre is: always only beneath art, always only something secondary, something made cruder, something twisted tendentiously, mendaciously for the sake of the masses. Wagner, too, did not change anything in this

respect: Bayreuth is large-scale opera—and not even good opera.—The theatre is a form of demolatry [worship of the people, of the masses] in matters of taste; the theatre is a revolt of the masses, a plebiscite against good taste.—This is precisely what is proved by the case of Wagner: he won the crowd, he corrupted taste, he spoiled even our taste for opera!—[35]

Here is something that must cast a shadow over Paulin's belief that there is a kind of "art" status to which film and film music might aspire but not attain without the deluding disguise of "Wagner." In a sense Paulin himself gets ensnared in the mechanism of fetishization, which he writes about when he implies that there might be an ideally unified "art" which film is not. To suggest that all that Paulin implies deconstructively about film, and (to be fair) about Wagner by extension, might also apply to the very concept "art" could be to liberate us and decenter the idealized "Wagner." In his place appears a historical figure who was a mediator of complex changes in the cultural practice and social signification of art, whereby the middle-class plunderers of the secret aesthetic treasures of privilege and power redistributed the goods while appropriating some of the privilege and power in and through the image of the Romantic Artist as a bestower of idealized cultural wealth.

Wagner's works, as reflections rather than complete realizations of his ideas, might be seen as tending toward and preparing the techniques, technology, and aesthetics of mass-entertainment film just as much as (or even more than?) they were the embodiments of a new class and canon of "high art" products. Perhaps we can accept that Wagner was, as Adorno occasionally implied, preparing the autonomous art of music for its "debasement" in film. Marc Weiner has nevertheless reminded us of Adorno's well-known *bon mot* (alluding to Nietzsche's Wagner-dedicated *The Birth of Tragedy out of the Spirit of Music*) about how in Wagner's works "we witness the birth of film out of the spirit of music."[36] The lesson we must learn from Wagner, Nietzsche, and Adorno is that "art" and "entertainment" always mediate each other even as they appear to be in conflict. That neither is quite what the other claims fuelled both Nietzsche's anger and Adorno's ambivalence. As for those misguided later film theorists: well, perhaps they were into something after all. The *Tarnhelm* was only theater magic, and we can all see through it. To uncover quite what it shrouded we need not worry about projecting Wagner onto film, but rather project what we know about film back onto Wagner.

NOTES

The first epigraph is from Scott D. Paulin, "Richard Wagner and the Fantasy of Cinematic Unity: The Idea of the *Gesamtkunstwerk* in the History and Theory of Film Music," in *Music and Cinema,* ed. James Buhler, Caryl Flinn, and David Neumeyer (Middletown, Conn.: Wesleyan University Press, 2000), 79; the second from Christopher Morris, *Reading Opera between the Lines* (Cambridge: Cambridge University Press, 2002), 205.

1. My citation is from the closing pages of Morris, *Reading Opera between the Lines,* which is about the symphonic interlude in Wagnerian and post-Wagnerian opera and not in itself committed to any "factional" position.

2. Something I attempted to address in "Movies as Opera (Behind the Great Divide)," in *A Night in at the Opera,* ed. Jeremy Tambling (London: John Libbey and Co., 1994), 71–110.

3. The susceptibility of leitmotivic practice to degenerate into "cinema music" is noted as early as the third chapter of Theodor Adorno, *In Search of Wagner,* trans. Rodney Livingstone (London: NLB, 1981), 46.

4. See Paulin, "Richard Wagner and the Fantasy of Cinematic Unity," 72, where he accepts that Adorno "unveils" the underlying heterogeneity of *Musikdrama.*

5. The best source of information here is Anno Mungen, "Bildermusik": Panoramen, Tableaux vivants und Lichtbilder als mutimediale Darstellungsformen in Theater—und Musikaufführungen vom 19. bis zum frühen 20. Jahrhundert (Remscheid: Gardez! Verlag, 2006). See also A. Nicholas Vardac, *Stage to Screen: Theatrical Origins of Early Film: David Garrick to D. W. Griffith* (originally Cambridge: Harvard University Press, 1949; repr. New York: Da Capo Press, 1987) and Jacky Bratton, Jim Cook, and Christine Gledhill, eds., *Melodrama: Stage Picture Screen* (London: BFI, 1994). The latter contains essays by Peter Brooks, Caryl Flinn, Laura Mulvey, Richard Maltby, and others.

6. A 1952 letter from Korngold to a German admirer, expressing the belief that his new Symphony in F♯ would prove "that monotony and 'modernism' . . . will ultimately result in disaster for the art of music" indicates his longstanding position. See Brendan G. Carroll, *The Last Prodigy: A Biography of Erich Wolfgang Korngold* (Portland, Ore.: Amadeus Press, 1997), 348.

7. See Paulin, "Richard Wagner and the Fantasy of Cinematic Unity," 73; he takes this idea fairly directly from Theodor Adorno and Hanns Eisler, *Composing for the Films* [1947] (London: Athlone Press, 1994), 5–6.

8. Richard Wagner, *Opera and Drama,* trans. W. Ashton Ellis (repr. Lincoln and London: University of Nebraska Press, 1995), Part 3, 330.

9. Ibid., 329 (Wagner introduces dance- and mime-related "pantomime"on p. 78, see also pp. 320–21).

10. Ibid.

11. From "On the Application of Music to Drama" [Über die Anwendung der Musik auf das Drama] (1879), in *Richard Wagner's Prose Works,* trans. William Ashton Ellis (London: Kegan Paul, Trench, Trübner and Co., 1897), vol. 6, 183.

12. See Wagner's letter to Liszt of Dec. 1874, in *Correspondence of Wagner and Liszt*, trans. Francis Hueffer, 2nd ed. rev. and ed. W. Ashton Ellis, vol. 2 (1854–1861) (New York: Scribner, 1897; repr. New York: Vienna House, 1973), 54.

13. See Thomas Mann, *Doctor Faustus: The Life of the German Composer Adrian Leverkühn as Told by a Friend*, trans. H. T. Lowe Porter (Harmondsworth: Penguin, 1968), 131–32 (here Leverkühn asks, "Why does everything seem to me like its own parody?").

14. Wagner, *Opera and Drama*, Part 3, 331.

15. Adorno, *In Search of Wagner*, 29.

16. See ibid., 30–31. There is a strong continuity of thought between *In Search of Wagner* and the Adorno and Eisler volume *Composing for the Films* (see n. 7 above).

17. Richard Wagner, *Tannhäuser*, ed. Egon Voss (Stuttgart, 2001), 9; author's translation.

18. *Tannhäuser* was originally designated as a "Grosser romantische Oper"; ibid., 81.

19. Translation from Oliver Strunk, ed., *Source Readings in Music History*, rev. ed., vol. 6, *The Nineteenth Century*, ed. Ruth Solie (New York and London: Norton, 1998), 152.

20. Richard Wagner, "Beethoven's 'Heroic Symphony,'" in *Judaism in Music and Other Essays*, trans. William Ashton Ellis (repr. Lincoln and London: University of Nebraska Press, 1995), 222.

21. Ibid.

22. Ibid., 224.

23. Ibid., 223.

24. See Peter Franklin, "The Boy on the Train, or Bad Symphonies and Good Movies: The Revealing Error of the 'Symphonic Score,'" in *Beyond the Soundtrack: Representing Music in Cinema*, ed. Daniel Goldmark, Lawrence Kramer, and Richard Leppert (Berkeley: University of California Press, 2007), 17.

25. The Ashton Ellis translation of "Beethoven's Choral Symphony at Dresden 1846" (1846) is cited from Albert Goldman and Evert Sprinchorn, *Wagner on Music and Drama* (New York: Dutton, 1964), 169.

26. "Overture to the *Fliegende Holländer*," in *Richard Wagner, Judaism in Music and Other Essays*, 229.

27. "Prelude to *Lohengrin*," ibid., 232. The text appears in French in John Deathridge and Klaus Döge, *Dokumente und Texte zu Lohengrin* (Mainz: Schott, 2003), 147; it was published in French for Paris concerts of February 1 and 8, 1860.

28. Paulin, "Richard Wagner and the Fantasy of Cinematic Unity," 59.

29. The translation (by Frederick Jameson) is taken from the Klindworth vocal score: Richard Wagner, *Das Rheingold* (G. Schirmer Opera Score Editions, New York/London [n.d.]). For the precise alignment in the full orchestra score, see Egon Voss, ed., *Richard Wagner Sämtliche Werke*, Band 10/1, *Der Ring des Nibelungen. Ein Bühnenfestspiel für drei Tage und einen Vorabend. Vorabend: Das Rheingold* WWV86A, Erste und Zweite Szene (Mainz: Schott 1988), 90–99.

30. Paulin, "Richard Wagner and the Fantasy of Cinematic Unity," 66.

31. Ibid., 68.

32. Is *Gone with the Wind*'s (1939) "Tara" theme, or that associated with King Richard in *The Adventures of Robin Hood* (1938), any less "mythic" than this is "realistic"?

33. Paulin, "Richard Wagner and the Fantasy of Cinematic Unity," 65.

34. Epigraph from Richard Wagner, "Art and Revolution," in *The Artwork of the Future and Other Works*, trans. W. Ashton Ellis (Lincoln and London: University of Nebraska Press, 1993), 53.

35. Friedrich Nietzsche, *The Birth of Tragedy, and The Case of Wagner*, trans. Walter Kaufmann (New York: Vintage, 1967), 182–83.

36. See Marc A. Weiner, "Why Does Hollywood Like Opera?" in *Between Opera and Cinema*, ed. Jeongwon Joe and Rose Theresa (New York and London: Routledge, 2002), 78; the Adorno quotation is found in Theodor Adorno, *In Search of Wagner*, 107.

THREE

The Life and Works of Richard Wagner (1913): Becce, Froelich, and Messter

PAUL FRYER

The rough magic of the silent cinema enables Wagner's characters to shimmer ectoplasmically into view . . .

PETER CONRAD, "HE'S TRICKY, THAT DICKY"

In the warm early summer months of 1913, a little over a year before the outbreak of the Great War in Europe, a short review in *The Musical Standard*, written under the seemingly unlikely pseudonym Euphilma, included the following critical comments:

an excellent production . . . most interesting and splendidly produced . . . well worthy of high praise.[1]

The work referred to here was not an opera, recital, or concert performance, but—probably for the very first time in a serious musical journal—a newly released motion picture. The review concerned the London premiere of the film at a private showing at The West End Cinema, on May 30, accompanied by the New Symphony Orchestra of London under the baton of the distinguished conductor and composer Landon Ronald. The film was *The Life and Works of Richard Wagner*, distributed by the Gaumont Company to mark the hundredth anniversary of the birth of the composer in 1913. An extraordinarily complex, detailed, and sophisticated film for its time, *The Life and Works of Richard Wagner*, directed by Carl Froelich and produced by Oskar Messter, was one of the earliest, if not the very first, feature-length biographical films ever made.[2]

"Biopics," as they became more commonly known, were becoming fashionable, and films about the life of Bismarck and Martin Luther had already proved very popular with German audiences.[3] The fashion originated with the very beginning of filmmaking itself, and both composers and performers have been well-represented as subjects. A shortlist would include Beethoven, Gershwin, Paganini, Grieg, Liszt, Johann Strauss, Schumann, Chopin, Vivaldi, Handel, Tchaikovsky, Lully, Marais, Rimsky-Korsakov, Mozart, and Mahler.[4] Each has appeared as a movie character, and their music, in one form or another, has featured in literally thousands of movie soundtracks. The best represented of all, however, has been Richard Wagner.

If we consider alone the number of movie scenes in which either the "Wedding March" from *Lohengrin* or "The Ride of the Valkyries" from *Die Walküre* has featured, it seems likely that Wagner has been the sometimes un-credited contributing composer to possibly thousands of movie scores. He has also featured as a central character on-screen: played by Alan Badel in William Dieterle's *Magic Fire* (1956), by Trevor Howard in Luchino Visconti's *Ludwig* (1973), somewhat less reverentially by Paul Nicholas in Ken Russell's *Lisztomania* (1976), and memorably by Richard Burton in Tony Palmer's highly detailed film of the composer's life, originally made as a television mini-series in 1983. Even considering the technical limitations of the time, however, Froelich's early film, if not the most searching or critical biographical exploration, remains in many ways the most important of all cinematic representations of Wagner. One central reason for this is the creative combination of the three most important figures involved in the making of the film: the producer, Oskar Messter, the director, Carl Froelich, and the composer, Giuseppe Becce, who also played the title role.

Oskar Messter, born in Berlin in 1866, is, in Deac Rossell's words, "widely known as the Father of the German Film Industry."[5] Using the business base of the family firm, which manufactured optical equipment, Messter had started working in the industry in 1896, designing and building film projectors. Later in that year he made his first films—described by Martin Koerber as "street scenes with parading soldiers, flowing traffic and railway scenes . . . generally reminiscent of the films made by Lumière"[6]—and built the very first German movie studio on the Friedrichstrasse in Berlin. During his first year he produced eighty-four short films, up to twenty-four meters in length,[7] which included several featuring the Kaiser and members of the German Imperial family filmed on location at public events. These became very popular and significantly helped to raise the profile of Messter's company.

Messter took over the lease of the first projection hall, which had opened on the Unter den Linden in Berlin in April 1896. Renaming the hall The Biorama, he began staging variety programs interspersed with his short films. These presentations became highly popular, and by the end of the year Messter had been invited to stage similar entertainments at Berlin's Apollo Theater, one of the city's most popular venues. He was one of the first filmmakers to experiment with time-lapse photography, helped to establish a star system in the German film industry with his promotion of the actress Henny Porten, and produced the first weekly newsreel in Germany, *Messter-Woche,* which first appeared in October 1914. He explored early close-up filming techniques, and his company later experimented with color film and three-dimensional projection. He was, in every sense, a true pioneer of the industry.

Perhaps Messter's most important contribution, however, was his early experimentation with synchronized sound films. These precursors of "the talkies" used a sound track recorded on large gramophone discs, which were then synchronized to the action as the film was projected live onto the screen.[8] Martin Koerber confirms that "[a]s early as 1896, in Messter's Biorama . . . a phonograph was used to provide a musical accompaniment to the 'living photography.' This was no arbitrary background music, but a series of pieces specially selected to accompany the images."[9]

In 1903, Messter presented the first program of projected synchronized sound films to a German audience at Berlin's Apollo Theater, and in the following year presented a similar program at the St. Louis World Fair. Within a decade Messter's company had installed his Biophon sound system in more than five hundred theaters. Although the early technology was fraught with many potential difficulties, Messter's company produced several hundred synchronized sound films, which he called Tonbilder. One of the earliest of these featured the tenor Siegmund Lieban, performing part of the Prologue from Leoncavallo's *Pagliacci;*

other operatic scenes included *The Death of Othello* (1909), a scene from Verdi's opera, with Franz Porten miming the title role, and at least one from a Wagnerian opera, the forging scene from *Siegfried* (1909). In 1907, the Messter Company released a severely abridged version of Wagner's *Lohengrin,* which also used a synchronized music track.[10] Messter went on to produce more than 350 films before his company, Projektions-GMBH Berlin, merged with the new UFA studios in 1917, for which he was paid more than five million marks. With such a pedigree, it seems hardly surprising that Messter would have instigated the highly ambitious project of creating a biographical film of Wagner to celebrate the centenary of the composer's birth.

Messter's original plan was that the film should be accompanied by a score arranged from Wagner's own music. However, although it appears that the Wagner estate raised no specific objections to the making of the film itself, they demanded a very high fee for the rights to use the music. Messter later noted in his autobiography that these were "extraordinarily high financial demands, reaching a sum close to half a million marks."[11] He was forced to adopt a different solution and employed a composer instead to write an completely original score.

The use of music of all kinds to accompany projected films is a practice as old as the moving picture itself,[12] probably originally employed to help to cover the excessive noise made by the operation of early, hand-cranked projection equipment rather than as an attempt to create a specific mood or atmosphere. The widely held and somewhat clichéd image of the piano player seated at an upright instrument, accompanying the on-screen action with improvised versions of favorite tunes of the day, is only a partly accurate one. Brian Coe reminds us that frequently in the early days, "films were shown as part of a music hall performance, and they were then usually accompanied by the pit orchestra . . . The travelling showman in the fairground would present his show to a background of music from the fair organs."[13]

Recognizing the emotive power of music and its ability to significantly add to the experience of the burgeoning movie audience, filmmakers were quick to adopt a less random approach. The practice of sending out cue-sheets which contained instructions on the specific music to be used for each scene, or a suggestion as to the kind of music that would work best, was superseded by the provision of a specific score with major movies, usually specially composed for the event, and often available in a range of orchestrations to suit the size of musical ensemble available. Movie theaters themselves became amongst the most prolific employers of professional musicians, with the grandest establishments maintaining full-sized orchestras capable of playing a very wide range of symphonic repertoire.[14]

There have been several claimants to the title of composer of the first original film score. The American composer Joseph Carl Breil is often credited thus for his score for Sarah Bernhardt's film of *Queen Elizabeth,* released in 1912. But he was by no means the very first. The French composer Camille Saint-Saëns had provided an original score for the 1908 film, *The Assassination of the Duc de Guise,* directed for the Film d'Art company by André Calmettes. For his new project, Messter chose a young Italian composer called Giuseppe Becce. Although Becce certainly cannot be credited as the first film music composer, he was to become one of the very earliest serious composers to specialize in writing music for the screen, and was to enjoy a long, fruitful, and influential career in the industry.

Born in the Veneto region of Italy in 1877, Becce had initially studied geography at Padua University, later moving to Berlin in 1900, where he studied conducting with Artur Nikitsch and composition with Leopold Schmidt and Ferruccio Busoni. Although he worked as a jobbing musician and conductor, Becce failed to make any significant impact as a serious composer. Neither of his two major early works, an operetta entitled *Das Bett der Pompadour* (1910) and an opera, *Tullia* (1912), found either public or critical success. Messter's commission must have intrigued the young composer, since it included the challenging instruction to create music that was Wagnerian in spirit, yet without ever quoting even the briefest phrase from any of Wagner's own compositions. In fact, Becce's final score is not comprised entirely of original music. The surviving piano reduction of the score, of which a copy exists in the Library of Congress in Washington, D.C., includes upon its title page the inscription, "Accompanying music arranged and partially composed by Dr. G. Becce."[15] The published score includes extracts from works by Haydn, Mozart, Beethoven, and Rossini, as well as Becce's own original music.[16]

The young composer's involvement in the project was, however, to extend a great deal further than creating the music. Unexpectedly, the unnamed actor who had originally been contracted to play the title role in the film withdrew from the project, and Messter proposed an unusual solution. He suggested that Becce should take the actor's place and portray the composer on screen. This was not as outlandish an idea as it might at first have seemed. The notion of any technique of film acting was entirely unthought of at this time. Actors were often described as *posing* for the film cameras rather than acting, which was considered to be a theatrical skill, and filmmakers frequently used non-professional performers, their selection being largely based upon a suitable physical appearance. Becce certainly possessed a physical resemblance to Wagner, which could easily be enhanced by theatrical makeup, and perhaps more importantly, because he was a genuine professional musician, he would be able to act conducting and playing the piano very convincingly (figure 3.1). With very little to lose, and equally little knowledge of the process of filming, Becce agreed, becoming not only the composer of the first complete score for a German film, but also the first and only real-life composer ever to play another in a motion picture.

This new career upon which he embarked occupied him for the remainder of his long working life. Between 1913 and 1960, Becce wrote music for almost two hundred films, which included some of the most influential German productions of the silent era: *The Cabinet of Dr. Caligari* (Robert Wiene, 1919), *Der müde Tod* (Fritz Lang, 1920), and *The Last Laugh* (F. W. Murnau, 1924). In the 1920s he was appointed head of the music department at the UFA studios, and positively welcomed the coming of the new sound-on-film technology. In 1929, he stated that "the development of talkies will go hand in hand with the development of film music, because sound film will help to evolve the style of film music that serious composers are already trying to achieve."[17]

Becce provided the score for Gustav Machaty's *Ecstasy* (1932), notorious for the inclusion of a nude scene featuring the actress Hedy Lamarr, and specialized in composing for "mountain films," a genre featuring mountaineering and emphasizing man's transforming struggle against the elements which became particularly popular with German audiences of the 1930s. He scored several of Leni Riefenstahl's films, including *The Blue Light* (1932). His final film score was for *Zauber der Dolomiten,* a documentary feature released in 1959.

FIG. 3.1. Becce as Wagner

The third and final figure in this creative triumvirate was the director, Carl Froelich. Born in Berlin in 1875, Froelich directed nearly eighty films in a career that spanned forty-five years and had begun with working as a cinematographer for Franz Porten in 1906. Although Froelich is credited with a short feature from 1912, *The Life and Works of Richard Wagner* was certainly his first substantial experience as a director, and as such, it shows the most extraordinary facility, not only for the effective and imaginative staging of scenes but also for composition, camera technique, and the ability to inject a real sense of movement and motion at a time when the majority of films were accused of seeming unduly static. Froelich certainly had a well-developed understanding of what film was capable of achieving, even at this early stage in the development of the medium.

This was probably due, as much as anything, to his early experiences as a camera operator, learning what the relatively primitive equipment of this time was able to achieve. He had worked as a cinematographer on almost twenty productions before he graduated to the director's chair. Messter, already a seasoned filmmaker by the time that he embarked upon his Wagner project, surely recognized Froelich's potential.

As well as being able to create a genuine atmosphere of "action" within his shots, Froelich also experimented with special effects, which, although primitive by modern standards and owing much to the pioneering work of colleagues such as Georges Méliès, still add a great deal to the overall dramatic impact of the film. For example, two characters from paintings come to life in an early dream sequence, illustrating the vividness of the young Wagner's imagination; the final montage sequence of the film shows the principal characters from the operas reappearing around the tomb of the dead master, forming a creative guard of honor in recognition of his artistic achievements.

Froelich also used location filming quite liberally, at a time when heavy and inflexible camera equipment could provide a major obstacle to such an enterprise. We are therefore shown the events of Wagner's escape into exile, including a most unusual scene on board a ship, with a long shot provided by a camera located on another boat some distance away creating a highly authentic wave motion. Scenes were also shot at the Villa Wahnfried and in the grounds of the Festspielhaus, as well as at several locations in Bavaria for the scenes involving King Ludwig.

Settings and costumes, although often quite theatrical, were designed to be as accurate as possible. Several sources about *The Life and Works of Richard Wagner* include a co-directing credit for William Wauer. Wauer had trained as an artist and was a well-known journalist and editor who had also shown a flair for directing in the theater. He staged a number of plays in Berlin, including several for Max Reinhardt's company. He later founded his own film production company and continued to work as both writer and director. Although the exact division of labor between Wauer and Froelich is not made explicit, it seems that Wauer concentrated on writing the scenario and designing the production, leaving Froelich to direct the cameras. This collaboration probably accounts for the level of visual accuracy in the film.

Froelich even used artificial lighting quite adventurously and subtly to create dramatic effect, at a time when the majority of films were still being shot in broad daylight to take advantage of the maximum intensity of natural light available. Considering the technical limitations of the time, Froelich's work on this film provides us with much evidence of the work of a highly skilled filmmaker. He later founded his own production company, frequently working with the popular actress Henny Porten, and continued to be involved in cinematic innovation, directing one of the first German talking pictures in 1929.[18]

The disintegration of Froelich's career after World War II was largely due to his association with the National Socialist Party in Germany. He had been a member of the Party since 1933 and was later appointed director of The Union of Film Manufacture and Film Evaluation. In 1939 he was appointed president of the Reichsfilmkammer and made a number of films for the Reichspropaganda Ministry. He was arrested at the end of the war, and although he underwent a process of de-Nazification, he was unable to re-establish an international career. After a gap of six years, Froelich made his final two films in West Germany in 1950 and 1951.[19]

The film that resulted from the collaboration between Messter, Becce, and Froelich is in many ways more sophisticated as an example of early filmmaking than it is as an exercise in creative storytelling. The linear narrative presents a series of snapshots of the great composer's life rather than any genuine attempt to "get beneath the skin" of Wagner the man or to subject his life or work to any form of meaningful analysis. In this respect the film may also be criticized for being hagiographical in its approach. Peter Conrad's somewhat unforgiving comments are not far wide of the mark:

> The ogre's life is piously sanitised: Wagner's affair with Mathilde Wesend-onck during the composition of *Tristan* is here an abstract Platonic infatu-ation, and he takes up with Cosima only after she leaves her husband, the conductor von Bülow (who, in reality, served as Wagner's obliging toady even after being cuckolded).[20]

However, there is humor (evident in the scene in which Meyerbeer dismisses the young Wagner with empty promises of assistance). There is drama (the flight into exile and the scenes of street battles), theatrical history (the staging of several scenes from Wagner's operas, which at least represent some evidence of early-twentieth-century staging tech-niques), and sensitivity (the relationship between Wagner and Ludwig, briefly sketched though it may be, suggests a real intimacy, affection, and understanding between the two men). Each of these qualities is evident within the framing of a number of small and stylish grace-notes, each of which preserves the sense of quality, even when the narrative itself appears to adopt a mechanical progression.[21]

Coming as it does from an era that long predates the contemporary obsession with the journalistic exposé and the unexpurgated biography, the film's sanitization of Wagner's story is not simply a matter of due reverence to a great artist. The film coincided with a resurgence of interest in the composer's work, and although Wagner himself had been dead for thirty years, his son Siegfried and his second wife Cosima, who both died in 1930, were highly regarded and influential members of the conservative musical establishment, maintaining the traditions at Bayreuth that the master himself had established.[22] It is unlikely that anyone wishing to operate effectively within the artistic establishment of Germany at that time would have deliberately provoked the Wagner family with the creation of an unnecessarily intrusive or critical version of the composer's life. Both Cosima and Siegfried appear as characters in the film and their dramatic representation would by necessity have been a matter for detailed consideration. Facts would need to be accurately retold, but without any unnecessary or inappropriate dramatic embellishment. A program for a screening of the film at the Theater am Moritzplatz in August 1913 describes the film as "a cinematic comment on the composer's life."

Even if Froelich and Messter had wished to make a more provocative and critical film, it is unlikely that it would have been publicly screened. Movie theaters in the German Empire were subject to state licensing and all films shown in Germany had to be approved by state-appointed censors. Both the Bavarian and the Prussian censors demanded certain changes before authorizing the film's release. These, however, seem to have been based upon the need to maintain public decency: a romantic scene between Wagner and Mina Planer, another between Wagner and Mathilde Wesendonck, and a shot which showed Wagner sitting in his bathtub, were all excised. The Bavarian censor also removed the scene in which Ludwig is impelled by his ministers to sign the document calling for Wagner's exile, although this was later reinstated. When the film reached Vienna the Austrian censors also reinstated some of the material that their German counterparts had seen fit to remove.

The film would have been seen as an educational tool as much as an entertainment, providing important factual details on the life of a composer about whom very little was then commonly known. Wagner had written his autobiography, *Mein Leben,* in 1880, and his collected prose works, supervised by the author, had appeared between 1871 and 1873 in nine volumes with a further volume appearing in 1883. Critical biographies were rare at this time, and although the correspondence between Wagner and Mathilda Wesendonck had been published in Berlin in 1904, critical editions of Wagner's letters did not appear in print until the 1960s. The relative accessibility of a motion picture would bring Wagner's life and work to a new and far wider potential audience. It is curiously coincidental that 1913 also marked the end of the thirty-year copyright restriction that had been imposed by the Wagner family, preventing performances of *Parsifal* outside of Bayreuth. The Stadttheater in Zurich became the first theater to stage an authorized production of the work.

The world premiere of Froelich and Messter's film was presented at the Union Theater Friedrichstrasse in the Bavariahaus in Berlin on 31 May 1913.[23] An unidentified press cutting suggested that there was "no better example of cinema's coming of age." Serious film criticism such as we would recognize today barely existed at this time, and journalistic coverage of a film's release generally consisted merely of a plot outline, some mention of the leading performers, and a few simple personal, and usually highly subjective observations on the overall quality of the production. Although this film was generally well received in the specialist press, some observers branded it amateurish, tasteless, unrealistic, and sometimes unintentionally humorous: the critic of the *Frankfurter Zeitung* noted that during the scene showing Wagner's father on his deathbed, he was not allowed to "pass away silently but instead seems to die a horrible death, suffocated by his family who trample all over him."[24] Other commentators suggested that the mere presence on screen of the character of King Ludwig of Bavaria was enough to raise the tone of the entire enterprise.

The use of music in the film caused a considerable amount of controversy. Leopold Schwarzschild, writing in the *Frankfurter Zeitung,* disapproved of the way in which Mozart's scores were used. Stating that "the music plays the minuet from *Don Giovanni* having disfigured the G minor symphony," he suggested that Becce was making obvious and thinly disguised attempts at imitating Wagner.[25] In complete contrast, O. T. Stein, writing about the Dresden premiere in *Das Lichtbild Theater,* noted that

> if it had not been for the highly tasteful musical arrangement done by Dr. Becce . . . well-played by a good orchestra . . . which reminded the listener of the magic of Wagnerian art and coincided beautifully with the screen images—one's interest in the film, because of its obvious faults, would not have been sustained. Here the music becomes a glorious helper, an artistic co-creator, just as it should be and will have to be in the cinema.[26]

It was not always clear from the limited contemporary journalistic coverage exactly which version of the score was used at each screening or in what form it was played. Messter Film GmbH published several different arrangements, which included full orchestra, and reduced orchestra and solo piano, to suit the facilities available at different theaters. The Berlin, London, Dresden, and Frankfurt premieres all employed orchestras, but W. Stephen Bush's review of the New York premiere only refers to an organ.[27] It is equally unclear if every performance actually used Becce's score, and it may well have been that some screenings were accompanied by improvised music. The London review clearly states that "the accompanying music has been specially arranged from the works of Wagner, by Mr. Landon Ronald,"[28] although this may have been a simple error.

No box-office receipts for the film were recorded; however, it was evidently considered both important enough and of sufficient earning potential to be given an international release, being distributed by Gaumont British Distributors in the United Kingdom and by Klaw and Erlanger in the United States. Presumably these versions were sent out with English-language intertitles, as was fairly common at the time, although there is no record of this and no copy appears to have survived.

The London premiere, given to an invited audience on the afternoon of May 30, drew the following response from *The Musical Standard:* "The way in which the principal events in Wagner's life have been filmed . . . is extraordinary and leaves nothing to complain of."[29] The reviewer went to considerable lengths to comment on the quality of the music accompanying the film, although the arrangement of the music was attributed to the conductor, Landon Ronald: "Although the New Symphony Orchestra only played at the invitation performance, yet at the succeeding performances the band was by no means inadequate; indeed the larger orchestra was too powerful for the size of the hall."[30]

The film premiered in New York at the New Amsterdam Theatre in November 1913. The U.S. distributors, Klaw and Erlanger, also recognizing the educational value of the film, used the premiere to launch a new initiative, as described in *The New York Times*, "to utilize their theatres at times when the more important houses of amusement are idle . . . a series of special matinees . . . at the New Amsterdam Theatre of the new motion picture 'The Life and Works of the composer, Richard Wagner' . . . with a narration by R. S. Pigott and an organ recital by W. H. Humiston."[31] Describing the film as "a drama of human interest," the *Times* writer was at great pains to assure his readers that this program would "in no way interfere with the run of 'The Little Cafe,' now playing at the same theatre."[32]

W. Stephen Bush, one of the first serious film critics, noted that the film "shows vast improvement, but it is not wholly free from jarring traces of that amateurishness which characterises so many German film productions."[33] Such reservations, however, did not prevent Bush from stating that "the subject, the music, the lecture and the acting of the principal characters hold out great hopes for the success of this feature. There are flashes of superb beauty in it."[34] He also speculated that the success of such a film might encourage other producers to explore the possibilities of making complete synchronized sound versions of Wagner's operas.

For all of its importance as a milestone in the development of the biopic as a cinematic genre, and the impressive array of technical and creative devices employed by the filmmakers, there is one additional aspect to *The Life and Works of Richard Wagner* that singles it out as worthy of particular consideration. At a time when the average "short" played for less than ten minutes, the notion of an hour-long film was considered highly ambitious. When this film was registered with the German censor on May 8, 1913, the running length was recorded as 2055 meters, with an estimated playing time of eighty minutes. The first Hollywood film to play for longer than seventy minutes, *The Squaw Man,* directed by Cecil B. DeMille, did not appear until a year after Froelich's film was released.

The version of the film that has survived is approximately sixty-nine minutes long. Even allowing for the inaccuracy of hand-cranked projection, this indicates clearly that approximately ten minutes of the original film is now lost. Such losses are not at all unusual in films from this period. Film damaged during a screening was often simply cut out of the print by the projectionist and thrown away without a second thought. Since no shooting script of any kind appears to have survived, there is no way of telling what is missing from the version that we have. It is tempting, though entirely futile, to speculate that this footage might include some further extracts from the operas: the staging of the *Ring* is virtually ignored in the surviving version. Although apparently "lost" films do occasionally re-emerge, it is perhaps unlikely that contemporary audiences will ever be fortunate enough to witness these ten additional minutes of Froelich and Messter's Wagnerian adventure.

Although Froelich's film must be credited as the most important Wagnerian cinema experience of its time, it was by no means the first. Prior to the release of Froelich's film, the most important Wagnerian property to make a transition to the screen was in some ways perhaps an even greater creative achievement: the Edison Company's film of Wagner's great music-drama, *Parsifal,* directed by one of the most effective filmmakers of the time, Edwin S. Porter, in 1904.[35]

Wagner's great masterpiece had been given in a concert performance by the Oratorio Society of New York in 1886, conducted by Walter Damrosch. However, it was not seen in a fully staged production at the Metropolitan Opera House until December 24, 1903. The cast of the American premiere included Milka Ternina as Kundry and two leading Bayreuth performers, Aloys Burgstaller in the title role and the Dutch baritone Anton van Rooy as Amfortas. This production was a huge public and critical success, but it also caused a major furore at the time: it was the first time that the opera had been staged outside Bayreuth, and the production was given in direct defiance of the instructions of Cosima Wagner. The German Wagner establishment considered such a production almost sacrilegious, and van Rooy, who had been much admired by Cosima and who had caused a sensation as Wotan during the 1897

Festival, was banished from the Festspielhaus and was never invited to sing at Bayreuth again. Porter's film *Parsifal* appeared in October 1904, barely ten months after the New York premiere of the opera. An English-language version of the opera opened at the Tremont Theatre in Boston only four days after Porter's film and came to the New York Theater in Manhattan at the end of October, and it seems fairly clear that Porter hoped that his film would capitalize on the considerable theatrical success that the opera was already enjoying.

The film of *Parsifal* is by far the most ambitious and expensive project that Porter completed during his time at the Edison Company. It was originally intended that special phonograph cylinder recordings of the opera could be made and synchronized to the action of the film, using the Edison Kinetophone system. This plan proved to be overly ambitious for the available technology, although some of the earliest screenings of Porter's film in New York are reported to have used synchronized sound.[36] Nevertheless, the performances on screen seem theatrically overexaggerated; one might say un-naturalistically operatic, perhaps intentionally so to give the impression that the actors are singing their roles. The staging appears to be conventionally theatrical; the scenery consists mainly of large painted backdrops designed by Harley Merry, and the camera is placed so that all shots appear to be seen from the point of view of an audience member seated in the orchestra stalls. The cast included Robert Whittier as Parsifal and Adelaide Fitz-Allen as Kundry, and eight scenes from the opera were included. Generally, the action of the film is faithful to the plot of the opera with the notable exception that in the first half of the film, Amfortas is given a wife and son.

After the problems caused by the staging at the Metropolitan, it seemed that America's experience of *Parsifal* was destined to continue to be dogged by controversy: the owner of the American copyright on the opera sued Edison for unauthorized use of the script of the opera, Edison lost the case and was forced to withdraw the film from release. But this did not prevent the company from reissuing the film five years later in a re-cut version.

What we see viewing Porter's film today is an extraordinarily ambitious work for its time—the first attempt to "represent" a complete, although highly abridged, Wagnerian work on film—and one of the very first films to make a serious attempt to present an operatic subject to the newly democratized audience created by the twentieth century's first great new art form, the cinema.

A NOTE ON THE RESTORATION OF *THE LIFE AND WORKS OF RICHARD WAGNER*

My own association with this extraordinary movie came about as the result of a commission for a film screening program by the Wagner Society of Northern California in San Francisco in 2003. This program investigated, in a fairly lighthearted manner, the use of Wagner in the movies, and covered a broad spectrum from Edwin S. Porter's *Parsifal* (1903) via Bugs Bunny (*What's Opera Doc?*) to later examples such as John Boorman's *Excalibur* (1981), Francis Ford Coppola's *Apocalypse Now* (1979), and Istvan Szabo's *Meeting Venus* (1991).

The success of this program led to a second commission and the suggestion that I might be interested in looking at Froelich's film. Although this seemed a particularly exciting proposition, I had never actually seen the film, nor was I in any way certain that the film still existed. Although frequently referred to, it appeared that few serious scholars had attempted any detailed analysis or description of the film. There have been so many occasions during my previous research when the disheartening phrase, "missing, believed lost," would constitute the only record of an early silent film's survival.

Enquiries revealed the existence of an archive copy of the film in the collection of the Friedrich Wilhelm Murnau Stiftung in Wiesbaden—a reconstructed version prepared for German television, with an orchestral score arranged by the Swiss conductor Armin Brunner in 1983. This version of the film was covered by copyright, however, and not available for further restoration, so we were forced to look elsewhere. My San Francisco colleagues eventually located a copy in a private film collection in the United States, and the owner agreed to allow us to use this for the creation of a new English-language screening version.

I have for some time worked with the British composer Barry Seaman, who has a particular interest in the composition of music for pre-sound films. Our first project had been the restoration of the 1915 silent film version of *Tsar Ivan the Terrible,* based on Rimsky-Korsakov's opera *The Maid of Pskov,* directed by Alexander Ivanov-Gai and featuring the great Russian operatic bass Feodor Chaliapin in his only silent film role. Froelich's film seemed like the perfect follow-up project for us to undertake.

Working from a digitized copy of the American version of the Wagner film,[37] we first edited out the original Gothic German script intertitles, replacing them with newly translated English titles. Apart from some minor grammatical changes and cuts to improve the comprehension for a contemporary audience, the new versions represent a faithful rendering of the old except for the correction of some errors in a few of the dates that do not correspond to the chronology of Wagner's life.

Barry Seaman then set about composing an entirely original sixty-eight-minute orchestral score to accompany the film. In keeping with the spirit of the original enterprise and the constraints of Becce's commission from Messter, Seaman accepted the challenge to produce a score that would complement and support the images on the screen without ever actually quoting from the music of the master himself; although it is fair to say that there are moments when Seaman's music distinctly evokes both *Parsifal* and *Tristan und Isolde*.

In the digital editing process, we also resisted the temptation to indulge in any further interventions into Froelich's original as it had been passed to us, incomplete though it is. With the exception of the removal of a few damaged frames, some minor attempts to improve the black and white "color" balance to enhance the sharpness of the image and achieve the best definition, and the inclusion of new intertitles and closing credits, every effort has been made to conserve the original.

The new version was premiered in San Francisco in 2004, and further screenings took place in New York City, Boston, Washington, D.C., Chicago, and London. Minor re-edits of the score and some changes to the orchestration have resulted in the production of three further versions, and further screenings in Seattle (as part of Seattle Opera's 2005 *Ring* cycle) and in Toronto (as part of the inaugural *Ring* cycle opening the new Four Seasons Centre for the Performing Arts in 2006). Projects such as this will always remain "work in progress," and I have no doubt that, time permitting, we will return to Froelich's film yet again as part of what has become a minor crusade to re-introduce this startling film to a twenty-first-century audience.

NOTES

The epigraph is from Peter Conrad, "He's Tricky, That Dicky," *The Observer* (October 2002).

1. "The Life of Richard Wagner—as Depicted by the Kinematograph," *The Musical Standard*, June 21, 1913, 555.

2. The exact definition of "feature length" is difficult to establish: The Academy of Motion Picture Arts and Sciences has set a minimum running time of forty minutes. The earliest European feature-length movies included the French productions *L'Enfant prodigue* (1907) and a version of *Les Misérables* (1909). The earliest American examples, which were released in 1912, included Frederick Warde as *Richard III* and an adaptation of Dickens's *Oliver Twist*.

3. The term biopic—simply a condensation of the descriptive "biographical picture"—probably originates from its use in *Variety*, the influential American entertainment publication. As early as 1899, the French pioneer filmmaker Georges Méliès made a film about the life of Joan of Arc.

4. Some major examples include Beethoven, *Das Leben des Beethoven* (Hans Otto, Allianz-Film, 1927) and *Immortal Beloved* (Bernard Rose, Icon Entertainment, 1995); Gershwin, *Rhapsody in Blue* (Irving Rapper, MGM, 1945); Paganini, *Paganini* (Heinz Goldberg, Conrad Veidt Film, 1923) and *The Magic Bow* (Bernard Knowles, Gainsborough Pictures, 1946); Grieg, *Song of Norway* (Andrew L. Stone, ABC Pictures, 1970); Liszt, *Liebesträume* (Heinz Hille, 1935), *Song without End* (Charles Vidor, Goetz Productions, 1960) and *Lisztomania* (Ken Russell, Goodtimes Enterprises, 1976); Johann Strauss, *Waltzes from Vienna* (Alfred Hitchcock, Gaumont British, 1934), *Wiener Walzer* (Emil Reinert, Cordial Film, 1951) and *The Great Waltz* (Andrew M. Stone, MGM, 1972); Schumann, *Song of Love* (Clarence Brown, MGM, 1947); Chopin, *A Song to Remember* (Charles Vidor, Columbia Pictures, 1945); Vivaldi, *Rouge Venise* (Etienne Périer, Clea Productions, 1989) and *Vivaldi* (Boris Damast, currently in production, expected 2010); Handel, *The Great Mr. Handel* (Norman Walker, G.H.W. Productions, 1942); Tchaikovsky, *Song of My Heart* (Benjamin Glazer, Symphony Films, 1948) and *The Music Lovers* (Ken Russell, Russ-Arts, 1971); Lully, *Le Roi danse* (Gerard Corbiau, Canal +, 2002); Marais, *Tous les matins du monde* (Alain Corneau, Film Par Film, 1993); Rimsky-Korsakov, *Song of Scheherazade* (Walter Reisch, Universal, 1947); Mozart, *Whom the Gods Love* (Basil Dean, Associated Pictures, 1936), *Mozart* (Karl Hartl, Cosmopol Film, 1955) and *Amadeus* (Milos Forman, Saul Zaentz Productions, 1985); Mahler, *Mahler* (Ken Russell, Goodtimes Enterprises, 1975) and *Bride of the Wind* (Bruce Beresford, Alma UK, 2002).

5. Deac Rossell, in Stephen Herbert and Luke McKernan, *Who's Who of Victorian Cinema* (London: British Film Institute, 1996), 97.

6. Martin Koerber, "Oskar Messter, Film Pioneer," in *A Second Life: German Cinema's First Decades*, ed. Thomas Elsaesser (Amsterdam: Amsterdam University Press, 1996), 54.

7. The actual playing time would depend on the cranking speed of both the cameraman and the projector operator—which might be anything between sixteen and twenty-four frames per second. One thousand feet (approximately 305 meters)

of film projected at twenty-four frames per second (now considered standard) would play for less than ten minutes. It is therefore likely that the playing time of Messter's short films would be no more than a minute.

8. In the 1920s, Warner Brothers developed a more famous synchronized sound system called the Vitaphone, which was used highly effectively for numerous serious and lighter musical subjects. This was the immediate predecessor of the sound-on-film technology that allowed the development of talking pictures from 1926 onwards.

9. Koerber, "Oskar Messter, Film Pioneer," 55–56.

10. The *Lohengrin* film no longer exists, but a copy of the *Siegfried* short has survived and has been restored (regrettably, without the accompanying sound disc).

11. Oskar Messter, *Mein Weg mit dem Film* (Berlin: Verlag Max Hesse, 1936), 63.

12. The first public film show given by the Lumière brothers in Paris in 1895 is said to have been accompanied by a pianist.

13. Brian Coe, *The History of Movie Photography* (Westfield, N.J.: Eastview Editions, 1981), 90.

14. The largest theaters would also employ soloists, singers, and choirs to further add to the effect. Several early screenings of Cecil B. DeMille's film of *Carmen* (1915), which starred the Metropolitan Opera star Geraldine Farrar, featured singers, who stood next to the screen and sang passages from Bizet's opera. The gala premiere of D. W. Griffith's *The Birth of a Nation* (1915) employed a symphonic orchestra and a choir to perform Joseph Carl Breil's original score for the film.

15. Gillian Anderson also lists the score in her definitive *Music for Silent Films: A Guide* (Washington, D.C.: Library of Congress, 1988).

16. Becce's original score was released on CD as *Giuseppe Becce: Music for the Silent Movie (1913)*, KOCH International GumH 3-6495-2, 1997.

17. Quoted in David Lewis, *All Movie Guide*, www.allmovie.com (accessed April 28, 2008).

18. *Die Nacht gehört uns* was based on a popular play and starred Hans Albers.

19. Froelich died in Berlin in 1953.

20. Conrad, "He's Tricky, That Dicky."

21. One example is the arrival of Ludwig to visit Wagner in exile. As the king's boat draws up at the landing stage, a single white swan swims in front of it.

22. Cosima ran the festival until 1906, when she handed the responsibility on to her son Siegfried.

23. There is some discrepancy here, since some sources record this date as May 13. If May 31 is indeed the correct date, the German premiere would have been preceded by the first private London screening, which is recorded as having taken place on the afternoon of May 30, one day earlier. It is possibly the result of a simple transposition of numbers.

24. Original review quoted by Ludwig Greve, ed., in *Hätte ich das Kino! Die Schriftsteller und der Stummfilm* (Munich: Kosel, 1976), 51.

25. Ibid. Leopold Schwarzschild (1891–1950) was a distinguished Jewish Berlin-based publisher, economist, critic, and co-editor of *Das Tage-Buch*. A prominent critic of Hitler and the rise of National Socialism, he sought exile first in Paris and later in the United States. His book, *World in Trance* (1943), a critical indict-

ment of the effects of the Treaty of Versailles, was said to have influenced Winston Churchill.

26. O. T. Stein, "A New Film Genre: The Richard Wagner Film Biography," *Das Lichtbild Theater,* June 5, 1913.

27. W. Stephen Bush, "The Life of Richard Wagner," *The Moving Picture World,* November 29, 1913, no page number.

28. "Notes," *The Musical Standard,* May 31, 1913, 485.

29. "The Life of Richard Wagner, as Depicted by the Kinematograph," *The Musical Standard,* June 21, 1913, 555.

30. Ibid.

31. "Moving Picture Matinees, Life and Works of Wagner at New Amsterdam First in New Plan," *The New York Times,* November 13, 1913, 11.

32. Ibid.

33. Bush, "Richard Wagner."

34. Ibid.

35. Porter was born in Pennsylvania in 1870 and had directed his first short film, *The Cavalier's Dream,* in 1898. His first "operatic" subject had been a two-minute film called *Faust and Marguerite* (1900). In 1903, Porter's great success, *The Great Train Robbery,* launched the Western movie genre that has retained its popularity right up to today.

36. Introduced in 1895, the Kinetophone system was the first real attempt to record and play back image and sound in one synchronized process by combining Edison's Kinetoscope with a cylinder phonograph. The Kinetoscope equipment was housed in a cabinet and watched by each individual viewer through a small window. Edison had first described this concept in 1888, and the first public exhibition was given in New York City in 1894. The first experimental Kinetophone films were made in the winter of 1894–95. The viewer would listen to the sound through rubber ear-tubes connected to the phonograph. It is generally considered that although image and sound would have started together, genuine synchronization would have been very minimal because of the lack of technology at that time. As such, Edison's system would only have provided background music. In 2001, the Library of Congress constructed a version of Porter's film using early Edison recordings for a soundtrack.

37. A frame-by-frame comparison with the Wiesbaden version of the film has subsequently proved that both versions are identical to each other, although the American version is a marginally clearer print.

FOUR

Listening for Wagner in Fritz Lang's *Die Nibelungen*

ADELINE MUELLER

In the preface to Gottfried Huppertz's published score for Fritz Lang's two-part film *Die Nibelungen* (1924), the composer implores movie-theater music directors preparing his music to follow his tempo instructions and the sequence of on-screen events with special attention "so that film and music . . . will merge into a *Gesamtkunstwerk*."[1] Wagner's loaded term was commonly, and often carelessly, invoked throughout the late silent film era to counterbalance the innate heterogeneity of the medium.[2] Huppertz, however, had more right than perhaps any other film composer of his time to misconstrue the term *Gesamtkunstwerk*. For while Wagner's influence on film music has occasionally been overstated, his shadow looms over *Die Nibelungen,* and not just because of its subject matter.

To begin with, director Lang and screenwriter Thea von Harbou based their film not on Wagner's *Ring* cycle but on the thirteenth-century *Nibelungenlied* and its antecedents. Although they claimed this was part of their renunciation of Wagner and a challenge to the supremacy of his work among Nibelungen adaptations, their imitation of Wagner's own eclectic, philological approach to the crafting of the story showed a deeper connection with the composer. Another echo of Wagner is found in the film's dedication, "dem deutschen Volke zu eigen" (to the German people to have as their own). In the souvenir program published to coincide with the film's premiere, Harbou wrote that for her and Lang, "the task suddenly stood before us to bring to the German people and to the world a glory that they possess together and [yet] hardly remember anymore, in a new form that speaks to the nature of our times and that requries no translation."[3] Harbou's words recall the revolutionary times in which Wagner commenced his own foray into the Nibelungen mythology. "In the stimulating recent past," he wrote in his 1849 essay "The Wibelungen: World-History as Told in Saga," "I too was occupied with the rewakening [*Wiedererweckung*] of Frederick the Red-beard, so longed for by so many, and strove with added zeal to satisfy an earlier wish to use my feeble breath to breathe poetic life into the hero-Kaiser for our acting stage."[4] Like Harbou, Wagner sought to reinvent the Nibelungen legend as an offering for his generation.[5]

For obvious reasons, it is in the accompanying music that the film's dialectical reaction to Wagner finds its most potent expression. In what follows, I trace several instances in which the music for *Die Nibelungen* appears at first to swerve away from, but then circles back to, a Wagnerian aesthetic. I will examine three versions of the two-part film, along with their scores: Huppertz's full-length original score for the 1924 premieres of Part 1, *Siegfried,* and Part 2, *Kriemhilds Rache* (Kriemhild's Revenge); a compilation score of Wagner excerpts for the 1925 American premiere of Part 1; and a Huppertz-Wagner soundtrack for a 1933 German re-release of Part 1, retitled *Siegfrieds Tod.*[6] Each score exemplifies a different attitude to Wagner and his legacy, "composing out" a specific reception history of the composer.[7] But in all three, the boomerang effect of Wagner's thorny allure epitomizes the complicated overlap of political détente and opera and film reception in the fragile interwar period.

VOLKER'S IMPOSSIBLE SONG: THE 1924 ORIGINAL SCORE

If Lang and Harbou's *Die Nibelungen* represented a limit case for the Wagner legacy in film music, no one felt that more keenly than Huppertz. The Cologne Conservatory–trained composer was working mostly as an actor and singer in the early 1920s, and had no experience with film scoring before receiving the offer to set Lang and Harbou's epic film.[8] Already at the outset, he was the studio's distant second choice: Universum-Film Aktiengesellschaft (UFA) had originally wanted to use Wagner's own music to score the film, but was prevented from doing so by the composer's heirs, a fact of which Huppertz was aware.[9] Huppertz's widow later told how he initially resisted the offer to compose the score for a film so closely associated with the *Ring* cycle.[10] And in the press, Huppertz tried to distance himself from Wagner. "For me," he observed in a special issue of *Filmwoche* devoted to *Die Nibelungen*, "the challenge was to connect an ancient legend with an ancient music. The extent to which I have succeeded may be judged by expert listeners."[11]

Huppertz's subtle plea for mercy failed to sway those "expert listeners." Music and film critics alike accused him of overloading the listener with too many themes in too short a time, of following the film too closely, and even of being a "Hindemith-Kopist."[12] The most damning criticism of all, that Huppertz had "shamelessly plundered" Wagner's own music, reveals the nature of the double bind he faced.[13] Huppertz had to create original music for a subject that seemed almost inseparable from Wagner's *Ring*, and furthermore, he had to compose within a mainstream film-scoring practice that relied heavily on quasi-Wagnerian thematicism. While it is true that Huppertz employs reminiscence motifs in an occasionally redundant manner, elsewhere he draws on Wagner's example without falling into cliché, foregoing obvious opportunities for illustrative mimesis in favor of a more liminal zone between diegetic and nondiegetic music (or, between source and mood music). The effect is similar to Wagner's "dissolution of barriers between music heard and unheard," even though the silent film medium does not allow for an easy analogue to Wagner's onstage musicians (e.g., Wolfram and his harp, Siegfried and his horn).[14]

The most explicit such blurring can be found in the climactic battle that ends Part 2, *Kriemhilds Rache*. The Burgundian knights and their leader, King Gunther, are entrenched in the hall of Etzel, while outside, Gunther's estranged sister Kriemhild leads the Huns' assault. As the hall begins to collapse in flames around the Burgundians, the bardic knight Volker von Alzey takes up a lute-like instrument and, as Gunther describes in an intertitle, "stimmt seine Fiedel zum letzten Sang!" (tunes his fiddle for one last song!)[15] Like many Wagnerian characters from Senta to Hagen, Volker has exhibited an erratic relation to his surrounding narrative throughout the film, wandering between the roles of participant, commentator, and narrative catalyst. Accordingly, in scenes that show him singing or playing, Huppertz often destabi

FIG. 4.1A. Volker begins to sing

lizes the expected agreement between score and image.[16] In the scene of
the Burgundians' annihilation from *Kriemhilds Rache*, the exaggerated
discrepancy between Volker's music and the screen image prompts the
viewer to fill the gap by participating imaginatively in the realization of
his elegy for the court of Gunther.

The first and most immediate manifestation of the "inaudibility"
of Volker's song is the lack of intertitles to indicate what he is singing.[17]
Harbou's novelization of her screenplay, *Das Nibelungenbuch*, provides
a text for Volker's song: a rhapsodic ode to the Burgundians' home at
Worms on the Rhine.[18] But no such text is included in the film version,
and the subject of Volker's ode is only alluded to when one of the Burgundian knights suddenly stretches out his arms and cries, "Ach wären
wir am grünen kühlen Rhein!" (Oh, if only we were back on the cool
green banks of the Rhine!) That the knight's brief outburst of *Heimweh*
is given an intertitle while Volker's extended song has none only serves
to highlight the latter's intangibility, while also implying that such sentiments were assumed to be so much a part of the German psyche as to
surpass verbalization.

EX. 4.1A. "Volker's Song"

The absence of a text for Volker's song is an inviting lacuna; when it comes to Huppertz's music, provocative omission gives way to out-right contradiction. The somber, faintly military sarabande identified in Huppertz's published score as "Volkers Gesang" bears little relation to Volker's contorted, defiant face as he nearly shouts his song (see example 4.1a and figure 4.1a). The clash between the music's dignified solemnity and Volker's grotesque physical expression initiates a slippage from mi-

FIG. 4.1B. Volker's song continues

mesis into commentary, even bardic sentimentalization. This effect is then heightened when Volker stops strumming his lute and holds it up at his side while continuing to sing unaccompanied (see example 4.1b and figure 4.1b). Although a brief detour into more unmoored chromatic territory seems at first to match Volker's abandonment of his accompanying instrument, the original diatonic melody soon returns (measure 9), revealing the chromatic passage to have been no more than a bridge in a standard AABA form. In other words, the silencing of the lute has not registered meaningfully in the score. Nor has the change in Volker's performing body: where earlier he could clearly be seen to sing words, once he stops strumming he begins to cry out the same syllable over and over. It may be "Rhein," or "Ah!"—there is no way to tell. Yet Huppertz's melancholy tune continues; detached from its singer, it now floats freely in the cinematic space, acting as a marker of—or a talisman guaranteeing—Volker's imperviousness to the flames that consume the hall. He should be burning to death as the building begins to collapse on his fellow knights, yet in his reckless defiance Volker lives on, his supernatural invulnerability mimicking that of his free-floating song.

EX. 4.1B. "Volker's Song," continued

Volker's "last song" does not appear in any of the medieval sources for Lang and Harbou's film, and Wagner left the character out of his *Ring* altogether. This scene, then, was entirely an invention of the filmmakers, providing Huppertz a rare opportunity to move out from under the shadow of Wagner, and even to thwart Huppertz's own stated *Gesamtkunstwerk* imperative. Yet the scene also demonstrates how compelling the Wagnerian gravitational force remains: in addition to Huppertz's

FIG. 4.2. Kriemhild, Hildebrand, and the Huns listen to Volker's song.

blurring of source music and mood music, the frequent cutaways to Kriemhild and her army listening, enthralled, to Volker's song from outside the burning hall blur descriptive and prescriptive effects (see figure 4.2). These reaction shots bring to mind the stage direction just before the vision of Walhall at the end of Wagner's *Götterdämmerung:* "From the ruins of the collapsed hall, the men and women, in highest emotion [in höchster Ergriffenheit], watch the growing firelight in the heavens." Just as Wagner's emotional onlookers acted as exemplars for the 1876 audience at Bayreuth, the transported listeners of Volker's song in *Kriemhilds Rache* cue the 1924 audience to assume an equally reverent attitude to the Burgundians' tragic end.[19]

Kriemhild's is the most reverent of all these responses—ironic, given that Volker, the bard who first sang to her of Siegfried, is now a mortal enemy. Her twice-repeated exhortation, "Hört ihr, Herr Volker singt!" (Hear ye, Herr Volker sings!), recalls the "Liebestod" from *Tristan und Isolde,* in which Isolde calls on her fellow characters, "Seht ihr's nicht?"

(Do you not see?) and "Hör ich nur diese weise . . . ?" (Do I alone hear this melody . . . ?).[20] Film and opera differ here, of course, in that no one else onstage or in the audience is privy to Isolde's vision except through her account of it, whereas Kriemhild's soldiers are shown hearing and reacting to Volker's song. But both songs remain, in their own way, "inaudible," with Isolde's and Kriemhild's awestruck responses creating a more powerful effect than could have been achieved with a more literal sounding object.

Volker's transcendent song encapsulates *Die Nibelungen*'s complex blend of fatalism and triumphalism, a blend that made it particularly attractive to a Germany reeling from the humiliating defeat of World War I and the international censure, rampant inflation, and political unrest that followed it. One reviewer even conflated Lang himself with Volker:

> Just as Volker von Alzey, the singer, once tuned his fiddle so that he might send the song of the Nibelungens out into the distance, so today Fritz Lang touches the mute strings of film, in order to answer the world's dominant reproach with that which has long rested in the dark womb of the prescient past.[21]

The reviewer could almost have been paraphrasing Wagner's own account of the attraction of the Nibelungen myth in the face of his political disillusionment. "I sank myself into the primal element of Home," Wagner wrote in his 1851 "A Communication to My Friends," "that meets us in the legends of a Past which attracts us the more warmly as the Present repels us with its hostile chill."[22]

The nostalgic retreat to an indeterminate, idealized past is a cliché of German nationalism, one whose enduring appeal peaked in the year *Die Nibelungen* premiered. 1924 saw revivals of numerous Nibelungen adaptations on stage and in print, and Lang and Harbou spoke openly about their film's role in the multifaceted effort to restore Germany's national pride.[23] In an elaboration on the film's bardic subtitle, "Ein deutsches Heldenlied" (A German Heroic Song), Harbou expressed the hope that *Die Nibelungen* would "become a singer, a bard-poet" to the "weary and overworked" German people.[24] This curious anthropomorphizing statement suggests that for Harbou, the film was no artifact but rather a living herald for all of Germany's postwar aspirations.[25]

SIEGFRIED'S APOTHEOSIS: THE 1925 COMPILATION SCORE

Along with prompting Germany's national renewal, *Die Nibelungen* promised to aid the restoration of its standing in the international community. Accordingly, the Berlin premiere of Part 1 of *Die Nibelungen* was followed by a speech from the German Foreign Minister, Gustav Stresemann, and UFA board chair Emil von Stauß's proclamation that "such a film will be and must be not just a national, but an international offering."[26] The real test of this second mandate was *Die Nibelungen*'s foreign tour, which included screenings in nearly a dozen of Germany's neighboring countries in Europe, followed by the United States. This last was undoubtedly the most crucial: America represented not just Germany's biggest competitor for film audiences back home, but its largest market for foreign export, and the American reception of *Die Nibelungen* would be a major test of Allied cultural détente with Germany following World War I.[27]

The film screened in the United States differed greatly from Lang and Harbou's original. In addition to the wholesale omission of *Kriemhilds Rache*, scene cuts, altered intertitles, and a new introduction shaded *Siegfried* as far more Wagnerian than Lang or Harbou had intended.[28] For example, the sequence depicting Siegfried's encounter with the dragon is preceded in the American print by the following intertitle: "In the heart of the wood lurked Fafnir the Giant, in the dreadful form of a dragon."[29] Wagner's *Ring* is the only other modern Nibelungen adaptation to conflate Fafnir and the dragon, and in Lang's original 1924 film, no intertitles accompanied the dragon sequence and nowhere was the dragon referred to as Fafnir.[30]

The American press furthered the conflation of Lang and Harbou's film with Wagner's *Ring* cycle. An advertisement in *The Nation* for the August 23, 1925, American premiere in New York City billed the film as "UFA's Great Music Photo Drama Based on the Norse Saga and Wagner's Ring Opera,"[31] and the cover of the New York premiere souvenir program described the film as "A Music-Photo Drama with Wagner's Immortal Score."[32] This referred to *Siegfried*'s new compilation score of Wagner excerpts, which had been arranged by music director Hugo Riesenfeld to take the place of the original by Huppertz.[33] Riesenfeld had impeccable credentials for the job: widely regarded as the preeminent film-music arranger and conductor of his time, he was the established music director for three New York picture palaces run by famed impresario Samuel "Roxy" Rothapfel: the Rialto, Rivoli, and Criterion theaters. Before that, Riesenfeld had been concertmaster at the Vienna Hofoper and the Metropolitan Opera, and he had even played violin at Bayreuth in 1901.[34] And Riesenfeld was no stranger to German films, having arranged the accompanying orchestral scores for four famous German imports in the early 1920s.[35]

Riesenfeld's *Siegfried* score was never published, and no manuscript score or cue sheets appear to survive, so for information about the music we must rely on contemporary reviews and in particular on Riesenfeld's own account in the souvenir program.[36] While he argues in the program that the exclusive use of Wagner's music was virtually a foregone conclusion, it was actually quite a bold risk on the part of the film's presenters. Just one year before *Siegfried*'s premiere, the Met had finally lifted a controversial seven-year ban on Wagner's works, one of a number of manifestations of the broad and lingering American opposition to Wagner and the German language that had begun during World War I.[37] *Siegfried* was thus burdened with yet another mission: the postwar rehabilitation of Wagner as an American cultural icon.

In order to maintain an all-Wagner score even for scenes that did not appear in the *Ring*, Riesenfeld chose music from elsewhere in Wagner's tetralogy, from *Siegfried's Idyll,* and even from *Lohengrin.* For instance, the scene of Brunhild and Kriemhild's confrontation on the church steps recalls a similar encounter between Elsa and Ortrud in Act 2, Scene 4 of *Lohengrin,* and it was precisely this music Riesenfeld used.[38] For another scene, the matrimonial contest at Brunhild's castle, Riesenfeld appropriated Wagner's "accompaniment for Hagen's announcement of the arrival of Gunther and Brunhilde in Gebichungenhall [*sic*]" (i.e., Act 2, Scene 3 from *Götterdämmerung*). Unlike the church steps sequence, this choice did not stem from any plot resonances with the opera but simply from the fact that the scene "called for a lengthy sequence of music expressing intense excitement."[39]

Riesenfeld also departed from compilation-score practice by arranging the music in freestanding sections, with brief pauses taking the place of the musical transitions found in a traditional continuous score.[40]

The resulting similarity to a concert of opera excerpts may have been intentional: unlike its Berlin premiere at the picture palace Ufa-Palast am Zoo, *Siegfried*'s American screenings were subject to a distribution contract stipulating that the film not be shown at "regular" movie theaters.[41] In other words, just as Wagner had reinforced the novelty and gravitas of his *Ring* cycle by designing a unique theater for its presentation at Bayreuth, UFA used prestige venues to set *Siegfried* apart from other blockbuster pictures. The London premiere on April 29, 1924, took place at the Royal Albert Hall with the London Symphony Orchestra accompanying. The West Coast premiere on November 23, 1925, at the Philharmonic Auditorium in Los Angeles, was accompanied by a pickup orchestra led by Adolph Tandler, the former conductor of the Los Angeles Symphony Orchestra. And for the United States premiere in New York City—the one for which Riesenfeld was responsible—the presenters chose the Century Theatre (a live music and theater venue) and handpicked their musicians from the Met orchestra. This last choice was as politically significant as it was culturally prestigious, given the Met's recent Wagner ban.

The connection to Wagner's *Ring* was cemented by a final innovation on the part of Riesenfeld and the premiere's conductor, Josiah Zuro, director of presentations at all of Riesenfeld's theaters. Riesenfeld and Zuro framed the film with a thematically connected live prologue and epilogue. Prologues, more so than epilogues, were regular features of film presentation at the larger theaters in the 1920s, and could involve singers, dancers, and actors as well as the house orchestra.[42] The Century Theatre's *Siegfried* prologue featured tenor Judson House in a staging of Wagner's "Forging Song," a move that further encouraged critical misinterpretation of the film as a *Ring* adaptation.[43] The epilogue was even more revealing. On the morning of the film's premiere, *The New York Times* described the concept as follows:

> A company of thirty persons will participate in the epilogue, and the ending of the film will be merged into this feature, showing Siegfried being conducted into Valhalla, the dwelling place of the gods, by the Valkyrie, while Kriemhilde, surrounded by her bodyguard [*sic*], looks on. As the strains of the funeral march from "Götterdammerung" [*sic*] die down— while the film chronicles the death of Siegfried—the curtain will rise on the epilogue, provided as a concession to a happy ending.[44]

Riesenfeld and Zuro were probably unaware that their revisionist epilogue actually brought *Siegfried*'s ending back in line with Wagner's original idea for the conclusion of *Siegfrieds Tod*. His 1848 prose résumé, "The Nibelungen-Myth as Sketch for a Drama," ends with a tableau nearly identical to the one staged at the Century Theatre in 1925:

> Midst solemn chants Brünnhilde mounts the pyre to Siegfried's body. Gudrun, broken down with grief, remains bowed over the corpse of Gunther in the foreground. The flames meet across Brünnhild [*sic*] and Siegfried:—suddenly a dazzling light is seen: above the margin of a leaden cloud the light streams up, shewing Brünnhild, armed as Walküre on horse, leading Siegfried by the hand from hence.[45]

In the final version of *Götterdämmerung*, of course, this ending is replaced by the engulfing of Walhall in flames. But in both Wagner's original prose résumé and the American epilogue, the medieval *Nibelungenlied*'s account of Kriemhild's revenge gives way to an apotheosis in which nearly all historical consequences of Siegfried's murder have been eliminated.[46]

One practical explanation for this epilogue is that it provided a more conclusive ending to *Siegfried*, given the absence of Part 2. Another motivation was that American preference for happy endings to which the *New York Times* account referred.[47] But the renunciation of revenge also suggests that the New York version of *Siegfried* sought to rewrite not just Lang and Harbou's film, but history itself—or perhaps to accelerate it, to speed the "healing of the wounds of war."[48] *The Moving Picture World* recommended seeing Lang's *Siegfried* as "a pleasant duty we owe ourselves," the begrudging tone reflecting a determined if equivocal optimism about the role the film stood to play in German-American reconciliation.[49]

HAGEN'S GUILT: THE 1933 SOUNDTRACK

The eventual collapse of the fragile goodwill between Germany and its former foes is of course all too familiar, and Lang and Harbou's film soon found itself once again appropriated to new cultural-political ends. Not long after the Nazi seizure of power in January 1933 and Joseph Goebbels's appointment as Propaganda Minister two months later, Goebbels made a speech to the Dacho-Versammlung, or Umbrella Organization of German Filmmakers, in which he cited *Die Nibelungen* as one of four model films: "Here is a film story not taken from our time, but crafted in a manner so modern, so close to the times, so topical that even the militants of the National Socialist movement were deeply moved within."[50] Two months after that, UFA—now an instrument of the Nazi party—released a re-edited version of *Siegfried*, retitled *Siegfrieds Tod*.[51]

As though adapting the approach taken during the film's initial foreign tour, UFA omitted *Kriemhilds Rache* altogether and shortened *Siegfried*. The most significant change, however, was the addition of a recorded soundtrack. This soundtrack does not include dialogue; the only spoken words are a brief opening voiceover in which Theodor Loos, the actor portraying King Gunther, reads a modern adaptation of the first stanzas of the medieval *Nibelungenlied*.[52] The remainder of the soundtrack is primarily Huppertz's original music, but with a major change: having now received the previously denied permission from Wagner's heirs, UFA hired Huppertz to revise his 1924 score to include selected excerpts from Wagner. This revision—which may also have been inspired by the foreign screenings—united epic poem, renowned composer, and beloved film into one towering monument to Germany's ancient and recent heritage.

The bulk of Huppertz's new score follows his 1924 original closely, with the occasional cut to accommodate edits in the shortened print. Wagner's music appears only sporadically, accompanying the most recognizable scenic analogues to well-known episodes from the *Ring*. For instance, the Dragon and Sword motifs appear during the scene in which Siegfried fights the dragon, and the Woodbird music and Siegfried's Funeral March accompany their respective appearances in the film. In addition, Huppertz occasionally repurposes Wagner in much the same manner as Riesenfeld had done. For instance, the Odenwald hunt sequence in which Siegfried is murdered begins with Wagner's extended horn soli passage from Act 2, Scene 3 of *Götterdämmerung*—which, while not a direct parallel in terms of plot, fits well with the images of the hunting party.

The most significant change made to the 1924 score—a change that alters the dramatic and political connotations of the entire film—involves not a quotation of Wagner's music but a more subtle emulation of his technique. In the original *Siegfried*, Lang and Harbou had been careful to emphasize Gunther's culpability in Siegfried's death. Frequent cuts to Gunther throughout the film showed his indecisiveness and weak moral character, emphasizing that despite Hagen's and Brunhild's influence, Gunther was ultimately to blame for ordering, and then failing to prevent, the murder of Siegfried. In the 1933 version, however, a surprising number of these cutaways to Gunther are eliminated, leaving his character's role in the murder much reduced and Hagen's amplified by default. Huppertz must have been aware of this new shading, because he accompanied it with a subtly compelling musical shift. In one of only a handful of instances of newly composed music in the soundtrack, Huppertz added multiple iterations of his own Hagen motif, an ominous rising whole-tone scale in the double bass (see example 4.2).

EX. 4.2. Huppertz's Hagen motif

Unlike the reminiscence motifs that otherwise dominate his score, Huppertz's new Hagen motif always appears in key scenes that establish Hagen's role in Siegfried's betrayal and murder, such as the ritual of blood brotherhood between Siegfried and Gunther, presided over by Hagen, and the moment in the Odenwald sequence when Hagen dares Siegfried to race him to the spring as Gunther looks on. In both scenes, Hagen is one of three characters taking part in the action, and the original score did not draw particular attention to him by including his motif. When the motifs appear in the 1933 version, then, the viewer's gaze is directed to Hagen in a kind of aural spotlight. Even when little has been changed visually, Huppertz's revised music emphasizes Hagen's villainy.

The first and most striking insertion of the Hagen motif occurs toward the beginning of the film, when Kriemhild sees Siegfried for the first time from her window and relates her prophetic dream of his doom. In 1924, this sequence, which shows a white falcon being pecked at by black eagles, was accompanied by a series of ascending diatonic major scales in the strings, with quietly fluttering tremolos in the background—an otherworldly music that simply signaled the shift to a dream state (see example 4.3a). In the 1933 *Siegfrieds Tod*, Huppertz replaced

EX. 4.3A. Kriemhild's Dream, 1924 version. Huppertz, *Die Nibelungen*, TK.

this innocuous bit of scene painting with a newly composed pairing of his Hagen motif and an agitated transformation of one of his motifs for Kriemhild. Layering Kriemhild's and Hagen's motifs in this way suggests to the viewer that it is Hagen who is to blame for the falcon's (i.e., Siegfried's) death, and Hagen who will present a threat to Kriemhild (see example 4.3b).

Making Hagen the principal villain was thus a joint effort of both editors and composer, resulting in a simplification of his characterization over the original film and its sources. Wagner made a similar move when drafting the *Ring*, altering his source materials to demonize Hagen and provide a more sympathetic treatment of Gunther. To give just two brief examples: in *Götterdämmerung*, Act 3, Scene 2, just before Siegfried is slain, Gunther changes his mind about the murder plot and tries (too late by a moment) to restrain Hagen's sword. In the following scene, Gunther dies while trying to protect the ring from Hagen, whom he calls a "shameless goblin's son," a reference to Wagner's wholly invented

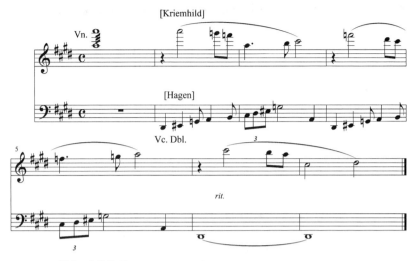

EX. 4.3B. Kriemhild's Dream, 1933 version

father-son relationship between Alberich and Hagen. The 1933 editors' decision to draw on Wagner's shading of these characters makes sense when one considers the political circumstances surrounding this earliest of Nazi films. Lang and Harbou's treatment of Gunther was clearly meant to be a critique of his character, perhaps even a broader social critique.[53] But for the pureblood Burgundian king to remain an ineffectual weakling who allows the murder of his truest friend would not have fit with the National Socialist ideals of German honor, fidelity, and strength of will. Gunther's disfigured half-relation, the relative outsider Hagen, made for a more convenient traitor.[54]

In its closing scene, *Siegfrieds Tod* departs both from Wagner's model and from its more immediate cinematic predecessors. The aftermath of Siegfried's death is not a vengeful battle as in *Kriemhilds Rache,* nor an apotheosis as in Riesenfeld's staged epilogue, nor an apocalyptic twilight of the gods as in *Götterdämmerung.* Rather, the film fetishizes Kriemhild's mourning for Siegfried, concluding with a shot in which she keeps vigil over her beloved's dead body. Perhaps the decision was motivated by more than time limitations. German viewers in 1933 would have remembered those previous versions' conclusions, either from having seen *Kriemhilds Rache* back in 1924, from hearing Wagner's *Ring,* or from learning the *Nibelungenlied* as schoolchildren.[55]

The ending of *Siegfrieds Tod* would thus have struck most German audiences as frustratingly unfinished. Vengeance, perhaps, was meant to be left to the German people to take on, "dem deutschen Volke zu eigen." That original dedication, however, was left out of the 1933 version, along with the film's subtitle, "Ein deutsches Heldenlied," and its division into "Gesänge" (songs). On reflection, these casual omissions are quite revealing: *Die Nibelungen* no longer belonged to the German people but to the Nazi party, and despite its soundtrack, it had ceased to sing.

NOTES

I would like to thank Anton Kaes, Elaine Tennant (and the other participants in her 2006 seminar on the *Nibelungen* tradition), Scott D. Paulin, Mary Ann Smart, and Richard Taruskin for their helpful comments on previous versions of this article. For research assistance I am indebted to librarians at the Pacific Film Archive, Berkeley; the Motion Picture, Broadcasting and Recorded Sound Division of the Library of Congress; the Film Study Center at the Museum of Modern Art, New York; and the Margaret Herrick Library of the Academy of Motion Picture Arts and Sciences; as well as to Gillian Anderson, Berndt Heller, Ross Melnick, and Aitam Bar-Sagi.

1. Quoted in Claudia Bullerjahn, "Von der Kinomusik zur Filmmusik: Stummfilm-Originalkompositionen der zwanziger Jahre," in *Musik der zwanziger Jahre,* ed. Werner Keil (Hildesheim: Georg Olms, 1996), 305. This and all subsequent translations from German are my own, unless otherwise noted (with thanks to Elaine Tennant for assistance).

2. Scott D. Paulin, "Richard Wagner and the Fantasy of Cinematic Unity: The Idea of the *Gesamtkunstwerk* in the History and Theory of Film Music," in *Music and Cinema,* ed. James Buhler, Caryl Flinn, and David Neumeyer (Middletown, Conn.: Wesleyan University Press, 2000).

3. Thea von Harbou, "Vom Nibelungen-Film und seinem Entstehen," in *Die Nibelungen: Ein deutsches Heldenlied* (premiere souvenir program) (Berlin: UFA, 1924), 7.

4. Richard Wagner, "The Wibelungen: World-History as Told in Saga" (1848), in *In Paris and Dresden,* Richard Wagner's Prose Works, vol. 7, ed. and trans. William Ashton Ellis (London: Kegan Paul, Trench, Trübner & Co., 1898; repr. New York: Broude Bros., 1966), 258. Legend had it that Frederick I Barbarossa (1122–90), the Holy Roman Emperor, was not dead but merely asleep, awaiting the right moment for his messianic return. See also Wagner, "A Communication to My Friends" (1851)," in *The Art-Work of the Future* (1892), Richard Wagner's Prose Works, vol. 1, ed. and trans. William Ashton Ellis (New York: Broude Brothers, 1966), 357ff.

5. See for example Harbou, "Vom Nibelungen-Film und seinem Entstehen," 7.

6. The premiere dates and locations of these versions are as follows: Part 1, *Siegfried,* February 14, 1924, Ufa-Palast am Zoo, Berlin; Part 2, *Kriemhilds Rache,*

April 24, 1924, Ufa-Palast am Zoo, Berlin; *Siegfried,* August 23, 1925, Century The-atre, New York City; *Siegfrieds Tod,* May 29, 1933, Ufa-Palast am Zoo, Berlin.

7. "Film music is nothing more than composed-out reception history." Hans-jörg Pauli, *Filmmusik, Stummfilm* (Stuttgart: Klett-Cotta, 1981), 230. See also Caro-lyn Abbate, "Wagner, Cinema, and Redemptive Glee," *Opera Quarterly* 21, no. 4 (2005): 599.

8. Huppertz is far better known for his score to Lang's *Nibelungen* follow-up, the 1927 *Metropolis,* but he also scored a number of films by Harbou and others until well into the sound era. For more on Huppertz, including the most complete works list and bibliography currently available, see Aitam Bar-Sagi, "The Gottfried Huppertz Home Page," www.fimumu.com/huppertz (accessed June 23, 2009).

9. Berndt Heller, private communication, December 12, 2007.

10. Berndt Heller, "Zur Rekonstruktion der *Nibelungen*-Musik von Gottfried Huppertz," in *Fritz Lang: Die Nibelungen,* ed. Enno Patalas and Fritz Göttler (Mu-nich: Kulturreferat der Landeshauptstadt, 1986), 48. Fritz Lang acknowledged the unique challenge Huppertz faced in his article, "Worauf es beim Nibelungen-Film ankam," reproduced in *Die Nibelungen: Ein deutsches Heldenlied,* 16.

11. "Was Jeder sagt," *Filmwoche,* no. 7 (1924): 133.

12. Hans Erdmann, Giuseppe Becce, and Ludwig Brav, *Allgemeines Handbuch der Film-Musik* (Berlin: Schlesinger'sche Buch- und Musikhandlung, 1927), vol. 12, 46–47; H. H. Stuckenschmidt, "Die Musik zum Film," *Die Musik* 8 (August 1926): 813; and Ernst Ulitzsch, "Die Nibelungen," *Kinematograph,* February 17, 1924, 14.

13. Wolfgang Schumann, "Kriemhilds Rache im Film," *Kunstwart und Kultur-wart* 37 (July 1924): 174. The few musicologists who have written in our own time about Huppertz's *Nibelungen* score echo this initial critical reaction: most identify and track the principal motifs, concluding that the score lacks Wagner's sophistica-tion and structural cohesion. See Rainer Fabich, *Musik für den Stummfilm: Analy-sierende Beschreibung originaler Filmkompositionen* European University Studies Series 36 (Musicology), vol. 94 (Frankfurt: P. Lang, 1993), 192–220; Bullerjahn, "Von der Kinomusik zur Filmmusik," 302–10; Ulrich Rügner, *Filmmusik in Deutschland zwischen 1924 und 1934* (Hildesheim: Georg Olms, 1988), 86–88; Christopher Hen-zel, "Wagner und die Filmmusik," *Acta Musicologica* 76, no. 1 (2004): 97; and Hell-er, "Zur Rekonstruktion der Nibelungen-Musik von Gottfried Huppertz," 43–48.

14. Carolyn Abbate, *Unsung Voices: Opera and Musical Narrative in the Nine-teenth Century* (Princeton: Princeton University Press, 1991), 122 and 131–34.

15. *Die Nibelungen* (DVD), dir. Fritz Lang, New York, Kino, 2002. The instru-ment's morphology is ambiguous: the intertitles describe it variously as a "Geige" (violin) and a "Fiedl" (fiddle), as does Thea von Harbou, *Das Nibelungenbuch* (Mu-nich: Drei Masken Verlag, 1923), but Huppertz's score refers to it as a "Laute" (lute). Two playing techniques (bowing on the lap and plucking) are used in the course of the film, though only the latter appears in this scene.

16. When Volker was introduced in Part 1, *Siegfried,* he was shown bowing his lute like a fiddle and singing of Siegfried's adventures; Huppertz, however, fore-grounded not sustained accompaniment lines in the strings but the plucked sound of harp arpeggios instead, and the melody came from a succession of three dif-ferent wind instruments, splitting and thus undermining the integrity of Volker's

voice. Even in the nickelodeon era, when musical accompaniment was not necessarily continuous throughout a film screening and verisimilitude had not yet been
standardized, scenes depicting music-making, dancing, or marching were almost
always considered to necessitate some form of matching musical "sound effect." See
Rick Altman, "The Living Nickelodeon," in *The Sounds of Early Cinema*, ed. Richard Abel and Rick Altman (Bloomington: Indiana University Press, 2001), 234–37.

17. I have adapted this concept of "inaudibility" from Béla Balázs, who wrote
the following about a silent film on Paganini: "The dumbshow of a great actor
made us imagine violin-playing so enchanting that hardened jailers dropped their
weapons . . . A merely visible, inaudible music, existing only in the imagination,
could have a magic effect." Béla Balázs, *Theory of the Film (Character and Growth
of a New Art)*, trans. Edith Bone (London: Dennis Dobson, 1952), 200. Balázs was
likely referring to the biopic *Paganini*, starring Conrad Veidt (dir. Heinz Goldberg,
1922/23).

18. Thea von Harbou, *Das Nibelungenbuch* (Munich: Drei Masken Verlag, 1923),
258–59.

19. Lang's reaction shots also reinforce the eerie disembodiment of Volker's
voice, which—like one of Michel Chion's *acousmêtres*—preternaturally carries
over the din of battle and through the huge wooden door to reach even the ears of
Kriemhild and her soldiers. Michel Chion, *The Voice in Cinema* [1982], trans. Claudia Gorbman (New York: Columbia University Press, 1999), 24.

20. The prescriptive undertones of the "Liebestod" are discussed in Abbate,
Unsung Voices, 134.

21. S. Wagener, "Der Nibelungenenfilm," *Die Filmwoche* 7 (1924): 122.

22. Wagner, "A Communication to My Friends," 357.

23. In addition to the premiere of Lang and Harbou's film, there was a new
production of Friedrich Hebbel's 1861 play *Die Nibelungen* at the Berlin State Theater; the reopening of the Bayreuth Festival (under Siegfried Wagner) with a tradi-
tionalist production of Wagner's *Ring* cycle; and the Vienna reprint of a children's
Die Nibelungen, illustrated by Carl Otto Czeschka, with a dedication similar to that
of Lang and Harbou's film (*Die Nibelungen, dem deutschen Volke wiedererzählt von
Franz Keim* [1909; Vienna: Gerlach & Wiedling, 1924]).

24. Harbou, quoted in Ulrich Müller, "'Das geistige Heiligtum einer Nation':
Die 'Grand Opéra Cinématographique' über Die Nibelungen von Fritz Lang und
Thea von Harbou (1924)," in *Alban Bergs Wozzeck und die Zwanziger Jahre: Vor-
träge und Materialien des Salzburger Symposions 1997*, ed. Peter Csobádi et al.
(Anif, Austria: Müller-Speiser Verlag, 1999), 647. Müller does not give the original
source of this quote. On this and other musical metaphors surrounding the film,
see David Levin, *Richard Wagner, Fritz Lang, and the Nibelungen: The Dramaturgy
of Disavowal* (Princeton: Princeton University Press, 1998), 104; and Tom Gunning,
The Films of Fritz Lang: Allegories of Vision and Modernity (London: British Film
Institute, 2000), 17 and 49–50.

25. On the broader nationalist subtexts of the film, see Anton Kaes, "Siegfried—A German Film Star Performing the Nation in Lang's *Nibelungen* Film," in
The German Cinema Book, ed. Tim Bergfelder, Erica Carter, and Deniz Gokturk
(London: BFI Publications, 2002); Müller, "Das geistige Heiligtum einer Nation";
and originally (and most famously) Siegfried Kracauer, *From Caligari to Hitler: A*

Psychological History of the German Film (Princeton: Princeton University Press, 1947), 94–95.

26. "Der Wendepunkt," *Lichtbild-Bühne*, February 16, 1924, 11.

27. For more on the unique blend of competition and interdependence between the German and American film industries in the 1920s, see Thomas Saunders, *Hollywood in Berlin: American Cinema and Weimar Germany* (Berkeley: University of California Press, 1994), especially chap. 2, "German-American Film Relations."

28. The jettisoned *Kriemhilds Rache* had garnered much less critical attention than *Siegfried* at the time of its German premiere. It finally premiered in the United States in 1928 at the small 55th Street Playhouse, three years after *Siegfried's* premiere. But it was largely ignored in the American press (no doubt due at least in part to the rapidly increasing popularity of, and studio investment in, sound films that same year). I have found no mention of the music that accompanied either the initial American run of *Kriemhild's Revenge* or its brief revival in 1930.

29. *Die Nibelungen* (VHS), dir.Fritz Lang, 1924; Chico, Calif., Blackhawk Films, 1981.

30. This feature originates in the Norse *Edda*, one of the earliest sources for the legend. John Flood, "Fafnir," in *The Nibelungen Tradition: An Encyclopedia*, ed. Francis G. Gentry et al. (New York: Routledge, 2002), 69. See also Victoria M. Stiles, "Fritz Lang's Definitive *Siegfried* and Its Versions," *Literature/Film Quarterly* 13, no. 4 (1985): 260.

31. Advertisement in *The Nation*, September 16, 1925, 311.

32. *Siegfried: A Music-Photo Drama with Wagner's Immortal Score* (New York: P. McNerny & Co., 1925), title page.

33. A comment by one reviewer suggests that some Americans might have at least been aware of the existence of Huppertz's score: "Just why the original score composed for the film was not used, was not stated." E. B. N., "Wagner versus Eddas in Screen Version of 'Siegfried,'" *Musical America*, August 29, 1925, 23.

34. Rick Altman, *Silent Film Sound* (New York: Columbia University Press, 2004), 291; and "Riesenfeld Joins Century Opera," *New York Times*, June 13, 1914, 9. The three Bayreuth productions in 1901 were *Der fliegende Holländer* (cond. Felix Mottl), *Parsifal* (cond. Karl Muck), and *Der Ring des Nibelungen* (cond. Hans Richter and Siegfried Wagner). It is not known in which production(s) Riesenfeld performed.

35. The films were *Deception* (originally *Madame Dubarry* [dir. Ernst Lubitsch, 1919]), *Passion* (originally *Anna Boleyn* [dir. Lubitsch, 1920]), *The Golem* (dir. Paul Wegener, 1920), and *The Loves of Pharaoh* (originally *Das Weib des Pharao* [dir. Lubitsch, 1921)]. None of these scores appears to have survived.

36. Hugo Riesenfeld, "Regarding the Score for 'Siegfried,'" in *Siegfried: A Music-Photo Drama with Wagner's Immortal Score*, 6.

37. See Myra Maxwell, "German Arms, Not Art" (letter to the editor), *New York Times*, November 11, 1917, 77; Ernest M. Skinner, "Metropolitan Ban on Wagner the Theme of Many Letters and Conflicting Views" (letter to the editor), *New York Times*, November 11, 1917, 77; and Glenn Watkins, *Proof through the Night: Music and the Great War* (Berkeley: University of California Press, 2003), 310.

38. Riesenfeld attributed his own conflation of the two scenes to Lang, writing that the encounter between Kriemhild and Brunhild was "a scene which the film

director took bodily from the second act of Lohengrin, and which naturally called for the accompaniment Wagner wrote for it." See Riesenfeld, "Regarding the Score for 'Siegfried,'" 6.

39. Ibid.

40. Ibid.

41. Flyer, Core Collection production file for *Siegfried*, Margaret Herrick Library, Academy of Motion Picture Arts and Sciences.

42. Roxy and Riesenfeld established the practice; see Altman, *Silent Film Sound*, 385–87.

43. "'Siegfried' at Century," *New York Times*, August 23, 1925, X3.

44. Ibid.

45. Richard Wagner, "The Nibelungen-Myth as Sketch for a Drama" (1848), in *In Paris and Dresden*, 311.

46. The *New York Times* account implies that projection of the film ended soon after Siegfried's death, thus bypassing the original closing scenes in which Kriemhild discovers Siegfried's body and vows vengeance on Hagen for Siegfried's murder.

47. Happy endings were even cited as one of the essential features that set American films apart from German films. See Benjamin De Casseres, "Our Domestic Movies and the Germans," *New York Times*, March 26, 1922, 54. The German trade press, reporting on *Siegfried*'s New York premiere, bestowed its blessing on the unorthodox epilogue, describing it as "highly applauded" and "even more beautiful" than the "impressive" prologue. "New-Yorker Premierenbericht," *Lichtbildbühne*, September 5, 1925, 34. However, at least one American critic concluded that the "rather foolish *tableau mouvant* afterpiece in the manner of the apotheosis of *Marguerite* added nothing to the general effect." E. B. N., "Wagner versus Eddas in Screen Version of 'Siegfried,'" 23.

48. Following a European tour undertaken a year before the New York premiere of *Siegfried*, the Austrian-born Riesenfeld observed, "The wound of the war is slowly healing." Hugo Riesenfeld, "European Impressions," *American Organist* 7 (February 1924): 97.

49. "'Siegfried'" (review), *Moving Picture World*, September 12, 1925, 169.

50. "Dr. Goebbels' Speech at the Kaiserhof on March 28, 1933," trans. Lance W. Garner, in *German Essays on Film*, ed. Richard W. McCormick and Alison Guenther-Pal, The German Library 81 (New York: Consortium, 2004), 154–55.

51. The new title recalls both Wagner's original title for *Götterdämmerung* and the title of part two of Friedrich Hebbel's 1861 trilogy, *Die Nibelungen*. With the help of Aitam Bar-Sagi, I recently discovered a rare print of the 1933 *Siegfrieds Tod* at the Pacific Film Archive, where it had been mistaken for the 1924 version (catalogue number 1616-108-8608). Neither Lang nor Harbou appears to have been consulted for the 1933 *Siegfrieds Tod*, although Harbou had since 1932 been a member of the Nazi party, and Lang had helped found the Directors' Group of the NSBO, or Nationalsozialistische Betriebszellenorganisation (National Socialist Factory Cell Organization). See Gösta Werner, "Fritz Lang and Goebbels: Myth and Facts," *Film Quarterly* 43, no. 3 (1990): 26. According to Ulrich Klaus, Franz Biermann supervised this sound-film version, although he is not listed in the film's credits. See Klaus, *Deutsche Tonfilme*, vol. 4, Jahrgang 1933 (Berlin: Klaus-Archiv, 1992), 164.

52. The only other time voices are heard is when a brief excerpt of choral polyphony accompanies the scene of Kriemhild and Siegfried's wedding. The music comes from Carl Thiel's "Motette im alten Stil," *Laudate Dominum,* op. 32, for six-part mixed chorus (1932), which is based on themes by the late-seventeenth-century Venetian composer Giovanni Gabrieli.

53. "Gunther . . . was never ignoble; he only had a weak soul. To say yes or no was difficult for him. In vain was his struggle against Brunhild's rigidity." Harbou, *Das Nibelungenbuch,* 91.

54. There was precedent for this treatment in the aforementioned 1924 revival of Hebbel's play *Die Nibelungen:* a contemporary review noted that that production shaded Hagen's character as far more monstrous than before. Alfred Klaar, *"Die Nibelungen"* (review), *Vossische Zeitung,* April 9 1924 (evening edition), in *Theater für die Republik, 1917–1933, im Spiegel der Kritik,* ed. Günther Rühle (Frankfurt: S. Fischer, 1967), 535. I am grateful to Anton Kaes for this reference.

55. "Since childhood days, the name of the Nibelungen resounds in all our ears . . . In school we read an excerpt from the epic, later we read it in its entirety, then we heard Wagner, saw Hebbel's drama, Ibsen's tragedy [*Haemaendene paa Helgeland* (The Vikings at Helgeland), 1858], the Nordic sagas. Now a film has usurped all these materials." Marianne Bruns, "Ein Nibelungenfilm," *Kunstwart und Kulturwart* 37 (May 1924): 84.

PART TWO

Wagnerian Resonance in Film Scoring

FIVE

The Resonances of Wagnerian Opera and Nineteenth-Century Melodrama in the Film Scores of Max Steiner

DAVID NEUMEYER

Max Steiner was one of the best-known composers working in Hollywood during the "golden" era of studio sound film production, roughly 1930–60. He was also among the first to work on the development of underscoring methods, or the use of musical accompaniments behind (or "under") dialogue. In early sound feature films, technical limitations on sound re-recording made it difficult to mix soundtrack elements effectively in post-production: drop-outs, brief but sharp losses of sound levels, were unpredictable and noticeable. An apparently simple solution—recording music on the set while the film was being shot—turned out to be both clumsy and expensive. Steiner's experience at RKO, one of the major studios, from the time he joined in 1929 through early 1932, was typical:

> [Most of the] music was still recorded on the set, causing a great deal of inconvenience and expense. Whenever the director, after the completion of his picture, made any changes, or recut his film, the score was usually ruined as it was obviously impossible to cut the soundtrack without harming the underlying continuity of the music. Occasionally we were able to make cuts that were not too noticeable.[1]

Under the circumstances, it was almost impossible to establish quickly an aesthetic practice for the soundtrack. As Rick Altman puts it, "bounded by the sound system's dynamic limits on the one hand, and the limits of human attention on the other, the soundtrack became an arena which multiple sound conventions sought to dominate."[2] The matter at hand was not simply a decision about the most appropriate ways to balance the different soundtrack elements: the traditions and practices of the various presentational and theatrical modes to which the cinema was heir jostled for priority as well. Again, Altman: "Not only did music, dialogue, and effects clash, but also differing traditions regarding the 'proper' way to present sound: live vs. recorded music, ex cathedra lectures vs. situated dialogue, narrative sound effects vs. vaudevillesque comic effects."[3] Given the mechanical limitations and the aesthetic confusion, it is not surprising that "music and dialogue often contested the right to the audience's attention, with each undermining the effect of the other"[4] (sometimes literally in the case of drop-outs, where the attempt to add one soundtrack element could momentarily cancel out the other).

By 1932, re-recording technology had greatly improved, allowing for an integrated soundtrack and therefore setting the stage for the development of a general soundtrack aesthetic, which was securely in place by the late 1930s.[5] Steiner also—and for the most part fairly—credited post-production mixing technology with a much improved situation for musicians in Hollywood, a change of circumstances he took full advantage of himself:

> With re-recording being rapidly improved, every studio again began to import conductors and musicians. At the time, I was general musical director for RKO Studios. I wrote *Symphony of Six Million* [1932], and *Bird of Paradise* [also 1932] soon after, the first of which had about 40 per cent, and the latter 100 per cent musical scoring. Both pictures had been shot for music. The directors and producers wanted music to run throughout, and this gradual change of policy resulted in giving music its rightful chance. One-third to one-half of the success of these pictures was attributed to the extensive use of music.[6]

Steiner's claim to chronological priority in orchestral scoring ("After this other studios followed suit and began to score their pictures")[7] does not bear up under scrutiny—Paramount had introduced extensive orchestral scoring into its feature films and short subjects in 1931, for example. It is true, however, that his work for producer David O. Selznick in the two films mentioned above, as well as in the hit fantasy-thriller *King Kong* (1933), was influential in encouraging extensive orchestral background scoring for certain types of feature films, in particular melodramas and high-budget spectacles.

Although the question of how to handle music was an important issue that reliable re-recording helped to resolve, it was overshadowed by the aesthetic question of how to balance dialogue with the other soundtrack elements. The answer was twofold, according to Altman: "Guarantee comprehensible dialogue [while at the same time constructing] a soundtrack with virtually constant total volume."[8] The latter, on the one hand, guaranteed a mode of aural continuity that was not disruptive or distracting (the analogue to the continuity editing that guaranteed a focus on narrative elements in the image track) and, on the other hand, contrived to keep the audience's attention at a generally heightened level. In the context of the continuous-level soundtrack, music plays an important role: "In its high-volume mode (when there is no dialogue to compete with), music thus serves a pseudo-narrative function, providing a relay between specific narrative events. In its low-volume mode (when it plays under dialogue or narratively important effects), music joins atmospheric effects in assuring continuity and a generalized sense of space."[9] With this, the foundation of an effective soundtrack aesthetic was firmly laid.

> Whereas early sound films simply transported to the soundtrack diverse and contradictory conventions derived from various pre-existing sound traditions (silent films, public address, legitimate theater, vaudeville, phonography), [feature films after 1932 offer] an integrated soundtrack dependent on a series of new principles. Earlier effects had been discontinuous; classical Hollywood sound effects can be continuous because they are embedded in a multiplane sound environment facilitating simultaneous presentation of foreground and background sounds. Dialogue and music can now share the same soundtrack without getting in each other's way thanks to systematic deployment of an intermittent strategy. Instead of conflicting, [speech, effects, and music] can be integrated into a single soundtrack through the serial or simultaneous application of realist or psychoacoustic principles.[10]

MAX STEINER, THE EARLY SOUNDTRACK, AND MUSIC'S PLACE

Steiner himself was especially interested in the interaction of speech and music: for him, a crucial step in the development of film music was that thanks to reliable post-production mixing, "we were able to control the respective levels between dialogue and music, thereby clearing the dialogue."[11] In other words, re-recording mixers could vary volume for individual channels (in accordance with the aesthetic priorities described by Altman above). Later in the 1930s, this process of adjusting music volume for dialogue was mechanized by the "up-and-downer," a device that raised and lowered music levels inversely with dialogue, in accordance with the fundamental tenet of the classical soundtrack aesthetic: when present, dialogue should always have priority. Combined with the method of recording music to a click track, which facilitated the close synchronization that Steiner favored, the "up-and-downer" made an efficient system that served him well in the dialogue-heavy melodramas for which he is particularly known, especially the cycle of Bette Davis films beginning with *That Certain Woman* (1937) and *Jezebel* (1938) and continuing with several well-known titles, including *Dark Victory* (1939), *All This and Heaven, Too* (1940), *Now, Voyager* (1942), and *The Corn Is Green* (1945); the series ended on a low note with *Beyond the Forest* in 1949.[12] As Kate Daubney observes, "Melodramatic plots often displayed a range of intensity and character development which was well suited to Steiner's carefully crafted characterization in music."[13] His "hyperexplicit" treatment of music could

> take different forms, such as mickey-mousing (the mimicry of movement) or intellectual signposting (the use of music as connotative or symbolic) . . . Steiner's methodical interpretation of action through placement of musical themes can also be read as hyper-explicit, leading us on a journey through the story as explained by the different themes. Such an approach arguably leaves little room for music to be an ambiguous narrative agent, and when the themes relate to particular characters, we have an almost complete version of the story in music.[14]

Despite Steiner's tendency to "overscore" a film (that is, insert a maximum number of minutes of music into the soundtrack), and even though he was enamored of close synchronization in dialogue underscoring (a manner of writing that suggests the "arioso" textures and continuities familiar from composers like Wagner and Puccini in particular), it is not quite correct to refer to his priorities or working methods as operatic. The diverse influences in Steiner's background put him in an unusually good position to draw upon a variety of sources while finding his way toward an effective treatment of music appropriate to the new medium of the sound film—that is to say, the feature film with recorded sound, a continuous-level soundtrack whose theatrical performance was conveyed through loudspeakers.

Steiner grew up in Vienna, where his father was a theater manager, his grandfather had been director of the Theater an der Wien, and family friends included Gustav Mahler and Richard Strauss (who was also Max's godfather). The young Max was certainly conversant not only with Wagner's operas but also with the post-Wagnerian milieu, yet he was often involved in performances of operettas and revues (he claimed to have conducted an operetta when he was only twelve years old, and an original operetta was produced at the Theater an der Wien when he was fifteen).[15] Later, Steiner worked in musical theater in London (1910–14) and New York (1914–29) before going to Hollywood, where he worked initially as an arranger, orchestrator, and conductor for film musicals. The depth of his theatrical experience is hard to overestimate. Tony Thomas recounts that "once launched as a conductor and arranger for stage musicals, he found one job after another," and in New York, "[b]y 1916, Steiner was established as a conductor on Broadway, and over the course of the next thirteen years worked on so many musicals he claimed he could not remember them all." Thomas emphasizes the limits on Steiner's activities during this period: "Despite the vast amount of theatrical music with which Steiner dealt in all these years in New York, he was involved in very little composition. His talent seemed to lie in arranging, conducting, and generally breathing life into other men's music. *Peaches*, the only show for which he wrote music, lasted only two weeks."[16] Steiner's first opportunity to write symphonic background music for a film came in 1930 (*Cimarron*), though, as we have seen, only in 1932 was he given the chance to compose large-scale scores.

It is tempting to set up an opposition, as Kate Daubney does, between Steiner, who moved from RKO to Warner Brothers in 1936, and Erich Korngold, who was hired by Warner as a "prestige" composer in 1935: "Unlike his contemporaries, particularly Erich Korngold, Steiner's background was not in the 'high art' of fin-de-siècle Viennese music, but in the harsher economic practicalities of entertainment theatre: twenty-five years of such experience would turn out to be an invaluable preparation for the constraints of Hollywood music-making."[17] I think this is too stark a contrast that undervalues Steiner's knowledge and goals, even if it is basically true that Korngold's scoring aesthetic was frankly operatic while Steiner's was more pragmatically grounded in the commercial realities of the musical theater and, one should add, more focused on the unique characteristics of sound film. It is better to say that Steiner balanced Wagnerian and post-Wagnerian conceptions of opera with underscoring methods derived from melodrama and operetta. Like his peers in the first decade of sound film, notably Alfred Newman and Herbert Stothart, Steiner was writing first to the new medium of the soundtrack, and he took advantage of whatever resources he found useful.

MAX STEINER ON WAGNER

In 1967, four years before Steiner's death, Myrl Schreibman, then a student at UCLA, interviewed the composer about *Gone with the Wind*. Schreibman, who was not a musician, asked whether Steiner wrote his themes for the actors or for the characters they played. The composer answered firmly that he wrote for the characters, but then qualified his answer. This led before long to an extended comment about his working methods:

> [The Tara theme belongs to the] plantation. The land. Scarlett has her own theme. It doesn't appear very often because there is no reason to play her theme. You play Melanie's, or Ashley's or Rhett Butler's. *Gone with the Wind*, like all my scores, is written like an opera. If you listen to Wagner's *Ring* you will find the same theme throughout. It goes from one end to the other, except *Meistersinger* doesn't have it. But it is in the others—*Götterdämmerung* and *Das Rheingold*. Any opera is like a symphony. A theme reoccurs in different ways. I did it with every one of my scores. If you listen to them carefully you will find they are all written the same way. I start out with a basic theme and then I keep going with it. Of course there are other tunes too.[18]

This is a remarkable muddle that speaks volumes about the shaky reliability of interview comments from Hollywood industry professionals, especially those who are recalling a time much earlier in their lives and who are anxious to establish their own legacy. In Steiner's case, the situation is further complicated by the fact that he did not age gracefully—although commissions had ceased coming his way several years earlier, a situation he attributed not so much to ill health as to the deterioration of industry practices, he still harbored the wish to write more film scores.

Many of the familiar tropes of the public discourse about Wagner and film music are raised in Steiner's comments, in particular, invoking Wagner as a tie to a high art tradition and invoking the leitmotif as legitimation for symphonic film scoring. Steiner specifically links the leitmotif technique to dialogue underscoring in the following:

> I said [to another interviewer] that Richard Wagner would have been one of the greatest picture composers that ever lived because he was underscoring dialogue just like I do. They [Wagner's characters] talk. They have these endless ad libs, if you know what I mean. [He sings and hums a bit of Wagner's music.] What the hell is that but underscoring? The same thing I was doing. He was underlining the whole action until he gets to a song, and then he gets to a song and he goes back again and he has the music accompany him to what we call a recitative.[19]

Finally, Steiner gives broad credit to the methods of nineteenth- and early-twentieth-century opera:

> I studied Wagner in my youth and I think I learned a lot. Puccini did the same darn thing. All of the opera composers always carried their melodies, and it came back and so forth. It is hard to explain unless someone is a musician. Anyway it is my way, which seems to have been successful.[20]

Steiner does himself a disservice by linking his complex, shifting, and subtle underscoring technique so tightly to the symphonic web of Wagnerian opera. In the interview, he ignores his own deep professional knowledge and experience in musical theater, a knowledge that he did draw on heavily during his tenure at RKO, where he was the music director for almost all of that studio's well-known musicals, including those starring Fred Astaire and Ginger Rogers. His late-life account flattens out the history of sound film by recalling only a selection of A-films (ignoring musicals), when in fact before the 1950s the great majority of films—by which I mean B-films, as well as serials and other shorts—were consumed by their audiences in the manner that television is consumed today. The musical conventions of these films mainly drew from popular melodrama, not opera. (I should add that not all A-films were smothered with music in the 1930s, either—a notable exception was filmed stage plays, which often had little if any music.)

The two fundamental problems for an operatic conception of film scoring are that (1) film actors, with rare exceptions, do not sing their dialogue—they speak it; and (2) background music is not continuous through a film's runtime (even heavily scored A-films from the later

1930s do not often go much beyond 50 percent). On the other hand, both of these traits fit well with the traditions of operetta and with the melodramas, monologues, and even pantomimes of operetta, musicals, and stage plays in the later nineteenth and early twentieth centuries. There is little doubt that beginning with the early scores for Selznick and continuing throughout his association with Warner Bros., Steiner did indeed look for some manner of "operatic" conception in films with high production values, but how much of that was Wagner, and how much Friml and Romberg, is still impossible to sort out in my view. I have written elsewhere about those aspects of Steiner's underscoring that seem to me to be closest to the theatrical melodrama.[21] Here I will discuss two examples that come closest to the opposite extreme, the continuous symphonic web of Wagnerian and post-Wagnerian opera. The first is a specific reference by Steiner to a Wagner opera (*Lohengrin*), the second is another concrete operatic reference (this time to *Tosca*). An additional, contrary example from *The Big Sleep* (1946) will show the weaknesses that eventually became apparent in Steiner's underscoring style.

LOHENGRIN AND A DISPATCH FROM REUTERS (1940)

In another late-life interview, Hugo Friedhofer picked out for special mention several pictures on which he had worked as an orchestrator for Steiner in the 1930s and early 1940s. Among them "was another picture that wasn't a big, wide, expansive score, but it was a very, very good one, and made its points very well. It was called *A Dispatch from Reuters . . .* Another standout of Max's, for me."[22] The sketches for this film include a number of marginal comments from Steiner to Friedhofer. The composer, who worked very quickly once he had music timings and his themes in place, was usually separated physically from his orchestrator. Although the substance of what must have been many phone calls is now irretrievable, the marginal notes have survived along with the sketches. These notes range from very pragmatic directives on orchestration options to puns and locker-room-level jokes to concise and often cutting critiques of the scene or film (or occasionally, its director or producer).[23] Specific references to concert composers are not common, but orchestral effects from specific compositions, perhaps not surprisingly, are mentioned more often, partly as aids to Friedhofer's work but partly also to

FIG. 5.1. *A Dispatch from Reuters* (1940), Julius Reuter and the sub-scribers to his news service spy the first homing pigeons arriving.

point out Steiner's musical allusions. The composer often mentions other films on which the two had worked (again, usually as aids for orchestration), but he also occasionally names operas, especially those by Wagner and Puccini.

One notable instance of an operatic reference is in connection with a scene in *A Dispatch from Reuters* (at about 00:30:00, or the beginning of reel 4 in the original). Julius Reuter (Edward G. Robinson) is at the height of his early success, before his news service based on homing pigeons is undermined by the telegraph. Reuter has just signed up subscribers to his stock quote service, and they arrive to await the first reports. Franz (Albert Bassermann) denies entry to Reuter's fiancée, Ida (Edna Best), on grounds that the timing of the news is so important that only subscribers are allowed in the room, but when Franz closes the door, she secretly ascends to the pigeon loft. Within the room, timing of the pigeon's arrival is the crucial issue. One subscriber notes the current time (1:15) and the delivery time (1:30). The bell suddenly rings, and Reuter rushes up the

EX. 5.1. a. *A Dispatch from Reuters,* trumpet call (my transcription);
b. Parallel passage in Wagner, *Lohengrin;* c. *A Dispatch from Reuters,*
main theme as heard against pigeons' arrival (my transcription)

stairs to find Ida waiting. Music enters with the abruptness of a stinger
and continues, high-pitched and repetitive, behind their conversation—
Steiner comments, "Hugo! I am trying to keep the Pigeons 'talking'
thruout!!" Music continues (in a lower register) when Reuter returns to
his subscribers to offer an explanation; one of the latter complains, but
a slow pan to a clock shows that the time is only 1:22. Unlike the earlier
sequence, which had no music, this offers a foreshadowing in an abrupt
shift to music that is both minor-keyed and foreboding. A horizontal
wipe (often used to show passage of time in early films) shifts the view
to the outside of the pigeon loft as Reuter peers into the sky nervously;
Ida asks the time and he replies that it is almost 2:00. Franz calls from
downstairs to say the subscribers are leaving. We see them walking outside (to music both active and dramatic); Reuter rushes out and begs
them to wait, then points to the sky and cries "There they are!" (figure
5.1). A reaction shot shows birds flying, and a rapid series of shots, cutting
back and forth, shows them arriving at the pigeon loft, the bell ringing,
and the subscribers hurriedly returning to the room.

Steiner comments about the moment of the pigeons' arrival, "A
pigeon a la Lohengrin?!" The joking avian reference is to Lohengrin's

FIG. 5.2. A *Dispatch from Reuters*, arrival of the first pigeon

arrival borne by a swan.[24] More than that, however, the immediate dramatic situation is parallel: in Act 1, Scene 2 of *Lohengrin*, trumpets are sounded, everyone awaits the arrival of Elsa's champion, and tension is palpable at the passing of time; suddenly he appears ("Seht! Seht!"; roughly, "There they are!"), and a noble and celebratory choral music follows on a brief polyphonic display of wonder. In *A Dispatch from Reuters*, Steiner inserts a trumpet call as the pigeons are sighted (see example 5.1a for a transcription; example 5.1b shows the equivalent moment in *Lohengrin*), and a triumphant, tutti presentation of the film's main theme (heard initially in the main title sequence) accompanies the arrival of the first pigeon (ex. 5.1c transcribes the theme; the screen still is in figure 5.2). Music fades out as the theme phrase finishes, slightly overlapping to a shot of the subscribers furiously writing down stock prices while Reuter reads them out.

Several observations can be made about this scene. First, Steiner obviously knew the opera well enough that the parallel occurred to him as he was watching the film and planning the music. Second, it is reasonable to assume that he was trying to make the scene as operatic as possible in order to exploit and fill out the allusion. The closely synchronized symphonic background music of classic Hollywood typically acts in a commentative manner, like a voiceover narrator—or like the Wagnerian symphonic web. In this case, Steiner maximizes that function and even achieves something like the musical form of arioso-chorus, the former in the underscoring of the dialogues between Reuter and Ida and between Reuter and the subscribers, the latter in the strongly foregrounded, expansive statement of the main theme, against which a very little dialogue—and even the pigeons' cooing—recedes. Finally, however, this is only a "moment" of opera (about two minutes and twenty seconds of music) that occurs in the context of a ninety-minute film whose multiplane soundtrack, in the typical manner, gives priority to speech. Nevertheless—and even if the effect here is more humorous than grand—this musical cue does show the potential of affinities that can be exploited in the treatment of dialogue underscoring.

TOSCA AND CASABLANCA (1943)

During a famously tense scene in *Casablanca,* Ingrid Bergman's character Ilsa Lund confronts Bogart's Rick with great emotion, demanding that he surrender exit papers that will save the life of her husband, the resistance fighter Victor Laszlo (Paul Henreid). She eventually pulls a pistol on Rick and all but calls him a cad and a scoundrel. Much of the music used in this scene is repeated from a closely parallel scene earlier in the film, when Ilsa returns to Rick's café after hours, tries to explain her abandonment of him in Paris at the time of the German invasion, and receives an embittered response (close-ups from their conversations in figure 5.3a–b). Under one of the prominent motives introduced in this earlier scene (and transcribed in example 5.2a), Steiner notes, "A poor man's Tosca."[25] He is apparently referring to a melodic resemblance either to the opening of Cavaradossi's Act 1 aria "Qual'occhio al mondo" (example 5.2b) or to the clarinet motive that precedes his "O dolce mani" in Act 3 and figures prominently throughout that act, most spectacularly at the end, the moment of Tosca's leap to her death (see example 5.2c). Whether Steiner deliberately introduced this motive in order to make a subtle reference to the plot parallel (Rick could save Laszlo, as Scarpia

FIG. 5.3A–B. *Casablanca,* first after-hours meeting between Rick and Ilsa, close-ups: *top,* Ilsa; *above,* Rick

EX. 5.2. a. *Casablanca* (1943), confrontation between Lisa and Rick, motive referred to by Steiner (my transcription); b. Parallel motive in *Tosca,* first option ("Qual'occhio al mondo," opening); c1 and 2. Parallel motive in *Tosca,* second option (1. clarinet before "O dolce mani"; 2. Tosca leaps to her death)

could save Cavaradossi) or simply noticed the resemblance after the fact is unknown. Because Steiner did not write the score in the chronological order of the film,[26] however, it is possible that he decided on the motivic citation while writing music for the final confrontation, a scene that might be misconstrued to suggest that Rick would ask for sexual favors in return for the exit visas (as Scarpia did of Tosca in return for Cavaradossi's release). Still, even then, the introduction of the motive does not align with any strongly parallel dramatic moment (such as revealing the gun, the analogue to the knife with which Tosca kills Scarpia); instead, the motive first appears when Ilsa makes another allusion to their time together in Paris ("Richard, we loved each other once").

Here again, Steiner's ready knowledge of operatic repertoire is apparent, even if the reference is much less specific than in *A Dispatch from Reuters.* And it is certainly true that in both of the confrontation scenes, music is given particular prominence, not so much by volume as by its consistent intensity and persistent motivic reference—but above all by the clarity of the formal parallels: the famous stinger chord that opens both scenes was originally used earlier in the film for the moment when Rick and Ilsa unexpectedly meet in his café (his attention having been drawn from across the café to a proscribed performance by Sam [Dooley Wilson] of "As Time Goes By"). On the other hand, these scenes, strictly speaking, are melodramatic; that is, they are scenes that foreground dialogue and that use music to underline and intensify shifting emotions. Martin Marks locates a more unequivocal operatic quality not here but in the last of *Casablanca*'s series of confrontation scenes—the film's ending:

> [S]everal key sound effects . . . figure prominently in the film's closing minutes . . . [T]he shrill sound of airplane propellers cues the start of Reel 11 Part 2 and leads to the final variation of "As Time Goes By" . . . The sight and sound of the propellers is followed by an altered version of the tense [stinger] chord we first heard when Rick saw Ilsa in his café—an appropriate parallel because once again Rick and Ilsa gaze at one another, this time as they prepare to part; then, delaying the inevitable, there comes a restatement of the sinking chromatic scale, the motive of doom. Finally the song is heard once more; and this time, unlike the previous two variations (and unlike the first scene at Rick's), no dialogue gets in the way. Knowing that his music would be out in the open, Steiner saw his opportunity to create a climactic variation in the manner of tragic opera; accordingly, the theme is now played by the whole orchestra at full volume, it is anchored to weighty minor key harmonies, and it is slowed down and extended with the most solemn of cadence formulas. (By way of precedent, consider the endings of *Carmen*, *Otello*, and *Tosca*, to name only a few famous examples.)[27]

OPERA AND NOIR: *THE BIG SLEEP* (1946)

Howard Hawks's film version of Raymond Chandler's detective novel, *The Big Sleep*, is a sprawling mess of a film whose narrative was muddled by indecision about the ending during production and by late post-production editing (initiated by the studio, not the director) that added ten minutes of new material designed to improve Lauren Bacall's faltering star status. To compensate, significant passages of expository material were removed and scenes with Martha Vickers, who plays Carmen, the murderer in the novel, were deleted or played down.[28] As David Thomson puts it, "Many commentators have reflected over the years on the density, and the nearly lyrical impossibility, of the plot in *The Big*

Sleep."[29] Thomson defends the film for its playfulness and the smoothness and effectiveness of its individual scenes.

> There's no denying, or escaping, the serene momentum of the picture, its slippery ease. There isn't a scene that doesn't play. The mounting sexual tension between the leads is heady, close to comic, yet very romantic, even if the prolonged double meanings of the horse-talk run a risk of being precious. The steady supply of new characters, or even bits, is life-enhancing: you feel the way Hawks cultivated those bits, if only to kid himself away from worrying about the fragile whole.[30]

Thomson decides that it is the developing romance between Marlowe and Vivian Greenwood (being carried out in real life at the same time by their actors, Bogart and Lauren Bacall) that holds the film together, but nevertheless, he too must finally admit that "the whole is ridiculous, and a commentary fifty years later cannot simply ignore that."[31] Unlike *Casablanca,* which mixed genres recklessly but fulfilled the minimum requirements of each and tied all its loose narrative ends together (amazingly, as its production history was, if anything, even more chaotic), *The Big Sleep* is at some moments a romantic drama, at others a romantic comedy, at still others a detective story (though only occasionally one with the gritty edge or deep-focus images of film noir, undoubtedly the proper cinematic venue for Chandler's story), but it never synthesizes those genres or even settles convincingly on any one of them.

Clearly Max Steiner saw the romance: from the start he plays down the darker elements of the story. His main title cue is bombastic rather than sinister, he assigns Marlowe a quixotic little scherzando theme, and he undermines the drug-addicted, mentally unbalanced Carmen by giving her a two-note motive that all too easily disappears into the musical texture. Only in the final thirty minutes does Steiner's familiar style of underscoring dramatic and romantic scenes with close synchronization come into full play, and even then it encounters obstacles: for example, the most expansive statement of the love theme in the film is heard while Marlowe is still tied up in the villains' home, before Vivian cuts him loose and they escape.

Perhaps there was little else Steiner could do but favor the romantic comedy angle. As the 1940s progressed, his scoring preferences fit less and less well with the carefully constructed realism of film noir in particular, but the general trend was away from the heavily scored films of the 1930s in any case. This change was not only a matter of aesthetic choice: continued improvements in microphones increased the quality of dialogue recording and re-recording, and other improvements reduced the level of background hiss, so that directors and sound editors felt more comfortable with a soundtrack whose "empty" spaces were not filled up with music. In such a context, it must have been particularly galling—but revealing as well—for Steiner to receive from the studio chief, Jack Warner, the following backhanded compliment for a film score completed only a few months before *The Big Sleep:* "I want to pay you praise for your intelligent scoring of *Mildred Pierce.* In my opinion it was the best you have done because most of all the music was not over done."[32] Steiner's instincts, whether they stem from opera or musical theater, were not congenial to a genre where the natural inclination was to limit music almost entirely to onscreen performances, often in bars or nightclubs.[33] Late in his life, he seems to have come to that realization himself, as the following interview comment intimates: "Some pictures require a lot of music, and some are so realistic that music would only interfere. Most of my films were entertainments—soap operas, storybook adventures, fantasies. If those films were made today, they would be made differently and I would score them differently."[34] Steiner's point is by no means so clear as one might like, but his remark does suggest that he was able to take a historical view, not only of generational change (especially noticeable in the 1950s and early 1960s) but also of aesthetically and technologically driven change.

The invention and consolidation of the continuous-level soundtrack happened gradually, starting with substantial improvements in re-recording technology in 1932 and progressing with both technological and aesthetic refinements through the mid-to-late 1930s. Max Steiner's work was part and parcel of that process. Early on, he saw the value in underscoring not only action but also dialogue, and the true distinctiveness of his method of dialogue underscoring was its strikingly effective manner of fitting some familiar theatrical devices into that novel system of reproduced sound that is the film soundtrack. As his models, not surprisingly, he took what was at hand for him, or what was familiar from his childhood and professional experience, the effective tools of arioso textures in opera and monologues and melodramas in musical theater. If eventually this anti-realistic or theatrical artifice proved too limiting, Steiner's extensive oeuvre showed that the method had been well suited for some corners of the feature film repertoire, in particular, historical films and romances, or "soap operas, story book adventures, [and] fantasies."

By the 1950s, a combination of economic and cultural shifts brought Korngold's bolder, broad-brush operatic style to the forefront. Competition with television pushed studios to focus more on high-budget films in order to distinguish their products and bring out audiences, and widescreen formats, combined with much better sound fidelity (which not only abetted but actually required larger orchestras), only encouraged the kind of spectacle one finds in historical films such as *The Robe* (1953), *Julius Caesar* (1953), and *Ben Hur* (1959). Steiner's last substantive score, for a western, *The Searchers* (1956), shows that he too understood the possibilities and, given more time and opportunity, would have known how to take advantage of them. As it stands, however, Steiner's distinctive contribution remains his early translation and transformation of the arioso mode and the thematic density of the Wagnerian symphonic web into the subtle, detailed art of underscoring dialogue and accompanying the narrative film.

NOTES

1. Max Steiner, "Scoring the Film," in *We Make the Movies*, ed. Nancy Naumberg (New York: Norton, 1937), 219–20. For more views on this question from the early 1930s, see Fred Steiner, "What Were Musicians Saying about Movie Music during the First Decade of Sound? A Symposium of Selected Writings," in *Film Music I*, ed. Clifford McCarty (New York and London: Garland, 1989), 81–107. Kate Daubney has additional information on Steiner's early years with RKO, with quotations from him, in Kate Daubney, *Max Steiner's Now, Voyager: A Film Score Guide* (Westport, Conn.: Greenwood, 2000), 8–9.

2. Rick Altman, with McGraw Jones and Sonia Tatroe, "Inventing the Cinema Sound Track: Hollywood's Multiplane Sound System," in *Music and Cinema*, ed. James Buhler, Caryl Flinn, and David Neumeyer (Middletown, Conn.: Wesleyan University Press, 2000), 357.

3. Ibid.

4. Ibid.

5. Rick Altman, "Sound Space," in *Sound Theory/Sound Practice* (New York: Routledge, 1992), 46–64, especially 55 ff.

6. Steiner, "Scoring the Film," 220. How Steiner came up with his influence figures is unknown. If he was not simply making the numbers up, they may have had their source in informal comments made by directors, producers, or other film personnel.

7. Ibid.

8. Altman, "Inventing the Cinema Sound Track," 353.

9. Ibid.

10. Ibid., 353, 356.

11. Steiner, "Scoring the Film," 220.

12. Steiner discusses his use of the click track in Tony Thomas, *Film Score: The Art and Craft of Movie Music* (Burbank: Riverside Press, 1991), 70–71. It should be understood that in using the term "melodrama," I am not referring to the nineteenth-century genre of stage play but specifically to the eighteenth- and early-nineteenth-century genre of works with spoken text and accompanying music, and—especially—to their persistence as "action" numbers in operetta and musicals (where the melodrama is obviously very closely related to the pantomime). Despite the narrow focus suggested by its title, the following article offers a concise, well-written summary of the historical relations between melodrama and cinema: Jon Burrows, "'Melodrama of the Dear Old Kind': Sentimentalising British Action Heroines in the 1910s," *Film History* 18 (2006): 163–73.

13. Daubney, *Now, Voyager,* 20.

14. Ibid., 46. The term "hyper-explicit" is derived from Claudia Gorbman's essay on *Mildred Pierce* (1945): "The musical score exhibits a pronounced tendency toward hyperexplication . . . The music is an element of discourse that magnifies, heightens, intensifies the emotional values suggested by the story. Just as melodrama displays a tendency to use the close-up on the female star's face . . . Steiner's music has a similar effect." See Gorbman, *Unheard Melodies: Music in Narrative Film* (Bloomington: Indiana University Press, 1987), 98.

15. Daubney, *Now, Voyager,* 3. For more details of Steiner's early life, see the same volume, 1–8.

16. Thomas, *Film Score,* 58.

17. Daubney, *Now, Voyager,* 1.

18. Myrl Schreibman, "On *Gone With the Wind,* Selznick, and the Art of 'Mickey Mousing': An Interview with Max Steiner," *Journal of Film and Video* 56, no. 1 (2004): 42.

19. Ibid., 46.

20. Ibid. Steiner makes it clear, however, that he is no unabashed fan or acolyte: "Wagner was undoubtedly a great composer. There is no question about that. I just don't particularly care for his music. I lean towards Tchaikovsky and Korsikoff [*sic*]. I like French music better" (ibid.). Wagner did not do terribly well at the hands of Hugo Friedhofer, Steiner's long-time orchestrator, either. Writing to Page Cook, Friedhofer acknowledged that style imitation was a necessary tool of the film composer and orchestrator and remarked that "[t]he trick is to remain well within the boundaries of whatever style you have chosen to simulate. Otherwise one runs the risk of starting—let's say—in the manner of Aaron Copland, only to wind up in a welter of Wagnerian schmaltz, something which is to me nothing less than abominable." Quoted in Linda Danly, ed., *Hugo Friedhofer: The Best Years of His Life, A Hollywood Master of Music for the Movies* (Lanham/London: Scarecrow Press, 1999), 169.

21. "Melodrama as a Compositional Resource in Early Hollywood Sound Cinema," *Current Musicology* 57 (1995): 61–94.

22. Quoted in Danly, *Hugo Friedhofer,* 46.

23. Daubney observes that "[t]his level of communication was extremely advantageous both to Steiner, who could have confidence in his orchestrator's ability, and to the smooth running of the postproduction system, for farming out part of the process to others was more likely to get the job done quickly than relying on one composer" (*Now, Voyager*, 13). Daubney discusses Steiner's sketches and their marginal comments in some detail (13–17).

24. I would like to thank my University of Texas at Austin colleague Michael Tusa for identifying this Wagner reference for me.

25. Daubney notes a similar instance in another film: "[I]n *They Died with Their Boots On* (1942), [Steiner] describes a dramatic moment of music for a scene as resembling 'A Warner Bros. "Tosca" at the end—verstehst!'" (*Now, Voyager*, 16).

26. Martin Marks, "Music, Drama, Warner Brothers: The Cases of *Casablanca* and *The Maltese Falcon*," in *Music and Cinema*, 163.

27. Ibid., 177.

28. David Thomson, *The Big Sleep* (London: BFI, 1997), 58–59.

29. Ibid., 42.

30. Ibid., 45–47.

31. Ibid., 42, 47.

32. Inter-office memo from Jack Warner to Max Steiner, June 14, 1945.

33. Roy Webb, who was Steiner's assistant in the latter's early years in Hollywood and thoroughly adopted Steiner's techniques and style, manages background scoring in film noir much better. For example, his score for *Murder, My Sweet* (1944), which is also based on a Chandler novel, is admittedly extensive but it remains effective because it is downplayed, both in level and in the much greater subtlety of its thematic treatment (which is to say that Webb plays to emotional synchronization first of all—it is quite possible to ignore the thematic references altogether with little loss in comprehension or appreciation).

34. Unpublished interview with Tony Thomas, quoted in Daubney, *Now, Voyager*, 18.

SIX

Wagner's Influence on Gender Roles in Early Hollywood Film

EVA RIEGER

The scenario of a typical Hollywood film might be as follows: Outside, a fierce storm rages. The camera pans to a room with a fireplace, a table, a bench, and a stool. A stranger tears open the door and stumbles in. His manner and his torn clothes suggest that he is on the run. He collapses unconscious onto the floor. The woman of the house looks at him anxiously, but also with interest. Is he sick, or just exhausted? He comes to, glimpses the woman, and explains to her that he is being pursued by bad fortune. A strange tension builds between them. This intensifies when he asks for water, because as she gives him some, they gaze intently at one another, seemingly sensing that something is happening. A conversation ensues during which both of them notice that they have fallen in love with each other. At the conclusion of the scene, the dark skies lift and spring seems to flood in—love has captured both of them and their happiness is complete.

What kind of film music would a composer of the 1940s have written for such a sequence? One person who took on this job accompanied the storm with agitated runs in the strings. As the woman hurries to fetch water for the thirsty stranger, a rising motif of parallel thirds played by the violins sounds for the first time (example 6.1).

EX. 6.1. Sieglinde's theme from *Die Walküre*

When the man looks at her intently, a cello plays a beautiful solo. It is repeated twice and followed by four more cellos joining to create a harmonically and sonically sublime moment, which makes us guess that the two will soon fall in love with each other. The motif associated with the man contains an augmented second, and the interval between the first four notes forms a tritone (example 6.2).

EX. 6.2. Siegmund's theme from *Die Walküre*

Her motif consists of a rising figure; his leads downward. Thus we suspect that the woman is the bearer of hope, while the man is dogged by misfortune. With his words, "But now the sun shines on me anew" ("Die Sonne lacht mir nun neu"), we know at once that his meeting with the woman makes him happy, because her motif is played four times in the violins, while bassoon, horns, and clarinets repeat the first part of it in triplets, thus increasing the intensity of the effect. As the skies brighten, the harps play pearly arpeggios and the woodwinds accompany "sweetly" (*dolce*), spreading an atmosphere of pure radiant joy.

But this is no film. Instead, it is the plot of the first act of Richard Wagner's *Die Walküre*. Nevertheless, the music could have developed along similar lines in a 1940s film. Wagner emphasizes a glance, imitates a movement, depicts a mood. One is reminded of Max Steiner, who musically depicted gestures, the minutest movements, and emotions so closely in *The Informer* (1935) that the technique prompted the expression "Mickey-Mousing" to describe it.

"The prevailing dialect of film-music language has been composed of the nineteenth-century late Romantic style of Wagner and Strauss," writes Claudia Gorbman.[1] This is only partially correct, because Wagner's method of characterization—apart from the leitmotif technique, which has roots as ancient as those of opera itself—is based on the tradition of affects, which in music can be traced back to the Renaissance. The unstoppable march of absolute music through the concert halls of the nineteenth century did not at all result in the disappearance of meaning.

It was assumed that images and feelings would be understood without any need for excessive explanation.

In his essays in *Oper und Drama* and *Über die Anwendung der Music auf das Drama*, Wagner explained that music needed to express everything which language could not, with the goal of combining both. His guiding principle was always to maximize the dramatic action on the stage. Wagner accomplished a great deal just by moving away from the preset units characteristic of earlier dramatic and instrumental works. He dispensed with set forms like the da capo aria, retaining only fragments of these traditions in exceptional circumstances. Instead, he developed themes "always in connection with or according to the character of a tangible appearance."[2] And indeed one can see how he perfected this technique as he developed from work to work. He operated with tiny musical elements which he would vary and modify as needed. The requirement for cadences was no longer the guiding criterion, and instead the musical-dramatic development would determine how he composed.

Total comprehensibility on stage was crucial for Wagner, and this was also true for the music. It is also clear that he was thinking cinematically well before the technology was available. For him, a "model staging" was more important than the printed score. The fact that only a staging of his works can fully reveal all their qualities has made his aesthetics a very rich source for film composers.

Besides using the leitmotif technique, Wagner drew on the tradition of musical affects in order to intensify the expressive capabilities of his sonic language. According to the music theory of the ancient Greeks, different feelings were inherent in certain modalities. For instance, the Phrygian mode was thought to spark a martial mood. During the Renaissance, this theory of musical affects from antiquity was again circulated. For the music theorist Heinrich Glarean, whose study *Dodekachordon* appeared in 1547, the Phrygian mode was wild and warlike, while the Lydian mode was feminine and soft. The Dorian mode conveyed for him the majestic and the weighty. Here already, we note gendered categorizations which are positively or negatively valued.

During the Baroque period, it was assumed that every human state of mind was determined by a certain emotion or mixture of emotions. These expressions of feeling were termed and typified as "affects." Baroque composers built on this tradition, perhaps foremost among them Johann Sebastian Bach, whose cantatas and oratorios are in turn a rich source for the musical interpretation of words and the development of an expressive harmonic language. In the course of the seventeenth and eighteenth centuries, the lyrical-expressive language of affect took on a leading role. Theorists and musicians like Heinichen, Marpurg, Quantz, Kraus, Mattheson, and others attempted to systematize the art of composition by publishing instructional guides, treatises, and educational manuals.

Since Wagner draws from this tradition, it is useful to understand some of its basic principles, especially since early film composers also appropriated elements from it. The easiest to hear are musical descriptions of physical movements like flying and running, or natural sounds such as thunder or birdsong. Haydn's oratorio *Die Schöpfung* (*The Creation*) is replete with such imitations, which are also easy for musical novices to understand. Equally identifiable are musical depictions of basic emotions (affects) such as sadness, anger, or joy. Sound painting, imitation of movement, the imitation of patterns of speech, and the representation of emotions: in Baroque opera, these four categories are omnipresent. The relevant affects for music can be traced back to Christian Wolff's system, developed in his *Psychologia empirica* (1732). Among the affects with positive emotive meaning (*affecti jucundi*) he included love, hate, joy, courage, merriment; of the affects with negative emotive meaning (*affecti molesti*) he counted sympathy, envy, regret, shame, fear, despair, pettiness, grief, boredom, and anger.

A feeling is expressed musically mainly by means of key (tonality), rhythm, tempo, instrumentation, inner movement, harmony, and intervals. Thus, some relics of the Baroque tradition were eagerly adopted by Wagner.[3] The interval of a second emphasizes feelings of pettiness or mourning. Descending chromatic steps represent despair or a frightening situation, in any event mournful affects, while rising chromatic steps suggest pleading or urging. If a rising fourth occurs at the beginning of a melody, it mostly represents feelings of heroism or determination, and in general rising melodies convey power and energy. An augmented fourth or a diminished fifth, also called *quinta deficiens* or the tritone, is used to portray pain, dejection, or lamentation. Evil or insanity are also often depicted using the tritone: for instance, the motif for the evil

Hagen from *Der Ring des Nibelungen* is constructed of two notes that form a tritone. When Wagner says of *Parsifal* that the "sensitive affect" did not fit the work, and thus he could not use the minor seventh,[4] he meant a very specific feeling, because it is exactly the seventh that is used in the *Ring* to describe the love of a woman: this has no place in his last work. The seventh is most powerful in its diminished form and paints feelings of despair and deepest agitation, especially when it accompanies an exclamation or is used to accentuate a single word. The interval is of course closely tied to the diminished seventh chord, which possesses a similarly intensive effect of suffering and passion. A falling seventh is used to express pain. The octave, on the other hand, emphasizes the grandiose or stands for strength.

Admittedly, the meaning conveyed doesn't just depend on the size of the interval, but is also a result of whether or not it rises, falls, or leaps, is played quickly or slowly, and what its melodic context is. Just as in a party game, a rule applies as long as it is not invalidated by a superior rule. Thus, for example, a fast tempo can have a greater impact on our awareness than the structure of an interval.

A minor scale represents sadness, but also suggests spiritual complexity. The major mode stands for positive, and often uncomplicated, naïve sentiments. While diatonic music can represent brightness and affirmation, as well as power and strength—meaning that it contains positive traits—chromatic music has since the seventeenth century been used to embody weeping, lamentation, suffering, the endurance of pain, as well as to depict evil, sinfulness, or misfortune. *Femmes fatales* such as Bizet's Carmen or Wagner's Venus, Ortrud, and Kundry belong to this category.

In the realm of instrumentation, the string section is often used as the foundation and thus is mostly neutral in terms of affect. The exception is when violins play *con sordino* or *pizzicato,* an effect that can convey tenderness or melancholy. In general flutes encompass the pastoral, idyllic, naïve, joyous, and tenderly lyrical, as well as the wistful, usually in the context of love. The horns signify hunting, or they underscore ostentatious, dignified movements, while the trumpet as the martial instrument is generally used to decorate ceremonial scenes such as elaborate parades. This hails from the traditional use of brass instruments dating back to the seventeenth and eighteenth centuries, when trumpeters enjoyed a privileged position, which in turn determined their identity. Trumpets can be read as male-identified.

Harmonically, dissonances produce mainly negative dramatic tension; the return to harmony signifies its resolution. At heroic moments or those of pomp and circumstance, fanfares are limited to standard triads. Untroubled moods are conceived using similarly simple harmonies. If conflict enters a love relationship, dissonances like diminished chords and suspensions appear. The minor subdominant region and the Neapolitan sixth are similarly used in conflict situations.

The following musical devices belong to the tradition of musical signification and were used—also by Wagner—for the musical depiction of happy, positive affects:

- Rising leaps and melodies
- Basic triadic motifs, or rising major triads/thirds
- Fanfare-like chordal progressions that expand beyond an octave
- Pure diatonicism
- Major keys
- Repetition of notes
- Simple or large leaps
- Dotted rhythms
- Loud volume (*forte*), full orchestra, dynamic changes
- An upward movement at the beginning of the phrase

For the representation of negative affects, the following are often used:

- Slow tempo
- Dissonance
- Minor keys
- Stepwise descending bass, in tragic situations the *passus duriusculus*
- Decreased volume (*piano*), little dynamic alternation
- Sinking/falling/descending intervals and melodic lines (especially at the end of phrases)
- Flute accompaniment (to convey longing)
- Vocal lines with small range, and small, usually descending, intervals (sadness)

- Sighing motifs, use of 4–3 suspensions (pleading, lamenting)
- Use of sarabande rhythm
- Long rests (tenderness, flattery)
- Songlike themes (*cantabile*)
- Small steps (sadness, sympathy)
- Chromaticism (despair, pain, longing, resignation)
- Dotted rhythms, $\frac{3}{4}$ time, sudden fermatas, and general pause (rage)

Wagner shapes his motifs according to this semantic tradition. Several of them describe motion or a movement, for instance the motif of the Giants in the *Ring,* which is ponderous and unwieldy, or Erda's rising motif, which ascends from the deepest depths. For motifs that are supposed to express grief or conflict, Wagner employs devices that have been in use for centuries: Woe motif, a descending half-tone; Renunciation motif, descending; Murder motif, descending; Brooding motif, a downward seventh leap; Twilight of the Gods motif, descending; Infidelity motif, a downward seventh leap. The Contract motif also descends (the necessity to honor contracts triggers Wotan's displeasure).

Not all motifs can immediately be interpreted unequivocally. For example, how can a motif which rises upward, and thus radiates a positive affect, actually spell death, as is the case with the motif in the *Ring* that solemnly appears when Brünnhilde announces to Siegmund that he is doomed to die? The combination of upward motion, minor key, and calm note values evokes the ceremonious and dignified announcement of the worst possible fate, which Siegmund takes with utmost poise. But the upward movement suggests that there is more to it than just death— namely, his strong love for Sieglinde.

The following two examples for the accompaniment of a sung text show with what subtlety and attentiveness Wagner composed. At the beginning of Act 1, Scene 2 of *Tannhäuser,* the hero laments that he longs for the normal world of mortals. Venus asks what is bothering him, to which he answers that he thinks he can hear the sound of bells. Appropriately, we hear the sound of bells; in addition, the calm chordal accompaniment signals a healthy normal world. When Venus answers, disjointed sixteenth notes convey her spiritual anxiety. Tannhäuser sings: "I cannot measure the time that I have tarried here" ("Die Zeit, die hier ich verweil', ich kann sie nicht ermessen"), and endless time is evoked by means of drawn-out chords in the accompaniment. He complains that he never gets to see nature, and the melody runs downward. Every new phrase begins higher and ends in a lower register—a tested indication for sadness.

Further enabling comprehensibility, Wagner most often combines his motifs with the stage action and less with thoughts and ideas. He never expressed himself definitively about his compositional approach to the motifs and the countless ways they are connected to and interwoven with each other. Since a motif is rarely repeated exactly the same way as it is first introduced, and instead is modified to always suit the person or the situation in which it is being (re)used, each musical idea is subject to endless variation. Although Wagner's technique of transformation and variation belongs to a long compositional tradition, he differs from his predecessors by the swift and agile way he molds his themes as needed. Since then, this practice has been a rich source of inspiration for film composers.

Despite continuing disputes about whether or not music conveys or contains specific meaning, the question posed in the 1980s about the gendered implications of music went too far for many musicologists. Still, a gender-specific reading of music has been used unhesitatingly for decades. For example, Kurt Overhoff, who as recently as 1967 wrote about the "masculine major" and "feminine minor" modes, linked the discussion of music with the idea of a "natural polarity" between the sexes.[5] The fact that the affects with positive emotive meaning were thus assigned to men and the *affecti molesti* to women was taken to be self-evident.

The dichotomous image of masculinity and femininity is a construction of the late eighteenth century and a consequence of the rise of the bourgeoisie.[6] People were irrefutably either masculine or feminine, with no subtle gradations between the two. Homosexuality was stigmatized as an evil degeneration. Lesbian love was all but unknown, because women were not considered to have their own sexuality. Men were taken to be public beings, and women were assigned to the private, domestic sphere. Within this dichotomy, women were overwhelmingly ascribed negative personal characteristics. Superiority was considered masculine and inferiority feminine, followed in turn by strength/weakness, norm/deviation, the "actual"/the complementary.

From the last third of the eighteenth century on, composers transcribed this construction into music, sometimes blatantly, sometimes less so. Nevertheless, this fundamental distinction between the sexes became ossified, in part because it was so convenient for the bourgeoisie. The feminine character—considered willing to sacrifice, endure pain, and accept renunciation—was restricted to the area of love or as the object of sexuality. Certain musical figures—traditionally used for conflict-ridden affects or moods, such as grief, sighing, sickness, hesitation, and despair—were applied to "pure" women and served to draw a predetermined personality which conformed to a female "nature." Masculine counterparts were assigned the musical equivalents of characteristics such as vivacity, decisiveness, impatience, irritability, and exuberance. "Evil" women were traditionally given "manly" characteristics, thus taking on the aura of deviancy and abnormality. In this way the supremacy of the male and the inferiority of the female character was established without anyone really noticing. Stereotypes developed which continued to be used in the twentieth century for film music and advertising jingles.[7]

The application of gender-specific music is easiest to hear in masses and oratorios. From Bach through Beethoven to Bruckner, the imposing sounds of trombones, trumpets, and horns represented masculine rulers, and were easily transferred to the heroes of profane music. By contrast, the Virgin Mary was described by flutes, delicate string sounds, harps, and woodwinds. At the end of the eighteenth century, bourgeois man assumed the divine legacy, a move Haydn set to music in exemplary works (*The Creation, The Seasons*). Wagner appropriates this tradition when, in *Rheingold,* he orchestrates the Valhalla motif (which, as Hans von Wolzogen and successive *Ring* analysts claim, describes the newly built castle)[8] with the magnificent sounds of the brass section: four tubas, two bass tubas, three trombones, and three trumpets; and again in *Die Walküre,* when he associates this motif with the appearance of Wotan. This music elevates the male protagonist Wotan by giving him an exalted, affirming character.

Are there parallels in early film music? Gender-specific orchestration is found both in Wagner's work and in film. Wagner feminizes the woodwinds throughout his work; for him, the oboes and the cor anglais express suffering. He frequently used these instruments to depict female figures, and implemented characteristics typical for the image of femininity back then. It is thus nothing unusual when Sieglinde is denoted by the clarinets and Siegmund by the cellos, or when Eva (in *Die Meistersinger von Nürnberg*) is represented by the oboe and clarinet during the fermatas in the opening chorale, while her lover Walther is characterized by the violas and cellos. Similarly, instrumentation in film music also reflects gender differences. In *The Wedding March (Der Hochzeitsmarsch)* (1928), J. S. Zamencik and Louis du Francesco used high instruments for women and sonorous ones for men; there are also countless examples of this practice in later films.[9] Romantic love is often associated with traditional feminine traits; when Frank and Nora fall in love in *Key Largo* (1948), we hear a solo violin.

Wagner associated dissonance, such as the sounds Beckmesser creates on his lute, with the negative. Even today, dissonance in film and television continues to accompany uncomfortable feelings such as danger, horror, or pain. This expressive immediacy necessarily appealed to the pioneers of film music, composers who were active during the "golden age" of film music, between 1930 and 1940. During this time, the basic conventions of Hollywood film music were established, to be further developed until about 1950. Above all, Max Steiner, who explicitly acknowledged Wagner's influence on his compositional praxis, adopted the leitmotif technique, which he varied and developed in accordance with the action on the screen. The degree to which Erich Wolfgang Korngold admired Wagner is evidenced by his decision to work on the soundtrack of *Magic Fire* (1955), a biopic about Richard Wagner. Bernard Herrmann also paid homage to Wagner by imitating Isolde's "Liebestod" from *Tristan und Isolde* in *Vertigo* (1958) when Judy, having been transformed into Scottie's dream woman, approaches him.

Siegfried in Wagner's *Ring* has a total of seven motifs, six of which begin with an upward fourth or fifth leap. Charlie Chaplin used this device in the musical score for *City Lights* (1931) to indicate male activity: the theme of the Tramp soars upward with dotted rhythms, while the Flower Girl's theme leads downward (example 6.3 and example 6.4).

Traditionally, the rising sixth expresses a pleasant feeling, often of love, and plays a significant role in the musical depiction of a "good" woman or blessed love, hence the term *Liebessexte* (love-sixth). This figure can be found in Alfred Newman's score for *Wuthering Heights* (1939),

EX. 6.3. The Tramp's theme in *City Lights*

EX. 6.4. The Flower Girl's theme in *City Lights*

Miklós Rózsa's *Spellbound* (1940), Maurice Jarre's *Dr. Zhivago* (1965) and countless other films. It is also part of Brünnhilde's love motif, which portrays the stripping of her identity as a Valkyrie and transformation into a loving woman. While the graceful flourish around the first note intensifies the expression of love, the motif ends with a diminished seventh drop: a clear sign for suffering, and—as evident by its use in the *Ring*—a sign for the love of a woman that ultimately fails (example 6.5). So the motif anticipates Brünnhilde's misfortune. This is no semantic wavering, but instead a layering of two levels of feeling, which nevertheless do not interfere with one another.

EX. 6.5. Brünnhilde's love motif from *Götterdämmerung*

The split between *femme fragile* (Elisabeth, Elsa, Irene, Sieglinde) and *femme fatale* (Venus, Ortrud) is not Wagner's exclusive specialty, but rather a cultural topos which finds its continuation in motion pictures. In films, the *femme fragile* usually gets small-stepped, regular, evenly phrased music. The similarity between Anne's theme in Max Steiner's score for *King Kong* (1933) and Madeleine's theme in Herrmann's *Vertigo* (1958) twenty-five years later (example 6.6 and example 6.7) shows how long-lasting such a feminine image was.

In *Rebecca* (1940, Franz Waxman), the new Mrs. de Winter has just such a simple theme (example 6.8), similar to Elsa's at the beginning of Wagner's *Lohengrin*. Venus is depicted without solid bass support,

EX. 6.6. Anne's theme from *King Kong*

EX. 6.7. Madeleine's theme from *Vertigo*

EX. 6.8. The new Mrs. de Winter's theme from *Rebecca*

EX. 6.9. Rebecca's theme from *Rebecca*

EX. 6.10. Mrs. Paradine's theme from *The Paradine Case*

exactly as Rebecca is in the eponymous film. Music which lacks lower sonorities has long been used to depict frightening situations, and it is no different in this case. Though attractive and seductive, she is also frightening: the nameless wife of Maxim wants to get away from her as much as Tannhäuser does from Venus. Chromaticism is also characteristic of the *femme fatale:* Rebecca's chromatically set, narrow-stepped theme slithers and undulates over harmonically unsure ground (example 6.9).

Venus is no different. When Tannhäuser excitedly interrupts the singers in order to instruct them that love is incomplete without sensuality and sexuality, Venus's acoustically seductive theme immediately slides in. Similarly, whenever Mrs. Danvers talks of the mysterious Rebecca, we hear her short theme, which frames the tritone and thus exudes wickedness. In *The Paradine Case* (1947), Waxman's melody ascends and descends chromatically and finds itself on harmonically unstable ground. The theme dedicated to Mrs. Paradine is strikingly similar to Rebecca's. Its lead-in is prepared by lush strings, giving it a romantic-longing sound in terms of orchestration. Despite the seemingly uplifting sixth leap at the beginning (which marks the domain of "love"), Waxman returns to a chromatically winding melodic line in order to depict the shadowy and dubious. After the upbeat, the melody arrives on a diminished seventh chord, thus emphasizing negativity (example 6.10). In addition, the bass contains evenly pulsating strokes, giving the whole theme a fateful tension. Again, the profligate actress Charlotte in *Stage Fright* (Leighton Lucas, 1950) is given a theme which connects mendacity and erotic seductiveness. The music underscores the idea that women who abandon the terrain of their "true nature" become morally corrupt.

Wagner loves to create extreme binary oppositions between the great representative world of power and the inwardly turned world of love. In other words, the male public sphere versus the private and erotic female sphere. This musical tradition is already evident among Wagner's predecessors; for instance, Christoph Willibald Gluck's opera *Iphegenie in Aulis* contains a dance performed by the slaves and slave girls. The men have dotted, upward-moving phrases, whereas the women are depicted with *legato* descending phrases (example 6.11 and example 6.12). Especially distinctive are the contrasts between the hunters and the bridesmaids in Weber's *Freischütz.* In Wagner's *Rienzi,* there is an "entrance of the virgins" during the "fight of the gladiators." The gladiators are announced with triplets in the trumpets. Huge broad chords with dotted rhythms conclude cadences that are reminiscent of marching music. By contrast, the virgins represent peace; they enter to the sounds of flutes, clarinets, and later, violins, playing tender trills. If we turn to the sailors and the weaving girls in Wagner's *Fliegender Holländer,* the male sphere is represented by rising motifs, rhythmic diversity, and increased volume, while the world of the women is characterized by calm, spiraling music.

EX. 6.11. "Dance of the Slaves" from Gluck, *Iphegenie in Aulis*

EX. 6.12. "Dance of the Slave Girls" from Gluck, *Iphegenie in Aulis*

Whether intensified or attenuated, these contrasts can be found in all of Wagner's operas. In *Tannhäuser,* the two poles of male activity are depicted in the dichotomy between the hunting party and the pilgrims' chorus, namely physical activity and spiritual contemplation. Female activities are relegated either to the sinful and scary underworld or to the pure world of self-sacrifice. Wagner here works with strict opposites that corresponded to the customary dichotomies of the time: soul/body, reason/emotion, and culture/nature. The idyllic bells, the joyful shepherd's song, the pilgrims' chorus, hunting music, the Count's hunting horse are coded as male (ceremonious, measure rhythms, regal fanfares, feudal grandeur), as is the use of low instruments. The seductive song of Venus, unbridled, infinite, chaotic sexuality, the Bacchanal and the song of the sirens are coded as female and use high instruments. When

Tannhäuser and Elisabeth are paired, only the former can indulge himself in all the activities necessary for personal development. He lives out his passions, satisfies his needs, and actively seeks happiness. Elisabeth is not permitted to live out her emotions, and her short upheaval ends with selfless love and a longing for death.

This distinction between the male-coded world of adventure and activity versus the female-coded world of love is most evident in swashbuckling or adventure films, as for instance in Erich Korngold's music for *The Adventures of Robin Hood* (1938), *The Sea Hawk* (1940), *Captain Blood* (1935), and *The Sea Wolf* (1941). In his introductory music for *The Sea Hawk*, brass instruments play a fanfare-like piece with festive trumpets and with tremendous volume and rhythmic diversity—the music depicts fighting men who plunge into adventure. The fanfares then give way to a contrasting B section featuring a *legato* love theme, which ends with a tremendous surge in the violins. Countless introductory pieces follow the same pattern: the man loves life's adventures, but always returns to the shelter of a woman's love.

To the extent that gender studies no longer looks exclusively at specifically male or female figures but rather examines male- and female-coded spheres, one can now see interesting intersections both in film and in Wagner's operas. For instance, Senta's betrothed, Erik, in the *Fliegender Holländer,* is presented as a sensitive and vulnerable man who remains fixed in bourgeois conventionality and fades before the impressive, imposing appearance of the Dutchman. His pleading aria, "Mein Herz voll Treue" (Act 2), is composed of regular phrases and has an even, inconspicuous accompaniment. He is introduced by the solo clarinet (the instrument that stands for love), and his melody is often ornamented by noticeable mordents, which convey the sense that he is a weak man. The film *Mildred Pierce* (Max Steiner, 1945) provides an interesting parallel. Mildred, the female lead, who despite many setbacks as a businesswoman nevertheless struggles through life, is accompanied by a male-coded theme with a rising seventh, dotted rhythms, and a stable tonal identity, whereas her husband, Bert, who divorces Mildred and leaves her without any support, gets a typically "female" theme which aimlessly turns in on itself and is composed of small steps in $\frac{6}{8}$ time.[10]

There are evident parallels between Wagner und Steiner in those cases where Steiner creates motifs that have a definite tonal identity. In

Mildred Pierce, the theme for the evil daughter Veda vacillates without any firm tonality, thus communicating that despite her strong will (her theme climbs upward), she is deficient as a person. In the transition music to the scene between Siegfried and Brünnhilde in the first act of *Götterdämmerung,* which alternates between the motifs of Siegfried and Brünnhilde, Siegfried's heroic motif is grounded in the tonic, has clear contours, is solidly constructed of triads which are stacked up on each other, stays tonally fixed, and is played by horns in unison under the score marking *kräftig* (robust). The opulent orchestration and development of the motif serves to demonstrate his strength, since the naïve young lad has turned into a grand hero. By contrast, Brünnhilde's motif is orchestrated for more tender, typically "feminine" instruments— woodwinds, violins, and cellos—and hovers around the dominant. The tonality fluctuates, and the motifs don't begin and end decisively (as in the case of Siegfried) but are threaded into one another, as if strung together, and are marked to be played *sehr weich* (very tenderly). The heroic motif forms the beginning and ending of the prelude, sandwiching Brünnhilde's motif. Most impressive is the buildup of Siegfried's motif. The scene begins at daybreak and portrays a sunrise. The Brünnhilde motif disappears, and Siegfried's motif experiences an unbelievably dynamic surge, played fortissimo by a dazzling array of eight horns, three trumpets, four trombones, and six harps. Brünnhilde comes across as musically subordinate to the hero. Despite her moral strength, which she retains to the bitter end of the tetralogy, she remains an appendage of men, and her entire existence is dedicated to serving them.

Since Wagner created *Gesamtkunstwerke* (total artworks) and was thus responsible for all aspects of his work, it is legitimate to ponder whether his influence on early film transcended a purely musical dimension (after all, film had become a popular form already by the 1920s, and thus Wagner's impact could still be felt some thirty years after his death). The danger of aestheticizing and thus rendering harmless violence and crime is, after all, not only contained in the subconscious effect of music, but also in the plot itself. Wagner's extremes of polarization had an impact not only on music but also on culture. Opera for him represented the epitome of metaphysical art, and he took it upon himself to announce universal truths through this medium, which he endowed as a sacred locus. While the nationalist and anti-Semitic aspects of his work have been prodigiously examined by scholars, the gendered coding of his musical language has been ignored, as has his conception of love, which has been accepted rather undifferentiatedly and applied to both sexes, as for instance by Jean-Jacques Nattiez.[11] But Wagner's thinking, his writings, and his compositions are infused with binary images and concepts. "Feminine identity is constituted as the 'lack.' Only in the act of living out her 'self' does the women find herself"[12]—this was the conventional conception of the bourgeois woman in the nineteenth century, when Wagner was writing his works. ("To be a woman is a crime," wrote one scholar about Hitchcock's films—an odd parallel.)[13] Many Hollywood films of the 1930s and '40s appropriate this traditional image of women. The music not only ennobles men as the active, motivated subject, whose deeds enhance his power, but also represents women as a timeless and anonymous femininity, undermining their historical reality. Frequently, they are the bearers of emotion. This may make them fascinating, but at a heavy cost, because they are musically tagged as negative figures and, in terms of the plot, must often suffer more than their male counterparts.

Parsifal had fatal consequences for conceptions of gender, because it suggested as a God-given natural law that spirituality is a masculine attribute while the libidinal-animalistic dimension is feminine. In Westerns, the woman waits at home for the hero to return, or functions as the prize to be won by him. One cannot eliminate the possibility that Wagner's racism and sexism also influenced the general culture. For the longest time, homosexuals were considered abnormal in American film, and Mexicans as primitive. The wholesale slaughter of native Americans and the degradation of Mexicans shaped film aesthetics for a long time. Using the example of the music for *King Kong,* Royal S. Brown shows how "it reinforces the stereotypes of cultural myth vis-à-vis 'primitive' cultures." He introduces Roland Barthes's term of "nativicity," which transcends implications of historical time and place.[14] If one considers how emphatically Wagner's writings and compositions served to set the standard for the national socialism that followed, one can certainly assume that his influence had a cultural impact even beyond it.

However, even though Wagner's influence on the work of early film composers is so evident, at least one of his practices was inimitable.

Wagner had control over the entire structure of his works, since he was responsible for both words and music. By contrast, in film, the conceptions of the director and the composer can diverge. Although the director Alfred Hitchcock was rooted in a patriarchal order, he was nonetheless able to recognize the suffering of the opposite sex. For instance, in the film *Marnie* (1964), the score of which was composed by Bernard Herrmann, he uses the nursery rhyme "Mother, mother, I feel worse" as diegetic music to indicate clearly that Marnie is not cured. Presumably, Hitchcock chose this song himself, since he shows that Marnie's misconduct stems from a childhood trauma and is curable. However, Bernard Herrmann labels her to the very end as a sick person by composing music filled with imposing seventh chords, a melody that leads downward in whole tones, and a chordal structure that oscillates between major and diminished triads. This reveals Marnie's ambivalently disturbed character, just as dissonant chords and downward-spiraling melodies also signify negative traits.[15]

Two examples from Wagner's *Götterdämmerung* and John Huston's *Key Largo* (1948, Max Steiner) show how women's song can have an existential impact well beyond its entertainment function. Both Brünnhilde's voice and her body are inseparably connected to her femaleness, because the voice is the locus of (linguistic) mediation between the individual's body and society. "Whether castrated or sexed in operatic arias, or genderless in the *Lied,* the lyrical encoding of the voice bespeaks us in our multiple aspects as biological creatures, psychological beings and cultural artifacts."[16] Wagner was well aware of the effect of the voice. By giving Brünnhilde inner strength he created the image of a woman who could demolish all conventional notions of gender identity. Admittedly, she pays a high price for all this since, as opposed to Siegfried's transformation into a hero, Brünnhilde must give up her identity as a Valkyrie. The strength she possessed as virgin and Valkyrie is lost after she yields to Siegfried; the musical motif that lays her heroic Valkyrie theme to rest—the whimsical embellishment of the first note and the upward sixth leap—is reminiscent of love and romanticism (see example 6.5 above). Wagner presents the split in Brünnhilde between warrior and lover as successive, not simultaneous. The new Brünnhilde is only possible at the expense of the old. But one element transcends this split: the voice. Wotan has been silenced and Siegfried is dead; she too will die, but she still has a voice and it is powerful. After surviving the violence done to her body and learning of the treachery against her, she enacts a revenge which culminates in the triumphant expression of an idealized all-encompassing love. Her closing song builds from measure to measure, overwhelming with musical espressivity that contains a breathtaking range of emotions. Dynamic leaps, intensity, and compelling declamation: Brünnhilde towers over the standard role given to women in the nineteenth century, and is thus a good example for Carolyn Abbate's claim that opera can give women a strong, "narrating" voice in spite of the fact that they are mostly doomed to die, as Catherine Clément stresses.[17]

In *Key Largo*, a woman's singing appeals to us quite differently, but with a similarly powerful effect. The gangster Rocco forces his former lover Gaye Dawn—an aging, alcoholic singer—to perform. He promises her whisky as a reward. As she badly needs a drink she sings a song from better times, and in so doing tries unsuccessfully to recapture her former charisma. Her voice breaks, and she can no longer find the right notes, which makes her look ridiculous. Max Steiner composes no musical accompaniment to this sequence. Instead of hearing straining violins, we hear only her broken voice, mercilessly compelling us to witness her demise. Rocco humiliates her even more by refusing to reward her for her effort. The woman as commodity, whose erotic charms formerly had value, is now in old age presented as worthless. Only when she gives voice to her despair does the music begin, and at this moment, the music transcends its function as a mere entertainment. In the end it is Rocco who is shown as cruel, as all sympathies focus on Gaye.

These examples show how music can also transcend the male domination so deeply rooted in Western culture, thus also having a humanizing effect—in Wagner's operas and in films alike—even contrary to the composer's intention. In Wagner's case, this is not a bad thing.

TRANSLATED BY NICHOLAS VAZSONYI

NOTES

1. Claudia Gorbman, *Unheard Melodies: Narrative Film Music* (Bloomington: Indiana University Press, 1987), 4.

2. Richard Wagner, *Sämtliche Briefe,* ed. Gertrud Stobel and Werner Wolf (Leipzig: VEB Deutscher Verlag für Musik, 1979), vol. 4, 241 (letter dated December 28, 1851–January 1, 1852).

3. See Henning Ferdinand, *Die musikalische Darstellung der Affekte in den Opern Georg Friedrich Händels* (Diss. Bonn, 1958), 61–85.

4. Quoted in Cosima Wagner, *Die Tagebücher* [Diaries], ed. Martin Gregor-Dellin and Dietrich Mack (Munich/Zurich: Piper, 1977), vol. 2, 333 (dated April 17, 1879).

5. Kurt Overhoff, *Die Musikdramen Richard Wagners. Eine thematisch-musikalische Interpretation* (Salzburg: Pustet, 1967), 38.

6. Karin Hausen, "Die Polarisierung der 'Geschlechtscharaktere'—eine Spiegelung der Dissoziation von Erwerbs- und Familienleben," in *Sozialgeschichte der Familie in der Neuzeit Europas,* ed. Werner Conze (Stuttgart: Klett, 1976), 363–93. The dichotomous image existed beforehand, but was intensified by the strong separation between home and waged work in Europe from the 1780s onward.

7. Eva Rieger, *Alfred Hitchcock und die Musik. Eine Untersuchung zum Verhältnis von Film, Musik und Geschlecht* (Bielefeld: Kleine, 1996).

8. Hans von Wolzogen, *Thematischer Leitfaden durch die Musik zu Richard Wagner's Festspiel "Der Ring des Nibelungen"* (Leipzig: E. Schloemp, 1878).

9. For an expansion on this subject, see Eva Rieger, *Leuchtende Liebe, Rachender Tod. Richard Wagners Bild der Frau im Spiegel seiner Musik* (Düsseldorf: Artemis & Winkler, 2009). See also Kathryn Kalinak, *Settling the Score: Music and the Classical Hollywood Film* (Madison: University of Wisconsin Press, 1992), 113–34; Caryl Flinn, *Strains of Utopia: Gender, Nostalgia, and Hollywood Film Music* (Princeton, N.J.: Princeton University Press, 1992), 115–18.

10. See Gorbman, *Unheard Melodies,* 91–98.

11. Jean-Jacques Nattiez, *Wagner Androgyne: A Study in Interpretation* (Princeton, N.J.: Princeton University Press, 1993). Wagner indeed aspired for unity of man and woman, but with man as the dominant sex. Woman's capacity to love is directed solely toward the male partner, for whom she is prepared to die.

12. Bettina Heinz and Claudia Honegger, *Listen der Ohnmacht. Zur Sozialgeschichte weiblicher Widerstandsformen* (Frankfurt/Main: Europäische Verlagsanstalt, 1981), 33.

13. James McLaughlin, "All in the Family: Alfred Hitchcock's Shadow of a Doubt," in *A Hitchcock Reader,* ed. Marshall Deutelbaum and Leland Poague (Ames: Iowa State University, 1986), 147.

14. Royal S. Brown, *Overtones and Undertones: Reading Film Music* (Berkeley: University of California Press, 1994), 41.

15. In *Psycho,* Herrmann similarly taints the female lead, Marion Crane, with his musical setting.

16. Nelly Furman, "Opera, or the Staging of the Voice," *Cambridge Opera Journal* 3, no. 3 (1991): 304.

17. See Carolyn Abbate, *Unsung Voices: Opera and Musical Narrative in the Nineteenth Century* (Princeton, N.J.: Princeton University Press, 1991); "Opera, or the Envoicing of Women," in *Musicology and Difference: Gender and Sexuality in Music Scholarship,* ed. Ruth Solie (Berkeley: University of California Press, 1993), 225–58; and Catherine Clément, *Opera, or The Undoing of Women* (London: Tauris, 1997). See also Ralph Locke, who is in agreement with Abbate, in "What Are These Women Doing in Opera?" in *En travesti: Women, Gender Subversion, Opera,* ed. Corinne Blackmer and Patricia Juliana Smith (New York: Columbia University Press, 1995), 59–98.

SEVEN

The Penumbra of Wagner's *Ombra* in Two Science Fiction Films from 1951: *The Thing from Another World* and *The Day the Earth Stood Still*

WILLIAM H. ROSAR

I could not be sure whether I had encountered
a ghost, an angel, a demon, or God.

GUSTAV DAVIDSON, *DICTIONARY OF ANGELS*

No sooner has the U.S. Air Force plane landed in the arctic snow then out jumps a reconnaissance crew that proceeds swiftly with a sled dog team to their destination—the site of a crashed aircraft of unknown origin. The screen action is accompanied by grotesquely melodramatic "hurry" music (à la silent film style) dominated by piano, culminating in a broad menacing octave motif banged out in the low register, doubled by tutti brass and capped *quasi-fanfare,* as the crew comes upon a very large circular shadow in a flat icy hollow—a flying saucer! (example 7.1) Its pilot is found frozen nearby in the ice and is, as it turns out, a very large vegetable in the shape of a man.

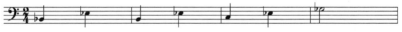

EX. 7.1. "Flying Saucer Sequence, Part 1," *The Thing from Another World*

An expansive grassy park in Washington, D.C., is the site of another flying saucer landing, from which emerges a tall man clad in a silvery spacesuit and helmet, whose name the audience later learns is Klaatu.

The *misterioso* music accompanying his entrance makes it clear that this is all pretty weird and unearthly. Then the music is abruptly silenced as the spaceman is shot down by a soldier who, it seems, felt under attack and reflexively pulled the trigger because the spaceman had raised an object in his hand that popped open (example 7.2). Moments later there appears from the saucer an even taller and imposing silvery robot called Gort that promptly destroys all the soldiers' weapons with a ray beam emanating from inside his head, melting pistols, rifles, bazookas, and even tanks in a blaze of light.

EX. 7.2. "Gort," *The Day the Earth Stood Still*

The slow menacing octave motif in the bass register that announces the robot's entrance, though longer, is, in character, quite like the one announcing the unseen saucer and its frozen occupant—and both sound like the Dragon motif (das Wurm-Motiv) in Wagner's *Der Ring des Nibelungen,* especially as it is first heard in the third scene of *Das Rheingold,* in which it features the use of tritones—the old *diabolus in musica*—when Alberich transforms himself into a giant dragon ("ein Reisen-Wurm"). The motif's later version, *sans* tritones, is heard in Act 2 of *Siegfried,* when the giant Fafner similarly transforms himself into a dragon (example 7.3).

EX. 7.3. Dragon motif, *Das Rheingold*

These anthropoid extraterrestrial visitors are from two science fiction films made the same year, in 1951.[1] Assuming that the similarity is not just mere coincidence, nor attributable to "meaningful coincidence" (or "synchronicity," to use C. G. Jung's term),[2] should historical inquiry proceed on the assumption that Dimitri Tiomkin, who scored *The Thing from Another World*, and Bernard Herrmann, who scored *The Day the Earth Stood Still*, were both looking over Wagner's shoulder, or, alternatively, that Herrmann or Tiomkin were looking over each other's shoulders? In the Hollywood film music scene of some fifty years ago Tiomkin was known for his "spies," who could infiltrate any studio music department.[3] But that cannot account for the similarity between Tiomkin's motif and Herrmann's, because Tiomkin wrote his first.[4] Chances are, too, that the two composers did not compare notes, since they were rather like rival tenors in an opera company. If Herrmann did not have his own spies, it is quite possible that he saw *The Thing from Another World* when it premiered in Los Angeles only two months before he scored *The Day the Earth Stood Still*. Thus it might have been the case that Herrmann was indeed imitating Tiomkin.[5]

The Thing from Another World and *The Day the Earth Stood Still* are influential exemplars of what film theorist Patrick Lucanio dubbed "alien invasion films," a subgenre of science fiction films that made its debut in the early 1950s, often lumped together with "monster movies."[6] The Dragon motif from the *Ring* would thus not have had a history of imitation in scores for such films, because in 1951 this subgenre was new. Though Lucanio argues that the alien invasion film is distinct from the horror film genre, William K. Everson, in his history of the movie villain, *The Bad Guy*, subsumes most space aliens under a category he calls "The Monsters," one category among twenty other kinds of villain. Everson writes:

> [I]n the wake of the atomic age, with the realization that interplanetary travel was becoming a distinct possibility, came the realization that other planets could produce monsters too—and that these could either invade earth en masse (as in one of the best of the science-fiction films, *War of the Worlds*) or arrive singly, as stowaways on rocket ships from earth that had made a successful round-trip. The bulk of these outer-space monsters were nightmares of modern art, human vegetables, "things" with giant eyes and long talons, and, in many cases, just huge blobs of self-enlarging jelly or slime. Earth-people tended to take them in their stride, and, when one of the first of them arrived in Universal's *It Came from Outer Space*, the townspeople knew exactly what to do. Grabbing the same lighted torches, the same [movie] extras (or their descendants) that had chased

the Frankenstein monster through the countryside for the previous quarter of a century, now set out to destroy the one-eyed blob—which, like the Frankenstein monster, would probably have been quite harmless and even sociable if left alone![7]

As a musical corollary, the "monster music" in alien invasion films to some extent echoes that in previous horror and fantasy films which, in turn, is rooted in the tradition of silent film "villain music," as I have noted with respect to the "Martian music" in Leith Stevens's score for *War of the Worlds* (1953).[8] Erno Rapeé in his *Encyclopedia of Picture Music* (1925) writes, "Sometimes you have a villain whose power to do evil is mighty but he achieves his evil deeds without any physical activities in which case chords slow and heavy should be proper synchronization."[9] The "intellectual carrot," known only as "The Thing," and Gort are both possessed of superhuman physical strength, but it is the power of their advanced technology that far exceeds that of human beings. Though Earthlings don't realize it, Gort is really a "good guy," a robot created by the inhabitants of other worlds for the express purpose of eliminating aggression, but he is perceived as a monster (= villain), whereas The Thing is clearly a "bad guy" in that he (or it) is apparently only interested in preying upon Earthlings for their blood, like a vampire.

Though not specifically consisting of "slow heavy *chords*" per se, as Rapeé would prescribe for villains having such mighty power, Wagner's ponderous, menacing Dragon motif is nonetheless slow and heavy, and shares characteristics of the "monster music" in classic horror films of the 1930s and 1940s. This is especially true of Max Steiner's theme for the gigantic gorilla in *King Kong* (1933) and the monster themes in Universal's Frankenstein films, particularly those scored by Franz Waxman, Frank Skinner, and Hans Salter.[10] (Boris Karloff, who initially portrayed the Frankenstein monster in the Universal films, actually disdained film scoring, and once commented about the music: "I know my films have it too—the heavy sinister stuff."[11]) That the music for monsters in the two alien invasion films discussed here should hark back to these horror films is in a way quite fitting, because as horror film historian Dennis Gifford observed, The Thing *looked* like the Frankenstein monster in the makeup created for Boris Karloff by Jack Pierce and imitated by other actors playing the role.[12] This was no coincidence. Lee Greenway, the makeup artist on *The Thing*, had tested a number of different concepts until director Howard Hawks told him to make The Thing "look like Frankenstein."[13] Similarly, the rigid, mechanical gait of Gort the robot also recalls that of the saturnine Frankenstein monster. Each shares in common with the music for the giant dragon a musical depiction of the *monstrous,* in the dual sense of something fearsome (or ugly) and abnormally large. Like a fire-breathing dragon, in *The Day the Earth Stood Still,* Gort the Robot destroys the army's weapons with a blazing ray beam, whereas the sheer brawn of the UFOnaut "Thing" renders him capable of dismembering a team of sled dogs that attack him in the snow, though through his advanced technology he had navigated a spacecraft across space to reach Earth.

The most obvious musical similarity shared by all three motifs is slow ponderous octave movement in the bass that gradually zigzags upward, prominently featuring tubas (though articulated by pianos in both Tiomkin's and Herrmann's motifs) and playing disjunct "angular" intervals. Could it be that the Dragon motif was actually imitated previously for "monster music" in horror films, and that this is the explanation for the similarity to the Herrmann and Tiomkin motifs? There is no indication of that, and neither Tiomkin nor Herrmann had scored horror films before. Yet clearly both composers were striving for something "monstrous sounding," and it may indeed just be fortuitous that each composer thought of what may well be the most famous monster in opera for their musico-dramatic inspiration—the Dragon in the *Ring*— rather than alternatively turning to the musical avant-garde for models. Ultimately, whether this was just an *Einfall,* or dramatic instinct on their part, or mediated by some shared secondary source known to both of them, who can say, as unfortunately their biographies and film history are mute on that question. The fame of the Dragon motif alone, though, is probably not sufficient to account for it possibly having served as a model in the context of the two science fiction films, given the maxim of expedience generally followed by most career film composers, namely, "*Use it if it works.*" The same pragmatic approach opts to "play it safe" by using "the tried and true."

How then does it "work"? Perhaps more than anything, by imitating the dragon's slow menacing movement the motif constitutes a simple instance of the *mimesis* or musical imitation commonly used in tone painting (*Tonmaleri,* or "Mickey-Mousing," as it is called in Hollywood film scoring parlance because of its common use in cartoons), even though the motif is heard well before the dragon is seen, and in spite of the fact that its menace and movement are described in the recitatives of Mime and Siegfried. John Deathridge noted that the motif's initial statement in Wagner's composition sketch for *Das Rheingold* is marked "Schlange" (snake) rather than "Wurm" (dragon, as noted above), and that an examination of the dynamic markings (e.g., "langsam u[nd] schneller" or "slow and then quicker") in the sketch indicates that Wagner "wanted the motif to accelerate as it unravels," as if depicting a serpent uncoiling.[14] It is arguable that even without Mime's and Siegfried's recitatives, Wagner's musical picture of the dragon readily conveys a sense of the monstrous menace, if not its actual form. As Albert Wellek maintained, "Tone painting . . . uses immediately obvious correspondences between sound and object or situation: the so-called primal synaesthesia (*Ur-Synästhesien*), and it needs no symbolism full of assumptions and conventions."[15] Accordingly, perhaps both Tiomkin's and Herrrmann's motifs may be seen as examples of the imitative practices characteristic of tone painting as well.

In addition to that, there is a venerable tradition in opera that links the Dragon motif with monster music and science fiction films alike, that of the *ombra* scene. In Italian *ombra* literally means "shadow" or "shade," and the term was introduced into opera studies by German musicologist Hermann Abert. Clive McClelland has succinctly characterized the *ombra* scene as one "involving the appearance of an oracle or demons, witches or ghosts," noting that early examples can be found in Monteverdi's *Orfeo* and Cavalli's *Giasone*. The most immediate antecedents to have influenced Wagner's *ombra* scenes would likely have been Weber's *Freischütz* and Marschner's *Vampyr* and *Hans Heiling*, as well as musical evocations of the demonic and diabolical by Berlioz and Liszt. McClelland notes that by the end of the eighteenth century, *ombra* scene music had "come to include a number of characteristic features, among them slow sustained writing (reminiscent of church music), the use of flat keys (especially in the minor), angular melodic lines, chromaticism and dissonance, dotted rhythms, syncopation, pauses, tremolando effects, sudden dynamic contrasts, unexpected harmonic progressions, and unusual instrumentation, especially involving trombones."[16] Common to the Wagner, Tiomkin, and Herrmann motifs are the low register favoring brass, the contrasting dynamics, the insistent rhythmic pattern, and lack of conjunct motion—all features of the *ombra* style tradition.

Underlying the musico-dramatic *ombra* tradition, and by extension its continued evolution in monster and science fiction films, may well be something deeper and more profound, as suggested by the title of a monograph by German musicologist Reinhold Hammerstein, *Die Stimme aus der anderen Welt: Über die Darstellung des Numinosen in der Oper von Monteverdi bis Mozart* (The Voice from the Other World: On the Depiction of the Numinous in Opera, from Monteverdi to Mozart).[17] The term "numinous" is from the phenomenology of religion, an adjective coined by the German theologian Rudolf Otto from the Latin word *numen,* meaning "local deity" in Roman religion. In his essay "The Numinous in *Götterdämmerung*," Christopher Wintle defines the numinous as denoting "the awareness of some divine or supernatural force for the good."[18] But this scarcely does justice to the term.

In his classic monograph *Das Heilige: Über das Irrationale in der Idee des Göttlichen und sein Verhältnis zum Rationalen* (translated as *The Idea of the Holy*), Rudolf Otto contended that religion ultimately has its origins not in rational and ethical ideas but in the non-rational, in emotional experiences of a very specific character, that which he termed *the numinous.* The "sense of the numinous" or "numinous consciousness" is something that psychologists today would call a kind of "altered state of consciousness" and is, Otto argued, the experiential basis of all religion.[19] At its most "primitive" stage the numinous manifests itself as the fear of demons, demonic dread, or "numinous dread," as Otto would say, and typically gives rise to ideas and images of earthly demons and monsters. At the opposite pole, in the highest state of numinous consciousness, there is the realization that the numinous is not of this world at all, that it is something otherworldly or transcendental, as depicted by the *sublime* in art and literature, and captured in Otto's phrase *das ganz Andere:* the "wholly Other."

Because the *ombra* tradition exemplifies features of numinous experience more than other operatic scene types, Reinhold Hammerstein looked to such scenes for the purpose of illuminating the *Klanglichkeit,* the characteristic musical sonorities (or symbols) that had been used in expressing the numinous which, in Western tradition, can partly be traced back to the angelic singing and blaring trumpets described in the

Bible.[20] For example, Hammerstein notes regarding the praise song of the seraphim and cherubim, "This praise is not perceived as 'beautiful' but as numinous sounding and ringing of over-powering volume."[21]

Der Ring des Nibelungen can be viewed as spanning virtually the whole spectrum of numinous experience, from experiencing the earthly goddess Erda and the monster Dragon to the sublime transcendental Valhalla. Yet largely on aesthetic grounds, Rudolf Otto was dismissive of Wagner's music dramas, believing that at most music could only be "analogous" to the numinous, as he was of the opinion that music constitutes a world of feeling unto itself, explicitly subscribing to Eduard Hanslick's views on the nature of musical beauty that he expounded in *Vom Musikalisch-Schönen* (On the Musically Beautiful).[22] Otto was perhaps blinded (and deafened) by his own neo-Kantian thinking,[23] because audiences and scholars alike have readily heard and seen the depiction of numinous experience in virtually all its various aspects in Wagner's music dramas, even without knowing much of the *Ring* saga itself.[24] For that matter, Otto does not actually deny that Wagner's music at times expresses the numinous—in fact he says nothing about it in this connection; rather, he cites passages in the works of Tomás de Luis Victoria, J. S. Bach, Mendelssohn, and Beethoven instead as exemplifying a "hushed" quality associated with what he calls "numinous sounds." Arguably, most of the musical effects and the "hushed" quality that Otto describes as epitomizing numinous sound can be found in Wagner's music as well—but that is a topic for another study.

C. G. Jung, who appropriated the term numinous from Otto in characterizing the archetypes or "primordial images" of the collective unconscious that are often given symbolic expression in myth through figures such as dragons, coined the noun *Numinosität* (numinosity) from it to describe their numinous quality: "Like the instincts, these images have a relatively autonomous character; that is to say they are 'numinous' and can be found above all in the realm of numinous or religious ideas."[25] As Jungian analyst Edward C. Whitmont succinctly wrote, whereas the numinous refers to "the awe, terror, energic and oracular impact of divine manifestation . . . [numinosity denotes] awesomeness, the quality that touches us and shakes us to the core, regardless of whether or not we understand it."[26] The oracular aspect of the numinous is perhaps particularly relevant here because of the role that has been played by oracles in the *ombra* scene tradition. For example, an oracle may be the ghost of a deceased ancestor or a demon. Thus it is from the oracular dragon (the giant Fafner, transformed) that Siegfried seeks knowledge of fear, and comes to understand the speech of birds after slaying him and licking his blood. In his monograph *Flying Saucers: A Modern Myth of Things Seen in the Sky,* Jung wrote of UFO occupants as reported through close encounters with them: "[T]hey possess frightful weapons which would enable them to exterminate the human race. In addition to their obviously superior technology they are credited with superior wisdom and moral goodness which would, on the other, enable them to save humanity."[27] The zealous but naïve scientist, Dr. Carrington in *The Thing,* hopes to learn the "key to the stars" and "secrets of a new science" from the vegetable man "Thing." Gort the Robot in *The Day the Earth Stood Still* embodies moral authority, as we learn from the spaceman Klaatu, who has come to Earth as a benevolent spokesman for advanced civilizations who have empowered such robots to act autonomously as a superordinate peace officers, patrolling the planets for the purpose of eliminating all aggression and destroying aggressors wherever they are found.

Interpreted from a symbolic vantage point, Jung saw flying saucers and their sage inhabitants as symbols of that archetype he called "the self," an archetype embodying order, psychological wholeness, and totality, one that unites and unifies all the conflicting attitudes and opposites found in the human psyche. Often "the self" archetype is only symbolized by geometrical forms such as the circle, sphere, and square, or in mandala designs, which are also often symbolic of the Deity.[28] Perhaps by no coincidence, Jung also saw the Dragon in *Siegfried* as symbolizing an aspect of the archetypal self. Of this he wrote, "When such symbols occur in individual dreams, they will be found on examination to be pointing to something like a centre of the total personality, of the psychic totality which consists of both conscious and unconscious."[29] Indeed, the very Ring itself has been interpreted as a numinous symbol of the self by Robert Donington in his now-classic monograph, *Wagner's "Ring" and Its Symbols.*[30] It is thus, too, that Patrick Lucanio's theory of alien invasions films draws upon Jung's conception of UFOs as being archetypal representations of the self. In his extensive study of UFO phenomena, *UFOs: Project Trojan Horse,* writer John Keel was among the first to suggest that angels and UFOnauts might be one and the same. That numinous entities might be difficult to differentiate from one another and are somehow dependent upon one's frame of reference was given expression by Gustav Davidson, author of *Dictionary of Angels,* who related a personal experience which Keel quotes:

> Suddenly a nightmarish shape loomed up in front of me, barring my progress. After a paralyzing moment, I managed to fight my way past the phantom. The next morning I could not be sure whether I had encountered a ghost, an angel, a demon, or God. There were other such moments and other such encounters, when I passed from terror to trance, from intimations of realms unguessed at to the conviction that, beyond the reach of our senses, beyond the arch of all our experience sacred and profound, there was only—to use an expression of Paul's in Timothy 4—"fable and endless genealogy."[31]

The controversial egocentric visionary who, it is reported, composed the *Ring* in a kind of trance, and perhaps thereby readily gave voice and expression to numinous archetypal contents in his music dramas—that little man with a big head—cast a giant shadow.[32] Whereas it has often enough been said that the composers of two generations stood in Wagner's shadow and then struggled to get out of it, as the essays in this volume attest, certainly four generations of film composers have stood in the penumbra of that shadow to this day.

NOTES

The epigraph is from Gustav Davidson, *A Dictionary of Angels—Including Fallen Angels* (New York: The Free Press, 1967), xii.

1. For an analysis of Herrmann's score, see E. Todd Fiegel, "Bernard Herrmann as Musical Colorist: A Musico-Dramatic Analysis of His Score for *The Day the Earth Stood Still,*" *The Journal of Film Music* 1 (2003): 185–215. Tiomkin's score for *The Thing from Another World* has not been a subject of published musical analysis, but the liner notes by Jeff Bond and Lukas Kendall for the Film Score Monthly CD release of music from the soundtrack contain useful production history on the film, as well as observations and descriptions of the music, including details about the instrumentation (see Dimitri Tiomkin, *The Thing from Another World,* Film Score Monthly CD, vol. 8, no. 1, 2005). The three musical examples in the text have been prepared by the author from the following sources: (1) "[Flying Saucer Sequence, Pt. 1] M27" (measures 12–15), from Tiomkin's sketches (1951) for *The Thing from Another World,* the Dimitri Tiomkin Collection, Cinematic Arts Special Col-

lections, Doheny Library, University of Southern California; (2) "Gort" (measures 1–8), from Herrmann's full score (1951) for *The Day the Earth Stood Still*, the Bernard Herrmann Papers, University of California, Santa Barbara; and (3) Richard Wagner, *Das Rheingold,* Klavierauszug zu zwei Händen von Richard Kleinmichel (Mainz: B. Schott's Söhne, n.d.), 97–98.

2. Elsewhere I have argued that synchronicity must be taken into account (if only to be ruled out) in the context of film music analysis so as to avoid the pitfall of spurious attributions of influence as well as other exegetical flights of fancy; see "The *Dies Irae* in *Citizen Kane*: Musical Hermeneutics Applied to Film Music," in *Film Music: Critical Approaches,* ed. K. J. Donnelly (Edinburgh: University of Edinburgh Press, 2001), 103–104.

3. James G. Stewart, interview by Craig Reardon, February 3, 1977, tape recording, Hollywood, California.

4. Tiomkin's score was recorded in March 1951, whereas Herrmann's was composed June–July 1951. A case could probably be made that Herrmann modeled certain elements of his score on Tiomkin's. For example, the instrumentation of Herrmann's orchestra, like Tiomkin's, calls for theremin (two of them in Herrmann's) and a large battery of percussion, including two pianos, harps, vibraphone, and organ (three organs in Herrmann's), with no string section (except for solo basses in Tiomkin's score and electric bass in Herrmann's).

5. *The Thing* premiered in Los Angeles April 27, 1951; see entry for *The Thing from Another World,* American Film Institute, *AFI Catalog,* http://gateway.pro-quest.com/openurl?ctx_ver=Z39.88-2003&xri:pqil:res_ver=0.2&res_id=xri:afi-us&rft_id=xri:afi:film:50336 (accessed August 25, 2008).

6. Patrick Lucanio, *Them or Us: Archetypal Interpretations of Fifties Alien Invasion Films* (Bloomington: Indiana University Press, 1987), 16–25.

7. William K. Everson, *The Bad Guy: A Pictorial History of the Movie Villain* (New York: Citadel Press, 1964), 110. Apparently Everson forgets that the Frankenstein monster was given the brain of a criminal, unbeknownst to his creator, Henry Frankenstein.

8. William H. Rosar, "Music for the Martians: Schillinger's Two Tonics and Harmony of Fourths in Leith Stevens' Score for *War of the Worlds* (1953)," *The Journal of Film Music* 1 (2006): 419–20.

9. Erno Rapeé, *Encyclopedia of Music for Pictures* (New York: Belwin, 1925), 14.

10. See *Bride of Frankenstein* (1935), scored by Waxman; *The Son of Frankenstein* (1939), scored by Skinner; *Ghost of Frankenstein* (1942) and *Frankenstein Meets the Wolfman* (1942), scored by Salter; *House of Frankenstein* (1944), scored by Salter and Paul Dessau; *House of Dracula* (1945), scored by William Lava; and *Abbott and Costello Meet Frankenstein* (1949), scored by Skinner.

11. Karloff, himself an amateur pianist, felt that "The mood [in films] should be conveyed by the action and not have to be underlined." See William H. Rosar, "Music for the Monsters: Universal Pictures' Horror Film Scores of the Thirties," *Quarterly Journal of the Library of Congress* 40 (1983): 419.

12. "The Thing reproduced itself asexually by podding, drank human blood, and was a vegetable. It was more intelligent than any man, stronger than ten, and was unshootable. And it looked like Boris Karloff." See Denis Gifford, *A Pictorial History of Horror Movies* (New York: Hamlyn, 1973), 168.

13. Bond and Kendall (see n. 1), 4–5.

14. John Deathridge, "Wagner's Sketches for the 'Ring': Some Recent Studies," *The Musical Times* 118 (1977): 389.

15. Albert Wellek, "The Relationship between Poetry and Music," *Journal of Aesthetics and Art Criticism* 21 (1962): 150; relative to the role of synaesthesia specifically in Wagner's works, see also Wellek's "Synästhesie und Synthese bei Richard Wagner," *Bayreuther Blätter* 52 (1929): 80–101.

16. Clive McClelland, "Ombra," *Grove Music Online, Oxford Music Online,* http://www.oxfordmusiconline.com.mcc1.library.csulb.edu/subscriber/article/grove/music/51808 (accessed August 25, 2008); and "Ombra Music in the Eighteenth Century: Context, Style and Signification" (Ph.D. diss., University of Leeds, 2001).

17. Reinhold Hammerstein, *Die Stimme aus der anderen Welt: Über die Darstellung des Numinosen in der Oper von Monteverdi bis Mozart* (Tutzing: Hans Schneider, 1998).

18. Christopher Wintle, "The Numinous in *Götterdämmerung*," in *Reading Opera,* ed. Arthur Groos and Roger Parker (Princeton, N.J.: Princeton University Press, 1988), 201, n. 5.

19. Rudolf Otto, *Das Heilige: Über das Irrationale in der Idee des Göttlichen und sein Verhältnis zum Rationalen* (Breslau: Trewendt und Granier, 1917), translated into English as *The Idea of the Holy: An Inquiry into the Non-Rational Factor in the Idea of the Divine and Its Relation to the Rational,* trans. John W. Harvey, 2nd ed. (New York: Oxford University Press, 1958); see also Charles T. Tart, ed., *Altered States of Consciousness* (New York: John Wiley & Sons, 1972), 1–2 and 414.

20. See Hammerstein's remarks about "numinose Klanglichkeit" in *Die Stimme,* 5–8.

21. Reinhold Hammerstein, "Music as a Divine Art," *Dictionary of the History of Ideas* (New York: Charles Scribner's Sons, 1973–74), 3 and 269.

22. Otto, *The Idea of the Holy,* 47–49.

23. For a discussion of Otto's debt to Kantian idealism, and its epistemological pitfalls, see Daniel L. Pals, "Is Religion a *Sui Generis* Phenomenon?" *Journal of the American Academy of Religion,* 55 (1987): 259–82. Though Otto admits a few sacred works can express the numinous "indirectly," Gerardus van der Leeuw argues strenuously and at length for the special power of music to indeed express the numinous; see his *Sacred and Profane Beauty: The Holy in Art,* trans. David E. Green (New York: Holt Rinehart & Winston, 1963); specifically on the visual depiction of monsters and the monstrous in religious art, see Mario Bussagli, "Terror and the Malign," *Encyclopedia of World Art* 13 (New York: McGraw-Hill, 1967), 1038–46.

24. Even the musical religiosity manifest in Wagner's *Tannhäuser* proved rapturous and transcendental to the poet Baudelaire, as he relates in his 1861 essay "Richard Wagner and 'Tannhäuser'"; for a discussion, see Bettina L. Knapp, "Baudelaire and Wagner's Archetypal Operas," in *Music, Archetype, and the Writer: A Jungian View* (University Park: Pennsylvania State University Press, 1988), 45–57.

25. C. G. Jung, foreword to *Complex, Archetype, Symbol* by Jolande Jacobi (Princeton, N.J.: Princeton University Press, 1959), x.

26. Edward C. Whitmont, *The Symbolic Quest: Basic Concepts of Analytical Psychology* (New York: Harper & Row, 1969), 312, n. 8.

27. *The Collected Works of C. G. Jung,* trans. R. F. C. Hull, vol. 10, *Civilization in Transition,* 2nd ed. (Princeton, N.J.: Princeton University Press), 317.

28. For a succinct definition of the self archetype, see the glossary in C. G. Jung, *Memories, Dreams, Reflections* (New York: Random House, 1961), 398.

29. *The Collected Works of C. G. Jung,* trans. R. F. C. Hull, vol. 20, *Symbols of Transformation* (Princeton, N.J.: Princeton University Press, 1956), 363–64.

30. Robert Donington, *Wagner's "Ring" and Its Symbols,* 3rd ed. (London: Faber and Faber, 1974), 16, 25–26, and 67.

31. John Keel, *UFOs: Operation Trojan Horse* (New York: G. P. Putnam's Sons, 1970), 225.

32. "Wagner composed like a man possessed—as if in a *trance,* with 'divine and demonic excitement,' receiving idea, tone, and gesture from his unconscious without any conscious direction on his part. His Dionysian side and his exalted spirituality took precedence over all else." See Knapp, "Baudelaire and Wagner's Archetypal Operas," 48.

PART THREE

Wagner in Hollywood

EIGHT

"Soll ich lauschen?":
Love-Death in *Humoresque*

MARCIA J. CITRON

Jean Negulesco's noir melodrama *Humoresque* (1946) uses portions of *Tristan und Isolde,* especially the "Liebestod," for the climax at the end of the film. Troubled socialite Helen Wright, played in characteristically arch style by Joan Crawford, commits suicide to the strains of Wagner's music by walking into the ocean at her beach house on Long Island. The music sounds in her ears from a fascinating interplay of sources. First it comes from the radio broadcast of violinist Paul Boray, her love interest (played by John Garfield), performing an arrangement from *Tristan und Isolde* with piano and orchestra. But as Helen becomes restive and moves away from the house, it is not possible for her to literally hear the radio emission. The music assumes a more generalized soundtrack function, divorced from the diegetic source. Yet the situation is more nuanced, involving memory, psychology, and music itself. Hearing not only relates to film-music categories, but involves the disposition of Wagner's music—what is heard and what is missing—and the musical focus of the film as a whole. For *Humoresque* is a biopic of a fictional violinist, and music, sound, and hearing figure prominently throughout.

In this essay I will focus on the final scene and the relationship between hearing, music, voice (or its absence), and the performer-biopic genre. Hearing bears more than an incidental relationship with Wagner's music, as the line "Soll ich lauschen?" ("Should I listen?") is a key phrase in the late-stage text of the "Liebestod," one of several lines centered on hearing. This reflexive relationship with the text is not made explicit in the film, however, as words and voice are absent in the instrumental arrangement. Yet the meaning of the unuttered words underpins the scene and the film. Helen comes to resent music and its obsessive pull for her virtuoso lover. In the final scene she clearly responds "no" to the question of her listening or attending to Paul Boray. The use of the "Liebestod" is thus brilliant on many levels—this even though the film is an overwrought melodrama, far from quality cinema, that may be most interesting for watching Crawford play to type. Perhaps Wagner's music "redeems" the movie. But regardless of one's opinion of *Humoresque*, the compelling use of Wagner's music crafts a strong ending that makes the film memorable.

WHAT HAPPENS

The film is structured as a flashback after Helen's suicide, and has Paul musing on his life. As in many Hollywood biopics, Paul comes from an impoverished immigrant background and has to overcome obstacles to succeed in the world of high culture, including his father's initial opposition to his playing the instrument. Meanwhile, the mother is highly sentimentalized as Paul's supporter who gets the violin and stands behind him. Once past childhood, Paul expresses himself more like a thug than an artist. He lacks sensitivity, utters curt one-liners, and recalls the gangster-like style of Edward G. Robinson. While this may be due to Garfield, an actor noted for tough-guy parts, the dialogue itself is aggressive. Perhaps the studio wanted to emphasize the contrast with socialite Helen Wright and the doomed nature of their relationship. The character also conforms to the hard-boiled male lead typical of 1940s noir melodrama.[1]

The plot of *Humoresque* is simple and predictable. After Paul grows up and gains musical proficiency, his pianist pal Sid, played in wisecracking style by Oscar Levant, introduces him to patron Helen Wright at a soirée in her swank apartment. After initial sparks fly—with "Flight of the Bumblebee" on the violin begun literally in her face—Helen becomes Paul's benefactor and launches his career. Soon he becomes a star of the virtuoso circuit. A romantic attraction develops, but the fact that Helen is married, has flings with protégés, and drinks heavily creates difficulties. Paul is torn, and sentimental ideals from boyhood give rise to conflict. Finally, Helen's husband says he will grant a divorce, she runs to tell

Paul, he ignores her (in the middle of a rehearsal), and she feels rejected. At the end Helen is to attend a big concert of Paul's with orchestra, but she does not show up. This becomes the scene of the broadcast of Wagner's music and Helen's walk into the sea to end her life.

The film uses a great deal of music. Most of what we hear are classical music pieces related to Paul's career. Among the works Paul performs are Lalo's *Symphonie Espagnole* for violin and orchestra, portions of the Mendelssohn Violin Concerto, and "Flight of the Bumblebee."[2] The title piece, Dvořák's *Humoresque* for violin and piano, appears in orchestral arrangement over opening and closing credits, and a few times with piano in the story. Notable are two opera potpourris for violin and orchestra arranged by Franz Waxman, composer for the film: a *Carmen Fantasy* and the *Tristan and Isolde Fantasy*.[3] Orchestral music without a solo part makes an appearance in Tchaikovsky's *Romeo and Juliet Overture-Fantasy*, the concert piece before the Wagner *Fantasy*. Sid has several performing opportunities, many of them brief rumbles on the keyboard in Levant's inimitable style. While a recording-studio rehearsal of Tchaikovsky's Piano Concerto No. 1, like the Wagner *Fantasy* at the end, shows Sid as a serious artist, most of the piano selections are virtuosic flourishes, as in excerpts from Khatchaturian's *Sabre Dance* and Gershwin's Prelude No. 3.[4] Only one section of the movie uses newly composed music by Waxman: a high-speed montage of New York City, with an exhilarating orchestral medley that captures the frenzy of modern life. The succession of images, marking the passage of time, is reminiscent of the famous sequence in Orson Welles's *Citizen Kane*. Moreover, the musical depiction of the machine age brings to mind the mechanist scenes in Fritz Lang's *Metropolis* (1927), a film Waxman probably saw as a youth in Germany.

The climactic scene of *Humoresque* cuts between Paul at the concert hall and Helen at the beach house, and lasts some thirteen minutes. First is a phone conversation between Paul backstage and Helen at home. Paul accuses her of wanting to upset him and ruin his career, and the camera registers her side of the call for quite a while. Meanwhile, the current work on the program, Tchaikovsky's *Romeo and Juliet Overture-Fantasy*, is heard in the background, first in the nearby concert hall and then over the radio in Helen's house. As their conversation becomes intense, the chordal death theme intones. In the one-way interchange from Helen's side, Helen becomes increasingly distraught, and when she thinks he did not hear her she says to him "Oh listen, listen." Then, after describing sky and water outside, she says, "What—you didn't hear." These lines form a fitting prelude to the theme of hearing in the *Tristan und Isolde* music to follow. Paul ends the conversation, almost hanging up on her, just before the final chords of the Tchaikovsky, at the end of the reprise of the love music. Retrospectively, this piece is a foretaste of the love-death connection played out more fully in Wagner's music, although the deaths of star-crossed youths in *Romeo and Juliet* seem more tragic than the expiration of metaphysical love served up in *Tristan und Isolde*.[5] After applause the next piece is announced: "Love Music from *Tristan and Isolde*, arranged by violinist Paul Boray." Helen pours a drink. The camera switches to the concert hall as the piece begins.

The *Fantasy* takes about ten minutes and consists of music from each act of *Tristan und Isolde*. It begins with the transitional bass-line passage from the end of the Prelude to the start of the opera proper. Next comes a truncated version of the opening chord progressions, highlighting violin and piano in duet, and then tutti orchestra on the famous deceptive resolution at measure 17 and its aftermath. Active transitional passages take us to Act 2, which starts with a few of the expectant riffs preceding the main action. About a minute later the music settles into the famous "O sink hernieder" section that starts the Love Duet. While the literal text is missing, semantic meaning comes from a voiceover Helen hears of her husband's earlier warning about her suitability to enter this relationship. She mentally re-plays Paul's accusation, "You want to ruin my career." Waxman follows the Love Duet with the "Ach, Isolde" music of Tristan from his Delirium Scene in Act 3, as Helen moves to the wind-swept parapet overlooking the beach.[6] Transitional music returns us to the concert venue, and Paul's angelic mother enters the hall: an obvious contrast to Helen, and a sense that Paul will be redeemed from the femme fatale ruining his life.

The "Liebestod" music is now underway—not its very beginning but the mid-to-final sections. A close-up of Paul bonded with his instrument dissolves into Helen's emoting face in close-up, wind tossing her hair about. From here to her death there is no cross-cutting with the concert hall. Graced by stunning black-and-white cinematography and lyrical shots of Crawford's tortured face, the gripping move to suicide against

Wagner's sexually charged music takes place.[7] At the final F♯ pedal point, Helen walks into the water. As she goes down we have a fish-eye view below water, and a wonderful sound effect kicks in: an immediate decrease in musical volume and intensity, mostly from the removal of waves' sound, as Helen loses hearing and life (we do not see her, however). At the final measures we are back in the hall and see Boray's mournful face next to the violin.

AMBIGUOUS HEARING: HELEN

The "Liebestod" text contains several references to hearing. Just before Isolde begins, Brangäne says to her mistress, "Hörst du uns nicht?" (Do you not hear us?) Isolde seems transfixed, unaware of her surroundings, and of course Wagner's original title for Isolde's expiring music was "Verklärung" (Transfiguration). The first few strophes center on seeing, as in the recurring line, "Seht ihr's nicht?" (Do you not see?) The "Liebestod" music in the film enters on the second iteration. From the start of the next strophe the text emphasizes hearing. Soon it transitions to waves and breezes, and then drowning. As I will detail, the film's staging of the "Liebestod" becomes a literal representation of its text and images.

Here is the unheard text that corresponds to the "Liebestod" music used in the film:[8]

Seht ihr's nicht?	Do you not see?
Wie das Herz ihm	How his heart
mutig schwillt,	proudly swells
voll und hehr,	and, brave and full,
im Busen ihm quillt?	pulses in his breast?
Wie den Lippen,	How from his lips
wonnig mild,	softly and gently
süßer Atem	sweet breath
sanft entweht—	flutters—
Freunde! Seht!	Friends, see!
Fühlt und seht ihr's nicht?	Do you not feel and see it?
Höre ich nur	Do I alone
diese Weise,	hear this melody
die so wundervoll und leise,	which, so wondrous and tender
Wonne klagend,	in its blissful lament,

alles sagend,	all-revealing,
mild versöhnend	gently pardoning,
aus ihm tönend,	sounding from him,
in mich dringet,	pierces me through,
auf sich schwinget,	rises above,
hold erhallend	blessedly echoing
um mich klinget?	and ringing round me?
Heller schallend,	Resounding yet more clearly,
mich umwallend,	wafting about me,
sind es Wellen	are they waves
sanfter Lüfte?	of refreshing breezes?
Sind es Wogen	Are they billows
wonniger Düfte?	of heavenly fragrance?
Wie sie schwellen,	As they swell
mich umrauschen,	and roar round me,
soll ich atmen,	shall I breathe them,
soll ich lauschen?	shall I listen to them?
Soll ich schlürfen,	Shall I sip them,
untertauchen?	plunge beneath them,
Süß in Düften	to expire
mich verhauchen?	in sweet perfume?
In dem wogenden Schwall,	In the surging swell,
in dem tönenden Schall,	in the ringing sound,
in des Welt-Atems	in the vast wave
wehendem All—	of the world's breath—
ertrinken, versinken—	to drown, to sink
unbewußt—	unconscious—
höchste Lust!	supreme bliss!

The second strophe personalizes Isolde's ability to hear something others do not hear, something meant only for her.[9] In "Höre ich nur diese Weise," the "Weise" is not just any melody but the "Weise" of Act 3 that traces Tristan's journey to his roots and imparts a sense of nostalgic timelessness. The "Weise" underlies his long soliloquy of reflection, the so-called Delirium Scene. In its first appearance after the Act's mournful opening music (a wonderful transformation of the *Tristan*-chord sonority), it becomes memorable through the plaintive timbre of solo English horn. Afterwards it weaves through Tristan's meditation in varied instrumental combinations, and by the time Isolde sings the "Liebestod" the melody is as memorable for the audience as for Isolde. Isolde's text describes the "Weise" as sounding gently from him, and that now it "pierces me through, rises above, blessedly echoing and ringing round me."

This describes what happens to Helen at this point in the film.[10] She hears and is pierced by the ringing tones of Paul's violin playing, which in Waxman's arrangement usually conveys the main melody. Paul's doleful lyricism is her "Weise." Unlike Isolde, however, Helen resists the tones. When the absent text intones "sounding from him, pierces me through," Helen places hands over ears to block the sound, even though she is far from the literal conveyor of the sound, the radio. More generally, Helen resists the power of classical music and its pull over her lover Paul, music being an unfair competitor for his attention.

The remainder of the text undergoes as literal a staging in the film as the first part. Now waves, breezes, and swelling guide and accompany Helen's movements. The text asks, "Shall I breathe them, shall I listen to them?" This suggests Helen's internal struggle over whether to yield to surging waves and kill herself. If she accedes to these sounds, which drown out Paul's music, she may escape the tyranny of music's hold on Paul. Wagner's text-music relationship encapsulates Helen's situation. The crucial line "Soll ich lauschen?"—Shall I listen?—occurs over a pivotal German augmented-sixth chord: a dominant-seventh sonority whose resolution is not certain until we hear the resolution. Once that occurs Helen's fate is sealed, and we know she will give herself over to the roaring noises.

Soon she walks into the water, a strewn concert poster drifting on the waves. The text continues to guide the action: "Shall I sip them, plunge beneath them, to expire . . . ? In the surging swell, in the ringing sound, in the vast wave of the world's breath—to drown, to sink, unconscious . . ." Helen (unlike Isolde) does not give herself over to the final line, "höchste Lust" (supreme bliss). It is hard to argue that Helen is transfigured to a higher spiritual realm. While the film displays a hypercharged quality in the scene because of Wagner's music and Haller's cinematography, Helen as a character does not rise to the level of transfiguration, of transcending her death into a state of supreme ecstasy. We adopt a neutral relationship to the event. Unlike the opera, Helen does not induce her own death so as to join her expired lover in a blissful state. She leaves the world on her own, alone, fleeing the power of music. The emotional aftermath redounds much more to Paul than to Helen.

After Helen goes into the waves we do not see her, but the camera shoots underwater and the sound decreases drastically.[11] We are in Helen's ears, and she (and we) still hear the music, including Paul's violin line. Now in its final measures, the heard "Liebestod" becomes a free-floating sound, without a definite auditory object in the fiction.[12] We return to the concert hall, the camera on Paul's face, for a diegetic conclusion.

Humoresque is not unique in connecting Wagner's music with water. Water imagery figures in other works associated with the composer. Wagner's comments on *Tristan und Isolde* provide a starting point. In his notes on the Prelude (with the Concert Ending), the composer writes of "the path into the sea of love's endless rapture" that drives the opera.[13] Wagner uses sea and water as a key metaphor in *The Artwork of the Future,* where the imagery frames the evolutionary voyage from Beethoven's symphonies to the fully formed artwork of the future, the music-drama.[14] *Tristan und Isolde* itself exploits water and voyage. Act 1 takes place on a ship that is crossing from Ireland to Cornwall. Act 3, including the "Liebestod," is set on a seacoast in Brittany, with water nearby.

Two more recent films also express the connection between water and Wagner's music. Don Boyd's operatic pastiche *Aria* (1987)—a collection of ten separate opera scenes, by ten different directors—includes a visualization of the "Liebestod." Directed by Franc Roddam and starring Bridget Fonda, the sequence shows two young lovers having sex in a Las Vegas hotel and slitting their wrists and dying in the bathtub. We watch their blood mingle with water as the reddened mixture snakes down the drain in a sickening spiral.[15] A second example is from 1983, in a famous biopic: Tony Palmer's film *Wagner,* created for public television in Britain and the United States.[16] The "Liebestod" music appears in a memorable place that aligns water and suicide. It accompanies King Ludwig, in episode seven, as he walks into a lake and drowns himself. As in *Humoresque,* the question of hearing is not clear-cut. Palmer may be suggesting that Ludwig the character is mentally rehearsing the searing music of his former idol and transferring it to himself: a paradigmatic use of psycho-diegetic music.[17] While historically it is not certain that Ludwig's drowning was intentional, Palmer shows us that it was. Ludwig's link with water has further resonance. The very name of his palace is Neuschwanstein, and the obsession with swans (shown frequently as palace decoration in the film) reflects the fact that swans were part of the Bavarian royal family's crest. In these two films, as in *Humoresque* and Wagner's opera, water suggests purification, cleansing, and re-birth.[18] Water also implies a return to the womb, a journey encouraged by the passive viewing conditions of film and of opera.[19] Both themes await further elaboration in another forum.

In *Humoresque* the relationship between the music's source and hearing is complex. Until Helen moves outdoors, the radio broadcast functions as the obvious musical source. This technological mediation within the story shows the significance of radio for the transmission of classical music in the pre-television era. As Royal S. Brown notes, this is the second time in the film that radio is connected with classical music: the first time it causes the cutting of sections of a broadcast piano concerto because of time considerations.[20] With the *Tristan and Isolde Fantasy*, the radio transmission is shown mostly on the perceiver's end, not the producing end, and a very specific listener and listening situation is involved. Helen is not hearing some impersonal, disembodied music, but music emitted by her lover. This inflects the status of that heard music, because an important narrative connection with the fictional emitter lies behind it. We might call it diegetic music with a strong psycho-diegetic component. The music interacts with Helen's psychological state and her conflicted, surging emotions. One could almost interpret the music-image interaction as a complex dialogue between music and Helen's emotions in which her emotional states, initially triggered by the music, become impetus to the unfolding of the music itself—as if her emotions "compose" the continuation of the music. Moreover, we in the outside audience recognize the piece as a special work, and it does special narrative work for us as well. It has been formally announced on the radio with a specific title. Even if we do not recognize "Tristan and Isolde" as a concept, by this point in the film we sense that it has major weight. After two hours and twenty-some classical pieces we anticipate a climax, and in the charged melodramatic atmosphere, something apocalyptic. Like Helen, we react to the music psychologically—a corollary to the psycho-diegetic status for characters in the fiction.

When Helen moves outdoors the "Liebestod" portion of the *Fantasy* blossoms. What is the status of the heard music? Helen cannot literally be hearing the radio transmission, and one might assume that the music is now sourceless music, or non-diegetic music. But that ignores important considerations that suggest that the music is anchored in sources within the film's fiction. One factor involves Helen's cultural position. As a wealthy classical music patron of 1940s New York, Helen would certainly be familiar with the "Liebestod," and it would form a basic part of her cultural literacy. When she literally hears earlier portions of the opera in Boray's *Tristan and Isolde Fantasy*, it is reasonable that she would tack on the most-performed section of the opera, the "Liebestod," in her mind, especially given her self-destructive bent. So from this point it is likely that she hears it in her psyche. In such a reading the music is psycho-diegetic and functions in a manner similar to the "Liebestod" in Ludwig's suicide in Palmer's film, mentioned above. The only way Helen can eliminate the sounds in her musical memory is by ending her life. In addition, a classical music aficionado such as Helen might even hear the absent words in her mind. They exhort her to enter the surging waves to sink, to drown, unconscious. In a fine-tuning of my earlier claim, I believe that in Helen's thinking this could be the only path to bliss in her troubled romance with Paul. As the music's volume wanes underwater, to herself she may be entering that transfigured state she has sought all her life. We viewers do not consider Helen to be transfixed. Helen has insufficient gravitas for a beatific altered state, and she remains a melo-dramatic caricature typical of film noir. But inside her reflexive narrative track, transfiguration is possible.

What we do know is that Helen dies. In this regard, Elisabeth Bron-fen's study of the relationship between film noir and Wagnerian "Liebes-tod" is suggestive.[21] Bronfen's main thesis is that Isolde and the femme fatale of film noir share many traits. Like the filmic femme fatale, Isolde uses seductive powers to ensnare a man, in this case magic potions, and to bring about his death (which does not happen). Although I do not entirely agree with this simplified comparison—Isolde does not qualify as a sexual temptress, unlike the femme fatale—Isolde in Act 1 does wish to see Tristan die, and the typical femme fatale of film noir wants to vanquish her mate. Nonetheless, Bronfen makes persuasive observations regarding the "Liebestod" that we can apply to *Humoresque*.[22] In film noir, narrative and generic considerations require the death of the femme fatale, and that is usually what happens. In *Tristan und Isolde,* however, nothing material causes the death of Isolde. She is not wounded, she does not have an illness, and thus there is no physical basis for her death during the "Liebestod." The opera glosses over this absence by ennobling the innocence of the lovers, whereas in film noir the femme fatale is guilty and pays with her life for her transgressive *jouissance.* If we extend this analogy to *Humoresque,* Helen the femme fatale has to die for the film to achieve narrative closure and ensure the survival of the masculine artist. She also must be sacrificed so that the masculinity of the male performer is purged of feminine associations, especially because music is coded feminine.[23] Earlier in the movie she was portrayed as the evil seducer by way of Waxman's *Carmen Fantasy,* performed by Paul as Helen attends a rehearsal. And as Susan McClary notes, Carmen has to die to contain female sexuality and protect mainstream society—goals that apply to Helen in *Humoresque.*[24] As for Helen's relationship to Isolde, we might say that Helen materializes Isolde's immaterial death in the "Liebestod," providing place, motivation, and details of death, and affirms the role of music in bringing about the death. Wagner's opera creates hypnotic music that privileges musical excess and glorifies irrationality. How appropriate that its apocalyptic ending becomes the climactic moment in a film about music-making.[25] Thus *Humoresque* offers an apt narrative context for a "resolution" of the indefiniteness of Isolde's death.[26]

SURE HEARING: PAUL

In the Wagner sequence we see Paul a few times: a lengthy stretch at the start of the *Fantasy,* in the middle when his mother enters the hall, and at the very end after Helen's death. Within the filmic fiction he emits the sound and hears it live. This renders his hearing more certain and knowable than Helen's, and the situation qualifies as diegetic music. But perhaps a special category should pertain when someone in the fiction listens to music they are producing: a sort of "auto-diegetic" relationship with the heard music. Of course, this pertains to the illusion of Boray producing these sounds. Isaac Stern, not John Garfield, is the actual violinist creating the music, and the performance was done to playback of the pre-recorded *Fantasy*.[27] Nonetheless, despite the use of instrumentalists' equivalent of singers' lip-synching, the reflexive relationship between hearing and emitting still holds in the fiction, and that is the operative framework for analyzing the type of diegesis that applies to the music.

The view of Paul finishing the *Fantasy* is especially striking. The music is the IV–I final cadence with the opening Tristan progression over it. We have just seen the long sequence of Helen's struggle and her decision to submit to the waves. And we have just heard, along with Helen, the hypnotic drive to climax of the "Liebestod" music. In the aftermath of this charged context, the camera shows a very tight close-up of Paul's face, and he has the most melancholy look of the character in the entire movie. He knows something decisive has happened to Helen and their relationship. The transfiguring nature of Wagner's music has affected him—not as a progression to bliss, as per the unheard text, but to a heightened sensibility regarding the doomed nature of their love. In addition to his angelic mother, another female figure in the hall witnesses his "conversion": a former girlfriend, Gina (Joan Chandler), a cellist, who serves as a Micaëla-like antidote to the femme fatale ruining his life. Unlike the opera *Carmen*, however, in which Don José dies, Paul lives on, and viewers are encouraged to think he will eventually end up with Gina. This is Hollywood, after all.

In addition to capturing the poignant look on Paul's face, the shot appears in soft focus and expresses a lyricism that suggests Paul's merging with the instrument itself. Given its location at the very end of the "Liebestod" and the musical drive that leads up to it, the shot exudes an aura of sexuality. It suggests Paul's bodily merging with the vibrations, the "body," of the instrument. The violin replaces Helen's body, which exists no more. This erotic act of displacement constitutes Paul's transfiguration. It also affirms Helen's view that Paul is wedded to the violin and has no room for her in his sexualized relationship with the instrument.

Erotic relationships between instrument and performer have been discussed in feminist terms by Suzanne Cusick, but the topic has not generated widespread exploration.[28] It does, however, resemble a connection that has received considerable attention: the vibrations and eroticism of the singing voice. Wayne Koestenbaum describes in rich metaphorical language the sexual connotations of the vocal apparatus and the ways in which it sets up patterns of desire with viewers and listeners.[29] He is particularly interested in the voice of the female diva and its resonance, literally and figuratively, with the body and psyche of gay male listeners. For *Humoresque* I am not bringing in the viewer/listener, but pointing out similarities between the eroticism of the violin's vibrations and those of the singing voice. Koestenbaum's opera queen experiences a metaphorical merging with the diva's voice that is ecstatic, and the erotic connection between performer and perceiver implies an eroticism that is also embodied within the singer her/himself. Paul experiences a merging with the vibrations of the violin, up close and next to him, that is similarly ecstatic. In this way, Paul as a solo violinist resembles the solo vocalist: each stands alone in front of the orchestra and audience, each undergoes a bodily connection with the mechanism emitting the vibrations. The singer has the built-in equipment, the violinist a near extension of his or her body. Hence Paul's hearing of what he plays, especially as seen in the extreme close-up, is shown to be as direct as that of a singer. Furthermore, the singer-violin analogy seems more plausible when one realizes that in the "Liebestod" portion of the *Fantasy,* the violin part usually replaces the vocal line of the original.

TRISTAN UND ISOLDE AS CONCERTO

Paul experiences another close relationship in the *Fantasy:* a musical connection with the solo piano part. The piano part is lush and romantic, and itself approaches the status of soloist in a piano concerto. The concerto genre, with one soloist or two, is extroverted and reaches out to an audience. It is a far cry from the rarefied inner-action domain of Wagner's opera. Aurally, it injects an easy-listening "pops" element into an icon of metaphysical art and builds on cultural understandings of Romantic piano music. I believe this is an important reason why the *Fantasy* works within the economy of the film, and why the staging of

Helen's death is so successful. Arguably, the piano and violin emerge as the real survivors of the Love-Death, and the male musician-friends that play them form the couple that will last. I am not suggesting an overt homosexual tie between Paul and Sid—the movie shies away from that idea—but rather a male bonding of two kids-from-the-wrong-side-of-the-tracks that trumps heterosexual love across classes.[30] One indication of the Paul-Sid bond is that they appear together in the scenes after the suicide.

Structurally and stylistically, the sense of a Romantic concerto is strong. The *Fantasy* displays a standard three-movement concerto layout. The first movement presents the Prelude music, develops the material, and builds up orchestrally. We experience the drama and sweep typical of first movements. The second movement opens with the start of the Love Duet, "O sink hernieder." A noticeably slower tempo and thinning of texture recall the second movement of many a Romantic concerto, such as the Grieg Piano Concerto or Brahms Violin Concerto. The finale gets under way with the pickup in tempo and the dominant pedal point at the start of the "Liebestod" music, and it pushes ahead with waves of orchestral and pianistic sound, which abate when Helen goes underwater.

The piano plays a major role in creating the feel of a concerto. The most important device is the piano arpeggio, up and down the keyboard, that Waxman deploys often. This more than anything converts Wagner's music from esoteric metaphysics to audience-friendly emotion. After all, the lush piano idiom in concertos of Tchaikovsky, Grieg, and Rachmaninoff has become common currency in the West and a trope of Hollywood scoring practices. Such "tabloid concertos," in K. J. Donnelly's marvelous phrase, figure prominently in 1940s melodramas.[31] In the *Fantasy*, the piano tips its hand when it serves up a rich arpeggio at the big deceptive resolution in the Prelude (measure 17). Our ears register Hollywood-style Wagner, not Teutonic Wagner. More full-bodied arpeggios, along with Tchaikovsky-like pianistic riffs, occur in the first movement. The second movement starts with a duet between violin and piano: a Chopinesque setting in which the piano's romanticized arpeggios depart from the ethereal string writing of the original, with its divided string sections and muted sound. The *Fantasy*'s foregrounding of the two solo instruments in the Love Duet conveys the special bond between the two male characters. After a while the piano is *tacet*, and a dramatic re-entrance of the instrument on the F♯ pedal of the "Liebestod" ushers in the final movement. For those familiar with the breezy passagework and skipping tempos of last movements, the arpeggios recall the sense of expectant conclusion found in concertos. In other words, the signifiers in the piano bring to mind comparable signifiers in finales of piano concertos. The writing transports the listener from the realm of Wagner (who did not write concertos or much piano music) to the more familiar realm of pops favorites, where many a Romantic piano concerto has a second home.[32]

The piano's arpeggiated push in the finale also accomplishes something crucial to the film: it provides the needed forward motion for Helen's struggle before she walks into the sea. Visually we see surging swells, blowing wind, romanticized Nature, melodramatic facial expressions. What better way to drive home emotional turbulence than to have insistent piano arpeggios added to a large orchestra? In concert-hall terms this would be unnecessary, but in Hollywood-scoring terms the semiotic force of the added sounds may indeed be needed. Furthermore, the absence of the vocal part as Helen dies may mean that the scoring requires a replacement—an element that pushes things over the top. The violin acts as a vocal replacement much of the time. But in filmic semiotics, some bigger musical sound or gesture is probably needed. Thus the presence of Levant in the film accomplishes several goals. Not only is he pal, accompanist, and member of the surviving couple, but he allows for a version of *Tristan und Isolde* that conforms to cinematic codes and maximizes the melodramatic effect of the suicide. I believe that without the participation of the piano in the *Fantasy*, Helen's death would be much less successful.

CONCLUSION

Waxman's *Tristan and Isolde Fantasy* presents a fascinating example of hearing Wagner's opera in film. For Helen, hearing is literal but also psychological, involved with cultural literacy and memory. For Paul, hearing is tied to performing and an erotic connection with his instrument. For viewers, hearing Wagner's music creates a memorable ending to a striking Hollywood melodrama, as powerful film signifiers guide our response to the film. Although the *Fantasy* is a classical music piece and the film offers a great deal of classical music, viewers are meant to filter Waxman's Wagner through Hollywood scoring codes, which transform Wagner into Tchaikovsky or Rachmaninoff. Not that there's anything wrong with that, as Jerry Seinfeld would say. But it is important to distinguish between Wagner's opera and its transformation into a Hollywood film score. Meanwhile, may audiences continue to enjoy a thrilling scene in which *Tristan und Isolde* crafts one of Joan Crawford's great moments in film.

NOTES

1. Paul Boray is a strong contrast to the fictional violinist of an earlier biopic, the popular film *Intermezzo* from 1939, directed by Gregory Ratoff. Leslie Howard plays the protagonist, a Swedish artist of great refinement—a far cry from Garfield's swagger. While *Humoresque* features melodramatic exaggeration and trades in alcoholism, depression, and suicide, *Intermezzo* idealizes music and its ability to shape noble sentiment. Both films feature illicit relationships, but *Humoresque* shows a depraved cheating spouse while *Intermezzo* offers a dignified artist who strays but does so under the spell of a fellow musician, noble-hearted pianist Ingrid Bergman. Another noted performer biopic, of a fictional pianist, is Max Ophüls's *Letter from an Unknown Woman* (1948), currently unavailable in NTSC format. For a study of biopics in which composer subjects may also be performers, see John C. Tibbetts, *Composers in the Movies* (New Haven: Yale University Press, 2005). For gendered elements in biopics of fictional performers, see Heather Laing, *The Gendered Score: Music in 1940s Melodrama and the Woman's Film* (Aldershot: Ashgate, 2007). For biopics generally, of people in all fields, see George F. Custen, *Bio/Pics: How Hollywood Constructed Public History* (New Brunswick: Rutgers University Press, 1992).

2. As explained in the featurette "The Music of *Humoresque*" on the DVD of the film (Warner Bros. DVD 67307, 2005), Isaac Stern's playing is what we hear when Boray performs, and Stern himself is fingering when Garfield is shown playing, with the actor's arms secured behind his back.

3. Franz Waxman (1906–67), a Jewish-German émigré to Hollywood in the 1930s, was a leading film composer from the 1930s to 1950s. Among his scores are those to *The Philadelphia Story* (1940), and Hitchcock's *Suspicion* (1941) and *Rear Window* (1955). He was also a classical music composer. Both fantasies for *Humoresque* were published and both are recorded, notably on Nadja Salerno-Sonnenberg's CD *Franz Waxman: Humoresque*, Nonesuch 79464-2 (1999), which includes other compositions used in the film. The disc is accompanied by excellent liner notes by Royal S. Brown.

4. Levant belonged to Gershwin's inner circle, and even after the composer's death was considered a leading interpreter of his piano music. The year before *Humoresque,* Levant portrayed Gershwin in the biopic *Rhapsody in Blue* and performed his music onscreen.

5. *Romeo and Juliet* and the "Liebestod" become entwined in Baz Luhrmann's updated film of Shakespeare's play, from 1996. The very end of the "Liebestod" is heard on the soundtrack as the lovers expire.

6. For an insightful discussion of the Delirium Scene, see Joseph Kerman, "Opera as Symphonic Poem," in *Opera as Drama* (New York: Vintage Books, 1956), 192–216.

7. Cinematographer Ernest Haller was a favorite of Crawford—he worked with her on *Mildred Pierce* the year before, a film that earned her an Oscar—and many have noted his visual love affair with her face in *Humoresque,* especially in the final sequence. See, for instance, Dan Callahan's review of the DVD (2005) in the online magazine *Slant,* www.slantmagazine.com/film/film_review.asp?ID=1651 (accessed November 19, 2007).

8. Text and translation—the latter modified by this author—come from the booklet for the CD set of the opera, *Tristan und Isolde,* Bayreuther Festspiele 1966, with Birgit Nilsson, DGG 449-722-2, © Polydor 1966, © DGG 1997. Robert Bailey presents a layout of the "Liebestod" text that is similar to mine (he considers the entire "Liebestod"); see his *Wagner: Prelude and Transfiguration from Tristan und Isolde,* Norton Critical Score (New York: W. W. Norton, 1985), 142.

9. Lawrence Kramer offers perceptive remarks on Isolde's personalizing of the sounds and how they embrace Tristan's voice (now dead), in *Opera and Modern Culture: Wagner and Strauss* (Berkeley: University of California Press, 2004), 226. Expanded discussion on the opera appears in his earlier study, *Music as Cultural Practice, 1800–1900* (Berkeley: University of California Press, 1990), 147–65.

10. Mary Ann Doane offers a perceptive feminist analysis of Helen and the scene, in *The Desire to Desire: The Woman's Film of the 1940s* (Bloomington: Indiana University Press, 1987), 96–105.

11. Doane considers water part of the theme of fluidity that characterizes Helen, which includes her heavy drinking, in *The Desire to Desire,* 104.

12. Kramer comments on the need for an absent object—namely, Tristan—in the "Liebestod": "Isolde's Transfiguration, which consummates her love and brings closure to the opera, occurs—and can only occur—once her desire is free to proliferate in the absence of its object"; *Music as Cultural Practice,* 147.

13. In Bailey, *Wagner: Prelude and Transfiguration,* 47; taken from *Richard Wagner's Prose Works,* trans. William Ashton Ellis (London: Routledge & Kegan Paul, 1899), vol. 8, 386–87.

14. Thomas S. Grey offers incisive remarks on the "aquatic imagery" in *Artwork of the Future,* pointing out associations between woman, womb, and water; see his *Wagner's Musical Prose: Texts and Contexts* (Cambridge: Cambridge University Press, 1995), 154–55.

15. For a study of the Roddam and another segment, see "Opera as Fragmant: 'Liebestod' and 'Nessun dorma' in *Aria,*" chap. 2 of Marcia J. Citron, *When Opera Meets Film: Aesthetic Perspectives as a Hybrid Medium* (Cambridge: Cambridge Universtiy Press, forthcoming). Jeongwon Joe address the entire film in "Don

Boyd's *Aria:* A Narrative Polyphony between Music and Image," *Journal of Musicological Research* 18, no. 4 (1999): 347–69.

16. For a lengthy discussion of Palmer's film, see Tibbetts, *Composers in the Movies,* 222–30.

17. The term "psycho-diegetic" was coined by Alexis Witt in an unpublished paper for a seminar at Rice University, "Opera and Film" (spring 2006). I have used it subsequently in published work, especially in "'An Honest Contrivance': Opera and Desire in *Moonstruck,*" *Music and Letters* 89, no. 1 (February 2008): 56–83. Psycho-diegetic, which refers to a remembered use of music, falls under the umbrella of "metadiegetic," Claudia Gorbman's term for larger-level functions of film music that go beyond diegetic and nondiegetic. See Gorbman, *Unheard Melodies: Narrative Film Music* (Bloomington: Indiana University Press, 1987), 22–23.

18. At least in episode seven of Palmer's *Wagner,* a recurring image shows characters bathing in a full bathtub: Wagner, King Ludwig, and the lead singers of *Tristan und Isolde,* Malvina and Ludwig Schnorr von Carolsfeld. The steam of the water is blamed for the vocal problems that prevent Malvina from performing in the opera's premiere, which was postponed from May 15 to June 10, 1865.

19. For regressive desires in film, see Kaja Silverman, *The Acoustic Mirror: The Female Voice in Psychoanalysis and Cinema* (Bloomington: Indiana University Press, 1988); Claudia Gorbman, *Unheard Melodies;* and Caryl Flinn, *Strains of Utopia: Gender, Nostalgia, and Hollywood Film Music* (Princeton, N.J.: Princeton University Press, 1992). I apply the concept to opera-film, especially Zeffirelli's *Otello;* see my *Opera on Screen* (New Haven, Conn.: Yale University Press, 2000), 96–106.

20. Brown, liner notes to CD *Franz Waxman: Humoresque.*

21. Elisabeth Bronfen, *Liebestod und Femme fatale: Der Austausch sozialer Energien zwischen Oper, Literatur und Film* (Frankfurt am Main: Suhrkamp, 2004).

22. See especially Bronfen, *Liebestod und Femme fatale,* 52–53.

23. Doane, *The Desire to Desire,* 96–104. The snuffing out of the feminine aspect of music in performer biopics is a major theme in Laing, *The Gendered Score.* For the demise of women in opera, see Catherine Clément, *Opera, or The Undoing of Women,* trans. Betsy Wing (Minneapolis: University of Minnesota Press, 1988).

24. Susan McClary, *Georges Bizet's Carmen,* Cambridge Opera Handbook (Cambridge: Cambridge University Press, 1992).

25. There is important literature on the hypnotizing powers of Wagner's music, especially by Thomas Mann and Theodor Adorno. With respect to Wagnerian phantasmagoria in film, see Marc A. Weiner's study on the charged opera scene in *Philadelphia,* "Why Does Hollywood Like Opera?" in *Between Opera and Cinema,* ed. Jeongwon Joe and Rose Theresa (New York: Routledge, 2002), 75–92.

26. Opinions on the scene are not uniformly positive. Irene Kahn Atkins, in her useful compact study of pre-existent music in film, finds the use of the "Liebestod" in *Humoresque* "too apt" from a cinematic perspective, and "so contrived that it does not function with any degree of subtlety." For Atkins, audiences in 1947 accepted the sequence because of "the unique and stylized talent of John Crawford." See Atkins, *Source Music in Motion Pictures* (Rutherford: Fairleigh Dickinson University Press, 1983), 98.

27. Statement by John Waxman, film-music historian and Franz Waxman's son, in the featurette "The Music of *Humoresque*" included in the DVD of the film.

28. Suzanne Cusick, "On a Lesbian Relationship with Music: A Serious Effort Not to Think Straight," in *Queering the Pitch: The New Gay and Lesbian Musicology*, ed. Philip Brett, Elizabeth Wood, and Gary C. Thomas (New York: Routledge, 1994), especially 79; and "Feminist Theory, Music Theory, and the Mind/Body Problem," *Perspectives of New Music* 32, no.1 (Winter 1994): 8–27. See also Elisabeth Le Guin, *Boccherini's Body: An Essay in Carnal Musicology* (Berkeley: University of California Press, 2006).

29. Wayne Koestenbaum, *The Queen's Throat: Opera, Homosexuality, and the Mystery of Desire* (New York: Poseidon Press, 1993). See also Cusick, "On Musical Performances of Gender and Sex," in *Audible Traces: Gender, Identity, and Music*, ed. Elaine Barkin and Lydia Hamessley (Zurich: Carciofoli Verlagshaus, 1999), 25–49.

30. Levant exudes urban Jewishness in this film and others, basically playing himself, while Garfield (a Jew who changed his name) plays a character in *Humoresque* whose Jewishness is largely concealed. While the character's impoverished Manhattan roots, admirable rise above his immigrant parents, and close friendship with Sid accord with the urban Jew, several key elements keep Jewishness below the surface and render him more of a generic urban tough guy than specifically a Jew. These include his very name (Boray is not a Jewish name), Garfield's chiseled looks and thuggish demeanor, his wasp-looking mother and sister (played by Ruth Nelson and Peggy Knudson), and the absence of Jewish ritual or symbols in the story. Of course, although Hollywood was founded and run by Jewish men, it purposefully downplayed or concealed Jewishness in films so as to appeal to mainstream America. See, for instance, Michael Rogin, *Blackface, White Noise: Jewish Immigrants in the Hollywood Melting Pot* (Berkeley: University of California Press, 1996); and Neil Gabler, *An Empire of Their Own: How the Jews Invented Hollywood* (New York: Anchor, 1989). For Jewishness in the plots and characters of the Broadway musical, see Andrea Most, *Making Americans: Jews and the Broadway Musical* (Cambridge: Harvard University Press, 2004). See also my earlier discussions, especially in n. 1, where I underline the gulf between Garfield's thuggish performer and the more usual biopic situation of a refined character as lead performer, for instance Leslie Howard's character in *Intermezzo* (1939).

31. K. J. Donnelly, "Wicked Sounds and Magic Melodies: Music in 1940s Gainsborough Melodrama," in *Gainsborough Pictures*, ed. Pam Cook (London: Cassell, 1997), 164. Donnelly notes the success of blockbuster pieces for piano and orchestra composed for the movies that popularized the given film and took on a life of their own, especially Richard Addinsell's *Warsaw Concerto* (for *Dangerous Moonlight*, 1941) and Hubert Bath's *Cornish Rhapsody* (for *Love Story*, 1944). Both probably influenced the style of Waxman's *Tristan and Isolde Fantasy*, especially the prominence of the piano. Moreover, both films are also biopics of fictional performers; for detailed discussion see Laing, *The Gendered Score*, 99–178.

32. Wagner's piano pieces are mostly early works and unimportant in his oeuvre. He did not compose any piano concertos.

NINE

Hollywood's German Fantasy:
Ridley Scott's *Gladiator*

MARC A. WEINER

Instinctively, his wounded, personal concerns shift
to the desecrated fatherland, and with the grand and
thundering words: "Are you still Romans?" he stands before
the degenerates like the avenging god of Rome.

RICHARD WAGNER, ON A SCENE FROM *RIENZI, DER LETZTE DER TRIBUNEN*

The war is over, Germania defeated, and the new Caesar returns to
Rome. But not all things German have been left behind, for as the imperial chariot passes the ranks of the Emperor's new and expectant subjects, a music is heard that was originally conceived and perceived as a
glorification not of things Italian and stately, but of their very opposite,
of the essence of the German soul made manifest in its most exalted,
and yet slain, superhero: Siegfried. Siegfried in a toga? And in a modern
film no less? Precisely: for the site of this merging of Roman image and
Teutonic sound is a key moment in Ridley Scott's 2000 epic blockbuster,
Gladiator, a box-office hit that earned twelve Academy Award nomina-
tions and five Oscars, including Best Actor in a Leading Role and Best
Picture of the Year. It is at this moment that the moviegoing audience
first sees Scott's vision of Rome, and the fact that this is also the moment
when the score by Hans Zimmer explicitly evokes Richard Wagner's
Ring cycle is of ideological importance.[1]

For those who can make the connection, this gives pause for reflection. For the rest of the cinematic audience—and that means for most of them—the music just sounds right because Wagner has so influenced the kinds of sounds we associate with grandeur and the large-scale clash of good and evil in the cinema. In what follows, however, I will argue that Wagner is not *only* used because of aesthetic considerations—orchestral texture and leitmotifs, say—nor primarily because of intertextual connections between the *Ring* cycle and the plot of *Gladiator* (though I will mention some of these later). Rather, I believe that Wagner is used in the film above all as but one of a number of signifiers that refer to German cultural and political history in general, and to America's experience of Germany in particular, as a means of unfolding their ideological operations.[2] In other words, approximations or evocations of Wagner's music are polyvalent, signifying not only artistic matters, but historical-political ones as well, and this simultaneous, multilayered signification may have contributed to the film's overwhelming success. For although *Gladiator* is no art film, its use of aesthetic signs as suggestive of political history is subtle and deserves attention. What's more, it is not unique in this respect, but constitutes only one example of how the Hollywood blockbuster of at least the past quarter century has employed Wagnerian music and quotes from Wagner's works as an emblem of his nation and of things associated with it in the modern American imagination.

THE FABULA

The film is set in AD 179–80, during which, according to the historical sources of Cassius Dio, Herodian, and the *Augustan History* upon which David Franzoni, John Logan, and William Nicholson based their screenplay, Commodus—the son of Marcus Aurelius—succeeded his father to become leader of the Roman empire.[3] *Gladiator* opens with a final victory of the Roman legions, under the direction of the general Maximus (played by Russell Crowe), over the forces of Germania, after which the aging Emperor (Richard Harris) asks Maximus to temporarily take over the leadership of Rome following his own death in place of his son, Commodus (Joaquin Phoenix), who has pride of place for succession to the throne within the Antonine dynasty. Marcus Aurelius fears that

Commodus would be too immoral to lead the empire well, and longs to annul the current form of government—the rule of Rome under the aegis of an Emperor who bequeaths his reign through primogeniture—and to return power solely to the Senate, the political institution representing the people that once formed the center of the Roman Republic.[4] When Commodus learns of this, he strangles his father and gives orders to have the general executed and his family murdered. Maximus escapes and flees to his home in Spain, only to find his wife and son slain.

What follows is the story of Maximus's rise from a hopeless, bereaved, and powerless cynic to a man driven by a thirst for revenge who comes to threaten the very foundations of Roman imperial rule. While unconscious and delirious on his family's graves, he is taken captive by mercenaries and brought to Zucchabar, a small city in the Roman province of Numidia in the north of Africa, where he is purchased by Proximo (Oliver Reed), an entrepreneur and trainer of gladiators. Maximus soon excels in his new profession. In the meantime, Commodus has inaugurated a series of daily spectacles of gladiatorial combat in the Colosseum intended to win his subjects' affection and to distract them from his plans to abolish the Senate. Proximo receives an invitation to have his combatants compete in the Roman games and takes his entourage to the capital city, where Maximus secretly hopes to find an opportunity to kill Commodus. At the conclusion of his first, victorious fight in the arena, his identity is revealed, and while the Emperor wishes him executed, Maximus is hailed as the people's favorite, forcing Commodus to spare his life.

In the following game(s), Maximus continues to be victorious. Commodus's sister, Lucilla (Connie Nielsen), who loathes her brother in part owing to his sexual advances, plots with Senator Gracchus (Derek Jacobi) to help Maximus assassinate the Emperor and return Rome to republican rule. The plot is unearthed, and Commodus has several members of the Senate, whom he perceives to be enemies, murdered in their sleep and Maximus and Gracchus imprisoned. He then decides to fight his adversary in the arena, and though he wounds him prior to their entrance into the Colosseum, Maximus kills him, gives orders that Senator Gracchus and all of the slaves be freed, makes public Marcus Aurelius's hope that Rome would once again be a Republic, and dies.

WAGNERIAN SOUNDS

So what, one might wonder, does all of this have to do with Wagner? After all, the composer viewed Rome as evincing all the corruption and failings of modern Europe.[5] The answer lies in the music of the film score, as well as in the commonalities and contrasts between the figures and machinations of *Der Ring des Nibelungen* and those of the cinematic drama set in Rome. For on more than one occasion, sonic passages from the film sound so similar to passages found in Wagner that they seem near quotations. The first of these accompanies a change of scene: immediately after Maximus surveys the small arena and the crowds of spectators at the conclusion of his first, victorious combat as a gladiator in Zucchabar, the images he beholds begin to blur and circulate, their vivid colors are gradually replaced by chromatic grays and blues, and visions of movement through clouds emerge and slowly give way to an aerial shot of what is obviously a model of Rome, gun-metal in color, until an emblem of the empire—an enormous stone eagle—fills the screen (see figure 9.1a), all the while underscored by a rich orchestral texture and arpeggiated triads (example 9.1).[6]

This passage, entitled "The Might of Rome" in a piano reduction of the film score, clearly evokes—sounds very much like, and, I would argue, is intended to call to mind—the rising and falling strings in the Prelude to *Götterdämmerung* (itself reminiscent of the Prelude to *Das Rheingold*) (example 9.2).[7]

For a listener who can hear the similarity with the music of the *Ring,* reception of this moment shifts to interpretation through comparison, begging the question as to what the Wagnerian tetralogy has to do with the film. What is the film's soundtrack pointing to here? It certainly underscores the grand proportions of the scene, depicting the larger-than-life figures it portrays and the vast power of the Roman Empire, both features similar to those of the Wagnerian universe. Both works concern rulers of, to say the least, questionable distinction, megalomaniacal in their ruthless accession of power and self-aggrandizing in their performative portrayal of it. The music seems to invite comparison of Commodus and Wotan, who are dangerous, brooding, scheming, and

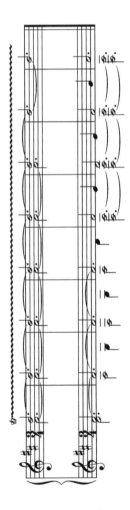

EX. 9.1. Commodus enters Rome

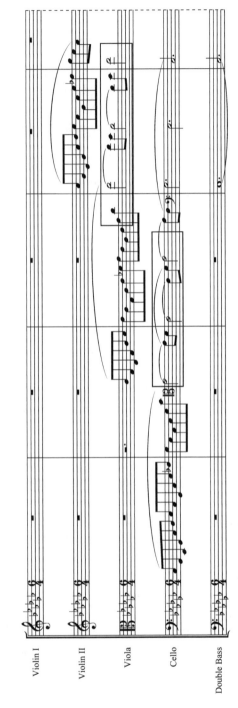

EX. 9.2. Götterdämmerung, Prelude

paranoid. Moreover, both Wagner's and Scott's works ultimately depict the demise of these corrupt leaders and the restitution of a preferable order, the natural state and the Republic, respectively.

But the similarities don't stop there, for this is not the only Wagnerian moment in the non-diegetic accompaniment to the new Emperor's entrance, and the next one points to yet another musical commonality that invites further ideational comparison. Following the wavelike motion in the strings, a repeated F♯-minor chord is heard that evokes a Wagnerian predecessor as well (example 9.3a and example 9.3b).

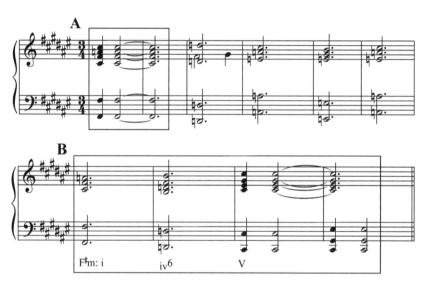

EX. 9.3A–B. Commodus and echoes of Wagner

Given the obvious affinity of the opening music in the scene with that of the opening sounds of *Götterdämmerung*, this brief repetitive iteration can be heard to echo a particularly celebrated passage from the final *Ring* drama, the beginning of Siegfried's portentous "Funeral March" from Act 3 of *Götterdämmerung*, with its repeated, thunderous C-minor chords signifying in the music drama the magnitude of the loss of the hero (example 9.4).[8] The note values are different, but the rhythmic configurations are similar and the sonic material readily calls to mind its operatic forebear for those already familiar with it.

It's as though the composer writing music for the movie was thinking not only of grandeur and tragedy per se, but specifically of the tragic

EX. 9.4. Siegfried's "Funeral March"

loss of Siegfried as of singular importance for understanding this scene in the film. Underscoring the connection between the "Funeral March" and Commodus, another evocation of the former appears, beginning just five measures after the repeated F♯-minor chords. At this point a three-measure harmonic progression (i–iv⁶–V) (example 9.3b) unfolds that bears a striking resemblance to one found in Siegfried's solemn and celebratory music, where it is heard in conjunction with the Tragic motif bewailing the Volsung's demise (example 9.5). (The i–ii$^{\emptyset 4}_3$–V progression in the Wagnerian material sounds very much like the i–iv⁶–V in Zimmer's passage because both share the descending bass progression of a major third followed by a semitone.)[9]

In other words, "The Might of Rome" refers to the funereal celebration in the orchestra of *Götterdämmerung* not once, but *twice*. Why? Is Commodus to be understood as a parallel to the German superhero, as though the Teutonic warrior lay dead on the wasted battlefield left behind in Germania, and his place as the most heroic of men has been passed on to the son of Marcus Aurelius? Hardly. While the aforementioned similarities between the rulers of the *Ring* and *Gladiator,* Wotan and Commodus, are straightforward, now the comparison is clearly, glaringly ironic, for here it parodies, ridicules, and denounces to the cinematic audience the man it non-diegetically portrays. In place of a funeral march, we have a pseudo-Wagnerian version of the "Triumphant March" from Verdi's *Aida*. In *Götterdämmerung* the repeated minor chords signify moments of musical nostalgia, recalling the glorious days of Siegfried's past, and thereby highlight the potential he had embodied for a more glorious, albeit unfulfilled or unrealized, future. But as Commodus makes his grand entrance, Senator Gracchus comments that the cowardly son of Marcus Aurelius returns to Rome as though he were "a conquering hero," and then asks rhetorically: "But what has he

EX. 9.5. Wagner, Tragic motif

EX. 9.6. Maximus, the Roman Siegfried

conquered?" Both before and after he does so, Zimmer's evocation of the *Ring* resounds as a mocking musical denunciation, as if the music were the expression of an ironic, judgmental narrator.

Nor is this the last time the music of *Gladiator* calls to the mind's ear the Wagnerian lament. At the climactic conclusion to the first, semi-staged battle in the Colosseum, in which the Emperor descends from his box to congratulate the new and still masked combatant, Commodus asks the unknown man his name. At first, the enigmatic warrior hesitates, and then answers simply: "My name is Gladiator." As he does so, the repeated E♭-minor chords enter ominously, followed by a descending and then rising melodic gesture—a vivid reminiscence of the opening of Siegfried's "Funeral March" (example 9.6).

The character of this music, engendered through the repetition of a minor chord and the subsequent ascending bass melodic line, after the initial falling of a minor second from E♭ to D, leading to the resounding of the same chord again, is one of tragic grandeur bordering on the mythic, a ghostly echo of the *Ring*'s glorifying elegy cited above (example 9.4). The two passages are not identical, but their affective power is virtually the same. There is nothing ironic here, for this is the moment in which Maximus reveals his identity, and the Wagnerian sounds lend him and his fury a degree of magnitude and pathos never afforded Commodus (as well as foreshadowing the Roman general's tragic end). Clearly the music here is not that of the Emperor who is, after all, one of the biggest slimeballs of recent cinematic memory. Instead, it serves, by virtue of both its affective character and its signification, to underscore the incommensurability of the two figures: the cowardly Roman Emperor and his adversary, the most terrifying and dangerous combatant in the film, the general known as "the greatest," Maximus.[10] *Gladiator* opens, after all, with a triumphant, final battle in a twelve-year military campaign intended to bring with it peace, the peace of victory, a "victorious peace," or "Sieg-fried." If Commodus is a poor man's Wotan, Maximus is the Roman version of Wagner's slain superhero.

The link between Maximus and Siegfried is not all that surprising if we consider that the ideational concerns of *Gladiator* and the *Ring* have much in common. Both are works concerned with the most serious and portentous themes of Western literary history: love (or the lack thereof), hatred, ambition, power, incest (consummated in the *Ring*, and in *Gladiator* Commodus's unfulfilled desire), murder, and revenge, all of which are portrayed against the backdrop of sweeping historical change. Siegfried is not, to be sure, the general's only model (another is obviously Spartacus), but he is an important one, or at least that's what Zimmer's music tells us.[11] When still a boy, the Wagnerian superhero is a "free spirit," at home in Mother Nature, befriender of birds, fox, bear, and deer, untutored in and completely ignorant of the ways of the world, and burdened only by his intermittent loneliness and longing for his deceased parents.[12] Similarly, when not functioning as a general, Maximus is a farmer, ignorant of urbanity and yearning for a reunion with his family. As he describes his home and farm to Marcus Aurelius, he can scarcely contain his glee in imagining his immanent return to a life there.

Nonetheless, through Zimmer's musical allusion he is presented as having far greater affinity with the older Siegfried, the boy-become-man slowly and cunningly deceived through the intrigues of a corrupt civilization, the court of the Gibichungs. In *Götterdämmerung,* a drama concerned with internecine political turmoil, the sacrifice of a super-hero, and the destruction of an authoritarian regime—all elements that reappear in *Gladiator*—Siegfried falls victim to the political machina-tions of Hagen, a monstrous and politically adept schemer intent on usurping power at all costs, who murders both the Volsung and his own half-brother, Günther, in order to acquire the ring. The similarities to Maximus as the victim of Commodus's sophistication, urbanity, duplic-ity, and malice are obvious.

Indeed, the entire film can be seen as a denigration of the figure of the politician and a glorification of the common, simpler man, both concerns of the Wagnerian tetralogy. If Commodus is a worst-case ex-ample of what a governing figure can be and do, Maximus is a man of the people, forced by circumstances to enter, however unwillingly, into the realm of politics. Not one member of the Senate, nor one of the Em-perors, comes off as unblemished: Gaius (John Shrapnel) has a mistress (and thus is the butt of derogatory teasing), Falco (David Schofield) is a scheming ally of Commodus, in the second draft of the screenplay Grac-chus is maligned by the Emperor as "that sodomite" (apparently not in-tended as a term of endearment), and Marcus Aurelius himself wonders if he, who has waged war for sixteen years of his twenty-year reign, will be remembered as a tyrant. Even his daughter, Lucilla, seems threateningly imposing to both her father and to Commodus, who recognize her scheming intellect and powers of adroit manipulation, and imagine that she would have been a formidable politician had she been born a man.

But Maximus is no politician; though he is Rome's greatest hero, his military prowess is not learned but seems a natural gift (and in this respect, also, he differs from Commodus, who is afraid to engage in a battle that has not been carefully rehearsed and staged), as is his spontaneous and heartfelt love of his family and his rural life. All of these attributes are portrayed as the opposite of those of a politician, which is made clear near the beginning of the film in a celebration following the defeat of Germania. Gaius, like his Emperor, clearly recognizes the political power Maximus could wield as the leader of an army devoted to him, yet the general is not interested in any political use of military force, nor in a position in the capital city that his control of the army might ensure. When Marcus Aurelius asks him, rhetorically, why they are in Germania, he replies: "For the glory of the empire, sire," revealing a naïve and untutored understanding of the workings of government, made clearer still in his answer to the Emperor's question as to what he thinks Rome is: "Rome is the light." Earlier, Falco—aware of the influential role Maximus could play—asks him: "Where do you stand, General? Emperor or Senate?" Maximus's reply is a straightforward rejection of the subtleties of political thought: "A soldier has the advantage of being able to look his enemy in the eye, Senator."

And yet, illuminating though these intertextual connections may seem to those able to recognize them—clearly a relatively small percentage of the modern cinematic audience, Wagner's growing popularity notwithstanding—we are still left with the question: Why Wagner? After all, any bombast would have served the same ends in the first scene, and given the conventions of cinematic dramaturgy, anything in the minor mode sounding somber and dramatic would have been deemed appropriate in the second. So why, given the extraordinary financial investment necessary to create and market a movie such as *Gladiator* that is targeted at a large and heterogeneous audience, imbue the film with references to Wagner that only a negligible number of viewing listeners would respond to with cognitive precision?[13]

FASCIST FANTASIES

I would suggest that the answer lies not solely in the aesthetic dimensions of the Wagnerian artwork, which means not solely or even primarily in the emotional power of the music or in the intertextual commonalities and ironies just discussed that emerge when comparing the *Ring* and the film, but somewhere else: in the associations that have come to attend Wagner's works in the modern Western imagination. I'd like to approach this issue by indirection, first citing a study of the role of gladiatorial combat in Rome by Lewis Mumford that is of use here:

> The inhabitants of modern metropolises are not psychologically too remote from Rome to be unable to appreciate this new form [of gladiatorial entertainment] . . . Every day, in the arena, the Romans witnessed in person acts of vicious torture and wholesale extermination, such as those that Hitler and his agents later devised and vicariously participated in.[14]

Of interest here is the presence of Hitler as the first thing that occurs to the modern mind when contemplating particularly horrific acts of violence and almost unfathomable evil. Since the end of World War II, Hitler has functioned in the Western imagination as the prototypical embodiment of the worst man is capable of, far more than is the case with such other twentieth-century rulers of, shall we say, questionable rectitude as Stalin, Mao, Pol Pot, or others. Hitler is the monster par excellence, the exemplar of evil against which all others must be measured, and as such he functions as one of the models for Commodus, lurking in the background throughout Ridley Scott's film, in which the evocation of Wagner's music is just part of a larger set of references to the Third Reich, be they textual, thematic, iconographic, or cinematic, as well as musical. In *Gladiator,* these diverse reference frameworks—the political and the aesthetic—coexist, and Wagner is part of both. I suggested at the opening of this essay that the use of Wagner as a signifier of things German in *Gladiator* is not unique; indeed, in one of the most popular film series ever, George Lucas's *Star Wars* saga, which also concerns the battle between (the forces of) good and evil, a conflation of pseudo-Wagnerian music and iconographies of Nazism must have struck audiences as appropriate as well, given the films' overwhelming popularity.[15]

FIG. 9.1A–B. Eagles of empire: *top, Gladiator; right, Triumph of the Will*

Where do references to Germany in general, and to Hitler in particular, show up in *Gladiator*? Let us return to the aforementioned bluish-black, gray, and white coloration of the clouds and the imperial eagle that accompany Scott's first visual depiction of Rome (figure 9.1a). This emblem—not only the figure of the eagle, but the way it is constructed and photographed—is obviously a reference to the work of Leni Riefenstahl, especially to her propagandistic documentary of the 1934 Nazi Party Conference rally in Nuremberg, *Triumph des Willens,* in which this very image plays a prominent role (figure 9.1b).

The similarity here is reinforced through comparison of the geometrically apportioned legions and spectators who accompany Commodus's appearance in Rome with similar images from Riefenstahl's film (figure 9.2a and figure 9.2b).[16] One unnamed source, citing production notes for *Gladiator* in a companion booklet to the film, makes this explicit:

FIG. 9.2A–B. Ceremonies of power: *top, Gladiator; left, Triumph of the Will*

"Ridley Scott wanted Commodus's grand entrance into Rome to echo Nazi-era propaganda films like Leni Riefenstahl's *Triumph of the Will*."[17]

Scott's colleagues and critics alike have recognized the visual parallels. For those interested in basing an argument on documented and verifiable intentionality, there are numerous statements by both the director and the composer that testify to their conscious decision to infuse *Gladiator* with aesthetic signs associated with National Socialism. Hans Zimmer stated candidly that the recognition of this gesture, not only to Riefenstahl in particular but also to the Nazism with which she was associated, was *the key factor* in his decision to employ Wagnerian material in his film score. That the use of Wagner at this point is no coincidence is borne out by Zimmer's remarks concerning the process he went through in fashioning his musical sounds for the modern image of the imperial power of classical antiquity:

> When I first looked at what Ridley had done with Rome, I suddenly real-
> ized that this was really a Leni Riefenstahl homage to Rome. And so I
> shamelessly put on my German hat and went into this Wagner territory.
> The scary thing was how easy it was for me to get into this sort of Wagner
> stuff. You know there's a fascist in all of us.[18]

That explains a lot, and it indicates some affinity with Herbert Windt's
purpose in his composition for Riefenstahl's film, which also was not
only based on but also, for those able to make the connection, *was to
be understood as* based on motifs from the *Ring* and *Die Meistersinger
von Nürnberg.*

It is very well known that Riefenstahl was Hitler's favorite film director and Wagner his favorite composer. In the 1920s, Hitler was a
regular guest of the Wagner family in Bayreuth and later in the 1930s, a
supporter of the festivals there; indeed, he even credited Wagner with
having inspired his vision of himself as the future *Führer* of a racially
pure German *Volk.*[19] A well-known anecdote linking the politician and
the composer has surfaced repeatedly in scholarship devoted to, as Don
DeLillo puts it in *White Noise,* "Hitler Studies," namely, Hitler's recounting of an experience he had while still a teenager when he attended a
performance of *Rienzi* in Linz together with a friend, August Kubizek. In
1939 Kubizek recalled that following the performance they had attended
in their youth, his friend "conjured up for me in grandiose, inspiring
pictures his own future and that of his people," and that when he later
reminded Hitler of the event, the Führer exclaimed: "In that hour it
began."[20] For our purposes, we have no need to go further into the role
that this specific work of Wagner's played in Hitler's self-understanding,
nor to enumerate all of the parallels between the text of this early grand
opera and the motifs found within the politician's later self-stylization;
suffice it to say they are numerous, and that fact is no arcane secret, but
part of common lore. That is the point: without these historical connections, both in the minds of the makers of the film and, to very differing
degrees, of the audience, I believe that the sonic, textual, and visual
makeup of *Gladiator* would have been very different.

It is also well known that Hitler was an enthusiastic devotee of all
things Roman.[21] Since the mid-eighteenth century, there had been a
tradition of profound interest in classical antiquity within German cul-

ture, from Winckelmann, Lessing, Goethe, Schiller, Hölderlin, Mörike, and Heine, to figures who, to greater or lesser degrees, influenced the development of National Socialist ideology: Wagner, Nietzsche, Spengler, George, and Houston Stewart Chamberlain, to name but the most prominent. (Though it should be added that for the most part, their interest had far more concerned the European image of ancient Greece than that of Rome, which was usually thought of as a civilization less pure, more modern, and more corrupt than its classical antecedent.)[22]

In the memoirs of the Führer's favorite architect, Albert Speer describes their plans for a monumental "great domed hall" unprecedented in its dimensions and intended to demonstrate for all the world and for posterity the grandeur of the Reich. Though larger in size, this imagined emblem of National Socialism, to be situated in the very center of Berlin's future "Adolf Hitler Platz," was based not on some refurbished, modern-day version of a castle, cathedral, or palace from the Teutonic architectural past, but on the Parthenon.[23] This new, Germanic vision from classical antiquity was to be 825 feet in diameter, 726 feet in height, and was to hold up to 180,000 of the devoted. Within and above this vast structure an image was to be displayed that appears at the opening of *Triumph des Willens,* an eagle with a swastika in its claws, of which Speer writes: "This symbol of sovereignty might be said to be the very fountainhead of Hitler's grand boulevard."[24] Obviously Scott's image of the eagle, sans swastika, appears at the opening of the transition in *Gladiator* from Numidia to Rome, at the very moment when the Preludes to *Das Rheingold* and *Götterdämmerung* are first evoked.

Nor was this the sole example of how Hitler's fantasies of his legacy dovetailed with his attraction to the legacy of Rome. In his biography of Speer, Dan van der Vat details a plan of Hitler's concerning how his accomplishments were to be perceived by later generations that makes the conflation of the Third Reich and the Roman empire explicit:

> It was at this time that Hitler and Speer formulated their so-called "law of ruins" whereby they built with distant posterity in mind. The remains of the Reich were to show the greatness of those who produced them, even when overgrown and worn 1,000 years hence. This morbid romanticism was inspired by the relics of ancient civilizations, such as the Pergamon Altar, the Pyramids and the monuments left all over Europe by the Romans.[25]

The key here is that for modern audiences, the portrayal of a decadent Roman imperium that brings with it associations of Nazism has its roots in the historical connection between the two, in the documented and well-known self-understanding of the Third Reich as a modern manifestation, a resurrection, of the defunct classical empire.

Zimmer's candid remark concerning Riefenstahl and fascism not only makes clear the function of one dimension of the soundscape of *Gladiator* (namely, its reference to Wagner at this point) but also helps us to identify and interpret the role played by a number of other aesthetic details and attendant ideas found in and associated with Scott's work. For upon examination, the world of *Gladiator*—the score, the screenplay, and the imagery—reveals numerous other references to National Socialism as well that were understood as such by the director. These are found in additional material available on both the two- and three-DVD versions of the film, such as an interview with Zimmer (quoted above) and a voiceover commentary with Scott and Russell Crowe:

1) When observing Commodus's entourage entering the imperial city between formations of Roman legions, Scott says: "This is the Wehrmacht" (the collective term used for all branches of the military under Hitler after 1934).[26]

2) Similarly, Scott characterizes a lengthier version of the scene than that viewed in the theaters in which the Praetorian guard effects a number of nocturnal surprise executions, thus:

> This is a scene of retribution, reaction in "the night of" what should have been "the long knives," but in fact, we didn't have enough actors to kill. [This is a reference not to Scott's actors, but to some of the dramatis personae, a group of Roman thespians in the film.] But these were the actors who had been outspoken against the Emperor and therefore were fire-bombed.[27]

"The night of the long knives" is a reference to the 1934 putsch against Ernst Röhm, the leader of the SA (*Sturmabteilung*), in which Hitler and Hermann Göring, the director of the German air force (*Luftwaffe*), had Röhm and several other key immanent and potential rivals murdered, and the SA disbanded and integrated into the SS (*Schutzstaffel*) under Göring. (Though the commentary refers to a longer version, the images of the Praetorians of which Scott speaks are identical to the version released in theaters. Of those elite Roman soldiers one commentator has observed: "The Rome Ridley Scott created was painstakingly researched, to be sure—but it was also imagined. From the fascist-overtoned armor of the Praetorian guard to the flowing manes of every horse ... Ridley's signature can be seen on every frame.")[28]

3) Immediately after the Praetorians are seen marching through the streets of Rome at night, an assassin is shown releasing a coral snake into Gaius's bed as the senator lies sleeping near his mistress, and Scott comments on the appearance of the assassin by describing him as a "snake-Meister."

4) When the scene of the initial confrontation between Commodus and Maximus in the Colosseum shifts to the Emperor's chambers, showing him discussing with Lucilla the general's reappearance in the arena, Scott remarks on the visual imagery by saying: "This is all very Teutonic, which is probably why the Germans based a lot of their architecture and uniforms on it anyway."

5) Toward the end of the film, once the assassinations have been carried out and the prisoners taken, Commodus, furious at Lucilla's betrayal, makes the following statement: "And as for you, you will love me as I loved you. You will provide me with an heir of pure blood so that Commodus and his progeny will rule for a thousand years." Two obvious references to National Socialism obtain here: the belief in the physiological purity of the Aryan "race," and the self-pronouncement of the new regime as the beginning of a "thousand-year Reich."[29] It is also typical of the post–World War II portrayal of Hitler as sexually, well, anomalous. From our first sight of him, Commodus exudes aberrance, megalomania, ambition, paranoia, emotional instability, a love of violence, a capacity for resentment and hatred, and sexual abnormality, all traits that have come to be associated with Hitler in the modern imagination.[30]

Clearly, the director's fascination with, and detailed knowledge of, National Socialism informed his conception of the plot, the characterization, and the visual makeup of the film. One may assume, therefore, that it also influenced his approbation of Zimmer's score, with its evocation and citation of Wagner.

THE MODERN COLOSSEUM

The National Socialist program was based upon the rejection of a politics of pluralism and of diverse forms of heterogeneity (not only political, but also national and racial) in favor of homogeneity (of a single nation united under one Führer, who rules over a racially homogenous realm). Seen in this light, within *Gladiator* the term "Republic" has a twofold valence: it refers overtly to the Roman model of a government through the Senate (which, as Gracchus and Gaius repeatedly emphasize, is supposed to represent not the interests of the wealthy and influential few, but of the people), a political form that antedated the establishment of primogeniture under the rule of the Emperors and thus, for all intents and purposes, exists in name only by the beginning of the film. But the term also refers more covertly to the *Weimar* Republic, a model of multi-party governance from 1919–33 that preceded the establishment of a fascist state under the Nazis. It is telling that in his commentary on the film, Scott refers to the formation of the Roman armies in the mud of Germania as similar to the conditions of World War I, a devastating event that led to the fall of the monarchical Wilhelminian empire and immediately preceded the formation of the Weimar Republic, and that shaped the psyche of a generation later to endorse Hitler. Thus, the allusions to the Weimar Republic, Hitler, National Socialism, Riefenstahl, and Wagner all function as pieces of a historical framework for the distribution of figures associated with laudable and common, versus venal self-interest, as well as the context in which these more general themes and motifs unfold.

But in saying as much I am not claiming that audiences have necessarily been *aware* of why they have responded to *Gladiator* with such enthusiasm.[31] Few of its viewers will have recognized the Wagnerian allusions, fewer still the resulting inter-textual connections, and probably not even all that many the references to Hitler and the Nazis, and therefore not to the Weimar Republic either, for that matter. But on the other hand, it is not enough to simply claim that the film's music "sounds like Wagner," for it can safely be said that that is the case with many, perhaps even most of the large-scale Hollywood productions these days. Of course there is something "Wagnerian" in the sound we have come to associate with the figure of the hero and with the concept of heroism as portrayed on film, but we do not need to recognize one source of such sonic and ideational associations in the nineteenth-century composer to be moved by examples of that association in the cinema today. If this is true, however, if recognition is *not* the key to understanding the use of Wagner in this Hollywood blockbuster (as source of dramatic configurations and historical figures), why has the conflation of these sounds and this story struck audiences as so forcefully persuasive?

This is a question that we can't get around, but that we also, ultimately, can only answer provisionally, hypothetically, and incompletely. That this is so is demonstrated by Lawrence Kramer's nuanced discussion of a similar phenomenon in a different film, namely the role of "The Ride of the Valkyries" in that famous scene from Coppola's *Apocalypse Now*, in which Lt. Col. Kilgore plays the Wagnerian passage over loudspeakers as his helicopter gunships attack a Vietnamese village. Kramer acknowledges the multiple possibilities within the reception process, without trying to overemphasize any one of these at the expense of the others, or failing to recognize the ultimately inexplicable nature of the means by which the work makes such an impact on the listening viewer. He recognizes a plurality of modes of reception and the fact that there is often something ineffable going on when audiences respond to the use of Wagner in the cinema, not only with respect to his music, but also to the associations he calls forth in the post–World War II era:[32]

> The effect [of the use of Wagner's music in the scene with the helicopters] is not simply—not primarily—conceptual. The armored choppers seem to look and move differently than they would otherwise, to be both more terrifying and more grotesque. The music will convey this effect whether it and its lore are recognized or not; but these things are also part of the story . . . The full force of the allusion remains esoteric for those who don't know the *Ring* cycle or the implications of associating Wagner with a racially charged triumphalism, but a wider semantic circle has nonetheless been drawn.[33]

I'd like to situate that "semantic circle" within what I've referred to as a cultural vocabulary of the modern Western imagination, within which Wagner can be understood as simply one component of a plethora of consistent references to a repertoire of associations attending the representation of Hitler and National Socialism. The function of Wagnerian music is shared by a number of other signs pointing to the same thing, be they textual ("pure blood"), motivic ("night of the long knives"), iconographic ("fascist-overtoned armor"), cinematic (*Triumph des Willens*), or musical (the *Ring*). There are still some, of course, who bemoan the association of Wagner's works with Nazism as a regrettable and unfair distortion or aberration of his dramas, but in terms of our understanding of his place in the modern film, such concerns are beside the point. For it is in part through their association with this nefarious reception that, for some, Wagner's works constitute "Artworks of the Future," even though, ironically, that connection may have become so ubiquitous that it is no longer even apparent in the spectacles of the modern, cinematic arena.

NOTES

The epigraph is from a letter to Albert Niemann, Venice, January 25, 1859, in *Richard Wagner: Werke, Schriften und Briefe,* ed. Sven Friedrich (Berlin: Digitale Bibliothek, 2004), 14,340. My translation takes some poetic liberties with the original, which is more stilted and verbose—it is Wagner, after all.

1. Zimmer acknowledges Lisa Gerrard as co-composer of other passages from the score.

2. A good discussion of the institutional agendas of the Hollywood dream factory is Geoff Kane, *New Hollywood Cinema: An Introduction* (New York: Columbia University Press, 2002), 49–84, 178–223. For an excellent introduction to the portrayal of modern-day concerns within the Roman past, see Maria Wyke, *Projecting the Past: Ancient Rome, Cinema, and History* (New York: Routledge, 1997); see also *Imperial Projections: Ancient Rome in Modern Popular Culture,* ed. Sandra R. Joshel, Margaret Malamud, and Donald T. McGuire, Jr. (Baltimore, Md.: Johns Hopkins University Press, 2001).

3. Passages from the sources are usefully contained in an appendix to Martin M. Winkler, *Gladiator: Film and History* (Malden, Mass.: Blackwell, 2004), 175–204. According to Jon Solomon, Marcus Aurelius's "Meditations" also served as a source for some of the film's final text; see his "Gladiator from Screenplay to Screen," in Winkler, *Gladiator: Film and History,* 8. I base my identification of the film's machinations as beginning in A D 179 on remarks found in Allen M. Ward, "Gladiator in Historical Perspective," in Winkler, *Gladiator: Film and History,* 31. For reasons I cannot explain, Scott says that "[t]he film must take you into this [Roman] world, so that you become part of 175 A.D. [*sic*]." Ridley Scott, "Introduction," in *Gladiator: The Making of the Ridley Scott Epic* (New York: Newmarket Press, 2000), 9. For most of his reign, the Emperor's official title was Imperator Caesar Marcus Aurelius Commodus; on other official titles he acquired during this time, see Dietmar Kien-

ast, *Römische Kaisertabelle: Grundzüge einer römischen Kaiserchronologie*, 2nd ed. (Darmstadt: Wissenschaftliche Buchgesellschaft, 1996), 146–51; however, in the second draft of the original script (co-authored with John Logan), which differs from the text of the film, Commodus refers to himself as "Lucius Aelius Aurelius Commodus." This version of the screenplay is available online at http://www.hundland.com/scripts/Gladiator_SecondDraft.txt (accessed January 15, 2008).

4. This is spelled out more expansively in the second draft of the screenplay, only parts of which were ultimately used in the film (see. n. 3); see T. P. Wiseman, "Gladiator and the Myths of Rome," *History Today* 55, no. 4 (April 2005): 37–43.

5. On Wagner's concept of Rome, see my *Richard Wagner and the Anti-Semitic Imagination* (Lincoln: University of Nebraska Press, 1995, 2nd ed. 1997), 46–52.

6. I would like to express my gratitude to Leah Branstetter, of the College-Conservatory of Music, University of Cincinnati, and Jonathan Yaeger, of the Jacobs School of Music at Indiana University, for generating the music examples used in this essay. For this example, Ms. Branstetter transcribed the passage from the film's soundtrack, while remaining music examples are based on the published piano arrangement of the film score (see n. 7).

7. Andrew Drannon is one of the few critics to have made note of the reference to the Prelude to *Das Rheingold* in this passage; see his 2000 review of the film at http://scoresheet.tripod.com/Reviews/gladiator.html (accessed January 15, 2008). This passage is also referred to in a CD recording of the film music, and the piano transcription of this piece is part of a series of selections from the score. See *Gladiator: Music from the Motion Picture*, piano transcriptions by John Nicholas, ed. Milton Okun (New York: Cherry Lane, 2000), 16–20 (measures 34–39); *Gladiator: Music from the Motion Picture* (CD), U.S. Decca, ASIN B00004STPT, 2000.

8. On the musical signification of Siegfried's "Funeral March" see Robin Holloway, "Motif, Memory and Meaning in 'Twilight of the Gods,'" in Richard Wagner, *Twilight of the Gods/Götterdämmerung*, English National Opera and The Royal Opera Opera Guide Series 31, ed. Nicholas John (London: John Calder, 1985), 35–36; for an unorthodox, albeit intriguing Jungian analysis of the passage, see Robert Donnington, *Wagner's "Ring" and Its Symbols* (New York: St. Martin's Press, 1974), 255–57, 297; for an empathetic and stirring reading, see also Lawrence Kramer, *Opera and Modern Culture: Wagner and Strauss* (Berkeley: University of California Press, 2004), 79.

9. I wish to thank Jeongwon Joe for bringing to my attention the similarities between the two passages, and Jonathan Yaeger for helping me describe specific, technical details of the similarities.

10. References to the text of the film released to theaters are to *Gladiator: Extended Edition* (3-DVD Video), DreamWorks Pictures, ISBN 1-4170-5778-5, 2005.

11. Some of the cinematic influences on *Gladiator* were, obviously, Mervyn LeRoy's *Quo Vadis*, William Wyler's *Ben-Hur*, Anthony Mann's *The Fall of the Roman Empire*, William Wyler's *Spartacus*, Bob Guccione's and Tinto Brass's *Caligula*, Joseph L. Mankiewicz's *Cleopatra*, and Federico Fellini's *Satyricon*, as well as many others; see Monica Silveira Cyrino, *Big Screen Rome* (Malden, Mass. Blackwell, 2005), 7–33, 59–158; Martin M. Winkler, "Gladiator and the Traditions of Historical Cinema," in Winkler, *Gladiator: Film and History*, 16–30; Solomon, "Gladiator from Screenplay to Screen," 9.

12. On the specific contours of Wagner's concept of heroism and the ramifications for its aesthetic representation, see Simon Williams, *Wagner and the Romantic Hero* (Cambridge: Cambridge University Press, 2004).

13. It bears at least mentioning that the film also contains some near quotations from the music of other classical composers, most notably Holst (the "Mars" music from *The Planets* in the opening battle scene) and Prokofiev. For pointing out the latter to me, I am indebted to Robynn Stilwell.

14. Lewis Mumford, *The City in History: Its Origins, Its Transformations, and Its Prospects* (New York: Harcourt, Brace and World, 1961), 230, cited in Winkler, "Gladiator and the Colosseum: Ambiguities of Spectacle," in Winkler, *Gladiator: Film and History*, 96, n. 30.

15. See Martin M. Winkler, "Star Wars and the Roman Empire," in *Classical Myth and Culture in the Cinema*, ed. Martin M. Winkler (Oxford: Oxford University Press, 2001), 272–90; Mary Henderson, *Star Wars: The Magic of Myth* (New York: Bantam, 2001), 144–47.

16. See Arthur J. Pomeroy, "The Vision of a Fascist Rome in Gladiator," in Winkler, *Gladiator: Film and History*, 114; Anthony Lane, "The Empire Strikes Back," *The New Yorker*, May 8, 2000, 125–26. Riefenstahl's 1936 filming of the Olympic games in Berlin, *Fest der Völker*, also constituted part of the repertoire of cinematic images from which Scott drew inspiration. On the games themselves, see Guy Walters, *Berlin Games: How the Nazis Stole the Olympic Dream* (New York: HarperCollins, 2006), 192–93, 199, 228–30, 267, 305–306, 314.

17. *Gladiator: The Making of the Ridley Scott Epic*, 120.

18. John Pattyson, "Gladiator: An Interview with Hans Zimmer," in *Gladiator: Music from the Motion Picture*, ed. Okun, unpaginated. In an interview contained in the bonus features on the 2-DVD release, Zimmer relates the same story verbatim, without however the final statement: "Hans Zimmer: Composing Gladiator," in *Gladiator* (Two-Disc Collector's Edition), U.S. Dreamworks Video, 2000, ASIN B00003CXE7, disc 2. For fear of digression and lack of space, I won't go into the problematic naïveté of the composer's statement that writing Wagnerian music makes one a fascist, but it's worth bearing in mind nonetheless.

19. On Hitler, the Wagner family, and Bayreuth, see (the largely apologetic) Brigitta Hamman, *Winifred Wagner, oder, Hitlers Bayreuth* (Munich: Piper, 2002); for an antidote, see Gottfried Wagner, *Twilight of the Wagners: The Unveiling of a Family's Legacy*, trans. Della Couling (New York: Picador, 1999). Literature on the association between Wagner and Nazism is, of course, legion. Among the more recent examples are George G. Windell, "Hitler, National Socialism, and Richard Wagner," in *Penetrating Wagner's Ring: An Anthology*, ed. John Louis DiGaetani (New York: Da Capo, 1991), 219–38; *Richard Wagner und das dritte Reich: Ein Schloss Elmau-Simposion*, ed. Saul Friedlander and Jörn Rüsen (Munich: Beck, 2000); and Joachim Köhler, *Wagner's Hitler: The Prophet and His Disciple*, trans. Ronald Taylor (Malden, Mass.: Blackwell, 2000).

20. August Kubizek, *Adolf Hitler, mein Jugendfreund* (Graz: L. Stocker, 1953), 140, 142. These events are discussed incisively in Berthold Hoeckner, "Wagner and the Origin of Evil," *The Opera Quarterly* 23, no. 2–3 (Spring–Summer 2007): 151–83.

21. Volker Losemann, "The Nazi Concept of Rome," in *Roman Presences: Receptions of Rome in European Culture, 1789–1945*, ed. Catharine Edwards (Cam-

bridge: Cambridge University Press, 1999), 221–35. See also Bettina Arnold, "'Arierdämmerung': Race and Archaeology in Nazi Germany," *World Archaeology* 38, no. 1 (March 2006): 8–31.

22. The classical study of the first part of this tradition is Walther Rehm, *Griechentum und Goethezeit: Geschichte eines Glaubens* (Leipzig: Dieterich'sche Verlagsbuchhandlung, 1936).

23. Albert Speer, *Inside the Third Reich: Memoirs,* trans. Richard and Clara Winston (New York: Macmillan, 1970), 152–58; see also Alex Scobie, *Hitler's State Architecture: The Impact of Classical Antiquity* (Philadelphia: Penn State University Press, 1990). For a wide-ranging reflection on Hitler's fascination with Rome, see Julia Hell, "Ruin Gazers: The Third Reich and the Re-Invention of an Imperial Imaginary," in *Ruins of Modernity,* ed. Julia Hell and Andreas Schoenle (Durham, N.C.: Duke University Press, forthcoming).

24. Speer, *Inside the Third Reich,* 153.

25. Dan van der Vat, *The Good Nazi: The Life and Lies of Albert Speer* (New York: Houghton Mifflin Co., 1997), 63.

26. Scott's commentary is found on *Gladiator: Extended Edition.*

27. "From the Cutting Room Floor," *Gladiator* (Two-Disc Collector's Edition), disc 2.

28. Walter Parkes, "Foreword," in *Gladiator: The Making of the Ridley Scott Epic,* 11.

29. See Friedemann Bedürftig, *Drittes Reich und zweiter Weltkrieg: Das Lexikon* (Munich: Piper, 2002), 485.

30. For an informative and insightful study of the use and omnipresence of Hitler in popular culture, and of the role sexuality plays in his portrayal, see Alvin Rosenfeld, *Imagining Hitler* (Bloomington: Indiana University Press, 1985).

31. In this respect Scott's and Zimmer's use of Wagner differs from the role of opera in other Hollywood blockbuster films from the recent past, in which the audience is intended to recognize the source of music as operatic, in order to mobilize a variety of associations attending the art form in the popular American imagination. See my "Why Does Hollywood Like Opera?" in *Between Opera and Cinema,* ed. Jeongwon Joe and Rose Theresa (New York: Routledge, 2002), 75–91.

32. That this is by no means a hard-and-fast rule is seen in the use of the "Ride of the Valkyries" in such movies as Fellini's *8½,* Wertmuller's *Seven Beauties,* Ken Russell's *Mahler,* and John Landis's *Blues Brothers,* in which the connection between Wagner and Nazism is either assumed to be understood or made explicit.

33. Lawrence Kramer, *Musical Meaning: Toward a Critical History* (Berkeley: University of California Press, 2002), 152–53.

TEN

Reading Wagner in *Bugs Bunny Nips the Nips* (1944)

NEIL LERNER

In its second minute the Hate rose to a frenzy. People
were leaping up and down in their places and shouting
at the tops of their voices in an effort to drown the
maddening bleating voice that came from the screen.

GEORGE ORWELL, *NINETEEN EIGHTY-FOUR*

I use Wagner. Scares the hell out of the slopes. My boys love it.

LIEUTENANT COLONEL BILL KILGORE, *APOCALYPSE NOW*

Can a Warner Brothers cartoon featuring a beloved cartoon character
like Bugs Bunny be seriously likened to a Two Minutes Hate? And if
a Hate had a musical accompaniment, would it sound anything like
Wagner? Both an Orwellian Hate and a cartoon like *Bugs Bunny Nips the
Nips* (directed by Friz Freleng, released in April 1944) have in common a
reliance on repetition as a rhetorical device, on a regularly recurring bar-
rage of ideas (often extreme and fictitious), images, and sounds designed
to sway mass opinion. In the case of *Bugs Bunny Nips the Nips,* Warner
Brothers' writers and animators caricatured and dehumanized the Japanese soldiers for a U.S. audience deep in war and not yet certain of what
would be their ultimate victory. The title of the cartoon, with its pun on

the word "nips"—the noun being the newly created and highly pejorative slang term in the United States for Japanese people, the verb meaning to pinch or bite—immediately signals an ostensibly comedic channeling of the collective rage that characterized so much of the national mood in the United States after the surprise attack on Pearl Harbor; the title also suggests that Bugs Bunny will do to the Japanese as the Japanese have done to others, and Bugs's sadism and cunning, normally reserved for purely fictional threats like Elmer Fudd, follow with that possibility. *Bugs Bunny Nips the Nips* includes within Carl Stalling's composite musical score two quotations from Wagner's music drama *Die Walküre*. Both of these brief quotations resonate subtly, if at all, without careful decoding, although the second of them offers an especially obscure reference that may connect the cartoon to an even more nationalistic tradition than is obvious from the surface level of dialogue and animation. When placed in the context of some of Stalling's other Wagner quotations (for instance, in his scores for the *Private Snafu* cartoons or in *Herr Meets Hare*), they provide further evidence of Stalling's sublime mastery of European concert hall and operatic traditions and the ways they can be employed in the service of comedic irony.

Daniel Goldmark begins an extended discussion of Wagner's music in Warner Brothers' cartoons in *Tunes for 'Toons: Music and the Hollywood Cartoon* (2005), drawing attention to Wagner's not infrequent appearances: from a study of Carl Stalling's cue sheets while at Warner Bros., Goldmark finds music from ten of Wagner's works appearing in 120 cartoons. Goldmark brings light to Stalling's propensity for employing Wagner in the service of satire, turning to Joseph Horowitz's study of Wagner's reception in the United States, and Goldmark proceeds to read the cartoon *What's Opera, Doc?* (1957) through a comparison with an earlier Warner Bros. cartoon obsessed with German culture, *Herr Meets Hare* (1945).[1] As Goldmark demonstrates, Stalling had both an encyclopedic knowledge of music (spanning popular and concert hall traditions) as well as a sometimes idiosyncratic sense of irony. Bearing Stalling's propensity for the occasionally opaque musical reference in mind, a close reading of the entire *Bugs Bunny Nips the Nips* and its score can venture towards some possible meanings that arise from the Wagner references. The cartoon indulges in numerous racist representations, some of which are amplified by the musical score and its intertextual connections to

Wagner, and at the same time, Stalling's use of the Wagner quotations injects further irony into this cartoon for those parts of the audience well versed in the world of Wagner's characters, stories, and melodies.

In her essay "Bugs and Daffy Go to War," Susan Elizabeth Dalton calls *Bugs Bunny Nips the Nips* "the most sadistic and unsettling of all the war cartoons."[2] After being adrift in the ocean, singing to himself, Bugs encounters a series of Japanese soldiers on a Pacific island, dispatching them with his characteristic wit, mischief, and cross-dressing, until he complains that with no more antagonists, he is confined to a world of "peace and quiet," which he hates. As a U.S. ship approaches and Bugs celebrates being rescued, a female bunny (feminine insofar as the bunny appears to be dressed as a female, for as both Bugs and Wagner force us to remember, outward appearances may not always be a true marker of interior gender identity) appears and ignites Bugs's passion. Howling and thumping his foot, with his eyes tumescently bulging from their sockets, Bugs leaps off in amorous pursuit as the cartoon ends.[3] Bugs's hyperbolic libido is but one marker of the exaggerated U.S./Japanese representations; Bugs the sexual aggressor, as seen at the end of the cartoon, parallels the penetrative role of the U.S. forces in the Pacific. Because of its anti-Japanese caricatures—the Japanese soldiers have exaggerated buck teeth, no shoes, and malevolent eyebrows, and Bugs refers to the Japanese soldiers as "Monkey Face" and "Slant Eyes"—the cartoon has been removed from formal commercial circulation, although it is rather easily available today via various internet sites.[4] W. Anthony Sheppard, in discussing anti-Japanese rhetoric in film music, observes that Hollywood largely ignored the Japanese until the U.S. involvement in World War II, at which point the U.S. film industry began to generate a large number of films offering negative depictions of the Japanese.[5] The period leading up to and including World War II saw a number of carefully constructed and widely distributed films of persuasion in many countries around the globe, as the relatively new medium of cinema gave governments and other political entities an efficient and efficacious means to communicate to the masses. Some of the most well-known examples include Germany's *Triumph of the Will* (*Triumph des Willens,* directed by Leni Riefenstahl, 1935) and *The Eternal Jew* (*Der Ewige Jude,* directed by Fritz Hippler, 1940), Britain's *Industrial Britain* (directed by Robert Flaherty, 1931/32) and *Night Mail* (directed by Harry Watt and Basil Wright, 1936), and the United States' *The Plow That Broke the Plains* (directed by Pare Lorentz, 1936) and *The River* (directed by Pare Lorentz, 1937).[6] These live action films fit within the parameters of Bill Nichols's expository mode; they also speak as part of a discourse of sobriety in which the wartime cartoons (as a medium associated with younger audiences) presumably do not engage, although the complexity of the Wagner references may argue for the need to allow for sober discourse even in supposedly banal forms of media.[7]

Carl Stalling's composite score for *Bugs Bunny Nips the Nips,* like most of his other scores for Warner Bros. cartoons, includes material borrowed from popular and concert hall traditions as well as his own original cues. The production file at the Warner Bros.' archive at the University of Southern California contains two cue sheets for this cartoon, one dated March 6, 1944, the other dated March 22, 1944. The earlier cue sheet refers to each of Stalling's cues as "Original A," "Original B," etc., and names for each of those are penciled in and then included on the later cue sheet (see table 10.1). Stalling turns several times to the pentatonic tune that since 1893 has served as Japan's national anthem, *Kimygayo,* using it in connection with various representations of the Japanese soldiers in the cartoon. Instead of using the United States' national anthem, other music—in particular, Wagner—performs the function of giving voice to a U.S. nationalistic message.

TABLE 10.1. Titles and Composers as Listed on the March 22, 1944, Cue Sheet

1. Merrily We Roll Along (Tobias-Mencher-Cantor)
2. Someone's Rocking My Dreamboat (Rene-Scott-Rene)
3. Adrift (Stalling)
4. Someone's Rocking My Dreamboat (Rene-Scott-Rene)
5. Trade Winds (Friend-Tobias)
6. William Tell Overture (Rossini, arr. Stalling)
7. Japs (Stalling)
8. Kimygayo (arr. Stalling)
9. Merrily We Roll Along (Tobias-Mencher-Cantor)
10. Honorable Bunny (Stalling)
11. Nipping the Nips (Stalling)
12. Kimygayo (arr. Stalling)
13. Happy Landing (Stalling)
14. Good Idea (Stalling)
15. The Magic Flute (Mozart, arr. Stalling)

16. Trade Winds (Friend-Tobias)
17. Die Walkure [*sic*] (Wagner, arr. Stalling)
18. Columbia the Gem of the Ocean (Shaw-Becket, arr. Stalling)
19. Die Walkure [*sic*] (Wagner, arr. Stalling)
20. Love Song of Kalua (Jerome)
21. The Island (Stalling)
22. Merrily We Roll Along (Tobias-Mencher-Cantor)

The cartoon opens with Bugs floating in a wooden crate "somewhere in the Pacific," singing his own version of the Ink Spots' song, "Someone's Rockin' My Dreamboat." The Ink Spots were one of the most popular African-American vocal groups during the 1940s, helping to pioneer the sound that would become known after World War II as doo-wop. Bugs's lyrics differ significantly from the words sung by the Ink Spots, as follows:

Bugs Bunny in *Bugs Bunny Nips the Nips:*

Someone's rockin' my dreamboat,
I'm captain without any crew,
We were sailing along, so peaceful and strong,
Suddenly something went wrong.
Someone's rockin' my dreamboat,
A rinky dinky . . .

Ink Spots:

Someone's rockin' my dreamboat,
Someone's invading my dream,
We were sailing along, so peaceful and calm,
Suddenly something went wrong.
Someone's rocking my dreamboat,
Disturbing the beautiful dream,
It's a mystery to me, this mutiny at sea,
Who can it be?

The third verse of the Ink Spots' song has the "captain without any crew" line, so what Bugs sings appears to be a composite of lines from several verses of the original. Particularly striking, though, is the change of "peaceful and calm" to "peaceful and strong." In this cartoon Bugs Bunny operates not just as an insouciant, wisecracking comic character, but also as a symbol of the entire U.S. military and democratic project. Indeed, the first buck-toothed and barefoot Japanese soldier that Bugs

FIG. 10.1. The Japanese soldier recognizes Bugs
as Bugs in an aside to the audience.

encounters quickly recognizes the disguised Bugs (despite the soldier's
myopia, as signaled by his glasses) as the character from Warner Bros.'
Merrie Melodies cartoons, speaking in broken English and reversing his
R's and L's in a manner clearly meant to ridicule: "That a Bugs Bunny.
I uh see in Warner Brother Reon Schresinger Merrie Melodie cartoon
picture. Oh, yes, he no fool me. Ahh, what ah up ah honorable doc"
(figure 10.1).

Paul Wells sees these cartoon characters as "bona fide cultural figures" whose symbolic identity "was well understood," explaining that
in these wartime cartoons, Bugs Bunny "was already established as a
character who would only respond when provoked, and then humiliate
always inferior opposition."[8] Bugs proceeds to win a series of battles
with Japanese soldiers, ranging from his beloved and frequent transvestism—Bugs briefly passes as a geisha to lull a large sumo wrestler
into a vulnerable position, hammering the Japanese giant on the head
as they puckered up for a kiss (perhaps the wrestler had time to think
"Das ist keine Frau!" before succumbing to Bugs's blow?)—to handing

FIG. 10.2. An angry Bugs Bunny complains about peace and quiet.

a parachuting Japanese soldier an anvil while proclaiming, with heavy irony given the United States's history of exporting scrap oil to Japan in the late 1930s, "Here's some scrap iron for Japan, Moto; happy landings."[9]

Stalling first borrows from the European operatic tradition in a sequence where Bugs attempts to conquer the numerous Japanese soldiers on the island by handing out ice cream bars with hand grenades hidden inside. Instead of Good Humor, the ice cream bars are labeled as Good Rumor, and Bugs drives an ice cream truck accompanied by Papageno's opening aria from Mozart's *Die Zauberflöte*, "Der Vogelfänger bin ich ja." (Stalling's instrumental arrangement of Mozart and Schikaneder's aria exploits its child-like innocence and sounds as though it were the ballyhoo music originating from the ice cream truck.) The (unheard) words in the aria reveal Papageno's knowledge and ability at bird-catching, a skill that finds a modern analogue in Bugs's devious technique of feeding enemy soldiers frozen, sugar-coated explosives; the intended comic effect of Bugs's weapons of mass destruction could resonate even more strongly to those aware of the extreme hunger experienced by

FIG. 10.3. Bugs tries to get the attention of the U.S. warship.

some Japanese soldiers. Sounds of off-screen explosions alert us to the efficacy of Bugs's ethnic cleansing program, and he ends the sequence in good humor, quipping cheerfully if not also chillingly that "business is boomin'."

After Bugs does away with all of the Japanese soldiers on the island—with each victory, he paints a Japanese flag on a palm tree—he finds himself in an unwanted "garden of Eden, so peaceful, so quiet," and he then declares, "and if there's one thing I can't stand, it's peace and quiet! Get me out of this place! I hate it!" (figure 10.2). At this point in the score, Stalling quotes a section from the famous first scene of the third act of *Die Walküre*, the "Ride of the Valkyries," that bit of now-hackneyed Wagner that made such memorable appearances in *Birth of a Nation* (directed by D. W. Griffith, 1915) and *Apocalypse Now* (directed by Francis Ford Coppola, 1979).[10]

Goldmark documents Stalling's tendency to respond with musical references in often literal ways to the visual material presented to him, even though at times, Stalling's quotations may be impenetrable to the casual viewer.[11] The music connects back to the role of Valkyries in taking fallen warriors up to Valhalla, although in this instance, the reference drips in irony—Bugs (and Warner Bros.) clearly did not view Japanese soldiers as honorable warriors worthy of an afterlife paradise. Yet another possible reason for quoting *Die Walküre* here may have to do with the fate of Brünnhilde, who, like Bugs on the island, finds herself trapped in a state of unwanted vulnerable isolation. As a U.S. ship approaches (accompanied by "Columbia, Gem of the Ocean"), Bugs waves a flag wildly to get its attention, shouting out, "A ship! I'm saved! I'm saved! Here I am. Hey, come and get me, here I am, I'm saved, hey, a ship, I'm saved, come and get me, here I am, hey. Hey, shake it up, step on it, what are you waiting for? You think I want to spend the rest of my life on this island?" (figure 10.3).

Brünnhilde: den   hehr - sten   Hel - den der   Welt   hegst du, o   Weib, - im   schir - men den   Schoß!

EX. 10.1. From *Die Walküre*, Act 3, Scene 1

Stalling accompanies those lines of dialogue with a brief passage (commonly known as the Tragic motif) from later in the same scene in *Die Walküre*, the moment when Brünnhilde tells Sieglinde of her pregnancy with Siegfried ("den hehrsten Helden der Welt hegst du, O Weib, im schirmenden Schoß"; "you have the noblest hero in the world, o woman, in your sheltering womb") (example 10.1).

Given his usual compositional habits, Stalling almost certainly had some reason for choosing that particular snippet of Wagner. Determining its significance, though, must rely on some speculation, for so far no primary materials have surfaced that would give definitive answers to these questions raised by specific quotations.

Stalling's cartoon scores possess an extremely tight coordination between the visual and musical gestures. Consider, for example, a brief twenty-three-second passage from the cue titled "Japs" (example 10.2). The initial descending melody and rising diminished seventh arpeggio hint at Bugs's diving and rising within the haystack in which he hides. The next melody serves, together with a clapping sound effect, to punctuate the act of the Japanese soldier's arm placing his hat on Bugs's head.

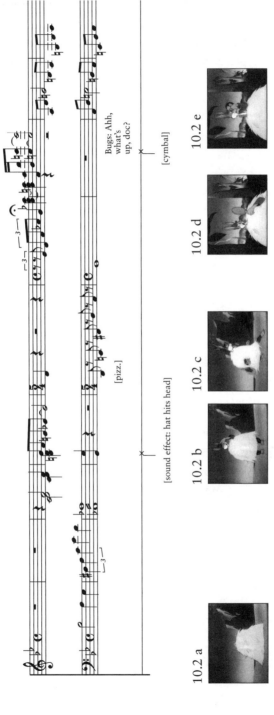

EX. 10.2. From "Japs" by Carl Stalling, transcribed by Neil Lerner

Then, as the legs of the Japanese soldier begin to tiptoe, the low strings play pizzicato notes with each step (Stalling was a master of the comic tiptoe effect). As Bugs and the soldier begin to realize they are sharing the same hiding place, and the arm of the soldier rises with a mirror, a D-diminished triad resolves to a D-minor triad; the tonal resolution mirrors the characters' growing realization of each other's presence. Finally, as the Japanese soldier comes into view, Stalling turns to several of the orientalist musical tropes available to him: a pentatonic melody in octaves, accompanied by a cymbal crash as Bugs and the soldier first gaze into each other's eyes.

With such close attention to matching music and image, what significance might come from the second Wagner quotation? Perhaps Stalling found the mention of Siegfried here compelling: Siegfried's very name (peace through victory) operates here with Bugs not as Teutonic myth nor as German nationalism; rather, it has been reappropriated in the context of U.S. nationalism, linking the victory of Bugs (symbolic of the United States) over the Japanese soldiers and the protection of the (U.S.) community through victory. Bugs—and the United States—shelter a coming peace with their victories, a peace that they will not allow to be nipped in the bud. Remembering Brünnhilde's isolation on the rocky mountain in *Siegfried* may provide an even more pointed connection between the moment of Bugs, trapped on the island, and the appearance of motifs from *Die Walküre* (Bugs and Brünnhilde are both characterized through their acts of disobedience).

That Wagner could be employed here in support of the Allies runs counter to what Goldmark finds in a later use of Wagner, including a similar form of the same motif from *Die Walküre,* in a Stalling cartoon score that appeared some eight months later. Discussing Freleng's 1945 *Herr Meets Hare,* a cartoon in which Bugs Bunny encounters Herrmann Göring in the Black Forest, Goldmark concludes "that the director clearly intended *all* of the German references as a comment against Hitler, the Nazis, and Germany as a whole, and Stalling clearly viewed Wagner as the suitable musical backdrop for such criticism."[12] In *Herr Meets* Hare, Bugs Bunny at one point imitates Hitler in order to confuse and assert control over the hapless Göring (this follows the earlier exchange in *Bugs Bunny Nips the Nips,* where Bugs imitates the Japanese general as a ruse to confuse the Japanese soldier), only Bugs-as-Hitler

FIG. 10.4. Image from Disney's *The Spirit of '43*, shown as the soundtrack plays the main motive from Beethoven's Fifth Symphony.

gets underscored by a similar Siegfried motif. Given the cartoon's strong anti-German sentiment, made overt through the ridiculing of Göring and Hitler, the use of Wagner in *Herr Meets Hare* simultaneously signifies Germany, high culture in general, and perhaps even Nazism, far different uses of Wagner than occur in the anti-Japanese cartoon, *Bugs Bunny Nips the Nips*.

Finding that Stalling more counter-intuitively used Wagner's music in support of the Allied side complicates Goldmark's conclusions. Stalling's use of Wagner in support of the United States falls within the same cultural logic that would allow the famous motive from Beethoven's Fifth Symphony, a musical icon firmly rooted in the Austro-Germanic tradition, to be appropriated by the Allied powers as a musical rallying cry: the rhythmic pattern of short-short-short long equals the letter "V" in Morse code, dot-dot-dot dash. (See figure 10.4 for an example of the "V for Victory" symbolism in a still from the Disney cartoon *The Spirit of '43* [1943]; that moment in the cartoon is accompanied by the Beethoven motive in the soundtrack.)

As Goldmark states, "[W]e can read Stalling's musical choices as his attempts to work with the cultural references the cartoons made."[13] The cultural choices here support what John W. Dower concludes about the U.S. racism directed against the Japanese during the war, a racializing of the enemy that was not duplicated when it came to European foes: namely, Stalling's use of Wagner in *Bugs Bunny Nips the Nips*, despite its heavy Germanic connotations, still fit within the larger project of dehumanizing the Japanese, which is not to forget that the Japanese had their own dehumanizing agenda when it came to the United States, a point that Dower argues.[14]

One paradox about these animated Japanese is their apparent mortality in the world of the cartoon. Even though the first soldier appears to survive bomb explosions, the rest of the Japanese soldiers succumb to Bugs's acts of violence. Normally, the rules of violence in Warner Bros.' cartoons permitted the constant revival of the characters; their reincarnations balanced out the violence. As Richard Thompson concludes at the end of his widely anthologized essay "Meep-Meep!":

> [W]hat is at issue in the Road Runner and other cartoons is not that rebirth occurs, but why it occurs. Not that death per se is a possibility in cartoons—although terminal catastrophe is a staple, for finishing sequences—but that resurrection at the bottom of every cartoon cycle exists solely and cynically so that the victim can proceed to his next debacle. More absolutely than zombies, vampires, and the undead are cartoon characters denied the solace of eternal rest.[15]

The caricatured Japanese soldiers may not appear again in Warner Bros.' cartoons after World War II, but the technique of dehumanizing the enemy as part of a government's war strategies does. We expect that Bugs cannot really be killed in a cartoon (even in *What's Opera, Doc?*, his death gets mitigated at the end by his final address to the audience), but what about the Japanese soldiers whom Bugs dispatches with such ease? In certain ways, these cinematic antagonists have the possibility and ability to return in their own way (like Alberich, whose death is not confirmed at the end of the *Ring*). For instance, a more recent cartoon that aired on *Saturday Night Live* ridiculed *Bugs Bunny Nips the Nips* and the parts of the U.S. populace swept along in the Bush administration's "war on terror" in the context of a more recent U.S. attempt to achieve peace through victory: the U.S. invasion of Iraq on March 20, 2003. On March 18, 2003, one of Robert Smigel's cartoon shorts (called "T.V. Funhouse") featured what Smigel calls the X-Presidents in an episode called "Iraq 2003."[16] In it, an animated Ronald Reagan complains about the lack of U.S. enthusiasm for the impending war in Iraq, and he snorts to an animated Jimmy Carter that "in my day, we had instructional cartoons to help people appreciate war." The cartoon within a cartoon that follows shows Bugs in the same Pacific island setting as we see in *Bugs Bunny Nips the Nips*. Bugs paints a toothbrush on a large missile, as a Japanese soldier with exaggeratedly huge buckteeth comes into the frame, gibbering nonsense (as the Japanese soldier in *Bugs Bunny Nips the Nips* also jabbered). Bugs says to the Japanese soldier, "Ahh, better brush, bow-legs," and the soldier starts to rub the missile over his mouth. Bugs holds up a sign that reads "Sirry, isn't he?" and then the soldier swallows the bomb, at which point Bugs takes his now missile-shaped body and uses it like a garden implement, with the buck teeth digging into the ground. As Bugs then waves a U.S. flag and the music switches to a rousing version of "You're in the Army Now," a skunk comes out, sees the Japanese soldier, and then puts a clothes pin on its nose while saying "pee-yew!" The cartoon within a cartoon ends with animated ex-presidents Reagan, Bush, Sr., and Ford laughing as Carter looks in disbelief. "Funny stuff," the animated representation of Reagan concludes, "it makes you laugh and hate." Does the fact that by 2003 there are those who can parody cartoons like *Bugs Bunny Nips the Nips* indicate any maturing as a culture? Or perhaps, just as in 1944, do we still have cartoon texts that some in the audience will read as ironic political demonology while others will be swept along in the laughing and the hating?

NOTES

In memory of Sgt. Leonard Lerner, U.S. Army Air Corps, 1943–45.

The first chapter epigraph is from Geroge Orwell, *Nineteen Eighty-Four* (New York: Harcourt Brace and World, 1949), 15. The second epigraph is from *Apocalypse Now* (dir. Francis Ford Coppola, 1979).

1. See especially pages 140–42 in Daniel Goldmark, *Tunes for 'Toons: Music and the Hollywood Cartoon* (Berkeley: University of California Press, 2005).

2. Susan Elizabeth Dalton, "Bugs and Daffy Go to War," in *The American Animated Cartoon: A Critical Anthology*, ed. Danny Peary and Gerald Peary (New York: Dutton, 1980), 161.

3. The Private Snafu cartoon *Operation SNAFU* (1945, and directed, like *Bugs Bunny Nips the Nips*, by Freleng) features a similar foot-thumping gesture, as a Japanese general demonstrates his attraction to Private Snafu in his disguise as a geisha.

4. Leonard Maltin determines that "subtlety was never the aim of these endeavors," referring to *Bugs Bunny Nips the Nips*'s dehumanizing characterizations; see *Of Mice and Magic: A History of American Animated Cartoons* (New York:

Plume, 1980), 250–51. Kevin S. Sandler discusses the "mobilization and policing of memory of Looney Tunes characters and cartoons" (9) in his introduction to *Reading the Rabbit: Explorations in Warner Bros. Animation* (New Brunswick: Rutgers University Press, 1998); he describes how "a single complaint about [*Bugs Bunny Nips the Nips's*] racial insensitivity from the Japanese-American Citizens League prompted its removal from store shelves" (9–10).

5. W. Anthony Sheppard, "An Exotic Enemy: Anti-Japanese Musical Propaganda in World War II Hollywood," *Journal of the American Musicological Society* 54, no. 2 (Summer 2001): 307.

6. For more on the use of music in these U.S. documentary films, see Neil Lerner, "The Classical Documentary Score in American Films of Persuasion: Contexts and Case Studies, 1936–1945" (Ph.D. diss., Duke University, 1997).

7. Bill Nichols, *Representing Reality: Issues and Concepts in Documentary* (Bloomington: Indiana University Press, 1991), 34–38.

8. Paul Wells, *Animation and America* (Edinburgh: Edinburgh University Press, 2002), 161.

9. Kevin S. Sandler discusses Bugs's fairly common transvestism in "Gender Evasion: Bugs Bunny in Drag," in *Reading the Rabbit*, 154–71.

10. Ulrich Müller has observed that "Wagner's music has been used up to the most recent times to represent national socialism" and also that "original excerpts from Wagner's music dramas have also been used for other expressive purposes such as indicating passion, secrets, battle and struggle, and so on." See "Wagner in Literature and Film" in the *Wagner Handbook*, ed. Ulrich Müller and Peter Wapnewski, translation ed. John Deathridge (Cambridge, Mass.: Harvard University Press, 1992), 388.

11. For instance, Goldmark quotes Chuck Jones's complaints that Stalling would sometimes be overly literal: "If there was a lady dressed in red, he'd always play 'The Lady in Red.' If somebody went into a cave, he'd play 'Fingal's Cave.'" See Goldmark, *Tunes for 'Toons*, 22. Also, Stalling had earlier turned to Wagner's music in his work for the Private Snafu cartoons. For example, Stalling quotes bits of *Rienzi* in both *Spies* (directed by Chuck Jones, 1943) and *Snafuperman* (directed by Friz Freleng, 1944). Both instances use the Wagner quotations to reinforce that we are seeing German submarines (in the case of *Spies*) or German bombs falling from the sky (in the case of *Snafuperman*).

12. Goldmark, *Tunes for 'Toons*, 145.

13. Ibid., 43.

14. John W. Dower, *War without Mercy: Race and Power in the Pacific War* (New York: Pantheon Books, 1986), especially pages 77–93.

15. The essay, which first appeared in 1976 in *Film Comment*, also appears in *The American Animated Cartoon: A Critical Anthology*, ed. Danny Peary and Gerald Peary (New York: Dutton, 1980), 225.

16. Occasionally this cartoon appears on sites such as YouTube before being thrust down the memory hole (to borrow Orwell's phrase).

ELEVEN

Piercing Wagner:
The *Ring* in *Golden Earrings*

SCOTT D. PAULIN

When Paramount Pictures released *Golden Earrings* late in 1947, the studio's publicity for the film promised "Gypsy kisses," intimate moments like the one illustrated in a print advertisement depicting the stars in ruddy makeup and "Gypsy" costume, Marlene Dietrich intently pinning a vaguely reluctant Ray Milland to the ground.[1] Revealing Milland's appearance to be plot-driven camouflage, the movie's promotional trailer tells of "a man from the civilized, conventional world, on a secret mission that plunges him into the primitive, passionate life of a Gypsy caravan."[2] What Paramount strategically failed to mention was that the "heart-pounding adventures" also promised by the advertisement are set against the recent war in Europe, and that Milland's mission is one of anti-Nazi espionage.

This omission was well-advised, considering some of the comments submitted by the movie's advance-screening audiences: "Not so much of the Nazis. I'm weary of the swastika"; "The war is over you know. Don't remind us too much."[3] By 1947, attitudes such as these had brought Hollywood's production of war-related films to its lowest ebb, their number sliding deep into single digits from an annual peak of over one hundred.[4] Downplaying the film's setting may have helped at the box office, but once spectators were in their seats, the approach to depicting the erstwhile Nazi menace must have been appealing. Unlike the espionage films of the early 1940s, *Golden Earrings* unfolds from the safe remove of victory, allowing a lighter, less urgent tone. Whatever threat the Nazis present within the narrative, their final fate is known, and the film's structure is reassuring: at least one of the protagonists has lived to narrate a flashback.

Music, like other elements of the film's promotion, put a calculated spin on the product. A recording of Victor Young's title song, performed by Peggy Lee, became a best-seller in advance of the film's release.[5] With lusty lyrics (even after being toned down to satisfy the Production Code office)[6] and an exotically coded sound, this song promised filmgoers a sensual experience, a selling point also noted in the ad campaign, in which the "Gypsy kisses" are echoed by "Gypsy music! A man would have to be more than human to resist the mad enchantment of wild tempos that set the blood afire!" In orchestral form, the song's melody plays over the movie's opening credits, and Young continues to plug it relentlessly, alongside other "Gypsy" melodies both borrowed and invented.[7] When a musical contrast arrives, as the credits fade into images of London, it takes the form of "British Grenadiers," a centuries-old military marching song and a default musical symbol for Britain in 1940s war films. This tune recurs throughout the score, but even on its first statement, Young presents a stoically reserved version of the usually jaunty melody, a meaningful variant of an original too familiar to require exact citation. The score thus sets up "Gypsy" music versus "British," precisely aligned with the mismatched romantic couple of the ads: sexy Gypsy meets uptight Englishman. But the soundtrack holds another element in reserve until music blasts forth from a Nazi radio, destabilizing the Gypsy/British binary with a third reference point: Richard Wagner.

This choice will seem predictable, even clichéd, as Carolyn Abbate has suggested of the cinematic use of Wagner's music "in ways that assume fascism, racism, menace, or simple, loathsome *Deutschtum* (bad Germanness *per se*) as default symbolism."[8] An association with Nazi Germany may be one of the most familiar points of intersection between Wagner and cinema, at least in the realm of soundtrack quotations and allusions. The intersection was real enough: Hollywood films of the 1940s did cite Wagner to signify Nazi Germany, if not on the level of convention that mandated musical references to "Deutschland über alles" (or, for France, "La Marseillaise").[9] But the history of this symbolism is not self-evident, and an investigation into its background will clarify the musical discourse of *Golden Earrings,* demonstrating that Young's use of Wagner is not the cliché it might seem, but rather a revisionist challenge to that cliché. Films since the 1940s have continued to score the Nazis with Wagner, but my focus leads strictly toward and through World War II; wrapping up a cycle of war-film production, 1947 marks a meaningful endpoint. An interpretation of Wagner's presence in *Golden Earrings* will follow this excursus.

MARCHES, MOTIFS, MEANINGS

The cinematic connection between Wagner and "loathsome *Deutschtum*" actually pre-dates the rise of National Socialism by many years, and it was forged through a composition ancillary to Wagner's own: the "Nibelungen-Marsch" of Bayreuth bandmaster Gottfried Sonntag (1846–1921).[10] Although it sounds like a pastiche of *Ring* leitmotifs, Sonntag's march is actually one step further removed from Wagner's scores, being based on the fanfares still used at Bayreuth to call audiences into the Festspielhaus before each act of the music dramas.[11] These fanfares reference the Donner, Sword, and Valhalla motifs, along with Siegfried's Horn Call, but most important, because most often cinematically employed, is the first strain of the march's trio, based on the Siegfried motif introduced by Brünnhilde in Act 3 of *Die Walküre*. Sonntag harmonizes this motif differently from the majority of its *Ring* appearances. The melody implies C minor, but Wagner (in the first instance) flirts with C major for a measure before making a swerve; Sonntag, working from the monophonic fanfare, dwells in C minor from the first downbeat. Both eventually reach an E-♭ major cadence, but Sonntag requires a second, consequent phrase to do so. This lingering away from the heroic tonic major may be a key to the grim images Sonntag's arrangement has sometimes supported.[12]

Anglicized as "Nibelungen March," Sonntag's potpourri found its way into American film accompaniment by the mid-1910s, appearing on silent-era cue sheets (where it is credited to Wagner, not to Sonntag) through the late 1920s. Aside from the ubiquitous *Lohengrin* "Wedding March," it is the most frequently demanded "Wagner" cue in these documents; in most cases the compiler specifically calls for the trio's Siegfried strain.[13] Other Wagner cues were assigned predictable functions—the *Fliegender Holländer* Overture for storm scenes, the "Magic Fire Music" for blazes—but the "Nibelungen March" was used to signify "Germanness" itself, a convention corroborated by Erno Rapée's *Encyclopedia of Music for Pictures,* where the category "German" includes "March Nibelungen."[14]

But this march was a malleable symbol; cue sheets reveal it being played both for *really* bad Germans and for comically bad ones. Among serious examples, *The Lone Wolf* (1917) synchs the march's trio to "The Headquarters of the German Spy System," *The Lost Battalion* (1919) to a shot of "German Officer at Desk"; *The Enemy* (1927) repeats it four times to represent the music of parading German troops. In *Lily of the Dust* (1924), it follows the film's pompous German villain as the "Colonel Theme." But the march also crops up in comedies like *Scrambled Wives* (1921) and, most tellingly, for satirical purposes in war farces, including *Lost at the Front* (1927) and *Buck Privates* (1928).[15] Whichever valence a film gave to the trio strain from Sonntag's march, a distorting mirror was held up to the German self-image, converting hero into menace or buffoon, and Sonntag's puffed-up arrangement lends itself easily to puncturing.

But in Germany itself, the "Nibelungen-Marsch" was taken very seriously in the 1930s, pressed into official service that left a mark on Hollywood's Wagner–Nazi equation. On December 8, 1936, the Propaganda Ministry restricted outdoor performances of the march to official Nazi events; in July 1937, another order mandated its performance at Nazi rallies.[16] Even before these orders, the march was performed in its entirety at the closing ceremonies of the 1934 Nürnberg rally, as documented in Leni Riefenstahl's *Triumph des Willens* (1935).[17]

Beyond the "Nibelungen-Marsch," the National Socialist media economy charged other music by Wagner with specific duties and meanings: the *Rienzi* overture for the opening ceremonies of *Parteitage,* Siegfried's forging song on the radio for Hitler's birthdays, Siegfried's "Funeral March" for memorials, the "Ride of the Valkyries" in newsreels reporting on Nazi air strikes.[18] These examples suggest how necessary it is to listen beyond the feature film in order to understand Wagner's place on soundtracks of this era, whether German or American; newsreels, documentaries, propaganda films, cartoons, and trailers all contribute to the context, as do other acoustic media, especially radio. One American instance of the latter is *The March of Time,* a long-running weekly radio broadcast (and theatrical newsreel series) that repeatedly dramatized mounting European tensions in the 1930s with Wagner's music.[19]

Whereas *The March of Time* took Wagner directly from his scores without re-composing him to sound uglier or more violent, a more militant musical attitude was enunciated in the *Why We Fight* propaganda series, created under the direction of Frank Capra and the sponsorship of the U.S. military. Constructed largely by excerpting and juxtaposing bits of newsreels and Axis propaganda films, adding narration and musical support to deconstruct the images, Capra's strategy for articulating the Allied position has been described as "re-present[ing] *Triumph of the Will* to an American mass audience."[20] The scores of these films "re-present" Wagner in a similar way. Analyzing the series' first installment, *Prelude to War* (1943), W. Anthony Sheppard notices that the Siegfried motif is labeled in the film's score as "Nibelungen March" and followed in quick succession by Italian and Japanese references, "suggesting that these national musics are equivalently dangerous."[21] But the "danger" of this Wagner fragment derives precisely from its mediation through Sonntag's march, as explicitly acknowledged in the score, and the Nazi appropriation of that march, of which Capra and series music director Alfred Newman were surely aware from Riefenstahl's film. This is a key to the function of Wagner in anti-Nazi film: in propaganda as in feature films, the Wagner repertoire choices replicated those made by the Nazis in their own propaganda. The effect was to challenge the Nazis in their own musical language: to undermine the meanings that German propaganda assigned to kernels of Wagner by reinterpreting that music in contrary terms.

As heard in *Prelude to War* and throughout the *Why We Fight* series,[22] the "Nibelungen" theme is a direct quote neither from Wagner nor Sonntag; rather, the motif is distorted, most often as a sinister, trudging march, a visceral sonic representation of what "we" fight against. When it appears in later U.S. propaganda films such as *Your Job in Germany* (1945) and *The Fighting First* (1945), this theme has accrued a great deal of meaning, actively created through years of use and re-use by propaganda-makers on both sides; not just any *Ring* leitmotif would do, although others might be cited in passing.[23] As a leitmotif signifying Nazism, it had migrated across many individual films; by 1945, audiences had been carefully taught how to interpret this music, whether or not they recognized its Wagnerian origin.

From propaganda shorts to wartime feature films is no great leap; the latter, too, were laden with propaganda, often with scarcely more subtlety.[24] But in feature-film soundtracks, Wagner's intersection with Nazism was managed according to different constraints. One point worth reiterating is that Wagner allusions remained the exception rather than the rule. It is possible to watch Nazis spying and slaughtering their way through dozens of 1940s dramas without hearing a single note of Wagner. Also, compared to the ceaselessly underscored propaganda films, virtually all Hollywood features are relatively sparing in their use of music. Here, Wagner's music is cited only upon carefully chosen occasions, and its presence is emphatically marked.

Typically, Wagner appears within the diegesis, and as in propaganda films, the references tend to be chosen from the Wagner excerpts already appropriated for Nazi propaganda.[25] The Siegfried motif, often in "Nibelungen March" form, remained the key musical reference. In *Arise, My Love* (1940), occupying Germans play Sonntag's march in the streets of Paris, beginning with the trio.[26] Heard through an open window but never seen, the marching band conveys the city's status as conquered territory in strictly acoustic terms. As if directly commenting on this scenario, the British film *In Which We Serve* (1942) sets a flashback in a movie theater. When a newsreel titled "Hitler in Paris" begins, the trio from the "Nibelungen March" is its soundtrack, serving again as the acoustic evidence of occupation. "He's got France now," says a sailor in the audience, "and France is only twenty miles from England."

Other musical selections work in similar ways. In *Reunion in France* (1942), diegetic Wagner again travels with the Germans, alerting listeners both inside and outside the film to Nazi-occupied space. "Robert, isn't that the March from the *Meistersinger*?" asks Joan Crawford, horrified, identifying the music with disgust as "Hitler's favorite melody" just before entering a room decorated with massive swastikas. This strategy is even used for comic relief: in *Above Suspicion* (1943), set in post-*Anschluß* Austria, the protagonists are warned that the evening's orchestral concert will be terrible: "You know how the Germans love noise." This opinion is validated with a sudden edit to a cymbal crash, ushering in the deafening bombast of the *Rienzi* Overture (another of Hitler's known favorites). Undercutting the German claim to musicality, the joke shows unsubtle Nazi Wagnerism invading Austria's acoustic terrain.

Framing Wagner in diegetic space has more than one effect. With Wagner confined to the narrative world, his music acquires the objective quality of reportage. This quality sometimes applies even when the music is technically nondiegetic. In *Arise, My Love,* just prior to the scene described above, three seconds of a "Nibelungen March" arrangement link the Siegfried motif to a montage of newspaper headlines and soldiers' tramping feet. A brief, distorted appearance of the same motif occurs in Max Steiner's score for *Confessions of a Nazi Spy* (1939), also amidst a newspaper montage, with the headline "German Advance in France Aided by Nazi 5th Column." In both cases, the music poses as a direct translation of the "news." All of these examples hold Wagner at a safe remove, blocking his music from any more expressive entry into the nondiegetic score, a boundary that other musical symbols, even "Deutschland über alles," cross with ease. It seems as if film composers may have wished to avoid speaking *too* overtly in Wagner's voice.

Finally, Wagner allusions are punctual rather than recurring, unlike their reiterative use in propaganda. This is true of the diegetic instances, but even in *Edge of Darkness* (1943), where Franz Waxman allows the opening of Siegfried's "Funeral March" into his nondiegetic score, the allusion is confined to isolated moments, framing a Nazi commander's suicide in the face of defeat by the Norwegian resistance. The music announces death, but it borrows only the march's opening rhythmic figures and not its apotheosis; manufacturing no heroism, it leaves the German demise devoid of glory or redemption. Waxman's allusion first seems to promise elegy—precisely the role of the "Funeral March" on Nazi radio—but then pointedly refuses to deliver it.

GERMANS, GYPSIES, GRENADIERS

The fate of Wagner's music in *Golden Earrings* is more nuanced than one might expect from the pattern established above, and some background on the film is required before tracing it. Adapted from Yolanda Foldes's recent novel of the same name,[27] the film uses its titular earrings as a pretext for Milland's character, Colonel Ralph Denistoun, to explain his piercings to an observant journalist. Denistoun's narration flashes back to 1939, the eve of war, with he and Richard Byrd (Bruce Lester) going undercover to obtain a poison gas formula from the scientist Krosigk (Reinhard Schünzel), an Oxford classmate of Byrd's father. They immediately fall into Nazi hands, but soon escape and split up to travel inconspicuously. Denistoun has the more eventful trip, falling in with the Gypsy heroine Lydia, played for deliriously high camp by Dietrich. She feeds the Colonel fish stew, claims him as her (initially unwilling) lover, and transforms him so convincingly with body paint and earrings that German soldiers are soon approaching him to have their fortunes told. An interlude, when Lydia leads Denistoun to her caravan, provides an opportunity for music-making (with *basso profundo* Gypsy chief Zoltan [Murvyn Vye] performing the title song). Having arrived in the same vicinity, Byrd is killed, but Denistoun ultimately gets the formula and reaches the border with Lydia's help. The film's ending returns to 1946, as Lydia and Denistoun reunite and ride off, apparently into an itinerant Gypsy life together.

A box-office hit despite tepid reviews, *Golden Earrings* has eluded serious commentary, partly because director Mitchell Leisen, a top name at Paramount in the 1940s, has rarely been the object of critical study.[28] (Dietrich scholars, perennially fixated on her early-1930s collaborations with Josef von Sternberg, have also ignored the film.) Composer Victor Young, music director at Paramount for many years, falls into a similar category as Leisen: the respected professional who is seldom singled out for special attention.[29] Professionalism may have been Young's problem, for his style is often described as the very model of self-effacing classical scoring. Even a sympathetic discussion of Young concludes as much: "One is never aware of music as an intrusive element in his films."[30]

Yet there *are* moments of musical intrusiveness in *Golden Earrings,* and one of these, the incursion of Wagner into the film's acoustic space, has already been mentioned. Given the plot context—*Deutschtum* most foul—Wagner's arrival fits an established pattern. However, Young's choice of Wagner is strikingly unusual. Eventually, he does cite the customary Siegfried motif/"Nibelungen March" theme twice in passing.[31] But he relies most heavily on a different *Ring* motif. This one is also associated with Siegfried, arriving in the *Götterdämmerung* Prologue as a majestic rewriting of his horn call, and coordinated with Siegfried and Brünnhilde's post-connubial emergence from their cave. Following

Paramount's pressbook for the film, which includes a soundtrack listing, I will distinguish between the usual "'Siegfried' Theme" and the "Helden Motive from 'Die Gotterdammerung' [sic]," the latter of which is most significant for *Golden Earrings*.[32]

Emerging only in the tetralogy's final installment, this "Helden Motive" has a limited lifespan. After several statements in the *Götterdämmerung* Prologue, it is withheld until the apex of the Act 3 "Funeral March." It appears once more, preparing Gutrune's entrance in the following scene and undergoing its only significant affective variation: here it outlines C minor, moving to a C♯ diminished triad. In borrowing this motif for *Golden Earrings*, Young refrains from cribbing it directly from Wagner, even in its first intrusion via radio (example 11.1).[33] This presentation of the motif is very close to a version heard in the *Götterdämmerung* Prologue (connecting Brünnhilde's first vocal paragraph to Siegfried's). The rhythm, harmonies, and bass line are nearly identical to Wagner, but Young omits a beat from the first bar and adds a B♭ bass pedal in octaves. Young typically notates this motif in some variation of the shifting meters shown here, which have no precedent in Wagner. (The deviations suggest that the motif may have been transcribed from a recording or from memory rather than a score.) Both Wagner and Young avoid repeating the "Helden Motive" precisely in any one form. In *Götterdämmerung*, its mostly consistent contour and tone are played out over subtle variations in rhythm and shifts in the bass line. But in order to convey the harshly negative affect required by *Golden Earrings*, Young needs to go further in deforming these heroic major triads.

EX. 11.1. *Golden Earrings*, "In Hands of the Germans," mm. 40–43

As the latter point suggests, Young's treatment of Wagner is unusual in another respect: unlike the examples already discussed, *Golden Earrings* makes recurrent, varied, nondiegetic use of a borrowed leitmotif. In a word, he uses it leitmotivically, at least in the sense that Hollywood composers understood the term, which is well known to differ from Wagner's own motivic practice.[34] Whether or not it was Young's intent— though I strongly suspect that it was—Wagner functions here less as a reflexive signifier of Nazism than as a signified in his own right. In other words, the score takes a position on Wagner, which unexpectedly turns out to be a position on Wagner's behalf, advanced through the musical transformations and audiovisual combinations within which the borrowed "Helden Motive" functions.

The film's screenplay introduces Wagner as the English agents plot their escape, waiting for their captors to become absorbed in a Hitler radio address. Suddenly, the signal: "a ponderous Wagnerian March Number filters up through the floor."[35] The ensuing Hitler speech is identified by Milland's voiceover as a "broadcast from Munich," but this is acoustic sleight-of-hand, for Hitler's voice has been lifted directly from the soundtrack of *Triumph of the Will*, once again a source of material for anti-Nazi recycling. Taken from the closing ceremonies of the Nürnberg rallies, this is the speech preceded directly in *Triumph* by the parade of Nazi banners *and* by Sonntag's "Nibelungen March."[36] The *Golden Earrings* scenario suggests precise modeling on these events, directly invoking a well-known moment in the Nazi instrumentalization of Wagner. But in place of the "ponderous Wagnerian March," where recent practice would have defaulted to the "Nibelungen March" trio, Young turned instead to a *Ring* motif with no significant pattern of either pro- or anti-Nazi appropriation in the cinema, ponderous indeed but not a march at all.[37] *Golden Earrings* is typical of the wartime practice of treating Wagner as a sonic invader of narrative space, but whereas earlier films had stepped gingerly around Wagner, the nondiegetic score of *Golden Earrings* soon proves permeable to a Wagnerian invasion.

As it jostles with the score's "Gypsy" and "British" material, the leitmotif's distinctive triadic texture frequently disappears, leaving an ominous bass-register melody line, ambiguously lacking its harmonic cushion. Trombones, bassoon, and bass clarinet, solo or combined, provide its typical color; rarely does it return home to the horn section. The

"Short Bridge" cue, lasting only three measures, is the most succinct variation (example 11.2): As a Gestapo officer points to a map, the motif is altered to outline a diminished triad on G, ending on a diminished seventh chord. Through most of the film, the "Helden Motive" is predictably linked to "loathsome Germans," dramatically so when a German officer kicks Lydia ("Almost Caught: Part I"), and when Byrd, after being shot, is tortured with a cigarette lighter ("Byrd's Death"). Roughly at the film's midpoint, a Wagner-saturated cue titled "A Close Call" surveys virtually all of Young's variations: intensifying sequences, spectral string tremolos, diminished and half-diminished sonorities abruptly pulling the rug out from any stray major triad, and a dank stench of Wagner hanging in the air as the Gestapo car finally drives away.

EX. 11.2. *Golden Earrings,* "Short Bridge" (complete)

More than the expressive extremes of these cues, it is Young's sheer persistence in developing the leitmotif's semiotic potential that makes his score unusual and begins to suggest an agenda on the composer's part, one possibly shared with Leisen.[38] The presence of Wagner on this soundtrack is far in excess of the narrative's needs, because Wagner's role here is not strictly to serve narrative. *Golden Earrings* openly reflects upon the historical conjunction of Wagner and Nazism: from the moment the film first represents Wagner's use at Nazi hands, it calls attention to Wagner as a token of symbolic exchange. The score will ultimately wrench Wagner's music out of these economies of meaning, and propose that it can be returned, purified, to a "natural" state—an ideologically loaded goal, to be sure, in its own right.

This objective is audible in Young's score, specifically in relation to another of its themes, which in turn clarifies the grounds for his choice of the "Helden Motive." I refer again to "British Grenadiers," a sign for wartime Britishness in countless other feature films: announcing the British success at Dunkirk in *A Yank in the R.A.F.* (1941); signaling British aid to the French resistance in *Reunion in Paris* (1943) and to the Norwegian resistance in *Edge of Darkness* (1943); whistled by a passing milkman on the home front in *Mrs. Miniver* (1943). But Young's treatment of "British Grenadiers" in *Golden Earrings* is just as exceptional as his Wagner; not only is its jaunty nature initially replaced by inwardness, but its subsequent leitmotivic guises range from tragic, at the death of Byrd, to heroic, when the mission is accomplished.

This latter apotheosis of "British Grenadiers" hints at an essential relationship: pitch-wise, the melody is virtually identical to Wagner's "Helden Motive." But Young persistently hides this identity. Nowhere does he didactically transform one into the other, as Wagner does (to cite the textbook example) with the Ring and Valhalla motifs after Scene 1 of *Das Rheingold*. A tentative, miniature gesture along these lines does occur early in the film, in a fourteen-second cue titled "Heavies' Bridge" (example 11.3). Measures 1–3 state the opening of "British Grenadiers" in A major; measures 4–6 state the "Helden Motive" as a trombone solo, also outlining A major. "British Grenadiers" begins by descending a fourth while "Helden" ascends a fifth, in either case to E; the subsequent C♯ of "Helden" is extraneous to "British Grenadiers," but after this point the pitches do not differ. Young's restriction of the "Helden" theme to its first nine notes maximizes its resemblance to the first phrase of "British Grenadiers," which is similarly manipulated to isolate its opening, "Helden"-like notes as a unit, landing on and sustaining the eighth pitch instead of respecting the original's forward motion.

Even in "Heavies' Bridge," there are significant enough differences in pacing and harmonization that a relationship between the themes never quite reaches the aural surface. (Further obfuscating a connection that is blatant on the page, the "Helden" phrase underscores dialogue here.) Still, "British Grenadiers" directs a magnetic attraction toward Wagner over the course of the film, gradually drawing the "Helden Motive" into its own orbit and away from the Nazi signification that distorts its features and darkens its meaning. In a final synthesis, "Helden" having faded out of the score, "British Grenadiers" will take on, for the first time, the Wagner motif's heroic tone. This moment of assimilation, even beyond the existing thematic affinity, seems to grant absolution to Wagner's music in a relatively painless denazification process.

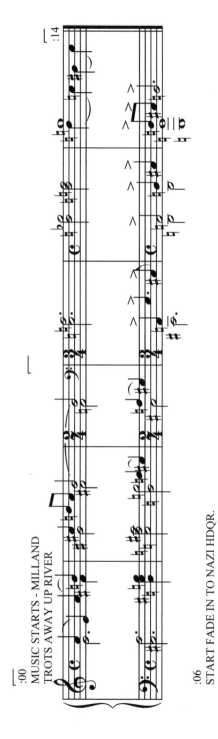

EX. 11.3. *Golden Earrings*, "Heavies' Bridge" (complete)

Locating a similar agenda in The *Great Dictator* (1940), Lawrence Kramer sees Charlie Chaplin's use of the *Lohengrin* Prelude as "a flat refusal to hand Wagner's music over to his [own] ideology."[39] Lutz Koepnick identifies other films that undertake revisionist appropriations of Wagner, including *Interrupted Melody* (1955), a biopic of soprano Marjorie Lawrence that challenges "Hollywood's essentializing view of Wagner as the dystopian archetype of decadence and destructiveness" by prescribing his music "as a cure that allows Lawrence to recuperate her body and voice."[40] But *Golden Earrings* has a more radical project than either of these films. *Interrupted Melody* confines Wagner to diegetic performances, and *The Great Dictator* to one culminating reprise after Chaplin's extended "globe ballet," but Young uses the nondiegetic score of *Golden Earrings* as a continuous engine for the leitmotivic resignifying of Wagner's music. Thus both Wagner's motifs *and* his techniques are put to work toward closing the hermeneutic cycle in which decades of politicized reception had left his music spinning. The last three appearances of the "Helden Motive" in Young's score are crucial for dramatizing this struggle over Wagner. In the second and third, Young's placement of the music supports a deliberate agenda on his part. But in the first, even more provocatively, it may have occurred by accident, as if the film were beginning the denazification proceedings of its own accord.

"Lydia Has a Plan," like the earlier "Heavies' Bridge," covers a segue from heroes to villains. Young's entire original cue is reproduced from the score as figure 11.1. In the fourth measure, a clear, triadic statement of the "Helden Motive" begins in B♭ major, to be coordinated with a "Start of diss[olve] to shot of [Gestapo officer] Reinman's hands." But the film's soundtrack fails to match the score. The solo "Gypsy" arabesques seen in measures 2–3 of this cue are omitted, displacing the "Helden Motive" relative to the intended images: its first two measures now face off directly with Lydia (figure 11.2), and the image fades to Reinman only as the cue itself fades out. This subtly destabilizes the motif's accrued significance, even if the moment passes quickly enough that the spectator may second-guess the combination of music and image that has occurred: Lydia, heroic within the film's narrative, momentarily acknowledged as such in Wagner's voice.

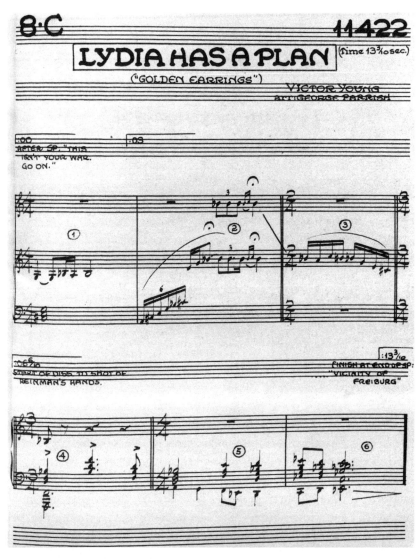

FIG. 11.1. *Golden Earrings,* "Lydia Has a Plan." Measures 2–3 are cut from the version heard in the film. Victor Young Collection, Robert D. Farber University Archives & Special Collections Department, Brandeis University.

FIG. 11.2. Lydia (Marlene Dietrich), accompanied
here by Wagner's "Helden Motive"

There is no obvious explanation for this change. If a cut in the music
became necessary for some reason, perhaps to agree with a belated cut
in the image-track, the decision of precisely *what* to cut may have been
up to Leisen, or someone else entirely, rather than Young. Technically,
the decision was wrong, as it places the thematic transition over images
other than what had been planned. This could be taken as an instance
of Adorno and Eisler's gripe—virtually contemporary with the release
of *Golden Earrings*—about the "special danger" of "arbitrary cuts" to
a film composer's work: "Such cuts are made with total disregard of
musical logic, and the composer's position in the industry is such that
his protestations have no chance of being heard, let alone heeded."[41]
But this audiovisual moment in *Golden Earrings* actually gives evidence
against Adorno and Eisler's anxiety that such conditions reduce music
to a distantly subsidiary role. Quite the opposite: whether intentionally
executed or a fortuitous accident, it is precisely this seemingly care-
less excision of two measures from Young's score that demonstrates

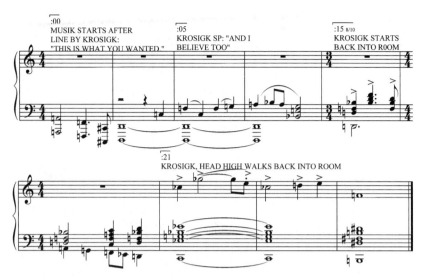

EX. 11.4. *Golden Earrings,* "Denistoun Gets Formula," mm. 1–9

music's potential power to reorient a film's semiotic economy. The film begins to dismantle the fallacious Nazi monopoly over Wagner when Lydia is granted equal claim to his music, a gesture made even more significant through this character's identification with a "race" to which Nazi ideology would prefer to deny any association with Wagner's music and the values attributed to it.[42] At this moment, intentionally or not, *Golden Earrings* begins to make good the rupture created by Wagner's instrumentalization.

There is no question of an accident at the second station of Wagner's passage out of Nazi hands. When Denistoun finally arrives at the home of "good German" Krosigk, the scientist proves wary of turning over the chemical formula, but when the Gestapo unwittingly inform him that Denistoun's far-fetched story is true, Krosigk has a change of heart. The cue "Denistoun Gets Formula" begins here, and the score (in agreement with the film) specifies careful synchronizations to dialogue and images (example 11.4). First: "Musik [*sic*] starts after line by Krosigk: 'This is what you wanted.'" Krosigk's speech continues, "for telling my fortune," as he passes a banknote on which the formula is inscribed. Krosigk's next line ("And I believe too") is also in the score, as the soundtrack offers a wistful "British Grenadiers" for Denistoun's exit. The "Helden Mo-

FIG. 11.3. Krosigk (Reinhard Schünzel), "head high," accompanied by Wagner

tive" follows immediately, in what may seem like another case of Wagner delimiting German space. But there is a substantial difference. The score makes it clear—and the filmed images even more clear—that the motif now attaches specifically to Krosigk, and this point is doubly reiterated. The motif enters, per the score, in full triads on B♭ when "Krosigk starts back into room"; sequenced up to an E♭ melody line, it repeats when "Krosigk, head high, walks back into room." "Bad Germans" are on the perimeter, but Krosigk is centered in the frame (figure 11.3), his moral victory as "good German" having contributed to Wagner's redemption.

The next and last appearance of the "Helden Motive" is also the most dramatically gratuitous, but as a gesture to complete the film's Wagnerian project, it is essential. It is also justified by geography, as the cue's title suggests: "Arrival at the Rhine." With Lydia and Denistoun on a hill overlooking the river (or rather, on a Paramount soundstage peering at a painted backdrop; figure 11.4), we hear the "Helden Motive" played in a manner unique within this film: softly, distantly (example 11.5). Perhaps Young's Wagnerian borrowings in *Golden Earrings* were motivated less by Nazi connotations than by this arrival, the target of

FIG. 11.4. Lydia and Denistoun (Ray Milland), arriving at the Rhine

a narrative orientation toward the *Ring* cycle's own point of origin and ending, the River Rhine. In the *Ring,* the Rhine Gold's return is required to rectify the age-old crime of its theft. *Golden Earrings,* too, casts a valuable but compromised object into those watery depths: Wagner's music itself. Could this renunciation release it from the bond to "loathsome *Deustchtum*," after years of use and abuse by Nazis and anti-Nazis alike?

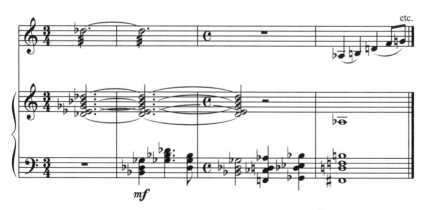

EX. 11.5. *Golden Earrings,* "Arrival at the Rhine," mm. 9–12

This would have been wishful thinking, if it was thought at all, for subsequent cinematic history has been more inclined to dwell upon Wagner's tainted past than to cleanse it, a decision difficult to begrudge considering the potent historical bond linking Wagner to this era of his reception. The juxtaposition of *Tannhäuser* and fascist-coded sadism in *Brute Force* (1947), the echoes of Valhalla amidst bombed-out Berlin in *The Young Lions* (1952), the decadent warbling of the "Liebestod" in *La caduta degli dei* (1969)—these, as Abbate has pointed out, are the rule: "default symbolism" for Wagner's music. As an alternative, consider a strategy closer in spirit to *Golden Earrings,* represented by films such as *The Stranger* (1946), *A Foreign Affair* (1948), and *Stalag 17* (1953). All are set during or just after the war, and the screenplay of each contains a potent speech or narrative moment in which Wagner is invoked. But none of them places a single note of Wagner on the soundtrack. This distinction is not negligible. When a film exploits a musical work for its pre-existing associations, it perpetuates and strengthens those associations; at the level of cliché, such associations may calcify into meanings that appear intrinsic to the musical sounds themselves. When we imagine Wagner's music as an icon inevitably linked to Nazism or even coterminous with it, we occlude the historically contingent means by which this music—and really only a few choice bits of it—came to function as a readily understood symbol within the representational economies of both Nazism and anti-Nazism. It is not my aim to protect Wagner from these vernacular hermeneutics, but I am struck by the latter group of films cited above and the objection they seem to raise. They activate powerful historical associations without asking Wagner's *music* to bear the uniquely weighty sonic semiotics of Nazism, a burden under which any musical sign cannot fail to collapse. To name the name and stop at that—to mute the music—may be a salutary act of reticence.[43]

Golden Earrings adopts a related attitude, and when Victor Young's score sinks the "Helden Motive" into the Rhine, the moment has an air of final leave-taking: a gentle Wagnerdämmerung. Alongside the denazification of Wagner, could this gesture also hint, as a collateral aim, at the de-Wagnerization of cinema? Here, the wishful thinking is doubtless my own, motivated by yet another urge: the de-Wagnerization of film music studies. I have contended elsewhere that Wagner's role in film music theory and practice has been a preeminently rhetorical, even fetishistic one, and my unease persists at this composer's resilient claim on centrality to scholarly narratives of music and film.[44] If my inquiry here has succeeded in specifying a narrow historical trajectory whereby the meanings of a handful of Wagner motifs became subject to a charged propagandistic debate, partially but not exclusively at the movies, I have perforce shortchanged the broader range of musical strategies pursued by this genre of films. Nevertheless, I maintain that Young's score for *Golden Earrings* rewards just this kind of close attention, and precisely because of the model it offers us: a model for how, after working through our issues with Richard Wagner, we might finally bid him farewell.

NOTES

For advice, feedback, and assistance of various kinds, I am grateful to Carolyn Abbate, Barbara Hall (Margaret Herrick Library, Academy of Motion Picture Arts and Sciences), Christopher Kim, Ryan Minor, Adeline Mueller, Sarah Shoemaker (Robert D. Farber University Archives and Special Collections Department, Brandeis University), Laura Tunbridge, and the editors of this volume.

1. One such full-page advertisement was placed in *Life*, October 13, 1947, 11.

2. The trailer is included with the film's DVD release. *Marlene Dietrich—The Glamour Collection*, Universal Studios, ASIN B000E6ESXK, 2006. I follow the screenplay's "Gypsy" nomenclature (rather than using a more historically sensitive designation), since the film is typical in representing a fictionalized "Gypsy" culture as "a figure of the European imagination," in Janet Lyon's words, "bearing little resemblance to—indeed, often obscuring—the historical lives and material conditions" of the Romani and other peoples on whom such representations are purportedly based. Lyon, "Gadže Modernism," *Modernism/Modernity* 11 (2004): 518. The language quoted from the trailer can trace its pedigree to a nineteenth- and early-twentieth-century construction of the "Gypsy" that had special durability in Britain as "an emblem of preindustrial nostalgia." Deborah Epstein Nord, *Gypsies and the British Imagination, 1807–1930* (New York: Columbia University Press, 2006), 60.

3. "Preview comments" collected on September 17, 1947. Paramount Pictures production records, Margaret Herrick Library, Academy of Motion Picture Arts and Sciences.

4. Chart of "American Produced Films by Year and War," in Russell Earl Shain, *An Analysis of Motion Pictures about War Released by the American Film Industry, 1930–1970* (New York: Arno Press, 1976), 31. Shain neglects *Golden Earrings*, but the pattern is clear even if his figures are not exact: a surge from thirty-two war films (addressing combat, espionage, and the home-front) in 1941 to 121 films in 1942, followed by a steady decline: 115, seventy-six, twenty-eight, thirteen, and two in successive years to 1947. A modest increase began in 1948.

5. Richard L. Coe's review in the *Washington Post*, December 4, 1947, notes: "Yes, this is the film which presents that current juke-box favorite, 'Golden Ear-

rings.'" The sheet music for this song featured the same illustration of Dietrich and Milland as the advertisement described above.

6. "The Hollywood Scene," *New York Times,* September 15, 1946.

7. The score's "Gypsy" elements are beyond the scope of this essay, but Young's "Gypsy" style draws on conventions with a significant nineteenth-century history. See Franz Liszt, *The Gypsy in Music* [1859], trans. Edwin Evans (London: New Temple Press, 1926); Jonathan Bellman, *The Style Hongrois in the Music of Western Europe* (Boston: Northeastern University Press, 1993).

8. Carolyn Abbate, "Wagner, Cinema, and Redemptive Glee," *Opera Quarterly* 21 (2006): 598.

9. Among many others, Adolph Deutsch's score for *All Through the Night* (1941) is heavily saturated with "Deutschland über alles," as Bronislau Kaper's music for *The Cross of Lorraine* (1943) is with "La Marseillaise."

10. A Carl Fischer edition was copyrighted in 1891, but the actual date of composition is unclear. A piano arrangement, subtitled "über Motive aus R. Wagners 'Ring des Nibelungen'," appears in *Das goldene Marschbuch: Beliebte Märsche aus alter und neuer Zeit für Klavier* (Mainz: Schott, 1953), 34–36. Herbert von Karajan recorded it with the Berlin Philharmonic Winds on *Preußische und Österreichische Märsche* (CD), Deutsche Grammophon, ASIN B000025I50), 1974, for which Johannes Schade's liner notes contain the only information on Sonntag I have found.

11. Another published arrangement indicates the march's origin in these fanfares. Preston Ware Orem, ed., *Opera Favorites for Piano Four Hands* (1913; repr. Mineola, N.Y.: Dover Publications, 2005), 46–49. A lithograph of the Bayreuth fanfares is reproduced in Hartmut Zelinsky, *Richard Wagner—ein deutsches Thema: Eine Dokumentation zur Wirkungsgeschichte Richard Wagners, 1876–1976* (Frankfurt am Main: Zweitausendeins, 1976), 24–25.

12. From Germany's defensive "Siegfried Line" in World War I to the German-American Bund's "Camp Siegfried" on Long Island in the 1930s, the name "Siegfried" itself acquired military and political associations that surely affected the reception history of this leitmotif.

13. My generalizations are based on roughly one thousand cue sheets in the Silent Film Music Collection and in the Collection of Thematic Music Cue Sheets for Silent Films, Performing Arts Special Collections, UCLA. Pieces by Wagner (including every stage work from *Rienzi* to *Parsifal,* but not counting the "Wedding March") appear on roughly 5 percent of these. Only the "Nibelungen March," with thirteen citations, approaches the status of cue-sheet standard.

14. Several of the cue sheets pre-date Rapée, suggesting a long-standing convention. Erno Rapée, *Encyclopedia of Music for Pictures* (1925; repr. New York: Arno Press, 1970), 226. For a chart summarizing Rapée's Wagner recommendations, see Christoph Henzel, "Wagner und die Filmmusik," *Acta Musicologica* 86 (2004): 108–109. Henzel misconstrues Rapée's listing of "March Nibelungen" as Siegfried's "Trauermarsch."

15. The cue sheets for all of these were compiled by James L. Bradford (the Cameo Music Service Corporation's most prolific employee by far) except for *The Enemy* (Ernst Luz) and *Lost at the Front* (Eugene Conte). Other cue sheets featuring the march include *A Regular Fellow* (1925), *Graustark* (1925), *The Great Deception*

(1926), and *Secret Orders* (1926). *The Man from Brodney's* (1923) atypically calls for the march's *opening* strain.

16. Joseph Wulf, *Musik im Dritten Reich: Eine Dokumentation* (Frankfurt: Verlag Ullstein, 1983), 134; Michael Meyer, *The Politics of Music in the Third Reich* (New York: Peter Lang, 1991), 105, 239, n. 34.

17. Commentary on the film often misidentifies this music, for example, as "Wagner's *Siegfried* motif" in "This Future is Entirely Ours—The Sound and Picture Outline for Leni Riefenstahl's *Triumph of the Will*," *Film Comment* 3 (1965): 16–22.

18. These examples are cited in Reinhold Brinkman, "Wagners Aktualität für den Nationalsozialismus: Fragmente einer Bestandsaufnahme," in *Richard Wagner im Dritten Reich*, ed. Saul Friedländer and Jörn Rüsen (München: C.H. Beck, 2000), 124–32; and Jens Malte Fischer, "Wagner-Interpretation im Dritten Reich: Musik und Szene zwischen Politisierung und Konstanspruch," in ibid., 145–46. See also Wulf, *Musik im Dritten Reich*, 248–49.

19. Many *March of Time* newsreels and radio broadcasts are accessible through Mary Wood, "The March toward War: The March of Time as Documentary and Propaganda" (2004), http://xroads.virginia.edu/~MA04/wood/mot/html/home_flash.htm (accessed November 23, 2007). Particularly rich with Wagner's music are "Hitler Sets the Stage for His Coup" (February 17, 1938) and "Hitler Takes Austria—Is Czechoslovakia Next?" (March 17, 1938).

20. Thomas Doherty, *Projections of War: Hollywood, American Culture, and World War II* (New York: Columbia University Press, 1993), 21–23. See also David Culbert, "'Why We Fight': Social Engineering for a Democratic Society at War," in *Film and Radio Propaganda in World War II*, ed. K. R. M. Short (Knoxville: University of Tennessee Press, 1983), 173–97.

21. W. Anthony Sheppard, "An Exotic Enemy: Anti-Japanese Musical Propaganda in World War II Hollywood," *Journal of the American Musicological Society* 54 (2001): 314–17.

22. The theme returns in *War Comes to America* and *Battle of Russia*. Other Wagner references are sporadic: *Divide and Conquer* and *Battle of Britain* cite the "Immolation Scene," and a *Fliegender Holländer* reference accompanies the Nazi invasion of Holland in *Divide and Conquer*.

23. On *Your Job in Germany*, see Sheppard, "An Exotic Enemy," 318.

24. Among the significant studies of war-era feature films, one of special relevance here is Jan-Christopher Horak, *Anti-Nazi-Filme: Der deutschsprachigen Emigration von Hollywood, 1939–1945* (Münster: MAkS, 1985).

25. This is also true of cartoons (especially Disney's): the "Ride of the Valkyries" in *Education for Death* (1943); the *Meistersinger* Prelude over the opening credits of *Der Führer's Face* (1942).

26. Like *Golden Earrings*, Paramount's *Arise, My Love* was scored by Victor Young, directed by Mitchell Leisen, and starred Ray Milland. This score identifies "Nibelungen (March)" as a public domain selection, arranged here by John Leipold. *Arise, My Love*, Victor Young Collection, Robert D. Farber University Archives and Special Collections Department, Brandeis University.

27. Yolanda Foldes, *Golden Earrings* (London: Robert Hale, 1945; New York: William Morrow and Company, 1946). The novel was optioned by Paramount prior

to publication, suggesting the perceived marquee value of its author (*née* Jolán Föl-des in Hungary), whose career had been established when *The Street of the Fishing Cat* sold over a million copies after winning the All Nations Prize Novel Competition in 1936. *Golden Earrings* was the first novel she published after emigrating (via Paris) to England, and its content may have been calculated to cater to Britain's longstanding "Gypsy lore" fascination, with Foldes playing the self-exoticized role of expert Hungarian witness on the topic. For a concise treatment of Foldes's literary context, see Lóránt Czigány, *The Oxford History of Hungarian Literature: From the Earliest Times to the Present* (Oxford: Clarendon Press, 1984), 378–79. The film departs from its source in countless ways, significant among which is the film's emphasis on the stereotype of Gypsy musicality, which is virtually absent from Foldes's book.

28. Leisen's *auteur* status is argued for by David Chierichetti, *Hollywood Director: The Career of Mitchell Leisen* (New York: Curtis Books, 1973); and David Melville, "Mitchell Leisen: Notes on an Exploding Star," *Senses of Cinema* (August 2005), http://www.sensesofcinema.com/contents/directors/05/leisen.html (accessed October 22, 2007).

29. The most detailed discussion of Young is William Darby and Jack Du Bois, *American Film Music: Major Composers, Techniques, Trends, 1915–1990* (Jefferson, N.C.: McFarland and Co., 1990), 267–302. See also Tony Thomas, *Music for the Movies* (South Brunswick: A. S. Barnes and Co., 1973), 43–48.

30. Darby and Du Bois, *American Film Music*, 301.

31. The cues "Dragging the River" and "Wake Up" quote this motif, in a form closer to the Wagner original than to Sonntag's march. Elsewhere, Young alludes ominously to the Fate motif from *Die Walküre*. All cue references are to the *Golden Earrings* score in the Victor Young Collection, Robert D. Farber University Archives and Special Collections Department, Brandeis University.

32. "Music," *Golden Earrings* pressbook, 2. Paramount Pictures press sheets, Margaret Herrick Library. Convention seems not to have settled on a single accepted label for this so-called "Helden Motive"; J. K. Holman considers it to be the "definitive" Siegfried motif, but also cites Ernest Newman's lable of "New Siegfried" and, from Robert Donnington, "Siegfried's heroic deeds as the ever-reborn spirit of youth." J. K. Holman, *Wagner's Ring: A Listener's Companion and Concordance* (Portland, Ore.: Amadeus Press, 1996), 156–57. Others refer to it as "Siegfrieds Heroenthema," following Hans von Wolzogen, *Thematischer Leitfaden durch die Musik zu Richard Wagners Festspiel "Der Ring des Nibelungen"* (Leipzig: Edwin Schloemp, 1876), 63–64. But Paramount's related label of "Helden Motive" must derive from its identification as the "Helden-Motiv Siegfrieds" in Lothar Windsperger, *Das Buch der Motive und Themen aus sämtlichen Opern und Musikdramen Richard Wagners* (Mainz: Schott & Co., 1921), vol. 2, 38.

33. Young's score is timed for twenty-six seconds of radio music, but the cue lasts only *five* seconds in the film, leaving unused a twelve-measure continuation based on other themes from the Siegfried-Brünnhilde duets.

34. Lawrence Morton observed that a "mere repetition of thematic bits," toward which cinematic practice tends, "does not make a film score Wagnerian, even if the composer thinks it does." While this sounds critical, it was meant as a defense against Adorno and Eisler's insistence that Hollywood film music debased Wag-

ner's technique, a comparison that Morton deemed misleading. Morton, "Hanns Eisler: Composer and Critic," *Hollywood Quarterly* 3 (Winter 1947–48): 210. Further distinctions have been drawn more recently: leitmotifs in film aspire neither to constitute large-scale form nor to be the primary carrier of filmic narration, according to Henzel, "Wagner und die Filmmusik," 101–102, 114; cinema forfeits the "mythic" function of the Wagnerian leitmotif, according to James Buhler, "*Star Wars*, Music, and Myth," in *Music and Cinema,* ed. James Buhler, Caryl Flinn, and David Neumeyer (Middleton, Conn.: Wesleyan University Press, 2000), 41–44.

35. *Golden Earrings,* Revised Final Script (July 20, 1946, with changes dated August 5, 1946), 10. Paramount Pictures scripts, Margaret Herrick Library. The screenplay is credited to Abraham Polonsky, Frank Butler, and Helen Deutsch, but Polonsky later denied that the released film included "a single word or scene" of his. William Pechter, "Abraham Polonsky and 'Force of Evil,'" *Film Quarterly* 15 (Spring 1962): 50.

36. Beginning from "Wir mussten als Partei in der Minorität bleiben." *Golden Earrings,* Release Dialogue Script (February 19, 1947), Reel 1A, pp. 9–10, and Reel 1B, pp. 1–2. Paramount Pictures scripts, Margaret Herrick Library. The film's later use of Liszt's *Les Préludes* is likely a similar gesture toward sonic authenticity, since this composition was used in Nazi Germany "to herald radio bulletins on the war in the east," precisely the role it plays here. Jonathan Carr, *The Wagner Clan: The Saga of Germany's Most Illustrious and Infamous Family* (New York: Atlantic Monthly Press, 2008), 177–78.

37. The only other appearance of this motif I have found in anti-Nazi film occurs in the Warner Bros. cartoon *Herr Meets Hare* (1945), where it is one among many Wagner references, heard as Bugs dons a Hitler mustache in order to outwit his German adversary.

38. Leisen is said to have possessed "complete understanding of all the major and minor aspects which make up a film . . . He knew exactly what he wanted in terms of costume design, art direction, sound recording and all the other elements of the cinematic crafts." His potential input on musical issues should not be underestimated. Chierichetti, *Hollywood Director,* 15.

39. Lawrence Kramer, "Contesting Wagner: The *Lohengrin* Prelude and Anti-anti-Semitism," *19th-Century Music* 25 (2001–2002): 205.

40. Lutz Koepnick, *The Dark Mirror: German Cinema Between Hitler and Hollywood* (Berkeley and Los Angeles: University of California Press, 2002), 247, 244.

41. Theodor Adorno and Hanns Eisler, *Composing for the Films* (1947; repr. London: Athlone Press, 1994), 111.

42. The Jewish composer Young, identifying as a member of another such "race," may well have had a vested interest in making precisely the kind of anti-essentialist moves that his score facilitates within the film. I would also argue that the marked excess of masquerade in Dietrich's performance critiques the "Gypsy" clichés in which her role is rooted; the film's heroine cannot be fully reconciled with the underlying stereotypes, and the vehemence with which she spits out the word *gadže* (non-Gypsy) when describing the hated Germans gives voice to a most unromantic acknowledgment of the historical plight of her character's people. Although the film has been criticized for its failure to acknowledge the Nazi genocide against the Roma and Sinti, Lydia does predict that "[o]ne day in thus accursed land

they will kill all of us." At the film's endpoint in 1946, we learn that Lydia has survived the war but no mention is made of the remainder of her caravan—an absence, combined with the persistence of their music (Zoltan's song, in instrumental form), that suggests something about the fate, unrepresentable in 1940s Hollywood, that her community would likely have suffered in reality.

43. On reticence as an aesthetic strategy, see Carolyn Abbate's forthcoming article "From Caligari to Operetta," which I am grateful for the permission to cite in advance of its publication.

44. Scott D. Paulin, "Richard Wagner and the Fantasy of Cinematic Unity: The Idea of the *Gesamtkunstwerk* in the History and Theory of Film Music," in *Music and Cinema,* 58–84.

PART FOUR

Wagner in German Cinema

TWELVE

Wagner as Leitmotif: The New German Cinema and Beyond

ROGER HILLMAN

Via the films of Alexander Kluge, Thomas Elsaesser pleads for a phenomenon which he calls "the Holocaust in West German cinema: absence as presence."[1] This notion demands a reassessment of much criticism of the New German Cinema. The claim that the New German Cinema did not completely sidestep the nadir of its nation's history, but that some of its directors treated that history in concealed form, is arresting (and sustainable too, I feel, for Edgar Reitz's *Heimat* trilogy [1984–2004], as I discuss in the last section of this essay). Also present in largely concealed form was Hitler, though this gap in the text remained in keeping with Nazi aesthetics.[2] The onscreen absence of Hitler, still ever present in the historical wings, implied as a corollary the absence from New German Cinema soundtracks of the figure appropriated by Nazi aesthetics, Richard Wagner.[3] A couple of major exceptions, to be explored below, prove the rule.

Wagner may be the cultural figure most resistant to transnational tendencies in identity politics, and to notions of world, or at least internationally nomadic, music. The hallowed counterpoint between Verdi and Wagner is worth recalling in relation to postwar identity politics in Italian and German films respectively. In the former case, Verdi bridged an unsustainable historical parallel between Italian Resistance in World War II and the Risorgimento.[4] This eliding function was underpinned by Verdi's credentials as an icon of democracy and a figure of the people, successfully blending artistic and public life. And Wagner? In the West Germany of the 1970s, Wagner seemed largely beyond redemption. Instead, film soundtrack references to the German musical tradition concentrated on the historically charged overtones of Beethoven's Ninth Symphony, in particular the "Ode to Joy," and a Haydn melody, better known by occupied Europe as the military band arrangement of "Deutschland, Deutschland über alles." Film soundtracks attempted to get beyond the recent patina of reception to restore these works' historical origins. No such attempt seemed feasible with Wagner, with the Promethean exception of Hans-Jürgen Syberberg's film discussed below, and a number of films by Werner Herzog, who in a sense disregards such debates.

SYBERBERG, *HITLER, EIN FILM AUS DEUTSCHLAND* (*HITLER, A FILM FROM GERMANY, A.K.A. OUR HITLER*) (1977)

This film is an idiosyncratic attempt to approach twentieth-century German history and cultural history via their common link in nineteenth-century Romantic nationalism.[5] Lasting over seven hours, the film avoids documentation, instead lending Hitler's features to a ventriloquist's puppets, even, drastically, to a dog-shaped puppet. The provocative alternate title in English, *Our Hitler,* foregrounds the uncomfortable link between him and us. Ventriloquism is the perfect dramatic means of suggesting the fulfillment of our desires. Against our wishes, we are plunged into audience identification with this Hitler, styled as a film from Germany.

The soundtrack uses music to interrogate the past. Wagner is contextualized alongside other composers from the Germanic canon: Mozart, Haydn, Beethoven, Liszt, Mahler. Wagner's domination tallies with expectations aroused by the film's title alone, a clichéd parallel that Syberberg challenges. The saturation of the film's soundtrack and its length suggest a dramatic kinship with the composer. But the film's balance diverges from that of opera in heavily favoring orchestral excerpts, which is characteristic of how Wagner's music is used in film (above all, as opposed to how Verdi's and Puccini's works are used).

The Bayreuth pit was unique among contemporary theaters in removing conductor and musicians from complete visibility. The lack of visual distraction for Wagner's audience compounds in Syberberg's film the standard effect of nondiegetic music, offscreen but directing our emotions, at the very least subliminally. This means we watch *Our Hitler* from the same viewing/listening situation as we would a Wagner opera, with a significant portion of the visuals accompanied by Wagner's music. Still more ambitious than Syberberg's assault on Hollywood as cultural agency is his attempt at the acoustic transformation of Hollywood into Bayreuth, the reclaiming of classical Hollywood's ideal of music being "invisible" to the spectator. Because Syberberg's Wagner is a non-vocal Wagner, it is as if we are watching his stagecraft enact the hidden orchestra—either sunk in the pit or offscreen—with its wash of Wagnerian sound. Apart from Alexander Kluge, none of the New German Cinema directors used classical music so expansively. Purely in terms of dramaturgy, Wagner functions here like the soundtrack of *Laura* (1944): there as here, the "theme" music continually evokes the absent title figure.

With Syberberg, the reduction of Wagner's Romantic aura by the tawdry attributes of Nazism becomes the real object of lament. While not an apologist for Hitler, Syberberg thereby aligns himself with a politically blighted nineteenth-century tradition. In his introduction to the script, he even links Wagner with Mozart as a common site of resistance to Hitler: "Hitler is to be fought, not with the statistics of Auschwitz or with sociological analyses of the Nazi economy, but with Richard Wagner and Mozart."[6] Music per se is viewed as legitimate irrationalism, the converse to Hitler's. Elsewhere Syberberg's Hitler figure, having emerged from the grave of Wagner, acknowledges the alien mold of the cosmic laughter of Mozart. This is a more realistic assessment of the ideological component of musical reception, and of course a Wagner opera, above all the Nordic myth-based *Ring,* is more "available" to ideology than a purely instrumental Mozart piano concerto.

In approaching the late–1970s identity crisis besetting (West) Germany and its filmmakers, Syberberg asks: "How is Hitler to be represented?" His chosen medium of film is closely allied to music. At the end of the opening credits, special thanks are given to Henri Langlois and the Cinémathèque Française, acknowledged as the spiritual progenitors of the film with the publication *Film—The Music of the Future.* The title evokes *Zukunftsmusik,* associated with Wagner and Liszt; film as latter-day *Gesamtkunstwerk,* a commonplace that for Syberberg functions as palimpsest, not effacement. As a re-creation of the Nazis' exploitation of the media for propaganda purposes, the soundtrack of *Our Hitler* frequently bombards the viewer with acoustic information, with art music examples but one element of a multi-strand soundtrack.

Early in the film, the circus barker lists representative highlights that are absent here because they belong to an "unrepeatable reality": "Stalingrad . . . the Twentieth of July plot . . . Riefenstahl's Nuremberg" (*Hitler*, 43). By implication we are instead to be offered repeatable reality, history primarily as myth, Wagner's Nuremberg, the leitmotifs of history. And yet of course this summary begs questions of representation, with Riefenstahl's Nuremberg no less artistically framed than Wagner's. Any historical unrepeatability of Riefenstahl's Nuremberg implies the uniqueness of her take on the city, both as art and as quasi-documentary. Nazi film had left Hitler as a mythical, and hence limitlessly allusive, gap in the text. Here the unrepresentable figure is reduced in stature, but not in chameleon quality, to Hitler-shaped puppets.

Syberberg's convergence of film and music relates the two as cultural history. His use of nineteenth-century music links with a view of music as an expression of the ineffable, while his film features the visual absence of the historical icon Hitler, a twentieth-century expression of the ineffable. The presence of often static-charged radio culminates in a famous broadcast of "Stille Nacht" on Christmas Eve 1942. Its rendition by German fighters from the uttermost reaches of the expanded Reich feigns a sovereignty that the imminent collapse of Stalingrad was to negate totally. By the end of Syberberg's film, the sentimental words "Sleep in heavenly peace" have been replaced by the death wish of the "Liebestod" from *Tristan und Isolde* (*Hitler*, 247).

The Wagner Syberberg is trying to rehabilitate is permeated with overtones of Nazi-directed reception, unavoidable in postwar German films. Among a host of Wagner quotations, *Our Hitler* avoids the more hackneyed "Hollywood" Wagner (of, say, "The Ride of the Valkyries" or the *Lohengrin* "Wedding March"). Instead the film opts for excerpts that have dramatic and textual significance (via the libretto they imply) for the whole opera or cycle, thereby reinvesting Wagner with musical value. Syberberg's editing of the soundtrack enabled a length of music excerpts which is rare in film. His handling of Wagner in particular is an acoustic equivalent of Wim Wenders's attempts to salvage images from the pace of Hollywood editing.[7] Wagner's original score remains more intact, less "chunked."[8] Music then functions less as a collage component and more as a primary source, a pro-filmic acoustic event.

At the same time as he confronts stereotypes of Wagner's kinship with Nazi excess, mythological obscurity, and anti-rationality, Syberberg uses Wagner as an iridescent weapon in his attack on Hollywood as cultural agency, a crucial subtext of this film. He tacitly addresses the historical irony of Hollywood film music of the 1930s and 1940s emanating largely from European émigrés (for example Max Steiner, Franz Waxman, Miklós Rózsa), in a style based strongly on late Romanticism, not least on Wagner.[9] In other words, the latter-day exponents of Wagner's musical lineage were in the United States, at the forefront of the dream industry. Syberberg's musical rehabilitation of Wagner from the trivialization of Hollywood then anticipates the attempted reclamation of German history at visual and dramatic levels by Edgar Reitz in his monumental *Heimat* cycles.

How, concretely, does Wagner look and sound with Syberberg? After an opening sequence in which Wagner permeates the soundtrack, potentially as highbrow mood music or operatic film narrative, there follows a section where his music is intercut with Nazi or at least Nazified songs (*Hitler*, 44ff.), so that the effect is of longer- and shorter-term cultural memory. The counterpoint is most striking when one of the narrators, Harry Baer, proclaims that "music . . . overcomes everything" while holding the puppet of Ludwig II. This statement is underpinned by the *Parsifal* Prelude, which yields to an archival record of the song "Today our Germany hears us." The hinge between the two worlds, as it must have been for the febrile imagination of the young Hitler, is the martial music of *Rienzi*. And a still more striking amalgam is created by the repeated funereal drumbeat of the roll call of the 1923 Nazi martyrs and the recurring evocation of the archetypal Germanic hero Siegfried with the "Funeral March" from *Götterdämmerung*. When the Hitler puppet says: "So long as Wagner's music is played, I will not be forgotten" (*Hitler*, 207), this is the musical example chosen. The "Funeral March" ruminates on the life of the dead hero (as a cluster of leitmotifs), and at the point where the exultant theme from Siegfried's Rhine Journey enters, Harry Baer takes up the narration with the words: "Thus spake the devil" (ibid.). Hitler the historical figure is demonized, shrouded in mythological mist, while the Wagnerian hero Siegfried is projected via Third Reich reception into the realm of the historical. With this degree of precision are the musical entrances planned in this film.

Syberberg quotes *Parsifal* extensively, with the quest for the Grail becoming synonymous with German Romantic striving for the transcendental. The first Wagner excerpt among many throughout the film is the Prelude, and this clearly stakes out Syberberg's Wagner, to be reclaimed from Hitler's.[10] The Hitler puppet's speech quoted in the last paragraph goes on: "(I will not be forgotten.) I've made sure of that. Branded forever in the history of Wagnerian music. The source of our, the source of my strength" (ibid.). Syberberg would ideally remove Wagner from the embrace of both the Right and the Left, although the weight he lends the nineteenth century might have led him back to the historically arresting phenomenon of the latter.[11]

The preponderance of Wagner from the outset stakes out an allusively rich acoustic terrain for this film. The Prelude to *Parsifal* is followed by excerpts from the forging of the Ring scene from *Das Rheingold,* the orchestral flourish and Donner's hammer blow before the entry of the gods into Valhalla, the final scene from *Götterdämmerung,* and a return to the *Parsifal* Prelude, all within the opening fifteen minutes. The unleashing by the Ring of such greed and destruction is perfectly positioned, as André Heller speaks of the legal claims advanced by thirty Hitler heirs (*Hitler,* 31–32).

The film's frames of reference arch still further. Musically the most dramatic of the above examples, a furious drum roll prefacing the gods' entry, is qualified by a yodeling voice, and the sequence of this intruder surrounded by the two Wagner excerpts is the same as that toward the end of the same director's *Ludwig—Requiem for a Virgin King* (1972). While the yodeler deflates the high pathos of Wagner's music, the musical combination signals the director's use of his own leitmotif cluster to combine film narratives. The title to Part 1 of *Our Hitler,* "From the World Ash-Tree to the Goethe-Oak of Buchenwald," links *Die Walküre* to the Weimar of Goethe and beyond. The name "Buchenwald" summarizes Syberberg's own lament, reducing a once highly poetic word to a single connotation and preserving the link between classical Weimar (the Goethe-Oak) and a concentration camp compound. The span of Syberberg's title, then, reflects his attempt to resuscitate archetypal myths which once fed into a great Romantic tradition and have since been hopelessly compromised. Wagner is a major player in advancing this thesis.

But the salvage operation is reversed with the appearance of *Rienzi*. Although the composer came to distance himself from this early opera, the latter-day orator Hitler embraced it. Its more martial instrumentation blends effectively with the marching songs of the Hitler era which feature in this section of the film. The "Funeral March" from *Götterdämmerung* undergoes similar recontextualization alongside jaunty renditions of military marches and song (*Hitler*, 108–109). Still more arresting are the occasional mini-dramas that Syberberg creates, parallel to and dramatically deriving from the Wagner he is citing. During ravings from the Man of Destiny about the Eros of ruling and of violence, culminating in an invocation of the charismatic leader (*Hitler*, 126), Donner's "He da! He da! He do!" rings out, leading into the orchestral flourish quoted briefly near the beginning of *Our Hitler*. The fanatical voice of invocation is joined by a crowd intoning "Sieg Heil, Sieg Heil," Goebbels's pledge of total submission to the Führer's will, and a hint of the "Deutschlandlied." The intoxication of the voices is matched by the upward surge of the music, resolving in Donner's hammer blow and the thunderclap of the kettledrums. The effect is a flash forward on the soundtrack to the foundations of the Nuremberg Rallies. And the Wagnerian viewer Syberberg is ideally addressing will make the further (dramatic/historical) connection that this music immediately precedes the entry of the gods into Valhalla, the mirage of grandeur penetrated only by Loge's prediction:

> Ihrem Ende eilen sie zu,
> die so stark im Bestehen sich wähnen.
> (They who delude themselves they will endure,
> are in fact hurtling toward their end.) (*Das Rheingold*, Scene 4)

In a film obsessed with German identity, the length and the textual and dramatic aptness of Syberberg's excerpts reclaim Wagner from Hollywood agency. But they also reclaim Wagner from Nazi appropriation. The Nazis' attempt to model history on Wagner's myths rebounds, with his myths penetrating the outcomes of their brand of history and outlasting their millennium.

THE DOCUMENTARIES OF WERNER HERZOG

Werner Herzog has continued to engage with Wagner well beyond the lifespan of the New German Cinema. But far more than in feature films, where Wagner's music might be expected on the soundtrack, Herzog employs it in his documentaries, indicating from the start his typically idiosyncratic perception of the genre. To complete a disregard for conventional genre boundaries, particular musical excerpts recur across both feature films and documentaries.

Herzog shares with Syberberg a close relationship with German Romanticism, a movement whose very aims would seem to point away from the direction of documentary. The tension between poetry and visual mimesis indicates the chasm between Herzog's conception of documentary and a more purist ethnography, likely to view "poetry" as an embellishment. And yet documentary theorists have also come to the conclusion that the genre is "a fiction (un-)like any other,"[12] but a fiction for all that. Point 5 of Herzog's Minnesota Declaration asserts that "poetic, ecstatic truth . . . can be reached only through fabrication and imagination and stylization."[13] Herzog's highly personal and unconventional statements about documentary magnify the creative consciousness behind the camera and the soundtrack.

What is the role of sound in the intensification of truth? Throughout the silent cinema era one level of sound was always present, namely music. Music supposedly fleshed out the images, lent them a third dimension, and hence made the viewing position more "heimlich." This is important to remember when we assess Herzog's return to Murnau—his creative adaptation (1979) of Murnau's *Nosferatu* (1922)—and the more general return of the New German Cinema to a pre-Nazi generation of German filmmakers. The earlier images were supported by music, and music functioned differently from that emitted through Dolby systems.

The link to Herzog's integration of Wagner into his own dramaturgy is the 1994 TV film *Die Verwandlung der Welt in Musik: Bayreuth vor der Premiere,* largely made up of a series of interviews with creative personnel both on- and off-stage at the Holy Grail for Wagnerians. The title alone, beyond functioning as his definition of opera,[14] indicates how

Herzog's Bayreuth is styled to become the German equivalent of the Hollywood dream factory. Whereas Hollywood transforms the world into images of the mind, the acoustic dream is so potent that it can transform the world into music. That also means that the classical Hollywood paradigm of visual supremacy is supplanted by nineteenth-century German music and music theater. This is established in the opening sequence, where the camera is given access to precious scores in the Bayreuth museum archives. Among these scores we see both *Tristan und Isolde* and *Parsifal*, but the soundtrack remains with the rhapsodic "Liebestod" from *Tristan*, in an unedited continuity of sound (ca. six minutes) that is unusual outside opera films.

Die Verwandlung der Welt in Musik features prominent conductors and other artists invited to Bayreuth. Their rehearsals surround an appearance by Herzog, reminiscing about his own production of *Lohengrin*, which had been in the Bayreuth repertoire from 1987 till his making of this documentary. At a rehearsal of the Sailors' Chorus from *Der fliegende Holländer,* the choristers are shot looking ostentatiously away from the stage action to follow their own conductor, who transmits tempi from his over-the-shoulder glances at the orchestra's conductor, Giuseppe Sinopoli. A similar effect is achieved with video monitors capturing different angles on the performance and by a montage of conductors from different productions. Images are dislocated while the body of music, the Wagner tradition, continues, from the early work *Der fliegende Holländer* to the summation of *Parsifal*.

In footage of rehearsals for *Lohengrin*, Herzog gives instructions to children. We hear of what Wolfgang Wagner rejected about Herzog's even grander conception for the production, styling Herzog as something of a latter-day Ludwig II, except that he is channelling his own conceptions through Wagner's opera rather than being a devotee in thrall to the composer's ideas. In this sense this film too has a narcissistic element—Bayreuth as a pretext for Herzog's visions. Paul Frey is interviewed about his role as Lohengrin, but when he actually sings, he is eclipsed in the foreground by the offstage Herzog and the fireman on duty, with Herzog even persuading the fireman to sing, from a viewer's perspective, over the voice of Paul Frey! A racking focus singles out them rather than the real performers, and their schoolboy irreverence extends to laughter, as the camera moves to a portrait of Ludwig II. Any transformation of the world into music, a claim perhaps applicable in the first place only to an acolyte's view of Wagner above all other composers, is briefly demystified by these pranks. After interviews with Heiner Müller and Daniel Barenboim, the film finishes with the end of *Tristan* and the crowd's response. This, then, is a documentary about staging the music of Wagner.

Elsewhere in Herzog's films, including the documentaries, music frequently becomes a kind of antipode to Beethoven, inasmuch as the outer world is deaf to the inner voices of the exalted and creative individual. Matching his confidence in seeing and articulating images that have never been seen before,[15] Herzog positions his listening viewer as the inner ear of Beethoven, hearing sounds that are only accessible to the happy few. The latter approach is exemplified by *Bells from the Deep: Faith and Superstition in Russia* (1995), in which pilgrims lying on the ice "hear" a sunken town's cathedral.

As an extension of this sonically charged universe, music alone is present for long stretches of Herzog's soundtracks. This ensures that Herzog's figures remain hermetically sealed images, still less anchored by "natural" sound than are singers under the stagelights of an opera house. The quality of an acoustic hothouse is crucial for Herzog's *Lessons of Darkness* (1991/92), with its apocalyptic footage of burning oil wells in the first Gulf War. The lack of ambient sound effaces what cultural anthropologist David Tomas calls "ephemeral and fragmentary histories."[16] When dialogue is also absent, sonic myth is created. Whatever the degree of empathy created with the devotees in Herzog's film *Pilgrimage* (2001), which features music by John Tavener, they are never represented from within or even fully located without, so that their world and the "normal" one (of the viewer) remain parallel, on opposite sides of the lens and of the sound barrier. Music is used here to immunize the viewer against anything other than the ecstatic truth, just as the impossible narrative weight borne by Philip Glass's scores in Godfrey Reggio's trilogy (*Koyaanisqatsi* [1982], *Powaqqatsi* [1988], and *Naqoyqatsi* [2002]) filters out the political commentary that seems to inhere in the images.

Wagner's music strengthens the palpable links between the themes and visuals of Herzog's documentaries and feature films. In *Little Dieter*

Needs to Fly (1997), the end of the "Liebestod" from *Tristan und Isolde* enters on cue when the pilot Dieter, recounting his crash landing in a Laotian jungle, uses the word "dream." Unsure whether it is "real" or "unreal," he speaks of death as a thick flow, pointing to floating jellyfish lit by an almost Marianic blue, images that recur in *Invincible* (2001). The musical "thick flow" is Wagner's orchestration of death, and anything further from a documentary depiction of Laos during the Vietnam War is hard to imagine. But when the "Liebestod" also swells at the end of *Schrei aus Stein/Scream of Stone* (1991), it signals that the ascent of a peak in the Andes has had all the glorious insubstantiality of opera. Such irony, viewed in more relaxed mode with the performance of Bellini at the end of *Fitzcarraldo* (1982), matches the sardonic quality attributed by William van Wert to the use of Wagner in *La Soufrière* (1977).[17] The same music used there, Siegfried's "Funeral March," appears behind burning oil wells throughout Section 7 of *Lessons of Darkness,* where it has no trace of irony, but functions rather as a threnody for the West.[18] In this sense Herzog's Wagner is Wagner at the service of Herzog's own transformation of the world through his *Gesamtkunstwerk* of the imagination.

The soundtrack of *Lessons of Darkness* combines long stretches of music as sole presence with a Wagnerian sense of theater, viewed as an aesthetic intensification of truth. The latter tendency is exemplified by *Julianes Sturz in den Dschungel/Wings of Hope* (2000), in which Herzog takes the sole survivor of a plane crash back to the crash site in the jungle and recreates her journey out. (The whole aspect of redemptive reenactment, as also in *Little Dieter Needs to Fly,* demonstrates a kinship between Herzog's documentaries and Wagnerian opera.)

In *Wings of Hope,* the *Rheingold* Prelude begins over the line "Das war wie ein Engel, der auf mich zukam" (That was like an angel approaching), just as there are entries of a Bartók work (*Buciumcana*) when the words "vision" and "dream" are uttered in *Little Dieter Needs to Fly.* Music transports the viewer beyond the visually representable world of the observational documentary. With reference to an angel, Juliane describes the effect of seeing her deliverer, and the Prelude continues for some minutes through to the last of the end credits. In Wagner's tetralogy the E♭ chord sustained in total darkness ushers in the transition from the social world of the theater foyer to the domain of Wagnerian myth. Herzog's use of the music here is almost a concession that for all the extraordinariness of the story he has recounted, he needs such a device to ensure a more general, mythical level to his documentary.

He prepares this with theatrical montage toward the end of the film. As a whole panel of the ill-fated plane is unearthed, Herzog's voiceover muses on whether this was the emergency exit through which Juliane was ejected (and saved). The music continues to swirl, while the camera takes us through the proscenium arch of the space in the hull, into the *Urwald* beyond, where the new Juliane stands as the unlikely center-piece, and Herzog retells her narrative. As the camera transports us through the stage curtain of the aircraft shell, the world is transformed into music drama. The effect is far more convincing than the incursion of Herzog's own drama into that of the story-to-be. Herzog interrupts the barely developed Juliane strand as he describes how at the time of the crash he was filming *Aguirre* in a nearby valley, with footage from that film gratuitously spliced into the film in process. So a montage of mythical theme and visuals within the new film does not work to lend it a mythical dimension, but the considered use of Wagner's music over images inherent to the film does, however much these images are con-structed around a stage effect.

In these final frames the *Rheingold* Prelude in no sense emerges from the jungle. Instead, it signifies the heightened consciousness and depths of the subconscious released by the extreme situation of Frau Juliane and this setting (back there, at the crash; its restaging calls for Wagnerian grandeur to lend it conviction). It is a clinching example of that isolation of music on the soundtrack discussed above. The sound of Wagner signals the filmmaker's hand in superimposing a mythical layer over the documented reality of the jungle. The same music has a similar dramatic function at the start of *Lessons of Darkness* (on the camera's magic carpet ride over Kuwait City), and above all when establishing the liminal space between civilization and the realm of Count Dracula in *Nosferatu*.[19] The latter example shows Herzog's interest in the inte-grated effect of Wagnerian theater beyond the opera score, as the figure of Jonathan Harker and the scenery and props are shot as if part of an opera production, for a Bayreuth stage at that.

By this line of reasoning, the documentary *Verwandlung der Welt in Musik* is central to an understanding of the theatrical use of music in Herzog's documentaries. According to anthropologist Steven Feld, "the idea of sound worlds is that social formations are indexed in sonic histories and sonic geographies."[20] Herzog's use of Wagner at the end of *Wings of Hope* transforms this notion into formations beyond the (merely) social. Feld qualifies this definition, since "we now all live in . . . 'sound worlds' [which] are simultaneously local and translocal, specific yet blurred, particular but general, in place and in motion."[21] This world-music quality facilitates Herzog's approach. In reinjecting Wagner with primarily mythical content, the music transcends the constraints of Germanic myth, and above all its reception as proto-Nazi and pan-Germanic. This far outstrips objections by ethnographic purists that any music other than what the ethnographic subject might perform is a breach of documentary conventions. Such a debate about "authenticity" is bypassed in the name, again, of an intensification of truth, of documenting culture and cultural memory in myth, behind their manifestations in the physical world.

These examples illustrate Herzog's take on opera: "[W]hen the music is playing, the stories do make sense. Their strong inner truths shine through and they seem utterly plausible."[22] We are left then with incompatible paradigms, with operatic ethnography. Herzog's documentaries challenge something more fundamental than genre categories. Their visual and acoustic representations exemplify much broader issues, such as cinematic "realism" and what that could possibly still mean; the relationship between the pro-filmic event and the edited footage and soundtrack; the way we see (while also being addressed through sound) and the way we dream, visions both. From the dramatic, technical, and choreographic issues emerging here, the affinity Herzog clearly feels to Wagner becomes self-evident.

HEIMAT 3

Edgar Reitz's three *Heimat* series bear comparison with Wagner's works on a number of fronts.[23] Their combined length dwarfs the monumentality of the *Ring*, exceeding three full productions. In over fifty-two hours, they cover eighty years of the history of Europe's most turbulent twentieth-century nation. Their individual dimensions, however, are those of a more chamber-music approach to Wagner. The closest parallel between Reitz and Wagner is probably their shared ground in navigating nothing less than an intellectual history of the nation, Reitz in the subject matter of his *Heimat* series, Wagner in the ongoing reception of his works. Reitz's view of twentieth-century Germany is full of social comment, with *Heimat 3* starting on the night the Berlin Wall falls and embedding in its plot many issues arising from German unification. But his film cycle also interweaves reflections on and through artforms—art history, literature, film itself, and music, for a start. At the level of content rather than form it is a *Gesamtkunstwerk*. The arts permeate German (big city) life, rather than being aesthetic extras, and a commitment to music reflects a longstanding thread of German intellectual history. Music at the core of Reitz's cycle shows a kinship to the prose works of Thomas Mann (with the filtering of Romanticism and philosophy, primarily via Wagner).[24] Where Mann's *Doktor Faustus* featured a diabolical retraction of German humanism as embodied in Beethoven's Ninth, Reitz's central figures cultivate their musicality to the end. Hermann leaves village life at the end of *Heimat 1* to study composition in Munich; he continues to compose and conduct throughout the second and third series. His partner Clarissa originally learns cello before becoming a singer in crossover and avant-garde styles, which challenge the German musical tradition in its national distinctiveness. This mirrors the dilemma of clinging to a concept of "Heimat" while allowing it historical flux. At the outset of *Heimat 2*, Hermann swears that music will be his sole love and his spiritual home.

Three decades on from the timeframe of *Heimat 2*, in a now-united Germany, *Heimat 3* highlights the difficulty of locating "Heimat" within Germany's Europeanization and globalization. Music, "the most German art" in Nazi propaganda, permeates *Heimat 3*, but as with cinema references, Germany is approached as part of Europe. At the acoustic level, Reitz's use of music without nationally specific markers parallels Wenders's global road movies, where U2 and others are prominent on the soundtrack. Hermann is invited to compose a Reunification Symphony. Its six movements seemingly make it a *chiffre* for Reitz's six-part film. But its fate, in never being performed onscreen, is also a comment on reunification not reaching completion in the historical script.

In this ongoing concern with the extreme case of a problematic twentieth-century national identity, reference to Wagner would seem both obligatory and impossibly fraught. About halfway through the final episode, a rare dream sequence situates Hermann in a liminal space, with a passing parade of ghosts from the past. His reveries in a field (Berlioz?!) precede the funeral of the publican Rudi, the heart and soul of Hermann's birthplace, Schabbach. At the funeral Hermann, still poised on the brink of reality (and in that sense, in an operatic space), surveys the graves of his own family. There is a strong sense of the passing of a town's dynasty, even before an earth tremor disperses the mourners. The brass band continues with its rendition of "Nearer My God to Thee." Reitz is confident that his audience will associate this melody with the sinking of the *Titanic*.[25] The tremor signals the subsiding of old slate quarries which provide the foundation for some of Schabbach. One of them has been converted by Hermann's late brother Ernst into a sub-terranean vault, where he has stored artworks—above all, art deemed decadent during the Nazi era. Ernst had despaired when parochial politics forced him to pursue a French offer to curate them, and ultimately they are lost altogether, as this tremor causes the vault to be flooded. A shortsighted salvage operation in which concrete is poured in seals the fate of the artworks.

The treasure is referred to on a number of occasions, with overde-termination, as Ernst's "Nibelungen hoard." The flooding of the under-ground lake destroys the bridge leading to the hidden treasure, and as it disintegrates, the Wagnerian viewer will be acutely aware of a super-imposed rainbow. Behind the lost German art treasures—lost first at home, in being deemed decadent, and then abroad in the aftermath of World War II displacement—one suspects this self-reflexive director is further lamenting the fate of so much film of the silent era, not confined to Germany. The notion of German originals having fallen into Russian hands dramatically parallels the tale of the Bosnian boy of Episode 5 who is wrongly suspected of being Ernst's biological son (and the object of deadly envy, in being deemed Ernst's heir). The boy's fate is a grim comment on the primacy up till the millennium of *jus sanguinis*, of German identity determined by bloodlines. His is one of two deaths in the heart of Lorelei territory, and he founders on contemporary rocks re-sulting from parochialism and greed, "made in Germany."[26] Far beyond Western triumphalism, greed, contested inheritances,[27] and betrayal are the leitmotifs of *Heimat 3*. When a return to German Romanticism (almost taking up Syberberg's project of a quarter century earlier) and multiple allusions to film history are added to an already complex mix of contemporary society and Germanic myths, the layered quality of the series becomes clear.

Heimat 3 in no sense attempts to transpose Wagner's *Ring* or its characters into the medium of a film narrative. But narrative links, such as those in the examples above, cry out for commentary, and once thinking along these lines, minor details seem to resonate, too. Although the Magic Fire surrounding Brünnhilde seems remote from the 1990s, in Episode 1 Clarissa does sing "Dido's Lament" at the Paris Opera, the music anticipating her being engulfed by flames from the funeral pyre.[28] When Hermann's older brother Anton dies, relatives discuss traditional burial as opposed to cremation, and Anton's daughter Marlies cannot conceive being suddenly surrounded by flames, as she puts it. Anton is ultimately cremated, and the urn buried in the country churchyard. But the novelty of the new ritual backfires, as Anton's cask melodramatically reappears after being lowered, bizarrely paralleling the final gesture of Siegfried's hand in *Götterdämmerung*.

One aspect of the soundtrack also resonates with the *Ring*. In Episode 4 new music is heard, preceded in the narrative by faultlines of disillusionment appearing within the Simon family dynasty. Scored for clarinet in its higher and bass registers, it is a circular, agitated motif that is strongly reminiscent of the Prelude to Act 1 of *Die Walküre*. Subsequent reappearances are elaborate variations, gradating into inventions. They serve as a unifying thread across a number of scenes in Episode 4, and then recur a single time in Episode 5. They accompany, for instance, Hermann's striding through the mist in the direction of Schabbach, his arrival at the grieving household in the wake of Anton's death, his heading for the gas station where he meets his other brother Ernst, and (in musically much freer form) his visit to his daughter's flat in Munich. In Episode 5, a guitar version accompanies Hermann's approach to the Lorelei, at the foot of which people have assembled to watch the forlorn figure of Matko, the Bosnian boy. His suicide from the top of the cliff (reminiscent of Ernst's earlier death as his plane crashes into the cliff) interweaves three strands, in a manner typifying the film: a latterday performance of the Lorelei legend; a variation of the *Ring*, with the family's feuding, greed, and envy culminating in the sacrifice of a false son, one wrongly deemed to be the only direct heir; and a contemporary reworking of this in the social reality of Germany at the end of the millennium, a Germany still struggling to accept concepts of identity other than ethnic ones.

The evocation of Wagner, and the way this allusion then emancipates itself while retaining the original link, mirrors Reitz's grand theme of reclaiming German culture. Wagner is rescued from Americanization (with a vulgarized concept of leitmotifs, or the "Ride of the Valkyries" from *Birth of a Nation* through to *Apocalypse Now*) and from Nazi overtones. The latter were classically present in the soundtrack to Leni Riefenstahl's *Triumph of the Will*, with music both by and in the mode of Wagner (in Herbert Windt's score). The Wagner allusion on Reitz's soundtrack anticipates the late twentieth century,[29] and this avant-garde quality continues with the inventions (in melody and instrumentation) wrought on the first statement. *Heimat 3* returns to what the New German Cinema was not historically in a position to reclaim, and at one level Reitz's summation of the twentieth century seems to be a salvaging of the nineteenth century. The nation of poets and thinkers, whose remoteness from politics was viewed as a primary facilitator of Nazism, has become an ideal nation of artists, filmmakers, and musicians, and its welcome back to the world stage is not without historical irony. But the embedding of Wagner in the narrative and his ghosting on the soundtrack complement the strong presence of Schumann, Günderrode, and Romantic iconicity (the Lorelei in legend, Caspar David Friedrich in some of the film's images). These function not as antiquated cultural treasures but as the seeding of new cultural blends, as in the film's final frames.

At the very end of the series, Hermann's daughter looks out at the new millennium. She has spent New Year's Eve with student friends, in desolate scenes by the river Main. The friend dying of AIDS prophesies a new "freedom" of gender, with man becoming woman and woman, man. This seems to be an elaborate parallel to the final sequences of Alexander Kluge's film *Die Patriotin* (1979), where Gaby Teichert and her colleagues worry away at Schiller's "Ode to Joy" ("All men shall become brothers"), New Year fireworks illuminate Cologne Cathedral, and finally she gazes calmly out through her window. Kluge's history teacher had sought a positive version of German history. Is this Reitz's verdict on Lulu/Simone's quest, now located in an era when the rest of the world is far more prepared to contemplate such a possibility? Is the sense of this ending the sum of those eighty years spanned by the three *Heimat* series, viewed in retrospect, rather than with apprehension at the future; or maybe with a Janus-gaze embracing both? The parallel film strand near the end of *Heimat 3* is provided by the former East German character Gunnar behind bars, unable to cope with freedom in the West; seemingly Reitz's attempt to connect his German–German theme with the larger East–West theme of Kieslowski's *Three Colors: White*.

One significant difference is that the New Year's gathering at the Günderrodehaus brings together the extended family, not the quarrelsome dynasty. In German, the "twilight" of Wagner's title *Götterdämmerung* is both crepuscular and pertains to first light. And that, visually and in narrative terms, seems to be Reitz's equivalent of the "redemption" theme at the end of Wagner's epic. "Pure" bloodlines have vanished with the deaths of brothers Anton and Ernst; Hermann had a different father. Hermann's daughter survives, her business acumen and growing maturity equipping her for her insecure outlook. Tears of apprehension reveal her emotion as her son plays Mozart on Hermann's piano, with Mozart, as in Syberberg's *Our Hitler,* having the last musical say. Reitz, too, still seems to need Mozart to act as the exorcist of Wagner.

NOTES

1. Thomas Elsaesser, "New German Cinema and History: The Case of Alexander Kluge," in *The German Cinema Book,* ed. Tim Bergfelder et al. (London: BFI, 2002), 183.

2. See Linda Schulte-Sasse, *Entertaining the Third Reich* (Durham, N.C.: Duke University Press, 1996). She states, "As a desired object beyond narrative representation, Hitler does not play a diegetic role in any Nazi feature film" (291). And Nazi-era film soundtracks in turn bypassed the most heavily propagandized composers. See Guido Heldt, "Hardly Heroes: Composers as a Subject in National Socialist Cinema," in *Music and Nazism: Art under Tyranny, 1933–1945,* ed. Michael H. Kater and Albrecht Riethmüller (Laaber: Laaber, 2003). He notes: "The gods from the pantheon of German music are missing. There is no Beethoven, Wagner, or Bruckner" (116).

3. On music in the New German Cinema, see Caryl Flinn, *The New German Cinema* (Berkeley: University of California Press, 2004); and Roger Hillman, *Un-*

settling Scores: German Film, Music, and Ideology (Bloomington: Indiana University Press, 2005).

4. See Deborah Crisp and Roger Hillman, "Verdi in Postwar Italian Cinema," in *Between Opera and Cinema*, ed. Jeongwon Joe and Rose M. Theresa, 157–76 (New York: Routledge, 2002).

5. The following analysis is based on sections of chapter 4 of my *Unsettling Scores* (see n. 3), where discussion of the film is not limited to Wagner. A single copy of Syberberg's film was made available for the German circuit, and it was not shown on German television till December 1979. The far more successful U.S. reception was helped by Coppola's distribution and a memorable review of the film by Susan Sontag in the *New York Review of Books*. See Anton Kaes, *From Hitler to Heimat: The Return of History as Film* (Cambridge, Mass.: Harvard University Press, 1989), 41.

6. Hans-Jürgen Syberberg, *Hitler: A Film from Germany*, preface by Susan Sontag, trans. Joachim Neugroschl (New York: Farrar Straus Geroux, 1982), 9. Subsequent references to this script in the body of the text are to *Hitler*, plus a page number.

7. Wenders's longer takes and altogether more meditative approach are characteristic of a number of European directors, as also of an exceptional U.S. director like Terrence Malick.

8. Wagner's score is elsewhere central to Syberberg's dramatic structure—his film *Ludwig: Requiem for a Virgin King* (1972) opens with the first E♭ chords of *Rheingold* and finishes with the end of *Götterdämmerung*.

9. See Slavoj Žižek, "There Is No Sexual Relationship," in *Gaze and Voice as Love Objects*, ed. Renate Saleci and Slavoj Žižek (Durham and London: Duke University Press, 1996), 221–23. Žižek traces Wagnerian features of Hollywood classicism that include "the invisibility of the apparatus that produces music," "emotions translated by music," and "narrative cueing" (222).

10. *Parsifal* is one example of dissension within the highest ranks regarding Nazi cultural politics. See John Deathridge, "Strange Love: Wagner's *Parsifal*," in *Western Music and Race*, ed. Julie Brown (Cambridge: Cambridge University Press, 2007), 79–81.

11. On Wagner and nineteenth-century socialism, see Frank Trommler, "The Social Politics of Musical Redemption," in *Re-Reading Wagner*, ed. Reinhold Grimm and Jost Hermand, (Madison: University of Wisconsin Press, 1993), 119–35.

12. See Bill Nichols, *Representing Reality: Issues and Concepts in Documentary* (Bloomington: Indiana University Press, 1991). Part 2 (105–98) is headed "Documentary: A Fiction (Un)Like Any Other."

13. See http://www.wernerherzog.com/main/index_html.htm (accessed February 2, 2008).

14. For the influence of music on Herzog, and in particular his elaboration of what "transforming a whole world into music" might mean, see *Herzog on Herzog*, ed. Paul Cronin (London: Faber and Faber, 2002), 255ff. On the opera stage he encounters "archetypes of emotional exaltation and purity" (259).

15. Andreas Rost, "Kinostunden der wahren Empfindung: Herzog, Wenders, Fassbinder, und der Neue deutsche Film," in *Positionen deutscher Filmgeschichte*,

ed. Michael Schaudig (München: diskurs film, 1996), 373: "I believe, or rather I am certain, that I have particular images, images I can see on the horizon and can articulate, which may be relatively new to the cinema, something that has never been seen before" (my translation).

16. David Tomas, *Transcultural Space and Transcultural Beings* (Boulder, Colo.: Westview Press, 1996), 105.

17. William van Wert, "Last Words: Observations on a New Language," in *The Films of Werner Herzog: Between Mirage and History,* ed. Timothy Corrigan (New York and London: Methuen, 1986), 70.

18. For a fuller analysis of music in this film, see Hillman, *Unsettling Scores,* 146–50.

19. There is a strong sense of liminality, beyond the water imagery, in the same music's bookending of Terrence Malick's *The New World* (2005).

20. Steven Feld, "Sound Worlds," in *Sound,* ed. Patricia Kruth and Henry Stobart (Cambridge: Cambridge University Press, 2000), 175.

21. Ibid.

22. *Herzog on Herzog,* 259.

23. What follows draws partly on http://www.rouge.com.au/6/heimat.html (accessed August 27, 2008), with thanks to *Rouge* editor Adrian Martin.

24. A key issue in Mann's œuvre informs the title of Episode 13 of *Die Zweite Heimat,* "Kunst oder Leben" (Art or Life).

25. See Edgar Reitz, *Heimat 3: Chronik einer Zeitwende. Erzählung nach dem sechsteiligen Film HEIMAT 3* (München: Knaus, 2004), 552–53.

26. At the head of each episode of the first series the viewer sees a stone bearing the inscription "Made in Germany."

27. Originally Reitz conceived *Heimat 3* as chronicling the last hundred days of the century, under the title of "Die Erben" (The Heirs). See Heiko Christians, "Edgar Reitz's 'Die zweite Heimat,'" *Weimarer Beiträge 47,* no. 3 (2001): 383, n. 8.

28. This in turn immediately follows on from a vast human chain of antinuclear protesters bearing candles, "Lichterketten," protecting what they call their meadow of peace and intoning a chorale.

29. See Peter Bassett, *A Ring for the Millennium: A Guide to Wagner's "Der Ring des Nibelungen"* (Adelaide: Wakefield Press, 1998), 36: "This startling operatic prelude would be considered audacious if penned by a composer in the late twentieth century—Wagner conceived it in 1854."

THIRTEEN

The Power of Emotion: Wagner and Film

JEREMY TAMBLING

I start from a film by Alexander Kluge, *Die Macht der Gefühle* (*The Power of Emotion*, 1983), about opera, Wagner, and "emotions." The film moves by an associative rather than a narrative logic; for example, at one moment moving from thinking about objects as opposite of emotions (objects perhaps last longer) to showing details of the Great Exhibition in London in 1851, in Joseph Paxton's Crystal Palace. Objects gained their museum, their place for display. The Crystal Palace was burned down a few years after the Reichstag was set on fire (in 1936 and 1933 respectively), says the voiceover, associating these two burnings. It adds that objects lost their Parliament: a statement to be taken in many ways, but associating people with things, that is, commodities.

Later, the film shows another sample of nineteenth-century architecture: the opera house as the "power plant of emotion." Opera is seen to be part of a process of urbanization, a modern phenomenon; this is a topic of Anselm Gerhard's *The Urbanization of Opera: Music Theatre in Paris in the Nineteenth Century.* But as it is said, from looking at the cables that carry electricity through the building, these are in a catastrophic state: emotions, then, are ready to burn up the opera house, in an example of what Derrida calls "archive fever," one of his terms for Freud's death drive; and emotions—affects—have a catastrophic impact within modernity.[1] (Though forced to use the terms "emotion" and "affect" interchangeably here because of Kluge's title, I prefer the term "affect." "Emotion" runs the danger of being almost fetishistic itself, in assuming a self generating emotions from itself; the word "affect" carries no such assumptions.)

Why does Kluge associate objects with affects, having first separated them? Affects have become commodities themselves, displayed in the opera house. Hans-Jürgen Syberberg, whose film of *Parsifal* (1982) predates *The Power of Emotion* (which at one point shows Michael Kutter, one of the two Parsifals—male and female—of Syberberg's film), knows that. *The Power of Emotion* at that point quotes the music for the Grail Knights in rehearsal and shows the conductor's control over this marching music. Military-style music produces a militaristic conducting. In an equivalent moment in *Parsifal*, during the music of the magic of Good Friday, Syberberg brings up behind the singers a kitsch-looking fountain, the essence of nineteenth-century religious and civic taste, and the Crystal Palace, with conductor Armin Jordan, directing the orchestra inside this space. The scene is redolent of Benjamin's Parisian "arcades," with all their implications for the display of the commodity.[2] The Crystal Palace was indeed to become a late-nineteenth-century venue for concerts playing extracts and excerpts, slices from operas and oratorios. Emotions are objects in nineteenth-century modernity.

For Arnold Whittall, discussing the diatonic and chromatic oppositions within *Parsifal*'s score, the Good Friday music "enshrines a pastoral spirituality totally absent from the Flower Maidens' seductive idyll: nature is not merely transformed from winter to spring, but from something dangerously artificial into something inspiringly real."[3] There is a difficulty in seeing how nature can be artificial, but Whittall's opposition between the inauthentic and authentic is critiqued by both directors, Kluge in seeing that an apparently "real" emotional effect is produced by the technics of the opera house, Syberberg by showing that. Both respond to Wagner. If Gurnemanz sings of "Karfreitages-Zauber," the point is that it is "magic" for Wagner, like the magic fire concluding *Die Walküre*. What is specially emotionally powerful in the music-drama *Parsifal* is produced by the power of prestidigitation, which for some critics gives the effect of the natural, but not for Syberberg or Kluge. These directors go further, because if emotions are magicked from nothingness, then objects are nothing. The Grail, in Syberberg's film, is the fetish-like wound borne on a cushion. In *The Power of Emotion*, before the opera house goes up in flames, the fire chief, curious, decides to uncover the Grail (an apocalyptic act during an apocalypse), only to see that it contains nothing.

What part does Wagnerian opera play in present modernity? Is it significant to recall Fredric Jameson saying that the postmodern is marked by loss of affect?[4] For Slavoj Žižek and Mladen Dolar, the epoch of European opera is over; they begin their psychoanalytic reading of opera noting that it could be seen as old-fashioned from the first, its time, like that of all art in Hegel's sense, as past, only manifestly more so than other art forms. For Dolar, "the opera is emphatically finished."[5] Perhaps it is too soon to be so certain, and there is in any case a distinction to be made between considering the power of some post-1945 operas and the idea that opera as an active force within a culture has gone. However, I have earlier argued that the crisis of nihilism associated with fascism marks the end of opera as a popular "power plant of emotions," and that the conditions of reproducibility, which imply the power of technology, which possess a complex relation to fascism, have altered the conditions for opera's reception and perhaps contributed to its end. The formative text is Walter Benjamin's "The Work of Art in the Age of Mechanical Reproduction" (1936) on the fading of the "aura" of the work of art: here, that which encases opera singers and opera houses, and which auraticizes emotions. The fit between advanced technology and fascist appropriations of it is noted when Benjamin's essay evokes Marinetti's Futurism, associating technology and war:

> '*Fiat ars—pereat mundus*,' says Fascism, and, as Marinetti admits, expects war to supply the artistic gratification of a sense perception that has been changed by technology. This is evidently the consummation of '*l'art pour l'art*.' Mankind, which in Homer's time was an object of contemplation for the Olympian gods, is now one for itself. Its self-alienation has reached such a degree that it can experience its own destruction as an aesthetic pleasure of the first order. This is the situation of politics which Fascism is rendering aesthetic. Communism responds by politicizing art.[6]

Fascism is the aestheticization of politics, but making politics aesthetic extends the tendency within bourgeois culture where reality is phantasmagoric, fetishised. "Phantasmagoria" is a word of the beginning of the nineteenth century, describing the images seen in the magic lantern; it associates with the pre-history of cinema, being used by Marx, in discussing the commodity, to show how "the definite social relation between men themselves . . . assumes the fantastic form of a relation between things": Marx calls this fetishism.[7] The "aura" attending the work of art implies what makes both opera and film examples of Adorno's "culture industry," where everything exists in terms that are unreal, fetishised. No cinema without aura; the problem for Kluge's work.

While film allows the removal of aura that opera attracts, perhaps making it more democratic in the way it is received, it also continues with the commodified status of opera, extending the aura, whose operatic symbol may be Bayreuth's invisible orchestra and darkened auditorium. The first removed the sense of opera as produced under material conditions, while darkness attracts the audience to the stage which makes things brighter, more vivid. That Wagnerian music-drama brings on film was Adorno's insight, upon considering Nietzsche's title *The Birth of Tragedy out of the Spirit of Music;* he says that Nietzsche "failed to recognize the artwork of the future in which we witness the birth of film out of the spirit of music."[8] Opera, on the basis of that argument, is not oppositional to film but produces it, developing the "phantasmagoria" that Adorno gives a chapter to in his book on Wagner. As Gurnemanz sings to Parsifal, as the latter says that they seem to be moving though he has hardly walked at all, "Du siehst, mein Sohn, zum Raum wird hier die Zeit" (You see, my son, time changes here to space). The enchantment within the operatic medium as practiced by Wagner means that the two are not entering consciously, under the power of a narrative impulse, but rather being brought into the halls of Montsalvat, the very sphere of the death drive, where music is a withdrawal and everything is in sympathy with death.[9]

Film has always commented on opera as its other, filmed it, parodied it, either seriously or with a sense of depending on opera to give it legitimacy, and has made it a reference point. Studying German cinema, Lutz Koepnick gives examples of the appropriation of Wagner. In Charlie Chaplin's *The Great Dictator* (1940), the opening of *Lohengrin* accompanies the fantasies of Adenoid Hynkel as he performs the globe ballet while thinking of imperial domination. This music returns when the Chaplinesque figure at the end, the Jewish barber, denounces the triumph of instrumental reason: "We have developed speed, but we have shut ourselves in. Machinery that gives abundance has left us in want. Our knowledge has made us cynical, our cleverness hard and unkind... The airplane and the radio have brought us closer together. The very nature of these inventions cries out for the good in man, cries out for universal brotherhood." Wagner here focuses an aspirationalism serving either fascism or humanism.[10] Similarly, Hollywood makes stories from the offstage experiences of opera stars, as with Curtis Bernhardt's *Interrupted Melody* (1955), the title taken from the autobiography of that name by the opera star Marjorie Lawrence, played by Eleanor Parker. Incapacitated by polio, she finds herself able to transcend it in singing Isolde's music from *Tristan und Isolde:* the music's power brings her to her feet in the "Liebestod."[11] The title puts together American optimism and Wagner's sense of writing "endless melody." In "Music of the Future" (1861), Wagner imagines the poet saying to the musician, "[E]xpand your melody boldly so that it pours like a ceaseless stream over the entire work: in it say what I refrain from saying because only you can say it, and silently I will utter everything because it is my hand that guides you."[12] Here the music's uninterruptibility is brought out by film as most able to show what opera can do.

Hollywood has used opera generally to disavow its own mystificatory tendencies. Marc Weiner, looking at films in the last twenty-five years of the twentieth century, discusses Jonathan Demme's *Philadelphia* (1993) in terms of a polar division between high and low culture. This, he says, lets the director displace onto the gay man who loves *Andrea Chenier* the associations of opera with disease, deviant sexuality, and extravagant difference: opera, not film, being allied with the phantasmagoric, with fetishised unreality.[13] The relations between opera, which has many interrogations of gender through the voice, and homosexual desire have been several times pointed out, and non-Hollywood film, as with the German filmmaker Werner Schroeter, has used opera as a figure of excess.[14] In *Philadelphia,* attention to opera functions as a way of criticizing such "excess," opera being taken as more unreal than film, displaying affects it has already fetishised.

Film's parasitic relation to opera shows when it uses the Wagnerian desire to be the *Gesamtkunstwerk,* Wagner's term in his manifesto "The Artwork of the Future" (1849). While creating the *Gesamtkunstwerk* may contain its own will to control, the suggestion is that where opera was the complete work of art for the nineteenth century, it was the aspiration of cinema to be that for the twentieth century. The limitation of film, for Adorno and Horkheimer in 1937, is in its "derisively fulfilling the Wagnerian dream of the *Gesamtkunstwerk*—the fusion of all the arts into one work."[15] But the *Gesamtkunstwerk* comes apart into manipulable sections for easy consumption:

> [E]ven in Wagner's lifetime, and in flagrant contradiction to his programme, star numbers [from *The Ring*] had been torn out of their context, re-arranged and become popular. This fact is not irrelevant to the music dramas, which had cleverly calculated the place of these passages within the economy of the whole. The disintegration into fragments sheds light on the fragmentariness of the whole.[16]

The fragments separable from "endless melody" show up its nature as commodity: Adorno speaks of the "fetish-character of music." The pretension to be writing the *Gesamtkunstwerk* turns out, through fragmentation, to be the display of opera as bourgeois commodity. But since everything of Adorno must be considered dialectically, turning Wagner back into fragmentariness is something which Adorno would welcome, since for Adorno (and for Benjamin in *The Origin of German Tragic Drama*), the work of art can only be a fragment, a ruin.

Wagner wanted not just the invisible orchestra, but the "invisible theatre" (so Cosima Wagner wrote, in her diary dated September 23, 1878).[17] Contrasting the ideal nature of sound with visual physical reality, Wagner desires to erase everything which cannot be manipulated by the work of art. The invisible theater finds its fulfillment in film. Wagner's desire resists the earlier statement that "the music sounds, and what it sounds you see on the stage." Jack Stein, quoting this, says that virtually all the motifs in *Parsifal* originate in the orchestra, independent of any vocal line. Hence the music is more symphonic than elsewhere in Wagner.[18] Yet wishing for the invisible theater implies something in opera which resists cinema: that sound cannot always have a visual equivalent. Writing about orchestral interludes in *Reading Opera between the Lines,* Christopher Morris says that the screen can never go dark. Hence every sound, in filmed or televised opera, must have a visual complement; if cinema is a visual medium, it exploits the possibility of the visual, tor-

turing everything to find a visual equivalent. Music withdraws the predominance of the visual while it fetishises sound as magically produced,
the orchestral interlude removing the agency of the voice. Morris speaks
of the Wagnerian and post-Wagnerian operas he studies (examples from
Delius, Massenet, Strauss, Debussy, Pfitzner, and Schreker) as mobiliz-
ing quasi-cinematic experiences

> while simultaneously seeking to transfigure and redeem them as some-
> thing more noble, uplifting, even metaphysical. This is the attitude that
> seems to underpin so many of the interludes when their fantasmatic ef-
> fects coincide with an idealistic appeal to Music's difference and tran-
> scendence. Hence music not only holds on to the lofty perch that the
> nineteenth century had granted it, but offers to elevate the tawdry effects
> of the theatre into its wordless, sightless domain. Applied to cinema, this
> metaphysics of music would mean repeatedly fading the screen to black
> while the film score continued in the darkness.[19]

Neither opera nor film can escape a fetishising quality inherent in
them both as part of the culture industry, one promoting the primacy
of the visual, the other fantasizing about going beyond that. Opera distorts film and film distorts opera, which may be a good reason for putting them together, because they work differently; but interestingly, the
operatic interlude seems to imply the limitation of the visual or scopic
regime, whereas film's attention to opera indicates how incomplete it is
to think of film as primarily a visual medium, while positively, it questions the metaphysics that surround music.[20]

The chief fetishising within opera and film, however, is in relation
not to their form but to the content: both are agencies for the production of emotion, as Kluge argues. Wagner's endless melody responds to
Schopenhauer's sense of music as a copy of the will.[21] Music voices not
ideas but that which is beyond representation, beyond conscious expression; that which is creative of mood (affect) that is constitutive of the
characters on stage. Such endless melody finds an analogue in cinema,
which, as Kluge considers it, has a relation to the unconscious. He writes
in an essay, "Utopian Cinema" (1979):

> Since the Ice Age approximately (or earlier), streams of images, of so-
> called associations, have moved through the human mind, prompted
> to some extent by an unrealistic attitude, by the protest against an un-

> bearable reality. They have an order which is organized by spontaneity. Laughter, memory, and intuition, hardly the product of mere education, are based on this raw material of associations. This is the more than ten thousand year old cinema to which the invention of the film strip, projector, and screen only provided a technological response.[22]

Affectual thinking, then, is cinematic. But not like Hollywood and mainstream cinema, as a complete work of art with narrative, filming, and sound all contributing to a single unified effect. Kluge's filmmaking follows through a tendency in cinematic thought to be discontinuous; he takes the elements of cinema apart, producing frictions (*Reibungen*), which disturb unity, and fractions (*Bruchstellen*).

Born in 1932 in Halberstadt (Saxony-Anhalt, Harz mountains) Kluge witnessed the firebombing of Halberstadt on April 8, 1945, which destroyed 80 percent of the town, including his parents' home. After the war, Kluge and his mother stayed in the West, his sister and the father in the East. A friend of Adorno in the 1950s, Kluge began making films in the 1960s, contributing to the 1962 Oberhausen Manifesto of "the New German Cinema" signed by directors such as Volker Schlöndorff, Werner Herzog, Wim Wenders, Helke Sander, Rainer Werner Fassbinder, and Edgar Reitz. The manifesto opposed the Hollywood entertainment industry of West German cinema, saying it had made no real break with National Socialism. Kluge's first film resulting from the Oberhausen Manifesto was *Abschied von gestern* (*Yesterday Girl*, 1966), giving the narrative of Anita G., played by Alexandra Kluge, Kluge's sister. Anita is a refugee from East Germany (Halberstadt passed to the German Democratic Republic in 1945), looking for a place in West German society. For Miriam Hansen, "both Anita and the people she encounters are products of the same history, albeit on different sides, and . . . neither she not they have access to, or engage in a meaningful relationship with that history."[23] That suggests Kluge's interest in a "counter-history," on which he speculates with Otto Negt in *Öffentlichkeit und Erfahrung* (*Public Sphere and Experience*, 1972). Kluge's methods have been called "montage (at best loosely tied to an episodic narrative) composed of images appropriated from other films (or paintings, or news photos, and so forth), set off by a title (. . . often written, as intertitles were in the silent film era) while the distinctive voice of a narrator speaks over strains of a forgotten piece of popular music or fragments from an opera, a text punctuated by some bit of aphoristic wisdom."[24]

Kluge's use of literary intertexts in his films distances the audience as reader from the film's diegesis; Lutze quotes him saying that the only reason he turned to cinema was because it offered him the opportunity to combine literature and music.[25] That combination steps back from film being seen as narrative, the apparent record of empirical experience; Timothy Corrigan quotes Kluge saying that "a dialogue with the real experiences of the audience demands a new filmic language, and this new language initially withdraws from the audience, because they're not used to it, and because the largest part of film language is stuck in the habitual grooves."[26]

Kluge's filmmaking years saw controversies over what Germany could tell itself about its past: with the American film *Holocaust* on West German television (1979) and the appearance of Edgar Reitz's sixteen-hour-long *Heimat* (1984) focusing attention on the life stories that Germans could tell each other, beginning after 1918.[27] This reawakening of memory, with a new attention to a personal memory, as opposed to American representations of it in the case of *Holocaust*, was followed by the controversy of U.S. President Ronald Reagan's visit to Bitburg in 1985, Claude Lanzmann's film *Shoah* (1985), and the *Historikerstreit* of 1986, when historians Ernst Nolte, Michael Stürmer, and Andreas Hillgruber used the Soviet gulags to relativize the reality of the death camps.[28] The question of Germany's disavowed past shows itself in Kluge's *Deutschland in Herbst* (*Germany in Autumn*, 1977) and *Die Patriotin* (*The Female Patriot*, 1979), which "work[s] on our history."[29]

The history teacher in *Die Patriotin* is researching German history: that she is a woman links her with *Abschied von gestern*, but since the woman in that earlier film was the filmmaker's sister, it brings out something potentially androgynous as well as autobiographical—the sister/history teacher "is" the brother/filmmaker. Anton Kaes draws attention to the firestorms in Halberstadt, saying "the image of the burning city" means that Kluge "returns obsessively to the motif of the individual's helplessness in the face of attacks from above in almost all his works."[30] Here, "history is the history of bodies," hence one "character" is a knee (an image of connection), which draws attention to what is ignored and disconnected from history. The knee is that of Corporal Wieland, killed at Stalingrad in January 1943. Caryl Flinn discusses how *Die Patriotin* excavates history, as that which can only be discussed from below (as opposed to the official versions), and how there is a dominant image of ice, of coldness, history as a "petrified, primordial landscape," as Benjamin calls it.[31] Kluge's technique of *Zusammenhang*—seeing things in their interconnection, seeing how they hang together—works through the film's montage nature, which gives images of the history of Germany, bringing out its victim status—that 60,000 were burned in bombing Hamburg. The film associates Hans Eisler's music for Resnais' *Nuit et brouillard,* not shown in West Germany until 1978, with German losses at Stalingrad. The absence of the death camps is problematic and is criticized, for instance by Eric Santner, who comments on Kluge's lack of affect.[32] No "power of emotion," then.

Thomas Elsaesser writes on Kluge's silence about the death camps, saying that his work shows what stopped the death camps from being represented; in *Die Patriotin*, the present exists as "performed failure," as parapraxis. History (*Geschichte*) appears as Freudian *Nachträglichkeit*—deferred reaction, relating to trauma—and subjectivity as *Eigensinn*—obduracy or obstinacy, not as the presence of affect. Obstinacy clings to subjectivity in the face of commodification.[33] The past cannot quite be spoken of, save that the phrase "saved thanks to someone else's fault" is used as a voiceover, in the context of a narrative in *The Power of Emotion* about a woman slumped unconscious in her car in a parking lot (she has taken an overdose), who is raped by a passing stranger but saved thereby her from suicide attempt. Elsaesser sees this as an allegory of another, historical situation, of guilt acquired through not rescuing someone in mortal danger.[34] He quotes the voiceover: "Die Narbe arbeitet nicht wie die Wunde" (A scar does not work like a wound). Elsaesser writes that this comment is followed by the interview of an RAF officer about air-raid bombings. He calls the firestorm "a necessary wound, tearing open the scar tissue of a grown city in order to make it bleed, because only fresh blood can clean a wound."[35] The wounding is to bring about a new access of feeling; the film cannot mourn; it is trapped in its loss of affect; it can only mourn that failure, in the hope that it may be possible to mourn later.

Syberberg treats the utopia of *Parsifal* —the Grail society—as a "society of the dead" and mounts the action on Wagner's death mask, suggesting that *Parsifal*'s theme is itself loss of affect. Santner writes that the Grail parts are performed as an "ascetic apotheosis" (quoting Syberberg), where "all separations, injuries, restlessness,—embodied by the wandering Jew and the 'evil' of woman—are overcome in the final sabbath celebrated by the death cult of the grail." Again, Santner quotes Syberberg, "what was divided for so long is thus finally reunited, at the cost of dissolution in the icy loneliness of this utopia of the last stage of our knowledge."[36] Diatonicism, then, is the marker of death, faring no better than the chromaticism to which Kundry kisses Parsifal (to the sound of the Tristan chord). She tries twice, once as the seductress and once as the woman. Parsifal refuses her twice, staying within the idea of seeing the woman as the commodification of the sexual, rejecting emotion or unable to sustain it. For Žižek, "he immerses himself in the bliss of the fantasmatic feminine by way of rejecting the real of the woman's desire."[37] Syberberg shows his critique of this by making Parsifal at that point become a woman. When Parsifal is kissed he remembers Amfortas's wound. With that, Parsifal remembers sexual desire and its pain: "O! qual der Liebe! Wie alles schauert, bebt und zuckt in sündigem verlangen!" (Oh, pain of loving! How all things tremble, quiver and shake in sinful, guilty yearning!). It is not clear whether this comments on male or female desire, whether the wound is male desire, or what the woman inflicts on the male by kissing him, threatening his masculinity. Syberberg's film has already shown such attention to the wound as a fetishism, so that Parsifal's breaking into a sense of the power of the wound shows him under the power of emotion as that which is culturally constructed. And that is related to the negativity of the words which Parsifal sings: the music-drama *Parsifal,* however sensuous and voluptuous the music is, is a refusal of the power of affect, save that of melancholia.

Freud separates mourning from melancholia, with the sense that the first can be worked through. Perhaps it can, though it is questionable whether Freud can maintain the distinction; but melancholia has more of ego in it in Freud's version.[38] *Parsifal* is melancholic, self-protective, as indicated by the armor of the warrior that Parsifal becomes in Act 3, and melancholia is inscribed in the opening phrases of the Prelude which are heard at the beginning of Kluge's *The Power of Emotion*. The music accompanies dawn coming up over the high-rise buildings of Frankfurt. This Prelude contains in its opening bars something of the motif of Amfortas's suffering, that which suggests the ego as wounded. It is an injured narcissism, which may mourn the loss of another but is ambivalent about that other, emphasizing its own affect.

The Power of Emotion begins with a thirteen-and-a-half minute sequence, which Peter Lutze analyses in his monograph on Kluge.[39] As already said, the first image is Frankfurt, with the Overture from *Parsifal* played on the soundtrack, and (in time-lapse photography) dawn coming up. The search for the life-giving sacred miracle in *Parsifal* associates itself with West Germany's "economic miracle." Two time sequences are implied: the slow ritualized Wagnerian hieratic time-scale, and the slow "natural" dawning which is speeded up through the power of technology, like the life of the modern city. After the title, shown over silence, there are shots of a World War I tank moving toward the spectator, of a burned baby's face wrapped in bandages, and shots from Fritz Lang's *Kriemhilds Rache* (*Kriemhild's Revenge*, 1924), with a voiceover commentary. The shots are of Hagen killing Kriemhild's child—before that, a voiceover says, "This child does not have much time to live"—and Kriemhild's revenge killing of Hagen.[40] This is followed by shots of a funeral (a ceremonious memorial service for the Hessian minister Heinz Herbert Karry, who was murdered by the Red Army in 1981, with the chancellor, Helmut Schmidt, attending) and shots from an old film *Stukas* (1941), directed by Karl Ritter, about fighter bombers dying in the battle against France in 1940. These shots are of a departing train, with an off-screen voice saying "Accept me, accept me into your ranks that I do not die a common death," adding, "Yet gladly will I sacrifice myself for the fatherland." After more of this, a voice comments, "Hölderlin, beautiful." It is succeeded by shots from another old film showing a uniformed man and woman, in which he says, "Yes, but a person notices just a minute before the departure of the train that he has forgotten the most important thing." The film is *Morgenrot* (*Dawn*, 1933), a U-boat drama of World War I made by the Austrian Gustav Ucicky, and the first film seen by Hitler in Berlin at its premiere after he become chancellor. (Kluge also quotes the famous line from the film, "A German knows how to die.") There follows shots from the father and daughter from *Rigoletto*, singing a cabaletta together, seen from the wings. If opera is "the classical project of a factory for intensified emotions," these must be seen "not frontally, from the perspective of the audience, but from backstage, where the work is being done."[41] If emotions are to be so intensified, the alienation effect must come in: the stage and singers are seen obliquely, not from the front.

Next we see a woman interviewing a singer, played by television actor Edgar Boehlke, in which the star says that in each performance of the first act he can appear optimistic because he does not know how Act 5, which is catastrophic, will turn out.[42] There are then shots of the Frankfurt skyline and the river, with the words from a 1939 song, "Sometimes One Must Say Adieu." The last moments of this sequence show the Eternal Feminine watching a sinking battleship, adding to the many suggestions here of leave-taking and of world wars as the fulfillment of the death drive. As the song ends, the voiceover says, "People who can no longer stand something endure it even longer; then they suddenly break out brutally and without warning." The power of trauma is enforced. And the sense emerges, reinforced through all the little narratives that appear in this film, of affects whose strange occurrence defies normative interpretations. There is the woman who is in the dock for having aimed a shot at her husband, but whose statements deny any malicious intention toward him; later there appears in a witness box the woman who has been raped while unconscious and who has no antagonism toward the rapist who saved her from death by an overdose by attacking her, using her lack of affect (the detail must have influenced the plot of Almodovar's *Talk to Her*). *The Power of Emotion*, according to Kluge, contains twenty-six stories, most in the form of preexistent footage with added narration. According to one reading, it is "concerned with the possibilities and impossibilities of love in a world regulated and destroyed by power systems and the laws of buying and selling."[43] Putting together the issues of *The Female Patriot* and the singer's words in *The Power of Emotion*, it seems that history is being excavated to see if there is any way in which its Act 5 need not have the catastrophic, *Götterdämmerung*-like effect of massive firebombings and torching of cities, including the opera house.

One voiceover draws attention to how much in the film has to do with heat and fire—there is a sequence called "The Opera House Fire": "One speaks of burning passions, never cold ones."[44] The opera house conjoins urbanism, the commodity, industry, and the sense of opera as manufacturing emotions. But since the power lines of the opera house "were flawed from the start," emotions never come out right; they are "overcooked." Opera manipulates: "There is an important change in *Tannhäuser* between Acts 1 and 2. A Christian castle is built in a pagan landscape in less than twenty minutes. Because of the abruptness of the historical process, there is no happy ending."[45] Three points are implicit. The first is the absence of time to work through loss and to mourn it. One thing is, instead, dumped on top of another. Second, there is the point that transformations are part of Wagnerian magic—they are not worked through in narrative terms. And third, opera thrives by ensuring no reconciliation between emotional states, only highly conflictual affects. This means that there is a link between this production of emotion and the desire to produce war, as seen in the murderous state of the knights who wish to kill Tannhäuser in the middle of the peaceful, artistic singing competition, which returns us to Walter Benjamin on how the aestheticisation of politics makes war look palatable.

Another voiceover brings associations between opera and war by discussing what Fredric Jameson would call nineteenth-century opera's "political unconscious," a revelation of what the text cannot talk about: i.e., warfare. So "*Aida* presents the story of two great peoples, the Ethiopians and the Egyptians, at war with one another for one hundred years. Opera cannot report these bloody events directly. The catastrophe must be transformed into an almost-could-have-had a happy ending. So, the war between two nations is turned into a story of three people . . . [But] because the opera is, in reality, about war, there can be no happy ending for the lovers in Act 5."[46] Affects become more powerful in being associated with the desire for the "happy ending." Kluge's interest in the impossibility of happy endings in opera informs his discussions of *Aida*, *Der fliegende Holländer*, *Die Walküre*, and *Carmen* (and includes a critique of Carlos Saura's film *Carmen*). He extends what he has to say about the subject of *Aida* being war: "[I]n the grandiose project of opera . . . the primal scenes, the carnage between nations, the failure of great political causes—are ennobled and raised to the level of a unified idiom of sound, communication, and meaning."[47] Then he argues that the point of *The Power of Emotion* was this: "[I]n the traditional alliances of feelings—that is, neither with passionate submission, nor entirely without it—human relationships do not thrive at all. War, as a sensual-practical critic of emotion, defeats our feelings at all levels." So wherever there are "'happy endings,'" these come out of the "absence of emotions."[48]

For Miriam Hansen, "in [Kluge's] most recent work, romantic love itself appears complicit with the catastrophes of German history, because it nourishes fictions of fate that prevent any alternative course of action and usually lead to murder, suicide, mass psychosis, and war." Quoting Kluge, "Operas are cruel by popular demand. It begins with being in love and ends with a divorce. It begins in 1933 and ends in ruins. The great operas begin with the promise of intensified feeling, and in Act 5 we count the dead."[49] Such language makes operas, and obviously especially Wagnerian ones, allegories of twentieth-century Germany. But of course, beginning in 1933 is flawed: it is not 1933 which begins the ruin; ruin is at and from the beginning of "modernity," and Kluge's sense of being able to find a moment of "origin" makes his analysis itself "Romantic" and simplifies it, along with the opera he critiques.

The linking of opera, emotion, and war appears in the Preface to Kluge's book *Die Macht der Gefühle:*

> The power of fate: the name of an opera which would fit almost all operas. But it remains doubtful whether there really is such a thing as fate. Perhaps there are really only a hundred thousand different causes which are *called* fate after the event . . .
>
> My last film was entitled *The Power of Emotion*. There *really* is such a power and there are also *real* emotions.
>
> *War* poses the greatest challenge to emotions. And incidentally it comprises the greatest challenge facing all power-based projects for such a time as it can prove that no power can hold it in check; and historically hitherto no power has been able to arrest it. I *wish* to tell stories of why emotions are not powerless.[50]

Something complex is being argued here about that title "The Power of Emotion." Kluge refers to the Fate motif in Bizet's *Carmen*.[51] This Wagner-like motif dictates what must happen to Carmen: she will be knifed by Don José, an ending which Kluge wishes to contest.[52] The "power of emotion" in the opera has become inseparable from "the force of destiny," title, of course, of a Verdi opera with Wagnerian motifs. Something in nineteenth-century opera invokes what Gertrud Koch calls "the feeling for irreparable tragedy"—while in contrast to opera, "the majority of films imagine themselves obliged to offer a happy ending."[53] While oversimplifying, Kluge wants to resist these drives toward resolution, and contests opera's alliance of itself with a death drive. In the book accompanying *The Power of Emotion* he comments that "for years I have been attempting through literary and filmic means to change the opera stories: to disarm the 5th act . . . I find a deep disbelief in the tragic; against the melancholy with which our culture appears to be infatuated."[54] If the antagonism is against the tragic, that must be its Aristotelian, not its Nietzschean version: the former type promotes the lonely hero, the latter gives no place to such individualism. If the melancholia is "infatuated," that implies a narcissism within it, which does not then relate to mourning. The melancholy would be post-Wagnerian, not mourning but self-protective about itself and its lack of affect. In that sense, the death drive, far from being a dissolution of identity, rather confirms it, as Derrida argues.[55]

The presence of a Fate motif in *Carmen* or the function of motifs in Wagner implies that something has been made absolute, given a full presence that memory can retrieve. Spontaneous emotion has been externalized as the power of fate, or destiny; hence Kluge must affirm that there are "real emotions"—through arguing that opera desexualizes these: as Gertrud Koch says, "[T]he passion opera demands is always one which has been deprived of precisely this sexual core."[56] "The Power of Emotion" acknowledges that emotions have been separated from a person: calling affects "Emotions" such as Love or Envy fetishises them and makes them absolute, separate from the person—part of the phantasmagoria where human relationships exist in abstract forms. Hence Adorno on the motif in Wagner: "[A]llegorical rigidity has infected [it] like a disease. The gesture becomes frozen as a picture of what it expresses."[57] For Adorno, the motif is the commodity, and the word "frozen" is significant. This works against the point that the power of emotion in opera is the music, like the music that only Isolde hears which stirs her as well as kills her. But put another way, although Hans von Wolzogen numbered the motifs in Wagner, another tendency in them resists the rationalizing and formalizing ability to name them, to bring them into a taxonomy of affects.

For Kluge, "the sharpest challenge for feelings is *war*." The last paragraph of the quotation from him makes three points. The first has to do with the observation that the nineteenth-century emotions which are brought into play by opera prove inadequate in the face of twentieth-century war, in the face of aerial bombings of cities like Halberstadt. If opera is an urban phenomenon, cities being targeted by aerial firebombing makes modern warfare city-based. And war is itself a powerful generator of feelings—hence the point about the heat of emotions, the power of the burning of cities, and bodies, in warfare. Opera manufactures affects, which are burned out by war, which targets the literal sites of emotional production. The third point is the utopian desire to be able to find affects which would go beyond war, but Kluge is not optimistic about the power of cinema to go beyond the twentieth century. The idea of war as the caesura of emotions explains why Kluge wants to write Germany's history, with special attention to World War II and the firebombing of German cities, which reveals in the bombers a particular alienation, a lack of emotion, as the men flying the planes know nothing of the cities they bomb.

On this side of the war, has opera "the power of emotion"? Can affectual intensity now even be created? Kluge seems to anticipate that question in a television opera, The First 140 Bars of the "Valkyrie," where he shows in conversation with a conductor how musicians must leave out parts of that passage, reducing Wagner to something more humanly possible to perform. Too much intensity.[58] Those first 140 bars are usually taken as the representation of a storm threatening the man who is running away from violence, but they are ambiguous because the Spear motif heard in them makes them not fearful but bringing on violence; they find a fuller, proleptic meaning in the idea of aerial bombing, a (fire)storm grander than the nineteenth century's imaginings. In that sense, Wagner needs the screen as a technology that exceeds that of the nineteenth century, a technology which has kept pace with the aerial bombings his music figures.

Perhaps affect is becoming harder. In a piece called "The Assault of the Present on the Rest of Time" ("Der Angriff der Gegenwart auf die übrige Zeit"), to accompany a film whose English title was The Blind Director (1985), Kluge calls cinema the equivalent in the twentieth century to nineteenth-century opera as a "power plant of emotion." Kluge says that his present project deals with elements of cinema, the illusion of the city, and people acting in the city who have all kinds of things moving through their heads: personal experiences, notions about cinema, the reality of the city. Cinema and the city have swapped over: the city is cinematic, and cinema and the experience of urbanism, whose essence may be that things are experienced in a state of simultaneity, go together. What brings the city and cinema together is "the category of time . . . Cinematic time, 'the condensed dramatic time of cities,' a lifetime—wrestling with time obviously occupies the course of our lives."[59] Kluge's film shows the desire to order things, not just "passing time." Kluge says that "one can also in three minutes tell a story which would be worth spending ninety minutes on. I give an hour and a half's time for a film, and in return get over eighteen hours of feeling alive." When the ability to take time to order stimuli is lost because the stimuli are pouring in and presenting themselves as the latest news, he says, that is the end of stories; "[T]ime no longer allows space for their development or for the perception of stories."[60] Believing in the importance of stories, which relates to the power of emotions, he moves away from filmmaking when they become impossible.

Could there be an opera equal to the devastation implied in war, which Wagner's narratives in the *Ring* seem to evoke, if not bring on? In the opening sequences of *The Power of Emotion,* all speeds and forms of time are experimented with: 1920s film shot too fast, a Verdian cabaletta which deliberately speeds up. There is no proper, no single time. The beginning puts the slowest piece of music—the opening of *Parsifal*—against a slow process, of the urban day, which has been speeded up. Wagner's Prelude begins with the phrase (the "Love Feast") played twice; Kluge plays it not the first time it is heard but the second, cutting out repetition, as if suggesting that this music already exists in the sphere of repetition, of quotation, that its affectual power now depends on its not being heard as a constructed piece for the opera house. There is a combination here of Wagner, where time, however apparently slow, has been made more urgent (it will not be repeated) plus Frankfurt, which is seen as speeded up, compressed. It makes the point that there is no natural time, or even single time.[61] The mythical time Wagner wants to evoke, marked by absence of immediacy, and the time of the modern city appear together with the sense that Wagnerian opera must be and can be made to speak in that different context; if not, there is the possibility that there will be no place from which to draw any affect. In that sense, Kluge does not leave Wagner behind, but also it seems that because they may be used, Wagner's music-dramas may be there before him.

NOTES

1. Jacques Derrida, *Archive Fever: A Freudian Impression,* trans. Eric Preno-witz (Chicago: University of Chicago Press, 1996), 12.
2. See Walter Benjamin, *The Arcades Project,* trans. Howard Eiland and Kevin McLaughlin (Cambridge, Mass.: Harvard University Press, 1999), 158–59, 167, 177, 182, 183, and 195.
3. Arnold Whittall, "The Music," in *Richard Wagner: Parsifal,* ed. Lucy Beck-ett (Cambridge: Cambridge University Press, 1981), 82. See my discussion of Syber-berg's film in *Opera, Ideology and Film* (Manchester: Manchester University Press, 1987), 194–212.
4. Fredric Jameson, *Postmodernism, or the Logic of Late Capitalism* (London: Verso, 1991), 10.
5. Slavoj Žižek and Mladen Dolar, *Opera's Second Death* (London: Routledge, 2002), 2.
6. Walter Benjamin, *Illuminations,* trans. Harry Zohn (London: Jonathan Cape, 1970), 244.
7. Karl Marx, *Capital,* trans. Ben Fowkes (Harmondsworth: Penguin, 1976), vol. 1, 165.
8. Theodor Adorno, *In Search of Wagner,* trans. Rodney Livingstone (London: New Left Books, 1981), 107. Further references in the text.
9. See ibid., 88 and 60 for these points.
10. See Lutz Koepnick, *The Dark Mirror: German Cinema between Hitler and Hollywood* (Berkeley: University of California Press, 2002), 140–41. On the Prelude's anti-semitism and Chaplin's use of it, see Lawrence Kramer, *Opera and Modern Culture: Wagner and Strauss* (Berkeley: University of California Press, 2004), 42–74. See also the discussion of Baudelaire on *Tannhäuser* and *Lohengrin* in Philippe Lacoue-Labarthe, *Musica Ficta (Figures of Wagner),* trans. Felicia McCar-ren (Stanford: Stanford University Press, 1994), 1–40.
11. Koepnick, *The Dark Mirror,* 234–58.
12. Quoted in Jack M. Stein, *Richard Wagner and the Synthesis of the Arts* (De-troit: Wayne State University Press, 1960), 154. Stein argues for an increasing em-phasis on the autonomy of the music in Wagner.
13. Marc A. Weiner, "Why Does Hollywood Like Opera?" in *Between Opera and Cinema,* ed. Jeongwon Joe and Rose Theresa (London: Routledge, 2002), 75–91.
14. See Alice A. Kuzmar, *The Queer German Cinema* (Stanford: Stanford University Press, 2000), 113–38 for discussion of Schroeter in this light.
15. Theodor Adorno and Max Horkheimer, *The Dialectic of Enlightenment,* trans. John Cumming (London: New Left Books, 1972), 124.
16. Adorno, *In Search of Wagner,* 106.
17. Quoted in Christopher Morris, *Reading Opera between the Lines* (Cam-bridge: Cambridge University Press, 2002), 9.
18. From "On the Term 'Music Drama'" (1872), quoted in Stein, *Richard Wagner and the Synthesis of the Arts,* 204; see also 210: the only motif originating in the vo-cal line is the Promise motif (212).
19. Morris, *Reading Opera between the Lines,* 207.

20. On the scopic regime, see Martin Jay, *Downcast Eyes: The Denigration of Vision in Twentieth-Century French Thought* (Berkeley: University of California Press, 1994).

21. Arthur Schopenhauer, *The World as Will and Representation,* trans. E. F. J. Payne, (New York: Dover, 1969), vol. 1, 262.

22. Quoted in Eric Rentschler, *West German Filmmakers on Film: Visions and Voices* (New York: Holmes and Meier, 1988), 54.

23. See Eric Rentschler, ed., *German Film and Literature* (London: Methuen, 1986), 213; for Miriam Hansen's essay on *Yesterday Girl,* see 193–216.

24. Stuart Liebman, "Why Kluge?" *October* 46 (1988): 6. He discusses *Die Artisten in der Zirkuskuppel* (*Artists under the Big Top: Perplexed*). See also on this film Marc Silberman, *German Cinema: Texts in Contexts* (Detroit: Wayne State University Press 1995), 181–91.

25. Peter C. Lutze, *Alexander Kluge: The Last Modernist* (Detroit: Wayne State University Press, 1998), 28.

26. Timothy Corrigan, *New German Cinema: The Displaced Image,* 2nd ed. (Bloomington: Indiana University Press, 1994), 92.

27. On *Heimat,* see Anton Kaes, *From Hitler to Heimat: The Return of History as Film* (Cambridge, Mass.: Harvard University Press, 1989), 161–92, and the special issue, devoted to *Heimat,* of *New German Critique* 36 (Fall 1985).

28. On the *Historikerstreit,* see Saul Friedlander, ed., *Probing the Limits of Representation* (Cambridge, Mass.: Harvard University Press, 1992).

29. On *Die Patriotin,* see Roger Hillman, *Unsettling Scores: German Film, Music and Ideology* (Bloomington: Indiana University Press, 2005), 89–109. He discusses the use of Eisler's music, concluding that Kluge is interested in "reinvesting the aura of music" (109); see also Caryl Flinn, *The New German Cinema: Music, History and the Matter of Style* (Berkeley: University of California Press, 2004), 107–37.

30. Kaes, *From Hitler to Heimat,* 109.

31. Walter Benjamin, *The Origin of German Tragic Drama,* trans. John Osborne (London: Verso, 1977), 156.

32. Eric Santner, *Stranded Objects* (Ithaca, N.Y.: Cornell University Press, 1990), 153–55. That absence of the former has been argued to be a problem in *Heimat,* too, contributing to a selectivity in the memory; though Santner argues that *Heimat*'s emotional drive sets itself against the Holocaust, and so with representations that critique Germany, instead of setting itself against a non-represented Auschwitz. Santner similarly criticizes Syberberg, saying of his film *Hitler: Ein Film aus Deutschland* (*Our Hitler: A Film from Germany,* 1977) that its melancholy only mourns that "Hitler gave the death drive a bad name." The thesis of Alexander and Margarete Mitscherlich in *Die Unfähigkeit zu trauern* (The Inability to Mourn, 1967) is crucial: Germany has not mourned because of new narcissistic fixes in the consumerist bacchanalia of the "economic miracle.'" See Santner, 57–102, and 147 for the comment on the "death drive."

33. See Christopher Pavsek, "History and Obstinacy: Negt and Kluge's Redemption of Labor," *New German Critique* 68 (1996): 137–63.

34. Thomas Elsaesser, in Tim Bergfelder, Erica Carter, and Denis Göktürk, *The German Cinema Book* (London: BFI, 2002), 182–91.

35. Ibid., 188.

36. Santner, *Stranded Objects*, 192.

37. Žižek and Dolar, *Opera's Second Death*, 165–66.

38. Sigmund Freud, "Mourning and Melancholia" (1917), in *The Penguin Freud*, vol. 11, *On Metapsychology* (Harmondsworth: Penguin, 1977), 245–68.

39. Peter C. Lutze, *Alexander Kluge*, 116–17.

40. See the discussion by Anton Kaes of "Siegfried—A German Film Star. Performing the Nation in Lang's Nibelungen Film," in *The German Cinema Book*, 63–70.

41. Quoted in Miriam Hansen and Sara S. Poor, "Kluge on Opera, Film, and Feelings," *New German Critique* 49 (1990): 109.

42. Flynn, *The New German Cinema*, 145.

43. Hans Günther Pflaum and Hans Helmut Prinzler, *Cinema in the Federal Republic of Germany* (Bonn: Inter Nationes, 1993), 82.

44. Quoted in Flynn, *The New German Cinema*,149.

45. Quoted ibid., 146

46. Quoted in ibid., 153.

47. Quoted in Hansen and Poor, "Kluge on Opera, Film, and Feelings," 101.

48. Quoted in ibid., 107–108.

49. Quoted in Miriam Hansen, introduction to special issue on Kluge, *New German Critique* 49 (1990): 9.

50. Quoted in Gertrud Koch, "Alexander Kluge's Phantom of the Opera," *New German Critique* 49 (1990): 85.

51. Quoted in Hansen and Poor, "Kluge on Opera, Film, and Feelings," 116.

52. Compare the arguments of Catherine Clément, *Opera, or The Undoing of Women*, trans. Betsy Wing (London: Virago, 1989); original edition published in 1979.

53. See Koch, "Alexander Kluge's Phantom of the Opera," 81.

54. Quoted in Lutze, *Alexander Kluge*, 103.

55. Jacques Derrida, *The Postcard: From Socrates to Freud and Beyond*, trans. Alan Bass (Chicago: University of Chicago Press, 1990).

56. See Koch, "Alexander Kluge's Phantom of the Opera," 84.

57. Adorno, *In Search of Wagner*, 46.

58. See Koch, "Alexander Kluge's Phantom of the Opera," 88.

59. See Alexander Kluge, "The Assault of the Present on the Rest of Time," *New German Critique* 49 (1990): 11–12.

60. Quoted in Koch, "Alexander Kluge's Phantom of the Opera," 82.

61. Pflaum and Prinzler argue that Kluge "thus condenses the hours of daybreak into a few seconds of a panorama of Frankfurt high rise buildings—by way of an extreme compression of time, which mediates a different experience as the 'real thing,' making progressive forms visible in a new way." See Pflaum and Prinzler, *Cinema in the Federal Republic of Germany*, 82.

FOURTEEN

Wagner in East Germany:
Joachim Herz's *Der fliegende*
Holländer (1964)

JOY H. CALICO

Joachim Herz's *Der fliegende Holländer* (1964), which he subtitled *Film nach Wagner,* is assured a place in film opera history because it is the first more-or-less complete Wagner opera on film. This unduly neglected film merits scholarly attention far beyond its novelty status as a cinematic first, however. Herz was first and foremost a stage director; in fact, the "film based on Wagner" was his only foray into that medium. It exerted considerable influence on subsequent stage productions that have since become landmarks, including stagings of other Wagner operas by Harry Kupfer and Patrice Chéreau at Bayreuth, and by Jean-Pierre Ponnelle at San Francisco. To date, the small body of literature on Herz's *Holländer* has focused on these two aspects of its history, but has not adequately considered the significance of the film's original context.[1] Herz's film is a product of Deutsche Film Aktiengesellschaft, better known as DEFA, which was East Germany's state-owned and only film studio; further-more, its production followed a public debate about Wagner's place in the culture of the German Democratic Republic (GDR). It is a distinctly *East German* cultural artifact, produced at the intersection of opera and film, and within the milieu of GDR social and cultural political policy. This essay has three parts: a contextual overview of GDR opera and film cul-ture up to the mid-1960s and Wagner's place in it; a general examination of Herz's film and his rendering of the character of Senta in particular; and an argument that Herz's *Der fliegende Holländer* is also an homage to F. W. Murnau's *Nosferatu,* making the high art of Wagnerian opera the Trojan horse whereby the horror film genre, otherwise virtually absent from DEFA repertoire, gained access to the East German screen.[2]

OPERA AND FILM IN GDR CULTURAL POLITICS

Opera and film, as two separate media, figured prominently in East German cultural politics from the very beginning, when that region was still technically the SBZ (Soviet Occupied Zone).[3] The primary role of opera houses was to produce Soviet opera and Russian and German classics, thereby preserving and promoting the classical *Erbe*, or German cultural heritage, on which the new socialist culture had to be based (although Verdi was also quite popular).[4] Despite the close association of Hitler with the Bayreuth festival and with the composer's descendants, and the resurgence of that festival just across the border in West Germany, there seems to have been little doubt early on that Wagner remained essential to East Germany's cultural heritage.[5] Already during the Allied occupation of 1945–49, the Berlin Staatsoper, the flagship East German opera house, had performed four Wagner operas: *Der fliegende Holländer* (1946), *Tristan und Isolde* (1947), *Die Meistersinger* (1948), and *Parsifal* (1949).

This was followed by a gap of six years at the Staatsoper, although when the company resumed residence in its newly reconstructed home on Unter den Linden in 1955, the work chosen to celebrate that event was *Die Meistersinger.* This hiatus also coincided with the founding of the East German state and the official transfer of power from the occupying Soviets to the SED, or the Socialist Unity Party. Some opera intendants (general directors) hesitated to stage Wagner in the zealously antifascist climate of SED-run denazification.[6] Some, such as Walter Felsenstein, founder and intendant of the Berlin Komische Oper from 1947 until his death in 1975, avoided Wagner for other reasons. He himself directed no Wagner operas after 1934 and none were staged at his house until he invited his former student Herz to stage *Holländer* in 1962; that production would become the impetus for Herz's film. Intendant Willy Bodenstein in Dessau had no such qualms, however; he programmed Wagner each season from 1950 onward and established the Richard Wagner Festival Week in Dessau in 1953.[7] Bodenstein's stated aim was to rehabilitate

Wagner and present him "free from the misinterpretations and falsifications of fascism." To that end he mounted twenty productions of Wagner's operas between 1949 and 1957, and by the end of the 1950s Wagner's operas were performed in the GDR more often than those by any other composer.[8]

A long-overdue discussion of Wagner's role in GDR culture finally got underway in the pages of the journal *Theater der Zeit* in July 1958,[9] at roughly the same time as the Fifth Party Congress of the SED met. Emboldened by a thaw in the wake of Khrushchev's visit to the GDR in August 1957, critics and readers alike voiced a wide range of opinions. *Theater der Zeit* continued to showcase the controversy through the December 1958 issue, one month after Khrushchev demonstrated unprecedented Soviet support of the GDR when he delivered an ultimatum to the western Allies demanding their withdrawal from Berlin in six months.[10] Critic Heinz Bär questioned the retention of *all* of Wagner's operas in the repertoire, noting the apparent compatibility of certain works with fascism during the Third Reich, and critic Erika Wilde agreed that some works remained in the repertoire *only* because they had become part of a sacred cultural heritage that needed to be questioned. Reader responses ranged from outrage ("First of all she is unmusical, and secondly she has either disowned her German-ness or she is no German at all") to pragmatism ("If one is committed to preserving German opera then one cannot abandon Wagner because the repertoire is limited, and he is beloved the world over") to strategic rehabilitation ("When the Nazis deified Wagner in order to monumentalize their own façade of culture, they had no concept of the changes Wagner had undergone in order to become a revolutionary fighter in 1848").[11] Of the themes that emerged in that debate, Wagner as Revolutionary found the most currency, and his early works—those that preceded his Swiss exile in 1849—were deemed relatively unproblematic; hence the enduring popularity of *Der fliegende Holländer*. According to statistics compiled by Peter Kupfer, there were 227 productions of Wagner operas in the Soviet-occupied zone and GDR between 1946 and 1965; fifty-six of those were productions of *Holländer*, in thirty-two different cities, resulting in at least 1,237 performances of *Holländer* in the first twenty years after the war.[12]

The cultural political agenda for *film,* however, was different. The occupying forces needed to control the public sphere, and while western

Allies focused on print media and radio, the Soviets turned their attention to film.[13] This was facilitated by the fact that SMAD (the Soviet Military Administration in Germany) controlled Potsdam-Babelsberg, home to the studios in which so many classic and Nazi-era Ufa (Universum-Film AG) films had been made. During the initial stages of the occupation the Soviets screened imports and even some Nazi-era films out of necessity, as resurrecting the production industry proved more difficult than jumpstarting theaters and distribution, but they quickly established that the DEFA aesthetic would make a clean break with that of the previous regime. In October 1945 the Central Administration for Public Education charged *Filmaktiv,* a group of experienced filmmakers, with developing a plan for the resurrection of the industry. Goals were clearly articulated: East German feature films were to be educational, but not manipulative; and they should be as entertaining as Hollywood movies. Dramatist Friedrich Wolf "appealed for a form of critical cinema that would address the problems of the transitional period and which would assist in bringing about a 'new and better Germany.'"[14] Walking this fine line produced a strong realist tradition with a commitment to contemporary social issues. Filming for the first project began on January 1, 1946, although SMAD did not grant DEFA a license for film production until May of that year, and the company released three feature films in its first year of operation, all of which exemplify this aesthetic: Wolfgang Staudte's *Die Mörder sind unter uns,* Milo Harbich's *Freies Land,* and Gerhard Lamprecht's *Irgendwo in Berlin.*

As with opera companies, however, once the SED assumed leadership in 1949, DEFA found itself in a new relationship with the state. The primary role of the opera companies was not to produce new works but to tend the standard German and Russian repertoire, which meant that intendants could invoke an opera's membership in the German canon as justification, even where Wagner was concerned. DEFA had a more serious problem, however, in that it needed appropriate *new* scripts, and under the SED it became increasingly difficult to obtain approval. After its promising start, the company released just thirty films in the first four years of the 1950s.[15] The film industry was particularly susceptible to the vicissitudes of Soviet bloc politics, and such events as Stalin's death and the June uprising, both in 1953, and Khrushchev's renunciation of Stalin in 1956 had immediate ramifications for DEFA. The thaw precipitated by the latter, and encouraged by the Soviet leader's 1957 visit to the GDR, ended for DEFA in July 1958—at the same time the Wagner debate got underway in the pages of *Theater der Zeit*—when Minister of Culture Alexander Abusch made it clear that allusions to other types of realism, such as Italian neo-realism, were inappropriate and would not be tolerated.[16] Allan notes that "Abusch's intervention marked the beginning of a new period of stagnation and a stark decline in the popularity of DEFA films, a decline that was to be exacerbated by the influence of television."[17]

The pendulum swung again in 1961, when East German artists experienced a certain creative emancipation with the building of the Berlin Wall. This liberation, and a new course at the Konrad Wolf Academy for Film and Television in Babelsberg-Potsdam designed to improve the quality of scripts, meant that Herz's foray into filmmaking coincided with, and was surely facilitated by, a historic moment of innovation in the industry. Screenplays had to be approved by the Minister for Culture, and that office was apparently amenable to audience-friendly genres such as comedies, thrillers, various musical films,[18] and reinterpretations of some classic texts, such as Heinrich von Kleist's *Der zerbrochene Krug* (*The Broken Jug*), revised as the script *Nachts sind alle Kater grau* (At Night All Tomcats Are Gray).[19] Herz's *Holländer* represented both a reinterpretation of a classic text and a music genre. It is certainly no accident that cinematic opera was enjoying something of a heyday in the USSR at the time as well.[20] That spirit of openness prevailed in the GDR until the Eleventh Plenum of the Central Committee in December 1965. The SED's vociferous criticism of DEFA at that time resulted in the banning of eleven films in 1965–66, all finished or nearly finished feature films, and threw the industry into paroxysms of self-criticism.[21] Herz's film was made in 1964 and spared the public humiliation of the eleven *Regalfilme*, also known as the *Kaninchenfilme* (rabbit films), because Kurt Maetzig's *Das Kaninchen bin ich* (I Am the Rabbit) was deemed the most egregious offender.

Despite East Germany's investment in both opera and film, it did not produce a tradition of opera *on* film.[22] Perhaps this is due to the fact that opera production was primarily a medium for preserving and reproducing the canon, while film was primarily a medium for new work. To the best of my knowledge, three such projects preceded Herz's *Holländer:*

Mozart's *Figaros Hochzeit* in 1949, screenplay and direction by George Wildhagen; Otto Nicolai's *Die lustigen Weiber von Windsor* in 1950, also directed by Wildhagen; and Albert Lortzing's *Zar und Zimmermann,* directed by Hans Müller in 1956.[23] The opera-film hybrid was not universally acclaimed, however; in 1951 eminent music critic Karl Schönewolf had complained about Wildhagen's productions. He feared that the combination of opera and film would destroy both media; that the artistic unity of the musical work would be irrevocably broken and dissolved when rendered in film; and that music would inevitably be reduced to a servant art, subservient to the film image.[24] It is no accident that the first three opera-films were works by canonical Austro-German composers, or that all three operas were comedies. Wagner and Beethoven may have outranked Mozart, Nicolai, and Lortzing in terms of musical cultural politics, but these choices are consistent with DEFA's charge to edify through entertainment by producing comedies that also happened to be, or could be said to approach the status of, German cultural *Erbe.* Musical edification and entertainment on film would take the form of classic operettas in the 1950s, and then a dozen or so *Schlagerfilme* (popular music films) in the '70s and '80s.[25]

HERZ'S *FILM NACH WAGNER*

Joachim Herz's film began life as a stage production. Recent accounts of his role as an opera director on the East German stage credit him with having single-handedly rescued Wagner in the GDR, beginning with his production of *Die Meistersinger* at the Leipzig opera house in 1960.[26] According to Herz, his work was not calculated to appease the state and its concerns about Wagner's late works or their prior association with the Nazis; rather, his agenda happened to manifest itself in an aesthetic that was consistent with, and therefore could be construed as supportive of, the realism expected on the stage at that time. He described his stage production style for Wagner as "theatrical realism," taking as his point of departure Felsenstein's notion of realistic music theater.[27] This style resulted in the invitation from Felsenstein to direct *Der fliegende Holländer* onstage at the Komische Oper in 1962. The success of that production, with its original 1843 ending, and a subsequent production in Leipzig with the revised 1860 ending, prompted an invitation to stage the opera at the Bolshoi on May 14, 1963, the 150th anniversary of Wagner's birth. This remarkable event signaled a number of firsts: it was the first production of *Holländer* in that house in nearly sixty years; the first staging of any Wagner opera at the Bolshoi since Eisenstein's *Die Walküre* in 1940; and it was the first time a foreign director had staged an opera there.[28] The fact that a production of *Holländer* at the Maly Theater in Leningrad in 1957 had been the first Wagner opera of any kind staged in the Soviet Union after World War II speaks to its significance in the Soviet bloc context.[29] Herz's successes with stage versions in Berlin, Leipzig, and Moscow led to the opportunity to commit his interpretation to film in 1964.

The film marks its share of firsts, as well. As previously noted, it appears to be the first more-or-less full-length Wagner opera on film (the score is judiciously pruned to a cinema-friendly 102 minutes in length). According to Herz, it was also the first time four-channel stereo sound was used in a European film, "enabling the 'voices' to issue from the separate cast of miming actors wherever they happen to be in the screen space" and "the ghostly crew [to be] heard as though from the rear of the cinema." The audio was pre-recorded by the Leipzig Gewandhaus Orchestra and Opera Chorus, with each soloist's voice on a separate track.[30] As was standard in Soviet cinematic opera of the time, the parts are played by actors rather than the singers whose voices are heard, and the occasional lapses in synchronization are minimal, given the film's vintage.[31] The truly astonishing technique of the film is not its audio, however, but its sophisticated cinematography, particularly for a neophyte director coming out of the stage tradition. (Herz's debts to the films of Murnau, Pabst, and Bergman are quite apparent; the homage to Murnau will be discussed in the next section.) The high level of technical skill is surely due to the fact that the DEFA system, which was modeled after that of the GDR theater, assigned a dramaturge and film advisor to each production, and those assigned to Herz were Lotti Schawohl and Peter Ulbrich, respectively.[32] While they were virtually unmentioned in interviews and reviews, the *Märkische Volksstimme* of Potsdam credited Herz's "apparently positive collaboration with talented cinematic advisor Peter Ulbrich" with "this unmistakably Wagnerian conception of cinematic solutions . . . such that one cannot imagine it more beautifully upon the screen."[33] More will be said about this below. Wagnerian opera may also have lent itself more easily to cinematic adaptation than some others because film is the medium best able to create the seamless transitions from one scene to another that the composer wanted. This is seen in the opening sequence, in which Senta and the viewer are transported through the boarded-up window out to the ocean below, and later into the flames of the fireplace.

Herz co-authored the screenplay with set designer Harald Horn and left the basic story intact, but drastically altered the perspective so that Senta displaces the Dutchman as the main character.[34] Wagner's Dutchman and his crew are cursed to wander the seas forever, and he may venture on land only once every seven years, when he can try to gain the love of a good and faithful woman who will save him (a favorite Wagnerian trope). He meets a man named Daland and asks for hospitality; Daland is delighted when the conspicuously wealthy stranger enquires about his daughter, and agrees to hand her over in marriage. As it happens, Senta is already obsessed with the legend of the flying Dutchman and, despite being in a relationship with Eric, she is drawn to the stranger and not opposed to this arrangement. Later the Dutchman hears Eric accuse her of infidelity and realizes that she may betray him also, so he returns to his ship to keep her from sharing his fate. In Wagner's opera Senta proves her love for him by throwing herself into the sea, whereupon they are united for eternity. Herz's Senta proves far more independent.[35]

The opera's opening sequence is entirely male dominated: Daland's ship casts anchor, the Norwegian soldiers come ashore, the Steersman sings his famous watch song, and the Dutchman is introduced with a powerful monologue about his fate, echoed by his crew. By contrast, the film opens with Senta reading the Dutchman legend alone in her room, and without music; the Overture and first scene are then reduced and drastically rearranged to draw the viewer's focus to her rather than to the Dutchman. When the action finally moves to the Dutchman, he is sometimes visibly singing and sometimes carrying on an internal monologue, and he a rather slight, unimposing figure. Herz's critique of the bourgeois society that traps Senta is evident from this opening sequence, when a shot with a wide-angle lens from on high creates a sense of extreme claustrophobia, exacerbated by the busy Biedermeier-era wallpaper. Her father and the housekeeper monitor her very closely at all times. The ambient sound of waves crashing on the shore grows ever louder; she runs to the window, which is boarded up; and the roaring wind eventually gives way to the D-minor music of the Overture. Senta fades away, and the camera takes the viewer through the window and outside to the ocean below. Her fascination with the story of the Dutchman triggers an obsessive dream, in which the power of her longing *literally* conjures him forth, so that most of the opera takes place in an extended dream sequence. Herz visually articulates the contrast between suffocating bourgeois reality, which is shot in standard ratio (approximately 4:3) and Senta's expansive fantasy world, which is shot using a widescreen process (approximately 1:2.35), identified by the filmmaker as CinemaScope. Anamorphic widescreen would also result in some distortion, particularly around the edges of the film, an effect that reinforces the unreality of Senta's fantasies. The ending is also important for Herz's conception of Senta. After the Dutchman returns to his ship in order to spare her life, she awakens in front of the fireplace to discover she has dreamt the whole thing. The Dutchman's portrait in hand, Senta exits the house into the liberation of the great outdoors, escaping forever the bourgeois constraints of patriarchal expectation.

THE UNDEAD

Far more unexpected than this refocused gender reading in a 1964 DEFA film is the introduction of elements from the horror film genre, although making the connection between the undead, a standard trope of horror, and Wagner's opera is not difficult. Herz even alluded to this in 1963, when he told an interviewer that the film was intended for people who have a horror of opera, and used the English word "horror" in a statement otherwise given in German: "viele Menschen, die vor der Oper einen Horror haben" (many people who have a horror of opera).[36] When Wagner composed *Holländer* in 1840–41 the undead were quite trendy as an element of the German Romantic fascination with the supernatural. The first literary account of the Flying Dutchman's story is probably still the most famous: Samuel Taylor Coleridge's "The Rime of the Ancient Mariner" of 1798. By 1812 the legend had cropped up in German literature, and Wagner's source was a treatment by Heinrich Heine. The undead were especially popular in German Romantic opera in the form of vampires; Wagner had conducted Heinrich Marschner's opera *Der*

Vampyr and certainly would have known Peter Josef von Lindpaintner's opera of the same name (both of 1828).[37] Marschner's opera exercised a particular fascination with audiences, and it remained in the repertoire of European houses throughout the nineteenth century.

Wagner's link to the undead is open to multiple interpretations. Perhaps the most literal is Ken Russell's version of Wagner *as* the undead in his 1975 film *Lisztomania*. Wagner drinks Liszt's blood as a metaphor for stealing his musical material and then creates a Frankenstein/Hitler creature to terrorize the world with his music until Liszt returns from heaven to destroy it in his "Love-powered, organ-piped spaceship."[38] Wagner associated his Dutchman's state of undeadness with a range of wandering figures as diverse as Ulysses, Prometheus, and Ahasuerus, the Wandering Jew. Michael and Linda Hutcheon analyze the symbol of the Wandering Jew for Wagner in 1842 as follows:

> [It] seems to have represented precisely this *positive* figure of the alien-ated artist, the outcast outsider, and the heroic rebel with whom Wagner himself clearly identified. However, there is no doubt that the composer's anti-Semitism led him to reinterpret the Wandering Jew in more negative terms within the next decade. But at this point, in 1842, this was still a figure that commanded Wagner's respect and engaged his imagination . . . The Wandering Jew, then, was the figure upon which Wagner consciously modeled his tortured undead Dutchman.[39]

This is in direct contrast to David Huckvale's analysis, which traces the vampire theme in Wagner's anti-Semitic vocabulary as part of a nine-teenth-century stereotype of the Eastern Jew and takes Marc Weiner's work as a point of departure.[40]

The continuous wandering is less relevant to the present argument than the requisite state of undead-ness that accompanies it. Slavoj Žižek describes this Wagnerian condition as "*the very opposite of dying*—a name for the undead state of eternal life itself, for the horrible fate of being caught in the endless, repetitive cycle of wandering around in guilt and pain."[41] He lists the Dutchman, Wotan, Tristan, and Amfortas as paradigmatic Wagnerian heroes whose past sins have condemned them to this fate and for whom the so-called second death of peace is their only desire. These characters do share the fate of suffering and the eventual second death, but only the Dutchman is truly appropriate in the context of Herz's attempt to bring opera to the big screen via horror. While the undead may be tragic, they are not horror material if they were not once human, or could not visit the same fate upon one of us. Wotan, Tristan, and Amfortas leave much suffering in their wake, but theirs is a solitary fate; their sin does not cause others to become undead. The Dutchman, however, has an entire crew of the undead, and stands to bring his curse upon women across the centuries.

German Expressionist cinema had had its own fascination with the undead. Barton Byg has written that the German Expressionist legacy manifested itself elsewhere in several genres—gangster films, film noir, and horror movies—but that the East German film company did not "do" horror. Rather, Byg sees the "stylized socialist realism" of DEFA film as the particular East German descendant of the Expressionist aesthetic.[42] That is precisely what happens in Herz's *Holländer*, in which Herz pairs his "theatrical realism" with a nod to that most famous of German Expressionist films, Murnau's *Nosferatu* (1922). To the best of my knowledge, only one review from 1964 makes this observation, but the homage is quite explicit.[43] The subtitle of Murnau's film is *Eine Symphonie des Grauens*, and it is not far from there to the obsession with the undead that characterized the original, Romantic musical context in which Wagner first conceived his opera. A review of Werner Herzog's 1979 *Nosferatu* pointed out that "the constant motifs of the horror film are all prefigured by both cinematic expressionism and German literary Romanticism," and in hindsight, that connection is apparent in Wagner's opera.[44]

Several plot elements facilitate this connection, because the story of the Dutchman is really a kind of vampire tale, but the literal, visual allusions Herz makes to Murnau's *Nosferatu* are quite specific. The visual tropes that associate the vampire with archways and the female protagonist with windows, for example, recur throughout. The use of on-location shots is another commonality. *Nosferatu* is atypical of most German Expressionist cinema because it is filmed outside, on location (compare the more typical *The Cabinet of Dr. Caligari*). The ability to stage action outdoors is a great asset when so much of the opera is concerned with nature, such as wind and sea, and Herz takes full advantage of this in his *Holländer*.[45] There is a beautiful scene in Murnau's film in which Ellen awaits the return of her husband at the beach, amid sand dunes and

FIG. 14.1. Nosferatu emerges from below deck.

FIG. 14.2. Herz's Dutchman on deck

FIG. 14.3. Herz's Dutchman zombie emerges from below.

burial sites marked with crosses; Herz's film has several seaside scenes, and the action passes repeatedly through a cemetery in the dunes as well. Murnau's film returns several times to images of characters reading *The Book of the Vampires*, and Herz frames his film with Senta's reading of the Dutchman legend; both books state that the sacrifice of a woman pure of heart is the only way the undead can finally die in peace.

Finally, the most explicit allusion to that classic film occurs on board the ship, in the scene in which the undead crew is roused from its sleep. The shot of the sailors emerging from below deck is virtually identical to the iconic scene in which Nosferatu climbs out of the ship's hold: the initial position of the hands on the deck, the close shot of the slowly rising ghastly white face, and then a view of the crewman on deck, filmed from behind and below. Herz capitalizes on the effect by having several members of the undead crew emerge in this way, and then lurch zombie-like toward the tavern where the sailors are carousing. Dressed in rags, wearing white makeup, and sporting skin in various degrees of decay, the undead stagger toward the unsuspecting revelers. The stark contrast, and separation, of good and evil shown in the night outside and the well-lit tavern inside is breached when the zombies begin breaking into the inn (figure 14.1–figure 14.3).

CONCLUSION

In Herz's *Film nach Wagner,* the cultural capital of Wagnerian opera is put at the service of another German medium with an equally distinguished, albeit shorter, tradition: Expressionist cinema. Each had been problematic at some point in early GDR history, and yet Herz's fusion was successful because he recognized yet another problematic genre, horror, as common ground, and then emphasized their respective horror features to mutual benefit. *Der fliegende Holländer* originated in German Romanticism's fascination with the undead, a theme that subsequently found its classic twentieth-century German manifestation in Murnau's *Nosferatu.* Horror was not among DEFA's approved genres, and the East German press ignored the obvious homage to Murnau's film, presumably because the fickle winds of cultural politics meant that the party line on Weimar-era culture was subject to change, but the references would have been apparent to anyone who had seen *Nosferatu.* Apparently the otherwise problematic horror genre was acceptable when it entered East German cinema in the Trojan horse of German high culture. There are plenty of ways to stage the Dutchman's crew that do not involve out-and-out horror elements; in fact, this author has never seen a production of Wagner's opera that made such extensive use of zombie effects as Herz's film does.[46] Conversely, the horror film genre may have been the Trojan horse whereby the problematic Richard Wagner was smuggled into GDR culture as well. As documented in *Theater der Zeit,* even some East Germans who valued Wagner's music conceded that its association with the Third Reich gave them pause. That regime's relative indifference to *Holländer,* coupled with the opera's irrefutable grounding in the German Romantic tradition, made it a safe choice as representative of *Erbe.* Happily for cinephiles, this particular piece of the German cultural heritage also happened to feature the undead.

NOTES

1. Sirikit Podroschko, "Senta, oder *Der fliegende Holländer* von Joachim Herz, ein Film nach Richard Wagner (1964)," in *Opern und Opernfiguren: Festschrift für Joachim Herz,* ed. Gerhard Heldt et al. (Anif/Salzburg: Verlag Ursula Müller, 1989), 227–39; Patrick Carnegy, *Wagner and the Art of the Theatre* (New Haven: Yale University Press, 2006), 323–29; Joachim Herz, "Wagner and Theatrical Realism," *Wag-*

ner 19 (1998): 3–33; and nominally, Lydia Goehr, "Undoing the Discourse of Fate: The Case of *Der fliegende Holländer,*" *Opera Quarterly* 21, no. 3 (2006): 430–51. No doubt the body of literature remains small because copies of the film are virtually impossible to locate and access.

2. This project would not have been possible without the generous assistance of several people. Paul D. Young, Associate Professor of English and Director of Film Studies at Vanderbilt University, viewed the film with me and first recognized the connection to *Nosferatu* and kindly advised on technical issues. I am grateful to Barton Byg, Evan Torner, and Hiltrud Schulz of the DEFA Film Library at the University of Massachusetts at Amherst for giving generously of their time, expertise, and research assistance. Renate Göthe, director of the newspaper clippings archive of Hochschule für Film und Fernsehen (HFF) "Konrad Wolf" Postdam-Babelsberg, very kindly responded to numerous queries and provided copies of their press clippings concerning Herz's film.

3. See Maren Köster, *Musik-Zeit-Geschehen: Zu den Musikverhaltnissen in der SBZ/DDR 1945 bis 1952* (Saarbrucken: Pfau, 2002); and Elizabeth Janik, *Recomposing German Music: Politics and Musical Tradition in Cold War Berlin* (Leiden: Brill, 2005).

4. Newly composed opera, on the other hand, was the subject of the first major cultural political crisis in the GDR, when Brecht and Paul Dessau were accused of formalism in their opera *Lukullus* in 1951. On this controversy, see chap. 4 in Calico, *Brecht at the Opera* (Berkeley: University of California Press, 2008).

5. See Gottfried Wagner, "Richard Wagner als Kultfigur 'rechter' und 'linker' Erlösungsideologien," in *Von der Romantik zur ästhetischen Religion,* ed. Leander Kaiser and Michael Ley (Munich: Fink, 2004), 71–88.

6. Sigrid and Hermann Neef, *Deutsche Oper im 20. Jahrhundert: DDR 1949–1989* (Berlin: P. Lang, 1992), 27.

7. Stephan Stompor, "Richard Wagners 'Ring des Nibelungen' in Dessau," *Musik und Gesellschaft* 4, no. 7 (1954): 268–69.

8. Recounted in Carnegy, *Wagner and the Art of the Theatre,* 316–17.

9. The role of Wagner in GDR culture and cultural politics remains surprisingly understudied. For a substantial recent study, see Elaine Kelly, "Imagining Richard Wagner: The Janus-Head of a Divided Nation," *Kritika* 9, no. 4 (2008): 799–829. I am grateful to her for providing a manuscript of her article before publication. Peter Kupfer conducted research on this topic as a Fulbright scholar but did not pursue the project as his dissertation (see his website cited below, n. 12). Other, less comprehensive studies include Ernst Krause, "Versuch einer Bilanz: Wagner-Pflege in der DDR," *Musik und Gesellschaft* 13 (1963): 272–75; and Werner P. Seiferth, "Wagner-Pflege in der DDR," *Richard-Wagner-Blätter: Zeitschrifts des Aktionskreises für das Werk Richard Wagners* (Bayreuth) 13, nos. 3–4 (1989), 89–113. See also Detlef Gojowy, "Richard Wagner und der europäische Osten," *Das Orchester* 31, no. 2 (1983): 118–23 for a token reference within the context of a discussion on Wagner in Russia and the USSR more generally.

10. This speech triggered the Berlin Crisis (1958–62). The full text is available in English translation as "Address by Nikita Khrushchev on GDR and Berlin (Moscow, 10 November 1958)" at http://www.ena.lu/ (accessed April 18, 2009).

11. Heinz Bär, "Wahllose Wagnerei," *Theater der Zeit* (July 1958): 22; Erika Wilde, "Der mystischer Gral deutscher Kunst. 'Lohengrin' von Richard Wager in

der Staatsoper Berlin," *Theater der Zeit* (August 1958): 35–36; multiple letters to the editor in *Theater der Zeit* (October 1958): 40–41.

12. See http://www.peterkupfer.com/gdropern (accessed Apri 20, 2009) .

13. Historical overview in this paragraph gleaned from Daniela Berghahn, *Hollywood behind the Wall: The Cinema of East Germany* (Manchester and New York: Manchester University Press, 2005), 11–55; and Seán Allan, "DEFA: An Historical Overview," in *DEFA: East German Cinema 1945–1992*, ed. Seán Allan and John Sandford (New York: Berghahn, 1999), 1–21.

14. Reported in the *Deutsche Volkszeitung* of December 6, 1945, cited in Allan, "DEFA: An Historical Overview," 3.

15. Ibid., 7.

16. Alexander Abusch, "Aktuelle Probleme und Aufgaben unserer sozialistischen Filmkunst: Referat der Konferenz des VEB DEFA Studio für Spielfilme und des Ministeriums für Kultur der DDR," *Deutsche Filmkunst* 6 (1958): 267, cited in Allan, "DEFA: An Historical Overview," 10.

17. Allan, "DEFA: An Historical Overview," 10. See also Wolfgang Jacobsen, ed., *Babelsberg: 1912 Ein Filmstudio 1992* (Berlin: Argon Verlag, 1992), 262–70.

18. Regarding the popularity of "Genre-Kino" in the early 1960s, see Rudolf Schenk, ed. *Das zweite Leben der Filmstadt Babelsberg: DEFA-Spielfilme 1946–1992* (Berlin: Henschel Verlag, 1994), 182–85.

19. See Sander L. Gilman, *Jurek Becker: A Life in Five Worlds* (Chicago: University of Chicago Press, 2003), 58.

20. Soviet cinematic operas included *Khovanshchina* directed by Vera Stroyeva (1959), *The Queen of Spades* directed by Roman Tikhomirov (1960), and several directed by Vladimir Gorikker: *Iolanta* (1963), *The Czar's Bride* (1965), *The Stone Guest* (1967). See Tatiana Egorova, Tatiana Ganf, and Natalia Egunova, "An Upsurge of Interest in Musical Cinema. Ways of Solving the Problem of 'Cinema and Opera': *Katerina Izmailova* by Shostakovich and Shapiro," in *Soviet Film Music: An Historical Survey* (Australia: Harwood Academic Pub., 1997), 186. They note that these inspired imitators throughout the Union republics but make no mention of the GDR.

21. Katie Trumpener, "*La guerre est finie*: New Waves, Historical Contingency, and the GDR 'Rabbit Films,'" in *The Power of Intellectuals in Contemporary Germany*, ed. Michael Geyer (Chicago: University of Chicago Press, 2001), 113–37. Trumpener focuses on two groups of filmmakers whose efforts were thwarted first by Abusch's intervention in 1958 and then by the Central Committee in 1965.

22. Wolfgang Thiel, "Opernverfilmung der DEFA," *Oper Heute* 9 (1986): 276–90. See also Karl Laux, ed., *Das Musikleben in der deutschen demokratischen Republik 1945–1959* (Leipzig: VEB Deutscher Verlag für Musik, 1963), 348–51.

23. For a list of DEFA films deemed important by the art music establishment up to 1959, see Karl Laux, ed., *Das Musikleben in der deutschen demokratischen Republik, 1945–1959*, 348–51. There were also two noteworthy composer biopics in this period: *Johann Sebastian Bach* (1950), directed by Ernst Dahl; and *Ludwig von Beethoven* (1952), directed by Max Jaap. The latter was made to commemorate the 125th anniversary of the composer's death and employed a host of prominent musicologists as advisors. It was awarded the national prize.

24. Karl Schönewolf, "Oper im Film," *Musik und Gesellschaft* 1, no. 4 (1951): 11–13. These complaints are not unique to film; some of the same anxieties surface

in critiques of live opera productions today, particularly those of the *Regieoper* persuasion. Detractors fear that the visual stimuli of interventionist stagings will undermine the integrity, primacy, and/or authority of the music.

25. *Rauschende Melodien*, directed by E. W. Fiedler in 1955, was based on Johann Strauss's *Fledermaus; Mazurka der Liebe*, directed by Hans Müller in 1957, was derived from Carl Millöcker's *Bettelstudent;* and Offenbach's *Die schöne Lurette* was directed by Gottfried Kolditz in 1960. Thiel, "Opernverfilmung der DEFA," 276–77; Andrea Rinke, "Eastside Stories: Singing and Dancing for Socialism," *Film History* 18 (2006): 73–87.

26. Carnegy, *Wagner and the Art of the Theatre*, 319–29. It should be noted that the section on Herz is the least objective segment of the entire volume.

27. Herz, "Wagner and Theatrical Realism," 4. See also Walter Felsenstein, *The Music Theater of Walter Felsenstein* (New York: Norton, 1975).

28. Carnegy, *Wagner and the Art of the Theatre*, 325.

29. Ibid., 419, n. 46. That production was conducted by Kurt Sanderling, who acted as translator for Herz's staging at the Bolshoi.

30. Ibid., 326.

31. Regarding the Soviet tendency to use a "double actor-singer cast" see Egorova et al., "An Upsurge of Interest in Musical Cinema," 187. The vocal and acting cast for Herz's *Holländer* is as follows: Gerda Hannemann and Anna Pracnal as Senta; Rainer Lüdeke and Fred Düren as the Dutchman; Gerd Ehlers and Hans Krämer as Daland; Mathilde Danegger and Katrin Wolzl as Mary; Herbert Graedtke and Rolf Apreck as Erik; Hans-Peter Reinecke and Karl-Friedrich Höltzke as Steuermann.

32. I am indebted to Hiltrud Schulz for this insight. Correspondence with the author, October 25, 2007. Schawohl was dramaturge on at least three other DEFA films: *Vom König Midas* (1962); *Der Tod des Professors* (1973–74); and *Das Graupenschloß* (1981–82). Ulbrich worked on at least five other DEFA films: as director and screenwriter on *Uns mahnt ein November* (1958) and *Sieben Sätzen über das Lernen* (1967); and as director of *Mit der NATO durch die Wand* (1961), *Acht Groschen (West)* (1968), and *Der Oktober kam . . .* (1970).

33. "Oper im Film: 'Der fliegende Holländer': Richard Wagners in filmischer Konzeption," *Märkische Volksstimme*, June 1, 1965. This is one of approximately fifty reviews held in the clippings file of the HFF Konrad Wolf, a copy of which Renate Göthe kindly supplied.

34. See Podroschko, "Senta, oder: *Der fliegende Holländer* von Joachim Herz."

35. Regarding women in DEFA film, see particularly Jennifer L. Good, "Women Who Showed the Way: Arbeiterinnen in DEFA Feature Film, 1946–1966" (Ph.D. diss., University of Massachusetts Amherst, 2004).

36. Joachim Herz, "Zur filmischen Gestaltung von Richard Wagners Oper 'Der fliegende Holländer': Gespräch mit dem Musikwissenschaftler Horst Seeger," *Joachim Herz: Theater-Kunst des erfüllten Augenblicks: Briefe, Vorträge, Notate, Gespräche, Essays*, ed. Ilse Kobán (Berlin: Henschelverlag, 1989), 107.

37. David Huckvale, "Wagner and Vampires," *Wagner* 18, no. 3 (1997): 127–41; Huckvale, "The Composing Machine: Wagner and Popular Culture," in Jeremy Tambling, ed., *A Night in at the Opera: Media Representations of Opera* (London: John Libbey, 1994), 113–42; and Linda and Michael Hutcheon, "The Undead," in *Opera: The Art of Dying* (Cambridge, Mass.: Harvard University Press, 2004), 146–83.

See also the way Thomas Grey ties the legend of Don Giovanni to the Romantic obsession with the undead in "The Gothic Libertine: The Shadow of Don Giovanni in Romantic Music and Culture," in *The Don Giovanni Moment: Essays on the Legacy of an Opera,* ed. Lydia Goehr and Daniel Herwitz (New York: Columbia University Press, 2006), 75–106.

38. Ross Care, Review of Ken Russell's *Lisztomania, Film Quarterly* 31, no. 3 (1978): 57.

39. Linda and Michael Hutcheon, "The Undead" 164–65. See also the link Simon Williams draws to the wanderer, particularly to Byron's Childe Harold, in "The Flying Dutchman: Vampire and Wanderer," in Williams, *Wagner and the Romantic Hero* (Cambridge: Cambridge University Press, 2004), 39. Regarding the comparison to Ahasuerus, see Dieter Borchmeyer, *Drama and the World of Richard Wagner,* trans. Daphne Ellis (Princeton, N.J.: Princeton University Press, 2003), 79–100.

40. Huckvale, "Wagner and Vampires."

41. Slavoj Žižek and Mladen Dolar, *Opera's Second Death* (New York: Routledge, 2002), 107.

42. Barton Byg, "DEFA and the Traditions of International Cinema," in *DEFA: East German Cinema 1946–1992,* 27–28.

43. "Der fliegende Holländer," *Neue Zürcher Zeitung,* March 6, 1965. The critic says that the ship scene in particular puts him in mind of *Nosferatu,* and notes that the enterior of Daland's house seems to come "straight out of the golden age of Swedish silent film." The critic's tone also suggests that, like me, he is dubious that Herz is entirely responsible for the result; he notes that Herz had said his only experience with film was as a filmgoer, to which this critic says "er ist ein sehr aufmerksamer Filmbesucher" (he is a very attentive filmgoer).

44. The horror genre traits are described as follows: "Normality is threatened by the monster; the nocturnal world intervenes in the diurnal; the familiar suddenly becomes uncanny; the 'monster' must be acknowledged and confronted, which often requires use of magic or forms of preternatural power that are denigrated by the scientific establishment." Kent Casper and Susan Linville, "Romantic Inversions in Herzog's *Nosferatu," The German Quarterly* 64, no. 1 (1991): 17.

45. Soviet cinematic operas were also "characterized by a passion for shooting on location," although those locations were typically interior rather than outside. Egorova et al., "An Upsurge of Interest in Musical Cinema," 187.

46. This fact, plus the recurring visual tropes cited above, persuade this reader that the homage is deliberate. It also suggests that Herz owed much to Ulbrich, Schawohl, and cinematographer Erich Gusko. Barton Byg, Director of the DEFA film library at University of Massachusetts, describes this film project as an anomaly, lacking the standard DEFA apparatus, documentation, personnel, oversight, and paper trail. As an opera scholar I was delighted to discover that Ruth Berghaus was the choreographer. Planet Film Productions is listed as the distributor in the United States on the following website: http://www.hollywood.com/movie/The_Flying_Dutchman/234419 (accessed April 16, 2009).

PART FIVE

Wagner beyond the Soundtrack

FIFTEEN

Nocturnal Wagner: The Cultural Survival of *Tristan und Isolde* in Hollywood

ELISABETH BRONFEN

STRAIGHT DOWN THE LINE

The seductive quality of the *Liebestod* narrative, with Richard Wagner's opera *Tristan und Isolde* undoubtedly the most resilient modern version, is contingent upon the reliability of its outcome. Even while the adulterous lovers are consumed by their forbidden passion, they are also framed by a predetermined narrative trajectory whose final stop is inevitably the cemetery. At the same time, the fatal love scenario raises the question whether the fantasy of a law-endangering and self-destructive enjoyment does not actually serve as a protective fiction, shielding from a traumatic knowledge whose scene is located elsewhere. The *Liebestod* scenario as such can be reduced to the following plot structure. A powerful older man hires a younger and more attractive man of superior strength to find the woman he wishes to marry. This representative is to watch her, court her in his name, and bring her to him. And yet the hero's name, Tristan, already anticipates the fateful outcome of any quest he might undertake. Indeed, what we discover within the first act of Wagner's opera is that Tristan's mission of courting a beautiful woman for another man is nothing other than a repetition of a series of earlier scenes of wounding and healing. Yet once these two lovers meet again on the ship, sailing to King Mark, something unexpected and yet fatefully predetermined happens. It is as though both of them were bewitched, for their anger at and disdain for each other suddenly turns into an equally violent and insurmountable romantic attraction.

They enter into the fantasy of *Liebestod*, in the attitude of one who says, "I know it's wrong, but I can't help it. I know you are bad for me but I don't care." The magic moment, when any enjoyment of revenge turns into the equally consuming fantasy of reconciliation, entails a transformation of Isolde's anger at Tristan's betrayal into a betrayal of their mutual master, King Mark, even as she now gives herself up completely to the very agent whom she had previously hated with such a passion. Their nocturnal love leads them to imagine for themselves an existence beyond space and time, beyond the constraints of symbolic laws, conventions, and codes, and they conceive of this future as the fulfillment of their preordained destiny. What they tell each other is that by transgressing the law, by crossing their master, they are simply following an old melody they heard prior to ever having met. Yet one must not forget, it was Brangäne who crossed her mistress's intentions by exchanging a death potion with a love potion, who is the one who, albeit unwittingly, sets into motion a chain of betrayals and delusions, of willful ignorance and fatal delaying, until both the law and death—or perhaps the law as death—finally catch up with the two fated lovers. Apodictically put: once Tristan and Isolde have fallen into each other's arms, it is straight down the line for both of them.

The wager this essay seeks to explore is that if Wagner's libretto for *Tristan und Isolde* is perhaps the most provocative modern version of the *Liebestod*, its most compelling postmodern refiguration occurs in the realm of what has come to be known as film noir. As Paul Schrader suggests, the label film noir does not refer to a genre but rather designates a specific, though unwieldy, period of film history. Including Hollywood films of the 1940s and '50s, "which portrayed the world of dark, slick city streets, crime and corruption," it also harks back to previous periods, notably the 1930s gangster films and German Expressionist crime films like Fritz Lang's *Mabuse*.[1] Indeed, seeking to isolate the conditions in Hollywood in the 1940s which were most influential in bringing about film noir, Schrader names the German influence, fed by the influx of German expatriates to Hollywood in the previous decades. As Schrader puts it, "[W]hen, in the late Forties, Hollywood decided to paint it black, there were no greater masters of chiaroscuro than the Germans."[2] In this essay I want to shift Schrader's argument slightly by suggesting a dif-

ferent German influence for film noir's negotiation of the transition between wartime and peace, namely, the late-Romantic pathos of Wagner's
Tristan und Isolde. For like the libretto by Wagner—with its emphasis
not only on a nocturnal setting but on a chiaroscuro tone enveloping
an entire plot revolving around the adulterous love of his two *Nachtge-
weihte*—the scripts of film noir play through a love of self-expenditure
beyond the law, where the lovers acknowledge that their story has been
predetermined by a fate they can't escape. As the noir scripts present
narratives about how the hero and his fatal seductress cede to this other
law, they deconstruct the *Liebestod* even as they play with our fascination for a romantic world beyond safe normalcy. The relation between
film noir and Wagner's libretto I am proposing focuses on the manner
in which the story of his tragic nocturnal lovers, as well as the encoding
of the relationships the various characters entertain amongst each other,
find a cultural survival, but also a refiguration in a different medium,
namely film. In so doing I am less interested in arguing for a definite
intertextual relation between the opera libretto and the film scripts.
Rather, I am interested in the manner in which film noir plots return to
the story of Tristan and Isolde, but do so in order to introduce significant
changes. By cross-mapping these films onto Wagner's libretto, the analogy I propose also highlights certain seminal differences, especially in
relation to the encoding of the feminine characters. It is thus not only
an exploration of the cultural survival of a particular story I am seeking
to explore but also the transformation this refiguration brings with it.

The noir inflection reintroduces two elements, which, though inherent to Wagner's libretto, are screened out by the overwhelming power of
a score whose aim is to call forth in the audience an experience of collective transfiguration in the face of a dual death. On the one hand, the
noir scripts argue that any narrative about an escape from the harsh constraints of the law requires a figuration of evil, while on the other hand,
they also insist that any transgressive enjoyment can only be thought of
as the inversion of an inconsistent, fallible paternal law. At the end of
the line what emerges is the impossibility of real transgression, for even
while the *Liebestod* scenario sustains a fantasy of stepping outside the
world of strife so as to shed all traumatic knowledge about one's past,
traces of this past prove to be ineffaceable; indeed, they return to haunt

the protagonists with a vengeance. Furthermore, in the noir world it ultimately is not fate that catches up with the fatal night-devoted lovers at all, but rather the law.

One aspect of the wager I am proposing is that both Wagner's libretto and the scripts of film noir devise narratives in response to a double crisis subtending modern culture. By presenting a fallible father who cannot speak for himself but must be represented by a son, they engage with a crisis in paternity. This younger man, in turn, is himself fallible, given his readiness to cede to the fatal woman's seduction, with her plan of double-crossing the very authority he allegedly represents. At the same time, however, these scripts also stage a crisis in feminine articulation within this system of masculine bonds. For as the fatal woman finds that she can't assert herself, her passivity turns into a vengeance which is both self-destructive and destructive of all representatives of the law.

Cross-mapping the scripts of film noir onto the libretto of *Tristan und Isolde* allows me, however, not only to trace the cultural survival of the Wagnerian couple. Teasing out the implications of the transformation that takes place in the noir inflection of Wagnerian *Liebestod* also allows me to deconstruct the grand narrative of atonement and salvation Wagner's opera installs, by privileging dimensions of the libretto that tend to be overlooked in favor of the all-engulfing score.[3] For what the noir scripts insist upon is that any nostalgic enactment of fated and yet liberating love is not merely a protective fiction but also an untenable fantasy. At the same time, reading Wagner's libretto against the noir script not only points to the impasse upon which this narrative of ecstatic salvation is based but also allows one to locate a fissure in Wagner's own libretto, out of which an alternative to his totalizing narrative of healing and redemption emerges. For within Wagner's libretto, Brangäne, who continually seeks to cross fate's master plan, gives voice to the question of whether, as one finds oneself irrevocably and inevitably bumping into one's past, one might not have a choice between embracing transgressive enjoyment and ceding to the laws of fate on the one hand, and on the other hand, acknowledging one's own hand in the outcome of all fatal events.

ACCIDENTALLY ON PURPOSE

The noir script usually begins in the second act of Wagner's opera, after Isolde has married King Mark. In Jacques Tourneur's *Out of the Past* (1947), the hero Jeff Bailey is hired by the gambler Whit Sterling to find and bring back the woman who ran off with $40,000 after having shot him four times with his own gun. Whit explains to the younger man, "When you see her, you'll understand." Indeed, the moment Jeff views her, coming out of the sun into the dark interior of the shabby café La Mar Azur in Acapulco, the fatal enchantment sets in, and though Kathie Moffett double-crosses him by returning to Whit even while Jeff tries to begin a new life in the small town of Bridgeport 350 miles outside Los Angeles, their past romance inevitably catches up with both of them. In Billy Wilder's *Double Indemnity* (1944), the hero Walter Neff finds that he suddenly can't stop thinking about the way an anklet cuts into the leg of the beautiful wife of one of his clients. What begins with an apparently innocent pass made at Phyllis Dietrichson, while trying to sell her car insurance, turns into a fatal scam, in the course of which he kills the husband, whose fatal accident he has also helped her insure.

Both of the noir scripts I have chosen as transformations of Wagnerian *Liebestod* use the voiceover of the hero, who, in an effort to explain a scene of violence revolving around theft and murder, conceives of a narrative to resolve the fundamental antagonism at the heart of his desire for transgressing the very law he also seeks to sustain. Even though the individual figurations of the *Liebestod* theme differ in significant ways, four elements structure both noir narratives. First, things that seem to happen accidentally prove to have taken place on purpose, although the events are sometimes orchestrated by the adulterous couple, sometimes the crossed husband, while sometimes the fatal events are the result of pure contingency. Second, in contrast to the Wagnerian libretto, here the femme fatal has no position outside the narrative her lover offers of these fateful events. Yet the noir script stages the way in which she infects the hero with her transgressive desire in a manner that both undercuts the masculinist prejudice it apparently installs even while it dismantles the romantic delusion upon which the hero's tale of fated love is based. Third, as in the Wagnerian libretto, the fantasy of perfect love conceived by the noir couple can only be sustained in a heterotopic realm outside symbolic reality, be this Mexico in *Out of the Past,* or the psychic journey Phyllis insists Walter must share with her in *Double Indemnity,* when she explains, "Nobody is pulling out. We went into this together and we're coming out of it together. It's straight down the line for both of us." Fourth, whereas in Wagner's libretto transgression is restricted to a betrayal of honor and a suicidal desire on the part of the adulterous lovers that ends in self-destruction, noir scripts redirect this destructive energy. Their plots hinge on the projected murder of the father as a strategy of survival on the part of the femme fatale.

In *Out of the Past,* tired of running and wishing instead to clean up the obligations that tie him to his former employer Whit, Jeff Bailey responds to his call to visit him at his home in Lake Tahoe only to find that the woman he once stole from Whit is "back in the fold now." As Kathie tries to seduce him once more by explaining, "I couldn't help it, Jeff," he responds by pointing out to her that she has always presented herself as one who is powerless before the law of fate. Yet in the narrative he offers to Ann, the woman he loves, he emphasizes his own tendency to relinquish responsibility and give in to fate. As we come to discover in the flashback, when Jeff, for example, finds that the post office is closed, so that he is not able to send a telegram to his employer Whit to inform him that he has found Kathie, he presents this as an accident he is nevertheless glad about. It allows Jeff to turn what is an issue of choice into a question of preordained destiny. Similarly, like Tristan, Jeff knows that the woman who has enchanted him with her beauty will not hesitate to betray and destroy those who cross her, and yet when Kathie asks him whether he believes that although she hates her husband she has not stolen from him, he laconically retorts "Baby, I don't care."

Indeed, as in Wagner's libretto, Kathie and Jeff's fantasy of transgressive love is both engendered and sustained by the heterotopia which Mexico, with its dark cafés, gambling halls, and beaches, represents to the two North Americans. In this place of interim exile, they can indulge in the fantasy that everything they do happens accidentally on purpose. Like Tristan and Isolde in the garden in front of King Mark's castle, they meet at night on the beach as though time were suspended. "What were we waiting for?" Jeff wonders in retrospect. "Maybe we thought the world would end." They could escape, and yet they seem to feed off being caught by the very man they also seek to betray. The logic of fate Jeff invokes, as he tells Ann of his past love for Kathie, serves to fuse any effort at escape with the return of past debts and obligations. During his confession to Ann, they are, furthermore, themselves in a heterotopic site. Jeff is driving through the night toward Whit, who has come out of the past to make his claim on his former employee.

Jeff closes his confession to Ann by describing how Kathie actually fulfills the violence Isolde only fantasizes about on the ship that is carrying her to her future husband. After they return to America and move to San Francisco, Kathie shoots Jeff's old partner Fisher, who has found out their hiding place and has come to blackmail them, while Jeff looks on in amazed horror. Crucial to the scene is not only the way it casts Kathie in the role of the ruthless woman who will destroy everyone who seeks to cross her plans. By insisting that she had to kill Fisher, she pits her ruthless drive for survival at all costs against Jeff's romantic delusion that their noir romance could be sustained against all odds. Her decision to kill allows us to recognize that she has a knowledge which exceeds that of the narrator. She acknowledges that they can never be free of the past. In so doing, however, Kathie points out to Jeff that her position exceeds both the scenario of fated love she has infected him with as well as the scenario of revenge that ties her to the husband she has betrayed, thus dismantling the very fantasy she has been sustaining on two scores. The manner in which Jeff narrates the story to Ann, however, suggests that he is seeking to cover over this fundamental antagonism inherent to his fatal romance. For he assures the woman, who trusts him unconditionally, that he no longer feels any passion for Kathie. Yet, drawn back into her seductive presence, Jeff once more succumbs to the fantasy of *Liebestod*. Against the pressing recognition that they can escape neither Whit's plan to turn Jeff into the fall guy nor the police, searching for Fisher's murderer, Kathie once more evokes the heterotopic scenario of a love beyond symbolic reality. "We can be together again, the way we were," she proclaims. "We can go back to Acapulco, start all over, as though nothing had happened."

Precisely because both lovers know that they will ruthlessly sacrifice the other so as to look out for their own interests—in Jeff's case the wish to get clear of the past and unite with Ann, in Kathie's case the wish to get clear of Whit, who pushes her around—they passionately embrace.

Jeff's ambivalence is such that he wants to be released from the past and he wants the past to consume him. Put into more radical terms, the noir inflection of the *Liebestod* is such that all the figures involved—the betrayed husband, his duplicitous representative, and the femme fatal—not only double-cross each other but constantly renegotiate whom to sacrifice to the law. At the same time, the two adulterous lovers are also irrevocably tied to each other, precisely because they know that consuming an enjoyment beyond the law and betraying each other to the law may end up converging.

If we then compare the relation of characters presented in this noir script with the Wagnerian libretto, several significant transformations emerge. The position of King Mark has been split into two figures. Tourneur presents to us a fallible representative of the law, Sheriff Jim, who is forced to accept that Ann prefers Jeff over him, even while he cannot bring himself to arrest the man his high school sweetheart loves. His counterpart, Whit Sterling, in turn represents the obscene figure of paternal authority, who gambles and withholds funds from the department of internal revenue. Kathie and Jeff cross both the legitimate and the perverted agents of symbolic law. Kathie, in contrast to Isolde, not only operates alone but also enters into different alliances, which she adroitly shifts according to her needs. Jeff, like Tristan, is supported by a helper, the deaf and dumb Kid, who, like Kurwenal, repeatedly warns him against danger. Indeed, as in the Wagnerian libretto, the Kid brings about the accidental death of Whit's helper Jo, who, much like Melot, has gone after Jeff to kill him, though in contrast to the Wagnerian plot, Jeff's partner does not follow him in his death. Instead, the Kid proves his love for his boss by refusing to resolve into a sentimental story the antagonism of desire, for which his master ultimately comes to pay with his life. To Ann's question of whether Jeff was going away with Kathie when the police caught up with them, he nods in affirmation, forcing her to recognize that she was not all there was to her lover's desire.

At the end of the film, as he watches Ann get into the sheriff's car, the Kid salutes the sign above the gas station carrying Jeff's name, as though to signal that their oblique homoerotic bond has won in the end against both the reality of Jeff's fatal embrace with Kathie as well as against the protective fiction of Ann's romantic trust. The disillusioned bride, in turn, takes on Brangäne's position, for throughout the noir script she is the one who pleads for a peaceful solution. She defends Jeff against Sheriff Jim, she repeatedly assures Jeff that she trusts in his love. At the same time she argues against the narrative of fated love by insisting that they can realize his fantasy of a home cleansed of all traces of the past, even while she refuses to accept Jeff's version of Kathie as an embodiment of evil. And like Brangäne, she is also the one who colludes with the constraints of the law, telling the sheriff about her love for Jeff, yet ultimately ceding to his authority once the Kid has shattered her belief in Jeff's fidelity.

Most striking, however, is the fact that the noir script endows its femme fatal with one significant attribute which Wagner had reserved for her helper. Kathie's desire undercuts the power of the men, who use her for their own gain, in part when she plays one man off the other but most significantly in the final confrontation with Jeff. For as she insists, "I never told you I was anything other than I am. You just wanted to imagine I was," she radically troubles the premises of his narrative of fated love by showing that in contrast to his willingness to abdicate choice and give himself up to accident, she actually could help it all along. At this point the noir script actually dismantles the misogynist encoding which its narrator installs by rendering visible the fact that men call the femme fatal evil precisely because of her insistence on agency. Kathie forces Jeff to realize that the stain of the past will always haunt him because it is the very motor of his desire. "You're no good and nor am I," she explains. "We've been wrong a lot, and unlucky a long time. I think we deserve a break." With his response, "We deserve each other," the script indicates that if his entrance into the noir world began when her beauty infected him with a fantasy of fated love, exit from this world occurs precisely when he acknowledges his own agency, in an act where accepting the constraints of symbolic law and ceding to a desire whose path leads to death proves to be the same thing.

Billy Wilder's *Double Indemnity*, in turn, begins in the third act of Wagner's opera. The film is framed by the wounded Walter Neff, who, having found refuge in his office, narrates his version of past events into a dictaphone before trying to get across the border to Mexico. The memorandum he addresses to his partner Barton Keyes, whom he describes as "wolf on a phony claim," begins with the confession of murder: "I killed Dietrichson. I killed him for money and for a woman. I didn't get the money and I didn't get the woman. Pity isn't it." The irony around which Wilder's film revolves is that the hero's narrative itself is a phony claim. For as the story unfolds, we are shown that what he desired was neither the forbidden woman nor her husband's money, but rather to cheat the law and get caught by the very man he sought to trick. The poignancy of Wilder's refiguration of Wagner's *Liebestod* scenario thus consists in the way he recasts his fated hero into a trickster.

In the flashback narrative, the evening after Phyllis has asked Walter to kill her husband and he initially appears shocked at this proposal, she visits him in his apartment. The manner in which Wilder stages their embrace, corresponding to the moment when Tristan and Isolde enter into the noir world of *Liebestod* at the end of the first act, brilliantly emphasizes the asexual nature of their attraction. After the initial kiss, Walter quite expressly disentangles himself from Phyllis's arms. Inspired by one of Walter's stories, Phyllis indulges in her fantasy of a fatal accident happening to her husband. Walter, in turn, counters with a double fantasy, for he not only assures her that his supervisor Keyes knows all the tricks, he also admonishes her that "if there is a death mixed up in it you haven't got a prayer. They'll hang you as ten dimes will buy a dollar." Only after having added, "and I don't want you to hang baby. Stop thinking about it," does he take her into his arms. The smile that suddenly lights up his face, as he presses her face to his right shoulder and looks out over her head, once more avoiding her kiss, thus signifies his pleasure at the thought that he can come up with the one trick his partner doesn't know, even while, by virtue of his explicit denial, the smile also implicitly refers to his pleasure at the thought of seeing her hang. The Walter Neff of the flashback story thus emerges as the Tristan of the first act, who desires Isolde for the death wish she embodies. He is also the Tristan who bonds with his friend Kurwenal to shame, taunt, and destroy the power of his female adversary.

Two things are particularly striking about the way Wilder films the deflection of a sexual consummation of passion on the part of his fated lovers. The camera draws back from their embrace and cuts to the wounded Neff of the framing narrative, speaking into his dictaphone in a dark room. It pans up to his face, which glows with some inner fire, as he explains the details of his fantasy of transgressive enjoyment: "It was all tied up with something I'd been thinking about for years, since long before I ran into Phyllis Dietrichson. Because, you know how it is, Keyes, in this business you can't sleep for trying to figure out all the tricks they could pull on you. You're like the guy behind the roulette wheel watching the customers to make sure they don't crook the house. And then, one night, you get to thinking how you could crook the house yourself, and do it smart because you've got the wheel right under your hand . . . and suddenly the doorbell rings, and the setup is right there in the room with you." Significant about this mise-en-scène is that while it postpones the second part of Neff's fantasy (his desire to enjoy Phyllis's corpse) by embellishing only the first part, it also screens out a visual rendition of their lovemaking. This is instead replaced with the image of the bond between him and Keyes. The camera doesn't cut back to the fated lovers until Walter is already leaning back on his couch, smoking, and watching Phyllis putting on her makeup, and we recognize that his adultery with Phyllis is the cover for a different enjoyment, namely, tricking the older man to whom he is also libidinally drawn.[4] As the cover object of desire, Phyllis must be sacrificed before the two men can finally unite in a forbidden homoerotic embrace, which proves to be coterminous with a lethal embrace.

Going through with their plan indeed successfully keeps Phyllis and Walter apart. Sometimes they meet accidentally on purpose in a designated supermarket, to discuss murder rather than love. However, Wilder stages this crisscrossed desire most poignantly in the scene where Keyes visits Walter one night to inform him that he is convinced "something has been worked on us in the Dietrichson case." Phyllis, who overhears their conversation as she too approaches Walter's apartment, hides behind the door as Keyes leaves. For several moments Walter remains suspended between his two partners, the woman with whom he has broken the law at his back, the man he has betrayed in front of him. After Keyes has left, Phyllis will once again stand behind Walter, place her arms around him and force him into an embrace, but only after he has already admonished her that "Keyes can't prove anything. Not if we don't see each other."

It was indeed Keyes who initially gave Walter a narrative about how transgressive desire inevitably leads to death. He assures Walter that the killers of Mr. Dietrichson will be digging their own graves: "They are stuck with each other and they have to ride together all the way to the end of the line. It's a one-way trip and the final stop is the cemetery." Wilder's version of the *Liebestod* script thus hinges on the way inflicting and healing a wound strangely correspond. For supported by Keyes's story, the cure Walter comes up with is to turn his murderous desire against the femme fatale so as to purify himself of the murderous desire she infected him with. In their final nocturnal confrontation, both Walter and Phyllis admit that instead of an eternal union with the other, they wish to enjoy the death of the other. Walter merely seeks to exchange one protective fiction for another. To motivate his own killing, he accuses Phyllis of having planned the murder all along. Phyllis, however, dismantles all romantic fantasy in what I want to call an ethical gesture, because it entails the recognition that she has nothing to lose in the loss of her life. After she has fired the first shot, she admits, "No, I never loved you nor anybody else. I'm rotten to the heart. I used you just as you said until a minute ago, when I couldn't fire that second shot. I never thought that could happen to me." In imitation of Tristan's hallucinatory transfiguration, Walter in turn is utterly caught up in a delusion one could call the sadistic reversal of *Liebestod*. "Sorry, I'm not buying," he answers, as his shots finally penetrate his lover.

But then, he was not only using her as she was using him. His desire was aimed at a different *Liebestod* scenario from the very beginning, making up the narrative frame of *Double Indemnity*. Indeed, the most compelling refiguration of the Wagnerian *Liebestod* offered by Billy Wilder involves the figure of paternal authority, who is once again split between the abusive, crude, and sexually indifferent husband, Mr. Dietrichson on the one hand, and Barton Keyes, the infallible detector of phony claims, on the other. The latter warns the hero against the fatal seduction of the woman, taunts her, and is willing to risk everything to destroy her. However, as many critics have noted, the fact that Keyes, who will not carry his own matches because "they always explode in my pocket" and repeatedly asks Walter Neff to light his cigar, is perhaps the key trademark of a homoerotic bond, related to the homoeroticism between Tristan and King Mark. With the exception of the first and the last exchange of fire between the two men, each instance implies the presence of Phyllis. If, then, Neff's narrative begins with the phony claim that he wanted a woman and money that didn't belong to him, it ends on a phony demand. Walter, who asks Keyes not to call an ambulance because he says he needs four hours to get to the border, collapses before he can even get to the elevator. If he had relinquished his desire to make a confession to Keyes and instead gone across the border into Mexico, he would have survived. Keyes kneels beside his wounded friend, while Walter, pushing a cigarette between his lips but finding that he no longer has the power to light his own match, turns to him. Then Keyes takes the match, lights it with his thumb the way Walter used to, and gives him fire. The last image of the film resonates with the full ambivalence of this exchange, for as Walter looks beyond Keyes, it is as though he too has recognized that there is nothing to lose in a loss. In this sense the femme fatale has succeeded in infecting him. Receiving Keyes's punishment as an oblique confession of love is, finally, the perfect plot, straight down the line. This is, of course, also the position in which Wagner's hero ends, with Isolde holding Tristan's corpse in her arms, through her hallucination reinvigorating his dead body. It was the two men's fatal love all along.

OUT OF THE WOUND

"There was one chance in a million we'd bump into our past," Jeff explains to Ann in *Out of the Past*. Yet what the noir scripts articulate so convincingly is that this enjoyment of pure contingency is the clandestine kernel of the *Liebestod* scenario. In a similar manner, both Isolde and Tristan obsessively reiterate a past scene of injury, where an inflicted wound never fully healed, designating this as the primal scene around which their *Liebestod* scenario revolves. Initially, in response to the song Kurwenal sings about the death of Morold, Isolde explains to Brangäne that her captor Tristan is the man who once came to her under the assumed name Tantris. Knowing him to be the murderer of Morold, she had wished to strike him dead with his own sword. But owing to the way his gaze penetrated her, she decided instead to heal the wound inflicted by Morold, so that in health he could travel homeward and trouble her no more with his powerful gaze. When Tristan returns to woo her for his king, this chain of woundings and healings takes another turn. Isolde is forced to recognize, "It was I who in secret brought this shame upon myself! Instead of wielding the avenging sword, I let it fall harmlessly!" (Act 1, Scene 3). If she is the creator of her own shame, she wishes him to fulfill the death she has designed for him, hoping thus to heal both the wound his gaze inflicted and the wound he inflicted by wooing her for another man. At the end of the first act, explaining to him that he may now utter his own fate, she offers him not his sword, however, but the drink of fatal atonement.

Their fantasy of a totally encompassing love is thus conceived as a release from this economy of psychic woundings. Having twice refused to wound him mortally with his own sword, and having failed to mortally wound them both with a drink of fatal atonement, Isolde has instead engendered a psychic state beyond any situation of recuperation. And yet—as the noir inflection of *Liebestod* so insistently plays out—any fantasy of escape must be thought as a phony claim. The economy of psychic recuperation is such that all therapy simply takes place on the level of after-pressures. Put another way, any real primal scene of wounding lies beyond the realm of representation. The dramaturgic value of a primal scene of wounding is purely structural. It functions as the point of departure, from which all subsequent psychic representations feed without ever having full access to this scene of originary shock, and as such exceeds all belated figurations. In the libretto, this chain of recuperative woundings is played out in the second act not only in the sense that Melot repeats Morold's act when he once more inflicts a mortal wound to Tristan's body. More crucially, Tristan and Isolde's delusion of escape wounds King Mark, who exclaims to Tristan, "Why, wretched man, have you now wounded me so sore . . . with never a hope that I could ever be healed" (Act 2, Scene 3). Referring to the betrayal of his trust more than to the actual adultery, Mark insists that the significant wounding occurs in relation to the infallibility of his symbolic authority, which is to say, in the introduction of deceit and suspicion on the symbolic level of exchange, not through any romantic desire for Isolde. In so doing Mark in turn wounds the fated lovers' delusional trust in the exclusive significance of romantic bonds.

In the third act, when Tristan offers his narrative to Kurnewal of how he got his current wound, he explicitly refers it back to the fatal wound of birth at the beginning of life. Fearing that Isolde will not arrive, he recalls that the old melody he now hears is the same as the one he heard as a newborn child, when it heralded the death of his parents. He recalls how Isolde healed and closed his wound, only to tear it apart again with his sword, before dropping this fatal instrument. In his confession he then moves on to the scene in which she gave him a poison draught to drink that instead of finally curing him of his fated yearning came instead to cast its dire love spell. In so doing, Tristan exposes the antagonism subtending human existence. Indeed, the *Liebestod* scenario he calls "Dying, still to yearn, not of yearning to die. What never dies now calls, yearning, for the peace of death" stages the psychic impasse Freud has theoretically formulated as a strife between the pleasure and the death principle. The former seeks to preserve a life-sustaining balance of tension and with it an economy of deferred desire, aimed at a release from this tension, while the latter aims at a tensionless state of existence, which is, however, coterminous with "deanimation."[5] Engendered in a heterotopic site between home and exile, first on a boat, then in a nocturnal garden, and finally on an island, the fantasy of *Liebestod* transposes a traumatic knowledge about the inevitability of contingency into a narrative of fate. It allows its two fated lovers to speak about the primordial loss subtending all efforts of recuperation, even while it functions as a protective fiction, allowing them to misrecognize, and thus continually transpose, the state of deanimation, of non-tension, at the beginning and end of existence.

There is, however, another voice in Wagner's libretto, based on the fact that, as I have already suggested, it splits the femme fatale into two figures—the vengeful Isolde, over whose body a protective fiction of enraptured ecstasy comes to be enacted, and Brangäne, who engenders this transformation of pure death drive into a fantasy of *Liebestod,* even while it is her role to warn against this all-encompassing drive. My own claim is that Brangäne's position is so compelling precisely because she speaks not beyond but from within the symbolic, whose harsh laws she keeps mitigating. In the first act she pits reason against Isolde's mad and vain frenzy, arguing first in favor of Mark's nobility and then invoking the power of her love potion. Finally, after having voiced her horror at Isolde's wish to administer the draught of death, she is the one who introduces the first duet of love between Isolde and Tristan by declaring that the narrative of enraptured passion they are about to proclaim to each other is nothing other than "foolish devotion's deceitful work," a lamentation of "eternal want and pain" (Act 1, Scene 5). In so doing, she offers us the possibility of ironic distanciation toward both Tristan's belief that his past rejection of Isolde was nothing other than the deceitful spell of malicious cunning, as well as Isolde's assurance that her anger at her lover was idle and foolish. From the start, the Wagnerian libretto positions Brangäne's repeated interventions so as to enact the sudden ecstasy of the two lovers as nothing other than the result of a draught of love, and thus not a necessity but a contingency.

In a similar manner, Brangäne warns Isolde in the second act that she hears only what she wants to, while remaining blind to those around her planning to betray her. In their debate over whether to extinguish the torch or not, Brangäne once more pits the voice of reason, pleading for a recognition that passion is a fiction, resulting from a deceptive draught ("Oh leave the warning flame, let it show you your danger") against Isolde's recklessness. Banishing Brangäne's light is meant to signify her total subjugation to the goddess of love—"I have become her property, now let me show my obedience" (Act 2, Scene 1). Indeed, Brangäne's intervention, admonishing the fated lovers, with her solitary voice, to "Take care! Soon the night will pass" (Act 2, Scene 1), seeks to break up their dyadic fusion. Yet her claim that the ecstasy they are experiencing cannot be indefinitely maintained only feeds their fantasy of an eternal life in death. Put another way, her voice of warning is what guarantees their fantasy of being able to foreclose the law, to renounce renunciation within the realm of social existence. Finally, in the third act, Brangäne's voice speaks out against the collective delusion that has taken hold of all those involved in the *Liebestod* scenario. She warns Kurwenal that King Mark and his court have come with peaceful intentions, and explains to Isolde that she has revealed the secret of the potion to the king. The ironic distanciation thus introduced by the libretto can be formulated as follows. Precisely because her voice not only offers an alternative to the tragic outcome, declaring that no one needs to die, but also represents the position no one heeds, it marks the voice of alterity, against which the delusion of fated love is erected. As such a mark of difference, however, it also gives voice to a contingency which undercuts the narrative of *Liebestod*. Things could have happened differently.

Brangäne's intervention is fruitless, of course, because the narrative promise sustaining any reworking of the myth of the "eternal love between Tristan and Isolde" works with the tacit understanding that the two lovers will abide by the script of fatality that has been preordained for them. Yet Wagner's inclusion of Brangäne's voice, engendering, supporting, guarding, but also warning against the totalizing fantasy of *Liebestod,* calls forth an ineffaceable fissure in Wagner's celebration of recuperative healings. Although the score seeks to seduce us away from the position of reason she represents, Wagner's libretto offers us her position as the one which is both catalyst of fantasy and that to which fantasy must be deaf and dumb, so as to play itself out straight down the line. She gives voice to the law of pure contingency, pitted against the preordained script of fated love—the old melody Tristan hears at birth, signifying the fatedness of his lot, only to hear it again as he lies dying, as well as the melody Isolde in her hallucination hears resonating from Tristan's corpse. Brangäne's voice declares: Take care! Precisely because night invariably gives way to day, everything could always still turn out differently. Her voice offers a different promise than the *Liebestod,* less enjoyable, perhaps, but also less circular; namely the promise of agency and intervention. She too knows there is nothing to lose in a loss, because the traumatic knowledge of our radical estrangement, our *unheimlich* presence in the world, is as irrecuperable as it is ineffaceable from all mortal existence. Yet renouncing a renunciation of this knowledge in her case means accepting the symbolic for what it is—the catalyst for viable narratives we construct so as to live, because without such a fallible protection against an unconditional and overabundant proximity to the erotics of the death drive there would be no representation of any kind: no score, no script, no fantasy. In her voice, though crisscrossed, the gesture of accepting our fate of radical alienation within the symbolic and the gesture of living an ironic distanciation from any one law of fate rest side by side.

NOTES

1. Paul Schrader, "Notes on *Film Noir,*" in *Film Noir Reader,* ed. Alain Silver and James Ursini (New York: Limelight Editions, 1996), 53. An earlier version of this essay appeared under the title "Noir Wagner," in *Sexuation,* ed. Renata Salecl (Durham, N.C.: Duke University Press, 2000).

2. Schrader, "Notes on *Film Noir,*" 54–56.

3. In so doing, I follow Catherine Clément's attempt in *Opera, or The Undoing of Women,* trans. Betsy Wing (Minneapolis: University of Minnesota Press, 1988)

to explore the ideologically encoded family romances played out in nineteenth-century opera libretti, divorced from the explicit intentions of the composer as well as the librettist, but without necessarily agreeing with the readings she offers.

4. Wilder's presentation of the bond between Keyes and Neff must be seen within the context of the Hays Production Code, forbidding any explicit presentation of homosexuality; see Leonard J. Leff and Jerold L. Simmons, *The Dame in the Kimono: Hollywood, Censorship, and the Production Code from the 1920s to the 1960s* (New York: Doubleday, 1990).

5. See Sigmund Freud, "Beyond the Pleasure Principle," in *The Standard Edition of the Complete Psychological Works of Sigmund Freud* (London: Hogarth Press, 1955), vol. 18, 3–66.

SIXTEEN

Ludwig's Wagner and Visconti's *Ludwig*

GIORGIO BIANCOROSSO

Luchino Visconti's filmed portrait of the last reigning King of Bavaria, *Ludwig* (1973), treats three main themes, each of which corresponds to an important facet of Ludwig's personality: his difficulties in performing his duties as leader of the kingdom; his homosexuality; and his absorption in and self-definition through art—especially Wagner's operas, of which he was a staunch and indefatigable promoter. Aside from showing Ludwig's genuine love for Wagner, as expressed through his acts of generosity to the composer and his words to his cousin Elisabeth, the film deals explicitly with the composer himself by showing his move to Munich with Cosima, Hans von Bülow, and their children, his preoccupations over the staging of *Tristan,* the scandal that prompted his dismissal from the Bavarian capital, and the growing involvement with what would eventually become the Festspielhaus in Bayreuth.

The music of *Ludwig,* all of which is either preexisting or adapted, is undoubtedly an important component of the dense grid of quoted, reconstructed, or referenced materials that make up the film as we know it. As the core element of the soundtrack, Wagner's works are symptomatic of the inherent dynamism and connotative potential of preexisting materials generally. They loom large over the first half of the film not only as a historical phenomenon that touches on the characters' lives but also as a symbolic, oblique presence in the narration, a rich field of subtexts that enter in relation to one another as well as to all the other innumerable texts, images, and symbols, which feed, enlighten, and also not infrequently obscure Visconti's ambitious and idiosyncratic biopic.

Possibly awed by the formidable baggage of associations Wagner's operas accumulated in their history, critics and scholars have often interpreted their role in cinema in the light of their reception history.[1] Insofar as that history informs the artistic intent of a filmmaker, our own horizon of expectations, and with it, inevitably, our encounter with the film, this is a necessary and laudable approach. What this leaves unexamined, however, is something equally important: namely, the extent to which Wagner's music, as it enters the world of a film, is itself transformed. Films are not static receptors but agents in the reception history of the music they employ. Far from merely dispatching ready-made meanings, preexisting music—and Wagner is no exception—partakes in the process of emergence that characterizes the meaning of music/image relationships in multimedia.[2] Put another way, preexisting music is more than merely "recognized" and then interpreted according to already acquired schemas of interpretation; it is also attended to in a temporal unfolding within a context of a strategically constructed narrative, an unfolding through which its programmatic and conceptual content may be nuanced, diluted, bent to fit a particular artistic or ideological agenda, or even utterly neglected.

In this essay I want to trace some of these transformations as they manifest themselves in *Ludwig,* in three successive stages. First, I will look at three instances of performances of Wagner's music in the context of Visconti's nostalgic reconstruction of nineteenth-century aristocratic culture. I will then examine a number of nondiegetic cues featuring Wagner's music as adapted by Visconti's collaborator, composer Franco Mannino. Finally, I will conclude by briefly addressing the questions surrounding the state of completion of *Ludwig* and their implications for the interpretation of the film presented herein.

MISE-EN-SCÈNE: MUSIC REGAINED

In an interview accompanying the DVD release of the so-called "restored" version of Visconti's *Ludwig,* Umberto Orsini, who plays Count von Holstein's role, tells the story of a typical, and revealing, moment of the production of the film.[3] Just as he was about to shoot the scene of the meal with which the Bavarian ministers celebrated the imminent deposition of Ludwig, Visconti asked Orsini whether the wine was cold enough. Aware that inside the flutes was real champagne, and not the cheap concoction actors are normally given when shooting, Orsini was amused by the question and jokingly replied that the champagne was still too warm and that it would take a few more minutes for it to be ready to serve. Visconti, unfazed and possibly unaware that Orsini was being playful, waited accordingly. What one sees on the screen, therefore, are the images of actors enjoying a glass of real champagne, chilled to perfection.

Having related the anecdote, Orsini goes on to suggest that the fact that the champagne was real and ready to drink gave the actors a sense of the "truth" of the meal they were reenacting. This is not only because of the awareness that the type of drink conformed to what was consumed on that fateful day. Orsini is also referring, I take it, to the fact that in so meticulously recreating the scene Visconti was affording the actors, through their very senses, a point of entry into a moment of the past. This, in turn, awoke in them a sense of the responsibility they had in conveying the historical and psychological truth of the moment they were reenacting.

Though rarely as probing and illuminating as Orsini's testimony, references to the perfectionism Visconti brought to bear on the costumes and sets in his period productions abound in both the scholarly literature and the press. Far from being a whim, Visconti's notoriously fanatical approach has an important and twofold purpose. On the one hand, it is meant to elicit from his actors acute awareness of the texture and materiality of the space being recreated (in something like the manner described by Orsini in the interview mentioned above). To achieve this goal, the accurately reconstructed historical detail need not be visible or hearable by the spectator. One thinks of Visconti's attention to the quality of the linens folded inside a closet, for instance, or the particular hue of the inside of a cup. The fidelity of the object or space to its presumed original manifestation, and the sensation it produces in the actors, is meant to affect their performance in such a way that something like the impression of inhabiting a certain milieu is conveyed to the audience as well.

When the carefully crafted object, configuration, or sonic detail happens to be a visible or hearable element of the mise-en scène, then the director may be said to be offering to the spectator, too, the chance to savor the sights and sounds of the past, however fleeting the experience may be, however mediated by the filter of memory, personal experience, and of course, the cinematic apparatus itself. There is nothing less at stake in this method than the obstinate, desperate desire to make the screen come alive through the miraculous re-creation of an irrevocably lost fragment of time past. The sustained close-up of the flute filled with chilled, bubbly champagne in *Ludwig* is rather like an act of faith in the objectivity of what is being recorded by the camera and the ability of cinema to perform the miracle of bringing the past back to life.[4]

Though this is far less recognized, throughout his career in both the theater and the film industry Visconti applied similarly exacting standards to musical performances. *Ludwig* features four onscreen performances, three of which involve Wagner's music. Wagner himself, played by a heavily made-up Trevor Howard, is seen performing only once, at the piano, during a conversation with the king (who is paying him a visit after the premier of *Tristan*). Ironically, it is not his music we see him playing but a transcription of the Prelude of *La Périchole* by the much-despised (by Wagner) Offenbach. The amusing sight of Wagner playing Offenbach is even more ironic when understood in the light of the previous sequence, set somewhat earlier in the Wittelsbach family's residence on the Island of the Rose, in Lake Starnberg. There, Elisabeth, Empress of Austria and cousin of Ludwig, puts on a tirade before the king for wasting money and endangering his reputation by staging *Tristan*. In the Offenbach scene, Howard is in front of the camera in a medium-long shot. His hands are not visible but we see him accompany with his torso the movement of the music, marking the end of his impromptu performance with the proverbial line, directed to the king, "This is the music Germans want to hear, not mine!" While in this instance uninterested in showing the visual aspect of the performance in painstaking detail, Visconti seems to have cared deeply about its musical quality. He was at pains to emphasize that composer and brother-in-law Franco Mannino, who was to perform the music and arrange it, refrain from playing too well, "for it is well known that Wagner was not a virtuoso at the piano."[5] The result is a very fine balance, the performance conveying something of the professional musician in Wagner yet just short of sounding like the work of a pianist.

Later in the film, Elisabeth's sister Sophie performs in her bedchamber Elsa's Act 1 narrative, "Einsam in trüben tagen," from *Lohengrin,* the opera that had a formative impact on Ludwig.[6] The sequence, which consists of one long, unedited shot, begins as if Sophie were performing to herself. In fact, she is sharing the room with Ludwig, but his presence is revealed only gradually as the camera first zooms out and then pans toward the right till Ludwig is seen in a dark corner of the room, reclining on a chair and visibly upset. The slow pace of the moving camera and the sustained image of Ludwig (Helmut Berger), head in his hands, makes the scene seem interminable, fatally exposing Sophie's fragile voice to Ludwig's, and our own, inspection. There is more than discomfort or contempt in Ludwig's reaction; solipsistically, he is not facing Sophie but registering his own profound embarrassment at her performance. That something so precious and familiar should now seem so unappealing throws him into despair and forces him to contemplate the terrible mistake he has made by promising to marry Sophie. He was soon to break off his engagement to her.

If Sophie's singing seems so painfully inadequate, this is because of the reaction we see on Ludwig's face. Her singing is not as unredeemably bad as some commentators would have it; it is, more simply, a plausible representation of how someone at her level of proficiency would sing. Indeed, once accustomed to it, one realizes that despite the limited range, hers is a not entirely unmusical voice. Ludwig's response notwithstanding, Sophie's voice seems so patently "below standard" because its quality is unexpected, as films feature by norm beautiful, resonant, and artificially enhanced voices. After all, moments of singing in cinema often take place in a fantastic or mythical realm that leaves little or no space to the imperfections of direct sound and the raw accents of the poorly trained, imperfect voice of an amateur.

Besides instigating Ludwig's emotional response and symbolizing his and Sophie's distance, such a voice is significant in that it is meant to ring true. Like a number of other episodes in *Ludwig,* the sequence is introduced without preparation and stands as a discrete moment in the king's life, meant to exemplify a state of affairs.[7] There are suggestions of what has led to it and intimations of what the future holds for the couple; none of these, however, is referred to explicitly, let alone shown. As such, and because it conforms to the physical and psychological attributes of the moment as Visconti understood it, this re-creation calls for contemplation as a self-standing *tableau,* reviving and not merely representing the past. It is like a recording of an event from another time with some of its elements, Sophie's voice among them, still intact.

Whether they come across as powerful, affecting re-creations or merely as lifeless, if faithful, reconstructions, Visconti's meticulously assembled canvasses are also representations of the work of memory. In his late films this is made apparent by depicting the main character as prone to being lost, as it were, in reverie. One thinks, in *Death in Venice,* of the flashbacks breaking through with increasing force into the seemingly smooth routine of Aschenbach's vacation in Venice; or, in *Conversation Piece,* the scene in which the professor suddenly remembers the study of his Rome apartment as it looked and felt on the day of his wedding, lit as if by the glow of youth and filled with opulent bunches of radiant flowers. In the stunning visualization of the professor's memory, the room looks the same and yet also different, the gulf between two distant moments in time brilliantly conveyed through lighting and set design.

These flashback sequences provided Visconti with yet another occasion for the exercise of complete control of the mise-en-scène. But the jolting roar of the booing crowd in *Death in Venice* or the impossibly vivid images of the flowers in the professor's room in *Conversation Piece* are not merely a function of a desire to depict things as they actually looked and sounded; they are also meant to express the force of involuntary memory. Proust's *Remembrance of Things Past,* which Visconti wanted to transpose to film, hovers like a giant shadow over all of his late films.

Visconti consistently treats his characters' reveries as a presentiment of death; therein lies their special poignancy. Another aspect of Proust's great novel that does find a nearly exact counterpart in Visconti's oeuvre is the relentless attempt to rescue from oblivion a slice of reality in the splendor and perceptual richness of its manifold details. In *Death in Venice,* Aschenbach's reminiscences are themselves contained within a formidable attempt to revive the look and feel of the Venetian Lido as the film director himself remembered it, having spent time there as a child just before the onset of World War I.[8] Visconti treated the historical film as a tool for remembrance and testimony independent of whether the subject of memory was made explicit in the course of the narrative or one of the characters actively engaged in remembering. *The Leopard* famously belongs to this group, as does *Ludwig*, the latter's status as testimony to a lost time boosted by the use, courtesy of the Wittelsbach and Habsburg families, of many of the original buildings and sites Ludwig himself built or visited.

For all the grandeur and impressiveness of the locales, however, the key to Visconti's belief in cinema as a medium of almost thaumaturgical powers lies in details of mise-en-scène found at the margins of the main action, hidden in the relatively obscure corners of the large canvas. While helping to "authenticate" the story and keep potential criticism at bay, historical research and the craftsmanship required to translate its findings into visible forms also inspired moments of genuine, if minute, scenographic invention. One thinks of the extraordinary detail of the ribbons scattered on the floor in *The Leopard*, as Count Salina walks aimlessly through his home as dawn approaches and the action of the ball subsides; or in *Ludwig*, the foregrounded chessboard in the scene where Ludwig pays a visit to Elisabeth's family in Bad Ischl; the worn-out, wet hound dragging its feet after a long day out, also in the Bad Ischl episode; or the sharp, calibrated sound of Elisabeth's shoes as she walks through Linderhof, reverberating against the walls of the castle's halls and bedrooms.

As ironic as this may seem, it is the significance of these details that justify the months of research and millions of dollars spent in pursuit of historical accuracy. What gives them their evocative power is their standing outside the forward thrust of the action. Freed from the tight fabric of the plot-driven mise-en-scène, they force upon the spectator an appreciation of the passing of time as such, above and beyond the fact that the medium of cinema imposes on them a temporal dimension. The contemplation of such "functionless details" as they emerge in the foreground against a background of time passing, unencumbered by pressing narrative needs, combined with the awareness of the accuracy of their reconstruction and the strangeness of their manufacture or appearance, produces a peculiar impression which is as close to the illusion of reliving the past as anything in big-budget, historically based cinema.[9]

The on-screen performance of the *Siegfried-Idyll* in *Ludwig* is a telling case in point (figure 16.1). The piece was famously performed on

FIG. 16.1. Visconti's *Siegfried Idyll*

Christmas day by a chamber orchestra, hired by Wagner for the occasion to mark the first Christmas of his newly born son Siegfried as well as Cosima's birthday (she was born on Christmas Eve). A celebration of fertility and family life, the sequence as a whole reads as a veiled commentary on Ludwig's inability to produce an heir and the extinction of the line of descendants of the main branch of the Wittelsbach family (this is followed, not coincidentally, by a scene depicting the late stages in the mental illness of Ludwig's as-yet unmarried brother, Otto).

Such reading is no more than adumbrated, however. Like the scene in which Sophie sings Elsa's number, the *Siegfried-Idyll* sequence stands, entirely self-sufficient, in splendid isolation. Like a moment of *ekphrasis*, it offers itself up to our appreciation as a virtuoso piece of descriptive acumen, impeccable taste, and historical reconstruction. Visconti's attraction to the tableau aesthetic in *Ludwig* follows quite naturally from the nature of the film's subject, the extravagant and meticulously reconstructed locales, and the king's own proneness toward contemplation. But that the subject was at all congenial to Visconti is hardly coincidental in light of Gilles Deleuze's observation that "in Visconti . . . objects and settings [*milieux*] take on an autonomous, material reality which gives them an importance in themselves."[10] Of these milieux, sound and music are an essential component, one that Visconti rarely, if ever, overlooked.

As indicated in the surviving evidence pertaining to the Christmas day performance of the *Idyll*, the ensemble is seen standing on the stairs leading from the antechamber to the sleeping quarters of Wagner's home in Tribschen (hence the term "stairs music" with which Wagner's children affectionately referred to it). Details of dress, design, and lighting are all carefully reconstructed and lovingly assembled in a complex that is as close to what must have been the original look of the locale as any afforded by the resources of modern cinema.[11] Silvana Mangano looks the part of Cosima more than ever and Howard's makeup is nothing short of miraculous. Visconti has a conductor, presumably standing for Hans Richter, lead the ensemble. As a bystander, the composer appropriately looks the part of the *metteur-en-scène,* the consummate man of the theater, looking on with apparent satisfaction at the spectacle he has managed to create in his own home. A glimpse of Wagner "directing" the couple's young girls so that they make the appropriate moves at the right time strengthens this impression.

It is a pity that the sequence as a whole fails to convey the awareness that Visconti was staging a staging. Dramatizing the tension between Visconti and Wagner, in equal parts responsible for what we see onscreen, might have animated a sequence that comes across instead as a frozen piece of stagecraft. This is the past as embalmed, not recreated. Two details redeem Visconti's *Siegfried-Idyll,* however. One is the awkward look of some of the musicians. Visibly uncomfortable, due the unusual venue in which they are being asked to perform, and also somewhat embarrassed at the extravagant characters they are playing for, their presence is a welcome touch of irony. Another detail is the degree of polish of the performance itself. Always sensitive to the quality of live performances, as opposed to studio recordings, Visconti asked and obtained from his musicians and collaborators both a very specific type of sound, grainy and with a warm room tone, and a style of performance that strikes a wonderful balance between accuracy and tentativeness (as is only too germane to a new piece performed under such unusual circumstances). Representing the effort and absorption necessary to producing musical sound in real time is of the essence to Visconti's understanding of onscreen performance.

All musical excerpts used diegetically in *Ludwig* share these qualities; all of them, moreover, are subject to stringent standards of historical accuracy in the name of "authenticity." This twofold set of requirements bespeak the aspiration to restore a sense of musical performances as unique, unrepeatable events, situated at a certain point in time and involving the physical effort of flesh-and-blood persons to produce sounds projected into a distinctive space. When used nondiegetically, Wagner's music sheds these qualities and is instead adapted, transformed, and manipulated in such a way as to enter a new, solipsistically conceived mythical realm, that of Ludwig himself. In this space, issuing as if from the recesses of the king's mind, the music ceases to have a concrete, tangible presence. Though its sounds reach our ears with equal force, it remains unclear whether we ought to interpret them as actual, recalled, or merely imagined. The difference between diegetic and nondiegetic music, then, finds in Visconti's *Ludwig* not only a moving dramaturgical justification but also a spectacularly apt elaboration.

SOLIPSISM AND DECADENCE: WAGNER AS FILM SCORE

In Visconti's best-known period reconstruction, *The Leopard,* the director's temptation to give a new lease on life to a milieu buried under the ashes of history nearly takes center stage at the expense of the lucid, rational exposition of the historical thesis which sustains the film (and which lifted it well above most historical dramas produced till then).[12] The thesis in *The Leopard* is expressed by the well-known dictum that "for things to stay as they are, they will have to change." Translated into more concrete terms, and as dramatized in the film, this means that there was continuity between pre- and post-unitary Italy, as the great landowners of the south, of whom the protagonist Salina is an outstanding representative, maintained their influence by agreeing to a pact with the emerging class of the new, mafia-friendly rich in the south and the industrialists in the north.

Ludwig is informed by no such thesis. True, the story of a king who not only rebels against the blind pragmatism of politics but defiantly embodies values antithetical to Bismarck's First Reich can be read allegorically as an indictment of a political trajectory that that culminates, and significantly for the worse, in Hitler's Third Reich.[13] But such a political message is at most implied. The film is firmly anchored in the private sphere. Among the subjects that enjoy at least some degree of elaboration, only the king's architectural projects and the gifts, through his patronage, of Wagner's music and the Bayreuth Festival amount to anything like a public contribution.

This was largely a posthumous legacy, however. As the historical documents suggest, and the film accurately if succinctly shows, Ludwig regarded Wagner, at least so long as he remained in his sphere of influence, as very much his own.[14] This has significant consequences as far as the role of Wagner in the film—both the man and the music—is concerned. Almost unique in the panorama of fictional works dealing with Wagner, and in striking contrast to Hans-Jürgen Syberberg's nearly contemporaneous *Ludwig: Requiem for a Young King* (1972), Visconti's *Ludwig* features Wagner's music as if the onslaught of later interpretations and appropriations had not yet affected its impact and meaning.

This, of course, applies first and foremost to Wagner's alleged last composition for solo piano (in fact, a fragment likely written in 1858 and revised while in Palermo in 1881).[15] The piece, dedicated to Cosima and often incorrectly referred to as the "Porazzi theme," is redolent in both style and technique of the beginning of the Prelude to *Tristan,* albeit in a form so concentrated as to anticipate one of Webern's symphonic miniatures. It is little more than a plaintive, slow-paced melody, harmonized in a characteristically chromatic fashion. Divided into three phrases evaporating, as it were, in quasi-cadential gestures, the melody comes to rest on a placid A♭-major chord. Visconti uses the melody to mark the beginning and the end of the film, as well as three of the most crucial junctures of the film: the departure from Munich of Richard Wagner; Ludwig's cruelly mocking coronation of Sophie, shortly before breaking off his engagement to her; and the moment of his arrest.[16] Like the unknown Verdi waltz in *The Leopard,* the thirteen-measure piano miniature became available to Visconti in a rather fortuitous fashion and, just like it, had hardly been publicly performed before the release of his film.[17] The work, therefore, lacked a reception history in the literal sense of the term. Its fate appears now to be sealed to *Ludwig* and, through the film, to Ludwig as well (see figure 16.2).

As to the excerpts from Wagner's better-known works, their gravitating toward the charismatic figure of the king reflects first and foremost the scope of the film's narrative vis-à-vis the chronology of the performances and reception of Wagner's works. *Ludwig* begins with the investiture of the young king in 1864 and ends with his death in 1886. Wagner and his works figure prominently only in the first half of

FIG. 16.2. The final freeze-frame at the sound of
Wagner's alleged "last composition"

the film. The composition of the *Siegfried-Idyll* and its presentation as a
gift to Cosima in 1870 mark the composer's last significant appearance.

The refreshing picture of Wagner's work that emerges from the film,
as yet unburdened by the meanings it took on in its long and checkered
history, is also a reflection of Visconti's single-minded focus on the figure of the king. Ludwig's deeply narcissistic understanding of Wagner's
work as a fulfillment of his own nature is given free rein by Visconti. So
strong is the king's personality, and so central his position in the film,
that *Ludwig* subsumes Wagner within the king's destiny. Given this, the
meaning of Wagner's operas oscillates between two contradictory yet
intertwined poles. They are the musico-poetic expression of a prelapsar-
ian state of grace, one to which Ludwig aspires, but also function as an
unremitting reminder of his own political and psychological decay.[18]

The inclusion of Wagner in the cast of characters eases the process
of abstraction of his music away from the mundane aspects of court life,
brutal dimensions of dynastic and national politics, and the scandal of
the ménage-a-trois between the composer and the von Bülows. As do
many of Visconti's characters, Trevor Howard's Wagner comes across
as an overwrought and theatrical figure.[19] Yet his physical presence on
screen, complete with the gesticulations, the whining, and excessive
talking appropriate to the case, does convey a sense of the unbridge-
able distance between a man and his creation, showing the persona as
inferred from the work to be incommensurate with the historical, flesh-

FIG. 16.3. Wagner and the von Bülows in Villa Pellet

and-blood person physically responsible for the coming into being of that work. On the evidence of his correspondence with the composer, it is both a person and a *persona* that Ludwig imagines himself associated with. Far from inhibiting it, the proximity to Wagner the man encouraged the king's proneness to idealize his work.[20]

Howard's first onscreen appearance gives, via the soundtrack, tangible expression to this process. The scene follows the testimony of one of the king's ministers that ends with a resentful reference to Ludwig's "extravagant" and costly passion for Richard Wagner. A cut to a new scene shows the composer in Villa Pellet, his new Munich home, in the company of Hans and Cosima von Bülow (figure 16.3).

As Wagner complains about his present situation, Mannino's instrumental adaptation of "So stürben wir, um ungetrennt," from Act 2 of *Tristan,* appears simultaneously in the soundtrack, accompanying a large portion of the ensuing dialogue. Hearing *Tristan,* soon to be premiered in Munich, over the film's first images of Wagner may seem no more than a didactic reference. Yet the undeniable pathos exuded by the music not only offers an immediate counter-argument to the petty remarks of the minister but also produces a movingly contrasting picture of the rather unpleasant person we are simultaneously watching onscreen. Far from creating a point of contact between the mythical realm conjured up by the music and the prosaic reality of the Wagner household, the use of music from *Tristan* propels the opera even further into a fantastic region that is already consistent with Ludwig's fanciful appropriation of it. It is as if we were looking at Wagner but listening to his music through the king's ears.

In *Ludwig*, it is as film music that Wagner's music becomes Ludwig's. The remarkable freedom enjoyed by Wagner's music from the overdetermined meanings attributed to it in the course of its reception history comes with a transformation of its aesthetic status, its subjection to an entirely different set of strictures and intertextual meanings, ones deriving from its newly acquired role as a score to a lavishly produced and sophisticated biopic. Far from being quoted as a monument of the past, a self-contained body external to the film and brought into it as a form of commentary or foreshadowing, Wagner's music is one with Visconti's portrayal of the king, becoming in the process another entity altogether.[21]

It is to three more important examples of this transformation that I would now like to turn. One such instance is the extraordinary sequence of Ludwig's encounter with his brother Otto during the war against Prussia in 1866. This begins, at the sound of "So stürben wir, um ungetrennt," with a shot of the Wittelsbach family flag hoisted atop the roof of the Berg residence.[22] The flag points to that hoisted by Ludwig in his chalet on the Island of the Rose while waiting for his beloved Elisabeth (which in turn echoes Isolde's signal to a dying Tristan in Act 3 of *Tristan und Isolde*). The music, transcribed for instruments only, continues as the camera goes on to show the residence, enhancing our impression that the building effortlessly combines elegance and grandeur. Once Otto is admitted inside, "So stürben wir" is replaced by the faint sound of a music box. Yet the spirit of *Tristan* endures.

Having first advised against the alliance with Austria against Prussia, Ludwig is in denial of the war. Upon entering his private quarters, Otto, and with him the audience, soon discovers that Ludwig is staging his own refusal to accept the war in a rather extravagant fashion. While a music box plays the "Abendsternlied" (Hymn to the Night Star) from *Tannhauser*, we see him contemplate images of the different phases of the moon projected onto the ceiling by a magic lantern. He has recreated, inside his own living room, a wholly artificial environment, a carefully crafted denial of the day. Ludwig is here performer, director, and sole member of the audience. While the magic lantern and the music box are a striking prototype of cinema itself, the manner in which he uses them resembles the solipsistic mode of reception afforded by contemporary home technology.[23]

The conversation with his brother is warm and affectionate till the two touch on the combined subjects of war and family. When Otto reminds him that the Wittelsbachs are related by blood to both their allies (the Habsurgs) and their enemies (the family of the King of Prussia), Ludwig abruptly shuts the music box and erupts in an outburst of anger. At this point, the instrumental arrangement of "So stürben wir, um ungetrennt" picks up again nondiegetically. The music of *Tristan* is here expressive of a cluster of feelings and ideas coexisting uncomfortably within the same consciousness: thoughts of promiscuity, madness, doomed destinies, and the awareness that his own attachment to Elisabeth, Empress of Austria, here referenced via *Tristan,* is yet another symptom of a malaise that runs deep in the family; in short, to paraphrase a well-known phrase by Wagner, deeds of Ludwig's inner life made tangible through the synchronization of music and the moving image. The return of the music of *Tristan* also suggests that although his brother is still there, Ludwig is once again alone, as he was at the beginning of the sequence. The darkened room is merely a physical manifestation of what is essentially a metaphysical isolation, a state of separated-ness that defies the actual physical proximity of other people but finds a sonic expression in the form of music.

As his brother leaves, Ludwig draws the curtains and drowns himself once again in the darkness of his room. A beautiful dissolve brings us then to an actual, as opposed to artificially re-created, nocturnal landscape. We see Ludwig walk through the forest surrounding the Berg residence at night as if, at long last, in his element, protected from even the slightest threat of personal contact. "So stürben wir, um ungetrennt" continues over the images of this environment, in one sense indistinguishable from it as both an element of its soundscape and a symbolic illustration of it. Something unexpected distracts Ludwig from his embrace of the night, however—a proof that such embrace is impossible. He notices one of his guards bathing in the lake. The music suddenly stops. The sound of crows flying by—an exquisitely executed sound over-

lap—makes the cut hardly noticeable. Ludwig is at first intrigued then visibly engrossed by the handsome, naked young man. The increasing urgency of his gaze is conveyed by one of the very few tracking shots in the film, the marvelous camera movement being all the more powerful here precisely for having being held up till this crucial point.

The scene is pivotal in terms of the destiny of the music of *Tristan* in the film. Its disappearance just as Ludwig discovers the extent of his attraction for the young man clarifies that *Tristan* occupies a sphere other than, perhaps even opposite to, that of sexual desire and its fulfillment.[24] This juncture also clarifies the meaning of *Tristan* as a subtext to Ludwig's relationship with his cousin Elisabeth. In retrospect, we know that the precondition of Ludwig's relationship to the cousin was the impossibility of its being consummated. The way in which the "Liebesnacht" underscores the sequences of Ludwig and Elisabeth walking, riding together, and even kissing would seem to lend support to Thomas Mann's view that "the act II of Tristan, I find now, with its metaphysical ambience of ecstasy, is more suited to young people who don't know what to do with their own sexuality."[25]

There is one more respect in which Wagner's opera, as a subtext, both specifies and amplifies the meaning of Ludwig's relationship with Elisabeth. *Tristan* is replete with both intimations and concrete instances of death. The film is similarly cast under images and actual occurrences of death: Ludwig's attraction to the night and his death-drive culminate in his suicide; Elisabeth's son's death and her sister Sophie's tragic death

FIG. 16.4A (*at left*) and B (*above*). Venus Grotto

in a fire in Paris, though never explicitly mentioned, marked important stations in the life of the empress as, naturally, did her own murder at the hand of the Italian anarchist Lucheni in 1898. The film hints at a possible death-drive on Elisabeth's part, too, during the Island of the Rose sequence mentioned above. During the conversation she has with Ludwig, Elisabeth segues from her firm warning against his championing of Wagner to the sarcastic remark that only a violent death brings glory to a monarch. This terrifying statement, accompanied by the notes of the "Liebesnacht," appears in hindsight rather like a startling prediction, a wish even.

The "Abendsternlied" recurs nearly as often as "So stürben wir, um ungetrennt," and is firmly associated with another aspect of the film: the idea of self-fashioning through a choreographed action in a scenographically conceived space. Like a Renaissance prince or a child who has not outgrown his desire to play with toys, on a number of occasions Ludwig reportedly staged re-creations of mythological, dramatic, or Wagnerian episodes *en plein air* (usually accompanied by music).[26] He also had permanent "sets" built where he could indulge his fantasies almost at will. The most spectacular of these is the Venus Grotto on the grounds of Linderhof castle (figure 16.4a and figure 16.4b).

The grotto is a fetishistic re-creation of the Grotta Azzurra in Capri and is frescoed with images drawn from the most memorable set of *Tannhauser*, the Venusberg (where the bacchanal that opens the opera takes place). Floating placidly on the water against the Naiads, Nymphs,

Graces, and Cupids depicted on the back wall of the grotto are the swans, a visual reference to the enduring presence of *Lohengrin*. Predictably, Visconti could not resist the temptation to set at least one important scene in this phantasmagoric locale, all the more so as plentiful iconographic evidence made the job of recreating the grotto in the studio relatively easy. To realize his vision of the king in the Venus Grotto, Visconti and his collaborators chose to shoot his meeting with the actor Keinz there. Infatuated with the declamation and the characters played by him, Ludwig is known to have invited Keinz to Linderhof castle for a few days. In the film he welcomes Keinz in the grotto, sailing a golden shell-shaped boat, a perfect copy of the original Münschelkahn. The king is surrounded by immaculately white swans, while the on-screen space is bathed in changing swaths of blue, red, and yellow light. The grotto was equipped with a light machine projecting strips of lights in different colors, and Ludwig on occasions also asked that music be played in it (despite the appalling acoustics). Accordingly, the film showcases the recreated grotto complete with a nondiegetic score.

As he did for "So stürben wir, um ungetrennt," Mannino transcribed the "Abendsternlied" for instruments only, the tenor voice replaced by a solo cello part. The composer stated that the director had asked him to eliminate the voice part so that the music would not interfere with the dialogue.[27] The rationale is, of course, perfectly understandable. Aside from the fact that there is almost no dialogue in this instance, however, the transcription does more than help achieve a desirable balance between different channels of sound. The cello tempers the Bellinian character of the aria while at the same time imbuing the music with a sense of pastness. It is almost as if the absence of the voice suggests a transformation operated on the music by the work of memory, the cello being the trace of a voice still present as a musical image rather than a sung text. The arrangement also allows the music to blend in with the set in such a way that it may be said to be an element of the grotto, issuing from the space depicted onscreen.

The way Visconti stages the encounter reinforces this impression in a surprising way. As Keinz enters this strange place, stranger than any set he had himself seen in the countless theaters where he performed, Ludwig slowly makes his way toward him on his boat. Having landed, he gazes repeatedly at the actor in a somewhat contemptuous way. He then feeds the swans in a deliberately slow, demonstrative manner, chagrin still on his face. Clearly, he is disappointed at seeing the flesh-and-blood Keinz—a mere actor—instead of one of the characters he was so well known for impersonating. Upon receiving the greatest actor of the age in a magic place that looks like a set but is in fact built through and through, Ludwig himself performs, erasing all possible distinctions between reality and fiction, flesh and image, history and myth.

The music is a constitutive element of this fantasy. As a learned reference, it suggests that in the form of the king himself, Keinz is meeting the evening star. But more importantly, while the music sustains the king's self-presentation it also unmasks it as delusional, a pure fantasy. The "Abendsternlied" thus occupies an ambiguous position, one that transcends the familiar ambiguity between the diegetic and the non-diegetic; the music sounds at the threshold between the heard and the unheard, illusion and delusion.

RECREATING LUDWIG

The scenographic excesses one sees in the Venus Grotto sequence are far from being an indulgence; they are essential to telling the story of Ludwig the designer, Ludwig the architect, Ludwig the stage director, and ultimately the mythomaniac (and sufferer).[28] The film stresses brilliantly the contrast between the ceremonies and rituals whose staging the king cannot control, like the investiture, and those that are entirely under his whim. Ludwig dreamt of being a director on an unprecedented scale, using the physical world as his stage. To this end, he employed the mountains and lakes of his kingdom, his buildings, and even human props—a hired actor. The film, as we have seen, completes this project to the extent that it includes Wagner's music in all those instances in which Ludwig could have only imagined it.

But is *Ludwig* itself complete? As is well known, the film was butchered before it went into distribution internationally in 1973. Visconti never wanted to see it and indeed disowned it. After his death, his collaborators bought back the surviving prints and discarded materials and re-edited *Ludwig* to its "intended" version. This was screened at the

Venice Film Festival in 1980 and released on VHS tape in the same year.[29] It is this version that is now commercially available on DVD.[30] But for all the claims of those involved in the restoration, the extent to which the final editing reflects the original plan remains unclear.[31]

The music provides tantalizing hints that the "restored" *Ludwig* may in fact be no more than an interpretation of the materials shot by Visconti and then left dormant as the film was released. Consider, for instance, the scene of Ludwig's conversation with his Cabinet Secretary Pfistermeister over his unsuccessful attempt to persuade Richard Wagner to take up residence in Munich. Ludwig's offer to Wagner, the importance of which is impossible to overestimate for the biography of the composer, was his first official act as a king. The exchange between the young king and the secretary is at once awkward, amusing, and illuminating. Ludwig complains about the fact that the state police are chasing Wagner. The Cabinet Secretary, not without irony, explains that it is not the police that Wagner fears most, but his creditors. Ludwig retorts that he does not care as long as Wagner is found and brought before him and then goes on to express his lack of interest for official functions.

The Prelude to *Lohengrin* accompanies the dialogue from the start, as if making Wagner's presence palpable even before his name is mentioned. The music calls up a whole world of cultural references, some of which were active forces in the shaping of Ludwig's identity. As an element unfolding in time and simultaneous with the dialogue between the king and his subordinate, it also becomes a suggestion of Ludwig's being somewhere else, dreaming of *Lohengrin* perhaps, or more prosaically, attempting to silence a conversation he does not wish to be engaged in. So palpably at odds with the mundane nature of the onscreen action, it gradually becomes the expression of an active attempt at disengagement, the evidence in the form of musical sound of a split attention.

The zooming camera near the beginning is a first indication of Ludwig's impatience with his secretary and increasing absorption in his own thoughts (zooming is a visual metaphor for a movement from the outside to inside of a character). This impression is also strengthened by the way in which music and the dialogue are mixed: the music is always a bit too loud, as if competing with the dialogue for the viewer's attention. The strongest evidence for this movement toward interiority, however, is the soaring, almost triumphant sound of the Prelude near the end of the sequence. This would indeed appear to mark the culmination of a trajectory toward greater and greater abstraction and self-absorption at the expense of the surrounding environment; and a prophetic one at that, too, since an important aspect of Ludwig's personality, as the film goes on to show, is his constant struggle to turn the physical and social reality around him into a static tableau for him to contemplate. Yet inexplicably, the last shot ends abruptly and prematurely, all the more so as there is a cut to another, very different piece of music: Schumann's *Kinderszenen,* used to underscore Elisabeth and Ludwig's first encounter.

There are several other instances of editing that, whether reflecting Visconti's original work done during post-production or what was redone in 1980, lack the polish characteristic of a finished film. Often a music cue lasts for as long as the corresponding sequence without any apparent thought given to whether it should accompany only a segment or stress an especially salient moment of it. In some cases one also senses that the original sequences were shortened at the fringes, resulting in somewhat rough beginnings and endings (especially apparent if one pays attention to the music). Entire episodes, moreover, are left without music. True, the distribution of scenes with or without music is not arbitrary and paces comfortably for the viewer the net of subtexts and allusions that the music inevitably produces. But whose choice was this? Is it a coincidence that most of the music-less sequences are those added to the version distributed in 1973—a sign, perhaps, that those who reconstructed the film did not have the heart to alter their audio-visual integrity? As to those sequences that do feature music, can we be sure that the choice of matching a certain piece, or portion of it, to a certain scene was not a posthumous re-creation, or even violation, of the initial score?

Ludwig remains, then, unfinished. The attempt by Visconti and his collaborators to clinch any argument about the meaning of Wagner's music in the film, by associating it so closely to the figure of the king, is fulfilled only partially. This applies especially to the cues used nondiegetically. Interpreting them as I have done here is as much an exercise in poetics as criticism, and by this I mean not so much the recovery of lost intentions as the exploration of the range of possibilities and effectiveness of the music-image combinations suggested, but only partially consummated, by the film. And because of this, as the afterlife apparition of a film that never was, *Ludwig* stands not only as a stage in the reception history of Wagner's music but also as an example of reception in the making, the very process of recontextualization and accrual of new meanings available for us not merely to observe but to shape through our own interpretations.

NOTES

I wish to thank the editors of this volume for their invaluable feedback during the preparation of this chapter. An early version of this essay was presented at the "Sound, Music, and the Moving Image" conference, held in London in September 2007. My thanks for the opportunity go to the members of the conference's Programme Committee (Julie Brown, David Cooper, Annette Davison, Miguel Mera, and Albert Riethmuller). Francesca Graneri and Emilio Sala have encouraged me to take up the topic of *Ludwig* and provided much needed help in refining my argument and locating materials. I thank them both.

To my father, "viscontiano della prim'ora," on his seventieth birthday.

1. See, for instance, Giuseppe Russo, *L'impossibile idillio* (Roma: Sideral Edizioni, 2006), especially chap. 5; and Roger Hillman, "A Wagnerian German Requiem: Syberberg's *Hitler,*" in *Unsettling Scores: German Film, Music, and Ideology* (Bloomington: Indiana University Press, 2005). In "Pivot Chords: Austrian Music and Visconti's *Senso* (1954)," Hillman also reads Visconti's *Senso* in the light of the twentieth-century reception of Bruckner's music, especially its Nazi appropriation (*Unsettling Scores,* 151–62). In the same essay, Hillman provides illuminating commentary on Visconti's use of folk and military songs (an aspect of *Ludwig* which lack of space prevents me from pursuing here).

2. See Nicholas Cook, *Analysing Musical Multimedia* (Oxford: Clarendon Press, 1998).

3. *Ludwig* (DVD), Medusa Video, N02SF00534, 2004.

4. This trait of the late Visconti, as so many aspects of his art, has its roots in nineteenth-century artistic practice. For a persuasive account of how the desire to recreate the past predates not only cinema but also photography, see Stephen Bann, *The Clothing of Clio: A Study of the Representation of History in Nineteenth-Century Britain and France* (New York: Cambridge University Press, 1984). For a fascinating study of the genre of the historical film interpreted alongside the practices of restoration and preservation in art and architecture, see Philip Rosen, *Change Mummified* (Minneapolis: University of Minnesota Press, 2001).

5. Franco Mannino, *Visconti e la musica* (Lucca: Akademos & Lim, 1994), 48.

6. On the significance of *Lohengrin* for Ludwig, see Franz Herre, *Ludwig II. von Bayern: sein Leben, sein Land, seine Zeit* (Stuttgart: Deutsche Verlags-Ansalt, 1986), 74ff.

7. Visconti most likely developed a taste for this style of storytelling from reading Tomasi di Lampedusa's novel *The Leopard* (*Il gattopardo,* 1958). And yet it is in *Ludwig,* rather than his 1963 version of *The Leopard,* that this style found its most thorough application.

8. There is a strong autobiographical impulse informing all Visconti's late work, which only the intrinsic significance of his subjects and the caliber of his collaborators prevented from overwhelming the representation.

9. On one aspect of the significance of the "functionless detail" in realistic literature, what he calls the "direct collusion of a referent and a signifier," see Roland Barthes, "The Reality Effect," in *The Rustle of Language,* trans. R. Howard (Berkeley: University of California Press, 1986), 141–48. In the cinema, and the visual arts more generally, the "functionless detail" does come across as less "functionless" than in literature, however, since its being integral to a holistically conceived set or milieu is never really in doubt. This would seem to point to a different understanding of the use of descriptive details in literature as well, one which, alas, cannot be pursued here.

10. Gilles Deleuze, *Cinema 2: The Time-Image,* trans. H. Tomlinson and R. Galeta (London: Athlone Press, 1989), 4.

11. Tribschen was reconstructed by the valiant technicians working for Visconti in the Cinecittà studios in Rome.

12. See Geoffrey Novell-Smith, *Luchino Visconti* (Garden City, N.Y.: Doubleday, 1968), 110–11.

13. Such a reading would be consistent with Visconti's first exploration of German history and culture, *The Damned,* a film so enmeshed with politics that it includes the Reischstag fire and the Night of the Long Knives as crucial pillars of its narrative structure. And yet considering the so-called German trilogy as a whole suggests rather a reverse trajectory, one in which *The Damned* already shows a regression toward the private sphere of which *Ludwig* is the culmination.

14. For Adorno, Ludwig's infatuation with Wagner is a symptom of "the relationship between Wagnerian mythology and the iconic world of the Empire, with its eclectic architecture, fake Gothic castles, and the aggressive dream symbols of the Neo-German boom, ranging from the Bavarian castles of Ludwig to the Berlin restaurant that called itself 'Rheingold.'" See Theodor Adorno, *In Search of Wagner,* trans. R. Livingstone (London: Verso, 1991), 123. Quite aside from his poorly informed judgment on the king and his musical, theatrical, and architectural taste, Adorno's thinking is circular here, as he projects aspects of the reception of Wagner's works back onto the works themselves.

15. See J. Deathridge, M. Geck, and E. Voss, *Wagner Werk-Verzeichnis* (Mainz and London: Schott, 1986), 460–61. Mannino's rendering of this piece on the piano as well as his transcription for string orchestra and wind quintet can be heard on the released recording of the film's original soundtrack (*Ludwig,* Philips 6323 021).

16. For an elaborate reading of the significance of the placement of the music and the way in which it resonates with several episodes of the film, see Russo, *L'impossibile idillio,* 102–107.

17. For the history of how the composition arrived on Visconti's desk, see Russo, *L'impossibile idillio,* 102–103. Russo's source, Franco Mannino himself, heard of the piece from Toscanini as early as 1946. Toscanini had accidentally seen it on the verso of the last page of a score of *Parsifal* given to him by Wagner's niece. The conductor donated a photographic copy of it to music critic Fedele D'Amico, who in turn passed it on to Mannino and Visconti's team. There is no reason to doubt this

reconstruction, but it is worth remembering that Russo does not seem to be aware that the piece is not, in fact, Wagner's last composition, nor that that it was hardly "discovered" by Toscanini (as Mannino would have it).

18. On this aspect of the relationship between Wagner and Ludwig, see Ernest Newman, "Wagner and Ludwig," in *The Life of Richard Wagner* (Cambridge: Cambridge University Press, 1976), vol. 3, 237–54; and Dieter Borchmeyer, "An Encounter between Two Anomalies: King Ludwig II and Wagner," in *Drama and the World of Richard Wagner,* trans. D. Ellis (Princeton, N.J.: Princeton University Press, 2003), 261–78.

19. This is not an isolated case. However thorough Visconti's casting method, virtuosic his makeup artists' work, and probing his manner of developing character psychology, the protagonists of Visconti's historical films are theatrical creations stiffened by excessively deliberate gesturing and too exacting a discipline. While understandable on commercial grounds, Visconti's preference for stars, too, is limiting, as the actors' off-screen personas often distract from the psychological qualities they are meant to project.

20. The correspondence between them, and the journal written by Wagner for the king, is collected in *König Ludwig II und Richard Wagner Briefwechsel,* ed. Otto Strobel, 5 vols. (Karlsruhe: G. Braun, 1936–39). For a selection of Wagner's letters to Ludwig in English translation, see *Selected Letters of Richard Wagner,* trans. and ed. S. Spencer and B. Millington (London and New York: Norton, 1987), 585–794.

21. I therefore disagree with film music historian Ermanno Comuzio, for whom Wagner's operas are used merely as a "beautiful backdrop." While it is possible that this may have been the initial motive behind the choice of the music, in my opinion the finished product, understood as the total product of music, dialogue, and visually realized narrative, far transcends Comuzio's characterization. See Ermano Comuzio, "Wagner e il cinema: itinerario di un rapporto," in *L'immagine in me nascosta—Richard Wagner: Un itinerario cinematografico,* ed. Ermano Comuzio and Giuseppe Ghigi (Venezia: Comune di Venezia 1983), 14.

22. Visconti and his crew actually used the castle where the young Elisabeth grew up, Possenhofen, made over to look like Berg. See G. Ferrara, "Giornale delle riprese in Austria e in Germania," in *Ludwig di Luchino Visconti,* ed. G. Ferrara (Bologna: Cappelli Editore, 1973), 62.

23. It is well known that the King attended countless theatrical representations staged for him, and him alone.

24. *Tristan* disappears from the film entirely after this point only to be reintroduced once much later, when Elisabeth decides to see for herself whether the rumors about the extravagance of Ludwig's castles are justified.

25. Thomas Mann, "Letter to Emil Preetorius," Dec. 6, 1949, in *Pro and Contra Wagner,* trans. A. Blunden (Chicago: University of Chicago Press, 1985), 210.

26. Among Ludwig's private performances outdoors it is worth mentioning the staging of the arrival of Lohengrin in the first act of the opera across the Alpsee, near Hohenschwangau, the Wittelsbach family castle. See Newman, *The Life of Richard Wagner,* vol. 3, 485; and Christopher McIntosh, *Ludwig II of Bavaria: The Swan King* (London: I.B. Tauris, 1982), 65.

27. Mannino, *Visconti e la musica,* 51.

28. For a view of the king's architectural projects, interpreted through the filters of his passion for Wagner and French culture, see Simon Jervis, "Ludwig II of Bavaria: His Architecture, Design and Decoration in Context," in *Designs for the Dream King: The Castles and Palaces of Ludwig II of Bavaria,* catalogue of the exhibition, Cooper-Hewitt Museum and Victoria and Albert Museum (London: Debrett's Peerage, 1978), 9–21.

29. *Ludwig* (VHS), Fonit Cetra Video, 1980.

30. Aside from the Medusa Video release (see n. 2) there is another DVD of the film produced by Arthaus (*Ludwig II,* 2001).

31. For the latest account of the tormented history of the film, see Russo, *L'impossibile idillio,* 18–33.

SEVENTEEN

The Tristan Project:
Time in Wagner and Viola

JEONGWON JOE

Some of the most sublime moments of my life were spent at
the side of a pond in the countryside of upstate New York,
recording singing frogs on a warm summer's night.

BILL VIOLA, "DAVID TUDOR: THE DELICATE ART OF FALLING"

"In the beginning was the Word . . ." provokes one to ask, where was
the image? But like the Biblical creation myth, Indian religion (for
example Yoga and Tantra) and later Asian religions (for example
Buddhism) also describe the origin of the world in sound . . .

BILL VIOLA, "THE SOUND OF ONE LINE SCANNING"

Bill Viola's comment on creation myths in the second epigraph epitomizes the essence of the sensorial hierarchy in his artistic world: sound
as the origin of images. His aesthetic focus on sound might seem ironic
for a visual artist, but it is not surprising considering that video is fundamentally an aural rather than a visual medium. Viola brings our attention to the ontological difference between video and film in terms of
their technological origins: whereas film depends on the photographic
process, video has evolved from audio technology. He notes that the
video camera is an electronic device that transduces physical energy into

electrical impulses and in this respect it is closer to the microphone than the film camera: "Film and its grandparent, the photographic process," he observes, "are members of a completely different branch of the genealogical tree."[1] Viola's interest in sound extends to its interaction with sight—"the crossover" between the two senses, hearing and seeing—and in this context he mentions his attraction to Wagner, who perceived his music in visual form. Viola quotes Wagner:

> My whole imagination thrilled with images . . . There rose up soon before my mind, a whole world of figures, which revealed themselves so strangely and plastic and primitive, that, when I saw them clearly before me and heard their voices in my heart, I could not account for the almost tangible familiarity and assurance in their demeanour.[2]

Given Viola's fascination with the sonic and visual "crossover," his engagement with Richard Wagner in *The Tristan Project* (2004) seems almost inevitable. As Lawrence Kramer discusses in detail in the following chapter, Wagner's *Tristan und Isolde* is replete with the intriguing interplay between sight and sound. In this chapter, I explore the affinities between Wagner's temporality and Viola's, drawing on Theodor Adorno's critique of Wagner's temporal world and theories of time in music and cinema developed by such scholars as Thomas Clifton, Mary Ann Doane, Jonathan Kramer, and Thomas Reiner. After I discuss the general aspect of the temporal affinities between Wagner and Viola, I examine how those affinities are manifested in *The Tristan Project*.

SCHIZOPHRENIA AND TIMELESSNESS: TIME IN WAGNER, VIOLA, AND CONTEMPORARY MUSIC

Here time becomes space.

RICHARD WAGNER, *PARSIFAL*

Time becomes a sculptural thing.

BILL VIOLA, "A CONVERSATION WITH BILL VIOLA, PETER SELLARS, AND DAVID ROSS"

> Listening to vertical musical composition can be like looking at a
> piece of sculpture . . . As with sculpture, the piece has no internal
> temporal differentiation to obstruct our perceiving it as we wish.

JONATHAN KRAMER, *THE TIME OF MUSIC*

Viola's special interest in sound, a temporal entity, explains the aesthetic primacy of temporal elements in his video art.[3] For Viola, the basic material of video is not the camera but time, and he finds that video art's kinship is closer to music than to space- and image-based arts such as painting and photography.[4] Viola does not have formal training in music, but he studied with David Tudor from 1973 to 1980 and worked as a member of Tudor's music ensemble Rainforest, which was later called Composers Inside Electronics. Before he undertook *The Tristan Project*, Viola was involved in several musical collaborations, including Tudor's *Rainforest IV*, a sound installation composed in 1973 and recorded in 1980 at the Berlin exhibition, "Für Augen und Ohren—Von der Spieluhr zum akustischen Environment" (For Eyes and Ears—From the Mechanical Clock to the Acoustic Environment).[5] Another music-related project Viola produced is a video film created in 1994 for Edgard Varèse's *Déserts*. It received its American premiere at the Hollywood Bowl in August 1999 with the Los Angeles Philharmonic under the baton of Esa-Pekka Salonen.[6] *The Tristan Project* was Viola's second collaboration with Salonen.

For Viola, the most fascinating aspect of video technology is its capacity for durational control—to play with and transform linear clock time beyond a naïve recording of it. In many of his works, he stretches, compresses, or re-orders what he has recorded. As many scholars and critics have indicated, cyclical temporality is a prominent element of Viola's works, including *Ancient of Days* (1979–81) and *Five Angels for the Millennium* (2001), to name a few among many. *Ancient of Days* is a depiction of the *creation* process in the biblical sense, but it was created by inverting the shooting of the *destruction* process—a reference to cyclical creation myths found outside of the Judeo-Christian tradition, such as in Hinduism.[7] *Five Angels for the Millennium* consists of five individual video sequences of an underwater human figure: "Birth Angel," "Fire

Angel," "Ascending Angel," "Creation Angel," and "Departing Angel." Viola originally intended to present a man sinking in water. But when he showed the finished work to photographer Kira Perov, his wife and artistic partner, he inadvertently ran the five films backwards, creating not a drowning man but a man coming out of the water, and the backward-running images became the final work.[8] Extreme slow motion, Viola's signature technique, also represents his visual strategy for intervening in the perception of natural, linear time progression in recorded moving images. In *Passage* (1987), for instance, he videotaped a four-year-old boy's birthday party, which was twenty-six minutes long, and stretched it to seven hours for his video-sound installation. In this type of work, the extremely minimized movement of images produces the effect of stillness—or the effect of "imprisoned time," in Viola's term.[9] This reverses the process of cinematic technology, which depends on the illusion of *motion* created by the rapid succession of *still frames* (the minimum rate to achieve the illusion of a moving image is about fifteen frames per second). Mary Ann Doane describes this process as cinema's "essential paradox."[10]

Viola's imprisoned time is a strong evocation of what Adorno finds in Wagner's temporal world, "the standing-still of time":

> The standing-still of time and the complete occultation of nature by means of phantasmagoria are thus brought together in the memory of a pristine age where time is guaranteed only by the stars. Time is the all-important element of production that phantasmagoria, the mirage of eternity, obscures.[11]

Adorno describes the Wagnerian phantasmagoria as "the earliest wonder of technology,"[12] which I will argue is comparable to (but without an ideological connection to) Viola's use of video technology. Adorno locates Wagner's phantasmagorical suspension of time in both his music and libretti. At the simplest level, Adorno discusses the dream or sleep motif as a manifestation of the oblivion of time, most prominently associated with the characters Kundry, Hagen, Wotan, and Brünnhilde. Beyond the narrative level, Adorno illustrates numerous examples of Wagnerian characters' refusal of time's progression at the more detailed level of the libretto; one example is Tannhäuser's song in the "Venusberg Scene" of Act 1:

The time I dwell here with thee, by days I cannot measure,
Seasons pass me, how I scarcely know,
—the radiant sun I see no longer ... [13]

In Adorno's view, Wagner's leitmotif technique is one of the musical elements of Wagner's work that contributes to the temporal stasis. He maintains that the leitmotif technique is essentially a non-developmental
repetition: although the reappearances of a motif are *disguised* through
modulation (and are thus illusionary and phantasmagoric), they are
no better than a sequential repetition, which is a "substitute for true
development."[14] Furthermore, leitmotifs obscure the progress of time
by their dispersed appearances throughout the opera. Another musical
example Adorno discusses is the harmonic stasis at the beginning of
the *Lohengrin* Prelude. He describes the lack of real harmonic progression in this music as "the phantasmagorical emblem for time standing
still."[15] In this respect, Adorno traces the non-functional harmony and
non-developmental motivic technique of French impressionism to Wagnerian practice (and he did not forget to indicate the irony of French
impressionist composers' efforts to avoid Wagner's "insatiable appe-
tite for dynamics").[16] He also finds the legacy of the Wagnerian "vacu-
ity of musical progress" in Stravinsky's music—another irony, given
that Stravinsky was a pronounced aesthetic opponent of Wagner.[17] For
Adorno, Stravinsky's relentless repetition of harmonic and rhythmic
motives eradicates the sense of temporal progression in the same way
Wagner's music does; he even calls Stravinsky "a Wagner"![18]

Although Adorno's musical criticism is heavily colored by his ideology—for instance, his equation of the lack of musical progress with that
of historical progress—some of his arguments are illuminating and can
be contextualized in the discourse of musical time developed by such
scholars as Jonathan Kramer and Thomas Clifton. As Kramer states
in the preface to his book *The Time of Music,* time in music can mean
many different things.[19] The focus of this chapter is the time that a musical piece "presents" or "evokes," as opposed to the "ordinary time" that
a musical work takes.[20] Since the beginning of the twentieth century,
more and more composers have shown strong interest in the compositional manipulation of time and have explored new temporalities, away
from linear time and metric regularity. Accordingly, most of the studies of musical time are devoted to contemporary composers, but Wag-

ner is occasionally discussed. Thomas Reiner mentions the legendary harmonic prolongation in the Prelude to Wagner's *Das Rheingold*—the extension of the E♭-major chord for 136 measures—as an example of Jonathan Kramer's idea of "harmonic stasis."[21] Thomas Clifton uses the term "static succession," which he defines as "the maximum motionlessness" that music can produce. He argues that *absolute stasis* does not exist in music because sound, unlike color, always produces a certain degree of movement.[22] In his view, it is almost impossible to find a pure form of static succession in pre-contemporary music, because the compositional conventions and restrictions at that time did not allow for such a pure form. Instead, static succession is combined with more typical motions in pre-twentieth-century music, and Clifton discusses the *Rheingold* Prelude as an example of the combined static succession.[23] From a strictly musical point of view, Clifton's concept of static succession is not exactly the same as Adorno's "standing-still of time," but the similarities are strong.

Wagnerian temporality as discussed by Adorno is also related to what Jonathan Kramer calls "vertical time": vertical music, he notes, "denies the past and the future in favor of an extended present."[24] He finds a remarkable resemblance between vertical time and psychopathological symptoms of schizophrenia. He quotes psychiatrist Frederick Melges's schizophrenic patient, who notes, "Time has stopped. There is no time . . . The past and future have collapsed into the present, and I can't tell them apart."[25] According to Kramer, vertical time makes us enter the timeless now of the extended present. Timelessness in vertical music, however, does not mean that time has ceased to exist, but that ordinary time has become frozen in an eternal now and is replaced by what he paradoxically calls the *time of timelessness*.[26] This eternal now is what is privileged in Stockhausen's compositional aesthetics of "moment form."

> An instant does not need to be just a particle of measured duration. This concentration on the present moment—on every present moment—can make a vertical cut, as it were, across horizontal time perception, extending out to a timelessness I call eternity. This is not an eternity that begins at the end of time, but an eternity that is present in every moment.[27]

The new musical temporalities discussed above—timelessness (or schizophrenia), vertical time, and moment time—all reject linear time.

As Kramer points out, the difference between linear and nonlinear time can be compared to the philosophical distinction between becoming and being, respectively.[28] The ontological condition of music is becoming, because sound unfolds in linear, clock time. In Thomas Clifton's words, "the essence of tones, unlike that of colors, is always to be in a state of becoming."[29] However, at the level of musical phenomenology (i.e., the level of the time that a musical piece "evokes"), either (linear) becoming-time or (nonlinear) being-time can dominate over the other, depending on compositional techniques, and the strongest representative of becoming-time is the teleological tonal progression.[30] Wagner stayed within the tonal tradition, but his harmonic "progression" is much less teleological than that of his contemporaries. Hence comes Carl Dahlhaus's description of Wagner's harmony as "wandering" or "centrifugal" in comparison to Brahms's "centripetal" harmony: he notes that "the characteristic function of Wagner's use of harmony is to establish not hierarchies but an order of succession," while Brahms's music is characterized by "tonal centrality."[31] Dahlhaus traces the "centrifugal effect" of Wagner's music to his frequent use of non-developmental sequence (in contrast to Brahms's "developing variation") and in so doing, he echoes Adorno's accusation that Wagner's music lacks true motivic and harmonic development, as discussed above.

Warren Darcy disagrees with Dahlhaus's analysis of Wagner's harmony and form: he even states that a central concern of his book, *Wagner's "Das Rheingold,"* is to deconstruct "the Dahlhaus myth" about Wagner.[32] According to Darcy's analysis, Wagner's harmony is more centripetal than centrifugal and his form is not devoid of architectural (i.e., teleological) structure. It is not within the scope of this essay to engage in the controversy between Dahlhaus and Darcy. But even if one subscribes to Darcy's theory, it is undeniable that Wagner's teleological tonal progression, motivic development, and architectonic formal structure are not transparent but are thickly disguised and concealed (and this concealment is the basis of Adorno's critique of Wagner, since he considers it the fundamental mechanism of phantasmagoria). Wagner's temporality is not as nonlinear as that of the twentieth-century music that Jonathan Kramer and other musical time specialists examine in their studies, but his technique of concealment produces at least the effect or illusion of nonlinear, schizophrenic time and timelessness—the "mirage of eternity," in Adorno's words.[33]

From Adorno's Marxist point of view, Wagner's privileging of the time of timelessness, the eternal now, is a regressive element, because Adorno regards lack of progress in musical time as reflecting lack of historical progress. For a similar reason, Fredric Jameson denounces the temporality of postmodern culture, which he argues is characterized by "schizophrenia," the collapse of past and future into the eternal present.[34] But for Jonathan Kramer, the new temporalities in contemporary music—whether spatial time, being-time, vertical time, or moment time—are an illuminating musical reconsideration of, if not a challenge to, "the hollow obsession with progress" promoted in the Enlightenment concept of modernity. For art historian Arnold Hauser, too, the "forward-looking expectancy" of the Western Enlightenment attitude is too "utopistic."[35] Many scholars consider the negation of linear time and the celebration of the present in various areas of twentieth-century art to be a reaction against the predominance of linearity and "becoming" in Western thought, which has lasted for centuries. Although a strict binary opposition between Western and non-Western traditions is problematic and too simplistic, one can differentiate their aesthetic and philosophical focus in the relative sense, and the idea of being and non-linear temporality, such as circular and reversible time, has certainly been more prominent in non-Western traditions—Hinduism and Buddhism, for instance. It is in light of this cultural influence that I begin the discussion of time elements in Viola's *Tristan Project* below.

TIME IN *TRISTAN* AND *THE TRISTAN PROJECT*

The sense of a palpable stillness and silence, reflected
in the serene image of the Buddha's face, was so
different from my memories of being in church.

BILL VIOLA, "THE LIGHT ENTERS YOU"

Buddhism has been one of the most influential philosophical, aesthetic, and spiritual inspirations for Viola's art.[36] On a Japan/U.S. Friendship Commission Fellowship, he formally studied Zen Buddhism in Japan for two years in 1980 and 1981 and became artist-in-residence at the Sony Corporation's headquarters. Among the Zen teachers he studied with in Japan was Daiju Tanaka, an independent priest (not associated with any temple) and artist. Viola notes that in spite of his teacher's limited knowledge of English, their communication was "deep, vivid, and clear." He recalls the first session he had with Tanaka over coffee at Mister Donuts near the Zen temple Eiheiji by calling it "The Mister Donuts Seminars on Zen Buddhism."[37] It is widely agreed that Viola's fascination with cyclical, reversible, and imprisoned time, discussed at the beginning of this chapter, constitutes the most prominent influence of Buddhism on his work. Like many of Viola's video-sound installations, *The Tristan Project* is conspicuous for its visual strategy of challenging the linear and irreversible temporality of clock time. My analysis focuses on three sequences: "The Darker Side of Dawn," "Passage into Night," and "Tristan's Ascension."

In *The Tristan Project*, Viola's video images are projected onto a giant screen during a live performance of the opera. The singers' acting onstage was minimized in the Los Angeles (2004 and 2007) and New York City (2007) productions to the extent that they were nearly concert performances. The 2005 Paris production, directed by Peter Sellars, was fully staged but the onstage action was extremely restrained and the stage setting was almost bare, so that Viola's video images became the main visual content of the opera. "The Darker Side of Dawn" appears during Act 2. It consists of a series of images of an old oak tree, which suggest the act's locational setting in the forest. A fixed camera was used to shoot the changing natural light, from daylight at around 3 p.m. to complete darkness surrounding the oak tree (figure 17.1). The time change in this act of Wagner's opera is a progression from night to dawn, but Viola visualized this temporal progression by reversing the sequence he videotaped from daylight to darkness, evoking cyclical time—the same process employed in *Ancient of Days* discussed above.

The sequence of the "The Darker Side of Dawn" is segmented into several parts that are presented not continuously but with other images—for instance, "Fire Man" and "Lover's Path"—that intervene between the segments. This mode of presentation further complicates and confuses the natural linear time progression. "Tristan's Ascension," the penultimate sequence in *The Tristan Project,* was also created by running the images in reverse. In other words, the *ascending* sequence was created from a *drowning* man, as in "Ascending Angel" discussed above

FIGURE 17.1. Bill Viola, "The Darker Side of Dawn" (2005). Color video projection on wall in dark room. Room dimensions variable. *Photo by Kira Perov.*

(in *The Tristan Project*, the character of Tristan was lowered into the water on a wire).[38] The two works are related to each other not only technically but also visually, since Tristan's drowning-up image in the bubbling water, which Ronald Blum describes as "the bodies dissolving like Alka-Seltzer,"[39] bears an unmistakable resemblance to that of the ascending angel.

"Passage into Night," which is first shown in the middle of the opera's "Love Duet" in Act 2, is a shot of a female figure gradually approaching across a desert plain.[40] The figure first appears as an extremely tiny, unidentifiable image that looks like an apparition in a mirage. As this tiny figure slowly grows in size, it becomes apparent that a woman is walking toward the front (figure 17.2). She approaches closer and closer until her dark robes fill the entire screen—a visual crescendo, one could call it.

Throughout *The Tristan Project*, the identity of the woman in this sequence remains unrevealed, as her face is tightly wrapped with a red scarf. In fact, even the figure's gender is ambiguous; the clothes suggest that it is a woman (and it *was* a woman Viola videotaped for this sequence), but it could be a man disguised in a woman's dress. The mysterious identity of the figure is further intensified by the glaring image around his/her feet created by the extremely heated air, which makes the

FIGURE 17.2.
Bill Viola, "Pas-
sage into Night"
(2005). Color
high definition
video on plasma
display mounted
on wall. *Photo
by Kira Perov.*

figure appear undulating and fluttering.[41] The temporal progression of
the "Passage into Night" sequence is as ambiguous as the identity of its
figure. Unlike "The Darker Side of Dawn," it is not presented in reversed
order; however, the discontinuous presentation of its segments with the
intervening images between them confuses and destabilizes the sense
of linear time (its video installation is exhibited continuously, the total
length of which is a little over fifty minutes). Each segment is a moving

image, but its movement in extreme slow motion creates the illusion of a still image and in so doing produces the effect of "imprisoned time."

As I discussed above, there is a strong parallelism between Viola's imprisoned time and Wagner's "standing-still of time," in Adorno's words. According to Adorno, the standing-still of time was "perfected" in *Tristan und Isolde*.[42] He does not enumerate examples from *Tristan*, but one can provide copious instances from the libretto, especially in the "Love Duet" of Act 2, in which the lovers' death wish is intermingled with their longing for the death of day and the eternity of night:

TRISTAN: The daylight, the daylight,
the envious daylight,
the hard-hearted foe, I
hate and loathe it!
You quench'd the torch
Could I quench the day
To revenge the suff'ring of lovers
And quench the day's cruel torment!
. . .
The day! The day
That shone all round
Where you shone
Like the glorious sun
In highest honour's
dazzling ray,
it stole Isold' away!
. . .
O hail the potion.
Hail that draught!
Hail all its magical mighty craft.
Through the doors of death
There flowed a tide,
When those portals
Were open wide,
Then they revealed my dream of delight,
The wondrous realm of night.
From the vision my inmost heart
Did enshrine,
Gone was the daylight's false lying shine;
And night-sighted, before me
I saw the truth in glory.

ISOLDE: By revenge the day
That you scorned was fired;
And with your sins
He then conspired.
What you perceived
In glory of night
To the empty pride
Of kingly might
You were forced to surrender.

TRISTAN: Oh, since we are
By night enfolded,
The envious day,
So keen and spiteful,
Still many keep us apart,
Yet not deceive our heart.
For his empty pomp,
And his glittering lies
Mean naught, after night
Has blessed our eyes:
And the flickering glare,
The flash of his lightning
Blind our sight no more.
When for death's dark night,
Loving have yearned,
When all her holy secrets have learned:
Then daylight's falsehood,
Fame and might,
Praise and renown
That shine so bright.
. . .
And the daylight's idle burning
All that remains is yearning
That yearning deep
For holy night,
Where endless and
Always true,
Love brings laughing delight?

BOTH: Oh, sink around us
Night of loving
Let me now
Forget I'm living,
. . .

BRANGÄNE: Lonely watcher
In the night,
You who dream
In love's delight,
Hear my warning
Call aright;
My foreboding
Makes me fear
Waken sleepers,
Danger's near!
Ah, beware!
Ah, beware!
Soon the night will pass!

TRISTAN: Let me die now!

ISOLDE: Envious watcher!

TRISTAN: I'll not awaken!

ISOLDE: Let the day
To death be given!

TRISTAN: Day and death
If they united,
They'd destroy
The love we plighted?
. . .

TRISTAN: So let us die
And never part,
Die united,
Heart to heart,
Never waking,
Never fearing,
Nameless,
Endless rapture sharing,
Each to each devoted,
In love alone abiding!
. . .

BRANGÄNE: Ah, beware!
Ah, beware! The night will soon be o'ver!

ISOLDE:	Let me die now.
TRISTAN:	Must I awaken?
ISOLDE:	Never waken.
TRISTAN:	With the day Must Tristan waken?
ISOLDE:	Let the day To death be given!
TRISTAN:	The daylight's menace Shall we now defy?
ISOLDE:	From his lies ever we'll fly?
TRISTAN:	His dawning ray Will fright us no more?
ISOLDE:	Ever guarded by night!
BOTH:	O endless night Blessed night Holy noble Night of love! When you enfold us, When we are blessed, How could we be wakend From you without dismay? Now banish all fearing Sweetest death, Longed for and hoped for Love in death![43]

As discussed above, the eternal now is a temporal characteristic of dreams and of vertical time. Wagner's *Tristan* does not present a dream motif as explicitly as the *Ring* cycle or *Parsifal* does, but alludes to it through the death wish—Brangäne: "Waken sleepers / Danger's near! . . ."; Tristan: "Must I awaken?"; Isolde: "Never waken"; Tristan: "With the day / Must Tristan waken?"; Isolde: "Let the day / To death be given!" As Wagner's lovers long to eternalize the ephemerality of night, Viola's images aspire to imprison fleeting time, to be in the state of the timelessness of time. Although it is not consistently so throughout the work, Viola's "Passage into Night" sequence is a visualization of the temporality that Wagner's nocturnal lovers wish for: the first segment of the sequence is presented during the opera's Act 2 "Love Duet" and the last segment appears in Act 3, accompanying Tristan's line, "She calls me from the night." At this point, the size of the figure in "Passage into Night" is huge, but its identity still remains uncertain; in fact, this figure adamantly refuses to be identified (recall that the face is tightly wrapped with a red scarf), and one cannot even tell for sure whether s/he is showing his/her front or back. This visual ambiguity between front and back suggests another layer of the confusion of temporal linearity: the sequence could be perceived as a shooting of the figure's receding from the camera, presented in reversed order, as in "The Darker Side of Dawn" and "Tristan's Ascension." As mentioned earlier, the dispersed appearance of the segments of the "Passage into Night" sequence and those of "The Darker Side of Dawn" further obfuscates linear temporality, and this visual mode of discontinuous presentation is analogous to Wagner's musical technique of leitmotif. Like the segments of Viola's visual sequence, the non-developmental (according to Adorno and Dahlhaus) reappearances of Wagner's motifs are scattered throughout the opera, thus obscuring the linear, directional time progress. Adorno singles out Act 2 of *Tristan* as an example of where "the musical content of the motivic models upon which the passages of intensification are based is hardly anywhere affected by sequential progressions."[44] The discontinuity of Viola's images and Wagner's leitmotifs is parallel to the discontinuity of moment time in Stockhausen's aesthetics.

Perhaps nonlinear temporality and other temporal elements shared by Wagner and Viola can be traced to their shared interest in Buddhism (and this connection is valid when one also considers Jonathan Kramer's view that Stockhausen's aesthetics of moment time and other nonlinear temporalities shown in contemporary music reflect the influence of non-Western aesthetics and philosophies, Japanese art and Buddhism in particular).[45] Viola's background in Buddhism was discussed above; in Wagner's case, Buddhist influences came through his infatuation with Schopenhauer's philosophy, which is permeated with Buddhism. Schopenhauer's influence on Wagner was visible for approximately the last thirty years of his life, during which *Tristan und Isolde* was composed. The death wish, the most prominent pathos in *Tristan,* is a reflection of Buddhism via Schopenhauer. In Buddhism, the freedom from all desires and suffering is the state of Nirvana, which can be achieved by willing a symbolic death as a renunciation of endless desire—a source of human sufferings. In a letter to Liszt, Wagner wrote:

> His [Schopenhauer's] chief idea, the final negation of the Desire of life, is terribly serious, but it shows the only salvation possible . . . If I think of the storm of my heart, the terrible tenacity with which, against my desire, it used to cling to the hope of life, and if even now I feel this hurricane within me, I have at least found a quietus which, in wakeful nights, helps me to sleep. This is the genuine, ardent longing for death, for absolute unconsciousness, total non-existence.[46]

Wagner had planned to bring the character Parzival into Act 3 of *Tristan* as a symbolic figure of self-renunciation. However, as the libretto of *Tristan* was developing along the lines of Schopenhauer's philosophy— not only in the concept of the death wish but also in the dualism at various levels of the libretto, between life and death, day and night, hatred and love—Wagner thought it unnecessary and redundant to introduce Parzival. Buddhist influence culminates in Wagner's last work *Parsifal,* which is widely known to be a blending of Christian and Buddhist symbolism. Another testimony to Wagner's strong interest in Buddhism is his plan to compose an opera on a Buddhist theme, *Die Sieger* (The Victors), for which he only left a short sketch.[47]

In addition to Buddhism, the shared interest in myth can be considered an element that contributes to the temporal affinity between Wagner and Viola. Anthropologist Edward T. Hall differentiates mythic (or sacred) time from profane time: while the latter is ordinary clock time, marking the passage of linear time—minutes and hours, days of a week, months of a year—the former is repeatable, reversible, and stoppable.[48] In this respect, myth is the opposite of history, in which the ruthless progress of clock time prevails. Another distinction between myth and history is the primacy of universality in the former and the primacy of particularity in the latter, which makes it possible to draw another parallelism between Viola and Wagner. In both Viola's oeuvre and Wagner's, the content of their works often represents primordial figures and experiences. The following statement epitomizes Viola's privileging of the mythic dimension of his art:

> As an artist, I feel that it will be the universal language of human practices like art, and the root commonalities and sources of religious practices, not our differences, that will get us through. These vital elements of human experience are not just some common ground that we can share in a social and political sense. They are the language of myth, the speech of the human heart. We need to recognize that the reality of things we share as individuals— the universal human experiences of birth, death, joy, hope, fear, sorrow, suffering, creativity, revelation—reside on this mythic level where poetry, not facts, speaks.[49]

In many of Viola's works, human figures appear not as particular people who carry particular stories but as people like us who share such primordial human emotions and experiences as pain, grief, birth, or death. In this context, the ambiguity and anonymity of the figures in *The Tristan Project* can be regarded as representing the primacy of universality. "Lover's Path" in Act 2 is an example. This is the sequence of the two lovers coming out of the nocturnal forest and walking into the sea, hand in hand. One cannot identify the lovers, since they were shot from the back: they could be the same couple who appeared during Act 1, presumably representing Tristan and Isolde, but they might not and need not be. Another example is "Passage into Night" (figure 17.2): as discussed above, the figure in this sequence remains unidentified throughout the video. Viola's privileging of universality extends to the spectator's viewing experience. Viola notes that people have been going to cathedrals for centuries to see icons of Mother Mary, "not necessarily to experience the story of a woman who lost a son, but to share their pain and grief with an image that accepts all human suffering equally and with infinite capacity. In other words, they bring the story to the image and not the other way round."[50]

As for Wagner's recourse to myth, it suffices to remember Adorno's accusation of its lack of historical consciousness and its advocacy of universality that transcends history. As many scholars have agreed, Adorno's arguments are often too strongly and inflexibly, if not blindly, overshadowed by his ideology; but notions of historical progress do illuminate the concept of time, including cinematic time. Mary Ann Doane

notes that time became increasingly reified, stabilized, and rationalized during the late nineteenth century and early twentieth century,
and argues that this rationalized time is in "complicity with notions of
the inevitability of a technologically induced historical progress." She
associates the desire to rationalize time with the desire to make time
"visualizable."[51] Movement is often represented as the embodiment of
time, and it has been the assumption of mainstream film and video art
that time is visualized through moving images on screen and that time
cannot be accessed without being mediated by movement.[52] Viola's art
challenges these assumptions through his aesthetics and production of
imprisoned time; it refuses the mode of visual representation of time
prevalent in mainstream cinema, in which time is subordinated to movement. Perhaps Viola's art can be aligned with the modernist cinema of
the 1960s and 1970s, which, according to Gilles Deleuze, is distinguished
by its capability to produce an image of pure time, liberated from movement.[53] And this pure time was already immanent in Wagner's *Tristan
und Isolde*. If Alex Ross believes Viola's images to "arise from the subconscious" of Wagner's score,[54] I propose that this subconscious of the
score is the temporality of Wagner's *Tristan*.

NOTES

This chapter was partially funded by the University Research Council of the University of Cincinnati. I wish to express my utmost thanks to Tom Kernan, who
worked as my research assistant during the academic year of 2006–2007. He gave
me immense help in the preparation of this chapter and in arranging my interview
with Bill Viola, included as the appendix of this volume.

The first epigraph to this chapter is from Bill Viola, "David Tudor: The Delicate Art of Falling," *Leonardo Music Journal* 14 (2004): 50. The second epigraph is
from Bill Viola, "The Sound of One Line Scanning," in *Sound by Artists*, ed. Dan
Lander and Micah Lexier (Banff, Alberta: Banff Centre, 1990), 40.

1. Viola, "The Sound of One Line Scanning," 44.

2. Richard Wagner, quoted in Viola, "The Sound of One Line Scanning," 49.

3. The first epigraph is from Richard Wagner, *Parsifal*, Act 1, Scene 1 (Gur-
nemanz); the second epigraph from Bill Viola, quoted in Holly Rogers, "Acoustic
Architecture: Music and Space in the Video Installations of Bill Viola," *Twentieth-
Century Music* 2, no. 2 (September 2006), 206; the third epigraph from Jonathan
Kramer, *The Time of Music: New Meanings, New Temporalities, New Listening Strat-
egies* (New York: Schirmer Books, 1988), 375.

4. Bill Viola, *Reasons for Knocking at an Empty House: Writings 1973–1994*,
ed. Robert Violette in collaboration with the author (Cambridge: MIT Press, 1995),

173. In relation to the technological difference that he finds between the ontology of video and film (see n. 1), Viola notes that film is not a time-based art unless it is "filming," while video is "videoing" all the time (62).

5. Viola discusses how David Tudor's aesthetics and work, including *Rainforest,* influenced him in his essay "David Tudor: The Delicate Art of Falling," *Leonardo Music Journal* 14 (2004): 48–56.

6. For detailed discussion of Viola's *Désert,* see Hans Emons, "Räume des Geheimnisses und der Einsamkeit: Bill Violas 'Désert,' Peter Mussbachs 'Kain ist Kain,' Hugo Niebelings 'Klage der Ariadne,'" in *Für Auge und Ohr: Musik als Film* (Berlin: Frank & Timme, 2005), 151–61. Varèse-Viola's *Désert* was one of the pieces on the program of the "Mostly Opera" concert, performed by Danish Radio Sinfonietta and conducted by Christian Eggen on October 5, 2007. For reviews of the concert, see http://mostlyopera.blogspot.com/2007/10/bill-violas-dserts-new-accordion.html (accessed November 12, 2008). The "Mostly Opera" concert was a part of the "Sound Around" festival, the Öresund Biennale of Contemporary Music, held in Copenhagen and Malmö with concerts, installations, and seminars.

7. Otto Neumaier, "Space, Time, Video, Viola," in *The Art of Bill Viola,* ed. Chris Townsend (London: Thames & Hudson, 2004), 64.

8. "Interview with Bill Viola," *Time,* June 3, 2003.

9. Viola, *Reasons for Knocking at an Empty House,* 214. His notion of "stopped-time" is well explored in his 1991 installation, "The Stopping Mind," which he describes as being based on "the age-old human desire to stop time" (213).

10. Mary Ann Doane, *The Emergence of Cinematic Time: Modernity, Contingency, the Archive* (Cambridge: Harvard University Press, 2002), 26.

11. Theodor Adorno, *In Search of Wagner,* trans. Rodney Livingstone, with a new forward by Slavoj Žižek (London: Verso, 2005), 76.

12. Ibid., 80.

13. Quoted in ibid., 76. Marc Weiner examines the "dream" and "sleep" scenes in the context of the phantasmagoric, seductive power of disembodied voice in Wagner's music drama. See Marc A. Weiner, "Primal Sounds," *Opera Quarterly* 23, no. 2–3 (Spring –Summer 2007), 217–46. One of the scenes Weiner analyzes is Alberich's appearance in Hagen's dream, which he also contextualizes in Wagner's manipulation of the interplay between seeing and hearing, between sight and sound.

14. Adorno, *In Search of Wagner,* 47. In a different context, Adorno compares the function of Wagner's leitmotif to that of advertisement in mass culture, describing it as music designed to be remembered by "the forgetful" (21).

15. Ibid., 76.

16. Adorno, *Philosophy of Modern Music,* trans. Anne G. Mitchell and Wesley V. Blomster (New York: Seabury Press, 1973), 189. He also discusses the parallelism between impressionist composers and Wagner in *In Search of Wagner,* arguing that it would be a "mistake" to discuss Wagner's harmonic practice "without further ado as impressionism" (53).

17. Stravinsky stated, "I do not want to discuss the music of *Parsifal* or the music of Wagner in general. At this date it is too remote from me. What I find revolting in the whole affair is the underlying conception which dictated it—the principle of putting a work of art on the same level as the sacred and symbolic ritual which

constitutes a religious service. Is not all this comedy of Bayreuth, with its ridiculous formalities, simply an unconscious aping of a religious rite?" See Igor Stravinsky, *An Autobiography* (New York: M. & J. Steuer, 1958), 162.

18. Adorno, *Philosophy of Modern Music*, 190. The double irony about Stravinsky lies in the fact that Adorno connects Stravinsky, who proclaimed himself to be "the anti-pope to Impressionism," with impressionist composers by arguing that he inherited musical stasis from impressionist composers as well as from Wagner (187). Adorno's discussion of Stravinsky in this book, which was first published in 1948 in German, is largely about Stravinsky's pre-neoclassical period, which started around 1923. Considering the line of Adorno's grouping of composers in terms of musical stasis, it would be a valid assumption that if he had survived the heyday of minimalism (he died in 1969), he would have considered it the ultimate stage of the evolution from Wagner, impressionism, and Stravinsky. (In this context, it is worth mentioning that for a listening question I gave several years ago, two students misidentified Philip Glass as the composer of the *Rheingold* Prelude). Indeed, Jonathan Cross argues for the kinship between Stravinsky and minimalism; see his "Minimal Developments," in *The Stravinsky Legacy* (Cambridge: Cambridge University Press, 1998), 170–92.

19. Kramer, *The Time of Music*, xiii. There have been extensive studies on musical time; see Jonathan Kramer, "Studies of Time and Music: A Bibliography," *Music Theory Spectrum* 7 (1985): 72–106.

20. See Kramer, *The Time of Music*, 7.

21. Thomas Reiner, *Semiotics of Musical Time* (New York: Peter Lang, 2000), 132–33. Reiner excludes Wagner's Prelude because his study focuses on musical time as a result of the "poietic process"—that is, musical time consciously intended by the composer.

22. Thomas Clifton, *Music as Heard: A Study in Applied Phenomenology* (New Haven, Conn.: Yale University Press, 1983), 104–105. He notes that absolute stasis does not exist in music because sound, unlike color, always produces a certain degree of movement, being in the state of becoming rather than being.

23. Thomas Clifton, *Music as Heard*, 105. Other examples he mentions are J. S. Bach's Toccata and Fugue in F major and Richard Strauss's *Also Sprach Zarathustra*.

24. Kramer, *The Time of Music*, 16.

25. Quoted in Kramer, *The Time of Music*, 375. Kramer acknowledges a difference between vertical time and the pathological disorder of schizophrenia in that the former does not force us to lose contact with external reality while the latter does; instead, vertical time provides a new reality (376).

26. Ibid., 378.

27. Quoted in Seppo Heikinheimo, *The Electronic Music of Karlheinz Stockhausen*, trans. Brad Absetz (Helsinki: Suomen Musikkitieteellinen Seura, 1972), 121.

28. Kramer, *The Time of Music*, 19.

29. Clifton, *Music as Heard*, 104–105.

30. See Kramer, *The Time of Music*, 19.

31. Carl Dahlhaus, *Between Romanticism and Modernism: Four Studies in the Music of the Later Nineteenth Century*, trans. Mary Whittall (Berkeley: University of California Press, 1980), 65–75.

32. Warren Darcy, *Wagner's "Das Rheingold"* (Oxford: Clarendon Press, 1993), 57.

33. Adorno, *In Search of Wagner,* 76.

34. Fredric Jameson, *Postmodernism, or the Cultural Logic of Late Capitalism* (Durham, N.C.: Duke University Press, 1999), passim.

35. See Kramer, *The Time of Music,* 17.

36. The epigraph is from "The Light Enters You" (Interview with Bill Viola), *Shambhala Sun: Buddhism Culture Meditation Life,* November 2004, http://shambhalasun.com/index.php?option=com_content&task=view&id=1357&Itemid=0 (accessed May 22, 2008). One of the most recent studies of the influence of Buddhism on Viola's art is Jamie Jewett, "Seeing the Mind, Stopping the Mind, the Art of Bill Viola," *International Journal of Performance Arts and Digital Media* 4, no. 1 (May 2008): 81–94.

37. "The Light Enters You."

38. See my interview with Viola in the appendix of this volume.

39. Ronald Blum, "The Sellars/Salonen/Viola Tristan Project Comes to an Extraordinary Culmination at the Opéra de Paris," *Andante: Everything Classical,* April 18, 2005, http://www.andante.com/article/article.cfm?id=25392 (accessed December 22, 2007). The bubbling underwater man is also a visual motif in *The Messenger* (1996). Some images used in *The Tristan Project* are related to Viola's previous works: for instance, "The Fire Man" and "The Fire Woman" in *Tristan* evoke the image of a man on fire in *The Crossing* (1996).

40. Some of the images of *The Tristan Project* were exhibited as video-sound installations at several places, including the Haunch of Venison Gallery and St. Olave's College in London (June–September, 2006) and the James Cohan Gallery in New York City (May, 2007), the last of which I saw. The three images exhibited there are "Passage into Night" (50 minutes and 14 seconds), "The Fall into Paradise" (9'58"), and "Isolde's Ascension" (10'30"). The installations at the James Cohan Gallery did not use Wagner's music but were shown with other sounds: "Isolde's Ascension" was accompanied by low-frequency drones from two small speakers and "The Fall into Paradise" was exhibited with the multidimensional sounds from six speakers of a surround system, starting with soft drones, which change into a thunderous explosion synchronized with the lovers' plunging into the water. "Passage into Night" was exhibited silently.

41. Bill Viola, *Love/Death: The Tristan Project,* a pamphlet published to accompany the exhibition at Haunch of Venison (London: Haunch of Venison, 2006), 45. This pamphlet contains color photos of main images Viola created for *The Tristan Project.*

42. Adorno, *In Search of Wagner,* 80.

43. English translation by Andrew Porter in *Tristan & Isolde,* ed. Nicholas John, English National Opera Guide 6 (London: Calder Publications Ltd., 1981), 68–72.

44. Adorno, *Philosophy of Modern Music,* 189.

45. Kramer, *The Time of Music,* 17 and 201–202.

46. Quoted in John Luke Rose, "A Landmark in Musical History," in *Tristan & Isolde,* 12.

47. *Die Sieger* was to be based on the story of Prakriti, who falls in love with a Buddhist monk and is eventually allowed by Buddha to be united with him as long

as their relationship remains chaste. This unrealized opera became the starting point for Jonathan Harvey's new opera, *Wagner Dream,* which was commissioned by the Netherlands Opera and premiered in Luxembourg in May, 2007. In Harvey's opera, Wagner's own life and Prakriti's story are intertwined. The characters of Wagner and his associates are played by non-singing actors, while all of the Indian characters are sung.

48. See Kramer, *The Time of Music,* 16–17.

49. Quoted in Mary Jane Jacob's interview with Bill Viola in *Buddha Mind in Contemporary Art* (Berkeley: University of California Press, 2004), 257.

50. Ibid., 255.

51. Doane, *The Emergence of Cinematic Time,* 5–7.

52. Ibid., 178.

53. Ibid., 179.

54. Alex Ross, "*Tristan* in Paris, and *Cyrano* at the Met," *The New Yorker,* May 30, 2005, 94.

EIGHTEEN

"The Threshold of the Visible World": Wagner, Bill Viola, and *Tristan*

LAWRENCE KRAMER

> The mirror-image would seem to be the threshold of the visible world, if we go by the mirror disposition that the imago of one's own body presents in hallucinations or dreams.
>
> JACQUES LACAN, "THE MIRROR STAGE"

The affinity between Wagner and cinema is such a familiar theme that we seldom pause to wonder at how strange it is. If we forget for a moment about a few received ideas—the supposedly proto-cinematic relationship between the stage and the hidden orchestra at Bayreuth, the misappropriation of leitmotif technique in classical narrative film—Wagner might well seem the least cinematic of composers. His operas are essentially accumulations of static tableaux, "deeds of music made visible," and the stage images afforded by this design are so permeated by his music that their visuality, even their visibility, is compromised. When Gurnemanz, in *Parsifal*, famously says, "Here time becomes space," he might as well be describing the Wagnerian corpus. And when the lovers in *Tristan und Isolde*, but especially Tristan, invoke the world of night, the night invoked is the very antithesis of the cinematic dark: it is a night without images.

What, then, brings Wagner and cinema together? How, that is, and how credibly, can we see, hear, read, grasp Wagner and cinema as a couple? The question, in its multiplication of verbs for sensing, carries part of what I take to be an answer. The guiding thread in this paper is the idea that Wagner and cinema come together on the ground, but it is shadowy and shifting ground, of a certain perception of presence, or, otherwise put, of the presentation, the making present or making a present of perception. This condition, I will suggest, is paradigmatically "present" in *Tristan und Isolde,* which also takes the constitution of its own perceptual presence as a part of its content. The explicit realization of this self-reflective condition, however, will turn out to have depended on the intervention of cinema, not in the movie house or on the DVD screen but in the opera house, in a kind of parallel *Tristan* composed cinematically by the American video artist Bill Viola.

By way of prelude, consider three statements as epigraphs—one for each interpretation of the *Tristan* chord in the opening measures of the opera's Prelude. The first is from Rilke's Eighth Duino Elegy: "Lovers, were it not for the other, who / blocks the view, are near to it and marvel" (Liebende, wäre nicht der andre, der /die Sicht vorstellt, sind nah daran und staunen).[1] The "it" that Rilke refers to, which he names the Open, is closely akin to the Wagnerian night, but Rilke gets its perceptual structure backwards. The lovers do not simply block each other's view; their mutually interfering presence is also what makes the view visible. The text's strange language performs this relationship in the act of denying it: the subjunctive "were not the other" is enclosed within the indicative "[they] . . . are near it" that the subjunctive supposedly curbs. What the lovers do is elude each other's grasp, even when grasped most closely. What cannot be touched appears as untouchable in visual form. As Rilke says in the Second Elegy, "*This* is ours, to touch each other *so;* the gods / can press us harder. But that is the gods' affair" (*dieses* ist unser, uns *so* zu berürhen; starker / stemmen die Götter uns an. Doch dies ist Sache der Götter).

Or music's affair. For in this way Rilke's lovers, Tristan and Isolde in all but name, echo or shadow the relation of music and image as described by my second epigraph, from Maurice Merleau-Ponty: "Music is not in visible space, but it besieges it, undermines [it]."[2] Wagner in general and *Tristan* in particular not only exemplify but also represent, make present, this musicalization or becoming-music of the visible. Viola's images perform the complementary process, "visualizing" the music not in the sense of adding a visual gloss to it (taking "gloss" in the senses of both commentary and shine), but by making the music's auditory presence present concurrently in visual form. And this is possible only because Tristan and Isolde, Rilke's lovers in all but name, are always blocking the view. The result is a continuous touching and parting, reinforcing and interfering, of sound and image, sound in motion and moving image, that touches on the conditions of experiencing presence as such.

But this presence, like each lover, is present precisely in its slipping one's grasp along the lines suggested by in my third epigraph. This one comes from Derrida, who seeks to envision or sound out an experience of presence not bound by what he calls the "continuistic postulation" of Western thought, that is, the presupposition of the continuous as a dimension of experience: "For the continuous is never given. *There is never any pure, immediate experience* of the continuous, nor of closeness, nor of absolute proximity, nor of pure indifferentiation." To reckon with this "*eidetic* law of experience and event, [this] very condition of desire," it is necessary to conceive—to touch?—"a living present [*a,* not *the*] that has to be interpreted differently from coincidence and fusion."[3]

Bill Viola's *Tristan Project* centers on a series of illustrative moving images designed to run concurrently with a performance of Wagner's *Tristan und Isolde,* though not necessarily a continuous performance. The images are also designed to be excerpted in exhibitions with or without the music present, and there is no single way in which their full form is supposed to combine with the opera. The premiere, in Los Angeles in 2004, spread the performances over three nights, one act per night. In 2007, a Los Angeles revival repeated the fragmentary presentation but also twice performed the opera plus images in full on a single night; in New York the same year there were no fragmentary presentations, only two full ones. All of these were semi-staged concert performances; they gave priority to the images.

Unlike these others, the production for the Paris Opera in 2005, directed by Peter Sellars, was fully staged. It is this production that my remarks primarily address. Although I will apparently be speaking of a durable "double *Tristan,*" the term may refer more to this singular event than to a repeatable work. "Event" here should be understood in the strong sense developed by both Jacques Derrida and Alain Badiou: an impossible thing that happens, an occurrence that cannot be confined within the established terms of understanding which, in turn, cannot plausibly survive the event.[4] (A hint or, if you like, a warning, an avowal: this is not the only way in which the peculiarities of this *Tristan* artifact—whatever it is—will affect the essay in hand.)

Viola's archive of images is, in advance and regardless of how it is used, the residue of an event. It does not constitute a work in the usual sense nor does it represent a means of reproducing a preexisting work. Seen in extracts or in the night-by-night form of a miniature *Ring* cycle, the images of *The Tristan Project* set *Tristan und Isolde* at a distance, troping on it, citing it, appropriating it, but never simply heeding its imperatives. Seen continuously and in their totality—a whole that is paradoxically a mere half—the same images expand their troping to constitute a new, collaborative *Tristan,* the double *Tristan,* a truer *Gesamtkunstwerk* than Wagner's technological means could allow.

But this collaboration also annihilates the collaborators. The conditions of this particular pairing make it impossible to identify a coherent authorial agency, even a double one. Neither music nor image, Wagner's work nor Viola's, can claim priority in the presentation; each is both text and gloss, substance and supplement. Viola's images are quite "true" to Wagner's combination of music and libretto—sometimes allegorically, sometimes illustratively, sometimes all too literally—but their effect is to deny semantic authority to both *Tristan* and the *Tristan Project,* to both Richard Wagner and Bill Viola.

The relationship of Viola's archive-supplement to Wagner's nominally original work is not one of reciprocity, nor of interpretation, except incidentally. The relationship is sensorial. What matters most about the full production, ideally the Paris production, is not how it might be repeated or what it might mean, but what its staging as an event has made perceptible, and perceptible more especially about perception itself. The juxtaposition of Wagner's nineteenth-century pace and scale with Viola's twenty-first century counterparts, even had it happened only once, would still be an exemplary demonstration of Walter Benjamin's famous thesis that perception is historically mediated by the technology of art: "It has always been one of the primary tasks of art to create a demand whose hour of full satisfaction has not yet come. The history of every art form has critical periods in which the particular form strains after effects which can be achieved easily only with a changed technical standard."[5]

Wagner's *Tristan* had incorporated its own straining after certain effects—of absorption, time dilation, and sensation—into the substance of its drama. Viola's changed technical standard presented itself as the hour of completion that gave Wagner's effects the acuteness and tangibility they had prematurely demanded. *The Tristan Project* sought to appropriate *Tristan und Isolde* by making it the beneficiary of what Benjamin called a "deepening of apperception across the . . . spectrum."[6]

In Paris, the singers appeared on a nearly bare stage, dwarfed by the images looming behind them on a cinema-size screen, but nonetheless performing the actions re-enacted and transformed by the image stream. Typically for Viola, the images move very slowly, sometimes hovering on the threshold of perceptible motion, almost as if their size were a kind of weight that slowed them down, although without their becoming any less apparitional. They do not break the condition of stillness but shed it by degrees.

This mode of motion holds good throughout the opera, absorbing the image stream into the musical action. Not that the pace of Viola's images is coordinated in Mickey-Mouse fashion with specific musical events; the independence of the visual and auditory streams is essential to the impact of those few moments when they do coalesce. But when the images move, both they and the eye movement they invite merge with the long-spanned ebb and flow of Wagner's music. Viola has spoken of a triangulation between the music, the images, and the bodies on stage; the music presumably mediates between the symbolic value of the images and the real presence of the bodies. Within this framework, which is itself continuously mobile, the images might be said to move, and better than bodies can, in time with the music of the Prelude in particular, especially of the first seventeen bars with their drawn-out languorous yearning, their climactic crest on a deceptive cadence, and their fragmentary recurrence at cardinal points in the drama. (The Prelude condenses the opera, all but the final Transfiguration; its recurrences condense the Prelude, only to slip away.)

In other words, the images move to the underlying or occult time that pervades Wagner's score, the time appropriate to its rhythm of continuously deferred harmonic and erotic satisfaction which is at the same time its own mode of satisfaction. Although Viola's images are illustrative, their primary reference is not to the musical or dramatic surface but to that which this surface makes appear beyond it. What registers most is the movement of the images and the music alike toward a depth of perception that is also a depth beyond perception. Both halves of the double *Tristan* spiral vertiginously inward, one vertigo compounding another, while the bodies on stage revealingly block the view. The apices of Viola's triangle all catch the primary pace and rhythm at which animation arises, at which we feel both ourselves and the world around us draw our sense of life from its source.

We can never see that source, but only see what divides us from it becoming translucent rather than opaque. This translucence arises in the presence of the other, the body to which the music of *Tristan* lays siege, or which the images of *The Tristan Project* draw out in a large luminous shimmer. At the same time, however, we can *hear* the source, or at least eavesdrop on it, thanks to the capacity of a certain music to mimic it, a music that it is the aim of this opera, perhaps uniquely, at least originarily, to discover. *Tristan* is about precisely this: not love or desire as such, however transcendent, but the absolute open, the endless night, that love and desire seek. In acoustic terms, the opera is not about the music we hear but about what the music would allow us to hear if only it would and we could, a latter-day version of the becoming audible of the music of the spheres. Or, to adopt the terms of Raymond Knapp's account, the opera seeks to make present the becoming audible of the world as world, or, in Heideggerian terms, the sound of the world worlding, or, as Isolde herself puts it, immersion "in the surging swell, / in the ringing sound, / in the world-breath's / billowing All" (In dem wogenden Schwall, / in dem tönenden Schall, / in des Welt-Atems / wehendem All).[7]

Wagner has a few other names for this impossible acoustic object, this primordially impossible object that becomes the music or that manifests itself as what the music becomes: a transfigured, continuously opening form of the unsignifiable presence that Lacan called the Real.[8] (My language means to echo this effect; the "this . . . object" of the previous sentence floats, disengaged, between reference to the music and reference to what the music expresses or embodies. The impossibility of doing otherwise is the point, and also the means—in the opera, too—of the object's dissemination.) The names Wagner uses are deceptively familiar except in their sheer insistence, their refusal of all mediation. Wagner calls his impossible object sometimes night, sometimes death, as his era taught him to, but his music presents it as the tidal flow of animation free of all circumstance, what he more accurately described as an expansion into infinite space. Interestingly enough, he does not call it love.

Within Wagner's *Tristan* the locus of this expansion is the irreconcilability between the movement of the music and the movement of the bodies on stage, the music paradoxically animating but inanimate, the bodies paradoxically animate but de-animating. In Wagner's terminology, the music belongs to the night and the bodies to the day. The music fills with a lifelike yearning that can frame its outcome only as death; the bodies deaden that very yearning with the material inertia of their living form. The key to this paradox is the body's incapacity to match the slow, endlessly transitional rhythm of the music, which it is nonetheless supposed to incarnate. By comparison with the music, even the most supple body—hardly the operatic norm—is clumsy. The extraordinary impact of *Tristan* derives in part from the persistence of this disjunction. The audience is at every moment drawn toward the horizon beyond the body that opens the view, and simultaneously, for the two movements are absolutely indistinguishable, drawn back to the beloved body, the same body, that eludes the grasp. In a sense, every experience of *Tristan* is an experience of the *Tristan* that one desires but can never have except in that desire—the very relationship between Tristan and Isolde themselves.[9]

Viola's images fundamentally change this situation. The point of reference is only proximately the character of Wagner, or Wagnerism, or *Tristan*. In the double *Tristan*, those terms, already transformed by the realized possibility of their imagistic doubling, become hermeneutic windows onto the character of human perception under the conditions of desire. This is a character that Wagner's original *Tristan* depends on and makes audible but without making it intelligible. The gap thus created is, again, one source of *Tristan*'s unusual power. It so happens, and this is what Viola happened on, that the power in question is magnified rather than diminished when its character does become intelligible.

By creating his oversize, slowly but variably fluid images, Viola makes visible what Wagner makes audible, the template of bodily movement that now feels as if it were always already immanent in *Tristan*, and may have become so precisely by this means. (We need not debate a phantom actuality; the effect is retroactive even if the immanence pre-existed it.) At times we can track the body's gain or loss of this plane of movement as the bodily images slowly alter from the very small to the very large or vice versa. Despite their own visibility as technological apparatus, these images at full size naturalize the bodily movement they depict, precisely because such movement seems natural to moving images, to cinema, even though it is not natural to the bodies depicted. Thus both listening and seeing merge into a sensuous form of embodied temporality that disperses itself across the phenomenal field to envelop the images, the music, and the bodies of both the performers and the audience.

This temporality also envelops the elemental landscapes of sea and forest, fire and water, moon and sunrise that fill Viola's image stream. These landscapes surround the lovers' bodies and merge the bodily-musical movement into an imaginary movement of nature itself. Yet it quickly becomes impossible to say which is primary, body or image or music or elemental nature; each term englobes all the others. The new media of presentation thus create a new medium of perception. A new prosthesis forms a new aesthesis, yet one that, if and as we enjoy it, seems to unfold what was always already immanent in the original opera.

Perhaps the best way to characterize this medium is to call it haptic. *Tristan* is the opera par excellence about that which cannot be seen. More: in the sense supplied by Merleau-Ponty's description of a visuality besieged by music, *Tristan* itself cannot be seen, or more exactly it seeks to become unseeable. So it has to be touched. Wagner's music forms an acoustic surrogate for that touch, which becomes metaphorically present in the erotic consummation that never happens except in that very music. Viola's images form a visual surrogate or supplement of this haptic music. They do so by enhancing—slowing down, dwelling on, lingering over—the peculiar intimacy that arises between the spectator and the full-size large-screen image, the cinematic image. They also do so by unfolding the haptic underpinning of that intimacy: the tendency of vision on the cinematic scale—things seen enlarged, as if from no distance—to become, itself, a modality of touch.

The languishing combination of music and image produces a haptic field that leaves neither image nor music untouched. Act 2, for example, in which Tristan and Isolde draw closest to each other and the music strikes its most sustained note of rapture, centers on a six-minute epi-sode in which, as the lovers embrace and caress one another, fragmen-tary images of their bodies fill the screen in a continuous stream into which the bodies ultimately seem to dissolve. The episode is shot in a blurry, grainy black and white (achieved by using an obsolete camera) that renders the bodies fluid, like water, fog, or fire, and renders the lov-ers' faces indistinct, virtually unrecognizable. This zero degree of color, the hue of blind or blinding touch, also accompanies the lovers as they pass through a series of forest scenes to the water's edge where, just be-fore submerging themselves in search of the ecstasy that will elude them at the last moment, their bodies do dissolve into a pair of luminous blurs.

There is a danger in this festival of touch. The haptic vision of *The Tristan Project* risks losing the condition of impossibility that is the opera's sine qua non, which is to say that the double *Tristan* risks creat-ing the illusion that *Tristan und Isolde* admits of a consummation that merely transcends the lovers' fate rather than being riven by it. Earlier in Act 2, the camera eye moves in slow circles around a close-up of the lovers' faces almost touching, almost kissing. It thus produces, know-ingly or not, an uncanny if more languid replay of the parallel moment in Alfred Hitchcock's *Vertigo*, Bernard Herrmann's score for which alludes to *Tristan und Isolde* throughout, especially at the pivotal juncture pre-ceding the kiss when we hear a paraphrase—surely a knowing one—of the climactic deceptive cadence closing the first period (those first sev-enteen measures) of the opera's Prelude. The moment in *Vertigo*, as we already know in secret and will know even better as the film goes on, is purely illusory, a false consummation. But the illusion is momentarily overwhelming, as the camera compels us to admit by making us dizzy, forcing us to share in the protagonist's vertigo.

Viola comes very close to embracing the same illusion, and not just here, where he ends by fading the image of the embracing lovers into the grainy back and white into which their bodies will subsequently dissolve. He has said unequivocally that "*Tristan und Isolde* is the story of a love so intense and profound that it cannot be contained in the material bodies of the lovers. In order to fully realize their love, Tristan and Isolde must ultimately transcend life itself."[10] His depiction of that transcendence as "Tristan's Ascension" during Isolde's Transfiguration (the "Liebestod," as it is usually mislabeled) arguably represents an exchange of the Lacanian Real for mere pictorial realism. But Viola holds back, as perhaps Wagner forces him to, by making the format of his images as important as their content. Each act in *The Tristan Project* has its own mode of imagery, and the changes from one act to another create a narrative that recovers—well, almost recovers—the very condition of impossibility that the more ecstatic of the images seem to abolish.

(One cautionary note: except for those actually shot in black and white, the images in *The Tristan Project* need to be seen in color; hence the lack of illustrative figures in what follows. Readers seeking illustrations will have no trouble finding an abundance of them with a Google Image search using the search terms "Viola" and "Tristan Project." Images of the lovers' ascensions are especially easy to come by.)[11]

Thus in Act 1, the lovers appear on a divided screen, performing parallel actions but without ever seeing or touching one another. Each half-screen frames one lover's body like a doorway and is divided from its counterpart by a distinct vertical bar. The act as a whole thus unfolds the lovers' encounter across two symmetrical columns of like images, uniting Tristan and Isolde in one sensory field and at the same time separating them in another. This pattern stops only once they have drunk the potion that allows them to reveal their true feelings, at which point a whirling pinpoint of light at the center of an otherwise black screen gradually rises toward the viewer and reveals itself as the lovers' bodies intertwined and ecstatically suspended underwater, the site and medium of their rapture throughout the work. Even at the peak of their ecstasy, however, when they sing each other's names to the music of the Prelude, the bar reappears in the form of the symmetrical positioning of their bodies. This positioning turns out to be a portent.

In Act 2 the bar that divided the screen in Act 1 is removed, yet the bar between the lovers, the mark of their impossible fulfillment, does not disappear. Or rather it *does* disappear, but it does not go away. The act is full of scenes involving the lovers, both apart and together, constructed around images of strict bilateral symmetry, some vertical, some horizontal. Act 2 gives the visible bar of Act 1 the sublimated form introduced at the latter's climax, the invisible line bisecting the symmetrical images.

This treatment reaches its acme, and also its closure, during the imagery for the closing passage of the love duet, which once again places the lovers underwater and gradually compresses their rhyming bodies to a perfect sphere, ultimately a pure whirlpool compressing to a point, a droplet, into which the bodies metamorphose—just in time for the famous scream from Brangäne to snuff out the imagery to solid black. This treatment transfers the whirlpool motion of the earlier faux-Hitchcock scene into another register in which the intimacy of touch approaches a point (literally a point) of transcendent consummation in exact proportion to the bodies' distance from the eye of the beholder. The later stages of this whirlpool-merging form one of the few moments in the work when (as in the haptic dissolution described above) bilateral symmetry is lost. The lovers' bodies in transition become a formless asymmetrical mass, what I long ago called an impossible object and what we have since become accustomed to recognizing as the mark, the blotch or stain, of the traumatic-transfiguring Real of desire.

As the process continues and the lovers approach their destined state, the eye or vertex of the whirlpool, we get a moment of transparent self-recognition that is a vision precisely of blindness. As Wagner knew, this consummation cannot be visualized, is that which cannot be visualized, cannot be seen; it exists only as a becoming-invisible. Long before the appointed climax is reached, or, in this case, forestalled by the famous scream, we know what shape it will take (or cease taking), so the episode's point—again literally—is unmistakable. But there is the further complication that the actual climax/disappearance marks an interruption, not a completion, leading to the further "insight" (the word is to be read "under erasure") that the climax of this desire and its curtailment are indistinguishable, that they form the only two in this whole work (the two of the *Lust*-trope, as I called it once[12]) that really do become one.

The remainder Act 2 is taken up by images of daybreak and of a burned-out wasteland, which prepare for the new imagistic modality of Act 3. Here the images appear within a narrow vertical oblong, produced by rotating the screen onto its side. The effect is almost as if the lovers were now being screened *within* the bar rendered visibly in Act 1 and invisibly in Act 2. The screen is an 18 × 36 oblong in the standard 1:2 widescreen aspect ratio. In Act 1 the split-screen doubling effect is created by unobtrusively adding black borders to produce diptych-like panels in the narrower 4:3 ratio typical of television before the advent of widescreen TV. Act 3 simply rotates the cinematic widescreen by 90 degrees.

The resulting 36 × 18 (2:1) space is literally still quite large; it also provides the vertical space necessary to accommodate "Tristan's Ascension." But in relation to what has been seen before the new screen space constitutes a sharp narrowing, suggestive not only of the bar in the diptych but also of the symbolic contraction of the two panels into one. At one level this contraction is a union, as is the contraction of the Act 2 love duet in the opera when Isolde, in her Transfiguration, recapitulates much of the duet as a solo. But at another level the contraction is a diminishment, even an obliteration. The screen of transcendence is indistinguishable from a field of compression and constraint.

Because Isolde's climatic Transfiguration occurs within this field, the screen's narrow aperture of longing keeps on constricting the visible even after the music has begun irreversibly to expand the audible into Wagner's long-sought region of "infinite space." This constriction *of* the visible is also a constriction *to* the visible, in keeping with the pictorial literalness of the sequence. We keep seeing what should escape our sight, keep on seeing when our vision should be dazed. "Tristan's Ascension" makes visible to all a sight that by definition Isolde alone sees or may see. We are supposed only to see her seeing so that we can *hear* more acutely what she sees. But as Isolde thus undergoes her fabled Transfiguration on stage, the transfiguration on screen is Tristan's. We see him through Isolde's eyes or, more exactly, we see (no longer touch, but see) him through her voice. We see too much; we see too much of him.

Or perhaps we see just enough. As the double transfiguration unfolds, Tristan's body is increasingly engulfed by the whirlpool into which we saw the lovers vanish in Act 2. The transfiguration, either transfiguration, Tristan's or Isolde's, once again takes the form of a becoming-invisible. But it does so, and perhaps can do so, only against the resistance of a surplus visibility exerted by the fixation of vision on the object of desire as (dead) body. Supervening on Isolde's vision (in both senses of the term), the engulfing imagery might be said to recreate the eye of the whirlpool as if from within, only to find, in Rilke's fashion, that the beloved keeps on blocking the view even after the sight of his body has been effaced and the body itself has floated away.

Once again: *Tristan und Isolde* is the opera par excellence about that which cannot be seen. The music of the opera symbolically emanates from the invisible, as its framing monodies, the sailor's song of Act 1 and the *alte Weise* of Act 3, do literally. The narrative reaches its climax and conclusion in the presence of a sight that, as just noted, Isolde can "see" but the audience cannot, and *also* cannot even when Viola's images *also* show it. Wagner's Isolde describes this culminating act of seeing as an act of hearing:

> Friends! Look!
> Do you not feel and see it?
> Can it be that I alone
> Hear this mild and wondrous tune?

> Freunde! Seht!
> Fühlt und seht ihr's nicht?
> Höre ich nur diese Weise,
> Die so wundervoll und leise?

The transfiguring sight remains a sound, a *neue Weise,* even when Viola's images besiege it. The premise, but also the goal, of this seeing through the ears is the opening of a shared interiority that is impossible to partake of in the realm of the visible. This opening necessarily takes the form of a rupture—with day, with bonds of loyalty and kinship, with memory, with life itself, with the tonality that was once the life of music. That is why Tristan tears at his wounds and why the lovers' non-reunion becomes Isolde's Transfiguration. Once again: this opera in a sense cannot be seen at all. It can only be heard. But to hear what cannot be seen, even though it is right before one's very eyes, changes what hearing is; the ear must reach out like some prosthetic hand to touch the skin of the inapprehensible. Do you not, Isolde asks rhetorically, *feel* and see it?

Her question explains in advance why the images of the lovers' bodies throughout the double *Tristan* must be gigantic and why they must seem to be both moving and still, discernible and indiscernible. They have to defeat the eye to free the ear. That is also why they must be cinematic but must not be cinema; a film version of *Tristan* could not do this. The solidity of the body must become the fluidity of the music. Nor can one *see* the Viola images, which absorb the gaze that cannot reduce or stabilize them. These images are the visible form of the blindness with which Wagner invested this opera. One has to grope for them.

Wagner's own name for this condition of perception is darkness, the realm in which the transcendental can speak unimpeded, though it may not speak at all and in any case we can't ever be sure of hearing it. In nineteenth-century terms it is a familiar name, but it is a theatrically inspired one: *Tristan* cannot be staged in the dark, but at best in a crepuscular light that only aspires toward the condition of its own impossibility. What the Viola images make us realize (or realize more acutely, since those of us mesmerized by this opera have always known it) is that this Wagnerian darkness does not require the absence of light. The Lincoln Center performance of *The Tristan Project* seemed to acknowledge as much by ending with the house lights fading up, not down. The opera is itself the darkness in which it must be heard.

And now for another image stream, utterance stream, to be juxtaposed with what you have just read, much as Viola's images and Wagner's opera are juxtaposed in the double *Tristan*. The two streams represent the same kind of doubling in another sphere, sometimes at one, sometimes not. The event I have been describing is a perfect frenzy of doubling. But no one should expect a Transfiguration—or not, at any rate, more than a touch of one.

During the portion of the love duet in which the bodies on screen fragment and dissolve, the image stream produces a continuous succession of what psychoanalysis designates as part-objects—real or fantasized body parts, or their symbolic equivalents, toward which desire is "directed without implying that the person as a whole is taken as a love-object."[13] In one sense this erotic register is nothing new: anyone who has seen a sex scene in an R-rated film will be familiar with the technique, which usually also involves steamy music distantly derived from Wagner and which has its own cinematic lineage in older Hollywood treatments of The Kiss such as Hitchcock's in *Vertigo*. So what makes this instance different?

For one thing, the bar of symmetrical division. The bar parts the part-objects, so to speak. Its persistent presence exposes and indeed reverses the concentration of libido and fetishistic glamour into the momentary object by making visible the fact that this process is always also going on elsewhere, diffusing itself across a visual field derived from the bodily totality that the stream of part-objects has temporarily obscured. But it is precisely this totality that bars the lovers from each other. The charm of the part-object in the double *Tristan* is its promise of an escape from the barred and barring logic of the whole, the logic of the body as "love-object." The lovers' haptic bliss is dominated by images of their hands, which replace or smudge away their faces—a study in itself[14]—and fills the screen with images of indistinct surfaces and crevices. The nocturnal journey that follows bathes the once-more symmetrical imagery on screen in the gray of blind touch. The lovers are heading toward the water where their submerged bodies will be touched everywhere at once. And once they enter the whirlpool there, in the segment of the love duet corresponding to Isolde's Transfiguration, the whirling vertigo consumes their bodies, suggesting—insisting, really—that the ultimate "object" of desire is not an object at all, not a body, but something indiscernible. But the object is, as it must be, impossible. The body always comes back, and with it comes the bar, the rigid and sometimes invisible support of the visible, including the bar between Wagner and Viola, who are never at one as to what these returns entail.

Another difference comes from the music. Music in the Hollywood scenario tends to function as the acoustic equivalent of a warm, enveloping body, a kind of musical flesh that does not so much "suture" the audience into the scene as enwrap and therefore enrapture them with it. The part-objects on screen do not part from the logic of the whole; they act as surrogates for the whole through the perceived wholeness of the music. But precisely this perception is what the music of *Tristan und Isolde* makes impossible, above all for the double *Tristan*.

The passing display of part-objects on Viola's screen marks the limit of visual representation in the sphere of desire. In concentrated form it echoes and mirrors the more comprehensive display of part-objects in Wagner's music: the endlessly recycled motifs and even more the continually recurring *Tristan*-chord and its derivatives as they whirl in the currents of a harmony that upholds their repetition by the denial of cadence. In the opera the visual equivalent of this denial is the presence of the bodies on stage, which deflect with their corporeality the music that besieges them. They "block the view" by being too visible, by declining to dissolve at the music's touch no matter how much we, and they, may want them to. In the double *Tristan*, the displacement of reference from the bodies on stage to the magnified body images on screen raises the stakes of this dilemma by doubling the desire involved. Viola's images are designed to rouse our desire to see them, and to see them intact, to see them as beautiful. That is one reason they continually return from the part-object to the body as love-object, which deflects with its intactness the proliferation of musical part-objects that it summons to besiege it.

But to deflect is not to deny. The logic of the part-object is not confined to the representation of part-objects onscreen; it permeates the double *Tristan* through the persistent indifferentiation of sight and touch. The framing logic here is the becoming-haptic of the optic based on proximity to the seen—the experience, noted earlier, that seeing things from very close up resembles or even converges with touching them. Derrida takes up this topic in *On Touching* with particular reference to the thought of Jean-Luc Nancy, a move in which we will follow him a bit later on.[15] As the lovers touch in Act 2, their dissolution into part-objects and the graying and blurring of their images reproduce the visual effect of proximity, of physical intimacy, with the eye up close to its object, too close to see it, so close indeed that the intimate suffers a disfiguration.

In Lacanian terms, this change in the object of desire, which results from the over-proximity of the Real, should be a debasement.[16] Yet here the dissolution of sight in the image presents itself as evocative rather than repellent, nebulous rather than glutinous. At least it seeks to; a great deal depends on who is seeing, and hearing, what. But at any rate it is precisely in hearing that sight and touch are brought into intimate contact.

Thanks to the music, which not only besieges the dissolving imagery but seems to be the force dissolving it, the over-closeness in this scene becomes beckoning, absorptive, welcoming. The process starts, symbolically, with a touch, as shots of the lovers' hands impel and guide the dissociation of their bodies until what we see becomes an image, not of the lovers, but of the music that has been drawing them toward a state for which there is no image. In this reciprocal becoming of touch and sight, touch becomes contemplative and sight becomes prehensile. Meanwhile, in what they sing, the lovers echo this reciprocity with a parallel or supplemental relation between symbolic and ecstatic union. They speculate on the language that divides them ("No more Tristan," "No more Isolde") and yet also provides them with the power of mutual recognition, the reciprocal naming in which their relationship as lovers begins (after they drink Brangäne's potion) and ends (as Tristan dies) to the same music, the languishing deceptive cadence from measure 17 of the Prelude. This strange indifferentiation between ending and beginning, meeting and parting, as rendered in the music, is as close anyone comes to totality in either *Tristan*. The music is how the lovers survive, or how their love does, but it is also what survives them.

The wedge idea for the double *Tristan*'s haptic design is Jean-Luc Nancy's claim that the existence, the possibility, of sensory indifferentiation means there is no "the" sense of sight or sense of touch, that each "touches" on the other. For Derrida this conception stands as a condition of possibility for the non-continuous presence toward which *On Touching* gropes. In this context the double *Tristan* might be understood as seeking, knowingly or not, to see (hear, touch on) what would happen if the zone of indifferentiation between sight and touch ceased for a while to be a perceptual outland, visited only occasionally, and instead became coextensive with the zone of perception as such. Thanks to the scale of Viola's images (a topic to which we will return), much of the double *Tristan* takes place within a simulation of this rezoning. The "zoning out" into blurry part-objects in Act 2 is not actually an exceptional episode but a consummating one.

What tends to confront the music, therefore, is not a stream of imagery but the touch of imagery, a touch that seeks the same relation to the music as do the lovers whose touch it images, the same relation that Wagner's lovers seek to each other with their voices: the becoming-one of two. But since there is no "the" sense of touch, or sight, or hearing, the indifferentiation of the senses cannot be limited to touch and sight; it affects the music, too. There is also a becoming-haptic of the auditory effected here, redoubled by the sensuous continuity of Wagner's harmony. So it is not simply that touch and sight intermingle in the hearing of the music. Touch also becomes the medium in which sight and sound become one and in which the music does not address from afar but touches the listener intimately, in the sensitive depth of the psyche, a more erogenous zone than anything found in the body.

But at the same time this does *not* happen. The condition of the impossible always intervenes; the bliss demanded by *Tristan*, either *Tristan*, demands a certain incoherence at its heart. None of these doublings or becomings ever arrives as an event, because the one is always two: one symmetrical fold and another, the music and the imagery, part-object and love-object, Tristan *and* Isolde.

Derrida argues that this non-arrival is the inevitable outcome of the silent dependency of continuity on acts of partition, that is, on the very doubling-as-splitting that is the obsessively redoubled state of the double *Tristan.* Nancy calls this process *syncope,* with a play on both the psychological fugue state and musical syncopation.[17] The syncope is both a perceptual delirium—a vertigo—and its denial. Just so: Hitchcock's rotation of the camera eye around the kissing lovers in *Vertigo* makes us as dizzy as the kiss does them, but the rotation is orbital, like the eye, and so is Viola's reenactment, albeit in Wagnerian time.

Derrida identifies this perceptual impasse-in-principle with the production and persistence of desire, in particular of the desire for immediacy, for presence, for contact, that seeks its satisfaction through touch. As a result, to touch on such immediacy requires what Derrida calls a long detour, one meant in particular to circumvent the resurgence of the opposition of the optic as law and rule to the haptic as the truth of closeness. Wagner in *Tristan* does whatever he can within the limits of his own musical and technological means to erase this limitation, to touch on touch in music without the detour. Viola's images do the same, although their bisymmetrical duality, like the meditation on the word "and" in Act 2 of Wagner's *Tristan,* acknowledges the limitation as a point of departure. The idea is to be swallowed up by a touch, which is the sum of being overwhelmed by what one hears and overpowered by what one sees.

This is also the idea that governs Isolde's Transfiguration, the idea of an extended moment, suspended between life and death, in which non-arrival becomes arrival itself. As we know, Viola represents *Isolde's* transfiguration primarily as *Tristan's* ascent through violently burbling water. The water becomes so agitated that it obscures the sight of Tristan's body even before the body breaks the plane of the upper screen space and disappears. Then, at the last minute, Isolde's body, replacing Tristan's at the midpoint of the latter's arc, breaks the surface of the sea and floats heavenward in a blissful field of blue. One might again demur that the all-important sense of impossibility has been lost here just where it is needed most, but against that stands the simple fact that in this consummation the logic of one and two inexorably prevails: we only ever see the one body, never the two as one.

Here once more the critical element is the doubling between the music and the image, the ultimate form of the doubling of Tristan and Isolde both on the screens and on the Wagnerian stage. Wagner provides the template by framing the opera as an extended chain of extended dialogues: Isolde and Brangäne, Tristan and Kurwenal, and above all, of course, the lovers themselves, with whom the dialogue form becomes a meditation on how to share, and thus to lose, a self. Wagner projects through voice what Viola projects into vision. Act 1 and especially Act 2 of the opera feature long periods in which nothing happens but the dialogue of the lovers as it is spun out into a musical interlocution without clear frame or edge, the protracted engagement of one voice merging with and parting from another. Condensed into voice, self can be dispersed by voice. But in Act 3 the voices never meet except, too late, at the moment of Tristan's death. The merging must thus take the very form of parting, and vice versa, and that is what happens during Isolde's Transfiguration.

This mutual (inter)voicing resembles the condition of non-fused proximity that Derrida seeks to identify as the condition of presence. It is also the condition established between Viola's images and Wagner's music, not because either accompanies or supplements the other, along the lines of narrative cinema, but because, and only because, the images and the music commingle—intimately, protractedly—but do not coincide. Of all the means employed to produce this "living present that has to be interpreted differently from coincidence and fusion," perhaps the most important is the distribution of voice. The fact may have seemed too obvious to dwell on until now, but Wagner's music is *sung*. Viola's images are voiceless. The double *Tristan* arises above all through the continuous non-identity between live singing voices and images that neither sing nor give any indication of aurality or auditory life. This disjunct conjunction is what prevents the music-image relation from being normalized, reduced, naturalized, or hierarchized as would be the case, for example, in the cinema.

The central instance is once again the love duet of Act 2, in which the voices come to relate, not as those of subject and interlocutor, but as the two registers of a single voice divided apparitionally into the figures of Tristan and Isolde. At least Wagner's lovers conceive of it this way, and although the paired singers on stage uphold the separation as real, bound by their bodies, the unbounded music continually insists on the opposite. In the double *Tristan,* the images superadded to the music drama redouble this doubling. Visually, cinematically, in the dissolution of intact oversize bodies into blurry part-objects and subsequently into amorphous masses of living substance, both the bodies and the persons of the imaged lovers merge. The imaginary Couple attains the state that Wagner's lovers, despite Wagner's music, can only seek to attain in their extended love duet before its interruption by the scream that, tearing at the ears, becomes the acoustic stain of the Real and aborts what promises to be the culminating cadence.

At this point in the double work yet another doubling/splitting occurs, as it does in the opera, where the interruption misses and therefore marks the point at which the duet must arrive when its latter portion is recapitulated in Act 3 as Isolde's Transfiguration. For the imaged lovers here do *not* become one at all. Recall that when they emerge from the bath of part-objects they hasten through the night to the sea and enter the whirlpool. As they go, their now-restored symmetrical positioning continually divides them into image and mirror-image, the elements of an erotic stereography, with the space between them again functioning like the Lacanian bar through the subject or the Derridean (re)mark of *différance.* The symmetry even lingers awhile after they submerge, but once undersea the bar becomes temporal rather than spatial: it disappears as the lovers' bodies sink and recede, symmetrically reversing its sublimated reappearance in Act 1 as they advance and rise. The one is two more than the two are one: another formula for desire at its metaphysical uttermost. Or, to state what we have already seen and touched on more than once, but at the level of a principle: every doubling is also a splitting. This is the leitmotif and leitbild of the double(d) *Tristan.* Without this shared partition there is nothing except the whirlpool of the Real, which, as we can see in the fate of the lovers once they have entered it, is nothing: nothing and no one. There can be no view without the other to stand in the way.

In Wagner's Act 3, this principle both devolves and evolves: devolves into the long scene of thwarted expectation in which Tristan bares his heart to Kurwenal while awaiting Isolde's arrival, and evolves from Tristan's death—which occurs just before he can hear the belated Isolde pronounce his name as he, with his last breath, has pronounced hers— into Isolde's Transfiguration. Each of these moments involves a musical doubling and splitting: of the *alte Weise*, of the big deceptive cadence from the Prelude, of the love duet. Yet with each splitting the ultimate communion comes closer. To grasp, in parting, what this strange movement of partaking in division does and does not, can and cannot accomplish, we can touch yet again on the last of these cardinal moments, along with its twin, while also doubling back to Derrida's *On Touching*.

This much is now familiar, another doubling and splitting: in both the original and the double *Tristan* the power of the lovers to open the view by blocking it peaks twice, in the broken love duet and its reparative sublimation in Isolde's Transfiguration. Why, the exigencies of plot aside, does the second peak succeed where the first fails?

In Wagner's *Tristan und Isolde,* the union of the lovers occurs only once they can no longer share a living touch. But this is not to say they cannot touch each other, only that they must not touch each other with their bodies nor, in the end, even with their voices. This is perhaps the deeper meaning of Brangäne's scream, since in most productions the love duet proceeds to a point where Tristan and Isolde are singing in one another's arms. The scream parts them, but in a sense they were already parted. Their union comes about through, or following, Isolde's Transfiguration in a music shared out between Tristan, dead and silent, and Isolde, alive and singing. This music in partition, in syncope, fulfils itself—how else?—twice: first in the recovery of the love duet's aborted cadence, and then perhaps even more in a symbolic act of touching that is also an act of mirroring. This touch, an acoustic stroke or caress, is the insertion in the cadential passage of the Desire motive first heard at the beginning of the Prelude—four rising semitones on the oboes linking the tonally cardinal pitches of G♯ and B.[18] The notes too are joined in their division at a point of harmonic repose. But by this time Isolde may no longer be able to hear them.[19]

In the double *Tristan* the split between visual separation and musical union is literally magnified thanks to the image of Tristan in submarine repose that persists during the Transfiguration scene. The Paris production is the touchstone here, its tiny live figure of Isolde facing the audience while the huge one of Tristan hovers apparitionally behind her back. The eye and the ear seem to heed different transcendental imperatives as the visual imagery of ascension falls out of sync with the auditory imagery of transfiguration, as if the wedding of the temporal flows between the twinned yet parted halves of the double Tristan were dissolving away. By the time the Desire motive touches the ear, Tristan's Ascension has long since been replaced by Isolde's and Isolde herself has all but disappeared. The notes are joined together; the lovers are not.

In the way they frame their conclusions, both the single and the double *Tristan* exemplify the condition that Derrida seeks to affirm by playing on Jean-Luc Nancy's concept of *partage,* sharing by division: "[It is necessary] to subtract sense, the senses, the senses of sense, the experience of sense and of the sharing out and parting of the senses, from any sovereignty of *presence,* immediacy, the proper and the proximate. Nothing, no presence whatever, without a detour."[20] This is not to say (repeating the standard misunderstanding of Derrida) that presence and immediacy are not real, do not really occur, but to say that they are not sovereign. Not even the most direct and intimate sensation will give us a *sovereign* presence because presence requires a detour; it is the gift and effect of the detour that at first seems to avert it. The end of *Tristan,* either *Tristan,* is an extended detour.

More generally, and in keeping with Derrida's critique of the presence-oriented identification of touch and closeness, the haptic with the proximate, Viola's images create the effect of proximity even though one views them from afar. This "even though" changes the character of proximity. The images create the effect, the sense (which is also sensory), of *proximity at a distance,* and thus challenge what Derrida critiques as the "continuistic postulation" of Western thinking. They do so by combining two modes of *partage:* by juxtaposing their slow, subaqueous, sometimes nearly imperceptible pace with the movement of the music, and by simultaneously (this concurrence also an act of *partage*) juxtaposing their spectral-cinematic appearance with the presence of the bodies on stage and with the latter's live voices.

So presented, take the term as you will, the images both absorb and interrupt the gaze and its auditory equivalent, and they do so both constantly and intermittently. They become present to excess and yet remain incapable of being intuited: they become *tangible* in a sense that is more than metaphorical but that also arrests them on the threshold of visuality, imperceptible except as assemblies of part-objects. Meanwhile, the embodied voices associated with but not belonging to these images make present—at a distance—the other person as a whole taken as a love-object. We know what the imaged bodies would look like if we could take them in with our gaze, but we cannot do so even when the imaged bodies are shown intact—for when they are actually shown at life size, their scale means that they are shown, precisely, at a distance, as the bodies on stage constantly remind us. Besides, each movement of the senses confronts us with a juxtaposition between two Tristans, two Isoldes, and with a movement of voice that ebbs and flows in between.

At the same time again, Viola's images disrupt any possible sense of an opposition between presence and meaning because, through every fluctuation of presence and its detours, the bodies—all the bodies, imaged and real—are surrounded by an elaborate iconography, especially of fire and water, an iconography loaded and overloaded with meaning from multiple traditions. So to draw out the beckoning inference with a formula in which Derrida's remains, retains, a spectral presence: nothing, no meaning without presence, no presence without meaning. But then, Wagner said much the same thing in the little program note he wrote for the concert version of the Transfiguration scene: "Over Tristan's body the dying Isolde receives the blessed fulfillment of ardent longing, eternal union in measureless space, without barriers, without fetters, inseparable!" No meaning without presence: Isolde receives her blessed fulfillment only through the sacramental medium of Tristan's body. No presence without meaning: the measureless space of eternity opens to Isolde only as the form in which she is inseparable from Tristan. The double *Tristan* ratchets this formula up to the point of its incoherence or collapse, especially in the Paris staging where the singers' bodies as well as their voices are not only present but part of the action. The music fills with too much presence, the images with too much meaning, yet each demands to be inseparable from the other in the measured space of a singular time.[21]

The foregoing considerations are meant to be independent of the two issues that dominated the immediate critical reception of the double *Tristan:* the "new-age mysticism"[22] of Viola's elemental images and the question of whether the images "overwhelm" the music because they, the images, are just so *big*. On either count the images might seem to produce a naïve reduction of Wagner's conception. Viola thinks of the three acts under the rubrics of Purification, the Body of Light (the two lovers' bodies merging into a luminous blur as they approach the water), and Dissolution (Tristan sinking into the watery element and rising transfigured from it). The conclusion of Act 3 follows the imagery of the Tibetan Book of the Dead, which states that hearing is the last sense to be lost and that the last sound that one hears is the sound of a mountain under a waterfall, for which Viola also provides a pictorial counterpart. The point at which the artist and critic part company is precisely here, where Viola's notion of unqualified transcendence comes into collision with the logic of sense that radically, more radically than Viola might like, de-authorizes the double work. This clash becomes, literally, most visible in the narrow oblong screen of Act 3, which Viola sees as oriented vertically toward the transcendental Above, but I see as a thickened version of the Lacanian bar.

These are not, however, the primary issues raised by the double *Tristan*. One might argue that the visual apparatus of virtually any production is necessarily reductive of Wagner's conception (which we need not, nevertheless, forget), and that rivalry between spectacle and music is as endemic to the multi-media genre of opera as rivalry between words and music. Regardless of whether complexity rules or size matters, the double *Tristan* is, was, an event in the strong sense because the mutually defamiliarizing combination of its cinematic apparatus with Wagner's music reissued the demand of the latter to make present, make a present, of the phenomenology of perception. Viola's paraphrase of Wagner via a changed technical standard reacts to the same problems in the logic of sensory life, which is also a logic of desire, that Wagner initially mobilized, or that mobilized him. Viola's supplement freshly exposes technology as the hidden hand in producing what Wagner called the "purely human," and it thus re-exposes and reorients Wagner's attempt to question the perceptual and metaphysical limits of expression, representation, articulation, and predication. Neither Wagner's opera nor its doubling by Viola is just another love story.

Nor is the double *Tristan* just another production; the sense in which it is, rather, another *Tristan* should by now be clear. The double

Tristan is not a compound of opera and illustration, opera and commentary, nor do the images constitute an interpretation of the opera. Instead, the single event of the double work is a disclosure of its own conditions of possibility, already latent in the opera but not necessarily discernible in the opera on its own. This second *Tristan* opens onto the Lacanian threshold of the visible world because it is no longer a presentation of its amatory narrative or the symbolic repercussions thereof, at least not primarily, but an intervention that touches on the field of vision, besieged by music, just where the view is blocked. The true author of the double *Tristan* is neither Wagner nor Viola, but the logic of the senses by which both of them were inexorably drawn.

NOTES

This chapter originated in an evening panel, "Visualizing Tristan: The Viola-Sellars Production of 2005," held at the Los Angeles meeting of the American Musicological Society in December 2006. The event was paired (aptly enough) with an afternoon panel in which Bill Viola and Kira Perov spoke about *The Tristan Project*. The technical and thematic information here derives from their remarks. I am also grateful to the Bill Viola Studios for making DVDs of *The Tristan Project* available for study. The other evening panelists were Beate Perrey, Esteban Buch, and Simon Williams, to all of whom I am indebted, as I am to a paper by Perrey, which was the stimulus for the AMS session, delivered in Paris in May, 2005, at the conference "Music, Poetry and Sense Experience," co-sponsored by the Centre for Research in the Arts, Social Sciences, and Humanities at the University of Cambridge and the Centre de recherches sur les arts et le langage at the École des Hautes Études et Sciences Sociales, Paris, and to Christopher Morris's paper, "Straight to Video: Staging *Tristan* in the Age of Widescreen," kindly provided to me by the author.
The chapter epigraph is from Jacques Lacan, *Écrits: A Selection*, trans. Alan Sheridan (New York: W.W. Norton, 1977), 3.

1. German text in my translation (here and throughout) from Stephen Mitchell's bilingual *The Selected Poetry of Rainer Maria Rilke* (New York: Vintage, 1984).

2. From Maurice Merleau-Ponty's *Phenomenology of Perception,* quoted in Jacques Derrida, *On Touching: Jean-Luc Nancy,* trans. Christine Irizarry (Stanford: Stanford University Press, 2005), 205.

3. Derrida, *On Touching,* all quotations from p. 124 except for the last, from p. 203.

4. See Jacques Derrida, *Without Alibi,* trans. Peggy Kamuf (Stanford: Stanford University Press, 2002), 71–75, 133–36, 233–37, 275–79; Alain Badiou, *Being and Event,* trans. Oliver Feltham (New York: Continuum, 2005), 173–90, 201–11.

5. Walter Benjamin, "The Work of Art in the Age of Its Technological Reproducibility, Third Version," trans. Harry Zohn and Edmund Jephcott, in Benjamin, *Selected Writings, Volume 4, 1938–1940,* ed. Howard Eiland and Michael W. Jennings (Cambridge, Mass.: Harvard University Press, 2003), 266.

6. Ibid., 265.

7. Raymond Knapp, "'Selbts bin dann ich die Welt': On the Subjective-Musical Basis of Wagner's *Gesamtkunstwelt*," *19th-Century Music* 29 (2005): 142–60; Martin Heidegger, "The Origin of the Work of Art," in Heidegger, *Poetry Language Thought*, trans. Albert Hofstadter (New York: Harper and Row, 1971), 15–88, at 44–46. Like Isolde, Heidegger finds the presence of world as enveloping All where the world as the scene of "blessing and curse" disappears: "In a world's worlding is gathered that spaciousness out of which the protective grace of the gods is granted or withheld. Even this doom of the god remaining absent is a way in which the world worlds" (45).

8. On the impossible object, see my *Music as Cultural Practice* (Berkeley: University of California Press, 1990; available online at California Digital Library), 72–101; on the Wagnerian Real, my *Opera as Modern Culture* (Berkeley: University of California Press, 2004), 221–28. On the Real, see Jacques Lacan, *Four Fundamental Concepts of Psychoanalysis*, ed. Jacques-Alain Miller, trans. Alan Sheridan (New York: W. W. Norton, 1981), 53–64 and 279–80; and Slavoj Žižek, *Looking Awry: An Introduction to Jacques Lacan through Popular Culture* (Cambridge, Massachusetts: MIT Press, 1993), 1–20.

9. See the chapter on *Tristan und Isolde* in Kramer, *Music as Cultural Practice*, 135–65.

10. Bill Viola, "Moving Image World for *Tristan und Isolde*," Program Notes for the Lincoln Center performance, accessed online at http://www.lincolncenter.org/programnotes/gp-tristan-050207.pdf (accessed June 30, 2008).

11. Viola clearly treats color as an expressive variable, like image size; it is essential to the images considered here, less so to those discussed in Jeongwon Joe's essay in this volume, where the process of Viola's visual composition is a primary factor.

12. For the *Lust*-trope, see Kramer, *Music as Cultural Practice*, 148–49.

13. Definition adapted and in part quoted from J. Laplanche and J.-B. Pontalis, *The Language of Psycho-Analysis*, trans. Donald Nicholson-Smith (New York: W. W. Norton, 1967), 301.

14. Largely missing from my account is any reckoning with the face, which has its own role to play in the double *Tristan*, especially in certain scenes of "purification" in Act 1 and in the "Vertigo" episodes in Act 2. Suffice it to say (without being too Levinasian about it) that the face, especially since the invention of photography, has typically been granted the power to stand in for the whole person, the whole body as love object. The face is the only part of the body that is virtually never a part-object. The rhetoric of the cinematic close-up depends on this exception, whereas opera has little use for it. Indeed, close-ups of singing faces in video representations of opera tend to bring the gaze uncomfortably close to the Real. Although Viola tends to idealize the faces of his Tristan and Isolde, he allows them to become masklike blurs when they need to, in the part-object sequence.

15. Derrida traces this idea from the work of Henri Bergson and Alois Riegl to its development in Maurice Merleau-Ponty, Gilles Deleuze and Felix Guattari, Jean-Luc Nancy, and himself (*On Touching*, 123–30). Hovering in the background is the Hegelian distinction between intellectual and non-intellectual senses, which parts the visual and auditory from the haptic, problematically so in Derrida's view. On

this topic see Derrida, "The Pit and the Pyramid: Introduction to Hegel's Semiology," in *Margins of Philosophy,* trans. Alan Bass (Chicago: University of Chicago Press, 1982), 69–108.

16. On this conversion of allure to debasement, see Lacan, *Four Fundamental Concepts,* 267–73; Slavoj Žižek, *The Plague of Fantasies* (London: Verso, 1997), 66–69; and Žižek, *The Abyss of Freedom* (Ann Arbor: University of Michigan Press, 1997), 21–24.

17. Jean-Luc Nancy, *Le discourse de la syncope* (Paris: Aubier-Flammarion, 1976); see also Derrida, *On Touching,* 105–15, 128–31.

18. On the structural significance of the relation between G♯ (=A♭) and B, which represent the "two tonics" of the opera, see Robert Bailey, "An Analytical Study of the Sketches and Drafts," in his *Wagner: Prelude and Transfiguration from* Tristan and Isolde, Norton Critical Scores (New York: W. W. Norton, 1985), 113–46; for the hermeneutic implications of Bailey's "double-tonic complex," see my chapter on *Tristan* in *Music as Cultural Practice.*

19. It is interesting to note in this connection that in the Metropolitan Opera's production of *Tristan und Isolde* in 2008, Isolde, played by Deborah Voigt, remained standing while the curtain fell. Her posture was almost defiant, and while the choice to leave Isolde standing (which is not unique) may have been in part a refusal to provide the mandatory Dead Soprano, it also seemed to suggest a more rigorous version of the impossible lovers' union, the burden of which a dead Isolde is spared but a living one would have to sustain indefinitely.

20. Derrida, *On Touching,* 130.

21. The quotation from Wagner is taken from Bailey, *Prelude and Transfiguration,* 48. The inseparability of presence and meaning that forms the leitmotif of these comments puts my text in implicit disagreement with Hans-Ulrich Gumbrecht's widely read *The Production of Presence: What Meaning Cannot Convey* (Stanford: Stanford University Press, 2004).

22. "New-age mysticism" is from Christopher Morris, "Straight to Video"; see unnumbered note.

Looking for Richard:
An Archival Search for Wagner

WARREN M. SHERK

An hour into John Boorman's 1981 film *Excalibur,* the scene in which Lancelot first lays eyes on Guenevere is underscored by Richard Wagner's Prelude from *Tristan und Isolde.* At the film's close, the solo music credit reads, "Original Music Composed and Conducted by Trevor Jones." Even though a list of Wagner's works eventually follows, the average filmgoer may be unable to tell which composer wrote which music.

Over the years, documenting the use of classical music in film has presented its own set of challenges. No single comprehensive source exists, though some credible internet sites are in development.[1] For further inquiries, there are places to turn. This essay surveys some of the archival resources at the Margaret Herrick Library for researchers, academics, and students seeking information on Wagnerism in cinema, and extends to the use of opera music in film as well.[2]

THE CORE COLLECTION AT THE
MARGARET HERRICK LIBRARY

For the researcher, a trip through the resources at the Margaret Herrick Library will reveal historical context and details of Wagner's music that may be useful alone or in conjunction with musical analysis. The Library collects a wide range of materials relating to motion pictures, including books, periodicals, scripts, photographs, posters, and other publicity materials. Extensive files of magazine and newspaper clippings can be found in the core collection, organized by film title, personal name, corporate name, and general subject.

The file for *Excalibur,* for example, includes a thick sleeve of reviews and magazine articles culled from dozens of local and national publications, from the *Village Voice* to UCLA's *Daily Bruin.* The critic Barry Brennan comments on the film's "operatic sweep" and "Wagnerian grandeur" but does not mention the use of Wagner's music itself as a contributing factor.[3] Scattered throughout the core collection are clippings about and photographs from Wagner-related films, including onscreen portrayals of Wagner, opera-films of Wagner, and films famous for their use of his music, from *The Birth of a Nation* (1915) to *Birth* (2004). The file for *Meeting Venus* (1991), a backstage drama that takes place during a performance of *Tannhäuser,* contains clippings ranging from *Screen International* to *Playboy,* reviews and credits, dozens of color slides and photographic prints, and most important, a music cue sheet and pressbook. The film composer Ernest Gold's file includes a number of articles he contributed to *Opera News,* such as "Wagner: Alchemist of Folklore."[4] Many of Gold's articles are unrelated to film music, but his perspective on opera may be of interest to researchers. In the "Opera on Film" file are clippings on *Porgy and Bess* (1959), the first opera to be filmed in 70mm; the growing popularity of stage operas shot in 3-D; and a list of operatic Vitaphone shorts dominated by Verdi arias.[5] The Vitaphone shorts were produced from 1926 to 1932 by the Vitaphone Corporation, a subsidiary of Warner Bros., and used a proprietary sound-on-disc motion picture system. At least sixty-four of these films, which range from four to ten minutes in length, feature opera singers. Vitaphone signed Metropolitan Opera singers and filmed at the Manhattan Opera House.

MUSIC AND RECORDED SOUND: USING SCORES AND ARCHIVAL RECORDINGS TO RESEARCH WAGNER

The Music and Recorded Sound collection holds sheet music, music scores, and recorded sound in various formats: disc recordings, tape recordings, and compact discs. Material also is located in the Sammy Cahn papers, the Ernest Gold scrapbooks, the Jerry Goldsmith music sketches, the Lux Radio Theatre collection, the Alex North papers, the Charles

Previn papers, and the Screen Composers Association records. Many studios—Disney, Fox, Paramount, and Universal in particular—still keep an enormous amount of scores, usually inaccessible to researchers. Fortunately, some studio archives are in university repositories and available for study: Republic (Brigham Young University), RKO (University of California, Los Angeles), and Warner Bros. (Univeristy of Southern California) among them.

A disc recording for the rehearsal of the "Abscheid" from *Lohengrin*, used in Scene 2414 of the MGM film *Luxury Liner* (1948), directed by Richard Whorf, was recorded on August 23, 1947, and on September 4, 1947. Nearly six weeks later, Siegmund's "Liebeslied" from *Die Walküre* was recorded for Scene 2430, as well as a short version of the "Liebeslied." To determine when the decision was made as to what Wagner music to use and where to use it might involve a look through the various scripts for *Luxury Liner*—there are more than a dozen versions—in the Library's Turner/MGM scripts collection. The production notes—studio-generated notes, dated October 12, 1948—reveal that a shortened version of the "Scene and Gavotte" ("Obéissons quand leur Voix appelle") from Massenet's *Manon* was selected to contrast with Siegmund's "Liebeslied." Both the "Gavotte" and the "Liebeslied" can be heard in the film. The tenor Lauritz Melchior's solo rendition of the latter, in concert form as arranged and conducted by George Stoll, "sounds almost like a different aria without the full orchestral accompaniment as is usually heard."

One of the more unusual music scores came to the Library from the director George Stevens. As head of the Special Coverage Motion Picture Unit of the U.S. Army Signal Corps during World War II, Stevens and his crew documented the taking of Hitler's Berchtesgaden headquarters, in Germany. Along with the footage, the director brought back to the United States a limited-edition reproduction of the original manuscript of the score for *Die Meistersinger von Nürnberg*. It was issued in 1922 and inscribed by Hermann Goering to Adolf Hitler on Hitler's birthday in 1935.

LOOKING FOR CLUES IN CUE SHEETS

As Roger Hillman writes, the closing credits of director Werner Herzog's Gulf War documentary *Lessons of Darkness* cite Wagner's music but do not elaborate on its use or placement in the film.[6] Still, for researchers, screen credits remain an ideal starting point. The next step is to access music cue sheets, which are found throughout the Library's collections and typically give the title of the work, the composer, method of use (instrumental, vocal, partial, etc.), timing, and placement of the music cue within a reel of film.

In recent years, more than eight hundred cue sheets have been placed in the Library's core collection production files, many submitted by composers as part of the Academy Awards nomination process. An example relevant to the topic of Wagner and cinema is a descriptive film music guide for *Lady Windermere's Fan* (1925): it suggests Wagner's music for the social reception scene, and a Fischer publication is recommended in the "taxable" column. Theaters paying a yearly fee to the American Society of Composers, Authors, and Publishers (ASCAP) would have unlimited use of music by ASCAP publisher members. Non-complying theaters had the choice of selecting a public domain version of the same Wagner work from another publisher. In the Harry Sukman papers, a cue sheet for the Franz Liszt biopic *Song without End*—in which actor Lyndon Brook portrays Wagner—lists more than five minutes of Wagner's music, including forty-one seconds of "Evening Star" from *Tannhäuser,* adapted by music director Morris Stoloff. The Library also has cue sheets, here called music reports (even though they are no different than standard cue sheets), for approximately one thousand titles in its Turner/MGM scripts collection.

For other sources of cue sheets, researchers can turn to film studios' music legal departments, which handle cue sheets as part of the clearance process, and performing rights societies such as ASCAP and Broadcast Music Inc. (BMI). Although film studios and performing rights societies normally do not release copies of cue sheets, a friendly inquiry may elicit information for U.S. and international versions of a film.

ARCHIVAL COLLECTIONS: FINDING WAGNER'S MUSIC AND MORE

Special Collections encompasses more than one thousand archival units—personal papers and organizational records—that include production files (budgets, call sheets, legal material, studio-based historical research, and schedules), scripts, correspondence, contracts, scrapbooks, and publicity materials. Among the major manuscript collections are those from Hal Ashby, George Cukor, Alfred Hitchcock, John Huston, Gregory Peck, Sam Peckinpah, Mary Pickford, Mack Sennett, George Stevens, Hal B. Wallis, and Fred Zinnemann. Collections of manuscripts and photographs from Metro-Goldwyn-Mayer, Paramount, RKO, 20th Century-Fox, and Universal, and other film studios are also available. There is a surprising variety of material relating to Wagner and opera music, including files in the Andrew Stone papers on several films directed by Stone that incorporate Wagner's music: *Stolen Heaven* (1938), *There's Magic in Music* (1941), and *Hi Diddle Diddle* (1943). For instance, a correspondence file for *There's Magic in Music* in the Paramount production records documents the involvement of the New York Metropolitan Opera in the film's production. Singers Richard Bonelli, Tandy MacKenzie, and Irra Petina appear in the film, as opera figures prominently in the story line. The main titles include the intriguing credit "Operatic Wrangle devised by Edwin Lester"—perhaps the only time such a credit appears. According to the legal file, one scene required arias from two different operas to be performed at the same time to evoke a "competition" between the performers. Composer, arranger, and lyricist Edwin Lester was brought in to "wrangle" the arias from *Carmen* and *Faust* into a dramatic yet musically harmonious result. That climactic scene is posted on YouTube.[7]

The Tom B'hend and Preston Kaufmann collection of theater material contains a file on stage prologues, including clippings from 1920s trade publications. At the Tivoli Theatre in Chicago, a "Wagneriana" overture with selections from "Richard Wagner's immortal compositions" was performed prior to a screening of *The Dark Angel* (1925). The voluminous programs in this collection are a treasure trove of information: for example, in the Wagnerian prologue to *The Last Payment* (1922), starring Pola Negri, twelve soli violinists played Walter's "Prize Song" from *Die Meistersinger* in unison, with full orchestral accompaniment.[8] The film exhibitor Sid Grauman said of Wagner, "This great revolutionist in music was also a revolutionist in spirit, and in an age devoted to the worship of Prussianism so fought the political battle of Democracy as to get himself exiled to Switzerland."[9]

Film aficionado Audrey Chamberlin kept meticulous scrapbooks that include clippings and miscellaneous pictorial material for *The Flying Dutchman* (1923) and *Siegfried* (1925). Two photographs from Niklaus Schilling's *Rheingold* related to a Los Angeles Filmex screening are in the Theatre Vanguard collection at the Library. The *Vertigo* music file in the Alfred Hitchcock papers contains contracts and specifics related to the scoring process, where the music was recorded, scoring costs, and an intriguing undated memo concerning a San Francisco Opera performance of "Die Walkuere" [*sic*].

Sometimes information ventures beyond the realm of music—for example, into the area of censorship. In 1954, a three-page letter from Joseph I. Breen, head of the Production Code Administration (PCA), was sent to a Republic studio official regarding the shooting script for *Magic Fire* (1955), a biopic of Wagner directed by William Dieterle, which re-created Wagner's opera music. Breen called for no excessive passion in the love scenes between Tristan and Isolde and the toning down of the suggestive dialogue spoken by Cosima and Richard. This was all in a day's work for the PCA. The production code was established in the 1930s to help the film industry regulate itself by adhering to certain moral guidelines. As part of the process, filmmakers submitted scripts and a variety of material to receive certification. The PCA was superseded in 1967 by the rating system of the Motion Picture Association of America (MPAA), which took over and maintained the PCA files. Those files—containing script excerpts, treatments, and material related to the censoring of song lyrics on approximately 20,000 films and properties—are now part of the MPAA Production Code Administration records at the Library.

THE INFLUENCE OF FILM SCRIPTS

The Library is home to two large studio collections of scripts, Paramount and Turner/MGM. As an aid to researchers, the Library maintains the Motion Picture Scripts Database: An Inventory of the Motion Picture Script Holdings of Six Los Angeles–Area Libraries (http://scriptlist.oscars.org/). Musical suggestions in the script may influence a composer's approach to a scene. For a wedding and honeymoon sequence set in

Las Vegas for *Flying Blind* (1941), the script called for a "wacky wedding march" and an onscreen rhumba orchestra. Although the cue sheet for this sequence lists simply Wagner's "Wedding March," Dimitri Tiomkin, the film's composer, came up with a clever and complex solution. In the full story, the cue opens with music to set the appropriate Vegas feel. Tiomkin then presents a tongue-in-cheek arrangement of Wagner's "Wedding March." Next, various musical quotes are incorporated, including an extended passage of Tiomkin's own "Cubanola," creating a seamless flow of musical ideas and ending with juxtaposed quotes from "La Cucaracha" and Wagner.[10]

Music by Wagner appears in at least eight films scored by Tiomkin. When Tiomkin received an Academy Award for his score for *The High and the Mighty* in 1955, he wanted to express his admiration and respect for classical music composers. (Tiomkin recently had been acquitted in a plagiarism suit due in part to the expert testimony of musicologist Sigmund Spaeth, who demonstrated that, taken to the extreme, nearly any musical theme can be broken down into short motifs that have antecedents in classical music.) During his acceptance speech, he started naming the long-dead composers, including Wagner along with Brahms, Strauss, and Beethoven. The audience burst into laughter, mistakenly believing Tiomkin was acknowledging that film music borrowed freely from classical music.

PERIODICALS AS A RESOURCE FOR WAGNER AND OPERA ON FILM

The Library houses a comprehensive collection of industry trade publications, fan magazines, scholarly journals, and house organs, as well as general, popular, and specialized serials. These materials are particularly helpful for research on early films. Before *The Jazz Singer* and the advent of sound, exhibitors of silent films received suggestions for musical accompaniment from house organs. The Library has extensive runs for a number of these studio publications, including the *Edison Kinetogram, Paramount Progress, Universal Weekly,* and *Vitagraph Bulletin.* For a wedding scene in *Frankenstein* (1910), the *Edison Kinetogram* suggested the "Bridal Chorus" from *Lohengrin* "till wedding guests are leaving."[11] That same year, the *Kinetogram* cited page numbers from an unspecified published Bizet score to accompany *The Cigarette Maker of Seville,* part of Edison's Grand Opera Series, featuring the pantomimist Pilar Moran as Carmen.[12]

In addition to cue sheets, periodicals were one of the primary sources disseminating information to musicians in the 1910s and 1920s. *Moving Picture World* included a bimonthly column, "Music for the Picture," which appeared from 1910 to 1919. Clarence Sinn, billed as the "Cue Music Man," was in charge of this column. In the days before blogging and the internet, the column provided candid editorial commentary and solicited input from readers. As some of the contributors to this volume have shown, Sinn's columns contain copious references to Wagner in relation to film scoring and accompaniment. One reference not cited in this volume includes musical suggestions for the accompaniment of *The Hypocrites* (1915) from a San Francisco accompanist, Adolph Rosenthal: "Prayer from Lohengrin until Political scene; the Tipperary March until appearance of Gabriel; then first bars of Lohengrin." Sinn takes Rosenthal to task over the selection of "Tipperary March," writing that "trivial popular stuff is good in its place, but when sandwiched between the 'Prayer from Lohengrin' and 'Raffs Cavatina' it is apt to jar on a refined sensibility."[13]

Hollywood Filmograph reported weekly film news in Los Angeles from the mid-1920s to the mid-1930s. In addition to covering early 1930s musicals, it documented the influx of composers of light and comic opera to Hollywood, including Sigmund Romberg, Rudolph Friml, and Oscar Strauss. The music critic Joseph O'Sullivan regularly wrote about film music in the *Motion Picture Herald* throughout the 1930s. A musician and composer himself, O'Sullivan specialized in opera and often would select a particular opera-related film to write about.

On the heels of Disney's *Fantasia* (1940), the use of concert and opera music in film grew in popularity, culminating with the release of *Humoresque* (1946) and *Carnegie Hall* (1947). The periodical *Film Music Notes* published significant material over the years related to film and opera, particularly in this post–World War II era. A special issue written by an elementary school superintendent of music considers the educational possibilities of *Carnegie Hall,* using music examples from the Prelude to *Die Meistersinger* as presented in the film.[14] The noted Canadian composer Louis Applebaum provides commentary on Franz

Waxman's adaptation of Wagner for *Humoresque*.[15] Opera sequences specifically composed by Mario Castelnuovo-Tedesco for the film *Strictly Dishonorable* (1951) are discussed by music theater historian Alfred E. Simon, later chief musical consultant for the Goodspeed Opera House in Connecticut.[16]

More obscure opera references in periodicals include a 1937 article in *Cinema Arts,* a short-lived New York publication, on the discovery and signing of opera singers.[17] Comments from the directors of the Tchaikovsky filmed opera *Christmas Slippers* appeared in an issue of *Cinema Chronicle,* published in Moscow by the USSR Society for Cultural Relations with Foreign Countries.[18]

Though it is not a film industry publication, *Pacific Coast Musician*—a complete run of which is at UCLA's Southern Regional Library Facility—deserves a mention. Billed as "the Oldest Musical Magazine in the West," it covered concerts, opera, and motion pictures, and at one time was the only weekly musical magazine west of Chicago. Although its publishing run was from 1911 to 1948, serious film music coverage did not begin until the mid-1930s and ended around World War II. Business manager R. Vernon Steele contributed a regular column on "Motion Picture Music and Musicians." Edoardo Sacerdote, an opera singer and head of the American Conservatory's voice department, wrote an article in which he discussed the possibilities of opera and music drama and film.[19] The magazine also published an interview with William von Wymetal, director of opera at MGM studios.[20]

DIGITAL IMAGES AND GRAPHIC ARTS

The Library's Digital Image Gallery has images of singers Geraldine Farrar and Gladys Swarthout, as well as the Manhattan Opera House during filming of the Vitaphone musical short *La Fiesta* in 1926. This film was screened before the premiere of *Don Juan* at Grauman's Egyptian Theatre. Also screened was another Vitaphone short featuring the Overture from *Tannhäuser* performed by the New York Philharmonic Orchestra, as documented in a program in the Hollywood Museum collection.

A German stone lithograph for Fritz Lang's *Die Nibelungen* (1924) and an offset print for *Tristan & Isolde* (2006) are available to Wagner researchers. These and other images are part of the Library's poster collection, the catalog for which is viewable online. The overture to *The Flying Dutchman* is advertised in the poster art for *The Bad Man* by the celebrated poster artist Batiste Madalena.[21] Conductors Vladimir Shavitch and Victor Wagner led the Eastman Theatre Orchestra when the film screened in Rochester, New York, in 1923. A later poster by Madalena announces the performance of the *Rienzi* Overture prior to a screening of *The Mysterious Lady* (1928).

Perhaps the most important contribution of film to opera has been increased accessibility and exposure. As the pressbook for *Big Broadcast of 1938* points out, the whole world, not just opera and concert audiences, is now able to see and hear Metropolitan Opera star Kirsten Flagstad sing Brünnhilde's "Battle Cry" from *Die Walküre*. In recent years, the introduction of the Library's online catalog, web-based scope and content notes for manuscript and photograph collections, and patron access to databases for Music and Recorded Sound, Manuscripts, Photographs, Graphic Arts, the Digital Image Gallery, and the Periodical index has only improved and increased public accessibility to this rich collection of film history.

NOTES

1. See, for example, "About.com: Classical Music: Classical Music in Movies and Television," http://classicalmusic.about.com/od/classicalmusicinmovies/ Classical_Music_in_Movies_and_Television.htm (accessed September 14, 2008); and "Classics from the Silver Screen," http://pachome2.pacific.net.sg/~bchee/ movies.html (accessed September 14, 2008). Beginning in 1998, the Naxos label published a list of classical works used in film that could be purchased on compact disc (http://www.naxos.com/musicinmovies). A similar list appears in Stewart Craggs, *Soundtracks* (Aldershot, U.K.: Ashgate, 1998).

2. The Academy of Motion Picture Arts and Sciences' Margaret Herrick Library is located in Beverly Hills, California. Visit the Library's website and catalog at www.oscars.org/mhl and catalog.oscars.org. Thanks to Library Director Linda Mehr and, in Special Collections, research archivist Barbara Hall and department coordinator Jenny Romero for their valuable input, and to graphic arts librarian Anne Coco and archival processor Bob Dickson for their helpful suggestions.

3. Barry Brennan, *Evening Outlook*, April 17, 1981.

4. Ernest Gold, "Wagner: Alchemist of Folklore," *Opera News*, January 24, 1955, 4–6.

5. William Shaman, "The Operatic Vitaphone Shorts," *ARSC Journal* 22, no. 1 (Spring 1991): 35–94. This article, published by the Association for Recorded Sound Collections, contains a history and filmography.

6. Roger Hillman, *Unsettling Scores* (Bloomington: Indiana University Press, 2005), 147.

7. At http://www.youtube.com/watch?v=Z16Sf70VcGw (accessed September 14, 2008).

8. In the collection's Million Dollar Theater file, see *Grauman's Magazine* 5, no. 2 (1922): 7.

9. Ibid.

10. See my online article, "The Story of 'The Prince and the Princess Waltz' and Other Wedding Music by Dimitri Tiomkin," http://www.dimitritiomkin.com/news.cfm?newsYear=2005, May 2005.

11. "Music Cues for Edison Pictures," *Edison Kinetogram* 2, no. 4 (1910): 11.

12. "Music Cues for Edison Pictures," *Edison Kinetogram* 2, no. 7 (1910): 12. *Faust* was the first in the series that also included *Aida*.

13. Quoted in Clarence Sinn, "Music for the Picture," *The Moving Picture World,* September 18, 1915, 1984.

14. Stanlie McConnell, "*Carnegie Hall:* Its Music and Its Teaching Possibilities," *Film Music Notes,* special issue (1947): 1–12.

15. Louis Applebaum, "Waxman and *Humoresque,*" *Film Music Notes* 6, no. 3 (1946/47): 5–6. Audio excerpts of Waxman's concert work can be heard with and without orchestra at http://www.tnv.net/cwax.html#vno (accessed August 26, 2008).

16. Alfred E. Simon, "*Strictly Dishonorable,*" *Film Music Notes* 11, no. 1 (1951): 12–13.

17. Mary Garden, "Music Comes to Hollywood," *Cinema Arts* 1, no. 1 (1937): 19.

18. "New Soviet Feature Films: *Cherevichki,*" *Cinema Chronicle,* no. 1 (1945): 1–7.

19. Edoardo Sacerdote, "Music and the Films," *Pacific Coast Musician* 25, no. 11 (June 6, 1936): 3–4.

20. William von Wymetal, "Opera in Motion Pictures," *Pacific Coast Musician* 26, no. 8 (April 17, 1937): 10, 13.

21. Margaret Herrick Library, Poster Collection, POST-18503. For more on *Madalena,* see Anthony Slide with Jane Burman Powell and Lori Goldman Berthelsen, *Now Playing: Hand-Painted Poster Art from the 1910s through the 1950s* (Santa Monica: Angel City Press, 2007).

Some Thoughts about Wagner and Cinema; Opera and Politics; Style and Reception

SANDER L. GILMAN

One of the most striking moments, often quoted and regularly evoked, that haunts the tale of Richard Wagner's relationship to the cinema (and to Western culture) took place at the Kaiserhof Hotel in Berlin on March 28, 1933. Joseph Goebbels, the newly appointed (March 13) Reich Minister for Popular Enlightenment and Propaganda (Volksaufklärung und Propaganda), addressed the "makers and shakers" of the German film industry. This debut performance marked Goebbels's commitment to the cause of both modernism and mass culture in the service of the Nazi state:

> I am grateful for this opportunity to discuss the state of film in Germany and the probable tasks of the German film industry in the future. I speak as someone who has never lost contact with film in Germany: in fact, I am a passionate devotee of the cinematographic arts. For many years I have seen what great heights the German film can attain as a result of the power and ingenuity of the German mind.[1]

Cinema, in the spirit of modernism, was the medium that he saw as most appropriate to serve as a basis for the reform of the German "spirit":

> We must rid ourselves of the idea that the present crisis is a material one: it is more a spiritual crisis, and it will go on until we are courageous enough to radically reform German films. For the past two weeks, I have been having discussions with representatives from every branch of the German film industry with very amusing results. These film gentlemen have the same picture of National Socialism as that given in the hostile

press. These people have no real idea of the National Socialist movement and its supporters, not even in their own minds.[2]

Here Goebbels is echoing Hitler's condemnation of modernism in all of the arts in *Mein Kampf* (1925): "The stage, art, literature, the cinema, the press and advertisement posters, all must have the stains of pollution removed and be placed in the service of a national and cultural idea. The life of the people must be freed from the asphyxiating perfume of our modern eroticism and also from every unmanly and prudish form of insincerity."[3] Yet it is clear that Goebbels finds a very special role for the cinema. German film had been unable to capture the sense of the emerging of the spirit of the November Revolution:

> German films are estranged from reality, without any contact with the actual situations of everyday life. It is indeed appalling that all the creative work in films was done in the pre-war era. Time and again the argument is heard that the kind of films that we demand would not fill the cinemas. I was told the same thing in 1926 when I first began discussing this. What is needed is imagination to bring to life the inner meaning and form of a new world. Many filmmakers still regard the seizure of power on the thirtieth as a phenomenon to which the only possible reaction is a shake of the head.[4]

But what films specifically does Goebbels evoke as models for the newly emerging revolutionary cinema, films that were not "estranged from reality"? It is the great films of the silent era (this well into the age of the talkies, which had appeared in Germany in 1928), such as Sergei Eisenstein's *Battleship Potemkin* (1925) and the first film version of Tolstoy's *Anna Karenina,* entitled *Love* (1927) and directed by Edmund Goulding and starring Greta Garbo. But centrally it was Fritz Lang's (and his wife Thea von Harbou's) two-part *Die Nibelungen: Siegfried* and *Kriemhild's Revenge* (1924):

> *The Nibelungen* is a film that is not far removed from our own epoch; it is so modern, so close to our own age and so topical that even the old fighters of the National Socialist movement were deeply moved by it. It is not the themes themselves that are important. Themes from Greek mythology can have just as modern an effect as themes taken from the present day. The important thing is the way in which these themes are treated.[5]

As I have noted, this evocation of Wagner (if once removed) and cinema has become a touchstone for much of the concern about the pleasures and dangers of this link.[6] But what was the actual response of the viewing public to this evocation? Publicity then and now meant that such official statements had an immediate reaction. The film, long buried in the vaults of the silent film studios, was resurrected with an added soundtrack by Gottfried Huppertz with the ideologically loaded addition of excerpts from Wagner, as Adeline Mueller discusses in her essay in this volume. It appeared on the screens of Berlin and people, especially the supporters of the new Revolution, flocked to see it:

> In this situation [after the Nazi advent to power] as one carefully places one foot before the other, the UFA—let us say in a pause to sniff the air—has undertaken a unique experiment, that is to present an old silent film, Thea von Harbou's first part of the *Nibelungen, Siegfried's Death.*
>
> Why? Only because the Minister of Culture Dr. Goebbels has recently remarked that this film belongs to the three most beautiful that he had seen in his life? I empathize with Dr. Goebbels's words. Perhaps I would have said the same on the spur of the moment.
>
> In an old volume of my Berlin notes there is an enthusiastic account of this film and its author, also of the direction of her husband Fritz Lang. Yet as it sometimes happens: one tells a woman for years about the extraordinarily delicious dishes that one's mother used to make, and then one actually goes home to mom and eats those dishes—and they turn out not much better that those one has had at home or in a restaurant.
>
> Something similar may well have happened for many in again viewing *Siegfried's Death.*
>
> The first purely fairytale scenes are even today totally wonderful, photographically masterful. Then the actual drama, this extraordinary feminine tale from wildest prehistory, occurs, triggered by Brunhild, which leads to Siegfried's murder, carried out by Hagen as the overly loyal servant of his King Günter, as it certainly must have taken place regularly during the era of the Merovingians. The result is again "Vengeance!" And we know from both tale and legend that the massacre by Attila the Hun's forces will follow. And here already the problem arises. One understands Brunhild as a modern person, the raging love-hate of her being betrayed, and one should actually imagine—that's how we were taught ever since school—that Siegfried's night of love with Brunhild, thanks to the cap of invisibility, betrays proud (!) Krimhild, who still loves him.
>
> Thea von Harbou does everything that she can in order to stress this devotion. But it no longer works, in spite of all of the beaming that the characters do . . .

Honestly, we were not inspired, rather we were depressed. Siegfried's biceps and resilient bounciness aren't enough. We think, taking a deep breath, that the old German tales did not represent the paean of loyalty but rather a chain of disloyalties. Nowhere had there been so many false kings, so much betrayal, and so many back-stabbings and spearings, from the earliest migrations to our November Revolution.

We always sought and spoke of loyalty as *the* ideal, because we did not have it. Neither historians nor novelists document its existence on German soil.

By the way, the silent film is still just as impressive as the talkies. To understand the plot one does not need the spoken word, no moaning of the queen, no spewing of the dragon, and no hammer blows of the smithy. The printed titles are sufficient.

Cleaning up literature and film is necessary, but with a return to the old recipes from mother's kitchen not everything can be accomplished![7]

This first-hand account is by Adolf Stein, who wrote a daily column under the pseudonym of "Rumpelstilzchen" from October 1, 1920, to August 8, 1935, for the widely circulated Berlin newspaper, the illustrated *Täglichen Rundschau*. Stein, a widely published antagonist to everything, politically and culturally, that the Weimar Republic stood for, was the media director of Alfred Hugenberg's massive right-wing media empire, which owned the paper as well as the film production studio UFA. Vituperative in his opposition to the Republic, he came to be a supporter of Hitler and the November Revolution (after Hugenberg came to back him in 1933) and a rather tepid fan of any of the cultural innovations of the Weimar film industry, even Wagner on film, a film that was reputed to have reduced Hitler to tears. (Hitler's taste in films was idiosyncratic—he loved Merian Cooper's *King Kong* [1933] as well as Disney animations.)

Yet it is interesting that Lang's film becomes unpalatable because of the question of loyalty—in a new Germany that will be in the future defined by the ultimate loyalty to state and Führer. The "archaic" nature of the silent film in a world dominated by the talkies seems still to be effective, at least to an arch-conservative filmgoer. How many viewers of the early 1930s would have responded to the silent world of Wagner in the same manner? Certainly, the fascist critic Hermann Haß saw the talkies in 1932 as "giving all the nuances of life to the characters [in the film]."[8] Stein's earlier enthusiasm for the film was within the world of Weimar culture in which Wagner and the myth of the Nibelungen had resonance, because it was an account of the absence of loyalty as well as the absence of fealty. It was the stench, if we can once again quote Hitler, of "every unmanly and prudish form of insincerity." In Lang's film Stein, unlike Hitler, read an absence of loyalty to the Hohenzollern monarchy. The film enacted the literal "stab-in-the-back" that the right wing saw as the reason for the collapse of the Empire and the abdication of the Kaiser (and, of course, attributed to the "Jews" and the "Left"). Yet it is striking that the film as noted in Stein's response is a film by its author Thea von Harbou and not by its "modernist" director Fritz Lang. The right generally detested Lang (and Hugenberg's UFA), seeing, for example, Lang's best-known film *M: A Murderer among Us* (1931) as a "blasphemous" attempt to "sensationalize" child murderers such as Adolf Haarmann.[9] Here Hitler's views in *Mein Kampf* that "the hideous productions of the cinema" written by "authors who were highly lauded" was a sign of what position one had to take on "Jewish questions. Here was a pestilence, a moral pestilence, with which the public was being infected."[10]

What went wrong with seeing Lang's film again in 1933? Was there something innately wrong with Paul Richter's (Siegfried's) biceps? Should not the response have been the joy of rediscovery, the sense of a new German cinema embedded in the world of the classic experience of the opera? Wagner and Cinema, certainly the stuff for a resurgent Nazi film industry, according to Goebbels. But this was never to be. That year the conservative critic Hans Traub described what he considered to be the inherent difference between theater (and one can substitute opera here)[11] and the cinema as follows:

> In 1932 there were an average of 9,000 movie showings, in contrast to 250 theatrical performances. But it would be premature to jump to conclusions and fault the theaters here. These statistics do not by any means present the theater as unpopular, or as something alien to the *Volk* or as a luxury no one can afford. Far more, this is evidence of the influence of the major linguistic institutions of the nation, independent of what is produced and presented [on stage]. The task of the theater is not to entertain, but rather to edify. Healthy instincts have always made distinctions between the theater and the operetta. Our task is to follow these instincts.

The theater has again become a genuine artistic institution—not in the sense of pragmatic moral didactics, but rather in the sense of profound inner edification and amusement that can only be satisfied by truly artistic production and the creativity that is truly bound to the *Volk*. Certainly, everyone in the population can and should have access to the theater; but not everyone will visit the theater all the time, on a daily or weekly basis. Theater should remain a highlight in people's lives. And these types of highlights require leisure and internal preparation.[12]

But the cinema is truly "just" entertainment:

The desire to forget one's own existence, a general sense of exhaustion, and a certain indifference toward all the urges of will drive the people in the big cities to the movies. There are a variety of reasons for this; this has been documented by scholars interpreting the matter from the perspective of social ethics to that of psychology. At any rate, this is de facto the situation we face today. We should be happy about that, for what could be more satisfying than the opportunity to present the people with pleasure and entertainment? We need only muster the courage to take a serious and healthy approach even to the un-heroic.[13]

Traub was certainly not alone in stressing the psychologically passive nature of the audience in the cinema rather than the result of live theater and opera—cultural catharsis. But what is central to the Nazi theory of the cinema is that it too demanded a "healthy" outcome in spite of the limitations of the medium. Major figures who examined and contributed to German high culture (from theater to opera) in the Third Reich, such as the critic Hermann Wanderscheck, agreed with this dichotomy.[14] As did, of course, figures quite removed from the Nazis, such as Arnold Schoenberg, in exile because of his being a Jew as well as for his "decadent" music: "I had dreamed of a dramatization of Strindberg's *To Damascus,* or the second part of Goethe's *Faust,* or even Wagner's *Parsifal.* All of these works . . . would have found the solution to realization in sound pictures. But the industry continued to satisfy only the needs and demands of the ordinary people who filled their theatres."[15] Schoenberg continues that "the drama of the future and the opera of the future cannot be art for the masses."[16] But of course, for the Nazis, this dichotomy meant the stripping of the "Jewish influence," represented by Weimar culture (and Schoenberg as well as Lang, a non-Jew), from both. Opera and cinema remain two very distinct worlds for those intellectuals shaped by the idea of *Bildung* (high culture)—in exile as well as under the Nazis. Yet of course, the implications of this juxtaposition after 1933 are very different in Berlin than in Los Angeles.

Initially Goebbels thought that the gap between "higher" and "lower" levels of culture could be bridged. According to a legend, he approached Fritz Lang late in 1933 to become head of the UFA, nationalized by the Nazis that year, the major cinema studio now under his ministry of propaganda. Lang fled to Paris soon thereafter, quite aware of what such a commitment to the November Revolution would mean:

> I will never forget it—Goebbels was a very clever man, he was indescribably charming when I entered the room, he never spoke at the beginning of the picture. He told me a lot of things, among other things that the "Führer" had seen *Metropolis* (1926) and another film that I had made— *Die Nibelungen* (1924)—and the "Führer" had said "this is the man who will give us THE Nazi film." I was perspiring very much at this moment, I could see a clock through the window and the hands were moving, and at the moment I heard that I was expected to make the Nazi movie I was wet all over and my only thought was "how do I get out of here!" I had my money in the bank and I was immediately thinking "how do I get it out?" But Goebbels talked and talked and finally it was too late for me to get my money out! I left and told him that I was very honoured and whatever you can say. I then went home and decided the same evening that I would leave Berlin that I loved very much.[17]

Thea von Harbou, who had sympathized with the Nazis well before the Nazi seizure of power and was a party member in 1932, remained in Germany after her divorce from Lang in 1933. (They had been legally separated in 1931.) Lang was a member of the Weimar avant-garde, even thought he admitted that he was highly "non-political" before 1933; Harbou a strong support of the New Order, who continued her film career under Goebbels. As Eric Rentschler shows in detail, much of the Nazi cinema was in fact entertainment with a bit of nasty propaganda—but little claim to the transcendental, to the aesthetic, to the spirit of the new Germany.[18] This was not because Goebbels did not see the utility of high art, cinema, and culture in the sphere of propaganda, but because the avant-garde cinema, to which Fritz Lang clearly belonged, seemed beyond the ideological pale, no matter how powerful its Wagnerian content. Here one can mention Thea von Harbou's *Der Herrscher* (The

Ruler, 1937), directed by Veit Harlan and starring Emil Jannings, that
praised absolute authority and total victory.

The model of appropriating the form of the avant-garde ironically
was Lenin's successful exploitation of Russian modernism (from Sergei
Eisenstein's cinema to Aleksander Rodchenko's Constructivism) in the
service of the Bolshevik Revolution and the building of the USSR; after
Lenin's death in 1924, Stalin took a much more conservative notion of the
boundaries of acceptable art. The irony of this should not be lost: as Dan
Diner points out, Goebbels always framed the struggle in Europe as that
between fascism and bolshevism.[19] In Mussolini's Italy the radical modernists, such as the Futurist Filippo Tommaso Marinetti (1876–1944),
were firmly on the fascist bandwagon, as Marinetti made clear in his
manifesto of 1924, "Futurism and Fascism" ("Futurismo e fascismo").
The German poet Gottfried Benn (1886–1956), himself an Expressionist as well as a supporter of the New Order, saw the need to merge the
new political and social revolution with the avant-garde in his *Art and
Power* (*Kunst und Macht*, 1934). In an odd way this view was advocated
by Joseph Goebbels in his talk at the Kaiserhof Hotel in Berlin on March
28, 1933—the same talk cited at the beginning of this essay—where he
acknowledged a propaganda advantage in expropriating the modern
cinema to the benefit of the Party.

At the end of the day Alfred Rosenberg's anti-modernism, in which
Wagner claimed a defining role, seemed to hold sway.[20] Rosenberg, the
self-styled "Philosopher of the Revolution" and later head of the Hohe
Schule, the Center of National Socialist Ideological and Educational
Research, spoke here for Hitler's own views. Hitler was a failed artist
as well as a film and Wagner fan. Indeed, he thought of himself often
as having been frustrated by the forces of modernism that dominated
the art schools in Germany and Austria and had refused to admit him
to the art school in Vienna in 1907 and again in 1908. His entire career
he felt compelled to comment on the visual arts and architecture of the
Third Reich as a specialist. Between Goebbels's pragmatic exploitation of
modernism and Rosenberg's disgust with it, there was only one choice:
the "Philosopher of the Revolution" won the day over the much more
powerful Minister of Propaganda.

So we are left with a conundrum that may well be the centerpiece
of any comparative study of Wagner and cinema: which Wagner, what

cinema, and how do the ideological and social contexts of both determine how they are to be understood? This present volume looks at a set of relationships while actually documenting various shifting meanings attached to both the figure and work of Richard Wagner, as well as the ever-changing meaning of "cinema."[21] Each essay explores a moment in their interaction, of their rapport or distance. The medium is not the message here—but rather the meanings that are generated when medium and content are paired. This seems self-evident. Carolyn Abbate evokes this in her brilliant essay on Wagner and cinema as a structural problem in the generation of meaning:

> Words like "echo" or "resonance," of course, are themselves fancy ways to describe inter-textual connection (or, in music analysis, to refer to formal repetitions). But an echo is also a gross physical, acoustic phenomenon; it is, after all, the sound that gives rise to the metaphors. These two aspects of echoing, the figurative and literal, are not as separate as the binarism might suggest. At the crossroads where they meet, there is a kind of re-literalized abstraction, itself shorthand for the epiphanic moments when intertextual echoes become manifest not via text alone (in the abstract sense), but via their realizations (in the gross, the physical, and whatever exactly assaults our senses in a particular here-and-now).[22]

Such interactions between the historical location of music and its analogs such as film demand a specific contextualization of both components. This is as needed as understanding the meanings associated with the Wagnerian snippets in the music of *The Thief of Baghdad* (1939), and the audience's as well as the composer's expectation of the "Orientalism" implicit in this in the 1930s. Yet when one examines the contentious debates about Richard Wagner and the Third Reich, which is why I selected the example of Goebbels and Lang, suddenly there is a reductivism that actually haunts much of the Wagner literature, for good or for evil, pro or contra.

Years ago, in the context of a *Ring* production at the Lyric Opera of Chicago, I ran a symposium which I provocatively called "Why Wagner?" A member of the audience, who had come to Chicago to see the production, asked me whether I would ever hold a conference entitled "Why Mozart?" The answer, of course, is that one should indeed ask ALWAYS not only "Why?" but also "Which?" And also, as in this present volume, "How?" Context defines in ways that are paramount to interpretation and reception. What Wagner are we seeing? How is that Wagner constructed and for what purposes? What is the medium through which we have access to this "Wagner"? If it is cinema, what is the intent of the film as medium and what is the reception of that intent—and intent here may well be articulated or implied, it may well be determined by the sense of the community or read by the community very much against the grain. Are we demanding an abandonment of the "purely" aesthetic appreciation of art, whether opera or film? Not at all, but we must also have a heightened awareness that such claims for aesthetics also have different meanings at different times. The aesthetics of "pure art" after the crushing defeat of the Nazis had quite different implications in the world of T. S. Eliot and his contemporary Gottfried Benn. Yet both were colored by their experience of the instrumentalizing of art during the 1930s and '40s. Must we not read Wieland Wagner's Bayreuth of the 1950s or the Wagner productions of the German Democratic Republic also in such a light? And that, in spite of Wieland Wagner's use of cinema in his 1937 production of *Parsifal* or the (relative) cultural thaw in the GDR after the ouster of Walter Ulbricht in 1971. Must we not ask, along with Karen Painter, why Beethoven, Wagner, and Bruckner were politicized in the Third Reich while Mozart or Haydn were not?[23]

All studies of culture depend on the sophistication of the reading of the context: not that such a reading can ever free itself from the perspective of the scholar making it. Thus ours is the pleasant work of an academic Sisyphus: always rolling the stone up the mountain of contextualization and interpretation so that others can take it, reshape it, reread it, and role it back again. Each reading adds to the sum; each reveals our own fascinations and preoccupations. Only at the end of days does the task end: remember that in 1945 it was not the cinema that registered the collapse of the Third Reich but Greater Germany Radio that marked it by playing the overture to Richard Wagner's *Twilight of the Gods*. Perhaps that tune will also echo in our own readings and re-readings then.

NOTES

1. Quoted in Gerd Albrecht, ed., *Film im Dritten Reich: Eine Dokumentation* (Karlsruhe: Duku-Verlag, 1979), 26–31, here 26. Translations in this essay are by the author.

2. Ibid., 28.

3. Adolf Hitler, *Mein Kampf,* trans. James Murphy (London: Hurst & Blackett, 1939), 123; this is the "official" Nazi translation into English. Cited after the Project Gutenburg online edition: http://www.scribd.com/doc/222119/Mein-Kampf-by-Adolf-Hitler-translated-by-James-Murphy (accessed March 4, 2008).

4. Albrecht, *Film im Dritten Reich,* 27.

5. Ibid., 30.

6. See especially Klaus Kanzog, "Der Weg der Nibelungen ins Kino: Fritz Langs Film-Alternative zu Hebbel und Wagner," in *Wege des Mythos in der Moderne: Richard Wagner, "Der Ring des Nibelungen": Eine Münchner Ringvorlesung,* ed. Dieter Borchmeyer (Munich: Deutscher Taschenbuch Verlag, 1987), 202–23; Gosta Werner, "Fritz Lang and Goebbels: Myth and Facts," *Film Quarterly* 43 (1990): 24–27; and David J. Levin, *Richard Wagner, Fritz Lang, and the Nibelungen* (Princeton: Princeton University Press, 1998).

7. Rumpelstilzchen, *Mang uns mang . . . 1932/33* (Berlin: Brunnen Verlag, 1933), 288–90.

8. Hermann Haß, *Sitte und Kultur im Nachkriegsdeutschland* (Hamburg: Hanseatische Verlagsanstalt, 1932), 179.

9. Ibid.

10. Hitler, *Mein Kampf,* 213.

11. A distinction between opera and film made by Ernst Bacmeister, "Die gesungene und die gesprochene Leidenschaft auf der Bühne," in *Der deutsche Typus der Tragödie* (Berlin: Albert Langen/Georg Müller, [1941]), 56–66.

12. Hans Traub, "Das Kino als Unterhaltungsstätte," *Der Film als politisches Machtmittel* (Munich: Verlag Münchener Druck und Verlagshaus, 1933), 5–7.

13. Ibid.

14. Hermann Wanderscheck, "Kulisse und Kamera," in *Dramaturische Appassionata* (Leipzig: Max Beck, 1944), 143–59.

15. Arnold Schoenberg, *Style and Idea: Selected Writings of Arnold Schoenberg,* ed. Leonard Stein and trans. Leo Black (Berkeley: University of California Press, 1975), 154.

16. Ibid., 337.

17. "Fritz Lang: The director talks about his life and work in this 1967 BBC interview with Alexander Walker," BBC Online, http://zakka.dk/euroscreenwriters/interviews/fritz_lang_521.htm (accessed February 24, 2008).

18. Eric Rentschler, *Ministry of Illusion: Nazi Cinema and Its Afterlife* (Cambridge, Mass.: Harvard University Press, 1996). See also Alan E. Steinweis, *Art, Ideology, and Economics in Nazi Germany: The Reich Chambers of Music, Theater, and the Visual Arts* (Chapel Hill: University of North Carolina Press, 1993); Richard Taylor, *Film Propaganda: Soviet Russia and Nazi Germany* (London and New York: I.B. Tauris, 1998); Robert C. Reimer, *Cultural History through a National Socialist Lens: Essays on the Cinema of the Third Reich* (Rochester, N.Y.: Camden House, 2000); Sabine Hake, *Popular Cinema of the Third Reich* (Austin: University of Texas Press, 2001); Lutz Koepnick, *The Dark Mirror: German Cinema between Hitler and Hollywood* (Berkeley: University of California Press, 2002).

19. Dan Diner, *Cataclysms: A History of the Twentieth Century from Europe's Edge* (Madison: University of Wisconsin Press, 2007), 52.

20. Alfred Rosenberg, *Der Mythos des 20. Jahrhunderts* (Munich: Hoheneichen, 1930), 426–31.

21. While we have not placed overt emphasis on the medium itself, our volume's contribution to Wagner scholarship lies in its focus on interdisciplinary issues involved in Wagner's multifaceted presence in cinema. In so doing, this volume extends what has been explored in a cluster of books published since the 1990s: Paul Lawrence Rose, *Wagner: Race and Revolution* (New Haven and London: Yale University Press, 1992); Marc A. Weiner, *Richard Wagner and the Anti-Semitic Imagination* (Lincoln: University of Nebraska Press, 1995); Frederic Spotts; *Bayreuth: A History of the Wagner Festival* (New Haven and London: Yale University Press, 1994); Michael Meyer, *The Politics of Music in the Third Reich* (New York: Peter Lang, 1991); Erik Levi, *Music in the Third Reich* (New York: St. Martin's, 1994); Pamela Maxine Potter, *Most German of the Arts: Musicology and Society from the Weimar Republic to the End of Hitler's Reich* (New Haven, Conn.: Yale University Press, 1998); Celia Applegate and Pamela Maxine Potter, eds., *Music and German National Identity* (Chicago: University of Chicago Press, 2002).

22. Carolyn Abbate, "Wagner, Cinema, and Redemptive Glee," *The Opera Quarterly* 21 (2005): 599.

23. Karen Painter, *Symphonic Aspirations: German Music and Politics, 1900–1945* (Cambridge, Mass.: Harvard University Press, 2008), 204.

APPENDIX

Interview with Bill Viola

JEONGWON JOE

JEONGWON JOE: Thank you very much for accepting my request for an interview.[1] I'm currently co-editing a collection, *Wagner and Cinema,* with Sander Gilman at Emory University, and two of the essays will discuss your *Tristan Project.* My contributors are from diverse disciplines of study, not only musicology but also cinema studies, literary criticism, gender studies . . .

BILL VIOLA: I'm happy to speak with you. That sounds interesting . . . Did you see my new exhibition at the James Cohan Gallery? There are six pieces on view from *The Tristan Project.* In total I made over twenty works from the opera materials but did not use the music. Some of the pieces have sound and some are silent.

JJ: I am actually more interested in totally silent pieces . . . I was glad that I saw the installations without Wagner's opera first at the Gallery before I see the opera. I'm going to see the opera performance tomorrow. I think it's more interesting than the other way around. The right order . . .

BV: Yes, the right order. Absolutely.

. . .

JJ: Did you know that Wagner's great-grandson Gottfried Wagner has worked as a video artist?

BV: I didn't know that. A video artist . . . beautiful! Wagner would have loved video. It naturally, ontologically, embodies his idea of the *Gesamtkunstwerk,* the place where all the senses are engaged and the various art forms coexist. The moving image—Grandfather

431

Cinema, children Television and Video, and their digital offspring High-Definition, Computer, Internet, Digital Cameras, Cell Phones, Youtube, etc.—are fast becoming the language of global culture. The legacy of Wagner's vision is embedded in today's media age.

There is another artist who had advanced these ideas in the twentieth century, the composer Edgard Varèse. His original idea was to make a film for his composition *Déserts*, to create a complete visual and sound experience. Unfortunately he was not able to fulfill his vision in his lifetime, the result of being too far ahead of his time. In 1994 I was invited to work with the Ensemble Modern, the Frankfurt-based contemporary performing ensemble, to fully realize this piece and make the visual component. I did not know at that time that I would later be making a four-hour video for *Tristan und Isolde*.

. . .

JJ: My first question about your *Tristan Project* is, do you have any special feeling about Wagner, compared to other opera composers?

BV: If you're an artist, it's hard to avoid Wagner's latent presence. But this project came up rather spontaneously. My experience with opera was mostly limited to contemporary work—people like John Adams, Phillip Glass, Kaija Saariaho, and of course director Peter Sellars, a close friend. I was aware of *Tristan* through literature, but I had never seen it before embarking on *The Tristan Project*.

. . .

JJ: I'm most interested in how the slow-motion images—a trademark of your video art—affect the perception of time; more specifically, how your visually created rhythm interacts with Wagner's musical time. It's going to be the topic of my essay.

BV: I think that in your essay, you should include human consciousness when you are discussing time, because we are beings of time. We live in time like the fish live in water; and like the fish we often take it for granted. Time determines everything about human beings. The still image we see in a photograph is not a really good representation of ourselves. As Buddha recognized 2,500 years ago, everything continues to change. So in music, the actual instrument that is being played is human consciousness, its continual transformation and reconfiguration. A work like *Tristan* goes beyond Aristotle's theory of drama. Instead, we need to look to Asian theater for similar models. The great fourteenth-century playwright and theorist Zeami, inventor of Japanese Noh theater, argues that the audience and the performers together create the art, while Aristotle's theory ignores the audience almost entirely—it's only what is on the stage that matters. In theater, unlike in the media, you have a direct, palpable connection to living consciousness. In Zeami's teachings, it is essential for the actors to learn how to use that energy in performance.

I traveled to Japan as a young man and was very influenced by Noh and its dreamlike quality of slowness. In *The Tristan Project*, the images slow down, which has a visceral effect on our preconceived notion of time. We live in a world where our perception of time is locked to a basic rate, measured by heartbeats, breaths, and lifespans. We know that if you drop a glass on the floor, it will fall within a certain time and will be broken. But in art we create a symbolic representation of our world, free from physical laws and constraints. In short, we add internal, subjective experiences and states of being to the equation. We can stretch out time to stillness and compress it to a blur of motion, and it is all a valid expression of human experience. We now have new technologies that can do this even more precisely and effectively.

So in my work when I slow down a sequence, my intention is to slow down a representation of experience that is real enough so that people can still recognize it as a glass falling, but unlike in human perception where it happens too quickly, the mind can experience the glass falling *consciously*. In other words, you become aware of what you're seeing while you're watching it; you have time to reflect and to experience perception as a memory. The relationship between perception and memory is a very special human experience, and my slow-motion pieces try to bridge that gap.

A traditional theater performance in Asia typically lasts as long or longer than a Wagnerian opera. I once saw an evening shadow puppet performance in Java, the Wayang Kulit, that was eight hours long, and a full Kabuki cycle in Japan that lasted for twelve hours, including two meals. If you consider Asian dramatic theories of the audience being a part of a performance, it is clear that duration is a critical component that physiologically changes human consciousness. By the end of the evening, audience members are physically exhausted, which dulls the rational mind and causes their emotions to respond more deeply. I don't know whether Wagner was consciously aware of doing that, but it's an important part of the experience of *Tristan*.

JJ: I don't think Wagner was, but I do see a parallel between his opera and your work—doing the same thing out of different motivations and different aesthetic considerations. The issue of consciousness and perception of temporal events remind me of some minimalist composers' intentions to make the process of their composition perceivable by the listeners. So the rate of musical change is very slow so that every single change can be perceived. I have been interested in the interaction between the aural and the visual, between time and space. When I had a talk with my film director friend Chanwook Park about his film *Oldboy* (it received the Grand Prix at the 2004 Cannes), he told me about what he did for the climax of the film—I think it is related to your control of time. He considered using slow motion for it, but he ended up creating the *effect* of slow motion by silencing the sound.

BV: That's great. Is the movie silent at that moment?

JJ: Not completely. He silenced ambient sounds entirely and it becomes a silent film for about three minutes, with very soft background music only. I found that it really creates an optical illusion in that the movement in that scene looks slower than when it's with sound.

BV: I've had that experience myself. I've done a lot of silent installations, and you do hear the inner sounds. It's like a psychological hearing. In the silent pieces, I think that when sound is absent you can focus better on the details and nuances of the image.

JJ: I watched three installations from your *Tristan Project* at the James Cohan Gallery, and I watched two of them—shorter ones—five times. And each time, my experience or perception was different, and each time, I was able to find something new. That was a very illuminating experience, artistically, spiritually, and intellectually.

BV: One problem that I think exists in video art compared to painting or sculpture is that people usually do not watch a work multiple times. They can stand in front of one painting as long as they want, and they constantly observe the same information over time, but when the images are moving, the work is only complete when it ends like a symphony does. We "observe" painting, but we "inhabit" video art. When you're *in* the piece experiencing it, the whole does not exist.

JJ: Yes, that's what video or cinematic art, dealing with moving images, shares with music. I know about your special interest in the musical or sonic dimension of your visual art. Can you tell me how you explored it in *The Tristan Project*?

BV: Let me first talk a little about how the piece was made. When I first started working, I tried listening to different performances of the opera to get an understanding and feeling for the music. Then as a test, I began to edit together some images from my own archive together with the music to see how this would work. But this became quite frustrating because, first of all, Wagner's *Tristan* is so vast that if you're working with individual phrases or motifs, you're only on the micro level and can get lost in minutiae. I realized that this was not the best way. So I put the music aside and I took out the libretto, and that was my guide for making visual images. I usually derive the images in my art from reading texts or writing. I thought a lot about the content, about the words, and the story. I gathered some books together—Gottfried von Strassburg, Nietzsche, Schopenhauer, Bryan Magee, and especially Roger Scruton.[2] I read the libretto multiple times and divided it up into what I felt were different sections, corresponding to emotional or spiritual zones. I had no intention of literally telling the story with my images, but I just wanted to feel the underground root system of the *Tristan* myth. I wrote and sketched for three months, and then we started shooting.

For some of the first sequences that I recorded, I used my simple camcorder, walking alone into a forest and shooting intuitively, following whatever my eyes were drawn to. Much of this material was used in Act 3. Then I came up with some ideas for "staged" set pieces—what I now call "The Fall into Paradise" (Act 1), "Fire Woman," "Tristan's Ascension," and "Isolde's Ascension" (Act 3). At the time I knew that all these images were related to certain themes in the opera, but other than Tristan's and Isolde's ascension in the "Liebestod," I didn't know precisely where they would be placed. When the shooting was completed (production began in February 2004 and finished nine months later on November 1), I then returned to the music once more and edited the images into the time form determined by the score. I didn't realize until I had finished the whole process that this was the right order to have done the work: to start with the content of the story—the source for my imagining the contents of the images—and then to use the time form to structure the images within the music. It was all a rather unconscious process.

JJ: How is the live music synchronized with the images? And how much accuracy do you intend?

BV: There are very few precise sync points, only a handful in the whole opera. And in performance they usually manage to hit very close. Generally speaking, the relationship between the image and the music is somewhat flexible and does not require precise synchronization. The playback system is set up in such a way that the images can follow the conductor's tempo. There are two high-definition hard drives for playback, each with the same program running in parallel in case of failure. Each section is individually cued up on alternative video servers so the next sequence can be cut in when needed. Each cue is indicated on the score and is called by the stage manager with the lighting cues. The video is pre-formatted in individual segments, with titles. Almost all of the sequences are open-ended and all have "heads" and "tails"—extra material before and after the key part of the sequence. That way if the conductor wishes to perform the music for that section a little faster or a little slower, there is enough video to continue the shot. There are over a hundred shots to manage, and there are three persons, director Alex MacInnis who designed the playback system and two technicians, who do a live mix every night.

JJ: What about the "Liebestod" sequence? How many visual cues are there?

BV: Not too many—three for Tristan and one for Isolde. The main sync point is Isolde's ascension. I visualized a kind of double structure in the "Liebestod," that of transfiguration and transcendence. Tristan has already died, but in the "Liebestod" we witness his transfiguration from his physical dead body into a spiritual being, and thus his ascension. Isolde is alive throughout this event, but she dies when the last crescendo comes in the music and achieves final release, along with the rest of us, when the Tristan chord resolves. Isolde has transcended life and she achieves her own ascension through sheer force of her will and desire. My visualization of Tristan's ascension and transfiguration is related to the *Tibetan Book of the Dead*, which was the source of many images of the union of opposites—fire and water, air and earth, light and dark, male and female—that are also present in Wagner's *Tristan*. I took from the *Tibetan Book of the Dead* the image of a human being falling and dissolving into the four elements: water, earth, water, fire, and air. According to the book, sound is the last sense to disappear at death, sometimes taking several days. The last sound that a human being hears after physical death is likened to the sound of a mountain under a waterfall, followed by the sublime sense of emptiness, or in Sanskrit, *moksa* (release), represented in the video as the image of Isolde falling upward into the void, trailing silvery points of light—the air from her last breath.

JJ: In the Paris production, how much interaction was there between live performers and your video images? And did your video images influence Peter Sellars's staging?

BV: There was quite a bit [of interaction], actually. Peter sometimes had the performers echoing in a simple way the performers' actions on the video. The stage, the platform or "bed," and the video screen are important geometric forms, and are echoed in lighting designer Jim Ingalls's square pools of light on the stage floor. The squares of light represented spaces, not only different parts of the scene physically (the front of the boat—Tristan's space) and the back of the boat (Isolde's space) in the first act, but also the isolation of the main characters from each other. In the video, the characters are physically isolated in different frames in Act 1. The color schemes in the lighting were also designed to echo or reflect the video.

At the end of Act 2, during King Mark's lament, the video shows dawn gradually breaking behind a huge oak tree from total darkness. By the end of the lament, the sky is brilliant and almost blinding. The stage lighting had to track the barely perceptible increase in luminosity over fifteen minutes. The shifting color of the lighting follows nature's shifting colors in the video and gradually lights up the singers, until all is revealed. In Act 3, when Tristan is delirious with fever, tearing off his bandages in a desperate gesture, the ten-meter-high video screen shows a struggling man drowning in water the color of fire and blood. The image dwarfs the performer and makes his actions appear futile, while both are bathed in the same color, making the video light appear to be pouring out of the screen and onto the stage. The whole scene evokes the image of a desperate, dying man's last attempt at transcendence. That was a real important corresponding point between the live performance and the video image.

JJ: How did you begin this collaboration?

BV: *The Tristan Project* began as a collaboration between conductor and Los Angeles Philharmonic music director Esa-Pekka Salonen and Peter Sellars, opera and theater directors. They were both invited to take on Wagner's opera by Gérard Mortier, who dreamed of having this work open his first season as artistic director of the Paris National Opera. Peter first mentioned it to me and Kira (my wife and work partner for thirty years) in early 2003, and Esa-Pekka made it official after he saw my exhibition at the Getty Museum that same year. The Los Angeles Philharmonic decided to bring it on board as a semi-staged concert version while we developed it into an opera, and invited Lincoln Center for the Performing Arts in New York to join in—hence *The Tristan Project* was born.

By the fall of 2003 Esa-Pekka had spent the summer delving even deeper into Wagner's score, which he had known since his student days. He described the riches and fresh inspirations he had discovered there to the three of us (myself, Kira, and Peter) at a lunch I don't think any of us will ever forget. This then set the stage for my work, which commenced right away. At the premier of the concert version at Disney Hall during the first two weeks of December 2004, Peter worked on the lighting with his longtime collaborator Jim Ingalls, and otherwise watched the video over and over in rehearsals and performances. He created a semi-staged version and worked on the emotional content of the opera with the singers. After this first run, it was his turn to take this knowledge and submerge [himself] into the material, which he did for the winter months of the new year. The fully staged version he emerged with in the springtime of April 2005 was beyond anybody's expectations. An austere black stage, its background framing the video images within an impenetrable void; a simple black platform that alternately becomes a seat, a lookout, a lover's bed, a witness stand, an infirmary, a pyre, a coffin, a tomb, or a path to heaven; costumes in shades of black with imprinted wisps of patterns derived from the video imagery; sharp, angled pools of light that alternately imprison or liberate the lovers; and moments of intense, blinding, white light that purify performers and public alike. Add to this the emotional intensity and inner depth he managed to impart to the performers, and the end result was a masterpiece, and personally for myself one of the greatest artistic experiences in my life.

JJ: Thank you very much for your generous time.

BV: My pleasure. Time is something I never seem to run out of.

NOTES

1. This interview was conducted in a lecture room at the Rubin Museum in New York on May 4, 2007. It immediately followed Bill Viola's public talk, which started at 1 PM in conjunction with the exhibition "The Missing Peace," which contained two of his works. The interview was about fifty minutes long. In this transcription, I have eliminated some portions of the interview that digressed from the main topic and have minimized my comments; Bill Viola subsequently expanded other portions of the interview. Thanks to Kira Perov for her help in editing the interview. There were two performances of the New York premiere of *The Tristan Project* at Avery Fischer Hall on May 2 and 5, 2007. The title roles were sung by Christine Brewer (Isolde) and Alan Woodrow (Tristan).

2. Roger Scruton, *Death-Devoted Heart: Sex and the Sacred in Wagner's Tristan and Isolde* (Oxford: Oxford University Press, 2004).

THE TRISTAN PROJECT: FACT SHEET

Bill Viola

A four-hour video was created by Bill Viola for Peter Sellars's new production of Richard Wagner's opera *Tristan und Isolde*. It was first presented in concert as *The Tristan Project* in December 2004 at Walt Disney Concert Hall with the Los Angeles Philharmonic, artistic director and conductor Esa-Pekka Salonen, and premiered as a fully staged opera at l'Opéra National de Paris in April 2005. It was reprised in Paris November 2006 with Valery Gergiev conducting, and in November 2008 with Semyon Bychkov conducting. The Paris Opera also took it to Japan in the summer of 2008. In May 2007 the concert version was presented at the Avery Fisher Hall in New York by the Lincoln Center for the Performing Arts with the Los Angeles Philharmonic, Esa-Pekka Salonen conducting. *Tristan und Isolde* (concert version) was also presented at the Gergiev Festival in Rotterdam (2007) and during the White Nights Festival in St. Petersburg (2008), both with Valery Gergiev conducting.

The video for the opera of *Tristan und Isolde* was produced by Bill Viola Studio, Kira Perov, executive producer, in collaboration with l'Opéra National de Paris, the Los Angeles Philharmonic Association, the Lincoln Center for the Performing Arts, the James Cohan Gallery, New York, and Haunch of Venison, London.

Individual video works and installations were produced from the various scenes in the video for the opera. They have been shown at the James Cohan Gallery, New York (2005 and 2007), Haunch of Venison, London (2006), and Kukje Gallery, Seoul (2008).

Over eighty people were involved in the production of this work. The principal team includes Kira Perov, executive producer; S. Tobin Kirk, producer; Harry Dawson, director of photography; Kenny Bowers, assistant director; Robbie Knott, special effects coordinator; and actors Jeff Mills (Tristan), Lisa Rhoden (Isolde), John Hay (Tristan), Sarah Steben (Isolde), Robin Bonaccorsi (stunt actor); Brian Pete, online editor; Mikael Sangrin, Becky Allen, Tom Ozanich, sound designers; Alex MacInnis, timeline coordinator/performance technical coordinator.

FILMOGRAPHY

COMPILED BY JEONGWON JOE,
WARREN M. SHERK, AND SCOTT D. PAULIN

The following filmography is arranged by alphabetical order of the titles. It focuses largely on English-language narrative feature films that quote Wagner's music rather than allude to it. Filmed opera (recordings of stage production) and opera-film (cinematic productions of Wagner's opera, such as Syberberg's *Parsifal*) are not included. Also excluded are silent films: please see Scott Paulin's postscript to the filmography, which provides some information about the cue sheets and cinema music collections relevant to research on Wagner in the silent era.

Film Title	Director	Music from Wagner
8½ (1963)	Federico Fellini	"The Ride of the Valkyries" from *Die Walküre*
100 Men and a Girl (1937)	Henry Koster	Prelude to Act 3 of *Lohengrin* (arr. Stokowski)
Above Suspicion (1943)	Richard Thorpe	Overture to *Rienzi*
Absolute Power (1997)	Clint Eastwood	Overture to *Tannhäuser*
Airplane II: The Sequel (1982)	Ken Finkleman	Overture to *Der fliegende Holländer*
All Forgotten (2000)	Reverge Anselmo	"Siegfried's Funeral March" from *Götterdämmerung*
Apocalypse Now (1997)	Francis Ford Coppola	"The Ride of the Valkyries" from *Die Walküre*
Apt Pupil (1998)	Bryan Singer	Prelude to *Tristan und Isolde*
		"Liebestod" from *Tristan und Isolde*
Aria (1987)	Don Boyd/Frank Roddam	"Liebestod" from *Tristan und Isolde*
Arise, My Love (1940)	Mitchell Leisen	"Nibelungen March" (Gottfried Sonntag)[1]
		Siegfried motif derived from Sonntag's "Nibelungen March"
The Bachelor (1999)	Gary Sinyor	"Wedding March"[2] from *Lohengrin*
Beaches (1988)	Gary Marshall	"Wedding March" from *Lohengrin*
The Big Broadcast of 1938 (1938)	Mitchell Leisen	"Brünnhilde's Battle Cry" from *Die Walküre*
Birth (2004)	Jonathan Glazer	Prelude to *Die Walküre*
		"Wedding March" from *Lohengrin*
The Blue Gardenia (1953)	Fritz Lang	Act 1 Prelude and "Liebestod" (orchestral arrangement) from *Tristan und Isolde*
The Blues Brothers (1980)	John Landis	"The Ride of the Valkyries" from *Die Walküre*

Bridget Jones's Diary (2001)	Sharon Maguire	"Wedding March" from *Lohengrin*
Brown Sugar (2002)	Rick Famuyiwa	"Wedding March" from *Lohengrin*
Brute Force (1947)	Jules Dassin	Overture and "Bacchanale" from *Tannhäuser*
Bugs Bunny Nips the Nips (1944)	Friz Freleng	"The Ride of Valkyries" from *Die Walküre*
A Bullet Is Waiting (1954)	John Farrow	*Die Meistersinger von Nürnberg* (excerpts)
La caduta degli dei (The Damned) (1969)	Luchino Visconti	"Liebestod" from *Tristan und Isolde*
Captiva Island (1995)	John Biffar	"The Ride of the Valkyries" from *Die Walküre*
Carnegie Hall (1947)	Edgar G. Ulmer	Prelude to *Die Meistersinger von Nürnberg*
Casanova Brown (1944)	Sam Wood	"Fire Music" from *Die Walküre*
Celebrity (1998)	Woody Allen	"Wedding March" from *Lohengrin*
The Cemetery Club (1993)	Bill Duke	"Wedding March" from *Lohengrin*
Chances Are (1989)	Emile Ardilino	"Wedding March" from *Lohengrin*
Charades (a.k.a. Felons) (1998)	Stephen Eckelberry	Entry of the Guests from *Tannhäuser*
The Chocolate Soldier (1941)	Roy Del Ruth	"Evening Star" from *Tannhäuser*
Christmas Holiday (1944)	Robert Siodmak	*Tristan und Isolde* (excerpts)
Citizen Kane (1941)	Orson Welles	Entry of the Guests from *Tannhäuser*
Confessions of a Nazi Spy (1939)	Anatole Litvak	Siegfried motif derived from "Nibelungen March" (Gottfried Sonntag)
Corpse Bride (2005)	Tim Burton and Mike Johnson	"The Pilgrim's Chorus" from *Tannhäuser*
Critical Condition (1987)	Michael Apted	"The Ride of the Valkyries" from *Die Walküre*

Film Title	Director	Music from Wagner
Counterpoint (1968)	Ralph Nelson	Overture to Tannhäuser
Davy (1958)	Michael Relph	Die Meistersinger von Nürnberg (excerpts)
Death to Smoochy (2002)	Danny DeVito	"Liebestod" from Tristan und Isolde
Der Führer's Face (1942)	Jack Kinney (for Disney)	Prelude to Die Meistersinger
Die—oder keine (1934)	Carl Froelich	Magic Fire and Sword motifs from Der Ring des Nibelungen
Do You Love Me (1946)	Gregory Ratoff	"Wedding March" from Lohengrin
Dracula (1931)	Tod Browning	Overture to Die Meistersinger von Nürnberg
Duet for Cannibals (1969)	Susan Sontag	Various
East of Eden (1955)	Elia Kazan	"Magic Fire" from Die Walküre
Education for Death (1943)	Clyde Geromini (for Disney)	"Ride of the Valkyries" from Die Walküre
Escape (1940)	Mervyn LeRoy	"Liebestod" from Tristan und Isolde (arr. for piano)
Excalibur (1981)	John Boorman	"The Ride of the Valkyries" from Die Walküre
		Prelude to Parsifal
		Prelude to Tristan und Isolde
		"Siegfried's Funeral March" from Götterdämmerung
A Farewell to Arms (1932)	Frank Borzage	"Liebestod" (orchestral arr.) from Tristan und Isolde
Father of the Bride (1991)	Charles Shyer	"Wedding March" from Lohengrin
The Fighting First (1945)	U.S. Army	Siegfried motif from Der Ring des Nibelungen
Five Fingers (1952)	Joseph L. Mankiewicz	Brünnhilde's Battle Cry" from Die Walküre
Flying Blind (1941)	Frank McDonald	"Wedding March" from Lohengrin

Film	Director	Music
Fogbound (2002)	Ate de Jong	Entry of the Guests from *Tannhäuser*
Forever Yours (1937)	Stanley Irving	*Lohengrin* (excerpts)
For Me and My Gal (1942)	Busby Berkeley	"The Ride of the Valkyries" from *Die Walküre*
Freddy Got Fingered (2001)	Tom Green	"The Ride of the Valkyries" from *Die Walküre*
Full Metal Jacket (1987)	Stanley Kubrick	"The Ride of the Valkyries" from *Die Walküre*
Giant (1956)	George Stevens	"Wedding March" from *Lohengrin*
The Gold Rush (1942 reissue of 1925 film)	Charlie Chaplin	"Evening Star" from *Tannhäuser*
The Great Dictator (1940)	Charles Chaplin	Prelude to *Lohengrin*
The Great Lover (1931)	Harry Beaumont	*Lohengrin* (excerpts)
		"Love Song" from *Die Walküre*
Hairshirt, a.k.a.Too Smooth (1998)	Dean Paraskevopoulos	Overture to *Der fliegende Holländer*
The Happy Time (1952)	Richard Fleischer	*Lohengrin*, Act 3 (excerpts)
Heaven's Burning (1998)	Craig Lahiff	"Liebestod" from *Tristan und Isolde*
He Died with a Felafel in His Hand (2001)	Richard Lowenstein	"The Ride of the Valkyries" from *Die Walküre*
Henry Aldrich's Little Secret (1944)	Hugh Bennett	"The Ride of the Valkyries" from *Die Walküre*
Herr Meets Hare (1945)	Friz Freleng	"The Pilgrim's Chorus" from *Tannhäuser*
Hi Diddle Diddle (1943)	Andrew L. Stone	*Tannhäuser* (excerpts)
Highlander II: The Quickening (1991)	Russell Mulcahy	*Götterdämmerung*, excerpts from Act 1
Holiday in Mexico (1946)	George Sidney	"Liebestod" from *Tristan und Isolde*

Film Title	Director	Music from Wagner
Humoresque (1946)	Jean Negulesco	"Liebestod," arr. for violin
I'm Going Home (2001)	Manoel de Oliveira	Prelude to *Lohengrin*
In and Out (1997)	Frank Oz	"Wedding March" from *Lohengrin*
Interrupted Melody (1955)	Curtis Bernhardt	Immolation Scene from *Götterdämmerung* "Liebestod" from *Tristan und Isolde*
In Which We Serve (1942)	Noel Coward and David Lean	Trio from "Nibelungen March" (Gottfried Sonntag)
I've Always Loved You (1946)	Frank Borzage	Prelude, "Liebestod," and other excerpts from *Tristan und Isolde*
King Solomon's Mines (1985)	J. Lee Thompson	"The Ride of the Valkyries" from *Die Walküre*
L.A. Confidential (1997)	Curtis Hanson	"Magic Fire" from *Die Walküre*
Lebensborn (1961)	Werner Klingler	Various[3]
Lemony Snicket's A Series of Unfortunate Events (2004)	Brad Silberling	Prelude to Act 3 of *Lohengrin*
L'Ennui (1998)	Cédric Kahn	*Siegfried-Idyll*
Lessons of Darkness (1992)	Werner Herzog	*Das Rheingold, Parsifal, Götterdämmerung* (excerpts)
Letter from an Unknown Woman (1948)	Max Ophüls	"Evening Star" from *Tannhäuser*
The Life and Death of Colonel Blimp (1943)	Michael Powell and Emeric Pressburger	*Lohengrin* (excerpts)
Lifeboat (1944)	Alfred Hitchcock	"Preislied" from *Die Meistersinger von Nürnberg*
Ludwig (1972)	Luchino Visconti	Various

Film	Director	Wagner work
Luxury Liner (1948)	Richard Whorf	"Siegmund's Liebeslied" from *Die Walküre* "Liebeslied Abscheid" from *Lohengrin*
Madame Spy (1942)	Roy William Neill	"The Ride of the Valkyries" from *Die Walküre*
Mad Love (1935)	Karl Freund	*Siegfried-Idyll*
Magic Fire (1956)	William Dieterle	Various
Manhattan Murder Mystery (1993)	Woody Allen	*Der fliegende Holländer* (excerpts)
March of Time—selected newsreel segments:		
Germany (Berechtsgaden, Bavaria) (March 1935)		Siegfried motif from *Der Ring des Nibelungen*
French Coal Miner Spy (April 1936)		Nibelung motif from *Der Ring des Nibelungen*
Inside Nazi Germany (January 1938)		Dance of the Apprentices from *Der Meistersinger von Nürnberg*
Meeting Venus (1991)	István Szabó	*Tannhäuser* (excerpts)
Meet the Parents (2000)	Jay Roach	"Wedding March" from *Lohengrin*
Men in White (1998)	Scott P. Levy	"The Ride of the Valkyries" from *Die Walküre*
Missing Daughters (1933)	Bud Pollard	"The Ride of the Valkyries" from *Die Walküre*
Murder! (1930)	Alfred Hitchcock	Prelude to *Tristan und Isolde*
Murder by Numbers (2002)	Barbet Schroeder	"Entry of the Gods into Valhalla" from *Das Rheingold*
My Big Fat Greek Wedding (2002)	Joel Zwick	"Wedding March" from *Lohengrin*

Film Title	Director	Music from Wagner
Naughty but Nice (1939)	Ray Enright	"The Ride of the Valkyries" from *Die Walküre*
Never Give a Sucker an Even Break (1941)	Edward Cline	"Wedding March" from *Lohengrin*
Nosferatu the Vampyre (1979)	Werner Herzog	Prelude to *Das Rheingold*
The Object of My Affection (1998)	Nicholas Hytner	"Wedding March" from *Lohengrin*
Once More, With Feeling! (1960)	Stanley Donen	Various
One, Two, Three (1961)	Billy Wilder	"The Ride of the Valkyries" from *Die Walküre*
Operavox (1996), "*Das Rheingold*"	Graham Ralph	Abbreviated animation of *Das Rheingold*
The Other Sister (1999)	Garry Marshall	"Wedding March" from *Lohengrin*
Out of Africa (1985)	Sydney Pollack	"Wedding March" from *Lohengrin*
The People vs. Larry Flynt (1996)	Milos Forman	Overture to *Tannhäuser*
People Will Talk (1951)	Joseph L. Mankiewicz	"Prize Song" from *Die Meistersinger von Nürnberg*
Primavera en otoño (1933)	Eugene J. Forde	*Tristan und Isolde* (excerpts)
Ready to Rumble (2000)	Brian Robbins	Prelude to Act 3 from *Lohengrin*
Rebel without a Cause (1955)	Nicholas Ray	"The Ride of the Valkyries" from *Die Walküre*
Repo Man (1984)	Alex Cox	"The Ride of the Valkyries" from *Die Walküre*
Reunion in France (1942)	Jules Dassin	March from *Die Meistersinger*
Reversal of Fortune (1990)	Barbet Schroeder	"Liebestod" from *Tristan und Isolde*
Romeo + Juliet (1996)	Baz Luhrmann	"Liebestod" from *Tristan und Isolde*
Runaway Bride (1999)	Garry Marshall	"Wedding March" from *Lohengrin*

The Running Man (1987)	Paul Michael Glaser	"The Ride of the Valkyries" from *Die Walküre*
Safe Passage (1995)	Robert Allan Ackerman	Prelude to Act 3 of *Lohengrin*
Say It Isn't So (2001)	James B. Rogers	"The Ride of the Valkyries" from *Die Walküre*
The Scarlet Empress (1934)	Josef von Sternberg	*Die Walküre* (excerpts)
Shadow of the Vampire (2001)	E. Eliza Merhige	Overture to *Der fliegende Holländer*
		Prelude to *Tristan und Isolde*
Shining Through (1992)	David Selzer	"Liebestod" from *Tristan und Isolde*
Small Soldiers (1998)	Joe Dante	"The Ride of the Valkyries" from *Die Walküre*
Snafuperman (1944)[4]	Friz Freleng	Overture to *Rienzi*
Song without End (1960)	Andrew L. Stone	Overture to *Rienzi*
		Overture to *Tannhäuser*
		"Pilgrim's Chorus" and "Evening Star" from *Tannhäuser*
Spies (1943)[5]	Chuck Jones	Overture to *Rienzi*
Stay Tuned (1992)	Peter Hyams	"The Ride of the Valkyries" from *Die Walküre*
Stolen Heaven (1938)	Andrew L. Stone	Various
Super Troopers (2001)	Jay Shandrasekhar	"The Ride of the Valkyries" from *Die Walküre*
Swing Kids (1993)	Thomas Carter	Prelude to *Tristan und Isolde*
The Talk of the Town (1942)	George Stevens	Prelude to Act 3 of *Lohengrin*
Tender Is the Night (1962)	Henry King	*Tristan und Isolde* (excerpts)
Testament of Dr. Mabuse (1933)	Fritz Lang	"Magic Fire Music" from *Die Walküre*
Testament of Orpheus (1960)	Jean Cocteau	Various

Film Title	Director	Music from Wagner
There's Magic in Music (1941)	Andrew L. Stone	Overture to Rienzi
Thirty-two Short Films about Glenn Gould (1993)	François Girard	Prelude to Tristan und Isolde
Three Hearts for Julia (1943)	Richard Thorpe	"The Ride of the Valkyries" from Die Walküre
Thrill of a Romance (1945)	Richard Thorpe	"Wedding March" from Lohengrin
Tomcats (2001)	Gregory Poirier	"Wedding March" from Lohengrin
Triumph of the Will (1935)	Leni Riefenstahl	"Nibelungen March" (Gottfried Sonntag) (allusion to "Wach auf" chorus from Die Meistersinger)
Tunisian Victory (1944)	Frank Capra	"Niebelungen March" from Der Ring des Nibelungen
Twenty Four Hour Party People (2002)	Michael Winterbottom	"The Ride of the Valkyries" from Die Walküre
Two Sisters from Boston (1946)	Henry Koster	Lohengrin (excerpts)
Unfaithfully Yours (1948)	Preston Sturges	Overture to Tannhäuser
Vegas Vacation (1997)	Stephen Kessler	"Wedding March" from Lohengrin
Verboten! (1959)	Samuel Fuller	Various
Wagner (1983)	Tony Palmer	Various
The Wagner Family: A Story of Betrayal (forthcoming in 2010)	Tony Palmer	Various
The Wedding Planner (2001)	Adam Shankman	"Wedding March" from Lohengrin
What Planet Are You From? (2000)	Mike Nichols	"Wedding March" from Lohengrin

What's Opera, Doc? (1957)	Chuck Jones	Various[6]
When Love Is Young (1937)	Hal Mohr	"The Ride of the Valkyries" from *Die Walküre*
When My Baby Smiles at Me (1948)	Walter Lang	"Wedding March" from *Lohengrin*
Where the Green Ants Dream (1985)	Werner Herzog	*Wesendonck-Lieder*
Why We Fight (1943–45), 7-part documentary series	Various[7]	
Part 1: *Prelude to War* (1943)	Frank Capra and Anatole Litvak	
Part 2: *The Nazis Strike* (1943)		
Part 3: *Divide and Conquer* (1943)	Frank Capra	
Part 4: *The Battle of Britain* (1943)	Frank Capra and Anatole Litvak	
Part 5: *The Battle of Russia* (1943)	Frank Capra	
Part 6: *The Battle of China* (1944)	Frank Capra and Anatole Litvak	
Part 7: *War Comes to America* (1945)		
The Young Lions (1958)	Edward Dmytryk	Valhalla motif from *Der Ring des Nibelungen*; "Träume" from *Wesendonck-Lieder*
Your Job in Germany (1945)	Frank Capra	"Nibelungen March" (Gottfried Sonntag); Motifs from *Der Ring des Nibelungen* in passing

NOTES

1. For information about Gottfried Sonntag, see Scott D. Paulin's section on "Marches, Motifs, Meanings" in chap. 11 of this volume.

2. The "Wedding March" is the same as the "Bridal Chorus."

3. "Johohoe! Traft ihr das Schiff" from *Der fliegende Holländer;* "Entrance of the Knights" (Chorus) from *Tannhäuser;* "Dich, theure Halle" from *Tannhäuser;* Overture to *Tannhäuser;* Excerpts from *Die Meistersinger von Nürnberg;* Prelude to Act 3 of *Tristan und Isolde;* "Wedding March" from *Lohengrin;* Prelude to Act 2 of *Lohengrin; Siegfried-Idyll;* and "Einsam in trüben Tagen" (Elsa's Dream) from *Lohengrin.*

4. *Snafuperman* is a short in the *Private Snafu* series of cartoon shorts sponsored by the U.S. Army and produced during World War II between 1943 and 1945. Most of the shorts were created at Warner Bros. animation studio.

5. *Spies* is a short in the *Private Snafu* series.

6. For details of Wagner quotes in *What's Opera, Doc?* see Daniel Goldmark, *Tunes for 'Toons: Music and the Hollywood Cartoon* (Berkeley: University of California Press, 2005), 151.

7. Siegfried motif derived from Trio of "Nibelungen March" (Gottfried Sonntag); Immolation Scene from *Götterdämmerung;* and Overture to *Der fliegende Holländer.*

POSTSCRIPT: WAGNER IN THE SILENT ERA: CUE SHEETS AND CINEMA MUSIC COLLECTIONS

Scott D. Paulin

Richard Wagner's name appears regularly, though far from ubiquitously, among the recommendations for musical accompaniment to be found on the cue sheets prepared for American silent films from the late 1910s through the 1920s. An account of the specific selections that cue-sheet compilers tended to cite not only offers clues into the meanings and functions associated with Wagner's works during this period, but also suggests which Wagner pieces local cinemas would have been assumed to have at the ready in their repertoires or libraries. The following generalizations are made on the basis of approximately one thousand cue sheets held in two collections at the University of California, Los Angeles.[1]

As might be expected, the *Lohengrin* "Wedding March" is recommended far out of proportion to any other Wagner composition—in virtually every film containing a wedding scene. Almost invariably, it is followed by the Mendelssohn "Wedding March," and in many cases, the cue-sheet compiler specifies a two-for-the-price-of-one arrangement by Leo Kempinski titled "Burlesque on Mendelssohn's and Wagner's Wedding March." (Typically, a third cue, most often Reginald DeKoven's "O Promise Me," intervenes between the two marches to accompany the exchange of vows.)

Excluding the "Wedding March," Wagner appears in some form on roughly five percent of the cue sheets examined; his music was thought suitable to accompany anything from the adventures of Rin-Tin-Tin in *A Hero of the Big Snows* (1926) to the sorrows of Lillian Gish in *The Enemy* (1928). In the case of some vague references, however, it is not entirely clear that the Wagner in question is *Richard*. Michael Hoffman's cue sheets for the Warner Bros. features of the mid- to late 1920s do not contain thematic incipits, and can thus be difficult to decode fully. Further, in material from the classical repertoire, Hoffman prioritized "tax-free" selections which sometimes carry titles other than those given by the composers themselves. His Wagner recommendations include not only recognizable entities such as "Entrance of the Gods" and "Flower Girls," but also more ambiguous ones including "Dreams" ("Träume" from the *Wesendonck-Lieder*?); "Playful Moments" (perhaps *Siegfried's* "Forest Murmurs"?); "Soft Breezes" (the "Spring Song" from *Walküre*?); and one of Hoffman's favorites for situations requiring "General excitement" or an *agitato,* the as-yet unidentified "Pangs of Passion."

Most other cue sheets of the era were prepared by the Cameo Music Service Corporation, which patented a "Thematic Music Cue Sheet" format including an incipit of several measures for each selection in addition to other identifying information. The majority of these cue sheets were prepared by James C. Bradford, but several other compilers, some of whom were tied to specific studios (Ernst Luz for MGM's films; Michael P. Krueger for Fox), are also represented. Within these cue sheets, by far the most common Wagner number is the "Nibelungen March," actually an arrangement by Gottfried Sonntag but not credited as such on the cue sheets. The theme called for is usually the Siegfried motif introduced in Act 3 of *Die Walküre,* which serves as the march's trio, and which most often functioned in film accompaniment specifically to signify Germanness, especially in a military context. Judging from the frequency with which it is cited, Sonntag's march (available in a Carl

Fischer edition copyrighted in 1891) must have been deemed an essential number for a well-stocked music library; it was also an economical one, as a half-dozen *Ring* motifs could have been extracted from it as needed.[2]

Cameo's thematic cue sheets also make reference to all of Wagner's stage works from *Rienzi* to *Parsifal*, in addition to the *Siegfried-Idyll*, and they tend to do so in semiotic agreement with the taxonomies found in sources such as Erno Rapée's *Encyclopedia of Music for Pictures*. Thus *Walküre*'s "Magic Fire Music" is recommended for situations involving fire (for example, in the 1928 semi-documentary *Chang*, linked to a title card announcing "Fire, the Friend of Man"); and the *Fliegender Holländer* Overture is called for in storm scenes. But not all Wagner citations were descriptive in nature. The "Entrance of the Gods" from *Rheingold* occasionally figured as a recommendation for a film's opening. From *Tristan*, both the Act 1 Prelude and "Isolde's Love Death" are sometimes recommended; the latter, for one example, is called for in *Sacred and Profane Love* (1921), although we are instructed that any "Passionate Love Music" may be substituted for it. From *Meistersinger*, the only reference I have discovered is the "Prize Song," indicated for performance by violin and piano in order to match a "diegetic" concert performance in the Jackie Coogan picture *Daddy* (1923).

In a few cases, Wagner's music is given a more special priority, recurring quasi-leitmotivically as an identified "theme": a "Das Rheingold Selection" is the "Monte Cristo Theme" in *Monte Cristo* (1922); the "Nibelungen March" trio is the "Colonel Theme" in *Lily of the Dust* (1924) and the "Gabriel Theme" in *Graustark* (1925). One especially interesting use of Wagner occurs in the cue sheet compiled by Rudolph Berliner for *The Red Kimona* (1925). This film, recently restored by UCLA, is framed by the appearance of the film's producer, identified as Mrs. Wallace Reid (Dorothy Davenport), who "addresses" the audience with a discussion of the social issues dramatized in the film's narrative. No doubt aiming to provide a properly earnest and edifying musical supplement to Mrs. Reid, the cue sheet recommends the "Swan Song" from *Lohengrin* when her name first appears in the opening credits, and the *Tannhäuser* "Pilgrims' Chorus" when she returns to offer didactic final words at the film's end.

Of course, most of these selections would not have been performed directly out of Wagner's scores in the cinema, but rather from a variety of editions used by theater orchestras. The surviving music collection of New York's famous Capitol Theatre includes a great many such arrangements, some of which are pre-cinematic versions for salon orchestra, others of which were created specifically for the movies (although this particular collection would have been used not only in film accompaniment, but also in the musical and theatrical preludes and interludes that were part of the Capitol's presentations, lasting into the sound era).[3] Consider just a few typical examples from this collection: William Axt's "The Night Riders," which specifies its function as "for Horseman Riding at Night, Night Attacks, etc." and acknowledges its provenance, "inspired by the immortal 'Ride of the Walkyries' by Richard Wagner"; Otto Langey's many arrangements, including a "Grand Fantasia on Richard Wagner's Music-Drama Parsifal" (1915) and a "Selection from Das Rheingold" (1922); Chas. J. Roberts's equally numerous "re-arrangements," including a *Tannhäuser* "Selection" (1914) and a *Tristan* Prelude (1915); and a "Siegfried-Paraphrase" arranged by Ross Jungnickel (1913), which is specifically asked for in Bradford's cue sheet for *Graustark* (1925). In order to gauge more carefully what Wagner sounded like in the silent era, a closer study of the proliferating published editions that were available at the time would be essential.

NOTES

1. Silent Film Music Collection and Collection of Thematic Music Cue Sheets for Silent Films, Performing Arts Special Collections, University of California, Los Angeles.

2. See my essay in this volume for further documentation on the "Nibelungen March."

3. Capitol Theatre (New York, N.Y.) Collection of Silent Film Music, Performing Arts Special Collections, University of California, Los Angeles.

CONTRIBUTORS

GIORGIO BIANCOROSSO is Assistant Professor in Musicology at the University of Hong Kong. He has published numerous articles in the area of film music, film criticism, and musical aesthetics. His recent publications include articles in the journals *Music and Letters* and *Music and the Moving Image,* and the monograph *Musical Aesthetics through Cinema* (forthcoming).

ELISABETH BRONFEN is Professor of English and American Studies at the University of Zurich. Her publications include *Hysteria and Its Discontents* (1998); *Home in Hollywood: Imaginary Geography of Cinema* (2004); and *Liebestod und Femme Fatale: der Austausch sozialer Energien zwischen Oper, Literatur und Film* (2004).

JAMES BUHLER is Associate Professor of Music Theory at The University of Texas at Austin. He is co-editor of *Music and Cinema* (2000) and co-author of *Hearing the Movies: Music, Sound, and Film History* (2009). His current project concerns the auditory culture of early American cinema.

JOY H. CALICO, Associate Professor of Musicology at Vanderbilt University, is author of *Brecht at the Opera* (2008). Her current book project, *Musical Remigration: Schoenberg's "A Survivor from Warsaw" in Postwar Europe,* is supported by an ACLS Frederick Burkhardt Residential Fellowship for Recently Tenured Scholars.

MARCIA J. CITRON is Lovett Distinguished Service Professor of Musicology at Rice University. She is author of *Opera on Screen* (2000) and *When Opera Meets Film* (forthcoming in 2010). Another area of research is gender, capped by the award-winning study *Gender and the Musical Canon* (1993; 2000).

PETER FRANKLIN is Professor of Music at the University of Oxford. His publications on film music include "Movies as Opera" in *A Night in at the Opera: Media Representations of Opera* (1994) and "The Boy on the Train, or Bad Symphonies and Good Movies" in *Beyond Soundtrack* (2007). He is currently co-editor of *The Cambridge Companion to Film Music* (forthcoming).

PAUL FRYER is Head of the School of Graduate and Professional Studies at Rose Bruford College (UK). His research specialty is in the area of opera, opera singers, and the pre-sound film industry, upon which he has published widely, including *The Opera Singer and the Silent Film* (2005).

SANDER L. GILMAN is Distinguished Professor of the Liberal Arts and Sciences at Emory University. He is author of *Fat: A Cultural History of Obesity* (2008); *Multiculturalism and the Jews* (2006); *Making the Body Beautiful: A Cultural History of Aesthetic Surgery* (1999); *Freud, Race, and Gender* (1993); *Jewish Self-Hatred: Anti-Semitism and the Hidden Language of the Jews* (1986); and many other publications. He has written widely on opera and culture.

ROGER HILLMAN teaches Film Studies and German Studies at the Australian National University, Canberra. A Humboldt Fellow, his recent publications include *Unsettling Scores: German Film, Music, Ideology* (Indiana University Press, 2005) and *Transkulturalität: Türkisch-deutsche Konstellationen in Literatur und Film* (as co-author, 2007).

JEONGWON JOE is Associate Professor of Musicology at the University of Cincinnati. She is co-editor of *Between Opera and Cinema* (2002) and has published articles on Milos Forman's

Amadeus, Philip Glass's *La Belle et la Bête,* David Lynch's *Blue Velvet,* Gérard Corbiau's *Farinelli,* and other works related to opera and film music. Her current projects include the monograph *Opera as Soundtrack* (forthcoming in 2011). She has served as a music consultant to Chanwook Park, the director of the Cannes award-winning films *Oldboy* (2004) and *Thirst* (2009).

LAWRENCE KRAMER is Professor of English at Fordham University and editor of the journal *19th-Century Music.* The most recent of his many books are *Why Classical Music Still Matters* (2007); *Opera and Modern Culture: Wagner and Strauss* (2004); and a collection edited with Keith Chapin, *Musical Meaning and Human Values* (2009), drawn from an international conference honoring his work.

NEIL LERNER is Associate Professor of Music at Davidson College. He is co-editor of *Sounding Off: Theorizing Disability in Music* (2006) and a contributor to *Aaron Copland and His World* (2005); *Off the Planet: Music, Sound, and Science Fiction Cinema* (2004); and *The Sounds of Early Cinema* (Indiana University Press, 2001).

ADELINE MUELLER is a doctoral candidate in musicology at the University of California, Berkeley, where she is completing a dissertation on late-eighteenth-century German opera. In 2007 she gave the introductory remarks at a screening of the Pacific Film Archive's newly rediscovered print of the 1933 *Siegfrieds Tod,* and she will be contributing an essay on Lang's *Die Nibelungen* to *A New History of German Cinema* (forthcoming).

DAVID NEUMEYER is Leslie Waggener Professor in the College of Fine Arts and Professor of Music in the School of Music, The University of Texas at Austin. He is co-editor of *Music and Cinema* (2000) and co-author of *Hearing the Movies: Music, Sound, and Film History* (2009) with James Buhler and Robert Deemer.

SCOTT D. PAULIN has most recently been Visiting Lecturer in the Department of Music at Dartmouth College. His publications include "Richard Wagner and the Fantasy of Cinematic

Unity," in *Music and Cinema* (2000), and "Cinematic
Music: Fallacies, Analogies, and the Case of Debussy," in
Music and the Moving Image (forthcoming in 2010).

EVA RIEGER taught at the University of Bremen. Her publica-
tions include *Frau, Music und Männerherrschaft* (1981; 1988); *Alfred
Hitchcock und die Musik: Eine Untersuchung zum Verhältnis von
Film, Musik und Geschlecht* (1996); and *Leuchtende Liebe, lachender
Tod: Richard Wagners Bild der Frau im Spiegel seiner Musik* (2009).

WILLIAM H. ROSAR is editor of *The Journal of Film Music* and
founder and former president of the Film Music Society. He
has taught history and analysis of film scoring at the University
of Southern California. His publications include "The 'Dies
Irae' in *Citizen Kane*" (2001) and "Music for the Monsters:
Universal Pictures' Horror Film Scores of the Thirties" (1983).

WARREN M. SHERK is a special collections database archivist and
music specialist at the Academy of Motion Picture Arts and Sciences'
Margaret Herrick Library. He also works in music preparation
for motion pictures as an orchestrator and music proofreader. He
serves as Secretary of the Film Music Society, and co-edited *Film
Music: History, Theory, Practice* (2004) with Claudia Gorbman.

JEREMY TAMBLING is Professor of Literature at Manchester
University and has published numerous books and articles on
film, opera, and opera-film. He is author of *Opera, Ideology and
Film* (1987); *Opera and the Culture of Fascism* (1997); and editor of
A Night in at the Opera: Media Representations of Opera (1994).

MARC A. WEINER is Professor of Germanic Studies and Adjunct
Professor of Comparative Literature, Communication and
Culture, and Cultural Studies at Indiana University, Bloomington.
His publications include *Undertones of Insurrection: Music and
Cultural Politics in the Modern German Narrative* (1993; 2008) and
Richard Wagner and the Anti-Semitic Imagination (1995; 1997).

INDEX

Italicized page numbers indicate illustrations.

Abbate, Carolyn, 7, 226, 244, 427
Above Suspicion (Thorpe), 230–31, 442
Absolute Power (Eastwood), 442
Abusch, Alexander, 298
Academy Awards, 6
accompaniment to silent films, 27–45;
   as added attraction, 30–31; allegorical
   character of, 38; cue sheets and cinema music collections from, 452–55;
   earliest known portrayal of Wagner, x;
   the face in, 38–39; leitmotif in, 27–28,
   33–37, 44n32; mechanically reproduced,
   44n35; mood as basis for, 34–35; narrative integration and development of accompaniment, 1908–1913, 27–45; as not
   necessary, 44n35; as not substituting
   for missing voice, 39; opera compared
   with, 37–38; scores provided for, 68–69;
   studio suggestions for, 414; tension
   between prescience and resignation in,
   37; typical program around 1910, 40n6;
   variety of music for, 68; villain music,
   155; Wagner associated with, 27; Wagner operas in, 4
Ackerman, Robert Allan, 449
Addinsell, Richard, 185n31
Adorno, Theodor: critique of Wagner's
   temporal world, 17, 361–62, 363, 364–65,
   369, 373, 375; on culture industry,

276; on fetish-character of music, 278;
on film as derisively filling dream of
Gesamtkunstwerk, 278; on film as heir
to Wagnerian music, 7; on Hollywood
film music debasing Wagner, 248n34;
on hypnotizing powers of Wagner's
music, 184n25; *In Search of Wagner,*
47; Kluge as friend of, 280; on Ludwig's
fascination with Wagner, 355n14; on
motif in Wagner, 288; on Nietzsche and
film, 1, 276; on phantasmagoria, 2, 276,
361, 364; on Stravinski, 362, 378n18; on
Wagner as bourgeois artist, 51; on Wagner as writing film music, 47, 50–51, 61;
on Wagner's leitmotif technique, 362,
377n14
The Adventures of Robin Hood (1938), 145
affects: musical, 132–37. *See also* emotion
Aguirre (Herzog), 264
Aida (Verdi), 286
Airplane II: The Sequel (Finkleman), 442
Albert, Hermann, 157
alien invasion films, 154–56, 160
All Forgotten (Anselmo), 442
All This and Heaven, Too (1940), 114
All Through the Night (1941), 246n9
Allan, Seán, 298
Allen, Woody, 443, 447
Almodovar, Pedro, 285

Stockhausen, Karlheinz, 363, 373
Stolen Heaven (Stone), 412, 449
Stoll, George, 410
Stoloff, Morris, 411
Stone, Andrew L., 412, 445, 449, 450
Stothart, Herbert, 116
The Stranger (1946), 244
Strassburg, Otto von, 435
Strauss, Richard, 132
Stravinski, Igor, 362, 377n17, 378n18
Stresemann, Gustav, 94
Strictly Dishonorable (1951), 416
studio archives, 410
Stukas (Ritter), 284
Sturges, Preston, 450
Sukman, Harry, 411
Super Troopers (Shandrasekhar), 449
Suspicion (Hitchcock), 182n3
Swarthout, Gladys, 416
Swing Kids (Carter), 449
Syberberg, Hans-Jürgen: classical music
 use of, 255; on film as music of the fu-
 ture, 1, 22n30; *Ludwig: Requiem for a
 Virgin King*, x, 258, 343; *Parsifal*, 22n30,
 274–75, 283; on Wagner as puppet, x.
 *See also Our Hitler (Hitler, ein Film aus
 Deutschland)* (Syberberg)
Symphonie Espagnole (Lalo), 169
Symphony of Six Million (1932), 112
synchronization, narrative, 36–37
Szabo, Istvan, 80, 447

The Talk of the Town (Stevens), 449
Talk to Her (Almodovar), 285
Tambling, Jeremy, 15
Tanaka, Daiju, 366
Tandler, Adolph, 96
Tannhäuser (Wagner): bacchanal ballet
 of, 51; Baudelaire on, 163n24; binary
 opposition between power and love in,
 144–45; in *Brute Force*, 244; in Capital
 Theatre music collection, 455; change
 between Acts 1 and 2, 286; characters'
 refusal of time's progression in, 361–62;
 filmography, 442–46, 449, 450; hero
 responds to Venus in diegetic song, 54;
 and *Meeting Venus* (1991), 409; motifs
 for representing affect in, 137–38; Over-

ture in Vitaphone short, 416; *Rebecca*
 compared with, 143; in *Song Without
 End*, 411; in Visconti's *Ludwig*, 346–47,
 349–51
Tavener, John, 262
Tchaikovsky, Peter: biographical pictures
 about, 66; *Christmas Slippers*, 416; piano
 concertos, 169, 180, 182; *Romeo and Ju-
 liet Overture-Fantasy*, 169, 170
Tender Is the Night (King), 449
Ternina, Milka, 78
Testament of Dr. Mabuse (Lang), 316, 449
Testament of Orpheus (Cocteau), 449
Testimony (Palmer), xiii
That Certain Woman (1937), 114
Theater der Zeit (journal), 296, 298, 307
There's Magic in Music (1941), 412, 450
The Thief of Baghdad (1939), 427
Thiel, Carl, 107n52
The Thing from Another World (1951), 12,
 152–56, 157, 160
Third Reich. *See* Nazism (National
 Socialism)
Thirty-two Short Films about Glenn Gould
 (Girard), 450
Thomas, Tony, 115
Thompson, J. Lee, 446
Thompson, Richard, 222
Thomson, David, 125–26
Thorpe, Richard, 442, 450
Three Colors: White (Kieslowski), 270
Three Hearts for Julia (Thorpe), 450
Three Tales (Reich), 9
Thrill of a Romance (Thorpe), 450
Tibetan Book of the Dead, 404, 437
time: Adorno's critique of Wagner's tem-
 poral world, 17, 361–62, 363, 364–65,
 369, 373, 375; becomes space in *Parsifal*,
 2, 276, 359, 381; cyclical temporality
 as element of Viola's works, 360–61;
 eternal now, 363, 365, 372; Kluge on cinematic, 290, 293n61; linear, 363–64, 365,
 374; as material of video, 360; moment,
 363, 365, 373; movement represented
 as embodiment of, 376; musical versus
 ordinary, 362–63; nonlinear, 364, 365,
 373, 374; pure, 376; rationalized, 376; in
 schizophrenia, 363, 378n25; temporal

Buddhism's influence on, 365–66, 373; on creation of the world and sound, 358; cyclical temporality as element of works of, 360–61; film and video contrasted by, 358–59; *Five Angels for the Millennium*, 360–61, 366; interview with, 431–40; "The Light Enters You," 365; on love story of *Tristan und Isolde*, 389; *Love/Death: The Tristan Project*, 379n41; modernist cinema aligned with work of, 376; on music and time, 16; musical collaborations of, 360; mythic dimension privileged in art of, 375; *Passage*, 361; on recording singing frogs, 358; slow motion as signature technique of, 361, 385, 432; temporal affinity between Wagner and, 374–75; on time as a sculptural thing, 359; on triangulation of music, images, and bodies on stage, 385, 386; on Wagner's latent presence in the arts, 1, 19. See also *Tristan Project* (Viola)

Visconti, Luchino: autobiographical impulse in late work of, 355n8; *La caduta degli dei*, 244, 443; *Conversation Piece*, 338; *The Damned*, 355n13; *Death in Venice*, 338; on historical film as tool for remembrance and testimony, 338–39; *The Leopard*, 339, 342, 343, 354n7; main characters as lost in reverie, 338; perfectionism of, 335–36, 354n4. See also *Ludwig* (Visconti)

Vitagraph Bulletin (periodical), 414
Vitaphone sound system, 83n8, 409, 416
Vitold, Michel, x
Voigt, Deborah, 407n19
von Wymetal, William, 416

Wagner (Palmer), ix, x, 7, 66, 174–75, 184n18, 450
"Wagner, Cinema, and Redemptive Glee" (Abbate), 7
Wagner, Cosima: American premiere of *Parsifal* defies, 78; Bayreuth tradition maintained by, 74; on her relationship with Wagner, xi–xii; in *The Life and Works of Richard Wagner*, 73, 74; *Siegfried-Idyll* played for birthday of, 340, 344; in Visconti's *Ludwig*, 333, 340,

341, 344, 345; on Wagner on invisible theater, 278; Wagner's last composition for solo piano (Porazzi theme) dedicated to, 343
Wagner, Gottfried, 431
Wagner, Richard, and cinema: affinity of cinema and, 381–82; American cinematic associations of, 14; cinematic imagination of, 2–3; cinematic presence beyond the soundtrack, 313–407; as forerunner of cinematic techniques, 47–48; gender roles in early Hollywood films influenced by, 131–51; in German cinema, 251–311; in Herzog's documentaries, 260–65; multivalent significance of, 48; music in soundtracks, 4–6, 8–9, 66, 211; and New German Cinema, 253–72; portrayals on film, ix–x; in Reitz's *Heimat* series, 265–70; as source of inspiration for cinema, 1–9; Steiner on film scores and, 116–18, 129n20; in Syberberg's *Our Hitler*, 254–59; two views of influence on cinema of, 46–47; in Visconti's *Ludwig*, x, 66, 336, 341, 343–45
Wagner, Richard, and Germany: denazification of, 14, 226–27, 234, 235, 236, 238, 241, 243–45, 259; in East German culture, 294, 295–96, 428; Hitler's relationship to, 200, 295, 426; Metropolitan Opera bans works of, 95, 96; Nazism associated with, 8, 47, 205–206, 209n32, 224n10, 226, 229–31, 235, 244, 257, 296, 307; post–World War I rehabilitation of, 11; revisionist appropriations of, 14, 238; as signifier of all things German, 187, 197, 227–29, 232; Stalin bans works of, ix
Wagner, Richard, archival resources for, 408–18
Wagner, Richard, characteristics of work of: Adorno's critique of temporal world of, 17, 361–62, 363, 364–65, 369, 373, 375; binary opposition between power and love in, 143–46; as bourgeois artist, 51; centrifugal harmony attributed to, 364; composes as if in a trance, 161, 164n32; compositional practice and stagecraft of, 55–60; control over entire structure

JEONGWON JOE is Associate Professor of Musicology at the University of Cincinnati. She is co-editor of *Between Opera and Cinema* (2002) and has published articles on Milos Forman's *Amadeus*, Philip Glass's *La Belle et la Bête*, David Lynch's *Blue Velvet*, Gérard Corbiau's *Farinelli*, and other works related to opera and film music. Her current projects include the monograph *Opera as Soundtrack* (forthcoming in 2011). She has served as a music consultant to Chanwook Park, the director of the Cannes award-winning films *Oldboy* (2004) and *Thirst* (2009).

SANDER L. GILMAN is Distinguished Professor of the Liberal Arts and Sciences at Emory University. He is author of *Fat: A Cultural History of Obesity* (2008); *Multiculturalism and the Jews* (2006); *Making the Body Beautiful: A Cultural History of Aesthetic Surgery* (1999); *Freud, Race, and Gender* (1993); *Jewish Self-Hatred: Anti-Semitism and the Hidden Language of the Jews* (1986); and many other publications. He has written widely on opera and culture.